IN PRAISE OF CHRISTIAN ORIGINS

Emory Studies in Early Christianity

General Editor
Vernon K. Robbins

Associate Editor
David B. Gowler

Editorial Board
L. Gregory Bloomquist, St. Paul University, Ottawa
Peder Borgen, University of Trondheim, Norway
H. J. Bernard Combrink, University of Stellenbosch, South Africa
David A. deSilva, Ashland Theological Seminary
Anders Eriksson, Lund University, Sweden
Thomas H. Olbricht, Pepperdine University, Emeritus
Russell B. Sisson, Union College
Duane F. Watson, Malone College

Original cover design by Gina M. Tansley
(adapted from Rick A. Robbins, *Mixed Media*, 1981)

The cover design introduces an environment for disciplined creativity The seven squares superimposed over one another represent multiple arenas for programmatic research, analysis, and interpretation. The area in the center, common to all the arenas, is like the area that provides the unity for a volume in the series. The small square in the center of the squares denotes a paragraph, page, or other unit of text. The two lines that extend out from the small square, perpendicular to one another, create an opening to territory not covered by any of the multiple squares. These lines have the potential to create yet another square of the same or different size that would be a new arena for research, analysis, and interpretation.

Emory Studies in Early Christianity

Volumes in this series investigate early Christian literature in the context of Mediterranean literature, religion, society, and culture. The authors use interdisciplinary methods informed by social, rhetorical, literary, and anthropological approaches to move beyond limits within traditional literary-historical investigations. The studies presuppose that Christianity began as a Jewish movement in various geographical, political, economic, and social locations in the Greco-Roman world.

1. David B. Gowler, *Host, Guest, Enemy and Friend: Portraits of the Pharisees in Luke and Acts*, 1991.

*2. H. Wayne Merritt, *In Word and Deed: Moral Integrity in Paul*, 1993.

*3. Vernon K. Robbins, *New Boundaries in Old Territory: Form and Social Rhetoric in Mark*, 1994. Ed. and introduced by David B. Gowler.

4. Jan Botha, *Subject to Whose Authority? Multiple Readings of Romans 13*, 1994.

5. Kjell Arne Morland, *The Rhetoric of Curse in Galatians: Paul Confronts a Different Gospel*, 1995.

6. Peder Borgen, Vernon K. Robbins, and David B. Gowler, eds., *Recruitment, Conquest, and Conflict: Strategies in Judaism, Early Christianity, and the Greco-Roman World*, 1998.

7. Mark D. Given, *Paul's True Rhetoric: Ambiguity, Cunning, and Deception in Greece and Rome*, 2001.

8. Anders Eriksson, Thomas H. Olbricht, and Walter Übelacker, eds., *Rhetorical Argumentation in Biblical Texts: Essays from the Lund 2000 Conference*, 2002.

9. James D. Hester and J. David Hester, eds., *Rhetorics and Hermeneutics: Wilhelm Wuellner and His Influence at the Close of the Century*, 2004.

10. Todd Penner, *In Praise of Christian Origins: Stephen and the Hellenists in Lukan Apologetic Historiography*, 2004.

*The second and third volumes were published by and are available from Peter Lang Publishing, Inc., 275 Seventh Avenue, 28th Floor, New York, NY 10001-6708; (212) 647-7700; FAX (212) 647-7707; customer service (800) 770-5264, (212) 647-7706.

All other volumes are available through T & T Clark International.

IN PRAISE OF CHRISTIAN ORIGINS

Stephen and the Hellenists
in Lukan Apologetic Historiography

Todd Penner

T&T CLARK INTERNATIONAL
A Continuum imprint
NEW YORK • LONDON

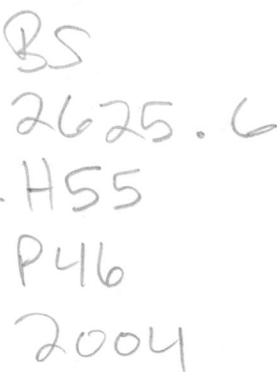

BS
2625.6
.H55
P46
2004

Copyright © 2004 Emory University

All rights reserved. No part of this book may be reproduced, stored in a retrieval system, or transmitted in any form or by any means, electronic, mechanical, including photocopying, recording, or otherwise, without the written permission of the publisher, T & T Clark International.

T & T Clark International, Madison Square Park, 15 East 26th Street, New York, NY 10010

T & T Clark International, The Tower Building, 11 York Road, London SE1 7NX

T & T Clark International is a Continuum imprint.

Cover design: Laurie Westhafer

Unless otherwise indicated, biblical and apocryphal quotations are from the New Revised Standard Version Bible, copyright 1989, Division of Christian Education of the National Council of the Churches of Christ in the United States of America. Used by permission. All rights reserved.

All Greek and Latin quotations are from the Loeb Classical Library.

Library of Congress Cataloging-in-Publication Data
Penner, Todd
   In praise of Christian origins : Stephen and the Hellenists in Lukan apologetic historiography / Todd Penner.
     p. cm. – (Emory studies in early Christianity)
   Includes index.
   ISBN 0-567-02620-5
   1. Bible. N.T. Acts VI, 1–VIII, 3–Historiography. 2. Bible. N.T. Acts VI, 1–VIII, 3– Socio-rhetorical criticism. 3. Church history–Primitive and early church, ca. 30–600. I. Title. II. Series.
BS2625.6.H55P46 2004
226.6'067–dc22
                                                        2003027920

Printed in the United States of America

04   05   06   07   08   09   10   9   8   7   6   5   4   3   2   1

...it's not some pilgrim who's seen the light
It's a cold and it's a broken Hallelujah.
— Leonard Cohen

In gratitude

for the generosity of my parents
Charles and Pauline Penner

and the once warm company of some feline friends
Tigger and Bert

Contents

Foreword: Acts as Epideictic History: A Recommendation of and Response to Todd Penner, by David L. Balch xi

Preface xxiii

Acknowledgments xxix

Abbreviations xxxv

I. Hellenists and *Historia*: Constructing Christian History and Theology in Modern Scholarship 1

II. Textualizing the Hellenists, Contextualizing Interpretation: Mapping the Exegetical Terrain 60

III. Writing History in Antiquity: Identity, Rhetoric, and Compelling Narration 104

IV. Jewish Apologetic Historiography: Cultural Identity and Rewriting the Past 223

V. In Praise of Origins: The Hellenists, Stephen, and the Christian Foundation Narrative 262

Epilogue: Historiography, History, and the Academy 331

Bibliography 339

Index of Ancient Sources 377

Index of Modern Authors 395

Foreword

Acts as Epideictic History

A Recommendation of and Response to Todd Penner

DAVID L. BALCH
Brite Divinity School (Fort Worth, Texas)

Todd Penner requested that I write this foreword knowing both that I am excited about his book and that I disagree with him on some points; I admire his insights as well as his nerve. While recommending his book as well as raising critical questions, I will certainly simplify the rich, complex presentation and reconfigure points he considers crucial. The reader should and will always make her own judgments.

Penner both criticizes modern, historical-critical interpreters of Acts and offers new perspectives on how to read the narrative rhetorically with what he now calls a "progymnastic poetics."[1] He studies Acts 6–7 in order to focus on the nature of *historia,* about which, he suggests, contemporary exegetes have had misconceptions. Many modern scholars seem more interested in historical facts behind the text than in Luke's narrative itself (chapter 1). Penner notes that scholars across a variety of approaches still, in the end, affirm the essential historical core in some way. For example, M. Hengel imports the "history of religions" school into Jerusalem. The Hellenists of Acts are the necessary bridge between a rural Jesus and the urban, universalist theology of Paul. H. Räisänen disagrees: the bridge is to be found in Diaspora Judaism, not in Palestine. In this dispute, however, the modern question about history behind the text has not changed, only the specific construal of the data. Although scholars such as M. Dibelius are often thought to represent an alternative to this historical-critical approach, issues related to history are not dispensed with as a result. Dibelius has argued, for example, that the speeches in Acts are historical examples of early Christian preaching. He separates Luke the historian from Luke the theologian. Penner argues rather that history and theology are flip sides of the same enterprise in Acts.

---

1. T. Penner, "Reconfiguring the Rhetorical Study of Acts: Reflections on the Method in and Learning of a Progymnastic Poetics," *PRSt* 30 (2003): 425–39.

The social historian P. Esler contrasts pro-temple Hebrews with anti-temple Hellenists. Further, God-fearers were marginalized because of their exclusion from the temple, but Christians, Esler suggests, allowed them full access to their communities. In contrast to these scholars' emphasis on theological and social history behind the text, Penner integrates classical rhetoric and historiography as well as the Lukan speeches and narrative to show that the epideictic rhetoric of Acts 6–7 focuses the self-identity of Christian readers. While Penner combines ancient rhetoric and modern literary analysis in this study, he also insists that the older historical-critical approach (e.g., F. F. Bruce, E. Haenchen, M. Dibelius, H. J. Cadbury, H. Conzelman, M. Hengel, C. J. Hemer, W. W. Gasque, J. A. Fitzmyer, C. K. Barrett) and newer literary approaches (e.g., R. I. Pervo, R. C. Tannehill, L. T. Johnson, W. S. Kurz, C. H. Talbert) can be and often are mutually exclusive.[2] Penner's later work criticizing the unreflective use of diverse methodology in the analysis of Acts has its roots in this study on the Hellenists, where his sometimes polemical proposal to address the need for thoughtful engagement of methodology finds its initial grounding.

In contrast to a contemporary scholarly consensus, Penner urges that Luke has not created a utopian text but rather narrates conflict (chapter 2; cf. chapter 5). He outlines the initial narrative as follows: founding the early Christian community (1:1–2:44), summary (2:43–47), conflict with outsiders (3:1–31), summary (4:32–35), conflict with insiders (5:1–11), summary (5:12–16), conflict with outsiders (5:17–41), summary (5:42), conflict with insiders (6:1–6), summary (6:7). When Hellenists complain against the Hebrews and the Twelve ask the community to choose (seven) wise men (Acts 6:1–6) to address the conflict, who are the latter? Luke does not use "Hebrews" to designate traditionalists, Penner argues; he also narrows the meaning of "Hellenists" to language, not geography (Diaspora origin) or theology (liberal view of the law). This significant move enables him to focus on the narrative, unlike Hengel and Esler, who focus rather on theological/social history.

There is a fair body of literature on the Hebrew versus Hellenist distinction in New Testament scholarship. This is one point where scholars will no doubt contend with some of the assertions that are put forward in this book. Outside the Acts narrative, "Hebrew" may refer to more than language (2 Cor 11:22; Phil 3:5; 4 Macc 5:2; 8:2; 16:15–16, all in polemical contexts); in the same way, "Hellenist/Hellenizer" may mean more than "Greek-speaking" (2 Macc 4:10, 13, also in a polemical context, and pseudo-Dio Chrysostom, *Oration* 37.26–27). "Hellenize" belongs to a group of words that has to do with speaking the language, but may also

---

2. See T. Penner, "Madness in the Method?: The Acts of the Apostles in Current Study," *CurBR* 2 (2004): 224–95.

refer either to political support or to adopting social customs, social meanings that Penner rejects when the terms occur in Acts. Debate will continue over whether Penner has established that historical-critical and narrative interpretations of Acts are indeed mutually exclusive.

Penner further deals with the relationship of speech and narrative in Acts. Does Stephen's speech in Acts 7 respond to the accusations in the narrative (chapter 2)? Dibelius thought the speech irrelevant, and subsequent scholarship has often agreed: Luke inserted a discourse that originally sketched the history of Israel into a narrative of the martyrdom of Stephen. But if Luke chose or created the speech, why does it fit the narrative context so poorly? Penner maintains rather that the speech does respond to the charges in 6:13, although in an unexpected way: rhetorically, the speech is a counter-accusation. The way forward, he argues again, is to access the rhetoric of the text, not the history or theology behind the text.

Discussion of the structure and the argument of Stephen's speech follows (chapter 2). Ancient historiography was transformed in the Hellenistic and early Roman periods; there was a turn from demonstrative to epideictic historiography, Penner observes. This shift was quite self-conscious in authors such as Pseudo-Hecataeus, Livy, Dionysius, and Josephus. Hellenistic and Roman expansion brought the issue of identity to the forefront. This book argues that epideictic rhetoric in Acts praises Jesus as a prophet like Moses and eulogizes the church bound together by friendship and service.

The relationship between historiography and rhetoric (chapter 3) was problematic in Hellenistic/Roman times. Was history nothing more than rhetoric (A. J. Woodman), or are the ancient histories of Thucydides, Polybius, and Luke comparable to their modern counterparts (C. W. Fornara, S. Hornblower, B. Witherington)? Aristotle contrasts tragedy and history, preferring the *former* because it provides values and virtues for human imitation, which history, being particular, cannot do. Penner suggests that Hellenistic historiography may reveal an attempt to merge history and poetics; or, at the very least, it reflects a more overt stage in the merger. The Romans bastardized all that was good about Greek historical writing, it is typically argued; but Penner suggests that the Romans developed the didactic function of examples already present in earlier historiography. Cicero connects history and rhetoric, especially epideictic. For Cicero, however, epideictic is related to deliberative oratory; the former praises what the latter advises. In revising his approach for this publication, Penner goes much further than just connecting historiography and rhetoric. He now argues that "genre distinctions [are] functionally irrelevant."[3] Analysis of Acts would

---

3. Penner, "Progymnastic Poetics," 436. I too have abandoned my earlier argument that Luke-Acts is exclusively historiography and now also compare Luke's two-volume work with biography. D. L. Balch, "ΜΕΤΑΒΟΛΗ ΠΟΛΙΤΕΙΩΝ. Jesus as Founder of the Church in Luke-Acts: Form and Function," in *Contextualizing Acts: Lukan Narrative and Greco-Roman*

profitably include not only historiography and rhetoric, but other genres as well, e.g., novel, epic, and biography.

Two questions for further discussion occur to me. Is our ancient author praising the church's friendship (epideictic rhetoric, as Penner argues) or does not Luke also presume that the house churches need to be persuaded to adopt the ethnic openness/*philanthropia* of the founders, as Luke reconstructs them (deliberative rhetoric)? The narrative in Acts 10–15 (see 10:28) may indicate that some among the Christian readers had a more ethnocentric view of the founders and of the church's boundaries than did our ancient author. Second, did not ancient history and biography also concern politics, collective values and action? If politics exclusively concerns the Roman state, the answer would be negative. But since contemporary writers employ the term politics to refer to the values and collective actions of subordinate groups within the state (Egyptians, Jews, the rich/poor, patricians/plebeians),[4] conflicts among Jewish-Christian insiders and between insiders and outsiders (some over ethnic and religious group boundaries) may be termed political. If so, would not the rhetoric at points in the text go beyond epideictic to deliberative? What is the nature of the conflict that Penner sees within the plot of Acts?

One of Penner's most important contributions concerns the nature of truth in ancient historiography, which was not the same as in modern historiography (chapter 3). Truth in history is truth as experienced in the *polis*. Penner argues that for Polybius the truth is that people get what they deserve and that Greeks and Romans are honorable in war; other ancient historians lie when they write otherwise. Truth in this understanding becomes not so much what really happened as what must have happened. Similarly, in *On the Malice of Herodotus,* Plutarch denies whole sections of Herodotus's history *because* he was pro-barbarian! History was didactic; historians trained leaders for the *polis,* inculcating Greek or Roman ethics in their readers/hearers.

Penner thus characterizes the relation between ancient historiography and truth, a question that begs further discussion. E. Gabba has written on the same issue. Dionysius of Halicarnassus's history and rhetoric promoted a classical, rationalist revival in the Augustan period, a rationalist revival that Dionysius claims was limited to the upper, European, non-Asian classes, which is a claim that Gabba accepts.[5] The conquests of Alexander introduced untutored masses into the Hellenistic political world, a social basis of unreason.[6] Christianity played a larger role in revitalizing classical culture,

---

Discourse (ed. T. Penner and C. Vander Stichele; SBLSymS 20; Atlanta: Society of Biblical Literature, 2003), 139–88.

4. Balch, "ΜΕΤΑΒΟΛΗ ΠΟΛΙΤΕΙΩΝ," 147, citing, for example, Dionysius, *Ant. rom.* 1.8.3.

5. E. Gabba, "True History and False History in Classical Antiquity," *JRS* 71 (1981): 55.

6. Ibid., 53, 55; cf. Balch, "ΜΕΤΑΒΟΛΗ ΠΟΛΙΤΕΙΩΝ," 150–54.

but at the same time admitted romantic and miraculous elements into its hagiographical texts.[7] According to both Dionysius and Gabba, Alexander's conquests (and thus Christianity originating in Asia) brought about a decline into irrational, false history.

There is an intriguing parallel between Greco-Roman rhetoric and art, which I introduce in order to question Gabba's characterization of true and false and in order to suggest one means of further expanding Penner's observations on the relation between truth, rhetoric, and biography/historiography. K. Schefold, one of the most important art historians of the twentieth century, insisted that rational thought, art, and religion are related.[8] In his *magnum opus*, published after seventy years as a historian of Greco-Roman art, Schefold argues that

> the end of Antiquity was not brought about by the victory of oriental religions. Far less did the orient defeat Hellenism through Christianity. The transformation of pagan into Christian Rome was more profound, a change not determined by external influences. Oriental and Hellenistic influences were incorporated only in so far as the Roman desire for a transcendental foundation of existence needed those elements. Christianity itself was decisively transformed by the [Roman] desire [for transcendence].[9]

This Roman desire for transcendence is visually overwhelming in the second and fourth styles of domestic art. Mythological frescoes tend to appear in the largest houses, where they would be seen by owner and slaves, males and females, patrons and clients.[10] Less expensive decoration is found in smaller houses and work shops, cupids, dancing women, nature scenes, etc. Dionysius wrote in the period of the second style, Luke-Acts was written during the time of the fourth style. Desire for truth in this sense goes beyond the *polis* experienced in everyday life. In the first century C.E., beginning with Nero, the *Roman* fourth style contrasted urban reality with ideal, sacred landscapes.[11] The Roman elite were patrons of this art; it did not originate with the Eastern lower classes (in Alexandria, Jerusalem, or Ephesus). Dionysius, Luke, and Plutarch addressed their biographical histories to a Roman culture that had such ethical, social, political interests, but also religious questions painted before their eyes in many *domus* and *insulae* in the form of myth.[12] Gabba's characterization of the rationalist, classical revival seeking truth

---

7. Gabba, "True History," 55, citing the *apocryphal* Acts.
8. K. Schefold, *Der religiöse Gehalt der antiken Kunst und die Offenbarung* (Kulturgeschichte der antiken Welt 78; Mainz: Philipp von Zabern, 1998), 20.
9. Ibid., 349 (my translation).
10. R. Ling, *Roman Painting* (Cambridge: Cambridge University Press, 1991), 23–42, 71–85, 101–43, 142–53.
11. Schefold, *Der religiöse Gehalt*, 326–27.
12. For myth in rhetorical education, see "The Exercises of Aellius Theon," 60 P, 66–67 P, 72–78 P, 92 P, 95 P, and 104 P (George A. Kennedy, *Progymnasmata: Greek Textbooks of Prose Composition and Rhetoric* [SBLWGRW 10; Atlanta: Society of Biblical Literature, 2003], 4, 9–10, 23–28, 39, 41, 68).

without myth ignores Roman art. New Testament scholars could thus profitably investigate further the interrelationship between Roman rhetoric, art, and biography/historiography with respect to truth claims.

I conclude that Penner's observations put the contemporary debate over the relationship between Thucydides, Polybius, and Luke in a different light. Dionysius of Halicarnassus would have disdained Luke-Acts as "Asian."[13] Heroes in the narrative are Jews—Abraham, Moses, Jesus, Mary, Stephen, Paul, many of whom speak Septuagintal Greek and are not European, neo-Attic Greeks or Romans who are better morally or politically more powerful than the barbarians. Dionysius's attitude toward such Asians is clear:

> In every city and in the highly civilized ones as much as any (which was the final indignity) the ancient and indigenous Attic Muse, deprived of her possessions, had lost her civic rank, while her antagonist, an upstart that had arrived only yesterday and the day before from some Asiatic death-hole, a Mysian or Phrygian or Carian creature, claimed the right to rule over Greek cities, expelling her rival from public life. (Dionysius, *Ancient Orators* 1)

Movement in Acts is not from Rome outward conquering the world (Polybius), but from Asian Jerusalem westward, eventually establishing religious/political beachheads (*ekklesiai*) even in Rome.[14] Neither Polybius nor Dionysius would have found Witherington's modern argument (Luke is like Polybius but unlike Livy) convincing, because Luke is praising Asians in Septuagintal style and even arguing that Athenians and Romans should worship this Asian God exclusively. For Polybius, Livy, or Dionysius, Acts could not be "true."

Penner then describes the ancient practice of writing *historia* (chapter 3). Persuasive and vivid narration (*narratio*) are both essential. To write persuasively can mean knowing when plausibility dictates silence. To write vividly can include the breakdown of *philia* in the family or of *philanthropia* in society, which generates fear and pity in the reader. For the historian this involves description (*ekphrasis*), putting something "before the eyes." This move correlates works of historiography with treatments of the exercise of description in antiquity, such as Philostratus the Elder's *Imagines*. I find it fascinating that the same term, *ekphrasis*, is used for both rhetorical history and Roman painting, the latter of which we New Testament interpreters have virtually ignored. Again, we might learn much about rhetorical (oral and

---

13. E. Gabba, *Dionysius and the History of Archaic Rome* (Berkeley: University of California Press, 1975), 27–29, 35–39, 53, 191–92, 199; and T. Hidber, *Das klassizische Manifest des Dionys von Halikarnass: Die Praefatio zu De oratoribus veteribus. Einleitung, Übersetzung, Kommentar* (Beiträge zur Altertumskunke 70; Stuttgart: Teubner, 1996), 18–19, referring to Dionysius, *The Ancient Orators* 1. Josephus (*Ant.* 5.220) refers to Israel as Asian.

14. Balch, "ΜΕΤΑΒΟΛΗ ΠΟΛΙΤΕΙΩΝ," 150–54, 162–70.

textual) *ekphrasis* from contemporary Hellenistic and Roman visual representation.[15] Painters, sculptors, and mosaicists portrayed many of the same scenes that Homer, Thucydides, Polybius, and Livy described verbally.[16]

Art can even help us understand the rhetorical terms used by the historians and orators. Demetrius, for example, distinguishes four rhetorical styles: simple, grand, elegant, and powerful (*On Style* 36).[17] They may all be combined, except that the grand and the simple styles exclude each other. Contemporary portraits of Pompey were powerful and elegant; portraits of Caesar were simple and powerful. The portrait of Pompey imitates Alexander the Great, emphasizing *pathos,* while that of Caesar emphasizes control.[18] The sculptor Stephanus created an athlete in neoclassical style (40–30 B.C.E.), a contrast to the famous sculpture of the priest Laocoon (writhing in pain while he and his two sons are being killed [martyred?] by Athena's snakes) in neo-Pergamonic style. Paul's own letters emphasize emotional appeals.[19] How would Demetrius have characterized Acts rhetorically? This question is essential for our examination of the text.

Besides persuasive and vivid narration, rhetorical historians describe the character's ethos that reveals moral choices. Again, not only rhetorical historians but also painters and sculptors portrayed characters' beauty and ethos.[20] This correlative adds support to Penner's observation that the ancient world classified people's status and character by geography, gender, and physical features. Finally, Penner treats Aristotle's *dianoia,* the thought or meaning of a work, here the speeches in relation to ethos; contrary to modern interpreters' opinions, he observes, the speeches are always related to the narrative. It is crucial that Penner discusses both Aristotle as well

---

15. J. J. Pollitt, *Art in the Hellenistic Age* (Cambridge: Cambridge University Press, 1986); and Ling, *Roman Painting.* The classic article is by K. Lehmann-Hartleben, "The Imagines of the Elder Philostratus," *Art Bulletin* 23 (1941): 16–44. See also C. Rietz and U. Egelhaaf, "Ekphrasis," *Der neue Pauly* 3 (1997): 942–50.

16. For example, the Casa del Criptoportico e Casa del Sacello Iliaco (Pompei I 6,2 and 4) in *Pompei: Pitture e Mosaici* (Enciclopedia Italiana; Rome: Arti Grafiche Pizzi S.p.A., 1990–2003), 1:193–329, has a series of eighty-three scenes, seventy-five of which are from the *Iliad.* The second-style paintings (40–30 B.C.E.) are reproduced on pp. 201–22 and the fourth-style reliefs (50–79 C.E.) on pp. 296–305. See further P. Zanker, *The Power of Images in the Age of Augustus* (trans. A. Shapiro; Ann Arbor: University of Michigan Press, 1990), 167–238.

17. I owe this comparison to S. Settis, *Laocoonte: Fama e stile* (Rome: Donzelli, 1999), 56–63.

18. K. Fittschen, "Pathossteigerung und Pathosdämpfung. Bemerkungen zu griechischen und römischen Porträts des 2. und 1. Jahrhunderts v. Chr.," *Archaeologischer Anzeiger* (1991): 253–70. See also D. L. Balch, "Paul's Portrait of Christ Crucified (Gal. 3:1) in Light of Paintings and Sculptures of Suffering and Death in Pompeiian and Roman Houses," in *Early Christian Families in Context: An Interdisciplinary Dialogue* (ed. D. L. Balch and C. Osiek; Grand Rapids: Eerdmans, 2003), 84–108.

19. T. H. Olbricht and J. L. Sumney, eds., *Paul and Pathos* (SBLSymS 16; Atlanta: Society of Biblical Literature, 2001).

20. K. Schefold, *Die Bildnisse der Antiken Dichter, Redner und Denker* (Basel: Schwabe, 1997). For the relation of Greco-Roman art to early Christianity, see Schefold, *Der religiöse Gehalt,* 417–34.

as the later *progymnasmata* by Theon, Hermogenes, and Aphthonius, typical of the manuals used to educate all ancient historians. Over and against the earlier, more formalistic approach of David Moessner that stresses arrangement and structure, Penner argues that the *progymnasmata* inculcate a culture of replication, teach a spirit of argumentation, and construct a plausible and ideal world rather than an actual and real one within the larger world of the *polis*.[21] Therefore, one who had learned a progymnastic poetics would not only create speeches but also write narrative drama in which to situate the speeches.

What audience(s) did this biographical historian address? Jewish apologetic historians rewrote the past (chapter 4). How hostile was the Roman society they were addressing? Apion represented strong anti-Jewish sentiments in Alexandria, and Greeks and Romans opposed conversion of their own to Judaism. There is, however, a near scholarly consensus that contemporary Judaism did not possess a missionary orientation.[22] G. E. Sterling's book has shifted the emphasis toward consideration of insider identity, although he still considers Jewish apologetic to be a response to outsider's negative perceptions.[23] Penner agrees rather with L. H. Feldman, who challenged the assumption of widespread Greco-Roman antipathy toward Judaism in this period, aside from an Alexandrian critic like Apion. Non-Jews like Strabo and Tacitus wrote less epideictic, more straightforward description (*ekphrasis*) with occasional negatives. Jewish apologetic is then largely epideictic, Penner argues, in concert with Roman historiography generally (see chapter 3). Defining the category more broadly than Sterling, Penner also discusses Esther and Daniel 1–6 as apologetic texts that compare pious Jews with non-Jews.

This discussion raises at least two questions for further discussion. Do Esther and the *Letter of Aristeas* belong in the same epideictic, apologetic category? The former is in some later additions hostile to Gentiles,[24] while the latter is assimilationist.[25] Additions A and F to Esther are so hostile to Gentiles that Josephus, writing for a primarily non-Jewish audience, omits them, whereas he knew and employed the other Additions.[26] Second, Penner concludes that the response to (internal and external) critics is occasional but

---

21. Penner, "Progymnastic Poetics," 432–38.
22. M. Goodman, *Mission and Conversion: Proselytizing in the Religious History of the Roman Empire* (Oxford: Clarendon, 1994), 8–9, 60-72; and L. H. Feldman, *Jew and Gentile in the Ancient World* (Princeton: Princeton University Press, 1993), 288–415.
23. G. E. Sterling, *Historiography and Self-definition: Josephus, Luke-Acts and Apologetic Historiography* (NovTSup 64; Leiden: Brill, 1992).
24. E. J. Bickerman, "The Colophon of the Greek Book of Esther," in *Studies in Jewish and Christian History* (AGJU 9; Leiden: Brill, 1976), 1:243–45.
25. J. M. G. Barclay, *Jews in the Mediterranean Diaspora from Alexander to Trajan (323 B.C.E.–117 C.E.)* (Edinburgh: T & T Clark, 1996), 138–50.
26. L. H. Feldman, *Studies in Josephus' Rewritten Bible* (JSJSup 58; Leiden: Brill, 1998), 530; cf. 518, 533, 535.

not extensive, except for Apion. Rewriting the biblical narrative functions primarily as retrenchment of Jewish self-perception. However, I observe that even Feldman agrees that Josephus's story of Balaam (*Ant.* 4.102–58) reflects internal, Jewish debates precisely in the narrative context in which Moses receives the laws from God.[27] These debates internal to contemporary Judaism include radical differences over how to relate to outsiders, disputes analogous to those in Acts 10–15, as well as to the deliberation in Dionysius over whether to grant citizenship to freed slaves (*Ant. rom.* 2.27). Are these not instances, as Penner agrees may happen, in which epideictic praise of the present community moves into conflictual, persuasive deliberation about the future? In summary, Penner adds additional support to the current scholarly assumption that Lukan apologetic is not addressed to outsiders, but rather primarily to insiders who are concerned with self-identity, as are Esther and Daniel.

The heart of Penner's contribution comes in chapter 5, where he focuses on ancient historiographical method and its import for the interpretation of Acts 6:1–8:3. The main plot device is conflict within and without (see his outline in chapter 2). Agreeing with David Moessner, Penner thinks the Gospel of Luke's travel narrative functions to contrast Jewish leadership with the prophet like Moses. Acts 1–7 similarly contrasts the household of Jerusalem Christians with Jewish leadership based in the temple. In comparison (*synkrisis*), friendship (*philia*) is at stake. Aristotle observed that when friendship breaks down, the audience feels pity and fear, especially when one brother kills another. There is a potential breakdown of *philia/philanthropia* within the early Jerusalem community and a second major tension between Jewish leadership and the newly formed community. Modern scholarship has often been more interested in the real nature of the theological and social conflict behind the text, but Penner examines the narrative itself: The primary function of this account is to depict the church coming together to address a need in its own community or in Jerusalem. Another contemporary historian, Dionysius of Halicarnassus, narrates Romans successfully mediating strife between rich and poor in their city. Both historians show an explicit interest in *stasis*; but in neither historian does conflict lead to chaos.[28] When E. Haenchen concludes that Luke reduces tension between Hellenists and Hebrews, he belittles the very conclusion Luke wanted his readers to draw!

There is constant interaction between the new Christian community and Jewish leaders; at every stage Jews are positively and negatively involved.

---

27. L. H. Feldman, *Judean Antiquities 1–4: Translation and Commentary* (vol. 3 in *Flavius Josephus: Translation and Commentary*, ed. Steve Mason; Leiden: Brill, 2000), 379–85, esp. n. 392 on *Ant.* 4.131. Cf. Feldman, *Josephus' Rewritten Bible*, 91–136; as well as G. Theissen, *The Religion of the Earliest Churches: Creating a Symbolic World* (Minneapolis: Fortress, 1999), 214.

28. Cf. Balch, "ΜΕΤΑΒΟΛΗ ΠΟΛΙΤΕΙΩΝ," 159–60.

Jewish rejection of the church is present throughout the narrative, but at almost every point some Jews also convert and support the movement. Penner here agrees with J. Jervell, G. E. Sterling, and L. C. A. Alexander: Luke deals with Jewish issues for a Jewish audience (perhaps especially in Rome), a thesis that will certainly generate further debate.

The entire narrative of Acts demonstrates increased mixing with the nations. Luke is concerned to demonstrate the *plausibility* of the manner in which the new people of the prophet incorporate this ever-increasing diversity. The historian Dionysius of Halicarnassus too had grounded Roman mixing with foreign nations into the very foundation of the Roman constitution.[29] Yet these foreigners do not change ancient Roman or Mosaic customs, or, if they do, God institutes the change.[30] The Hellenists in Acts represent a stage in this intermixing of nations, foreseen by God's prophets.

On the other hand, there is a breakdown of friendship with outsiders, with resultant *misanthropia* among (other) Jews. The Stephen narrative articulates conflict between the Mosaic prophet's new *politeia* and the *politeia* of (other) Jews, a polarization that causes discomfort among modern Christian scholars and theologians. The core of the narrative occurs in the accusations in 6:11, 13–14 on law and the temple, the centerpiece of Acts 6–7 and, for that matter, the whole book. Why does Stephen not directly address the charges? Quoting Theon's *Progymnasmata*, Penner brilliantly shows that to do so would have changed the speech from epideictic to judicial. Thus, the contrast between Stephen and the Jewish leadership is an argument from ethos; Luke narrates the persecution of the righteous by the unrighteous. The encomium on the righteous Stephen further reflects on the Christian community, which he represents.

Finally, Penner analyzes Stephen's speech as an invective. My summary and question-raising ends here. Penner continues to interpret the narrative and speech as an Aristotelian tragedy in which brother kills brother, arousing pity and fear in the reader. The rhetoric does not persuade readers to adopt a particular set of values (deliberative) or defend the new movement against hostile attackers (judicial). Luke affirms members of the house churches in their knowledge that Christianity represents the true line of development from Abraham to Joseph, Moses, David, Jesus, the apostles, Stephen, and Paul, representing the best of Greek and Deuteronomic values (epideictic). In summary, Penner disputes the consensus that Luke's narrative in Acts tones down conflicts in the early church. On the contrary, the plot emphasizes conflict, the breakdown of friendship to the point that brother kills brother, which would induce pity and fear in the audience. Acts is an example of progymnastic poetics in action.

---

29. Ibid., 167–70.
30. Ibid., 174–83.

Penner concludes that the historical-critical tradition from Baur to Hengel has misdirected discussion of the Stephen narrative and speech. Dibelius's distinction between Luke the historian and Luke the theologian too is a misconstrual. Todd Penner has thoroughly reshuffled categories that modern scholars have constructed, surely stimulating further lively discussion of the rhetorical *narrative* of Acts.

To conclude, I return to the correspondence between Roman rhetoric and art. Euripides wrote *Iphigenia at Aulis* in 405 B.C.E. After he died, there was a competition to paint Iphigenia, and Timanthes won over Colotes.[31] Timanthes' visual representation of Iphigenia voluntarily giving her body for Greece was so moving that a later editor has rewritten the conclusion to Euripides' tragedy. Euripides' narrative now concludes in the way that the viewers of Timanthes' fresco of Iphigenia expected. Todd Penner has helped us to ask how Luke, a biographical historian narrating conflicts among the earliest house churches, would have rewritten the story in an argumentative, ideal, political, progymnastic style, as his Christian audience in Roman culture would have expected.

---

31. Balch, "Paul's Portrait of Christ Crucified," 88–99.

Preface

This study represents a revised version of my doctoral dissertation, submitted to Emory University in the summer of 2000. It is the final product of nearly ten years of study that began at the University of Manitoba in 1989. In the course of this journey I developed a fascination with the literature of Hellenistic Judaism, the history of New Testament scholarship, the book of Acts, and, finally, the Greco-Roman sociocultural and literary background of early Christian texts. In writing this study, I managed to incorporate all of these loves so that a chapter is essentially devoted to each. In a sense, this study also stands as a testament to the profound influence that my teachers (Larry Hurtado, Carl Holladay, Luke Johnson, Vernon Robbins, and Hendrik Boers) have had on me; anyone knowing their work will see reflections of it throughout. Moreover, the methodology in which I was baptized — the *Religionsgeschichtliche Schule* approach to the study of early Christianity — bears an indelible mark on my scholarship, and lies at the center of this current study.

I cannot now remember precisely how I landed on the subject of the Hellenists in Acts 6:1–8:3 as the topic over which I would struggle for the remaining years of my doctoral studies. Given my interests stated above, however, the selection has turned out to be quite a logical one, as the Hellenists have been a key element in the history of scholarship dealing with both the influence of Hellenism on early Christianity and the reconstruction of Christian origins. The Greek-speaking Jews of Acts 6:1–8:3 have been viewed as the progenitors of the early mission to the Gentiles (also responsible for initiating some of its essential theological and sociological content), providing the lynchpin linking the Jerusalem traditions of Jesus with the message of Paul. The Hellenists are considered to have provided the nexus in which the original Jewish message of Jesus was transformed into a Greek universal proclamation of redemption. Although their appearance in the story of Acts is relatively brief, they play a critical role in the modern reconstructed history of early Christianity from behind the Lukan narrative. As I found when I conducted my research for chapter 1, the Hellenists are so fundamental for the history of scholarship on Christian origins that we can hardly now imagine a version of an incipient Christianity that dispenses with them.

Several key encounters with particular scholars have played a formative role with respect to the approach taken in this study. Working on Hellenistic Judaism with both Larry Hurtado and Carl Holladay, I was quickly introduced to the seminal work of Martin Hengel related to the influence of

Hellenism on Second Temple Judaism. Despite the importance of his work on Hellenistic Judaism, and although Hengel had done work on Acts and historiography, as well as on the Hellenists in particular, his place in this current study was solidified much more so by a personal encounter with him at Emory University in the early stages of this project. On that occasion I had the opportunity to query Hengel on the various "problems" related to the dual representation of Stephen before the council, focusing particularly on the inclusion in the text of both an orderly trial scene and a mob lynching. It was the general nature of his response that surprised me the most. At a particular point in the conversation Hengel abandoned his original position, that the trial scene was the more historically authentic feature of the account, and suggested that it probably was rather the mob lynching. In that moment I realized that, for Hengel, the historical fact of the existence of the Hellenists was much more important than any one particular scenario. Chapter 1 of this study represents my attempt to make sense of my conversation with Hengel on the Hellenists. The trajectory of scholarship I trace, set in a broad context, accounts for why the Hellenists have assumed such a critical role in our conversations, despite their brief and rather momentary appearance in the Lukan narrative itself.

My study of ancient rhetoric in a doctoral seminar with Vernon Robbins was perhaps the most critical component early on for the framing of this study. At this point Robbins was working on his *Tapestry of Early Christian Discourse*,[1] which implicitly shaped the manner in which we studied ancient rhetoric. It was in this seminar that I produced my first study of the Hellenist narrative, grappling with the speech and narrative from a rhetorical standpoint and focusing particularly on the ancient rhetorical Handbook tradition. Although my dissertation topic had not yet been set, I had a sense that trying to integrate speech and narrative in Acts would preoccupy a good portion of my academic energy in the years that followed. I thought it useful for this purpose to seize on what was clearly a long-standing scholarly convention — that the speech of Stephen did not fit well with the narrative setting in which it was placed — and to reevaluate whether or not there might not be a greater connection than had been realized by previous scholarship.

The paper I presented a year later for the "Rhetoric of the New Testament" session at the AAR/SBL Annual Meeting in 1996 in New Orleans, published in the *SBL Seminar Papers*, became the groundwork for the subsequent dissertation, although in large part for its failures rather than successes. Two encounters happened around that time that shaped the "dialogue" in this text. First, shortly after presenting the paper in New Orleans I offered the paper again at a doctoral colloquium at Emory University.

---

1. V. K. Robbins, *The Tapestry of Early Christian Discourse: Rhetoric, Society, and Ideology* (New York: Routledge, 1996).

Carl Holladay, who would become my *Doktorvater*, provided a response to my essay. His reply was a fair but devastating critique of my use of the Handbook tradition for analysis of a *narratio* outside of a speech, arguing that the rhetorical manuals are most clearly applicable to oratorical composition and practice. Particularly problematic was my attempt to treat the narrative of 6:7–15 with the speech of Acts 7 as a seamless whole based on rhetorical elaboration. It made me realize that if this project were to succeed I would need to reformulate my rhetorical approach. I had not yet at that time fully appreciated the avenues that socio-rhetorical criticism could provide, and I had yet to study more carefully Theon's *Progymnasmata*, which was, finally, the missing link I needed to understand that, while formal rhetorical analysis might fail at many points, the rhetorical culture of which the Handbooks were just one part was pervasive. Rhetorical composition was taking place in manifest ways and locations, but in contexts of which biblical scholars were largely unaware. One of the two prongs undergirding the discussion in chapter 3 was born out of this pointed critique of my earlier work. This broader observation, coupled with the passion that Luke Johnson gave me for Greco-Roman moral philosophy, particularly the dynamic duo of Plutarch and Lucian, helped me realize in my reading of ancient historiographical discussions, particularly Plutarch's treatise on Herodotus and Lucian's on writing history, that rhetoric and sociocultural *topoi* were intricately bound up together in ancient thinking about the task and "duty" of the historian. Chapter 3 of this study represents my attempt to come to grips with the broader implications of this intersection for the conceptualization of the writing of ancient *historia*.

A second memorable encounter was with Margaret Mitchell in a chance meeting early on in this project, in which she happened to ask me about my dissertation topic. I explained, quite proudly as I recall, that I was revisiting the Stephen narrative and making the argument, based on rhetorical analysis, that the entire unit functioned epideictically rather than judicially, the latter being the nearly unanimous consensus on the designation of the species of rhetoric in the text. I had not realized in that moment, of course, that I was speaking to someone who probably knew as much about epideictic rhetoric as any scholar and more than most. She pointedly remarked, "It's not epideictic, it's judicial! The speech is contextualized in a trial narrative!" It was clear to me after we parted ways a few minutes later that her words would hang over this study from beginning to end. In retrospect I consider Margaret Mitchell's words a gift, because knowing how others would likely respond in advance made me all the more determined to shore up the argument in chapters 4 and 5. The larger epideictic focus I proffer here may still not convince all readers, and many will no doubt be skeptical about its larger application to Acts as a whole, but I did persuade myself much more thoroughly as a result!

As it now stands, this study is the result of these larger "stories": In the first chapter, I lay out the evolution of the modern "story" of the Hellenists, reconstructing the essential lines of development from Baur to Hengel and beyond, tracing how the Hellenists became such a critical lynchpin in scholarly tradition, and assessing why the convention is still assumed as an assured datum of historical inquiry. The "story" reflected in chapter 1 does not arise in a vacuum but is in many respects the result of rather complex (and sometimes convoluted) narrative features in the Lukan text. In chapter 2 I lay out those components of the narrative in Acts 6:1–8:3 that have been critical for modern scholarly assessment of the role of Stephen and the Hellenists both in early Christian history and in the Lukan narrative, especially paying attention to the gaps and fissures in the Lukan account that have given scholars from Baur onward pause in the reading of the text.

In chapter 3 I make the shift to the sociocultural world of "Luke," the writer of Acts, examining both the sociocultural aspects and literary characteristics that were formative for the composition of the Lukan narrative. It is such a long chapter because I address some fundamental questions about the nature of ancient *historia*. First, I seek to blur modern conceptions and delineations of the "genre" of ancient historiography, situating Acts within the tradent of ancient *historia* but also making the argument that this designation still leaves open questions of meaning and the connection of the narrative to "history" as we traditionally understand that term. The third chapter therefore deals with the rhetoric of historiography, as well as the sociocultural and ideological underpinnings that shift the genre away from explicit moorings in "real," "brute" facts toward the literary elaboration of narratives within historical frames of reference, making the argument that *historia* must finally be considered to be the narrative in and of itself, irrespective of its actual ties to those features we generally assign to the term "historicity." Second, in the chapter I also set forth several key literary techniques that help support the broader historiographical ethos outlined in the earlier portion of the chapter. In short, then, I promote an essential distinction between ancient conceptions of *historia* as narrative and modern uses of the same *historia* both in historical and theological constructions of nascent Christianity.

In chapter 4 I extend the insights of the third chapter to the Jewish practice of rewriting biblical narratives, arguing for sociocultural and literary connections to the broader context set in the preceding chapter. The raison d'être for chapter 4 is that the historiographical context for Acts cannot be established simply in concert with the Greco-Roman tradition, but needs to be fleshed out more fully within its Jewish (particularly Hellenistic Jewish) context, since many of the themes raised in Acts 6:1–8:3 are readily understandable in this trajectory. Further, the emphasis on epideictic historiography that surfaces in chapter 3 is more explicitly tied to Jewish historiography in the fourth chapter, thereby setting the precedent for understanding "apologetic" historiography as being essentially, although not necessarily solely, about the establishment of personal and group identity through the sociocultural, literary, and ideological tropes of praise of one's own history and culture, as well as the possible denigration of an established or implied opposition. This attempt to read Jewish historiography, and then Acts in particular, through this larger epideictic lens represents one of the essential reconfigurations of more traditional readings of the Hellenist narrative. Moreover, the fourth chapter contributes substantially to my reading of Stephen's speech in chapter 5, particularly with respect to the reconfiguration of the Jewish foundation narrative in Hellenistic Jewish authors. In the fifth and final chapter, then, I tackle the Lukan narrative of Stephen and the Hellenists, seeking to situate a reading of that textual unit within the Greco-Roman and Jewish sociocultural and literary contexts established in chapters 3 and 4. The rereading of the narrative in light of the prior chapters is intended to provide an alternative contouring of the issues considered essential for interpreting the text. The resultant position articulated in the final chapter is that Stephen and the Hellenists perform a critical narrative function for Luke, serving to highlight the praiseworthy features of the newly formed community in Jerusalem.

The final product, then, is essentially a study of both modern scholarly uses of the Hellenist narrative and the Lukan "use" of the Hellenists read against the Greco-Roman and Jewish literary and sociocultural contexts delineated in this study. I have thus argued for a broad but fundamental distinction in the questions we often ask of the narrative and the "answers" the material itself may in fact yield. But more than that, this study suggests that there is also a connection between the way we read the material and the manner in which it was written, and that, given our own modern ideological predilections, there is something in and/or about the narrative that feeds, but on another level also creates or at least controls to a degree, our scholarly assumptions and movements. A hermeneutical dance of sorts takes place between text, interpreters, and respective historical and cultural contexts: We are shaped by the text inasmuch as we shape it. If correct, this observation ultimately attests to the literary and rhetorical power and prowess, as well as the historical force, of the Lukan narrative itself.

In explaining some of the study's unique contours based on various formative encounters, I suppose I have produced something of a "foundation narrative" for this current monograph. Of course, there are other stories, larger and smaller, that would explain in a fuller way the issues raised and the positions taken in this study. Moreover, the trajectory of scholarship that begins here has not ended, but has continued to develop in the ensuing years. New encounters bring new issues and, in a truly socio-rhetorical spirit, this study would no doubt be reconfigured in significantly different ways were I to start over from the beginning. I have resisted rewriting it, however, mostly because I am not sure it could be done, at least in the way that would be true to its original intent. As I have looked back on this study in the past months, realizing it is the culminating product of my graduate work, I see many aspects I can appreciate as being formative for me as a scholar, but I also observe numerous features I would now reformulate (and some I would abandon). Yet I know that as far as stories go, the one I am currently writing would not be possible (let alone conceivable) had this one here not been told (what now seems) long ago.

Acknowledgments

Scholarly works do not appear in a vacuum. They partake of the ebbs and flows of life over a period of years. Both professionally and personally numerous individuals and communities have contributed to the coming-into-being of this current study. I am grateful for all that I have received, great and small, from so many, near and far, all of whom have contributed in some way to this project.

This monograph represents the culminating stage of the six years I spent at Emory University in the Graduate Division of Religion pursuing a Ph.D. in New Testament and Christian Origins. Emory proved to be a most welcoming place for a Canadian looking for an adventure beyond the border. My work on Acts 6:1–8:3 was initiated in Vernon Robbins's seminar on the New Testament and ancient rhetoric. He strongly encouraged this project from the beginning, and contributed helpful criticisms and insights along the way. His imprint is evident throughout, and I am grateful to Vernon for his friendship and generosity over the years. Hendrick Boers's seminar on New Testament interpretation kindled my interest in the perennial questions of biblical studies, and I am appreciative for his work with and on me. Roberta Bondi exemplified the model of scholarship I hope someday to approximate more fully: a passionate engagement of ancient texts and traditions arising out of one's own personal commitments and experiences. John Hayes embodied the ideal of the scholar who really does "know it all." He taught me that there are rarely any new ideas, cultivating, in the process, a love for the history of scholarship. Gail O'Day stepped in at critical stages in my studies to provide support and encouragement. She also rendered numerous valuable criticisms and insights on the dissertation as one of its readers. Most important, she made me laugh on more occasions than I can count, constantly reminding me of the deep-rooted humanity of my scholarly endeavors.

Luke Johnson was a mentor throughout my time at Emory. My encounters with him in and out of class were formative both academically and personally. I have learned much about writing, reading, and thinking from Luke. His high level of engagement and commitment to intellectual rigor have left an indelible impression. Finally, Carl Holladay, my adviser in this project, inspired its growth throughout. He was there to spur me on when I seemed to languish, and he encouraged ever higher levels of engagement with the material. My first seminar at Emory in the fall of 1993 was his course on Jewish backgrounds, and I have tried to emulate his passion for this study ever since. Carl has provided outstanding guidance over the years, keeping me from making numerous errors in judgment. His eye for detail and nuance has greatly enhanced not only this study but my other scholarly pursuits as well.

My time at Emory was marked by the establishment of new friendships. I am grateful to those fellow students in the department who provided much needed release from the pressures of studies. During the ardor of researching and writing, Michael Hyrniuk and Ingrid Haus afforded memorable breaks, which enriched my academic experience by reminding me of the relativity of the pursuit of knowledge and the futility of scholarship as an end in itself. Cameron McKenzie always made coming home feel a little less strange, and the stimulating conversations we had on biblical studies over the years have helped shape my thinking about the Bible and "story" in the ancient and modern worlds. Leigh Lytle and Michelle Malone proved to be "neighbors" in the truest sense of that word, providing me with one of the major highlights of my time in Atlanta: house-sitting their furry family (Tigger, Tookey, Wheezy, Peanut, and Lucy). For those of you who can appreciate the kindred nature of animal spirits, these felines proved to be among my closest allies, and the hours I spent with them gave me some of the most revitalizing breaks from writing that I have ever experienced.

The original dissertation reached its conclusion a fair distance from Atlanta. In 1999 I began teaching at Austin College in Sherman, Texas. The support I have received from colleagues at Austin College has been outstanding. I could not have found a better home in which to begin my professional career. It was here at Austin College that I was able to come out of the closet as a humanist in the study of religion and culture. Although such affirmations are still too rare in the field of biblical studies, this institution embraced me as its own and gave me the courage to explore, at my own pace, the ramifications of this commitment and calling. I am indebted particularly to Max Grober, who took on the sometimes daunting task of being a mentor and friend, eliciting some of the highest levels of academic engagement even in the short walks to the men's room. Bill Moore taught me by example that Sauron (and perhaps even the Balrog) is still best challenged in and through the materials we study and teach and that evoke our own passionate engagement. Moreover, the concurrent deans of the Humanities, Dan Setterberg and Bernice Melvin, and the vice president for Academic Affairs, Michael Imhoff, have been highly supportive of and helpful in my efforts to pursue research as a constituent element of my pedagogical commitments at the institution. Further, I am grateful to the staff of Abell Library, who, under the direction of Larry Hardesty, have been most helpful in securing materials over the past few years, making my research endeavors so much easier as a result. The students at Austin College have also proved themselves to be challenging and engaging, patiently allowing me to work out in class some of the broader implications of the research embedded herein. Special mention goes to Stacy Smith, Mary Newburg, Abby Wood, Amy Summers-Minette, Alex Stehn, Caty Locke, Sloane Franklin, Lindy Olsen, Rebecca Napier, Michele Kennerly, Ann Melton, and Anne Jernberg, all of whom have reminded me again and again that learning is a wonderful thing and that it goes in both directions. I am grateful also to Lindy Olsen and Michele Kennerly for their editorial eyes on various drafts of this manuscript. I feel fortunate to have had such extraordinary undergraduate students, whom I felt I could entrust with such labors. Bonnie Roos came to Austin College as this work was taking its current shape. Her companionship has proved most stimulating, and her rants, which are tremendously amusing, have brightened some darker days. Finally, my colleague in the Religion Department, Steve Stell, deserves special recognition. The opportunities that have come my way ultimately have been possible to pursue largely because of his collegiality and support. If Platonic forms actually exist, Steve is without a doubt the "ideal" colleague and mentor. I will always owe a great debt to him, who has made me laugh hard and ruminate long and reflect deeply over what it means to be human in this and other worlds.

Between the finishing of the dissertation and the current reconfiguring of that study into this book, I had the most extraordinary experience as a participant in a workshop on "Teaching and Learning for Undergraduate Religion Faculty" sponsored by the Wabash Center for Teaching and Learning in Theology and Religion. The hospitality and friendship and mentoring that I experienced in that year-long period was beyond what I, as a hardened skeptic, could have imagined. Special recognition goes to both Paul Myhre, who thankfully understood the intimate connection between laughter and learning, and Milton Moreland, who read my dissertation early on and has been a strong advocate of this project. Finally, Patricia Killen was the leader of the workshop for Wabash. Patricia gave me so much more than I had expected; most of all she gave me confidence to pursue my academic and pedagogical commitments and visions unbounded and unfettered. For that I will always be grateful.

This project also received some strong interaction and engagement by several noted scholars in the postdissertation phase. I am grateful in particular for Larry Hurtado's critical challenges to an earlier draft of the manuscript, as well as the interest and encouragement of Samuel Byrskog. Special thanks goes to three individuals, all of whom provided extensive feedback on this work in its original incarnation. Harold Attridge offered helpful comments and kept me from making some embarrassing blunders, displaying patience along the way with some unfortunate phrasing by this junior scholar. David Moessner supplied the most substantive feedback. He and I disagree on many points with respect to ancient historiography and literary poetics, but I have learned much from his scholarly research, and he has kept me on my toes throughout the rewriting process. Finally, this work may well not have seen the light of publication had it not been for the strong support of David

Balch. I have admired David's work for many years, and it proved fortuitous that our paths crossed in the fall of 2001. I am most grateful for his willingness to engage the issues of critical importance to the ancient world (and our own) with a quiet intensity, a humble spirit, a prodigious intellect, and an open mind. He has provided a model of scholarly engagement I will strive to emulate.

The publication phase of this project was enthusiastically supported by the Emory Studies in Early Christianity board, especially Vernon Robbins and David Gowler. I am also appreciative of the efforts of Henry Carrigan and Amy Wagner to see this manuscript through to publication. Particularly helpful was Amy's persistence and final negotiations, which proved critical in finally getting this book out! Special thanks to Don Parker-Burgard for the superb copyediting of the manuscript, which significantly improved the final product. As well, John Eagleson did a speedy and excellent job of typesetting the manuscript providing along the way much needed last minute aid to a scholar in stress. I am grateful also to Jason Carl, and especially Michele K. and Jacqueline K. for their efforts in indexing the manuscript in the final hours. Further, Caroline Vander Stichele gave an earlier version of this manuscript a thorough read and offered substantive interaction over many of the issues herein. Over the past four years Caroline and I have been engaged in various ancillary projects that have also greatly informed and shaped my current research agenda and this final product. The generosity in friendship and rigor in academic engagement of this "colleague in action" have been a constant source of inspiration.

I would like to express my deepest gratitude to my parents, Charles and Pauline Penner, for their unwavering support and encouragement over my (what seemed like endless) years of study. The completion of this project would not have been possible without their generosity and support; it is for this reason that I have dedicated the book to them. Further, Jacqueline Klassen has been there for the ride — up and down — over the past ten years as this project took shape. She has been a source of strength and encouragement throughout much of this work, and I will always be indebted to her for her many kindnesses, those seen and unseen. Jacqueline has taught me by example that the past will always be a part of the future, affirming what the Canadian novelist Margaret Laurence once observed: "The river flow[s] in both directions."

Sad news came as this project drew to a close in the fall of 2003, when I learned that two former mentors of mine had passed away. Carl Ridd (University of Winnipeg) and Gordon Harland (University of Manitoba) died within several months of each other. While both shaped me more than I will ever fully recognize, I do know that I could not have written what is here now if I had not learned so much about reading texts and cultures from them before.

Finally, although they cannot fully comprehend it, Eli, Efi, Hank, and Buzz, my current furry friends, have been an enormous source of hope and life in the writing of this monograph. It was with deep sadness that Cuthbert, who provided immense delight in the final stages of the dissertation, left so suddenly and with such seeming ease. I also want to pay special tribute to my other muses, especially Carrie Brownstein, Corin Tucker, and Janet Weiss, aka Sleater Kinney. Their ability to stay true to themselves in the midst of the world as it is, and to image a world that might yet be, has provided inspiration from the inception of this work (*Dig Me Out*) through to its culmination (*One Beat*). Their music kindles that desire to join Macbeth in his clarion call: "Lay on, MacDuff, and damn'd be him that first cries, 'Hold, enough!'"

Abbreviations

Primary Sources

Aelius Aristides
- *Or.* — *Orationes* / *Orations*

Aphthonius
- *Prog.* — *Progymnasmata*

Aristotle
- *Poet.* — *Poetica* / *Poetics*
- *Rhet.* — *Rhetorica* / *Rhetoric*

Arrian
- *Anab.* — *Anabasis of Alexander*

Cicero
- *De or.* — *De oratore* / *On the Orator*
- *Fam.* — *Epistulae ad familiares* / *Letters to His Friends*
- *Inv.* — *De inventione rhetorica* / *On Invention*
- *Leg.* — *De legibus* / *On the Laws*
- *Off.* — *De officiis* / *On Duties*
- *Or.* — *Orator*

Demetrius
- *Eloc.* — *De elocutione* / *On Style*

Dionysius of Halicarnassus
- *Ant. rom.* — *Antiquitates romanae* / *Roman Antiquities*
- *Comp.* — *De compositione verborum* / *On Literary Composition*
- *Lys.* — *De Lysia* / *On Lysias*
- *Pomp.* — *Epistula ad Pompeium Geminum* / *Letter to Gnaeus Pompeius*
- *Thuc.* — *De Thucydide* / *On Thucydides*

Epictetus
- *Diatr.* — *Diatribai (Dissertationes)* / *Discourses*

Isocrates
- *Hel. enc.* — *Helenae encomium*
- *Nic.* — *Nicocles*

Josephus
- Ant.   Antiquitates judaicae / Jewish Antiquities
- C. Ap.   Contra Apionem / Against Apion

Lucian
- Hist.   Historia / How to Write History
- Philops.   Philopseudes / The Lover of Lies
- Ver. hist.   Vera historia / A True Story

Maximus of Tyre
- Or.   Orationes / Orations

Philo
- Abr.   De Abrahamo / On the Life of Abraham
- Ios.   De Iosepho / On the Life of Joseph
- Migr.   De migratione Abrahami / On the Migration of Abraham
- Mos.   De vita Mosis / On the Life of Moses
- QE   Quaestiones et solutiones in Exodum / Questions and Answers on Exodus
- Virt.   De virtutibus / On the Virtues

Pliny the Younger
- Ep.   Epistulae / Letters

Plutarch
- Adul. amic.   Quomodo adulator ab amico internoscatur / How to Tell a Flatterer from a Friend
- Her. mal.   De Herodoti malignitate / On the Malice of Herodotus
- Thes.   Theseus / Life of Theseus

Quintilian
- Inst.   Institutio oratoria
- Rhet. Alex.   Rhetorica ad Alexandrum
- Rhet. Her.   Rhetorica ad Herennium

Sallust
- Bell. Cat.   Bellum catalinae / The War with Catiline

Seneca
- Ep.   Epistulae morales / Epistles

Sextus Empiricus
- Adv. Gram.   Adversus Grammaticos / Against the Grammarians

Suetonius
- Aug.   Divus Augustus

Tacitus
- *Ann.* — *Annales / Annals*
- *Hist.* — *Historiae / Histories*

Secondary Sources

AB	Anchor Bible
ABD	*Anchor Bible Dictionary.* Edited by D. N. Freedman. 6 vols. New York, 1992.
ABRL	Anchor Bible Reference Library
ACS	American Classical Studies
AGJU	Arbeiten zur Geschichte des antiken Judentums und des Urchristentums
ALGHJ	Arbeiten zur Literatur und Geschichte des hellenistischen Judentums
AnBib	Analecta biblica
AnG	Analecta Gregoriana
ANRW	*Aufstieg und Niedergang der römischen Welt: Geschichte und Kultur Roms im Spiegel der neueren Forschung.* Edited by H. Temporini and W. Haase. Berlin, 1972–
ATS	Altertumswissenschaftliche Texte und Studien
BAFCS	*The Book of Acts in Its First-Century Setting.* Edited by B. W. Winter. Grand Rapids, 1993–
BBB	Bonner biblische Beiträge
BETL	Bibliotheca ephemeridum theologicarum lovaniensium
BibIntS	Biblical Interpretation Series
BS	Biblical Seminar
BTB	*Biblical Theology Bulletin*
BZ	*Biblische Zeitschrift*
BZNW	Beihefte zur Zeitschrift für die neutestamentliche Wissenschaft und die Kunde der älteren Kirche
CA	*Classical Antiquity*
CBET	Contributions to Biblical Exegesis and Theology
CBQ	*Catholic Biblical Quarterly*
CBQMS	Catholic Biblical Quarterly Monograph Series
CPJ	*Corpus papyrorum judaicorum.* Edited by V. Tcherikover and A. Fuks. 3 vols. Cambridge, 1957–64.
CRINT	Compendia rerum iudaicarum ad Novum Testamentum
CurBR	*Currents in Biblical Research*

EBib	Etudes bibliques
EKK	Evangelisch-katholischer Kommentar zum Neuen Testament
ESEC	Emory Studies in Early Christianity
FCNT	Feminist Companion to the New Testament and Early Christian Writings
FGH	*Die Fragmente der griechischen Historiker.* Edited by F. Jacoby. Leiden, 1954–64
FRLANT	Forschungen zur Religion und Literatur des Alten und Neuen Testaments
FzB	Forschung zur Bibel
GR	*Greece and Rome*
HCS	Hellenistic Culture and Society
HDR	Harvard Dissertations in Religion
HNT	Handbuch zum Neuen Testament
HTKNT	Herders theologischer Kommentar zum Neuen Testament
HTR	*Harvard Theological Review*
HTS	Harvard Theological Studies
HUCA	*Hebrew Union College Annual*
ICC	International Critical Commentary
ITS	Innsbrucker theologische Studien
JBL	*Journal of Biblical Literature*
JETS	*Journal of the Evangelical Theological Society*
JRS	*Journal of Roman Studies*
JSJ	*Journal for the Study of Judaism in the Persian, Hellenistic, and Roman Periods*
JSJSup	Journal for the Study of Judaism in the Persian, Hellenistic, and Roman Periods: Supplement Series
JSNT	*Journal for the Study of the New Testament*
JSNTSup	Journal for the Study of the New Testament: Supplement Series
JSOTSup	Journal for the Study of the Old Testament: Supplement Series
JSPSup	Journal for the Study of the Pseudepigrapha: Supplement Series
JTS	*Journal of Theological Studies*
KEKNT	Kritisch-exegetischer Kommentar über das Neue Testament (Meyer-Kommentar)
LD	Lectio divina
LSJ	Liddell, H. G., R. Scott, H. S. Jones, *A Greek-English Lexicon.* 9th ed. with revised supplement. Oxford, 1996.

MJS	Münsteraner judaistische Studien
MnSup	Mnemosyne, bibliotheca classica Batava, Supplement
NIGTC	New International Greek Testament Commentary
NovT	*Novum Testamentum*
NovTSup	Supplements to Novum Testamentum
ns	new series
NTAbh	Neutestamentliche Abhandlungen
NTS	*New Testament Studies*
PA	Philosophia antiqua
PEQ	*Palestinian Exploration Quarterly*
PRSt	*Perspectives in Religious Studies*
QD	Quaestiones disputatae
RelSRev	*Religious Studies Review*
ResQ	*Restoration Quarterly*
SBAB	Stuttgarter biblische Aufsatzbände
SBL	Society of Biblical Literature
SBLDS	SBL Dissertation Series
SBLMS	SBL Monograph Series
SBLRBS	SBL Resources for Biblical Study
SBLSemS	SBL Semeia Studies
SBLSP	SBL Seminar Papers
SBLSymS	SBL Symposium Series
SBLTT	SBL Texts and Translations
SBLWGRW	SBL Writings from the Greco-Roman World
SBS	Stuttgarter Bibelstudien
SCHNT	Studia ad corpus Hellenisticum Novi Testamenti
SCJ	Studies in Christianity and Judaism; Etudes sur le Christianisme et le Judaisme
SFSHJ	South Florida Studies in the History of Judaism
SH	Studia Hellenistica
SHC	Studies in Hellenistic Civilization
SHR	Studies in the History of Religion
SJLA	Studies in Judaism in Late Antiquity
SNTSMS	Society for New Testament Studies Monograph Series
SP	Sacra pagina
SPB	Studia post-biblica

SSEJC	Studies in Scripture in Early Judaism and Christianity
StBL	Studies in Biblical Literature
STDJ	Studies on the Texts of the Desert of Judah
Str-B	Strack, H. L., and P. Billerbeck. *Kommentar zum Neuen Testament aus Talmud und Midrasch*. 6 vols. Munich, 1922–61.
SUNT	Studien zur Umwelt des Neuen Testaments
SVTP	Studia in Veteris Testamenti pseudepigraphica
TANZ	Texte und Arbeiten zum neutestamentlichen Zeitalter
TAPS	Transactions of the American Philosophical Society
TDNT	*Theological Dictionary of the New Testament*. Edited by G. Kittel and G. Friedrich. Translated by G. W. Bromiley. 10 vols. Grand Rapids, 1964–76.
TF	Theologische Forschung
TSAJ	Texte und Studien zum antiken Judentum
TU	Texte und Untersuchungen
TZTh	*Tübinger Zeitschrift für Theologie*
WMANT	Wissenschaftliche Monographien zum Alten und Neuen Testament
WUNT	Wissenschaftliche Untersuchungen zum Neuen Testament
ZNW	*Zeitschrift für die neutestamentliche Wissenschaft und die Kunde der älteren Kirche*

I

Hellenists and *Historia*

Constructing Christian History and Theology in Modern Scholarship

History in/of Acts

Over thirty-five years ago W. C. van Unnik pointed out that one of the great storm centers of debate in New Testament scholarship was over whether Luke ought to be treated as a historian or a theologian, arguing that only a thorough study of Luke's relationship to the historians of antiquity would reveal the answer.[1] In this debate, the choice between theologian and historian carried with it direct implications for understanding Acts as *historia*. In their response to the more skeptical German tradition on the matter of the reliability of Acts, earlier British scholars (e.g., W. M. Ramsay) had argued that in most details Acts was an accurate historical record of the events of the early church. The emphasis on Luke's reliability in Acts received some support from German scholars as well, most notably the New Testament critic A. von Harnack, who brought to the forefront of discussion and debate the question of sources used in the composition of Acts. Acts could be read as a reliable historical narrative precisely because the writer relied on historical sources.

With H. J. Cadbury's 1927 groundbreaking study, however, a significant shift took place. Luke-Acts began to be viewed as a literary product. In other words, the process of writing itself came to the foreground. As Cadbury stated, "We should inquire what the author thought took place before we ask what took place. We should ask why the author narrates it as he does before we ask whether it is true as he narrates it. The study of the making of a book is a prerequisite to its evaluation."[2] Despite making this significant shift, Cadbury's own conclusions on the nature of Lukan *historia* were more conservative. Cadbury argued that, for the most part, the writer relied on sources and that these, arising in early Christian communities, were largely reliable, providing a high degree of control over the production of

---

1. W. C. van Unnik, "Luke-Acts: A Storm Center in Contemporary Scholarship," in *Studies in Luke-Acts* (ed. L. E. Keck and J. L. Martyn; Nashville: Abingdon, 1966), 15–32.
2. H. J. Cadbury, *The Making of Luke-Acts* (2d ed.; London: SPCK, 1958), 362.

the two-volume work. The only significant place for Lukan creativity then, according to Cadbury, came in the speeches.[3]

While Cadbury's work was significant for its stress on understanding the *historia* of Acts in its historical and literary contexts, his German contemporary M. Dibelius laid the groundwork for the emphasis on Luke as a theologian. For Dibelius, the meaning behind the presentation of particular events — not the accuracy of those historical events — was crucial. Although Dibelius still thought of Luke as having been Paul's actual traveling companion, in numerous essays he accented Luke's particular theological vision that shaped and controlled his material through the creation of speeches, the shaping of narrative, the emphasis on the typical, the art of description, and the linking of particular episodes in sequence.[4] Beyond this, Luke was also perceived as a "herald and evangelist, a rôle which he fulfils completely in his first book and wishes ultimately to fulfil also in Acts."[5] In a similar way to Cadbury, however, Dibelius remained fairly conservative in his historical conclusions. Nevertheless, he came down on the other side of the line: While Luke was no doubt an ancient historian, his role as "preacher" in the speeches indicated that he could never fully abandon the kerygmatic thrust of early Christian tradition in order to become absorbed fully in the process of writing history.[6] With Dibelius, then, the line between Luke as historian and Luke as theologian was drawn, although clearly that line was grayer as a result of Dibelius's research. *Historia* could no longer entail for the modern interpreter simply the impartial recording of events, but involved interpretation and the imputation of meaning into past actions.

H. Conzelmann gave fullest expression to this particular trajectory in his study on the theological program of Luke-Acts.[7] Departing from the more conservative conclusions of Dibelius, Conzelmann argued that the writer of Luke-Acts was more concerned with portraying a particular view of *Heilsgeschichte* than providing an accurate representation of the past. Conzelmann's study solidified in many quarters the primacy of Luke's role as theologian, evangelist, and preacher. In his commentary, E. Haenchen developed in more detail the initial program of Conzelmann and firmly

---

3. See H. J. Cadbury, "The Speeches in Acts," in *The Beginnings of Christianity: The Acts of the Apostles* (ed. F. J. Foakes Jackson and K. Lake; London: Macmillan, 1933), 5:426–27. On the still conservative nature of Cadbury's conclusions, see B. R. Gaventa, "The Peril of Modernizing Henry Joel Cadbury," in *Cadbury, Knox, and Talbert: American Contributions to the Study of Acts* (ed. M. C. Parsons and J. B. Tyson; Atlanta: Scholars Press, 1992), 15–16, 25–26.

4. See particularly M. Dibelius, "The First Christian Historian," "The Speeches in Acts and Ancient Historiography," and "The Acts of the Apostles in the Setting of the History of Early Christian Literature," in *Studies in the Acts of the Apostles* (ed. H. Greeven; London: SCM, 1956), 123–37, 138–91, 192–206.

5. Dibelius, "First Christian Historian," 134–35.

6. Dibelius, "Speeches in Acts," 183–85.

7. H. Conzelmann, *The Theology of St. Luke* (trans. G. Buswell; New York: Harper & Row, 1961).

established the dividing line between Luke as historian and Luke as theologian.[8] The historical reliability of much of the Acts account was in question, but this was, in Haenchen's view, not the real point of Luke's work in the final analysis. Luke wanted to "capture and edify" his readers, contributing to the spread of God's word through the retelling and reshaping of the past.[9]

Van Unnik's outline for future study on the problem of Acts should be understood in this context. In the mid-sixties the views of Conzelmann and Haenchen were just gaining widespread support. The reaction by more conservative scholarship was also achieving momentum. Following upon van Unnik's advice, scholars began to study Luke-Acts against the backdrop of ancient historiography, picking up where Cadbury had left off several decades earlier. E. Plümacher, for example, wrote one of the first substantial treatments comparing Luke with the historians of antiquity.[10] Numerous other studies appeared in the ensuing years. However, despite the ongoing research, Luke-Acts in many respects still remains a storm center in modern New Testament scholarship. Debate over some of the fundamental issues endures, especially with respect to the nature of Acts as *historia*. Framed by this discussion in the 1960s, the issue of whether Luke should be viewed primarily as a preacher/theologian or a historian is still a matter of contention.

As in many cases of such ongoing debates, the earlier issues have received new contours in the process of discussion.[11] One of the hallmarks of recent investigation of the nature of *historia* in Acts centers on the treatment of the genre of the work as a whole. Since it is recognized that the genre of a work has a direct bearing on its content and function, researchers have sought to elucidate the import of genre for understanding the nature and character of the Lukan text. As a result of this trajectory of inquiry, various primary genres have been set forth for Luke-Acts, including biography, history, and novel.

One of the foremost proponents for viewing Luke-Acts as a form of ancient biography is C. H. Talbert. Based upon his analysis of the literary patterns shared by the gospel and Acts and drawing upon the similarities between Luke's two-volume work and Diogenes Laertius's *Lives of the Philosophers*, Talbert argues that Luke-Acts displays the same pattern that

---

8. E. Haenchen, *The Acts of the Apostles: A Commentary* (trans. R. Mcl. Wilson et al.; Philadelphia: Westminster, 1971).
9. E. Haenchen, "The Book of Acts as Source Material for the History of Early Christianity," in *Studies in Luke-Acts* (ed. Keck and Martyn), 260, 278.
10. E. Plümacher, *Lukas als hellenistischer Schriftsteller: Studien zur Apostelgeschichte* (SUNT 9; Göttingen: Vandenhoeck & Ruprecht, 1972).
11. See my recent assessment of the current shape of discussion in T. Penner, "Contextualizing Acts," in *Contextualizing Acts: Lukan Narrative and Greco-Roman Discourse* (ed. T. Penner and C. Vander Stichele; SBLSymS 20; Atlanta: Scholars Press, 2003), 1–21; and idem, "Madness in the Method? The Acts of the Apostles in Current Study," *CurBR* 2 (2004): 224–95.

is reflected in Laertius's sources: the life of a founder (A) followed by a succession list or narrative of his followers (B).[12] Talbert views this A/B pattern combined with a third element — summary of doctrine (C)[13] — as one trajectory in the ancient biographical tradition. While some such biographies were of purely literary interest, many others, according to Talbert, served specific didactic functions. Luke-Acts, in his view, belongs to that latter type.[14] In this case, the *historia* of biography takes on a particular shape: The A/B pattern is narrated in such a way so as to highlight the essence of an individual and the tradition that he established, with a view toward attacking foes or inculcating values.

Few scholars, however, have followed Talbert's designation of Luke-Acts as ancient biography.[15] Rather, the majority has adopted the most obvious generic identification for Luke's work: ancient historiographical writing.[16] Within this larger category, however, there are numerous subgenres proffered for Luke-Acts, based predominantly on how the function of its content is construed. Here the nature and, more important, the character of *historia* are intricately connected to what is perceived to be the overarching motivation and intent in writing. As a result, some of the more prominent designations are historical monograph, political historiography, universal/general history, apologetic history, institutional history, kerygmatic history, biblical history, typological history, and historical *hagiographa*. In each of these designations the literary influences and projected aim of Luke-Acts differ. Part of the reason for this range of opinion is primarily the diversity that exists among

---

12. See C. H. Talbert, *Literary Patterns, Theological Themes, and the Genre of Luke-Acts* (SBLMS 20; Missoula, Mont.: Scholars Press, 1974), esp. 125–39; and his most recent defense of his thesis in "The Acts of the Apostles: Monograph or *Bios?*" in *History, Literature, and Society in the Book of Acts* (ed. B. Witherington; Cambridge: Cambridge University Press, 1996), 58–72.

13. According to Talbert, Luke-Acts lacks this third component (*Literary Patterns*, 131).

14. See further C. H. Talbert, "Biographies of Philosophers and Rules as Instruments of Religious Propaganda in Mediterranean Antiquity," *ANRW* 2.16.2 (1978): 1619–51; and C. H. Talbert and P. L. Stepp, "Succession in Mediterranean Antiquity, Part 1: The Lukan Milieu; Part 2: Luke-Acts," *SBLSP* 37 (1998): 148–79.

15. For critical appraisals of Talbert's thesis, see D. L. Barr and J. L. Wentling, "The Conventions of Classical Biography and the Genre of Luke-Acts: A Preliminary Study," in *Luke-Acts: New Perspectives from the Society of Biblical Literature Seminar* (ed. C. H. Talbert; New York: Crossroad, 1984), 63–88; D. P. Moessner, "And Once Again, What Sort of 'Essence'? A Response to Charles Talbert," *Semeia* 43 (1988): 75–84; and J. B. Chance, "Talbert's New Perspectives on Luke-Acts: The ABCs of Ancient Lives," in *Cadbury, Knox, and Talbert* (ed. Parsons and Tyson), 181–201.

16. L. C. A. Alexander has argued that such a designation is not as obvious as many scholars have made it out to be and that the preface of Luke-Acts has little in common with the Greco-Roman historiographical tradition as a whole. See her *The Preface to Luke's Gospel: Literary Convention and Social Context in Luke 1.1–4 and Acts 1.1* (SNTSMS 78; Cambridge: Cambridge University Press, 1993); and "The Preface to Acts and the Historians," in *History, Literature, and Society* (ed. Witherington), 73–103; as well as the recent response by D. E. Aune, "Luke 1:1-4: Historical or Scientific Prooimion?" in *Paul, Luke, and the Graeco-Roman World: Essays in Honour of Alexander J. M. Wedderburn* (ed. A. Christophersen et al.; JSNTSup 217; Sheffield: Sheffield Academic Press, 2003), 138–48.

the ancient writings frequently categorized as "history." The matter is further complicated in that Luke-Acts is always both similar to and different from its literary predecessors and supposed models. Nevertheless, despite the seeming disparity in specific subgeneric classification, overall there is some essential agreement. In particular, most scholars who view Luke-Acts as a form of ancient historiography understand that Luke has written an account that seeks to place the story of Jesus and the early church within the historical, cultural, and social context of the Roman world. As opposed to biography, the focus in historiography is on events — and usually events of profound significance — rather than on individuals per se. Moreover, it is the interpretation and slant placed on these events that becomes important for ancient history writing. Thus, most scholars would also agree that the *historia* of Luke-Acts involves much that previous scholarship has labeled as theological. While the precise nature and function of *historia* differ depending on the specific subgenre that is adopted, overall there is a common pattern: The function and character of the narrative are in large part an expression of the larger literary aims of the writer as a historian of the early Christian movement. The main issue then is how the generic designation "history" affects the presentation of the narrative and the function of *historia*. In other words, classifying Luke-Acts as ancient historiography may imply little about its historical veracity in and of itself, but rather say something about its intent and purpose.[17] As G. E. Sterling observes,

> [T]o place Luke-Acts into the framework of ancient historiography does not presuppose a settlement of the issue of veracity. The relevance of this to that

---

17. There are some scholars who insist that aligning Luke with certain "model" ancient historians necessarily implies something about Luke's own ability and veracity in the details. The attempt to associate Luke with Polybius and Thucydides, thereby distancing Luke from his nearest contemporaries (Livy and Josephus), carries with it the misplaced notion that there is veracity by association. For example, see B. Witherington, "Editing the Good News: Some Synoptic Lessons for the Study of Acts," in *History, Literature, and Society* (ed. Witherington), 324–47; and idem, "Finding Its Niche: The Historical and Rhetorical Species of Acts," *SBLSP* 35 (1996): 67–97. For the correlation more generally between "accuracy" and "history," see the following representative studies: W. M. Ramsay, *Was Christ Born at Bethlehem? A Study on the Credibility of St. Luke* (London: Hodder & Stoughton, 1898), esp. 34, 47–48; C. J. Hemer, *The Book of Acts in the Setting of Hellenistic History* (ed. C. H. Gempf; WUNT 49; Tübingen: Mohr Siebeck, 1989; repr., Winona Lake, Ind.: Eisenbrauns, 1990), 94–99; and R. Riesner, *Paul's Early Period: Chronology, Mission Strategy, Theology* (trans. D. Stott; Grand Rapids: Eerdmans, 1998), 332–33. Scholars who turn to other genres for assessing Acts frequently reflect similar notions of ancient historical composition. Thus, R. I. Pervo, in his discussion of the Jewish Hellenistic writer Artapanus, clearly identifies his understanding that history does not depart — dramatically or intentionally — from the known details (in the case of Artapanus, from the details of Scripture). See his *Profit with Delight: The Literary Genre of the Acts of the Apostles* (Philadelphia: Fortress, 1987), 131; cf. 118–19. Similarly, M. Palmer Bonz (*The Past as Legacy: Luke-Acts and Ancient Epic* [Minneapolis: Fortress, 2000]) argues that Luke-Acts should be viewed as epic instead of history since "in instance upon instance Luke can be seen creating seemingly plausible historical details... to advance his literary and theological themes" (186). She suggests that the "high degree of literary creativity and control" evidenced in Luke's work is an obstacle to viewing it as historiography (184). Epic, she argues, provides a framework for the primacy of literary imagination and creativity in Luke-Acts (187–88).

question is to ask what we mean by the category of history into which we place Luke-Acts. The issue of reliability can only be fully addressed once we understand the historiographical tradition of Luke-Acts and comprehend what the tasks and expectations of that tradition were.[18]

The third generic category — that of ancient romance — highlights the novelistic features of Acts.[19] The work of R. I. Pervo has been influential here.[20] Separating the Gospel of Luke from the book of Acts in terms of genre, Pervo focuses on the latter's dramatic episodes and the legendary quality of character representation. In his view, Acts is a type of historical novel and represents a literary work that fictionalizes — primarily for the purposes of entertainment and edification — core historical events and personages. Unlike our modern literary genres, the line between history and fiction was often permeable in antiquity. As was the case with "history," the mere designation of a work as a "novel" says less about its fictional character and more about its overall purpose, although its "fictionalizing tendency" is often still prominent.[21] Thus, the real dividing line for scholars between the novel and the historical work vis-à-vis their respective *historia* is in regard to function: In the novel the emphasis is on pleasurable and entertaining communication, with the shape of the narrative being placed in the service of this larger purpose.

The lines between the three genres — biography, history, and novel — are both fluid and somewhat artificial in the classification of ancient literary productions. For instance, historical works contain numerous features of biography, and the presence of dramatic episodes is just as prevalent in Roman historiography as it is in the later novels.[22] Rhetorical invention, fictional representation, idealization of the past, and characterization were features of the ancient mode of communication and not specific to one particular branch of ancient literature. At stake in this debate over the genre of Luke-Acts, then, is the way in which *historia* is conceived. While most agree that Luke-Acts is *historia*, the disagreement is rather over the character and function of *historia* in Luke-Acts. Is Luke-Acts a didactic biography

---

18. G. E. Sterling, *Historiography and Self-definition: Josephus, Luke-Acts, and Apologetic Historiography* (NovTSup 64; Leiden: Brill, 1992), 3.

19. Another classification left out of this present discussion is epic, which mediates the historical and romance classifications. On Luke-Acts as ancient epic, see Palmer Bonz, *Past as Legacy*; D. R. MacDonald, *Does the New Testament Imitate Homer? Four Cases from the Acts of the Apostles* (New Haven: Yale University Press, 2003); and M. Moreland, "Jerusalem Imagined: Rethinking Earliest Christian Claims to the Hebrew Epic" (Ph.D. diss., Claremont Graduate University, 1999).

20. See Pervo, *Profit with Delight*, as well as S. M. Praeder's earlier, groundbreaking study, "Luke-Acts and the Ancient Novel," *SBLSP* 20 (1981): 269–92.

21. See Praeder, "Luke-Acts and the Ancient Novel," 278–79.

22. On this latter point see Plümacher, *Lukas als hellenistischer Schriftsteller*, 80–136; as well as W. C. van Unnik, "Luke's Second Book and the Rules of Hellenistic Historiography," in *Les Actes des Apôtres: Traditions, rédaction, théologie* (ed. J. Kremer; BETL 48; Leuven: Leuven University Press, 1979), 55–57.

of succession, aimed at locating the "true voice" of the religion amid rival claimants? Is Luke's two-volume work intended to provide a continuation of biblical history, or is it focused on reconfiguring native traditions so as to respond to the critiques of outsiders and encourage the faithful? Is the Acts of the Apostles a work that dramatizes episodes and re-presents historical events and personages for entertainment? These are questions that are critical for understanding Luke-Acts as a whole.

The issue of genre has dominated analysis of Luke-Acts over the past several years. This discussion, however, is yet another means of addressing the matters involved in the earlier treatments of Luke-Acts: the relationship between the historical and the theological in Luke's work. In recent studies, scholars have tended to articulate this relationship less in terms of the theologian versus historian distinction and more in terms of generic influence on the presentation and function of *historia*. Nonetheless, in varying degrees and ways, modern critics are still addressing the questions posed by earlier scholarship: What is the nature of *historia* in Luke's two-volume work? How does it relate to the purposes of the writer? What is the function of the material? How does arrangement reflect meaning and intent? Thus, new contours have been given to earlier discussions, although some of the fundamental questions have remained the same. Therefore, one of the particular hotbeds of discussion identified by van Unnik in 1966 remains one of the key issues in Luke-Acts studies today. These and related issues have a direct bearing on the interpretation of various units of narrative in Luke-Acts, one of the most intriguing of which is Acts 6:1–8:3 — the account of Stephen and the Hellenists.

Modern New Testament scholarship has expended a great deal of energy examining this text, attempting to delineate the precise nature and function of the *historia* in the narrative.[23] For the most part, the issue has often been articulated in terms of earlier debate: What is history and what is theology in the Hellenist account? Yet the contrast between history and theology is only one way of framing the issues in the narrative, and ultimately the central matter of concern is the character of the *historia* that Luke relates/(re)produces. Was Luke's intention to provide a detailed historical account of the first early Christian "martyr"? Is Stephen's speech essentially a faithful rendering of the theology of the early Hellenist community? Or, conversely, is there a distinction to be made between the historical content of the material — the source of the highly stylized, dramatic episode — and the literary and artistic character of Luke's work? If this is the case, can one recover the original *Grundschrift* or its gist from what is extant? Or, taking the matter one step further in the other direction, if history and theology can be separated, can one recover the theology of Luke and the function

---

23. See H.-W. Neudorfer, *Der Stephanuskreis in der Forschungsgeschichte seit F. C. Baur* (Giessen, Germany: Brunnen, 1983), for a full discussion of the history of scholarship.

of the material for the readers of his own day? One way or another these questions address the fundamental issue raised in this study: What is the character and function of the Hellenist account in Acts? Moreover, I hope to illuminate how contemporary constructions of Acts 6:1–8:3 provide an excellent avenue through which one can engage the power of ideology to shape both the text and the interpreter, often resulting in a causal connection between the discursive character of the text and its mimetic reinscription in contemporary scholarly analysis.

Constructing Christian Origins: F. C. Baur's Philosophical-Historical Configuration

Modern study of the Hellenist narrative has its genesis in the work of F. C. Baur, upon which much of the critical analysis done in the twentieth century was built. Through a study of the relations among early Christian groups as reflected in the Pauline letters, Baur came to believe that there were two specific and competing segments in early Christianity: a Petrine and a Paulinist group. Essentially, these two groups disagreed over the nature and implications of the gospel message. The Petrine group was Jewish-Christian, a conservative segment that failed to break free completely from the strictures of the law. The Paulinist group, by contrast, represented the liberal wing of early Christianity: free from the law and moving outward to the Gentiles. According to Baur, these two groups were in constant opposition during a good portion of Paul's ministry. It was this particular construal of early Christian history that was foundational for Baur's overall methodological approach to the New Testament. Already in his classic 1831 article,[24] Baur was developing a methodology that would later come to be known as *Tendenz* criticism, by which Baur understood that the study of early Christian materials ought to be conducted by examining a particular text's theological or ideological stance within the broader historical and theological landscape of earliest Christianity. In other words, Baur could map early Christian texts and traditions by associating them with particular factions of the early church. This approach proved formative for Baur's understanding of Acts.

Thirteen years later in his study of Paul and Peter, Baur had already come to formulate a fairly strong disregard for the historical value of Acts.[25] For Baur, the image of Paul throughout Acts is distorted, as the writer attempts to bring Paul into line with the Jerusalem apostles and to establish a harmony

---

24. F. C. Baur, "Die Christuspartei in der korinthischen Gemeinde, der Gegensatz des petrinischen und paulinischen Christentums in der ältesten Kirche, der Apostel Petrus in Rom," *TZTh* 4 (1831): 61–206.

25. F. C. Baur, *Paul the Apostle of Jesus Christ, His Life and Works, His Epistles and Teachings; A Contribution to a Critical History of Primitive Christianity* (ed. E. Zeller; 2d ed.; London: Williams & Norgate, 1873, 1875; repr., Peabody, Mass.: Hendrickson, 2003), 1:1–252.

and hegemony that never actually existed in the early church. Adopting M. Schneckenburger's argument that Acts is an apologetic text, a position based largely on the establishment of the parallels between the apostles and Paul in the text,[26] Baur argued that Acts was written in the second century by a follower of Paul in order to come to the aid of a beleaguered Paulinism. This aim was accomplished, in Baur's view, by toning down the harsher elements of Paul's doctrine and linking Paul to some of the theological tenets of the Petrine Jewish-Christian group: "[T]he Pauline doctrine was so severely repressed that it could only maintain itself through a concession, which modified the hardness and bluffness of its opposition to the law and Judaism, and by this means put itself into a position as far as possible harmonizing the antagonistic views of the powerful Jewish-Christian party opposed to him."[27] Acts thus represents an attempt to militate against some of the second-century critique of Paul by showing the apostle to the Gentiles to be in agreement with the Jerusalem church and his mission to the Gentiles to be sanctioned by the Jewish-Christians, including Peter himself.

This particular view of Luke-Acts obviously had a strong effect on Baur's reading of the Hellenist narrative in Acts 6:1–8:3. In 1829 Baur delivered an address on Acts 7 in which he assumed the basic historical reliability of the account related to Stephen. While this position was established before his shift toward *Tendenz* criticism, he had already aligned the content of Stephen's speech with a more pessimistic view of the relationship between Judaism and Christianity, contrasting this stance with the more positive assessment of Peter.[28] By the time Baur published *Paul the Apostle*, his position on Stephen and the Hellenists was much more developed, and these later notions would prove foundational for succeeding scholarship.[29]

Baur reflected little on the incident in Acts 6:1–6 — the problem between the Hellenists and Hebrews over the former's widows — other than to assert that the dissension resulted because of deeper ideological differences between the two groups. It was the presence of two distinct ideological groups in early Christianity that interested him the most; this became an essential premise in Baur's reconstruction. In the earlier stages of Christian origins

---

26. M. Schneckenburger, *Über den Zweck der Apostelgeschichte* (Bern: Fischer, 1841). While Baur adopted the notion that Acts was an apologetic writing, he did not view it as a strict defense of Paul, and he rejected Schneckenburger's view that Acts was still, on the whole, a trustworthy document despite its apologetic aims (see Baur, *Paul the Apostle,* 1:1–14).

27. Baur, *Paul the Apostle,* 1:12.

28. F. C. Baur, "De orationis habitae a Stephano Act. Cap. VII. Consilio, et de Protomartyris hujus in christianae rei primordiis momento," *Festum Christi Natalitium (Tübingen)* (1829): 1–40. See the brief note on this address in W. G. Kümmel, *The New Testament: The History of the Investigation of Its Problems* (trans. S. M. Gilmour and H. C. Kee; Nashville: Abingdon, 1972), 127.

29. See Baur, *Paul the Apostle,* 1:39–62. Baur's ideas were, of course, not totally new, as similar sentiments were already expressed earlier by, for example, English Deists such as Thomas Morgan (on Morgan, see H. G. Reventlow, *The Authority of the Bible and the Rise of the Modern World* [trans. J. Bowden; Philadelphia: Fortress, 1984], 397–404).

these two groups were allied, even though the Hellenists were more liberal than their Judaizing counterparts. The Stephen episode represents a transition point, however, as the persecution that followed (8:2–3) is understood to be directed primarily at the Hellenistic wing of early Christianity. Baur focused on two elements in Acts 6:1–8:3: the charges brought against Stephen and the content of the speech. These two elements provide mutual support for the position that Stephen had formulated opinions that had offended the Jews. Baur acknowledged that the charges brought against Stephen are said to be false (7:13), yet he insisted that the speech, offered in defense, confirms in part the truth of the charges: Stephen did speak against the temple and the law. Thus, the precise form of the charges may have been false, but their essence was undoubtedly true.

By 1843 Baur had abandoned his earlier contention that Stephen's speech came from a historical source that the author of Acts used. The writer of Acts has, like a good historian, placed a speech in the mouth of Stephen. Nevertheless, Baur understands that the essence of the speech — particularly those elements that confirm the charges that Stephen spoke against the temple — reflects the views of the historical figure. Further, in Baur's analysis, the writer of Acts has fabricated the Sanhedrin trial; it provides a forum for the expression of Stephen's particular Hellenist views and comes about because the writer is modeling this episode on the trial of Jesus in Luke. The "indisputably... best established fact" is that Stephen's words against temple worship prompted a "tumultuous insurrection," leading to his stoning. Finally, sorting out the work of the creative historian from the historical kernel behind the present narrative, Baur suggests that the charges and the parallel confirmation in the speech itself provide the best access to the historical event behind the current narrative.

Baur was never troubled by his inability to detect a clear source behind the narrative; he also did not think that because one part of the narrative was fictive doubt should therefore be cast on other aspects of that same account. The reason for this was simple: His prior formulation of the character of the Hellenists and the nature of their theology guided his interpretation of the text. Within the narrative of Acts 6:1–8:3 his argument was clearly circular: The charges and speech confirm the Hellenist ideology, which in turn confirms the charges and the speech. Yet his prior work on the Pauline letters had provided him with the primary data for his formulations in Acts: If such theology can be detected in Paul, when it then surfaces elsewhere in the New Testament it can be assigned to the Pauline trajectory. This basic delineation illustrates quite well the *Tendenz* methodology at work: Having established the prior tendency, it could now be detected in non-Pauline texts.[30]

---

30. See P. C. Hodgson, *The Formation of Historical Theology: A Study of Ferdinand Christian Baur* (New York: Harper & Row, 1966), 209.

Based on this method, or more precisely, on his previous reconstruction of the theological nature of Paulinism, Baur was able to situate the ideological nature of the content of Stephen's speech. According to Baur, the oration of Stephen represented an attack on the temple as the locus of worship in Judaism. Baur argued that the entire speech addresses the proper place of the temple, even though the temple itself surfaces only in the final verses: The promises offered to Abraham only have their proper fulfillment in the establishment of the temple, so that throughout the retelling of the history of Israel there is a subtle underlying critique of the temple. The mention of the "tabernacle of witness" in Acts 7:44–45 provides the key for Baur:

> [T]he "tabernacle of witness," free, movable, wandering from place to place, bound to no particular spot, and therefore keeping the worship connected with it in constant motion, fulfilled much better the aim of a spiritual service of God, than the massive, stationary Temple, with its stern fixed worship — in which the real, external, material phenomena were so much more predominant, because they were no longer kept down and penetrated by the invisible Ideal — the Heavenly "Form" which Moses had seen.... That the essence of true religion did not consist in outward ceremonials, connected with a temple service confined to an appointed spot, was the one great idea, through which, at that time, Judaism saw itself superseded by Christianity.[31]

This combination of nineteenth-century Protestant interpretation of Judaism and German Idealism, especially the tradition connected with Friedrich Schelling,[32] found its concrete expression in the symbolic interpretation of the tabernacle as the spiritual dwelling par excellence. The temple was a symbol of outward observance and ceremony, while the religion of the "spirit" was represented by the tabernacle. This classification, of course, resulted in no naïve retreat into the simplicity of tabernacle worship for Baur. Rather, the tabernacle and temple were representative of "spiritual" and "sensuous" worship respectively. In the end, the real point of Stephen's speech for Baur was not that temple worship had been replaced, but that Christianity, with its emphasis on spiritual worship beyond the limits of law and cult, had superseded the faith of the Jews, overturning the "Jewish monopoly on religion."[33] In Baur's opinion, even if this speech did not come

---

31. Baur, *Paul the Apostle*, 1:49–50, 59.

32. On the connection of Baur and Schelling, see especially K. Berger, *Exegese und Philosophie* (SBS 123/124; Stuttgart: Katholisches Bibelwerk, 1986), 28–48.

33. Baur's words are harsh on this matter: "This inevitable rending asunder of Christianity from Judaism, whereby Judaism would be rendered negative as an absolute religion, and by which its final extinction was threatened, had been realized by Stephen; the high, liberal standpoint which he assumed, fostered in him the energetic zeal with which he laboured in the cause of Jesus" (*Paul the Apostle*, 1:59). In Baur's opinion, the "ingratitude and disobedience" of the people was "their truest and most characteristic nature" — indeed, it was an "innate and natural passion" (1:51) — and thus the real point of the speech was simply to point out that the Jews were "not capable of receiving the Messianic salvation" (1:62 n). The anti-Jewish nature of these sentiments have their roots in earlier German Protestant scholarship, which was later "canonized" in F. Weber's *System der altsynagogalen palästinischen Theologie aus*

effect, but the detection of what constitutes the revelation of the divine Spirit in a given historical instance: the union of ideal and manifestation. Furthermore, Baur sought the historical significance of key individuals of the past. Therefore, in regard to Stephen, Baur focused primarily on his "historical importance."[38] For Baur, this meant much more than the role that certain characters performed in history. Rather, as P. C. Hodgson points out, the stress is

> on the function of the success with which they lay hold of and express the ideas shaping the age in which they live — the success with which they become the medium and instrument of the course of history.... [I]t is clear that Baur does not dismiss the importance of historical persons but rather sought to discover the true ground for the significance of their respective individualities.[39]

Therefore, the historical importance of Stephen rests precisely in the "fact" that he saw what God was doing in his present — the movement from outward ceremony to true spiritual worship inclusive of all — and articulated the new work of God in Christianity at the cost of his own life. Stephen, in this perspective, was important for Baur precisely because this early Christian figure perceived the manifestation of the "Absolute Idea" or "World Spirit" in the historical process at work in his own day. Peter, by contrast, is of less historical significance precisely because, in Baur's view, he did not grasp what God was doing in his present.

Obviously the determination of who is historically important and who is not rests upon a priori interpretations of what is the underlying historical process and manifestation of the divine Spirit in any given historical instance. In essence, Baur's conclusions with respect to the Hellenists rest upon his prior reflection on the meaning of history and the relationship of Stephen to this overarching divine process. Yet if one grants the philosophical principles at work, Baur's particular approach to the Stephen narrative makes perfect sense. The historian must delve beneath the surface and penetrate to the historical core, attempting to establish that aspect of the "Absolute Idea" being made manifest at this point and time. Separating the later interpretation and additions of the writer of Acts is exactly the appropriate task for the historian, because only in this way can one grasp the underlying principle at work. This effort receives further legitimization through the belief that what one finds is not only the revelation of the divine Spirit but the process of the Spirit coming to consciousness of itself. Thus, history is a process of development, with each succeeding historical revelation in effect superseding the former. The framework out of which Baur was operating thus necessitated his interpretation of Stephen's speech as being supersessionist in nature. Stephen would have no historical importance in

---

38. Baur, *Paul the Apostle*, 1:62.
39. Hodgson, *Formation of Historical Theology*, 187.

this system if, in fact, the core of his speech confirmed the prior revelation of the Spirit in Judaism.

Given his prior theological views, Baur's approach to *historia* in Acts 6:1–8:3 thus requires precisely the method he used and the conclusion he reached. Therefore, whatever one thinks of his specific reading of the Stephen narrative and speech, anyone who wishes to challenge him must first contest the underlying framework of interpretation. There is a problem that arises, however: What becomes of this method and interpretation once the premises and framework of the German Idealistic tradition have been abandoned by subsequent scholarship? One would have to consider that this approach to *historia* and the specific interpretation of the Hellenists would have to be reevaluated, if not completely reformulated. Needless to say, this rethinking did not take place. The prominence of the German Idealistic premises and framework waned over time, but the approach to the narrative — including Baur's specific conclusions — remained.

From Philosophy to History: Scholarship after Baur

Much of the scholarship on the Hellenists after Baur rearticulated his emphases, although there was some opposition to Baur's particular reading of the speech.[40] For Baur, the connection between Paul and the Hellenists was critical for understanding Paul and for reconstructing Christian origins. Once this connection had been made — and tacitly assumed in subsequent scholarship — it garnered only occasional mention in the writings of some of the more influential scholars of the period. In contrast to Baur, W. Bousset believed that one could not so simply identify Hellenistic influence on Palestinian soil with that which Paul found outside Palestine.[41] He also did not regard the information in Acts to be all that reliable. The Hellenists of Acts 6:1–8:3 thus play no role at all in Bousset's study of the origins of the Christ cult in early Christianity. Paul's connection is with the primitive Hellenistic communities of Tarsus, Damascus, and Antioch — not with those of Palestine.[42] The Hellenists receive more attention in R. Bultmann's treatment of the theological tendencies of early Christianity. For Bultmann, Hellenistic

---

40. C. C. Hill, *Hellenists and Hebrews: Reappraising Division within the Early Church* (Minneapolis: Fortress, 1992), 8–17, has summarized much of the scholarship on this point. See also the longer but similar treatment by H. A. Brehm, "The Role of the 'Hellenists' in Christian Origins: A Critique of Representative Models in Light of an Exegetical Study of Acts 6–8" (Ph.D. diss., Southwestern Baptist Theological Seminary, 1992), 10–105.

41. W. Bousset, *Kyrios Christos: A History of Belief in Christ from the Beginnings of Christianity to Irenaeus* (trans. J. E. Steely; Nashville: Abingdon, 1970), 120n. 3.

42. Ibid., 119–20. This view represents a significant shift from the earlier *Religionsgeschichtliche Schule* position, such as one finds in W. Heitmüller, "Zum Problem Paulus und Jesus," *ZNW* 13 (1912): 320–37. Heitmüller still insisted that Acts 6:1–8:3 offers valuable information about pre-Pauline Christianity, and, with Baur, concurred that the Hellenists pro-

Jews in Palestine "as a matter of course took a more liberal stand toward the Law." Thus, Stephen did criticize the law and temple, illustrating that the Hellenists were not simply "serving table, but that they were proclaimers of the word." In other words, for Bultmann the Hellenists represented a "party" within early Christianity — a specific ideological movement.[43] On the one hand, it is evident that Bultmann's position here is very much influenced by Baur's previous formulation of the relationship — even developed further insofar as the nature of Hellenistic Judaism is concerned. On the other hand, Bultmann places little emphasis on the Hellenists of Acts 6:1–8:3 in particular. In Bultmann's view, the Hellenistic Christianity of Syria is most important. Acts 6:1–8:3 contains some data regarding the early Hellenistic Christians,[44] but in his actual reconstruction of the theology of the Hellenistic church Bultmann hardly uses Acts. For Bultmann, as was the case with Bousset before him, the role of Hellenistic Judaism was much more important in the formation of Gentile Hellenistic Christianity than the Hellenists of Palestine per se. The interpretation of the role of the Hellenists of Acts is noteworthy only insofar as it confirms their particular configuration of Hellenistic Judaism more generally and Hellenistic Gentile Christianity specifically. Their approach thus represents a fundamental shift: Whereas Baur moved from the text outward, albeit under the influence of a very specific interpretive framework, Bultmann and Bousset move from the general religious background toward the text. The Hellenists in this approach are not so much the "bridge" between Jesus and Paul but represent one manifestation of a larger religious spirit widespread in this period, which had a variety of expressions.

In contrast to the work of Bousset and Bultmann stands the work of those scholars who placed a high value on the sources behind Acts 6:1–8:3. In North American scholarship B. W. Bacon provided significant impetus in this direction. In a posthumously published work, Bacon postulated that with respect to the Gentile mission in Acts there were two primary sources used by Luke: the Petrine source and the Pauline one, both emphasizing the formative role of their respective figure in the founding of the Gentile mission.[45] Acts 6:1–8:3, however, represents neither source; it is an independent witness to the founding of the Gentile mission. Although skeptical of

---

vided a critical link between Paul and Jesus. Also significant for this strand of interpretation is W. Grundmann, whose essay, "Das Problem des hellenistischen Christentums innerhalb der Jerusalemer Urgemeinde," ZNW 38 (1939): 45–73, outlines the critical link the Hellenists form in the movement from Jesus to Paul, especially in terms of establishing the theology at Antioch. Much of what Grundmann wrote in 1939 anticipated later German developments.

43. R. Bultmann, *Theology of the New Testament* (trans. K. Grobel; New York: Charles Scribner's Sons, 1951), 1:55–56.

44. Ibid., 1:64.

45. B. W. Bacon, *The Gospel of the Hellenists* (ed. C. H. Kraeling; New York: Henry Holt, 1933), 74–76.

the Lukan additions to, and reworking of, the source, Bacon argued that behind Acts 6:1–8:3 lay a clear and recognizable tradition from the church(es) of Antioch.[46] Like Baur, Bacon argued that, despite the Lukan attempt to conceal it, this account reflects the existence of an independent Hellenistic body in early Christianity. The Hebrews and Hellenists formed two separate groups, organized independently of one another. In Bacon's interpretation, the writer of Acts portrays the seven elected Hellenists as "servers," when in fact they were much more — namely, the "pillars" of the community. In line with Bultmann, Bacon maintained that the movement to evangelism was a natural outcome of their role in the community.[47] Luke, in this view, attempted throughout to bring the Hellenists into conformity with the Jerusalem church by, for instance, portraying the Hebrews and Hellenists as an organic unit or having Peter and John sanction the ministry of Philip in Samaria.[48] Nonetheless, beneath the veneer of Lukan redaction one can detect the Hellenist source throughout this section. Of particular interest to Bacon was the "Hellenistic motive" of this source: "From Stephen down, the Hellenists stood for a universal gospel free from the particularistic barriers of Jewish nationalism."[49] Like Baur, Bacon believed that once the Hellenist role in early Christianity is properly understood, particularly insofar as their theology is construed as being universalistic in thrust, then the subsequent Pauline and Johannine developments in early Christianity are more easily explained.[50]

Bacon's approach is interesting both for the way in which it connects with the scholarship that preceded him and the manner in which it distinguishes itself. On the one hand, Bacon's approach is very much in the tradition of Baur's earlier work: For Bacon, the writer of Acts has harmonized traditions, attempting to reconstruct Christian origins as a peaceful and organic movement. Beneath Acts 6:1–8:3, however, one detects a more powerful religious force that comes into conflict with the conservative Hebrews in Jerusalem; the essential nature of this force was the supersession of the temple and the law and the dislodging of the gospel of Jesus from its Jewish particularistic constraints through the movement out to the Gentiles. This earlier Hellenist movement was the precursor to the development of Pauline Christianity.

---

46. This particular formulation already precedes Bacon in the work of A. von Harnack on the sources of Acts, and Bacon is obviously influenced by Harnack at this point (Harnack, *The Acts of the Apostles* [trans. J. R. Wilkinson; New York: Williams & Norgate, 1909], 170–75): Acts 6:1–8:3 largely stems from an Antiochian tradition that had Stephen and Barnabas as its focus. Harnack and Bacon do differ over where they situate the Phillip narrative; the former places it within the Jerusalem tradition (*Acts of the Apostles*, 178), while Bacon views it as an essential element of the Antiochian/Hellenist source (*Gospel of the Hellenists*, 76).
47. Bacon, *Gospel of the Hellenists*, 78.
48. Ibid., 76–77.
49. Ibid., 79.
50. Ibid., 80.

Clearly Bacon has been influenced by the scholarship in Baur's tradition. At the same time, there is an important shift. While Baur was aware of the problem of sources in his study of the Hellenists, and indeed addressed this in part, he also knew of the difficulty of attempting to reconstruct that which underlies the account in Acts. Baur knew that the so-called "Hellenist theology" existed from his previous research on Paul and the letters, and thus he could postulate the significance of the Hellenists in Acts 6:1–8:3 based upon his prior reconstruction of Christian origins. There was no need to establish a source or even defend its existence. Moreover, for Baur it was a particular philosophy of history that gave one access to the true meaning of events in early Christianity, while in Bacon's work that role is ascribed to historical sources. In other words, the emphasis now shifts to the modern scholarly task of sifting through redaction and tradition, reducing the former to a veneer covering the real events reflected in the latter. This redirection had already gained momentum since Baur's work nearly a century before, and it did not originate with Bacon. Yet the shift to the primacy of sources in the prewar period would indelibly mark in many quarters subsequent work done on the Hellenists in particular and on Acts as a whole.

Since the earlier work of Baur, source-theory approaches to Acts 6:1–8:3 had gained significant ground.[51] Even those scholars who were quite skeptical regarding the use of sources in Acts more generally affirmed the presence of underlying traditions in Acts 6:1–8:3. E. Haenchen, for instance, who argues that the speech and the specific narrative setting essentially come from Luke's hand, nevertheless posits, on the basis of deduction and analysis of alleged Lukan redaction, the existence of Hellenist material that guides Luke's writing of the narrative in question.[52] For Haenchen, the bare details are as follows: Stephen and the Hellenists formed a distinct group from the Hebrews (a premise deduced from the fact that while the Hellenists were persecuted the Jerusalem apostles were not); Stephen and the Hellenists headed up a mission to their Hellenistic compatriots in Jerusalem (an element Luke conceals because in Luke's theology only the apostles can proclaim the word); the Hellenists appear to have been more willing to exercise freedom in relation to the law than their Hebrew counterparts (this is what caused the uproar against them); and as a result of their dispersion they moved to Syrian Antioch, where they began accepting uncircumcised Gentiles into the Christian community.[53] This is a bare sketch, which Haenchen is unwilling to flesh out in more detail. Yet, while its relative brevity is apparent, it is clear that its presence as a historical datum is critical for Haenchen,

---

51. For a general summary of the various source positions and criticisms of each, see Hill, *Hellenists and Hebrews*, 92–101.

52. Haenchen, *Acts of the Apostles*, 266, 273. See also H. Conzelmann, *Acts of the Apostles* (ed. E. J. Epp and C. R. Matthews; trans. J. Limburg et al.; Hermeneia; Philadelphia: Fortress, 1987), 44, 57.

53. Haenchen, *Acts of the Apostles*, 266–68.

and this despite his overall stress on Luke's overt theological agenda in writing Acts 6:1–8:3. While he readily argues that Luke's theological creativity has caused the reenvisioning of his original material, the Hellenists themselves cannot be a Lukan fiction. The priority that this assumption is given in Haenchen's work goes a long way in demonstrating just how important the Hellenists have become for understanding and reconstructing Christian origins.

M. Simon's study (1958) represents another milestone in the scholarship on Acts 6:1–8:3. Although perhaps more dominant in North America and England, this approach assumed that the information in Luke's composition connected readily with historical reality, reflecting the actual Hellenist movement. Even the speech is assumed to reflect the general gist of the "Hellenist tradition of thought."[54] Thus, for Simon, Acts 6:1–8:3 as a whole represents a fairly accurate picture of Stephen and the Hellenists in early Christianity. Interpreting the speech, Simon asserts that

> we shall be led to the conclusion that Stephen understood the message of Jesus more completely and more accurately than the first disciples, who "continued daily with one accord in the Temple." ... [T]hat Stephen's disciples were the real initiators of the Christian mission outside Jerusalem is pretty sure. Their message, by shaking off, as perverse and idolatrous, important elements of the ritual Law, and by disjoining Christianity from the Jerusalem cult, had indeed provided the starting point for a universalistic outlook.... [T]hus, the Hellenist message undoubtedly represents one step towards Christian emancipation.[55]

These fairly strong statements are clearly reminiscent of Baur's earlier formulation. The most notable shift is in the treatment of the narrative as a source for historical reconstruction. Simon moves with relative ease between the content of the narrative/speech and the reconstruction of the historical role of the Hellenists in early Christianity. Moreover, there is a close relationship in his work between the *historia* of the narrative and the

---

54. M. Simon, *St. Stephen and the Hellenists in the Primitive Church* (London: Longmans, 1958), 40. Simon assumes the results of E. Norden's brief analysis of the speech. E. Norden (and others) argued that the speech is characteristically un-Greek, and thus could not have come from the hand of Luke (see Norden, *Die antike Kunstprosa* [Stuttgart: Teubner, 1958], 2:484). The distinctive character of Stephen's speech in contrast to many of the other speeches in Acts has often been noted. U. Wilckens, for instance, argues from the content of the speech that it could not have been written by Luke but had to have come from a Diaspora Jewish-Christian group, which he narrows to the "Hellenists" (*Die Missionsreden der Apostelgeschichte: Form- und traditionsgeschichtliche Untersuchungen* [WMANT 5; 3d ed.; Neukirchen-Vluyn: Neukirchener Verlag, 1974], 208, 219). This position has become almost axiomatic in scholarship on Acts 6:1–8:3; the speech does not come from Luke and it cannot necessarily be traced back to Stephen directly, but it "undoubtedly" comes from the Hellenistic Jewish strand of early Christianity (see R. Scroggs, "The Earliest Hellenistic Christianity," in *Religions in Antiquity: Essays in Memory of Erwin Ramsdell Goodenough* [ed. J. Neusner; SHR 14; Leiden: Brill, 1968], 182–200).

55. Simon, *St. Stephen and the Hellenists*, 110–12.

historicity of the data beneath the surface of Lukan composition. As a result, the Hellenists become relatively insignificant for understanding Acts and fundamentally important for understanding and reconstructing Christian origins, particularly the movement of the gospel from Jerusalem to the Gentiles. For Baur, philosophical notions guided his particular interpretation of the text and history; for Simon, all that is left is history. This change is no small shift in emphasis, since the consequences for interpretation and ideologies in the approach to the text are significant: Elements of Acts 6:1–8:3 are now *historia* only insofar as they reveal something about the actual events in early Christian history.

More recent source-critical approaches to Acts 6:1–8:3 have continued in this same vein, separating tradition from redaction as the main method for understanding the narratives of Acts. The underlying logic is simple: Since Luke used tradition in his composition of Acts, one can go back and sift out the original material from the Lukan additions and later accretions, arriving at more primitive and original data on the early church. Although few scholars reflect in a conscious and critical manner on this particular approach to Acts as *historia*, it is apparent that in its practice the following principle is at work: If the redaction is theological in nature, then the historical character of the work must rest in the so-called traditional material that allegedly lies beneath the Lukan veneer. Within this framework, *historia* is implicitly viewed as being the historical kernel of the Lukan composition. Accordingly, while the redaction is an interesting element for study, its relevance for *historia* is minimal: Redaction tells us something about the author; tradition reveals something about history.

This particular understanding is aptly illustrated in G. Lüdemann's recent study of tradition and redaction in Acts.[56] In his analysis of the Stephen narrative, for instance, he focuses on 6:11 and 6:13, arguing that the historical kernel of the Lukan narrative can be discerned in the charges brought against Stephen. He maintains, in regard to 6:13, that Luke would not have placed these charges in connection with Stephen unless they were already present in the tradition. If they were based on the charges brought against Jesus in Mark 14:58, as many scholars have argued, then it is hard to understand why Luke would have left them out of the gospel but included them in the Hellenist narrative. The charges must therefore stem from the historical tradition. Moreover, since Luke would have been averse to the nature of the charges themselves, the attribution of the false character of the charges must be Lukan redaction in this case. Their revolutionary nature, as well as the fact that Luke attempts (in this portion of the narrative) to depict the Christian community as a harmonious entity, suggests to Lüdemann that the

---

56. G. Lüdemann, *Early Christianity according to the Traditions in Acts: A Commentary* (trans. J. Bowden; Minneapolis: Fortress, 1989). Also see his "Acts of the Apostles as a Historical Source," in *The Social World of Formative Christianity and Judaism: Essays in Tribute to Howard Clark Kee* (ed. J. S. Neusner et al.; Philadelphia: Fortress, 1988), 109–25.

charges reflect the reality of Stephen's theology and that Luke has attempted to tone down this radical critique of law and temple.[57] The conclusion that the charges are not false but that the historical Stephen actually spoke against the temple and the law, justifies in turn the assumption that the basic conflict between Stephen and the Hellenist synagogues was historical as well. It would also be obvious that an individual with the radical views of Stephen would provoke first verbal and then physical conflict. The "split" in Acts 6:1 can then be viewed as caused by this radical critique of the temple and law. For Lüdemann, the redactional elements, while trying to domesticate Stephen and the Hellenists, cannot completely conceal this historical core.[58]

Recent studies of Acts 6:1–8:3 have persistently maintained this tradition of interpretation. Two seminal German commentaries on Acts in recent years have both moved between tradition and redaction in their reconstruction and interpretation of the Hellenist narrative.[59] C. K. Barrett, in one of the more recent English commentaries on Acts, follows a similar approach, arguing (in line with the older hypothesis) that Luke used two independent, divergent accounts related to Stephen. The account in Acts 6:1–8:3 has two conflicting traditions of charges (6:11 and 6:13) and two different renderings of the setting for the speech (one before the Sanhedrin, the other a mob scene).[60] Throughout he provides a fairly traditional reading of the role of Stephen and the Hellenists in early Christianity. The most recent French work on Acts similarly follows this pattern, although it is more complex in its formulation.[61]

---

57. Lüdemann, *Early Christianity*, 82–83. This particular position is fairly common. Baur already raised the issue of the historical validity of the "false" nature of the charges (*Paul the Apostle*, 1:43–44). Harnack maintained the same position but even more forcefully (*Acts of the Apostles*, 172–73). This tradition of interpretation has continued particularly in German scholarship on Acts 6:1–8:3 (see more recently N. Walter, "Apostelgeschichte 6.1 und die Anfänge der Urgemeinde in Jerusalem," *NTS* 29 [1983]: 371).

58. Lüdemann, *Early Christianity*, 84–85. It is interesting in this light that Lüdemann understands the speech in Acts 7 to be largely a Lukan creation based on traditional Jewish exemplars. He considers the speech to be fairly conservative in character, evidencing no direct break with the temple but something to be read in the context of the mission to the Gentiles, foreshadowing a movement from the chosen people to all people (86–89).

59. See G. Schneider, *Die Apostelgeschichte* (HTKNT 5; Freiburg: Herder, 1980), 1:420–22, 432–34; and R. Pesch, *Die Apostelgeschichte* (2d ed.; EKK 5; Neukirchen-Vluyn: Neukirchener Verlag, 1995), 1:230–36.

60. While Barrett maintains that, because of the literary artistry of Luke, it is difficult to separate out the original sources, he nonetheless goes on (without much trepidation) to divide the Stephen narrative into three sections. See C. K. Barrett, *A Critical and Exegetical Commentary on the Acts of the Apostles* (ICC; Edinburgh: T & T Clark, 1994), 1:319–21. This recognition of doublets in the Stephen narrative was already propounded earlier in the century by F. J. Foakes Jackson and K. Lake ("The Internal Evidence of Acts," in *Beginnings of Christianity* [ed. Jackson and Lake], 2:149).

61. In view here is primarily the work of the École Biblique. M.-É. Boismard and A. Lamouille have attempted to establish a complex theory regarding the use of traditions, sources, and redaction in Acts. In their work on Acts 6:1–8:3, for instance, they argue that three basic levels of material have come together: a core account in "Document P," a major expansion of this by the writer of Act I (60s C.E. Jewish Christian writer), and further additions by the

Interest in the use of Acts for the reconstruction of Christian history has clearly increased from Baur to the present. As the work edited by F. J. Foakes Jackson and K. Lake between the years 1920 and 1933 demonstrates, in order to gain access to the historical events of early Christian history one must first peel away the later layers of that movement. In the preface to the first volume of their work they observe:

> The great literary achievement of the last fifty years of New Testament scholarship was the discovery and the general solution of the synoptic problem. It is the task of this generation to translate these results into the language of the historian; to show how literary complexities and contradictions reveal the growth of thought and the rise of institutions.[62]

Despite the fact that scholars vary in the particulars of what is considered tradition and redaction, the methodology of each differs little. Thus, Barrett and Lüdemann find common ground not in their specific renderings of the Stephen narrative but in the methods implemented and the goals that guide their research. As Foakes Jackson and Lake maintained earlier in the century, the aim of this particular course of study is to uncover the underlying currents of history that lay beneath the surface of the literary product. In this way, these later scholars have much in common with Baur's earlier analysis. Fundamentally different, however, is the particular goal of their respective investigations. If for Baur this endeavor was at least in part philosophical in nature, for later scholars the motivation, although obviously shaped by theological implications, is largely driven by the aim of recovering early Christian historical data. In all of this, true value and meaning is ascribed to that which lies closest to what "actually happened" in early Christian history.

To understand this shift more broadly it is helpful to assess, for heuristic purposes, the specific development in historiographic conception that took place in subsequent scholarship after Baur, wherein there was a move from an organicist conception of history toward a more contextualist approach.[63] Baur can be considered an organicist, which means, in essence, that he understood the particulars of history as part of a larger synthetic

---

writer/redactor of Act II (traditional writer Luke) and the redactor of Act III (90s C.E. later writer in Rome). See the literary breakdown in their *Les Actes des Deux Apôtres: III Analyses Littéraires* (EBib ns 14; Paris: Gabalda, 1990), 103–12. The point of this particular approach is to reconstruct the original sources, separate out the redaction, and move as closely as possible to the history reflected beneath the final narratives. That this is the goal of the three-volume series by Boismard and Lamouille is made apparent in the sibling work by J. Taylor, who provides an explicit historical commentary on the source analysis in the former volumes (see Taylor, *Les Actes des Deux Apôtres: IV–VI Commentaire Historique* [EBib ns 23, 30, 41; Paris: Gabalda, 1994–2000).

62. Foakes Jackson and Lake, *Beginnings of Christianity,* 1:vii.

63. These particular terms are drawn from the work of H. White, *Metahistory: The Historical Imagination in Nineteenth-Century Europe* (Baltimore: Johns Hopkins University Press, 1973), 15–19.

process. As H. White suggests, "[A]t the heart of the Organicist strategy is a metaphysical commitment to the paradigm of the microcosmic-macrocosmic relationship... [in which] individual entities [are viewed] as components of processes which aggregate into wholes that are greater than, or qualitatively different from, the sum of their parts."[64] The previous discussion of Baur's program of historiography places him squarely within this tradition. The contextualist conception by contrast maintains that events and individuals can only be understood by placing them within the context in which they initially occurred. The reason for particular actions is explicable by tracing the relationship between an event or individual and the entangled relationships of that given historical epoch. As White describes, " 'What happened' in the field can be accounted for by the specifications of the functional interrelationships existing among the agents and agencies occupying the field at a given time.... [T]he aim of explanation is to identify the 'threads' that link the individual or institution under study to its specious socio-cultural 'present.' "[65] The contextualist approach describes much of modern academic historiography. Particularly important for the analysis here is the emphasis placed on "tracing the threads," which is exactly what the source-critical approach is attempting to accomplish. Since history inevitably deals with concrete events of the past, the Lukan redaction is certainly less interesting than the historical kernel behind the composition, unless, of course, one is interested in studying Luke in his own sociocultural present.

Needless to say, much of the scholarship on Acts 6:1–8:3 has focused on the history of earliest Christianity. In so doing, the stress has naturally been placed on tracing the threads of events behind the narrative composition by the author of Acts. This move entails not only looking at events with a view to their sociocultural relationships but also constructing those events and personages by sifting through the available data and by sorting out source from redaction. In order to understand, then, Stephen's relationship to the earliest apostles in Jerusalem or to the other Hellenists, one first needs to reconstruct the "historical" Stephen from Luke's account. It is for this reason that not only the search for sources but also the presupposition of their very existence are so fundamental for a great amount of scholarly study of Acts 6:1–8:3.[66]

---

64. Ibid., 15.

65. Ibid., 18.

66. One notices this insistence on the use of sources by Luke even by those scholars who have done much to advance the position that the Stephen episode and speech have largely been composed by Luke. E. Richard (*Acts 6:1–8:4: The Author's Method of Composition* [SBLDS 41; Missoula, Mont.: Scholars Press, 1978), for instance, has presented a strong case that Acts 6:1–8:3 is largely the product of Luke's creative hand (278, 307). Yet Richard also maintains (largely based upon Luke's use of the Old Testament in the speech) that Luke used "trustworthy annals of the period." Repeatedly, Richard makes claims that certain parts of the narrative belong to tradition (often without much supporting evidence). In other words, even someone like Richard, who sets out to demonstrate why the redaction-critical sifting of Lukan creation from tradition will not work in Acts 6:1–8:3, comes around to assert the existence

The consequences of this methodology, rather than the results, are of special interest for the present study. If one separates the historical kernel from the Lukan redaction, the relationship between the two is overlooked. In fact, in the models outlined above the redaction is most often construed as being at cross-purposes with the historical kernel. Clearly, in this case, an understanding of *historia* as the representation of the whole narrative is not possible. Rather, only one element — either tradition or redaction — comes into focus. Scholars thus must choose between using the material in Acts to study Lukan theology or to reconstruct early Christian history. What scholars achieve through this particular method is nothing short of the bifurcation of *historia* itself. M. Hengel's work provides the best demonstration of this scholarly tradent.

From History to Theology: Hengel, Hellenists, and *Historia*

The trajectory of scholarship on the Hellenists that begins with Baur culminates in Hengel's work on Acts 6:1–8:3. Hengel not only provides the most systematic interpretation of the Hellenists in the tradition of Baur; he also fuels the debate over the reconstruction of early Christian origins. The influential nature of his treatment of the Hellenists — which has had far-ranging impact on discussions of both Jewish and early Christian history — justly earns Hengel a special place in the analysis of the history of scholarship. The "tracing of the threads" methodology outlined above has borne extensive fruit in the work of Hengel, whose formative and perhaps dominating description of Hellenistic Judaism can best be understood as his attempt to reconstruct an origin of Christianity wherein the Hellenists of Acts shine brightly and definitively.

To begin with, Hengel's work on Acts 6:1–8:3 must be placed within the larger context of his work on Second Temple Judaism. Through numerous books and articles, Hengel has taken up the *Religionsgeschichtliche Schule*'s earlier distinction between Hellenistic and Palestinian Judaism.[67] Whereas older German scholarship (e.g., Bousset) had maintained that there was a deep gulf between the Judaism of the Diaspora and the Judaism of Palestine — a gulf that was based largely on more and less conservative positions on Torah, the land, and the people — Hengel argues that

---

of older traditions and sources despite offering little proof (cf. 286, 288–89, 291–92, 297–98, 300, 305–9, 311).

67. The major works by Hengel in this area are *Judaism and Hellenism: Studies in Their Encounter in Palestine during the Hellenistic Period* (2 vols.; trans. J. Bowden; Philadelphia: Fortress, 1974); idem, *Jews, Greeks, and Barbarians: Aspects of the Hellenization of Judaism in the Pre-Christian Period* (trans. J. Bowden; Philadelphia: Fortress, 1980); and idem, with C. Markschies, *The 'Hellenization' of Judaea in the First Century after Christ* (trans. J. Bowden; Philadelphia: Trinity Press International, 1989).

any such distinction based on one being more "hellenized" than the other simply cannot be supported by a close reading of the primary sources. While the older view held that the Judaism of the Diaspora was highly influenced by the prevailing Hellenistic syncretism of the period and that the Judaism of Palestine remained an isolated enclave of rigid commitment to Torah, Hengel argues that all Judaism of the period — in both Palestine and abroad — came under extensive Hellenistic influence. Moreover, in Hengel's configuration, Hellenism provided the opportunity and tools (including the linguistic framework) necessary for the formulation of the Jewish faith in this period and thus should be construed as a positive rather than negative force. Furthermore, syncretism, although clearly present in the Judaism of the time, essentially caused Jews of both Palestine and the Diaspora to rally around their traditions rather than to depart from them:

> [T]he Hellenistic environment represented a certain danger, though its effects should not be over-estimated. In warding off the "reform attempt," the Judaism of Palestine and the Diaspora had found a firm centre in the law which, despite all alien influences and an astonishing multiplicity, at least enabled it to present a relatively closed front to the outside world.[68]

Thus, the unique combination of the "reception and reworking of Greek thought side by side with self-assertion against alienation"[69] led to a dynamic and vibrant Jewish life in both Palestine and the larger Greco-Roman world. According to Hengel, "the almost complete fusion of religion and nationalism not only prevented any assimilation, but at the same time gave the Jewish minority, particularly in the Diaspora, a political importance which even the Roman rulers after Caesar had to take seriously."[70]

This particular understanding of Judaism is important for Hengel's treatment of the Hellenists. On the one hand, it allows him to undercut the arguments of older German scholars such as Bousset that the innovative step toward worshiping Jesus in the Christ cult could only have developed outside Palestine on Hellenistic soil. If Judaism in Palestine were hellenized, there is no reason early proponents of the faith in Jerusalem could not have made that first move to worshiping Jesus. On the other hand, it enables him to formulate the great advance the early church made in Jerusalem that would lead to dramatic new emphases in Christianity: the mission to the Gentiles that moved Christianity beyond the closed system of Judaism. Thus, besides providing Judaism with the tools necessary to continue to thrive in the Greco-Roman world, Hellenism also forced the Jews of the period to close ranks, resulting in a focus on Torah and nationalism in both Palestine and the Diaspora. Consequently, Judaism became a closed system, lacking the

---

68. Hengel, *Judaism and Hellenism*, 1:308.
69. Ibid., 1:309.
70. Ibid., 1:313.

impetus to assimilate with the surrounding world, paving the way for Christianity as a religion of liberty from the law. Hengel has thus accomplished two fundamental sweeps in his study: He has hellenized Palestine and palestinized the Diaspora. In other words, those aspects usually associated with Hellenistic Judaism (language and culture) are seen to be active in Palestine, and those aspects usually associated with Palestinian Judaism (a conservative view of Torah and a strong sense of nationalism) are understood to be just as influential in the Diaspora. Moreover, Hengel has deemphasized for the most part the syncretism and assimilation often touted as a significant feature of Hellenistic Judaism. The liberal spirit toward the Torah that was viewed to be one of the hallmarks of Hellenistic Judaism has been transferred to early Christianity, a movement characterized by its prophetic and spirit-inspired nature.[71]

This last point is particularly significant. Since in Hengel's view the Judaism of Palestine and the Diaspora closed its ranks due to the impetus of Hellenism, early Christianity provided the "way out" that was previously associated with Hellenistic Judaism. In other words, the early Christian movement undertook a critique of Jewish particularistic and nationalistic focus on Torah from within Judiasm. It was precisely its prophetic, spirit-inspired criticism that managed to undercut the enclosed system of the Judaism of the period. Hengel's book on Judaism and Hellenism thus culminates with reference to the Hellenists in Jerusalem:

> [The] revolutionary consequences [of the Christian message] were recognized above all by the group of "Hellenists" in Jerusalem who were familiar with the self-contradictory nature of the Jewish mission — the protective attitude of Judaism over against its environment, which had been developed in the controversy with Hellenism and was most strongly expressed by the absolutized place of the Torah, was shattered in pieces. Christology took the place of "Torah ontology" as an expression of the free and sovereign saving revelation of God in history, which no longer recognized national or historically conditioned limitations.[72]

This statement by Hengel is significant since it firmly links his massive reevaluation of the relationship of Judaism and Hellenism with his interest in the Hellenists of the primitive church in Jerusalem. It is not a coincidence that these Hellenists are now those who enact many of the tenets often attributed by the *Religionsgeschichtliche Schule* to Hellenistic Judaism. Through the Hellenists, Hengel is able to move the most significant developments of early Christianity into Jerusalem in the formative period of

---

71. It is fairly clear that strong theological concerns dominate Hengel's particular presentation and interpretation of the data. Some of these are readily detectable in the statements made above. For further assessment of this aspect of Hengel's work, see J. J. Collins, "Judaism as *Praeparatio Evangelica* in the Work of Martin Hengel," *RelSRev* 15 (1989): 226–28; and L. H. Feldman, "Hengel's *Judaism and Hellenism* in Retrospect," *JBL* 96 (1977): 382.

72. Hengel, *Judaism and Hellenism*, 1:313–14.

Christian history. The association of the Hellenists with Hellenistic Judaism goes back to Baur. Hengel has taken the position one step further, however, by arguing that the Hellenists did not borrow their torah-critique from Hellenistic Judaism but came up with it themselves under the influence of the message of Jesus: They were the progenitors of the Christian view of the Jewish law. The innovative notions advanced in Acts 6:1–8:3 originated with the early Christians, sharply distinguishing this Jewish sect from its larger religious heritage. One would rightly anticipate, then, that the Hellenist view of the law would dominate Hengel's discussion of Acts 6:1–8:3.

Hengel's specific conclusions appear all the more surprising since he fully realizes and accepts that Luke is a tendentious historian and that therefore his account must be used with caution. Hengel adopts the theory of an Antioch Source underlying the narratives in Acts 6:1ff., but argues that Luke has revised the source throughout to the degree that the actual source is now no longer open to reconstruction: "The ancient historian took pride in so reshaping his sources that his model could no longer be recognized, and the mark of his own original style emerged all the more clearly. This basic rule in the ancient use of sources is often too little noted by the sophisticated analysts who very neatly set tradition off against redaction."[73] Moreover, Hengel similarly insists that the actual speech of Stephen can only be used cautiously, as the hand of Luke can be detected throughout, reworking older traditions that can no longer be reconstructed with confidence. According to Hengel, only those portions of the speech that cohere with the charges brought against Stephen in the narrative can be used to reconstruct the theology of the Hellenists.[74] At the same time, Hengel also believes that Luke has shaped the narrative to a large degree, especially in the use of the Sanhedrin as the setting for the trial, providing the Lukan framework for the speech and the charges.[75] Here one observes the strong influence of Baur's earlier work on the Stephen narrative, particularly the emphasis on the historical reliability of the charges and the Jewish mob scene, with both elements being viewed as the primary components of the original narrative and both mutually reinforcing one another. Thus, the actual incident involved words uttered by Stephen that led to a Jewish lynching. According to Hengel, these words must have cohered with the actual charges if one is to understand the nature of the Jewish response. It is easy to see how this particular path then leads to an anti-temple and anti-law reading of the speech itself. Thus,

---

73. M. Hengel, "Between Jesus and Paul: The 'Hellenists,' the 'Seven,' and Stephen (Acts 6:1–15, 7:54–8:3)," in *Between Jesus and Paul: Studies in the Earliest History of Christianity* (trans. J. Bowden; Philadelphia: Fortress, 1983), 4. Also see Hengel's more recent comments, where he refers to the "harmonizing tendency" of Luke as axiomatic (Hengel, with A. M. Schwemer, *Paul between Damascus and Antioch: The Unknown Years* [trans. J. Bowden; Louisville: Westminster John Knox, 1997], 181).

74. Hengel, "Between Jesus and Paul," 19.

75. Ibid., 19–21.

directly from Stephen, the ideas behind it certainly did. Thus, Stephen was clearly a forerunner and predecessor of the apostle Paul, and this was his true *historical* importance: Stephen expressed the initial tenets that Paul, in his "breach with Judaism" (i.e., his conversion), would develop even further.[34]

Baur's work on the Hellenists was foundational for later scholarship. Baur not only raised the issues that would be addressed after him, but he also formulated the discussion in a way that would, for the next 150 years, determine the shape and direction of the research and results from analysis. The importance of Baur thus rests not only in his conclusions but also in his method. Since the latter so fundamentally influenced the shape of subsequent scholarship, his approach to Acts 6:1–8:3 as *historia* is thus worth discussing in more detail.[35]

The influence of German Idealism on Baur, his *Tendenz* method, and his general conception of history are well studied.[36] For Hegel, history was the ongoing manifestation of the divine Spirit, as well as deity coming to consciousness. Thus, at any given point in history there was both a revelation of the divine in historical time and space and also a development over previous revelations as "God" came to further consciousness. For Baur, then, the main aim of the historian was to penetrate beneath the mere hodgepodge of events to their inner core, in order to elucidate the historical process at work.[37] This approach is not simply the search for connections of cause and

---

Targum, Midrasch, und Talmud (ed. F. Delitzsch and G. Schnedermann; Leipzig: Dörffling & Franke, 1880). See further G. F. Moore, "Christian Writers on Judaism," *HTR* 14 (1921): 197–254; S. Heschel, *Abraham Geiger and the Jewish Jesus* (Chicago: University of Chicago Press, 1998), 106–26; S. Kelley, *Racializing Jesus: Race, Ideology, and the Formation of Biblical Scholarship* (New York: Routledge, 2002), 66–80; and J. B. Tyson, *Luke, Judaism, and the Scholars: Critical Approaches to Luke-Acts* (Columbia: University of South Carolina Press, 1999), 12–29.

34. Baur acknowledges that Paul in fact never mentions any predecessor such as Stephen. Baur argues that Paul's breach with Judaism was so great and his theology so original that one can really only consider Stephen a predecessor in hindsight; from Paul's own perspective, there could be no predecessors (*Paul the Apostle*, 1:62 n). Later scholarship would make this connection between Stephen and Paul much more explicit.

35. For a summary of Baur's approach to history, see Hodgson, *Formation of Historical Theology*, 142–201.

36. Kelley, *Racializing Jesus*, provides a general discussion of the broad German Idealistic context and influence, although Baur departed from the Hegelian system in significant ways as well (on this point, see E. P. Meijering, *F. C. Baur als Patristiker: Die Bedeutung seiner Geschichtsphilosophie und Quellenforschung* [Amsterdam: Gieben, 1986], 51–84; and Berger, *Exegese und Philosophie*, 41–46). For Baur, Lutheranism was part of the unfolding of the Spirit in world history and was (and continues to be) an undeniable theological (and historical) reality. Indeed, Baur was operating out of a particularly Christian understanding of the Hegelian philosophical system. Thus, for Baur, his vested interest in Acts 6:1–8:3 and Paul had come about by the very existence of the ideas of Luther. Consequently, he had much less at stake in the historical realities of his *Tendenz* critical approach to New Testament origins than is often appreciated. At the same time, given his particular philosophical commitment, the emergence of German Lutheranism demanded the de facto existence of earlier traces of these later ideas: His entire program of historical studies was based on the Hegelian axiom that later ideational developments are preceded by earlier, partial expressions.

37. See further Hodgson, *Formation of Historical Theology*, 162.

relying almost solely on the charges and the brief notice in Acts 6:8–10 regarding Stephen's character and power, Hengel concludes the following:

> The charge of blaspheming Moses and God...is basically a consequence of Stephen's spirit-inspired preaching (6:10). In Luke's redaction this feature is toned down by the insertion of the speech, and the connection between 6:15 and 7:55 is interrupted. Here we probably have a historical foundation. The criticism of law and temple is connected with the eschatological enthusiasm of the Hellenists, inspired by the spirit.[76]

For Hengel, then, the Hellenists function as the bridge between the teaching of Jesus and the theology of Paul. They are Paul's predecessors insofar as Stephen and his circle establish the initial insights into the significance of Christ's death and resurrection. Moreover, since they were Greek they necessarily must have taken the initial steps to translate the message of Jesus into Greek, making the transition to a language that had much more powerful forms and capacity for expression of the Christian message than Aramaic.[77]

It is striking that for all of Hengel's previous efforts to demonstrate that one cannot easily distinguish between Palestinian and Hellenistic Judaism, he himself frequently differentiates between the Hebrews and Hellenists in Acts 6. The contrast is based on their language (Greek and Aramaic), their respective rural and urban roots (the Hebrews were "backwoods men," while the Hellenists reflected the more cosmopolitan view of the city), and their theology (the Hellenists were more universalistic and less tied to the temple and Torah than their Hebrew counterparts).[78] In Hengel's work, the approach to the Hellenists first solidified by Baur is now firmly entrenched within a very similar framework; what for Baur was the work of the universal divine Spirit in Hengel becomes the work of the Holy Spirit. Hengel has taken the bold initiative of Christianizing the philosophical language of Baur. This move allows Hengel to view the innovative measure of the Hellenists as *sui generis* in their historical context: The Hellenists translated the message of Jesus into the language of Paul and by so doing formulated the

---

76. Ibid., 29.
77. Ibid., 26–28. See further the assessment and critique of Hengel's position by L. W. Hurtado, *Lord Jesus Christ: Devotion to Jesus in Earliest Christianity* (Grand Rapids: Eerdmans, 2003), 207–10.
78. Hengel, "Between Jesus and Paul," 25–26. It is thoroughly surprising that Hengel should here appeal to the theological differences between the Hellenists and Hebrews (he makes the same point, but less tentatively, in *Acts and the History of Earliest Christianity* [trans. J. Bowden; Philadelphia: Fortress, 1979], 73, where he states that the Aramaic Christians were more restrained and conservative in their attitude toward the law [cf. also 74]). Obviously he himself sees no inconsistency in this statement. What causes the Hellenists to shift position is the Spirit, not their commitment to Hellenistic Judaism (in fact, according to Hengel, the Hellenistic Jews in Jerusalem during the feasts were quite conservative; they were Jews for whom land, Torah, and temple were key facets of their religious commitment ["Between Jesus and Paul," 18]). Nevertheless, this particular formulation looks suspect, in that what was once viewed as the distinctive contribution of Hellenism now becomes the distinctive contribution of the Christian Hellenists.

gospel message in such a way that it dramatically and resolutely departed from the Jewish expressions of the early Aramaic-speaking church in Jerusalem. Hengel does attempt to smooth over the gap he inadvertently creates between the Hellenists and the Hebrews in Jerusalem, arguing that in effect the differences are really only of a minute character. Yet everything he writes on the Hellenists belies this claim.[79] Indeed their message — "the eschatological abolition of Temple worship and the revision of the law of Moses in the light of the true will of God"[80] — and their mission — a movement out to the Gentiles because of the rejection the Hellenists faced from their Jewish compatriots[81] — in his view represent radical departures from any previous expressions of the Christian faith. In Hengel's scheme, it is precisely the Hellenists' recognition of the authority granted to them by the "gift of the spirit... [,] a sign of the dawning of the eschatological age,"[82] that enables them to make these bold and provocative advances in the sphere of the early Aramaic-speaking community in Jerusalem.

It is fairly evident that Hengel's speculative account is based on a few short references and relies on a priori assumptions to undergird the skeletal outline from the narrative itself. If the source behind the passage has been taken over seamlessly by Luke and reworked, then one would not be able to distinguish between the source and the Lukan additions because any aspect of the story could presumably belong either to Luke or to the source. One could argue, for instance, that the charges are in fact a creation by the author *and* that the Sanhedrin trial is the original part of the tradition. There is no real way of proving or disproving any number of variant histories of Stephen and the Hellenists. Furthermore, even if one could isolate the original material that Luke has reworked, or attempted to cover up, there is no way of verifying the historical reliability of this material. It would have to be assumed.

Yet, despite the serious problems with this approach, it is necessary to reiterate that Hengel's work on the Hellenists is paramount for contemporary scholarship precisely because he thoroughly grounds the earlier position of Baur that the Hellenists perceived and grasped a new work being manifested by God. The original nature of the Hellenist enterprise is so important to

---

79. One of the oddities of Hengel's work is that he should so adamantly claim that the distinctions, if any, between the Hellenists and the Hebrews were minor, and yet so strongly maintain the older Tübingen school's sharp division between the mission of the Jerusalem church and that of Paul (see his "Der Jakobusbrief als antipaulinische Polemik," in *Tradition and Interpretation in the New Testament: Essays in Honor of E. Earle Ellis* [ed. G. F. Hawthorne and O. Betz; Grand Rapids: Eerdmans, 1987], 248–78), who, in Hengel's view, was influenced by the Hellenists. In effect, Hengel's reconstruction of the conflict between Paul and the Jerusalem church has direct implications for his reading of the Hellenist material; it follows for him that there would also have been a sharp conflict between the Hellenists and the Hebrews over the issue of law-observance. Hengel's method of *Tendenz* criticism is thus quite similar to Baur's.

80. Hengel, *Acts and the History*, 73.
81. Ibid., 74–78.
82. Ibid., 73.

Hengel that much of his previous work on Judaism in fact sets up the framework in which his claims for the Hellenists must be understood. For Hengel, the Hellenists are more than simply the bridge between Jesus and Paul; they are also the link between the revelation of God in Christ and the fuller exposition of the meaning of this event in the so-called law-free theology of Paul. They represent, in effect, a segment in the trajectory of the true and faithful manifestation of God's divine Spirit in human history. Hengel has simply developed what was latent in much of the scholarship influenced by Baur, but it is still an important development as the focus shifts more decidedly to the historicity of the Hellenists and their reconstructed theology. Within Baur's scheme, if this theology were to be attributed to Luke instead of Stephen, the manifestation of the divine Spirit would still have been grasped by some individual of that historical epoch. Within Hengel's view, however, that individual must be a historical figure named Stephen; otherwise, the critical link between the Jesus event and Paul's interpretation would be lost. Hence, despite obvious contortions in his use of Acts 6:1–8:3, and despite the seemingly more nuanced positions in his work on Judaism and Hellenism, Hengel "canonizes" the results of Baur. The historicity of the episode in Acts 6:1–8:3 is now firmly established in modern scholarly discourse. To challenge this premise is both to dispute the heart of Christian theology as Hengel understands it and to undermine the Judaism of the Hellenistic period he has deftly constructed to cradle the origins of this Christian message.[83]

Entrenching the Hellenist Construct: Post-Hengelian Developments

In the studies following Hengel, there is a fundamental entrenchment of the core of Hengel's Hellenist paradigm. Scholars continue to emphasize the temple and cult critique in the theology of the Hellenists.[84] Moreover, the connection of the Hellenists to the first Christian community in Antioch becomes an increasingly important emphasis. Acts 12:19 mentions the spread of missionaries after the persecution of Stephen, detailing that certain men from this group first preached the gospel to "Hellenists," probably Gentiles,

---

83. In his critique of J. Bihler's study of the Hellenist narrative (*Die Staphanusgeschichte im Zusammenhang der Apostelgeschichte* [MTS 1.16; Munich: Hueber, 1963), Hengel accuses Bihler of having abandoned the study of the historicity of the account for a focus on redaction. This move, in Hengel's view, has serious consequences: "Luke becomes basically the writer of a theological romance. If this tendency is maintained, the whole history of early Christianity vanishes into nebulous obscurity" (Hengel, "The Origins of the Christian Mission," in *Between Jesus and Paul*, 173 n. 44). For Hengel, it is clear, historicity has epistemological primacy over Lukan theology.

84. See, for instance, A. Weiser, "Zur Gesetzes- und Tempelkritik der 'Hellenisten,'" in *Das Gesetz im Neuen Testament* (ed. K. Kertelge; Freiburg: Herder, 1986), 146–68; and K. Berger, *Theologiegeschichte des Urchristentums* (2d ed.; Tübingen: Francke, 1995), 160–61.

in Antioch. This feature is significant in Hengel's work precisely because it allows him explicitly to associate the Hellenists of Jerusalem with an outreach to the Gentiles. K. Berger's recent attempt to write a theological history of early Christianity continues in this same vein, laying stress on the Antioch connection.[85] With Hengel, Berger agrees that this link is central precisely because Antioch will become "the starting point of the later mission travels of Paul" and therefore "here, not in Jerusalem, lies the most important center of the early Christian history of theology."[86] The focus on Antioch is crucial because this is the assumed original context for Paul's first mission work among the Gentiles, and it is presumed that he was influenced here by the theological atmosphere created by his predecessors in that city.

Another important feature that develops from the Hengel/Baur synthesis is the emergence of the connection between the Hellenists and the gospel tradition. N. Walter, for instance, in accounting for Paul's contact with particular elements of the Synoptic Jesus tradition, argues that the Hellenists (the "Hellenistic Jewish movement") were likely some of the earliest transmitters of Jesus tradition. Two tenets are critical for Walter. First, Paul, while at first persecuting this group, later joined it after his conversion experience. Second, the Hellenist theology, over against that of Peter, James, and the Jerusalem church, more openly and clearly challenged the "basis" of Judaism, allowing "only relative importance to remain attached to the Torah and Temple" and indeed initiating the first steps toward accepting Gentiles on the same basis as converted Jews. With this framework in view, Walter makes the following claim:

> This group certainly had contact from the start with Jesus-tradition (in a more or less fixed form). But for them those sayings and other traditions which revealed an implicit criticism of the Torah or Temple would probably have been especially important. So many of the apophthegms which show Jesus in conflict with the norms of Judaism may have taken shape and then have been handed on within this circle.[87]

Walter is forced to admit that Paul reveals little acquaintance with this type of Jesus tradition, but argues nonetheless that Paul has been influenced in part by summaries of Torah in the "double commandment" and notions of Jesus having done away with the Jewish system of impurity (cf. Rom 14:14a with Mark 7:15).[88] This sayings material, Walter points out, "which

---

85. Berger, *Theologiegeschichte*, 166–67. Berger's entire summary of the Hellenists is completely indebted to Hengel's work, including his emphasis on the pneumatic and charismatic qualities of Stephen and his circle (164–67).

86. Ibid., 167 (my translation).

87. N. Walter, "Paul and the Early Christian Jesus-Tradition," in *Paul and Jesus: Collected Essays* (ed. A. J. M. Wedderburn; JSNTSup 37; Sheffield: Sheffield Academic Press, 1989), 74.

88. Berger, *Theologiegeschichte*, 168, elaborates in more detail the specific types of Synoptic traditions that likely go back to the Hellenists, among which are the law critique of Mark (and

questioned Jewish values either wholesale or in detail, may well have been taken up with special interest and transmitted in early Hellenistic Jewish Christianity."[89] He then concludes:

> It seems to me to follow from these observations and considerations that the Hellenistic Jewish part of the early church and then, in continuity with it, Paul had a use for and actively "cultivated" such material from the Jesus-tradition as could help to justify their Law-free gospel which was open to the Gentiles. Apart from that, any sayings which were relevant to the "apostolic existence" of their missionaries were also, of course, important within this line of tradition.[90]

This statement is remarkable for what it both states and implies. First, Walter's entire treatment of the Hellenist Jewish movement's connection to the Jesus tradition and to Paul rests on a series of "givens" that are simply assumed to have been proved by previous scholarship on the Hellenists:[91] (1) The key elements of Hellenist ideology are the critique of Jewish values and customs, including but not limited to the temple and Torah; (2) the main thrust of their message was to undermine the fundamental features that defined the Judaism of their day; (3) they originally began a law-free mission to the Gentiles in Antioch; and (4) they formed a key link between the message of Jesus and the ministry of Paul.[92] Walter elaborates on the last point in more detail: Not only did the Hellenists' message influence Paul, but in fact the Hellenists transmitted "in fixed form" sayings and stories about Jesus that would have been formative for Paul's own formulations of a law-free mission to the Gentiles. One further element in Walter's presentation is striking for its tacit assumption that the Hellenists in effect provided the model for Paul's missionary enterprise, not simply in their message of a law-free gospel for Gentiles but in their practice as well. Walter clearly states that the Hellenists had a concern to support and defend the "apostolic existence" of their missionaries. What in Acts is simply a by-product of persecution against the church after the death of Stephen has become a full-blown mission with an "apostle-like" existence, presumably influenced by the stories of Jesus and his "missionaries" in the tradition. This point is

---

consequently that of Matthew and Luke as well), the understanding of law in Mark, and possibly even the title "gospel" as it is to be linked to the Hellenists as the first "evangelists."

89. Walter, "Paul and the Early Christian Jesus-Tradition," 75. Alongside this material Walter observes that this group likely also used sapiential Jesus-traditions, detailing the way Christians ought to live. This material, however, is clearly less significant for Walter as it is not at "variance with Jewish tradition" (75).

90. Ibid., 76.

91. See his brief comments in N. Walter, "Hellenistische Diaspora-Juden an der Wiege des Urchristentums," in *The New Testament and Hellenistic Judaism* (ed. P. Borgen and S. Giversen; Aarhus: Aarhus University Press, 1995), 52–54.

92. Walter comes very close to attributing the rise of the institutional church to the Hellenists as well, a by-product of their having been the first to grasp fully the message of Jesus ("Apostelgeschichte 6.1 und die Anfänge," 387).

most significant for what it reflects about the state of scholarship rather than what it reveals about the history of earliest Christianity. What in Hengel and previous scholarship is still a point to be proved — the degree to which the Hellenist account in Acts 6:1–8:3 reflects historical reality — no longer needs to be argued now; rather, the preceding reconstructions become the point of departure for ever more elaborate deductions and inferences. There is little in Walter's comments on the Hellenists and the Jesus tradition that can be said to be anything more than speculation, most of which cannot even be challenged simply for lack of evidence. Yet once the original premises have become axiomatic, the results of elaboration based on these "givens" seem less dubious than they really are.

The problem with the underlying premises in the study of Acts 6:1–8:3 becomes increasingly acute the further scholarship attempts to go beyond the fundamental story. The recent study by T. Seland illustrates this particular problem well, demonstrating once again the real difficulties inherent in this method of reading Acts 6:1–8:3. Seland begins his work assuming that Luke has used sources in the composition of this textual unit.[93] His conclusion is that the charges against Stephen, the trial scene, and the final martyrdom narrative (6:8–15 and 7:54–60) go back to a pre-Lukan source. Moreover, as is quite common in scholarship on the speech, he simply asserts that the speech is a Lukan rendition of something that in some form goes back to Stephen and the Hellenists.[94] Seland approvingly cites P. Dschulnigg in this regard: "Without the assumption of larger traditional material this speech can hardly be understood."[95] His conclusion to the brief discussion of sources is that "Luke most probably worked with source materials, i.e., he

---

93. T. Seland, *Establishment Violence in Philo and Luke: A Study of Non-Conformity to the Torah and Jewish Vigilante Reactions* (BibIntS 15; Leiden: Brill, 1995), 224. Also see Seland, "Once More — The Hellenists, Hebrews, and Stephen: Conflicts and Conflict Management in Acts 6–7," in *Recruitment, Conquest, and Conflict: Strategies in Judaism, Early Christianity, and the Greco-Roman World* (ed. P. Borgen, V. K. Robbins, and D. B. Gowler; ESEC 6; Atlanta: Scholars Press, 1998), 169–207.

94. Seland, *Establishment Violence*, 225.

95. P. Dschulnigg, "Die Rede des Stephanus im Rahmen des Berichtes über sein Martyrium (Apg 6,8–8,3)," *Judaica* 44 (1988): 195 (my translation). This assertion, despite the work of Richard in arguing a good case for the contrary, is clearly the majority opinion in contemporary scholarship. One could cite numerous examples of agreement on this point from recent scholarship. See especially H.-W. Neudorfer, "The Speech of Stephen," in *Witness to the Gospel: The Theology of Acts* (ed. I. H. Marshall and D. Peterson; Grand Rapids: Eerdmans, 1998), 275–94; E. Larsson, "Temple-Criticism and the Jewish Heritage: Some Reflexions on Acts 6–7," *NTS* 39 (1993): 384; and P. Stuhlmacher, *Biblische Theologie des Neuen Testaments I: Grundlegung, Von Jesus zu Paulus* (Göttingen: Vandenhoeck & Ruprecht, 1992), 160–61. Larsson's position is further nuanced by his wariness over how much of the speech to ascribe to Stephen and the Hellenists, maintaining that the tradition-history of the speech is complex. The major reason why scholars cannot move beyond this position is simply that they find it inconceivable that there would be such a perceived incongruity between speech and context if Luke were to have been responsible for composing the speech (see Larsson, "Die Hellenisten und die Urgemeinde," *NTS* 33 [1987]: 217).

relied upon tradition. These findings are quite consistent with his methods as expressed in Luke 1:1–4."[96]

Seland's overall argument could hold regardless of whether Luke created the Stephen narrative *ex nihilo* or relied upon an earlier Christian tradition. Seland's fundamental position is that the Jewish mob violence against Stephen is not "illegal" according to Jewish law. Rather, based on his reading of Philo's *On the Special Laws* 1.54–57, he argues that there was an appropriate place for "establishment violence" — "legitimate killing of an irregular nature" — against those apostates who were viewed as blaspheming God.[97] This framework for understanding the action against Stephen neither stands nor falls with the presence of sources in Acts 6:1–8:3, and certainly Seland's insights are significant for understanding the larger interaction of early Christians and Jews. However, as Seland's actual discussion of the Stephen narrative reveals, he has simply taken over many of Hengel's assumptions without qualification or demonstration. For instance, Seland summarizes his assessment of the narrative as follows: "The primary agents instigating actions against Stephen were Diaspora Jews.... Stephen [was considered] a problematic former colleague whose preaching was felt to strike at the very heart of the reason for their settlement, i.e., the Temple and its cult."[98] Seland identifies these opponents as "conservative" Jews rather than liberal ones: They moved to Jerusalem precisely because they wanted to be close to the temple. This argument closely resembles Hengel's. Moreover, what makes Seland's case particularly interesting is not the traditional elements of scholarship on Acts 6:1–8:3 that are apparent, but the lack of critical reflection on the implication of redactional analysis and source criticism for his thesis. Seland maintains, for instance, that while the preaching of Stephen was not for certain coupled with non-observance of the law, "according to Luke Stephen's preaching was considered related to such attitudes by the Diaspora Jews."[99] Yet, according to Luke, the agitators are jealous (6:10), lying (6:10, 12) troublemakers (6:11). From Luke's "normative" perspective there is no basis for the charges brought against Stephen, and the killing is portrayed as anything but legitimate.[100] If Luke were interested in portraying the Jews negatively here, as he clearly is, then this has implications for how one uses specific elements in the Acts narrative. The issue of source and redaction cannot be passed over lightly: Understanding the passage historically and analyzing it narratively are two different

---

96. Seland, *Establishment Violence*, 227. Seland does add, however, that the Lukan creative hand makes it difficult to sort out tradition from redaction, implicitly contradicting what he has tried to establish up to this point.

97. Ibid., 252; cf. 256.

98. Ibid., 250.

99. Ibid., 252.

100. Seland recognizes this latter point in part (ibid., 236). See also Hill, *Hellenists and Hebrews*, 57–58.

movements, but in Seland's work they are combined and elided. The shift back and forth between historical "facts" and literary narrative is so swift and deft that it almost seems like sleight of hand: Now Seland argues from historical referentiality (Jewish vigilante action as reflected in Philo), and now he argues from the existing narrative (Luke's particular portrayal of an event). Yet these are quite different steps that have here been collapsed, and Seland's lack of reflection on the issue of sources — indeed his deliberate downplaying of the matter — while lending an air of credibility to his argument, ultimately undermines his larger aim.

Hengel's work on Acts 6:1–8:3 should not be blamed entirely for this situation — after all, there is a long history of scholarship on the Hellenists prior to Hengel that he simply takes up and rearticulates. Yet Hengel's failure to reflect adequately on his method, especially the inherent problematic nature of using "feeling" for reconstructing historical realities,[101] has proved detrimental for the study of the Hellenist narrative in Acts and, in fact, for the interpretation of Acts more generally. The axiomatic nature of the enterprise has become particularly problematic, as key stages in the line of argument are simply sidestepped, and somewhat dubious propositions turn into cornerstones for the reconstruction of early Christian history. In the final analysis, this methodological approach simply does not deal at all with the nature of *historia*, and the features of redaction, sources, historicity, and literary reading are collapsed together in a largely unreflective manner. Of course, part of the problem has been the recognition of the tenuous nature of attempting to separate tradition from redaction (Hengel himself argues for this difficulty), but simply to sidestep the issue is to end up with a completely new set of problems. If tradition cannot be separated from redaction, it is difficult to believe that the solution lies in collapsing history and theology.

The problems with the discursive nature of this construction of the Hellenist narrative perhaps reaches its fullest expression in precisely those studies that seek to overturn Hengel's work in this area. H. Räisänen, for example, establishes one of the main critiques of Hengel's position, offering his own assessment of the account of the Hellenists in Acts 6:1–8.[102] He argues that the narrative was composed largely by Luke, who, using a few fragments of historical tradition, constructed the episode on Old Testament models.[103] Thus, as far as Räisänen is concerned, the basis of Hengel's

---

101. Hengel, "Between Jesus and Paul," 134 n. 7.

102. H. Räisänen, " 'The 'Hellenists': A Bridge between Jesus and Paul?" in *Jesus, Paul, and Torah: Collected Essays* (trans. D. E. Orton; JSNTSup 43; Sheffield: Sheffield Academic Press, 1992), 149–202. See also Räisänen's recent summary and evaluation in "Die 'Hellenisten' der Urgemeinde," *ANRW* 2.26.2 (1995): 1468–1514.

103. Räisänen, "Hellenists," 151–52. This position is also found in Richard, *Acts 6:1–8:4*, 273–74, who argues that, despite a few historical details, the major emphases of the unit must be attributed to Lukan theological interests. A similar position was put forth earlier by D. Daube, who argued that the Hellenist episode in Acts 6:1–7 was composed almost solely on the basis of Old Testament models ("A Reform in Acts and Its Models," in *Jews, Greeks, and*

position — the existence of an Antiochian source underlying the events surrounding the Hellenists — is undercut; Luke did not have access to sources for the Hellenist episode in Acts 6:1–8:3, only fragments of historical tradition. Otherwise, Räisänen argues, Luke surely would have included notes on the founding of the church in Antioch.[104] While Räisänen's own methodological approach and subsequent conclusions may be questionable, the major import of his conclusion should not go unnoticed: Luke has barely any historical information on the Hellenists.

This conclusion becomes significant because of Räisänen's next move: While Luke had no record of the founding of the church in Antioch, his connection of the dispersed Hellenists with the founding of that church (cf. Acts 11:19–20) is probably accurate, as the "men of Acts 11.19–20 have come from somewhere... [and] the 'Hellenists' of Jerusalem, too, must have *gone* somewhere.... [E]ven if Luke did nothing more than speculate in some such way, the odds are that he guessed right."[105] This statement is made precisely in light of the "fact" that Luke himself had no access to any firm historical details on the Hellenists, according to Räisänen.

As Räisänen moves on in his study, his position becomes increasingly tenuous and, at the same time, revealing. First, he argues that apart from the killing of Stephen (an assured historical detail since "Luke could not invent by himself the fact that Stephen was arrested and killed"),[106] there was no general persecution against the church in Jerusalem — the Stephen episode was an isolated event. Nevertheless, the remaining Hellenists in Jerusalem left the city because of the open hostility. This move is critical for Räisänen, as he needs "liberal" Christians to found the church in Antioch; Paul's adoption of the "liberal life-style" is inexplicable apart from the influence of the Hellenists or "like-minded" individuals.[107] One may well wonder what this "like-mindedness" would be based on, since it has been established by Räisänen that the speech and most of the Hellenist episode was constructed by Luke without a source. Thus, while attempting to undermine Hengel's argument by dispensing with the Antiochian source, Räisänen has in effect undercut his own position as well. Yet the prevailing assumption remains: Someone must have influenced Paul. This affirmation necessitates a return to the fundamental premise of Baur that Paul's message has antecedents in the sphere of Hellenistic Jewish theology.

Christians: Religious Cultures in Late Antiquity; Essays in Honor of William David Davies [ed. R. Hamerton-Kelly and R. Scroggs; SJLA 21; Leiden: Brill, 1976], 151–63).

104. Räisänen, "Hellenists," 153–54. This "certainty" that Luke would have included notes on the founding of the church at Antioch had he possessed the information rests on the primacy of Antioch (and Antiochian theology) in reconstructions of early Christian history.
105. Ibid., 155.
106. Ibid., 166.
107. Ibid., 157.

Räisänen's next move is to suggest that Hengel's view of the Hellenists as mediators between Jesus' critical stance on the law and Paul's later formulation is wrong. Particularly problematic for him is the association of the Hellenist stance with spirit enthusiasm, as this is a strongly Lukan theme. Especially important in this regard is Räisänen's skepticism. For instance, after analyzing the Stephen narrative in Acts 6:8–7:1, he concludes that there is actually very little evidence to go on for reconstructing the nature and accuracy of the charges in 6:14, particularly, again, because Luke does not seem to be using a source.[108] Moreover, Räisänen argues that the speech is largely a Lukan composition (although it may preserve some fragments of the early Christian memory of Stephen). Consequently, very little can be gleaned from the speech for the reconstruction of Stephen's own theology. This formulation includes the assertion that, while the anti-temple accusation is probably a Lukan recollection (i.e., Luke did not, or could not, invent it), it is not necessarily a historically accurate one.[109] On the issue of the law, however, Räisänen is willing to make a stand: Stephen must have said or done something that challenged the basic understanding of Jewish law. There is absolutely no evidence in the text to support this claim, since Räisänen, in his attempt to undermine Hengel's position, has largely ousted the narrative as a reliable guide. Rather, something quite different seems to direct Räisänen's argument, namely, his pre-understanding of Paul's theology. Starting from the assumption that fundamental for Paul was the spiritualizing of Torah, Räisänen believes that the way to account for the rise of this view in early Christianity is to have this position propagated earlier by liberal Hellenistic Jews. Here he does part ways with Hengel, as the latter's work seeks to challenge this approach to early Christian theology. Räisänen, by contrast, revives the older position on this point of contention: Liberal Hellenistic Judaism influenced early Christian conceptions of the law. For Räisänen, the essential issue is circumcision, and it was the Hellenists of Jerusalem who first dropped this as a requirement for Gentiles.[110] Räisänen, however, does not inspire much confidence in his own interpretation when he states, "With all this, we have surely moved a good step into the realm of uncertain speculation, though not necessarily any farther than is the case with some other recent reconstructions of the mission and message of the Hellenists."[111]

---

108. Ibid., 170.
109. Räisänen still believes it is possible that Stephen may have criticized the temple (ibid., 201); thus, he wavers on the issue.
110. Ibid., 187–88. Räisänen uses the episode of Philip and the Ethiopian eunuch as an example here; indeed, it is one episode in which Räisänen seems to place great stock. Here is a case — likely before Stephen's death — of a Jew accepting the baptism of an uncircumcised Gentile (188).
111. Ibid., 188.

Räisänen concludes by suggesting that the connection to Hellenistic Diaspora Judaism should be maintained for the Hellenists, particularly the "spiritualizing tendencies" at work in Hellenistic Judaism:

> The experience of the "Hellenists" among non-Jews probably prepared them for the decision to give up those parts of the law which were most offensive to would-be converts. The experience of Christ as the Lord then somehow freed them to join the "allegorizers" in dropping the outward observance of some commandments and thus to take the step which Philo, for all his liberal theory, refused to take.[112]

It may seem odd that Räisänen's attempt to revise Hengel's proposal has ended up here. It certainly shows a lack of critical reflection on the use of Acts 6:1–8:3 as a whole. It also demonstrates that the role of the Hellenists in the early Christian community has come to the point that even if this group did not exist, it would be necessary to invent them.[113]

For Räisänen, then, the "spiritualizing" views of the Hellenists — characterized by their dropping of circumcision as a requirement for entrance into the community — becomes the basis for Paul's later rationalizations of these principles. As Räisänen continues, one observes that the Hellenists in fact have become formative not only for Paul but also for early Christianity in general. They are, for instance, the assumed founders of the Christian community in Rome,[114] and we meet them again as troublemakers in the Gospel of Matthew.[115] In light of all this, it may seem surprising that Räisänen has opposed Hengel's reconstruction of the role of the Hellenists in early Christianity to begin with. However, he primarily objects to Hengel's failure to connect the views of the Hellenists with their liberal Diaspora Jewish background (i.e., Hengel's distancing of the origins of Christianity from Judaism). Notwithstanding his claims to the contrary, it is difficult to see how he can really criticize Hengel's position; the Hellenists are still the "bridge" between Jesus and Paul, only in a less direct sense.[116] They simply founded the community on principles that Paul would later develop and reformulate in light of his own experiences and convictions. In the end, this situation reflects the degree to which the original views of Baur have become entrenched in subsequent scholarship. Despite the complete lack of source material in Acts 6:1–8:3 — or at least the inability to reconstruct an Ur-text with any

---

112. Ibid., 190.
113. As A. J. M. Wedderburn notes, "The Hellenists *may* not be the 'bridge,' but a 'bridge' there must be, even if it has been submerged without trace beneath the onrushing stream of past history" ("Paul and Jesus: Similarity and Continuity," in *Paul and Jesus* [ed. Wedderburn], 130).
114. Räisänen, "Hellenists," 193.
115. Ibid., 200.
116. For similar appraisals, see the more recent studies by E. Rau, *Von Jesus zu Paulus: Entwicklung und Rezeption der antiochenischen Theologie im Urchristentum* (Stuttgart: Kohlhammer, 1994), esp. 82–86, 96–100, 115–16; and W. Kraus, *Zwischen Jerusalem und Antiochia: Die "Hellenisten," Paulus und die Aufnahme der Heiden in das endzeitliche Gottesvolk* (SBS 179; Stuttgart: Katholisches Bibelwerk, 1999).

certainty — scholars have advanced oversimplified theories based largely on intuition regarding their sense of what must have been present in the formative period of Christian origins. The philosophical underpinnings of Baur have been replaced with a rather simplistic cause and effect approach, which reduces historical critics to uncovering — if not inventing — the *historia* that remains hidden from view. The critical question in all of this is whether the narrative of Acts 6:1–8:3 is really concealing anything at all.

The natural result of this post-Baur trajectory is best illustrated by the recent analysis of F. Vouga, who takes the above trajectory to its extreme, arguing that there is almost nothing in Acts 6:1–8:3 that can be taken as accurately reflecting the early history of the Hellenists. Indeed, except for the mere mention of the existence of Hebrew-speaking and Greek-speaking congregations and the brief note in Acts 11:19–20 about the preaching of the Hellenists as they returned to Antioch, the rest of the account in Acts 6:1–8:3 is fiction, reflecting Lukan "salvation historical" aims.[117] Were Vouga to leave the analysis there, he might be fine. But, despite his deconstruction of the Acts narrative (or perhaps in light of it), he goes on to make the following claim:

> The following is historical: the development of early Christianity cannot be understood without autonomous groups of Greek-speaking followers of Jesus with a Hellenistic education; these Hellenists had a distinctive understanding of the death and resurrection of Jesus; their Christology was connected with a particular interpretation of law, which brought them into conflict; and they were the first to preach the gospel outside of Palestine.[118]

This set of claims represents the "historical" given for constructing the history of earlier Christianity. It does not need to be proven; it is simply assumed. This statement is remarkable precisely because, while much of it has largely been argued before, in those earlier cases the premises were based on reading the narrative in Acts 6:1–8:3 as a reflection of historical realities. Because the metanarrative has become so entrenched in scholarship, Vouga can now dispense with the narrative in Acts (so much so that his details on the Hellenists must be teased out from the Pauline letters), and yet he still arrives at the same conclusions.[119] Vouga's work at this point has obviously

---

117. F. Vouga, *Geschichte des frühen Christentums* (Tübingen: Francke, 1994), 42. Vouga observes that the list of names is unsubstantiated outside of Acts 6:1–8:3; the narrative of Stephen's martyrdom is simply based on *topoi*; the association with the temple is made by Luke; and the speech is most likely a Lukan creation, as is the connection of the preaching of the Hellenists with the first mission to the Gentiles (Acts 9). In the final analysis, very little if any reliable information about the Hellenists can be gleaned from the Acts account. Indeed, the unreliability of Acts in general is attested by the fact that Vouga completely leaves it out of his treatment on the history of early Christianity.

118. Ibid., 42 (my translation). See similarly W. Schmithals, *The Theology of the First Christians* (trans. O. C. Dean, Jr.; Louisville: Westminster John Knox, 1997), 77.

119. Overall, Vouga's precise construction of Hellenist history follows similar lines as earlier scholars. Noteworthy elements in his presentation are the following: Liberal Diaspora Jews

moved beyond its pertinence for reading the narrative of Acts 6:1–8:3, and his analysis rightfully needs to be challenged at its source: his reading of the other literary documents of early Christianity (especially the Pauline letters). Nevertheless, the insistence that the one given historical fact of early Christianity is that these Hellenists must have existed illustrates the enduring effect of past scholarship. In Acts, the existence of the Hellenists may at the very least be required narratively, but New Testament scholarship has made their existence a historical necessity.

In the final analysis, the research from Hengel to the present on the Hellenists has left New Testament scholarship with a somewhat paradoxical situation. When the interest in Christian origins is reduced to the quest for historical cause and effect, the narrative of Acts 6:1–8:3 is either overinterpreted (as in Hengel) or ignored altogether (Vouga). The results, curiously enough, come out the same: Consistently the Hellenists are understood to be the link between Jesus and Pauline Christianity through their emphasis on a law-free mission to the Gentiles. From Baur to Vouga there exists a particular construal of early Christian history based on assumptions regarding the influence of a more liberal Hellenistic Judaism on early Christian theology and practice. The historical axiom in this model is that early Christians must have had a precedent in practice (or at least "spirit") that provided the impetus for an openness to Gentiles. Once this is granted, then one must simply look for this "link" in early Christian texts. The reading of the Hellenists supported by the majority of scholars from Baur to the present is thus necessitated by the historical model underlying the research: It is historically impossible to conceive of early Christian history without a thread like the one that more liberal Hellenistic Jewish Christians in Acts provide. More important, the vagaries, complexities, and nuances of historical relationships are ignored in favor of a more simplistic approach: the assertion of a core historical datum such as the presence of seven men or a group represented by the Hellenists. Some counter voices have been offered, however. C. C. Hill's research on the Hellenists in early Christianity, for example, confronts many of these issues, challenging the results of earlier scholarship. The question remains, though, to what degree even the counter approaches in fact overturn the dominant methodological framework and the conclusions established therein.

---

were actually followers of Jesus and were witnesses to Jesus' final conflict with the Pharisees in Jerusalem, his last table fellowship, his violent death, and the Easter experience. Going back to their synagogues and homes after their experience of Jesus, they preached a message of the forgiveness of sins in the synagogues. Moreover, they brought with them the practice of table fellowship and articulated it in connection with Jesus' death as a salvific act, developing it into a cult form. Furthermore, their real conflict came with the Jewish Christians of Jerusalem, as these opposed the Hellenists for their law-free mission to the Gentiles (Vouga, *Geschichte des frühen Christentums*, 45–46).

Different Direction? Hill on Hengel and History

In many respects, Hill's work on Stephen and the Hellenists should be viewed as a direct and critical response to earlier scholarship on Acts 6:1–8:3.[120] He offers it as a challenge to the work of Hengel and, more indirectly, to the Baur tradition as a whole. More generally, Hill engages the major branch of New Testament scholarship that has continued to insist upon recovering a particular and distinctive Hellenist theology from the account in Acts.[121] Although Hill is not explicitly focused on the account of Acts 6:1–8:3, he is interested in analyzing the common assertion that there existed in early Christianity a distinct group of Hellenistic Jewish Christians who had a more liberal attitude toward Torah, including an anti-temple or temple-critical position. This frequently proffered detail represents, for Hill, the most questionable aspect of Hengel's legacy and in his view contradicts some of Hengel's main contributions elsewhere: for example, that Palestine was a fully hellenized region, making distinctions between "liberal" and "conservative" Judaism problematic. Of course, Hengel indeed accounts for, even if implicitly, such distinctions himself and they appear to be crucial elements underpinning some of his larger theological interests in early Christian history in general and the Hellenists in particular.

Hill's analysis of the Stephen/Hellenist narrative contains three key elements: (1) The persecution in 8:1–4 is ultimately a Lukan literary device and does not reveal the existence of ideologically distinct groups in Jerusalem (resulting in the Hellenists being persecuted, while the Hebrews were not); (2) the speech of Stephen, including the charges leveled against him in the introductory narrative of 6:8–15, is largely a Lukan creation and should not be read as anti-temple and anti-law in orientation; and (3) the basis of the account of 6:1–7 does rest on historical grounds but does not emphasize theological differences between the "Hellenists" and "Hebrews" (it only details community problems arising from the neglect of widows). Thus, in an attempt to undercut over a century of scholarship on Acts 6:1–8:3, Hill simply turns to an analysis of the narrative, suggesting that most scholars, based on numerous a priori assumptions, half-truths, and misreadings on a massive scale, have grossly exaggerated the historical significance of the Hellenists. Hill's conclusion is that the portrait of Acts 6:1–8:3, when read in light of the internal evidence of the text itself and the external evidence regarding the history of early Christianity gleaned from Paul's letters, does not support the division of early Jewish Christianity in Jerusalem into two

---

120. Hill, *Hellenists and Hebrews*, 41–101. For a summary of his position, see C. C. Hill, "Acts 6.1–8.4: Division or Diversity?" in *History, Literature, and Society* (ed. Witherington), 129–53.

121. Although left out of the main discussion here, Brehm's study, "Role of the 'Hellenists,'" undertakes a similar, albeit more detailed, analysis of the history of the discussion, focusing on the theological models that influenced the Hellenist interpretive trajectories of Baur, A. Neander, and A. Ritschl.

distinct ideological groups — one liberal, the other more conservative in its respective attitude toward Jewish law and practice.

Hill's specific arguments are of less interest for the aims of this study, but there is much in his work that is commendable, including his analysis of Stephen's speech. It is, however, more important for the argument in this chapter to address the following question: Has Hill advanced the discussion of Acts 6:1–8:3 significantly beyond where Hengel has left us? If the problem with Hengel's reading of Acts 6:1–8:3 is more fundamentally a flaw in the conception of *historia* in Luke-Acts, then a rereading of Acts, however accurate it may be, really does not address the larger issue at stake in the Hellenist question. It is precisely at this juncture that Hill's analysis fails to move contemporary scholarship significantly forward: Hill indeed shares Hengel's view of history in Acts, while attempting to demonstrate that Acts 6:1–8:3 in particular cannot shed much historical light on the Hellenists. Hill differs from Hengel only in a specific detail, not in overall conception. Hence, his argument with Hengel is essentially historical in nature. If one can demonstrate that the speech, the trial scene, and the subsequent persecution are highly reworked, perhaps even invented, by Luke on the basis of either Old Testament models or narrative necessity, then the material does not aid in reconstructing this aspect of early Christian origins; one needs to turn to Paul for help in this case. Nevertheless, Hill's conception of the material is still essentially referential in nature (i.e., one can move, with caution, from the details in the narrative back to a reconstruction — albeit rudimentary in some cases — of the social and historical realities of the early church), even if in a particular instance he argues against referentiality.[122]

A good example of Hill's overall approach is his treatment of Acts 6:1–7, the account describing the initial problem between the "Hebrews" and the "Hellenists" in Jerusalem, a narrative often viewed as reflecting underlying theological differences but which Hill takes at face value as a description of economic problems in the early Christian community. While Hill accepts D. Daube's suggestion that the narrative of the appointment of the seven has been modeled on the Numbers 11 passage describing the appointment of the seventy elders, he also contends that this is not reason in and of itself to suggest that Luke has invented the tradition. He then goes on to outline several tests that can be employed to verify the historical authenticity of the Lukan account. Two of these are particularly pertinent for the analysis here: (1) the historical probability of the event related and (2) the impression one has of Luke's veracity and/or historical accuracy.[123] In Hill's view, the account of the appointment of the seven is not only historically

---

122. It is thus not entirely true that Hill argues against referentiality altogether in the Stephen narrative. Rather, those elements that conflict with his historical model are viewed as Lukan additions. This approach is remarkably similar to those Hill criticizes: Those elements that conflict with the specific model adopted are considered to be Lukan elements.

123. Hill, *Hellenists and Hebrews*, 25–26.

probable, but it also bears the distinct impression of Lukan accuracy. Hill bases his conclusions on two points: (1) Greek-speaking Christians would most likely have had their own leaders and (2) two known Jewish practices are reflected in this text, namely, the establishment of boards of elders (especially "boards of seven") and the exercise of charity (more specifically, the daily food distribution in Jerusalem by the wealthy for the poor).[124] The fundamental challenge to the older view that is offered by Hill in this case is that the division in the early church came about through problems resulting from economics rather than theology: The "Hebrews" simply stopped helping the "Hellenist" widows.

The point here is not to take issue with particular aspects of the interpretation of Acts 6:1–8:3. Rather, I observe that Hill has not moved the discussion fundamentally beyond Hengel's formulation. Given such criteria as "probability" and "impression of historical veracity," one is left with the same methodology Hengel used. The ancient historians had a penchant for verisimilitude in describing events and persons, and thus probability in and of itself tells us very little about the historicity of the narrative. In fact, in terms of probability and impression, the narratives of Acts 6:8–15 and 8:1–3 are as seemingly historical as 6:1–7. There is nothing intrinsically historically unlikely or improbable about either of them. Rather, Hill's overarching model is unity in the early church in Jerusalem, just as Hengel's dominant premise is disunity in the early church. Hill reinterprets the significance of 6:1–7 in light of unity, and thus emphasizes the economic basis of the problem. But here Hill becomes as selective and arbitrary as those scholars whom he criticizes, only he chooses to regard 6:1–7 as historically accurate, while arguing that the remainder of the account is essentially a Lukan theological product. Hill's advance, then, is not the offering of a new method but the reapplication of the earlier method through the use of a new starting point. Instead of moving from a point of division in the early church toward even further Christian cultural and theological diversity (the Baur model), he begins from a point of unity in the community and a commitment to fundamental cultural and theological congruence in the development of nascent Christianity, a position arising out of the classic binary opposition between orthodoxy and heresy as two fundamental options for construing the point of origin for Christianity.[125] The questions being asked of the narrative have

---

124. Ibid., 26. N. Hyldahl, *The History of Early Christianity* (trans. E. M. Arevad and H. Dyrbye; Frankfurt: Peter Lang, 1997), 171–76, follows a similar line, taking it one step further on the basis of the earlier suggestions of Billerbeck: The "Hebrews" are not Jewish Christians but Jews, and the early church thus responds to the failure of the Jews in Jerusalem to support Hellenistic Jewish widows.

125. Hill's study is dedicated to a reassessment of the role of the Jerusalem church in Christian origins, not to its removal from history (*Hellenists and Hebrews*, 196–97). In fact, his real interest is in the Pauline materials, especially the oft-proffered thesis that the earliest opponents of Paul were Judaizing missionaries connected with the Jerusalem church. His primary aim is, in fact, to push the insights of Hengel even further: Hellenism had such a profound impact in

not changed, only the specific construal of the data. Thus, if one were to inquire as to the nature of *historia* in this model, one would have to admit it still represents, as in Hengel, historical events and personages. Hill simply rejects some parts of Acts 6:1–8:3 as unhistorical, while accepting others as having a historical basis.

In fairness to Hill, he never presents his study as anything other than an attempt to challenge the tradition of interpretation that has emphasized diversity in theological outlook among the early Christians in Jerusalem. He has little interest in Luke's theology in its own right and, as a consequence, in Luke's overall narrative and historical aims. Yet it is precisely in Hill's critique of former scholarship that the weakness of this entire trajectory of interpretation is underscored once more, namely, the inadequate reflection on the nature of Lukan *historia*. The fundamental problem with previous scholarship — the underlying conception of history and history writing — is left out of the discussion altogether. Indeed, not only has Hill failed to move beyond the older approach, he inadvertently and unwittingly has entrenched it further.

The history of interpretation from Baur to Hengel has thus left a legacy of speculation and conjecture regarding the narrative of Stephen and the Hellenists. Most scholars following this line of inquiry agree that the narrative and speech, as they now stand in Acts 6:1–8:3, present problems for the interpreter. Furthermore, most proceed on the premise that it is possible to separate out the more historical from the less historical in Luke's presentation. Where one draws that precise line — between what is historical and redactional — varies from scholar to scholar, generally based on more or less conservative views of the place and purpose of historical writing in early Christianity. The results often seem arbitrary and historically problematic in terms of the rather linear and often flat construction of Christian origins

---

Palestine that the early Christian community in Jerusalem was a pluralistic and diverse group of people, not easily reducible to facile theological camps. While Hill is committed to unity in the early period of Christianity (contra Hengel), he promotes an ethos of diversity as well, but one that cannot be categorized simplistically (and certainly not theologically). Ultimately, Hill understands that to bring unity to the conception of the Pauline churches vis-à-vis the Jerusalem church one has to undercut the assumed Hellenist versus Hebrew theological rift (as Tübingen *Tendenz* analysis has fundamentally shaped both sides of the debate — anti-Pauline missionaries versus Paul; Hebrews versus Hellenists — as two prongs of the same essential tension). By so doing, all motivation for the theological tensions with Pauline opponents disappear at a primary level (Paul still had opponents, but they were not representative of real disunity in the larger church; they were simply local annoyances). Thus, as odd as it may seem for someone who so thoroughly argues for Lukan composition of the Stephen narrative and speech (in the end, we know "probably very little" about the Hellenists [Hill, *Hellenists and Hebrews*, 101]), the existence of the Hellenists is still a known and significant datum for Hill. It is, in fact, one of the key points of his argument; without the existence of the Hellenists Hill's argument about the full impact of Hellenism on the diversity of early Christianity (and hence the diversity of problems in the Pauline churches) falls short, and as a result a monolithic view of the Hebrew community in Jerusalem once again becomes a tantalizing option.

that results. Even Hill's approach falters on this same ground. As interesting as it may be to many and even theologically and historically imperative to others, it is questionable whether a historical narrative such as Acts 6:1–8:3 can be sifted through as easily or as palpably as many New Testament scholars have done from Baur onward. Indeed, the history of scholarship on the Hellenists reveals a complex movement between different epistemological models of history and the use of diverse frameworks for the construction of Christian origins, often with an interplay between epistemology and historical reconstruction. Despite attempts to understand and appreciate the "Lukan view" of *historia* (both Luke's own conception of what *historia* is and the specific manifestation of his own historiographic-literary art in the text), in the end one receives the distinct impression that the final constructs of both conception and practice often appear rather modern and, ultimately, rather arbitrary.

Moving in the Other Direction: Dibelius and Lukan *Theologia*

While the overwhelming majority of scholars of Acts 6:1–8:3 have been interested in recovering the historical traditions underlying the Hellenist narrative, the rise of redaction criticism, and especially the influence of Dibelius on Acts studies, paved the way for scholars to move in the other direction: away from history to theology, making a methodological distinction between materials that belong to the sphere of historical investigation and those that belong to the realm of theological and ideological analysis. For the most part, the scholars surveyed above accept this basic division. Yet in most cases they have attempted to separate out the Lukan redactional elements only to ignore these in favor of the historical kernel.

Despite this one-sidedness in the study of Acts 6:1–8:3, Dibelius's contribution is significant. Just as Hengel must be singled out for his methodological approach, particularly for the way he breaks down the unity of *historia,* Dibelius also must be criticized for achieving the same thing, albeit working from the opposite direction. In particular, Dibelius introduced a potentially problematic conception into Luke-Acts studies by making a distinction between Luke the historian and Luke the theologian, a tension that has remained in New Testament criticism ever since. A look at Dibelius's work as it relates to the Hellenists will help illustrate this point and provide a fuller context for my own reassessment of ancient historiography later in this study.

Resulting from his interest in literary genres and their development, Dibelius moved the discussion of Acts ahead significantly in his time by comparing this work to ancient historiography more generally, concluding that

Acts must be read in light of the literary practices of the ancient historians.[126] In this way, Dibelius felt that some of the so-called incongruities that were so often pointed out as evidence for viewing Acts as an inferior literary product in fact suggested the opposite, namely, that Acts was to be read in light of the great historical works of antiquity:

> [T]he ancient historian does not wish to present life with photographic accuracy, but rather to portray and illuminate what is typical, and this practice of aiming at what is typical and important allows the author of Acts partly to omit, change or generalize what really occurred. So it is that, where he sometimes appears to us today to be idealising, and describing what was typical, he was really trying to discharge his obligations as an historian. Thus, through literary methods of the historian, he was able to discharge his other obligation of being a preacher of faith in Christ.[127]

Despite what some scholars may think, Dibelius was clearly not trying to make an argument about the unhistorical character of Acts. Haenchen pushed this element further, but even with him, this fundamental belief remains: Luke is operating as an ancient historian. Like Cadbury, Dibelius understood the connection between historiographical composition and literary artistry; therefore, the assertion that Luke was a historian meant first and foremost that scholars had to attend to the unfolding of the historical aims in the narrative itself. For Dibelius, this meant that elements of Luke's composition that appeared, from a modern perspective, to be out of place in a work of history (e.g., idealizing and the highlighting of the typical) were in fact at home in the world of ancient historical writing. Fundamentally, then, much like Cadbury's work, Dibelius's analysis was in some sense an apologetic for Luke's literary effort.

Dibelius also goes further, however, separating the task of the historian from that of the theologian or evangelist.[128] It is perhaps to be expected that someone who appreciated so well the connection of Acts to ancient history should so thoroughly make the division at the point of "theology"; after all, this element went beyond the interest of the ancient historians, as they were unconcerned about events that took place "according to the will of God."[129] Yet there is discernable here another level of apologetic: a concern to protect the message of Luke from being absorbed into the ideology of the

---

126. Dibelius, "First Christian Historian," esp. 133–37.
127. Ibid., 136–37.
128. Dibelius repeatedly makes the distinction between the two. See "Speeches in Acts," 166, 178, 180–81, 183, 185.
129. Dibelius, "Speeches in Acts," 181. This is an overstatement, especially when one compares Luke to Jewish historians such as Josephus or Greek historians such as Diodorus Siculus and Dionysius of Halicarnassus (see J. T. Squires, *The Plan of God in Luke-Acts* [SNTSMS 76; Cambridge: Cambridge University Press, 1993]), but Dibelius was more interested in the "classical" Greek historians. Indeed, it was imperative for his apologetic that Luke be associated with the great Greek historians such as Thucydides, as he was attempting to elevate Acts to the status of the "high" literature of antiquity.

great Greek and Roman historians (i.e., Luke is not *just* the same as them). Dibelius is difficult to read on this point, as he becomes increasingly vague the closer one gets to his conception of the disjunction between the respective tasks of the historian and theologian. Clearly, however, he believes that Luke departs from ancient historiographical practice in a fundamental way by "sermonizing" in the speeches and displaying an interest in the kerygma of early Christianity.

This issue comes into clearer focus in Dibelius's analysis of the speeches in Acts. Dibelius is aware that in the production of ancient history writers were obligated "to illuminate and somehow present the meaning of events."[130] Indeed, Dibelius fully appreciates that by ordering various stories a historian such as Luke turns these independent narratives into history.[131] The speeches are important in this light; they frequently provide the author's interpretation of the significance of specific events or of the larger historical narrative that is unfolding. At key turning points in the narrative of Acts, speeches are used to interpret the significance of the events at hand.[132] Dibelius is clear that the speeches are shaped and elaborated by Luke, although he is reticent to say that Luke freely invented them *ex nihilo*.[133] There are, however, speeches that occur in the narrative that do not fit the specific narrative occasion. These are of particular interest to Dibelius. Stephen's speech is one such example, wherein the larger context of the book rather than the actual narrative (historical) situation — the trial before the Sanhedrin — accounts for the significance of the speech.[134] In this framework the speech is designed to further the overarching themes of the book as a whole rather than to relate key information for the Stephen episode itself. Dibelius argues that the loose connection between speech and context suggests that Luke has inserted the speech into a story about a Jewish mob-lynching of an early Christian martyr.[135] According to Dibelius, the speech supports the burgeoning conflict between Christianity and Judaism, providing the motivations for the impending breach in the narrative.[136]

---

130. Dibelius, "First Christian Historian," 125 (cf. "Speeches in Acts," 138–40). See the earlier and similar assessment by P. Wendland, *Die hellenistisch-römische Kultur in ihren Beziehungen zu Judentum und Christentum* (HNT 1.2; Tübingen: Mohr Siebeck, 1912), 331. M. Wilcox, "A Foreword to the Study of the Speeches in Acts," in *Christianity, Judaism, and Other Greco-Roman Cults: Studies for Morton Smith at Sixty* (ed. J. Neusner; SJLA 12; Leiden: Brill, 1975), 1:206, traces this emphasis back to J. G. Eichorn (1810). Cf. H. J. Cadbury, "The Speeches in Acts," in *Beginnings of Christianity* (ed. Foakes Jackson and Lake), 5:426–27.
131. Dibelius, "First Christian Historian," 129.
132. Dibelius, "Speeches in Acts," 164.
133. Ibid., 164 n. 55. This situation holds true also for the kerygmatic speeches (see 165–66).
134. Ibid., 174–75.
135. Ibid., 168–69. This particular line of argument was enormously influential on subsequent scholarship, including more historically conservative critics such as Hengel.
136. Ibid., 170, 175.

For Dibelius, then, the speeches represent the primary medium by which Luke as historian manifests the literary elements of the genre of historical writing. Yet there is a further complication to this picture, arising in particular from the missionary speeches. These represent a third type of speech in Acts, one in which there is no connection between the themes of the speech and either the immediate or macronarrative context of Acts. These speeches, for Dibelius, represent the writer's attempt either to produce a sermon the way it was preached in his own day or to "sermonize" for the readers themselves — to preach to his audience on everything from the dangers of Gnosticism to the importance of belief in the resurrection for Christian faith.[137] In this latter use of speeches, according to Dibelius, Luke has departed from the role of historian, since not only is the speech unrelated to the immediate context, but it also does not relate to the more general themes of the work as a whole. Dibelius pronounces, "Here the analogy of historical writing fails, and the kerygmatic aim of the book, i.e., not only to narrate but also to proclaim, comes into evidence."[138] For Dibelius, the movement from speech in context to speech apart from context illustrates a shift from historian to theologian.

There are therefore three types of speeches in Acts: speeches that explain or interpret their narrative context; speeches that are unrelated to their narrative context but develop larger themes of the book; and speeches that are unrelated to their context, do not develop larger themes, and are intended to "preach" to the reader. In the first type of speech, Dibelius sees the historian at work. In the third type, there is no doubt for Dibelius that the historian has disappeared and we are now presented with a theologian. The second type of speech, which includes the speech of Stephen, is transitional. It represents a fluid stage wherein the functions of historian and theologian are combined. Dibelius states, "[I]f I have stressed frequently the fact that in many instances the speeches by-pass the situation of the time, this is because such license has in the first place been suggested to the author by the example of the great historians; but it is from his sermonizing attitude that we understand why and how he availed himself of this liberty."[139] Thus, the occasion for these types of speeches arises from the literary repertoire of the ancient historian, but the content is shaped largely by the task of the theologian: to present the speech not as a "part of the story, but as a living proclamation and as an exhortation."[140] Despite his attempt to have us read Acts in the context of ancient historiography, Dibelius insists on drawing a sharp line in those instances he deems Luke to have gone beyond the boundaries of

---

137. Dibelius, "First Christian Historian," 132; and "Speeches in Acts," 178, 180. The speech of Stephen straddles the line at this point. In terms of content it belongs to the category of "mission speeches," but in terms of function it falls into the class of "thematic speeches."
138. Dibelius, "Speeches in Acts," 178.
139. Ibid., 180.
140. Ibid.

ancient history, that is, when Luke "forgets" his narrative and preaches to his readers.[141]

For the purposes of this study, two elements of Dibelius's work in particular are significant. First, Dibelius not only introduced the disjunction between historian and theologian into the discussion of Acts, he emphasized this repeatedly, making this feature one of his enduring contributions to the study of Acts. Indeed, he formally and thematically identified the points at which Luke began moving from one sphere to the other. For Dibelius, the writer of Acts was a literary master, wearing two different hats at various times. At certain points, the writer was a historian, using all the various literary devices available in that genre. At other times, the writer was a theologian who, using the literary devices available to the ancient historian — particularly the speeches — was able to move beyond the merely historical shaping of his narrative in order to preach the word of God to the readers of his text. Thus, the movement toward theologian was made possible and indeed occasioned by the historical practice of placing speeches in narrative contexts. But the writer of Acts moved beyond the merely banal into the kerygmatic realm of the Christian faith, which transcended historical contingency. Dibelius never viewed this as a negative feature of Luke's historical work; in fact, all the evidence, meager as it may be, suggests that Dibelius found this facet to be praiseworthy. Herein we see some perceptible traces of Dibelius's own faith commitment showing through; Luke the theologian used a historical genre to incarnate the kerygma of the faith.[142] Yet, as commendable and understandable as this may be, inadvertently Dibelius drove a sharp and seemingly irreversible wedge between the historical and theological tasks in ancient Christian writing. In essence, what appears to be a unitary narrative is now divided between *historia* and *theologia*. Whereas the previous trajectory of scholarship constantly sought to reduce *historia* to that which has a factual basis, this latter position, while clearly identifying *historia* as something much more than that which is merely or only historical, suggests that the theological must not be reduced to the level of *historia*. Despite its emphasis in the opposite direction, it is every bit as misdirected as the previous approach, as it too inevitably breaks down the unitary narrative function of *historia*.

Second, Dibelius drove a wedge, particularly in Acts, between speech and its narrative context. One of the features of the theologian's task, for Dibelius, is the elaboration and development of speeches that have no apparent

---

141. Dibelius's failure to consider any of the second or third types of speeches as epideictic in nature or function (ibid., 182) kept him from relating these speeches more clearly to ancient historiographical practice. Earlier in his essay (ibid., 144) Dibelius identifies epideictic speech as that one type that is not clearly connected to its narrative context or even necessarily to the work as a whole but that is intended to inform or instruct the reader directly.

142. See further Dibelius's own articulation of the relationship between faith and history in *Geschichtliche und übergeschichtliche Religion im Christentum* (Göttingen: Vandenhoeck & Ruprecht, 1925).

connection to the narrative context. This assertion has serious implications for the analysis of the Stephen narrative and speech in Acts 6:1–8:3. Stephen's oration belongs to Dibelius's second category of speech, and as such relates to the larger themes of the historical work. Nonetheless, according to Dibelius the speech is completely irrelevant to its narrative context. As such, either the narrative or the speech can be analyzed in turn without reference to the other. Although Dibelius clearly saw himself as articulating a position diametrically opposed to that of Baur's — that Luke was not interested in the politics of the actual nascent Christian church but in the grander theological kerygma of the early faith[143] — he inadvertently fueled the latter's position with this argument by allowing scholars to reconstruct either the core of the speech or the narrative any way that best suited their particular historical and/or theological agenda. Furthermore, and more seriously, Dibelius's position furthered the breakdown in the unity of Lukan *historia*. Rather than attempting to account for the perceived disjunction between speech and narrative in terms of literary design, historical purpose, or even the Lukan conception of *historia* itself, he simply accounted for it in terms of the cross-purposes of the theologian and historian. Clearly, by separating theological purpose from the goal of history writing, Dibelius arbitrarily curtailed the possible ways of defining that relationship. In fact, one can make a very good case for viewing the two elements as inseparable in the context of the distinctive combination of "Christian" and "historian" in Acts. What we have is not theology versus history, but a particular type of ideology adopted by an ancient historian that results not in a different function of the material but in a distinctive manner of explaining and interpreting the historical material itself.

Dibelius's view has left an indelible stamp on the discussion of the Hellenist narrative in Acts. Some scholars followed Dibelius's lead wholeheartedly, using the speech almost entirely as a means for elucidating the theology of the writer. Indeed, many scholars have pushed Dibelius's more nuanced observations much further, particularly emphasizing the theological over against Luke's historical contribution. J. Bihler, for instance, argued that the narrative as well as the speech were shaped by concerns for believers contemporary with the author. For example, the relationship between the apostles and the seven reflects later theological issues related to heretics, while the role of Stephen and Philip in the narrative reinforces the importance of subordination to the apostles, particularly to their successors. According to Bihler, "The representation in Acts 6–8 is therefore not written from the standpoint of a historian; but from that of a theologian and servant of the church. Luke does not merely want to collect and order the somehow

---

143. Dibelius clearly states his opposition to the Tübingen approach to the study of Acts ("First Christian Historian," 132; and "Speeches in Acts," 174). Indeed, much of what Dibelius says either about Luke as a historian or Luke as a theologian can be understood as an implicit critique of Tübingen *Tendenz* criticism.

retrievable traditions related to the beginnings of the church; much more so he wants to exhort the Christians in his own time regarding what they have to do."[144] Haenchen offers a complementary observation regarding Luke's use of the Stephen episode:

> [I]t was not only the historian in Luke who welcomed a Sanhedrin trial-scene at this point, but also the author. Here alone — not before any howling mob! — was there scope for the great speech which would enable Luke to make the Christian position vis-à-vis Judaism plain. It goes without saying that in the circumstances the moderating Gamaliel and the Pharisees who (according to Luke!) to some extent sympathized with the Christians do not make themselves heard — Luke possessed the happy gift of forgetting people when they might interfere with his literary designs.[145]

Haenchen, with evident sarcastic overtones, makes the point that Luke has shaped not only the speech but also the narrative so as to advance his goals as a theologian and preacher in the church. Naturally, there are other, more nuanced appropriations of Dibelius's research, but the lasting effects are still perceivable. One of the first issues that often arises from an analysis of Acts 6:1–8:3 thus relates to how both Stephen and his speech advance the larger theological themes of the writer of Luke-Acts.[146]

History after Theology: Dibelius's Legacy

Dibelius's conclusions gave significant impetus to the existing tendency — held over from the Tübingen school — to view Luke's narrative in Acts with historical suspicion. While there are various points on the spectrum regarding this issue, Dibelius has forced every scholar to recognize that theological interests have pertinence for understanding Luke's historical narrative. It is telling that even the most conservative scholars — those who adamantly defend Luke's historical accuracy throughout Acts — must also pay appropriate attention to the theological elements shaping Luke's account. Yet few scholars have readily identified the way in which theology and history are so intricately connected in Luke's narration of history. This problem can be traced back to the work of Dibelius himself, who was never able to reconcile fully the theological and historical aspects of Acts. The lack of precision at this point has a direct effect on the interpretation of the narrative and speech in Acts 6:1–8:3. If the direction of inquiry is not the recovery of

---

144. Bihler, *Stephanusgeschichte*, 241 (my translation).
145. Haenchen, *Acts of the Apostles*, 274.
146. See N. A. Dahl, "The Story of Abraham in Luke-Acts," in *Studies in Luke-Acts* (ed. Keck and Martyn), 142–48; and G. Stanton, "Stephen in Lucan Perspective," in *Studia Biblica 1978: Papers on Paul and Other New Testament Authors* (ed. E. A. Livingstone; JSNTSup 3; Sheffield: Sheffield Academic Press, 1980), 345–60.

the historical tradition, what then about moving in the direction of Lukan theological interest? But the inability to define adequately the relationship between these two movements results in serious problems for interpretation.

Dibelius's problematic legacy for the interpretation of Acts 6:1–8:3 becomes especially apparent in the analysis of the speech. In particular, the process for identifying the elements that are to be viewed as specifically Lukan theological concerns deserves further consideration. The alleged anti-temple nature of Stephen's speech (especially in 7:44–50) represents a good test case. The Baur tradition offered an extreme reading of the speech, arguing that it reflected an anti-Jewish stance on the part of the Hellenists. Indeed, in this view Luke attempts to muffle the extreme nature of the Hellenist sentiment in the interest of Jewish-Christian rapprochement. Yet, when one turns to the speech as an example of Lukan theology, this entire scheme is turned on its head. If anti-temple slander exists in the speech, then does it represent the position of Luke? Some scholars, realizing the implications of this assertion for a larger reading of Lukan theology (particularly Luke's position vis-à-vis the Old Testament view of the temple), have argued that the speech is not actually anti-temple in nature,[147] or that Luke is not responsible, fully at least, for the polemic, since it is preexistent in the tradition.[148] Others, in a similar vein, redirect the polemic of Acts 7, arguing that the speech is concerned not with the temple per se but with improper worship of God,[149] or with a critique of Jewish leadership.[150] Yet the function of the speech in the context of the narrative is often left to one side in this discussion. In other words, does Luke intend to depart from his historical narrative and provide the reader with a summary of his own position on the temple? Is this speech intended to interpret the narrative of Acts? Is it intended to characterize Stephen or, conversely, the Jewish leaders and/or people? In the latter case, one must ask whether Luke could invent a speech for a narrative without necessarily having any theological investment of his own in it. Or, even more dramatically, could Luke invent a speech that in fact contradicts his own theological aims and convictions? This question is important because it reveals the possibility that attempts to reconstruct

---

147. Räisänen, "Hellenists," 176–80; and B. Witherington, *The Acts of the Apostles: A Socio-Rhetorical Commentary* (Grand Rapids: Eerdmans, 1998), 262.

148. See, e.g., C. K. Barrett, "Attitudes to the Temple in the Acts of the Apostles," in *Templum Amicitiae: Essays on the Second Temple Presented to Ernst Bammel* (ed. W. Horbury; JSNTSup 48; Sheffield: Sheffield Academic Press, 1991), 365–66; and O. H. Steck, *Israel und das gewaltsame Geschick der Propheten: Untersuchungen zur Überlieferung des deuteronomistischen Geschichtsbild im Alten Testament, Spätjudentum und Urchristentum* (WMANT 23; Neukirchen-Vluyn: Neukirchener Verlag, 1967), 268–69.

149. See, e.g., J. B. Chance, *Jerusalem, the Temple, and the New Age in Luke-Acts* (Macon, Ga.: Mercer University Press, 1988), 39–40.

150. H. A. Brehm, "Vindicating the Rejected One: Stephen's Speech as a Critique of the Jewish Leaders," in *Early Christian Interpretation of the Scriptures of Israel: Investigations and Proposals* (ed. C. A. Evans and J. A. Sanders; JSNTSup 148; SSEJC 5; Sheffield: Sheffield Academic Press, 1997), 295.

Lukan theology may be using material never intended for that purpose. So, the arbitrary nature of historical reconstruction that was a problem in the scholarship of the previous section finds a parallel here with respect to the arbitrary readings of Lukan theological themes and emphases. In the terms that Dibelius set, one can (indeed must) raise this critical issue: If we grant the division between historian and theologian, how do we determine when, in fact, Luke is one or the other?

The relationship of Stephen's speech to the surrounding narrative reveals the continuing nature of the problem. Dibelius suggested that there was no relationship between the speech and its narrative context but that there was a connection between the speech and the larger themes of Acts. The ambiguity of the speech in relation to its narrative context continues in more recent scholarship. J. Zmijewski, for instance, takes the failure of the speech to relate to the preceding narrative situation as an indication that Luke could not have been completely responsible for the composition of the speech (or otherwise he would have made it relate more directly to the charges brought against Stephen).[151] But, irrespective of whether or not Luke created or edited the speech, the failure to connect the speech with its context breaks down the unity of speech and act as intricately related elements of ancient historiographical practice. Even those attempts to unify (reify?) the narrative and speech through an analysis of Lukan tradition and redaction[152] ultimately falter on the grounds that they do not satisfactorily integrate the traditional — historical or literary — and redactional elements. Illustrating that Luke has shaped and modeled the narrative and/or speech is still a long way from appreciating either Luke's theological or historical vision, and especially the interrelationship of the two. Moreover, just as scholars such as Lüdemann have come no closer to the *historia* of Acts 6:1–8:3 by separating out tradition from redaction, so those scholars who seek Luke's unique theological vision by sifting out redaction from tradition — particularly in the speeches[153] — are essentially no closer to Luke the theologian.

Whereas those scholars insistent on recovering the historical kernel of the text erred by reducing *historia* to that which is merely historical, scholars on this side of the divide err by separating the tasks of theologizing and historical writing so thoroughly that Lukan theology becomes precisely that which does not advance the historical aims of Acts. It is clear by now that both of those emphases are wrong, as they do not account fully for the complexity of historical narrative in Acts 6:1–8:3. I believe that a better appreciation of

---

151. J. Zmijewski, "Die Stephanusrede (Apg 7,2–53) — Literarisches und Theologisches," in *Das Neue Testament: Quelle Christlicher Theologie und Glaubenspraxis* (Stuttgart: Katholisches Bibelwerk, 1986), 88. See also Pesch, *Apostelgeschichte*, 1:244; and Wilckens, *Missionsreden*, 208.

152. Richard, *Acts 6:1–8:4*; and J. Kilgallen, *The Stephen Speech: A Literary and Redactional Study of Acts 7,2–53* (AnBib 67; Rome: Biblical Institute Press, 1976).

153. See particularly K. Kliesch, *Das heilsgeschichtliche Credo in den Reden der Apostelgeschichte* (BBB 44; Bonn: Hanstein, 1975).

the unitary conception of Luke's narrative can be gained and, subsequently, a fuller understanding of how one is to evaluate and assess the actual historical nature of Stephen and the Hellenists can be achieved, by turning to a more detailed analysis of the character of *historia* in Acts 6:1–8:3.

What Is at Stake and Why It Matters

It is a long, convoluted road leading from Baur to Hengel and beyond, and the discussion here has by no means been exhaustive. It would be unfair to suggest that all scholarship concerned with the Hellenist narrative in Acts 6:1–8:3 can rightly or easily be painted with the same broad brushstroke. Even when one looks at the scholars who are concerned with questions of history and historicity, it is evident that varying concerns and emphases naturally exist. Yet some larger patterns also emerge, and these are worthy of attention because they belie more significant problems in the history of Acts scholarship.

Baur's approach to the Hellenists, although obviously indebted to a history of Lutheran Protestant scholarship on Judaism, was also shaped substantially by his philosophical roots in German Idealism. While his conclusions regarding the Hellenist narrative in Acts 6:1–8:3 have proved foundational for subsequent scholarship, his view of history as the coming-to-consciousness of the Spirit has not. In Baur, however, these two movements cannot be separated. As a result, what was at stake in Acts 6:1–8:3 for Baur was a particular religio-philosophical system. The ideas are much more essential in this framework than the specific historical details. Thus, the historical existence of Stephen is ultimately much less of an issue of focus for Baur than is the presentation of the ideas existing in the speech and narrative of Stephen.[154] Of course, Baur's *Tendenz* criticism shaped his presentation of the details. Luke could not have composed the speech, since Luke, in Baur's scheme, belonged to the realm of early Catholicism — something seemingly incompatible with the ideas of Acts 6:1–8:3. Therefore, there must have been another singular figure behind the ideas coming to expression in this text. But again, Stephen and the Hellenists per se were not the real crux for Baur. Rather, he had much more invested in his particular interpretation of the narrative, especially the emphasis on the supersession of nascent Christianity from ancient Palestinian Judaism.

After Baur, however, there were some significant shifts in the conception of historical study. In particular, the historicity of events increasingly became a matter of concern and debate. For many scholars, the Hellenists as

---

154. J. B. Tyson ("From History to Rhetoric and Back: Assessing New Trends in Acts Studies," in *Contextualizing Acts: Lukan Narrative and Greco-Roman Discourse* [ed. T. Penner and C. Vander Stichele; SBLSymS 20; Atlanta: Society of Biblical Literature, 2003], 27) argues that Baur is still clearly interested in history but that a shift has occurred to the ideas of the author as a new form of historical reconstruction.

the link between Paul and Jesus took on greater importance, and, well before Hengel, they worked this out in a variety of ways on the basis of Baur's initial insights. Throughout, the historicity of the narrative, in some form, became a matter of scholarly debate. One thing is apparent: Whether liberal (e.g., E. Haenchen) or more conservative (e.g., F. F. Bruce) in orientation, the conception of history was the same, that is, the "historical" is that which is factually true and which has actually happened. While Haenchen and many others in the German school of interpretation continued to emphasize that Luke had altered a story detailing the lynching of Stephen by an angry mob, inserting a speech and developing the narrative, the more conservative scholars, by contrast, maintained the basic historicity of the account as it now appears in Acts. Where these two sides find unity is in their shared view of what makes something "history." The reason why this position is important to them, however, differs from scholar to scholar. Perhaps surprisingly, the more conservative interpreters often have seemed to have less theological stake in the discussion than scholars such as Haenchen. For the latter, at issue was a particular understanding of the nature of Christian origins: a historicized version of Baur's ideational framework. The ideas that were crucial for Baur are now turned into events that are the medium for early Christian revelation. Despite such differences, however, at the center is a shared view of history as the plane of significant human activity. One can gain knowledge of the past by tracing the threads behind accounts, attempting to reveal that which represents real and factual human actions in particular historical contexts. Historical works have value precisely as factual records of past human events, and those sources that provide access to the past understood in this way are given priority over those that do not. In this context, Hengel's interest in the Hellenists as the link between Paul and Jesus represents yet a further development. Hengel also values history as the medium of "real" and "factual" data on the past. Even more so, however, Hengel's work makes explicit that history mediates revelation, and this confession fundamentally shapes his understanding of Judaism, early Christianity, and especially the Hellenist narrative in Acts. Whereas for Baur the ideas themselves expressed that which was quintessential, for Hengel it is the contextualizing of those ideas in real people and factual historical events that is most significant. In some ways, there are striking similarities between Hengel's overarching framework and Baur's, particularly with respect to the movement of the spirit/Spirit in human history and the presence of a conservative law-abiding Judaism necessitating, perhaps even demanding, a Christian emphasis on freedom from the law. For Hengel, however, there is a shift in focus as the factuality of Stephen and the Hellenists becomes more essential: The links cannot be merely philosophical/ideational; the ideas must be tied to actual occurrences in human history. History as the medium of God's revelation thus becomes the starting point of Hengel's research and accounts for why the Hellenists are so critical to his scheme: They are the only known links between Paul and Jesus, without whom Jesus is left to the law-abiding Jewish-Christians of Jerusalem and Paul becomes nothing more than an interesting but ultimately misguided mystagogue. Hengel can demonstrate the continuity of divine revelation in human history precisely by tracing the threads that connect Jesus to Paul, linking Jesus as interpreted and experienced through the lens of (a somewhat muted) Hellenistic Judaism to the early Christian Hellenists in Jerusalem and then the Christianity of Jerusalem to the expression of the same in Antioch.

At stake in the debate about the Hellenists, then, is the question of origins. In particular, the critical issue involves the grounding of earliest Christian theology. This observation is as true for Hill as it is for Hengel. Although it is easy to read Hill and other scholars who argue against early theological diversity in Jerusalem (contra Baur and Hengel) as departing significantly from this scheme, in fact they reinforce it, even if inadvertently. The argument is no longer whether Stephen can be interpreted as anti-temple or not, but whether unity or diversity grounds earliest Christian theology. Hill argues that Paul's letters do not reveal a theological diversity among early Christian communities, and hence his reading of Christian origins — and particularly Acts 6:1–8:3 — is articulated in this light, but this shift does not change the fundamental methodological approach. Thus, a scholar such as Räisänen, who puts forth a position ostensibly opposed to that of Hengel's, inevitably offers only a differently nuanced version that still grants the Hellenists — or an entity that stands in for them — an axiomatic importance in early Christianity. Even those scholars who insist that Luke's hand can be detected throughout Acts 6:1–8:3 still maintain that underneath it all lies a discrete historical reality. Although it may be difficult to recover and interpret the historical core, this approach nonetheless offers the security that despite all literary artifices, both historical and, for many, revelatory realities are inevitably affirmed. The task of recovering and describing the nature of earliest Christianity is, therefore, a matter of that which grounds earliest Christian theology, which not inconsequently also forms part of the basis for modern scholarly identity (i.e., scholars have a large stake in the outcome of the constructive task). The Hellenists have played a key role in this discussion, whether or not they are always clearly and centrally identified as having done so.

But not all scholars took the path of least resistance. Seeing the difficulties particularly with Baur's position — or the way Baur's historical reconstruction of Christianity became a beginning datum of Luke-Acts inquiry — Dibelius tried to skirt the issues involved by focusing on the theological and literary aspects of the text. Here not history but kerygmatic expression becomes the medium of revelation. Thus, Dibelius was most interested in those aspects of Luke's presentation that either expressed the primitive Christian kerygma or, as some later scholars maintained, represented the preaching of the gospel in Luke's own day. The other details were comparable to the literary achievements and methods of the classical Greek and Latin historians. Dibelius's interest in the speeches was therefore foundational rather than incidental to his overall approach. Indeed, in many respects his conclusions, while different from Baur's, have the same stress: the movement away from concrete history to ideas. Scholars like Haenchen, who believed they were furthering Dibelius's research,[155] in critical ways were moving in a different direction; after all, for Dibelius, Luke the historian was still the traveling companion of Paul.[156] Yet Dibelius's belief that the speeches reflected the earliest Christian kerygma also indicates a historicizing interest: The preaching that was grounded in earliest Christian theology was of greatest and lasting value. Dibelius thus stands somewhere between Baur's religio-philosophical emphasis on the historical expression of ideas and the trajectory that sees concrete history as the ultimate and often only medium of reality.

From this brief synopsis, it is easy to appreciate why the Hellenists have become such a *crux interpretum* for scholarship on Acts. Much more is involved here than a particular interpretation of Stephen's speech and determining whether or not the Hellenists form a bridge between Jesus and Paul or confirm a particular reading of Pauline theology. Rather, at issue are fundamental matters such as the nature of historical knowledge and the role of history in divine revelation. Yet the secondary issues are just as important and relevant for this discussion, as they reveal that at stake also is a particular vision of Christianity itself: That which grounds earliest Christian theology and which is closest to the point of origin has historical and theological priority. Thus, despite efforts by Hill and others to put this issue to rest, by offering their own reconstruction of the basis of early Christian theology they have, in the end, fueled the debate rather than quelled it. That the Hellenists have been used as a tool and discursive subject in this context is clear. Irrespective of one's particular view of the Hellenists, it is patently clear that they are a critical historical and theological datum for modern scholarship. That it will continue to be so for some time is quite likely. The *Anchor Bible Dictionary* has recently canonized the critical consensus on the Hellenists in the following summary:

> Thus, it is now thought that it was this community of Christian Hellenists who accelerated the transferal of the Jesus tradition from Aramaic into Greek, who helped bring Christian theology fully into the realm of Greek thought freed

---

155. Haenchen, *Acts of the Apostles,* 34–35, points out that Dibelius had moved away from reconstructing the early history of Christianity to an appreciation of its literary history. Haenchen's commentary, although sometimes appearing unappreciative, in fact was a major advance toward the application of Dibelius's insights to the whole of Acts.

156. Dibelius, "First Christian Historian," 136. Haenchen and Conzelmann are best understood as representing a synthesis of Baur and Dibelius: taking their cue from Dibelius's literary approach to Acts, but with a much more *Tendenz* critical bent.

from Aramaic pre-acculturation, who were instrumental in moving Christianity from its Palestinian setting into the urban culture of the larger Empire, who first saw the implications of Jesus' resurrection for a Law-free Gospel for the gentiles (and for Jews), and who were the bridge between Jesus and Paul. These Christian Hellenists were the founders of Christian mission outside Palestine, and a theological tradition capable of articulating a gospel for the Greco-Roman world.[157]

The issue van Unnik addressed in his seminal essay in the mid-1960s was as much prophetic as it was a summary of the current state of Acts study in his own time. In many respects, the treatment of the Hellenists and Stephen in modern New Testament scholarship is a microcosm of the larger issues surrounding Acts interpretation as a whole. Modern academics may attach an overinflated importance to the Hellenists, but what they have come to represent more broadly in the study of Christian origins and in the study of Acts is, if anything, underappreciated. The small narrative unit of Acts 6:1–8:3 has a direct bearing on how one interprets history, understands Christian origins, and grounds New Testament theology.

Going Forward: Back to History

Dibelius's legacy is an important one in Acts research, and the issues raised in his studies have ongoing value. On the one hand, Dibelius, along with Cadbury, moved scholarship beyond the question of sources and focused attention on Acts as a literary work. Dibelius's rejection of any sustained source aside from an itinerary or travel narrative that formed the basis for the central section of Acts (not to be confused with the "we" source), and his postulation of small, fragmentary units that formed the *Grundschrift* of the rest of Acts,[158] shifted focus toward the literary activity of the writer, which, for Dibelius, meant an interest in those aspects of Acts that reveal the historian at work. On the other hand, this approach brought the question of genre to the forefront. For instance, Dibelius's work on the speeches in Acts consisted primarily of a comparison between Acts and the ancient Greek and Roman historical works: One could learn what the writer of Acts had done with the speeches by comparison with other literary writers of antiquity. Dibelius understood that some sense of the larger literary context had to be grasped in order to appreciate fully the nature of what Luke was attempting to accomplish in individual narratives and as a whole. This component represented the legacy of form criticism that influenced Dibelius's style-critical approach to Acts.

---

157. T. W. Martin, "Hellenists," *ABD* 3:136.
158. Dibelius, "Style Criticism of the Book of Acts," in *Studies in the Acts of the Apostles*, 5–11.

The most recent scholarship has continued in this particular direction, attempting to locate and establish the genre of Luke-Acts as novel, biography, or history, among others. With each of these generic designations, particular reading strategies are established for interpreting the material in Acts.[159] It is for this reason that so much is perceived to be at stake in identifying the genre of Luke-Acts. As Dibelius knew long ago, appropriate and accurate comparison of the material in Acts with similar types of literature sharing the same literary, social, and cultural context can illuminate texts that often seem opaque to the modern reader. Or, if the texts are clear at one level, such comparison may help elucidate aspects of authorial intention or particular features of a writer's work that otherwise might go unnoticed. Even particular themes that may seem rather banal within the larger structure of an early Christian text may be enlivened in their comparison with similar themes in contemporary writers, highlighting elements and patterns that were important for the writer but have escaped our notice. The question posed at the core of this study is also bound up with the larger issue of genre: What is one to make of *historia* in Acts? In particular, past scholarship has paused too infrequently to pose the all-important query: What did the writer of Acts intend by the Hellenist narrative? Was it to provide access to factual data on the early Christian movement? Was it to provide his own particular theological or kerygmatic version of religious dogma? Was it simply a narrative device? If so, to what end? These are critical questions, and all of them are wrapped up with the discussion of the Lukan genre. Even within a given genre, there are issues that divide yet further. For instance, what does it mean to say that Luke-Acts is "history"? There is still much about intention and purpose left unstated, let alone questions about the utilization of traditional materials that remain. For instance, whether Luke has an apologetic (defending the Christian movement to the Roman government) or a polemical (undercutting particular Christian heretical doctrine) purpose changes the way the narratives are read. Moreover, if Luke is a theologian, or, better, a theological or hagiographical historian, then the orientation of both narrative and speech will be contoured in this light.

---

159. This premise lies behind the recent work of D. P. Moessner, who has attempted to delineate the particular "poetics" of Lukan narrative strategy, placing emphasis on the nature of reading and interpreting that is thereby evoked. See, e.g., D. P. Moessner, "Dionysius's Narrative 'Arrangement' (οἰκονομία) as the Hermeneutical Key to Luke's Re-Vision of the 'Many,'" in *Paul, Luke, and the Graeco-Roman World* (ed. Christophersen et al.), 149–64; idem, "The Lukan Prologues in the Light of Ancient Narrative Hermeneutics: Παρηκολουθηκότι and the Credentialed Author," in *The Unity of Luke-Acts* (ed. J. Verheyden; BETL 142; Leuven: Leuven University Press, 1999), 399–417; idem, "The Appeal and Power of Poetics (Luke 1:1–4): Luke's Superior Credentials (παρηκολουθηκότι), Narrative Sequence (καθεχῆς), and Firmness of Understanding (ἡ ἀσφάλεια) for the Reader," in *Jesus and the Heritage of Israel: Luke's Narrative Claim upon Israel's Legacy* (ed. D. P. Moessner; Harrisburg, Pa.: Trinity Press International, 1999), 84–123; and D. P. Moessner and D. L. Tiede, "Conclusion: 'And some were persuaded...,'" in *Jesus and the Heritage* (ed. Moessner), 358–68.

In what follows I will argue for historiography as the primary genre for our analysis of Acts. While recently I have been promoting the promise and possibility of a cross-generic approach to the study of Acts,[160] which does not limit the conversation to one particular genre, for the purposes of this study I will focus on the genre of historiography, without intending to imply that this is in any way a hard and fast boundary for engagement of Lukan narrative dynamics. Rather, herein genre becomes the point of departure for a discussion that must necessarily continue beyond the bounds of these published pages. Despite these caveats, however, I believe that, by analyzing the Stephen/Hellenist narrative in light of the goals and aims of ancient historical writing, Luke's perspective on *historia* and the role of the Hellenists in Acts will be both tempered and illuminated as a result. Furthermore, in what follows I aim to illustrate the way in which the narrative of Acts 6:1–8:3 helps one understand the relationship between theology and history in Acts, especially the manner in which a proper appreciation of Luke's historical aims underscores the relationship between these two oft-separated functions. The analysis of Hellenist narrative I undertake in this study will help shape the understanding of these categories of discourse, showing not only that they are essentially flip sides of the same enterprise (contra Dibelius) but also that there are important limitations on what can be considered historical (i.e., related to the historicity of events) vis-à-vis early Christianity (contra Hengel) and what is understood to be Lukan theology/ideology proper. Thus, as van Unnik suggested over thirty years ago, we can only move forward in our understanding of Luke-Acts by moving backward, examining more fully the relationship between Luke and ancient historiography (Greco-Roman as well as Jewish) and exploring more completely the implications of that relationship for the reading of Lukan narrative.[161] Before making this move, however, it is critical that some of the essential exegetical issues in the interpretation of Acts 6:1–8:3 be laid out in more detail, in order to facilitate further discussion and engagement of broader features of Lukan narrative composition.

---

160. See esp. Penner, "Madness in the Method?"; idem, "Contextualizing Acts"; and idem, "Reconfiguring the Rhetorical Study of Acts: Reflections on the Method in and Learning of a Progymnastic Poetics," *PRSt* 30 (2003): 425–39.

161. van Unnik, "Luke-Acts," 27.

II

Textualizing the Hellenists, Contextualizing Interpretation

Mapping the Exegetical Terrain

Texts and interpreters are intricately linked in the process of analysis and interpretation. The predominant theories related to the Hellenists that I delineated in the first chapter are themselves not solely the invention of modern ideology and historical interests. There is in fact a textual basis for the particular moves that scholars have made in this respect. This observation need not imply that texts necessarily dictate certain interpretations; rather, there is a complex interplay between ideologies at work, wherein the text both evokes and also affirms particular ideological commitments by modern scholars. It is therefore worth examining more closely the textual details, as well as the gaps and fissures, which have as much baffled scholars as they have pushed them in particular directions of interpretation. In what follows, I am interested in mapping the exegetical terrain of the Hellenist and Stephen narratives. In particular, there are features of the larger narrative and speech that have both been shaped by but in turn have also shaped the metanarratives that scholars have constructed for the elusive Hellenists. To this end, in what follows I will examine the three major units of Acts 6:1–8:3 (the Hellenists and the widows in 6:1–7; Stephen and his opponents in 6:8–7:1 and 7:54–8:2; and Stephen's speech in 7:2–53), highlighting the critical textual and syntactical features that have been the focus of discussion and debate in contemporary scholarship.

Textual Markers I:
The Hellenists in Narrative (Acts 6:1–7)

Acts 6:1–7 represents the *locus classicus* for the study of the Hellenists and their role in Christian origins, as well as for the larger critical study of Lukan composition. Herein so many of the theories applied to the larger narrative — particularly the delineation of the so-called Hellenist theology — find their origin, focusing on the suscint opening verse: "Now in those days, when the disciples were increasing, there came about grumbling on the part of the Hellenists toward the Hebrews" (6:1, author's translation).

Up until this point in the narrative, Luke has dealt with the formation of the new community in Jerusalem, from the ascension of Jesus and the commissioning of the apostles to their subsequent preaching and the consequent increasing conflict with the Jerusalem/temple establishment. The relationship between conflict and community growth is as important in these opening chapters as it is for the rest of Acts. After Peter's speech to the crowd in 2:14–36, followed by the first conversion account in Acts, Luke places a summarizing statement in 2:43–47, indicating the growth and prosperity of the Jerusalem community. Following the conflict between Peter and John and the temple authorities in 4:1–31, Luke includes a similar type of statement in 4:32–35, detailing the communal sharing of goods. Immediately following this second summary statement regarding the communal life of the first adherents to the "new faith" in Jerusalem there is conflict within the community, offsetting the conflict without in 4:1–22. Thus, in 5:1–11 one finds the story of Ananias and Sapphira, who threaten to cast a shadow on the ideal portrait of the early Jerusalem community that Luke has drawn, especially as it relates here to the communal sharing of goods and the idealized nature of early Christian friendship.[1] Subsequent to their punishment, Luke places a third summarizing statement in 5:12–16, this one emphasizing the signs and wonders of the apostles (as also in 2:43), particularly their healing of the sick and demon possessed. As with the healing of the crippled man in 3:1–10, the general note on healing in Luke's summary statement is followed by further persecution at the hands of the high priest and Sadducees (5:17). The Hellenist episode in Acts 6:1–7 then follows the escape and subsequent flogging of the Jerusalem apostles in 5:18–42. After the Hellenist narrative in Acts 6:1–8:3, the Jerusalem community fades into the background, as the account moves from Jerusalem to Samaria and then outward toward other parts of Judea — fulfilling the programmatic statement of 1:8. This Lukan interest in conflict and opposition, as well as resolution and absorption, is an important element of his historiographical technique.[2] Moreover, beyond the oft-noted geographical outline provided in 1:8, Luke appears also to be

---

1. See G. E. Sterling, "'Athletes of Virtue': An Analysis of the Summaries in Acts (2:41–47; 4:32–35; 5:12–16)," *JBL* 113 (1994): 679–96; A. C. Mitchell, "'Greet the Friends By Name': New Testament Evidence for the Greco-Roman *Topos* on Friendship," in *Greco-Roman Perspectives on Friendship* (ed. J. T. Fitzgerald; SBLRBS 34; Atlanta: Scholars Press, 1997), esp. 236–57; idem, "The Social Function of Friendship in Acts 2:44–47 and 4:32–37," *JBL* 111 (1992): 255–72; and S. S. Bartchy, "Community of Goods in Acts: Idealization or Social Reality?" in *The Future of Early Christianity: Essays in Honor of Helmut Koester* (ed. B. A. Pearson; Minneapolis: Fortress, 1991), 309–18.

2. Luke's own historical presentation is congenial to the philosophical model adopted by Baur. Baur's focus, of course, was not on the narrative per se; he was more interested in the historical/historic tensions that Luke was attempting to resolve.

interested in a finely structured ethnic progression in the narrative, beginning with 2:8–11 as a pattern for what is to follow.[3] The ethnic dimension clearly follows the geographical outline in 1:8, but in some respects adds more nuanced elements that are omitted from the general summary in 1:8.[4]

In this larger context, the reference to the "increasing number of disciples"[5] in 6:1 connects this opening of the narrative unit to the summary

---

3. With a focus on Jerusalem as the center, the list of names in 2:9–11 reveals groups of people associated with the principal directions (see D. R. Edwards, *Religion and Power: Pagans, Jews, and Christians in the Greek East* [New York: Oxford University Press, 1996], 88). For the relationship of 1:8 and 2:9–11 to the Table of Nations (Gen 10), see J. M. Scott, "Luke's Geographical Horizon," in *The Book of Acts in Its Graeco-Roman Setting* (ed. D. W. J. Gill and C. Gempf; BAFCS 2; Grand Rapids: Eerdmans, 1994), esp. 499–543; and idem, *Geography in Early Judaism and Christianity: The Book of Jubilees* (SNTSMS 113; Cambridge: Cambridge University Press, 2002), 56–96. Also see the excellent discussion of the relationship of this material to Roman imperial geography by G. Gilbert, "Roman Propaganda and Christian Identity in the Worldview of Luke-Acts," in *Contextualizing Acts: Lukan Narrative and Greco-Roman Discourse* (ed. T. Penner and C. Vander Stichele; SBLSymS 20; Atlanta: Society of Biblical Literature, 2003), 233–56; and idem, "The List of Nations in Acts 2: Roman Propaganda and the Lukan Response," *JBL* 121 (2002): 497–529.

4. Alongside these features, one should also observe the repetitive nature of the larger literary context, since Acts 6:1–7 is part of a crescendoing pattern in the preceding narratives in Acts 1–5 (see R. C. Tannehill, "The Composition of Acts 3–5: Narrative Development and Echo Effect," *SBLSP* 23 [1984]: 217–40; and D. Marguerat, "La mort d'Ananias et Sapphira [Ac 5.1–11] dans la stratégie narrative de Luc," *NTS* 39 [1993], esp. 211–17; J. B. Green, "Internal Repetition in Luke-Acts: Contemporary Narratology and Lucan Historiography," in *History, Literature, and Society in the Book of Acts* [ed. B. Witherington; Cambridge: Cambridge University Press, 1996], 283–99). This feature relates to the oft-noted phenomenon of parallels between specific characters in the narrative. On these, see C. H. Talbert, *Literary Patterns, Theological Themes, and the Genre of Luke-Acts* (SBLMS 20; Missoula, Mont.: Scholars Press 1974), 15–65; S. M. Praeder, "Jesus-Paul, Peter-Paul, and Jesus-Peter Parallelisms in Luke-Acts: A History of Reader Response," *SBLSP* 23 (1984): 23–39; and D. P. Moessner, "'The Christ Must Suffer': New Light on the Jesus-Peter, Stephen, Paul Parallels in Luke-Acts," in *The Composition of Luke's Gospel* (ed. D. E. Orton; Leiden: Brill, 1999), 117–53.

5. This instance is Luke's first use of μαθητής in Acts. He will use it numerous times after this point (twice more in this narrative [6:2, 7] and twenty-nine times in all, considerably less than in the gospel, however). The term should be contrasted with οἱ δώδεκα, used here as a synonym for ἀπόστολοι (cf. 6:6). The traditional view is that Luke has created (or maintained) this distinction in terminology in order to subordinate others — read here Paul — to the authority of the Jerusalem leaders (i.e., the "twelve" in Lukan perspective). On this, see G. Klein, *Die zwölf Apostel: Ursprung und Gehalt einer Idee* (FRLANT ns 59/77; Göttingen: Vandenhoeck & Ruprecht, 1961), esp. 202–3. This view fits well with the mediating function of Lukan narrative, which the Tübingen school promoted as Luke's attempt to bring unity to the historical representation. Luke domesticates Paul, who uses the "apostle" terminology to refer to himself frequently (cf. Rom 1:1; 1 Cor 1:1; 2 Cor 12:12; Gal 1:17). Luke's use of the terminology to describe only the Jerusalem "twelve" seems to carry with it a certain subordinating function, and thus there is some legitimacy to the earlier view. Whether Luke is attempting to domesticate/subordinate Paul is questionable, however, given the larger context of Paul's activity in Acts. The view that Luke's usage reflects traditional Palestinian elements (cf. J. Roloff, *Apostolat-Verkündigung-Kirche: Ursprung, Inhalt, und Funktion des kirchlichen Apostelamtes nach Paulus, Lukas, und den Pastoralbriefen* [Gütersloh: Mohn, 1965], 232), which are shaped by the author, rests on source theories that are difficult to substantiate. In this view Paul's use of ἀπόστολος to refer to himself in his letters would have been an apologetic move on his part, to assert his status on par with the Jerusalemite originals. Some scholars thus interpret 1 Corinthians 15:3–8 to be traditional Palestinian material altered by Paul in v. 8, who is promoting himself as an apostolic equal (with rhetorical effect

statements in 2:47 ("increasing number of believers") and 5:14 ("increasing numbers of believers"; cf. 5:16, "great numbers of people seeking healing"). In 6:1, then, as with the incident involving Ananias and Sapphira in 5:1–11, one again finds conflict in the community,[6] here concerning the distribution of food (linking this event with the theme of communal fellowship in the first two summary statements). Thus, running from Peter's sermon to the end of the Hellenist "problem" in 6:7, one can outline the literary structure thus: founding of the Jerusalem community (1:1–2:44); summary statement (2:43–47); conflict with outsiders (4:1–31); summary statement (4:32–35); conflict with insiders (5:1–11); summary statement (5:12–16); conflict with outsiders (5:17–41); summary statement (5:42); conflict with insiders (6:1–6); summary statement (6:7).[7] The juxtaposition of both internal and external conflict with the more idealizing summarizing statements belies any suggestion that Luke has created a simple utopian view of the early community.[8] It is at this point, since the subject matter begins to diversify (focusing less on the apostles and more on other early heroic figures), that scholars have not surprisingly proffered the presence of a new source or tradition.[9]

---

in v. 9). See further G. Lüdemann, *Opposition to Paul in Jewish Christianity* (trans. M. E. Boring; Minneapolis: Fortress, 1989), 72–73.

6. F. S. Spencer, *Acts* (Sheffield: Sheffield Academic Press, 1997), 64, argues that this reveals a growing movement from initial harmony to disharmony in the community.

7. The pattern continues with a subsequent "conflict with outsiders" section (Acts 6:8–15; 7:54–8:3). This represents the final conflictual account of the Jerusalem portion of Acts. Indeed, 8:2–4 represents the final "summary statement" of the opening unit of Acts 1–8. This summary statement, however, portrays a more hopeless state for the Jerusalem community, necessitating movement outward from the Holy City. J. T. Squires has recently argued that 8:4–12:25 functions as the Lukan narrative preparation for the "turn to the Gentiles" that will dominate the rest of the book (see "The Function of Acts 8.4–12.25," *NTS* 44 [1998]: 608–17). The Hellenist narrative, therefore, and especially the Stephen portion of it, forms the Lukan segue into the next major section of the book.

8. R. P. Thompson, "Believers and Religious Leaders in Jerusalem: Contrasting Portraits of Jews in Acts 1–7," in *Literary Studies in Luke-Acts: Essays in Honor of Joseph B. Tyson* (ed. R. P. Thompson and T. E. Phillips; Macon, Ga.: Mercer University Press, 1998), emphasizes the idealized nature of the image of the *ekklesia* in Acts 1–7 (334–37) and finds it surprising that Luke has included the narratives of Ananias and Sapphira and the Hellenists and Hebrews. But this position is overstated, despite the clearly idealized view of the Christian community in the summary statements. The pattern of outer/inner conflict juxtaposed with growth and positive portrayal is a key literary device of Luke in Acts; see W. S. Kurz, "Narrative Models in Luke-Acts," in *Greeks, Romans, and Christians: Essays in Honor of Abraham J. Malherbe* (ed. D. L. Balch et al.; Minneapolis: Fortress, 1990), 187–88; and A. Rakotoharintsifa, "Luke and the Internal Divisions in the Early Church," in *Luke's Literary Achievement: Collected Essays* (ed. C. M. Tuckett; JSNTSup 116; Sheffield: Sheffield Academic Press, 1995), 165–77.

9. C. K. Barrett states that "almost all students of Acts" postulate that Luke is following a new tradition (or, in Barrett's case, "source") here (*A Critical and Exegetical Commentary on the Acts of the Apostles* [ICC; Edinburgh: T & T Clark, 1994], 1:52, 54–55, 305; cf. T. Seland, "Once More—The Hellenists, Hebrews, and Stephen: Conflicts and Conflict-Management in Acts 6–7," in *Recruitment, Conquest, and Conflict: Strategies in Judaism, Early Christianity, and the Greco-Roman World* [ed. P. Borgen, V. K. Robbins, and D. B. Gowler; ESEC 6; Atlanta: Scholars Press, 1998], 28). Barrett posits the use of μαθητής and οἱ δώδεκα—the first use of the former and the only use of the latter in Acts—and the new subject matter as definitive evidence

Historical questions aside for the moment, there are several noteworthy features of this text. First, the unit 6:1–7 is constructed on a chiastic pattern. The opening with mention of the problem (v. 1) — the lack of proper distribution among the Hellenist widows — is to be contrasted with the closing of the unit, with the theme of the increasing size of the community (v. 7). The middle section of vv. 2–6 is also patterned in a similar manner. Verse 2 narrates the "twelve" gathering the community, while v. 6 depicts the "apostles" appointing the seven. Verse 3 contains the call of the "twelve" to select "seven men," while v. 5 lists the names of these individuals. Finally, the middle unit (v. 4) represents the lynchpin of the account: the key roles of prayer and preaching in the increase of the Jerusalem community detailed in vv. 1 and 7.[10] In response to the problem in v. 1b, the "twelve" gather the entire community together (τὸ πλῆθος τῶν μαθητῶν), and the whole community is then "pleased" with the "word" of the apostles in v. 5 (ἐνώπιον παντὸς τοῦ πλήθους).[11] The community (τὸ πλῆθος τῶν μαθητῶν is still in view) then selects seven of its members. The text is not entirely clear at this point, but the "seven" are often understood to have come from the Hellenist group itself. As B. Capper observes,

> The solution to the dispute over care for the hellenists' widows was the appointment of the seven officers (6:5). All seven have Greek names and appear to be drawn from the hellenist community alone. This implies that the solution to the dispute was *not* the integration of the "hellenist" widows *into* the "daily distribution" of the "Hebrew" congregation but rather the establishment of offices to organise care within the hellenist community itself, which clearly had no arrangement of any kind for the care of the poor.[12]

---

for this position. Barrett makes much of the fact that Luke does not use οἱ δώδεκα elsewhere in Acts. οἱ δώδεκα is found several times in the Gospel of Luke (9:1, 12; 18:31; 22:3) and in some cases in Luke's so-called special material (Luke 8:1).

10. E. Richard, *Acts 6–8:4: The Author's Method of Composition* (SBLDS 41; Missoula, Mont.: Scholars Press, 1978), 215–19, 268, adduces significant linguistic evidence for the parallelism of vv. 2–4 and vv. 5–6 with an inclusio formed by vv. 1 and 7 (similar to the suggestion made here). Verse 4 is significant precisely because of the stress laid on prayer (1:14, 24–25; 2:42; 4:24–31) and preaching (2:14–36; 3:11–26; 4:17–20; 5:27–32, 40–42) in the expansion of the Christian movement in Jerusalem, as well as in the increasing conflict between the authorities and the members of the Jerusalem community. See the brief note on this verse as a "rededication" in J. N. Collins, *Diakonia: Re-interpreting the Ancient Sources* (New York: Oxford University Press, 1990), 230.

11. The scribe of MS D clarifies the text with the addition of τῶν μαθητῶν; the entire community is "pleased," not just the Hellenists.

12. B. Capper, "The Palestinian Context of Community of Goods," in *The Book of Acts in Its Palestinian Setting* (ed. R. Bauckham; BAFCS 4; Grand Rapids: Eerdmans, 1995), 353–54. Despite Hill's attempt to demonstrate the lack of divergence in the early community, he comes surprisingly close to Capper's position: The Greek names indicate that the "seven" all came from the Hellenist community and that they were set in charge of distribution only in their own community (Hill, *Hellenists and Hebrews: Reappraising Division within the Earliest Church* [Minneapolis: Fortress, 1992], 46–48). Hill also adds the detail that the seven must have been leaders in the Hellenist community before their selection (26, 46).

Yet the narrative does not actually indicate the origin of the seven, although it seems to imply that these seven would provide the daily distribution for both the Hellenists and the Hebrews. The only statement in Capper's citation that can be supported with assurance on the basis of the narrative is that the appointment of the seven was done in response to the problem of distribution. The rest is either conjectured or based on the assumption that 6:1–7 attests to the formation of a second group within the Jerusalem community. Rather, the main focus seems to be the mirroring of the choosing of the twelfth apostle in 1:15–26.[13] Just as in that former passage, where the establishment of the apostolate in Jerusalem leads to witnessing and rejection, the installation of the ministry of the seven also leads to a similar — albeit even more violent — end.

Unlike the selection of Matthias, however, here the community as a whole selects the "seven men" at the behest of the apostles. Stephen is characterized most fully, as one filled with faith and the Holy Spirit (the fulfillment of the requirement in 6:3: "full of the Spirit and wisdom"), while the six others are mentioned simply by name, with the exception of Nicolaus, who is described as a "proselyte." The seven men are then brought by the community and placed before the apostles. Although the grammar of this verse is somewhat awkward,[14] in light of the declaration in v. 3 — "whom we shall appoint" — it seems that the apostles are the ones who pray and lay their hands on the seven in the act of commissioning for service (v. 6). The community then responds to the command of the apostles, puts forth a group of seven men, and these are then commissioned/appointed by the apostles for the ministry of distribution. Once this task is completed, Luke adds the characteristic

---

13. In light of this parallel, the ecclesial language used in each case is striking. In 1:20 ἐπισκοπή is used, and in Acts 6:1–7 the language is akin to διάκονος (διακονία διακονέω), and may, perhaps, be an allusion to the office (S. G. Wilson, *Luke and the Pastoral Epistles* [London: SPCK, 1979], 60). It is worth pursuing whether Luke intends to invoke the offices of the church that, although clearly not established in the time reflected in the narrative, existed in his own, or, at the very least, whether or not church offices may have given Luke the model for the presentation of the characters in the narrative (although the precise meaning of διακονία in this text remains elusive and therefore makes such associations difficult). Many scholars have pointed out the similarity between the character of the "seven" and Stephen in 6:3, 5, 8 and the character demanded of those aspiring to church office in 1 Tim 3. That the title "deacon" represents someone who is subordinate to the "overseer" has now been thoroughly established by Collins, *Diakonia*, 235–37 (see also R. A. Campbell, *The Elders: Seniority within Earliest Christianity* (ed. J. Riches; Edinburgh: T & T Clark, 1994], 134). Collins's argument (230–32) regarding 6:1–7 fits closely with the suggestion here, and bears further investigation. This link would also support the suggestion by some scholars that what is going on in the narrative is the transfer of power from the apostles (overseers) to the "seven" (who function as deacons). It is important for Luke that there be explicit human connections drawn between characters in the narrative — a chain of both command and contact. If the model of overseer-deacon works, then the "seven" are actually subordinate representatives of the twelve apostles, which could explain why they naturally take on preaching duties *alongside* the distribution ministry (it is questionable whether Luke ever intends for the reader to infer that the former has been abandoned for the latter).

14. The participial phrase could refer to the community as a whole (so Barrett, *Acts of the Apostles*, 315).

community summary statement in v. 7 (cf. 2:43-47; 4:32-35; 5:12-16; 5:42) to close off this narrative of internal conflict and its resolution. Playing off λόγος in v. 2 ("the word of God"), v. 4 ("the ministry of the word") and v. 5 ("the word/matter"), the narrative unit concludes with the phrase "the word of God grew" (v. 7). In line with the statements in 2:41, 47 and 5:14-15, Luke notes the increase in the number of adherents to the new community in Jerusalem. In an interesting addition to the statement in 6:7, Luke attests as well to the conversion of priests to the "faith." This element demonstrates further the rapid pace of growth in the early Christian movement that Luke is trying to establish in Acts 1-6. In 4:1 the priests (part of the temple establishment), who initially opposed the apostles, quickly and in great number ("many") switch allegiance to the burgeoning faith (and then just as quickly disappear from Luke's narrative). This notice in 6:7 regarding the priests is part of Luke's larger interest in both the opposition from and also the receptivity of the Jewish people to the new message preached by the apostles.

While the narrative features are intriguing in their own right, the history of scholarship has instead focused rather on those elements that lie beneath a surface reading of the text. Clearly the one element that has dominated discussion is the precise identity of the Ἑλληνιστής and Ἑβραῖος mentioned in 6:1. For most scholarship on this passage, these terms have been the starting place for thoroughgoing speculation. The terms are literally translated "Hellenist" and "Hebrew," but from the seemingly obvious reference to spoken language,[15] especially with respect to the category "Hellenist," the terms have come to take on much greater significance. The difficulty

---

15. At one level, nearly all scholars of 6:1-7 maintain the position that the "Hellenists" speak the Greek language, and the "Hebrews" Aramaic. Indeed, frequently one finds this articulated in terms of the liturgy of the respective communities (see P. F. Esler, *Community and Gospel in Luke-Acts: The Social and Political Motivations of Lucan Theology* [SNTSMS 57; Cambridge: Cambridge University Press, 1987], 143, 159, following Hengel). Yet this would be an overly simplistic characterization of scholarship, since very few scholars mean only "language" when they refer to "language." As is the case with Hengel, other aspects — cultural, religious, economic, or social — are brought into conjunction with linguistic expression. Strictly speaking, the designation of the spoken language of the "Hellenists" is the plain or explicit meaning of Ἑλληνιστής. The same, however, cannot be said for the referent Ἑβραῖος, as most scholars maintain it bears a greater ethnic dimension. In terms of the precise component of each group, it is almost always assumed that Ἑβραῖος designates Jews belonging to the newly formed messianic community described in Acts. It may also be read, however, as a designation of Jews in general. In this case, Aramaic-speaking Jews in Jerusalem ceased distributing to Hellenist Jewish widows, and the community had to intervene (in this configuration, it would not be an inner-community conflict; see N. Hyldahl, *The History of Early Christianity* [trans. E. M. Arevad and H. Dyrbye; Frankfurt: Peter Lang, 1997], 174-76). Johnson's overall argument — that language of possessions in Luke-Acts functions to delineate the people of the prophet (hence, representing insider terminology; L. T. Johnson, *The Literary Function of Possessions in Luke-Acts* [SBLDS 39; Chico, Calif.: Scholars Press, 1977], 220) — would suggest that this position is untenable, as would the fact that Luke explicitly connects the Hebrew/Hellenist problem with the temporal clause "in the days of the increasing of the disciples," which provides the setting for the dispute. Luke's point seems to be that the problem is internal to the community and is in some way connected to the rapid increase (described in Acts 2-5) of converts to the new movement.

with Ἑλληνιστής and Ἑβραῖος in 6:1, and, indeed, in the passage as a whole, is the circular nature of the arguments frequently proffered. On the one hand, the passage posits a clear problem in the Jerusalem community: The Hellenist widows are being neglected in the daily distribution (6:1b). Yet scholars, largely in light of their previously adduced conclusions based on the Stephen portion of the narrative (and a particular interpretation of the speech), have determined that the real problem could not have possibly been "neglect in daily distribution." Thus, when the term Ἑλληνιστής is analyzed in light of the larger reconstructed scenario, this seemingly innocuous designation suddenly takes on extraordinary depth of meaning, referring to Diaspora Jews with a more liberal theological stance than the "Hebrews."[16] Haenchen's analysis is fairly typical: "[T]hat these distributors began to 'overlook' the Hellenistic widows...accords with the hypothesis that the Hellenistic Christians had become suspect to the others and began to sense the fact on some such tell-tale occasion as — precisely — the distribution of poor-relief."[17] Thus, the lack of distribution to the widows has taken on much greater import as it becomes an indication (perhaps even a cipher) for deeper theological differences and divergences.

Given the importance of these details for generating the dominant paradigms of interpretation, we must look more closely at Luke's use of these two all-important terms. The term Ἑλληνιστής occurs two other times in Acts. In 9:20 the word refers to Greek-speaking individuals but not adherents to the

---

16. This position is that of Baur, and shared, with some modifications, by Hengel. While many scholars have concurred that Ἑλληνιστής is primarily a linguistic designation, most have infused this "speaking" with cultural elements as well (see also H. A. Brehm, "The Meaning of Ἑλληνιστής in Acts in Light of a Diachronic Analysis of ἑλληνίζειν," in *Discourse Analysis and Other Topics in Biblical Greek* [ed. S. E. Porter and D. A. Carson; JSNTSup 113; Sheffield: Sheffield Academic Press, 1995], 182). Admittedly, this particular characterization of modern scholarly views on the "Hellenists" combines a variety of positions. Some scholars do in fact emphasize the language aspect (Barrett, *Acts of the Apostles*, 308–9), others the geographical distinction (Diaspora versus Palestine), others strictly the theological, while still others the ethnic component (i.e., "to live like a Greek" in terms of either Jews who adopt Greek lifestyles [O. Cullmann, "L'Opposition contre le Temple de Jerusalem, Motif Commun de la Theologie Johannique et du Monde Ambiant," *NTS* 5 (1959): 161] or Gentiles themselves [H. J. Cadbury, "The Hellenists," in *The Beginnings of Christianity: The Acts of the Apostles* (ed. F. J. Foakes Jackson and K. Lake; London: Macmillan, 1933), 5:59–74]). See further Brehm's synopsis of the various positions ("Meaning of Ἑλληνιστής," 180–84), as well as E. Ferguson, "The Hellenists in the Book of Acts," *ResQ* 12 (1969): 159–80; J. B. Tyson, "Acts 6:1–7 and Dietary Regulations in Early Christianity," *PRSt* 10 (1983): 155–58; and S. Légasse, *Stephanos: Historie et Discours D'Étienne dans les Actes des Apôtres* (LD 147; Paris: Cerf, 1992), 185–89.

17. E. Haenchen, *The Acts of the Apostles: A Commentary* (trans. R. Mcl. Wilson; Philadelphia: Westminster, 1971), 268. Those readings that seek to place the blame on noncommunity "Hebrews" (outsiders), who are neglecting the Jerusalem community's Hellenists (insiders) for the reason that they are viewed as being outside the purview of traditional Judaism, are essentially making the same argument, except that the Jerusalem community is here portrayed as uniting with the Hellenists against the external threat (thereby preserving the unity of the assembly). See further W. A. Strange, *The Problem of the Text of Acts* (SNTSMS 71; Cambridge: Cambridge University Press, 1992), 125–26.

new faith (quite possibly Jews) living in Jerusalem, who seek to kill Paul.[18] In 11:20 the word becomes even more problematic. This narrative picks up where 8:1–4 leaves off: the scattering of the Jerusalem community after the death of Stephen and their subsequent preaching abroad. Some "men of Cyprus and Cyrene," having left Jerusalem because of the persecution, speak to "Hellenists" in Antioch, some of whom convert to the new faith. The problem here is that these "Hellenists" would seem, in part at least, to include Gentiles, as the larger context of the subsequent issues in Antioch clearly implies a Gentile presence (cf. 15:1–5, 22–35).[19] The contrast with Ἰουδαῖοι in 11:19 would make some sense in this light, particularly as the missionaries from Jerusalem are portrayed as breaking with those others in 11:19 who spoke only to Jews. Thus, the implication is that "Hellenists" in 11:20 are in fact Gentiles. In Acts the three occurrences of Ἑλληνιστής appear to carry different connotations in each case (i.e., there is no consistency in use). Thus, Luke does not seem to have a particular party or group in mind at any time when the word is used.

Brehm's analysis of Ἑλληνιστής is particularly useful at this juncture. He suggests that the term carries with it an intersecting range of meanings, beginning with the primary ancient usage: "speaking Greek."[20] Brehm further suggests that for Luke the term Ἑλληνιστής is not important in and of itself. Rather, it must be interpreted in light of Luke's apparent interest in specifying and distinguishing different groups in the narrative (cf. 2:9–11) and especially his use of pairings in the presentation of different characters in Luke-Acts. This observation is as true for 6:1 as it is for 11:19–20, since in both cases Luke distinguishes between two groups: "Hellenists" and "Hebrews" in 6:1, and "Jews" and "Hellenists" in 11:19–20. As for the meaning of Ἑλληνιστής in 6:1, Brehm's conclusion, based on his analysis of the syntagmatic relationships of the word in Acts, is simply that it refers to Jews who speak Greek. Since Ἑβραῖος can be used as a synonym for Ἰουδαῖοι (an ethnic designation; cf. Paul's use of Ἑβραῖος in 2 Cor 11:22 and possibly also in Phil 3:5), one must be careful about simplistically equating Ἑβραῖος with "those speaking Hebrew." Nevertheless, Brehm is most likely correct in making this connection in the case of Acts 6:1, as this association provides the counterpart for the "Hellenists," who spoke Greek.

---

18. R. Pesch et al., "'Hellenisten' und 'Hebräer': Zu Apg 9,29 und 6,1," *BZ* 23 (1979): 87–88.

19. The debate about 11:20 is complicated by the textual variant Ἕλληνας, which seems to have been placed in the text by a scribe to contrast this group with the Ἰουδαῖοι of 11:19; thus, these figures are Greeks/Gentiles (see B. M. Metzger, *A Textual Commentary on the Greek New Testament* [New York: United Bible Societies, 1975], 386–89). It is likely that the reading of Ἑλληνιστής is the correct one, but the problem of defining its meaning does not so easily recede as a result; it could be that it still means Greek/Gentile regardless.

20. See Brehm, "Meaning of Ἑλληνιστής," 185–99; and "The Role of the 'Hellenists' in Christian Origins: A Critique of Representative Models in Light of an Exegetical Study of Acts 6–8" (Ph.D. diss., Southwestern Baptist Theological Seminary, 1992), 106–74.

Delimiting the meaning of Ἑλληνιστής is difficult because it is not even clear that Stephen and the seven belong to this group. Although they are often assumed to be part of the Ἑλληνιστής designation — based largely on the fact that they all have good Greek-sounding names! — it is not entirely evident in the narrative whether they belong to the "Hebrews," "Hellenists," or a combination of both. Since the precise delimitation of the group is ambiguous, it is difficult to see how one can use Stephen's speech and consequent martyrdom to reconstruct a distinct Hellenist theology or mission. The narrative simply does not allow for any inferences regarding the meaning of "Hellenist" based upon later narrative developments in Acts 6:1–8:3.

G. Harvey's recent treatment of the use of the designation "Hebrew" demonstrates further the difficulties inherent in 6:1–7.[21] After analyzing the various positions on the "Hellenist" versus "Hebrew" conflict, he asserts that "all that is left is the seemingly banal observation that the author must have had some commonly understood difference between the two labels in mind."[22] Thus, Harvey agrees with most scholars that Luke intends some differentiation between the two, but also maintains that the context does not reveal precisely what the writer's understanding of those differences in fact were. Indeed, the context does not even allow for the supposition that the difference is purely language based. Harvey's analysis is also significant because of the way he goes about establishing the meaning of these terms. From his study of the use of "Hebrew" in Jewish literature, he suggests that it most often was used to designate a "true Jew" such as Abraham, conservative and traditional, albeit the definition of what this ascription differs from text to text.[23] Harvey uses the meaning in other texts to determine the definition intended, or most likely implied, in Acts 6:1–7:

> It is probable that the languages referred to in the designations do indicate, as is generally accepted, a difference of culture. The "Hellenists" speak Greek as an expression of their acceptance or participation in the then predominant culture. The "Hebrews" are associated with "traditional," more parochial values. In the case of these Christian "Hebrews" and "Hellenists" perhaps the "overlooking" of the widows was due to a suspicion of some contamination from "foreign" influences. It may, however, simply have been that the dominant (at least in this situation) Hebrew or Aramaic speaking group did not understand (or want to understand) the needs of the Greek-speaking group.[24]

---

21. G. Harvey, *The True Israel: Uses of the Names Jew, Hebrew, and Israel in Ancient Jewish and Early Christian Literature* (AGJU 35; Leiden: Brill, 1996), 104–47.
22. Ibid., 135.
23. Ibid., 146–47, 270–71. Also see G. Harvey, "Synagogues of the Hebrews: 'Good Jews' in the Diaspora," in *Jewish Local Patriotism and Self-Identification in the Graeco-Roman World* (ed. S. Jones and S. Pearce; JSPSup 31; Sheffield: Sheffield Academic Press, 1998), 132–47. See also the similar discussion by D. Georgi, *The Opponents of Paul in Second Corinthians* (Philadelphia: Fortress, 1986), 41–46, esp. 42–44.
24. Harvey, *True Israel*, 135–36.

This treatment reveals the basic problems with most studies on this passage. Since the context does not allow for inference, Harvey employs the meaning of "Hebrew" from other Jewish sources. Having established that meaning as "traditional" and "conservative," he then reconstructs the opposite of that (liberal and nontraditional) and mirror-reads an inferred definition for "Hellenist." While Harvey is more reserved in drawing conclusions than many other scholars, the problems with his position are clear.

For the most part, Harvey is correct; the term "Hebrew" implies "good Jew." Moreover, while the designations "traditional" and "conservative" are partly true, the meaning of these words (as Harvey admits) differs from text to text. There is no unified conception of "Hebrew" but only one defined by the author who is using it. Overall the term functions as a way of characterizing positively those who belong to the "true Israel" over against those who are viewed as outsiders. It is often a polemical and rhetorical *topos* as a result. Since the construction of identity is primary, the problem for inquiry into Luke's use is that nowhere in Luke-Acts does the precise issue of identity arise (or at least in the way framed in other Jewish texts), and it is uncertain that the purpose is to delineate the nature of being "Hebrew" in 6:1 as equivalent to being a "good Jew." Moreover, there is no indication that the conservative Jews of 15:5 and 21:20 are to be identified with the "Hebrews" of 6:1 (especially given Luke's varied use of "Hellenist"). Considering also that Philo predominantly uses "Hebrew" to refer either to past ancestors or those who speak Hebrew/Aramaic ("ancestral language in distinction from the use of 'Greek' by other people of similar descent"),[25] there is some precedent for regarding "Hebrew" in 6:1 as predominantly designating language.

The silence of the text in 6:1–7 allows one to go only so far. Clearly the writer intends to make a distinction of some sort, and all scholars recognize this function. That language is primarily in view is a position that involves the least amount of speculation. Where Luke does refer to conservative Jewish clashes in his construction of origins of the Christian movement, he does not use the term "Hebrew" to characterize the traditionalists (cf. 15:1–2). Where the adjective Ἑβραΐς occurs, it does so with an explicit reference to language (cf. 21:40; 22:2; 26:14; cf. Ἑλληνιστί in 21:37).[26] The range for inference is still minimal, but the designation of "language" in 6:1 seems most reasonable (although possibly with overtones of geography: Palestine versus Diaspora). Overall, as I will suggest later, the precise nature of the distinction is much less important for Luke than the fact that the terms are intended to include all Jews. Luke's intention is not to point out dissimilarity but to establish diversity amid adversity in the composition of the Jerusalem

---

25. Ibid., 124.
26. The extension of the adjective to include cultural aspects seems unwarranted (but see Georgi, *Opponents of Paul*, 42).

community. For the moment, however, it is helpful to narrow the association of "Hellenist" to "language."²⁷ While the position that only language is intended in 6:1 does not find unanimous support, most scholars will at least agree that nothing is stated *explicitly* about geography (Diaspora origin)²⁸ or theology (liberal view of the law) in the designations.²⁹

Despite the relative lack of textual clues, speculation has not been muted as a result. From Haenchen's comment above, for instance, it is clear that many scholars are not inclined to keep the discussion of Ἑλληνιστής and Ἑβραῖος at the level of linguistic designation. The recent treatment by Esler illustrates this larger trend,³⁰ as he goes to great lengths to demonstrate that the "Hellenists" spoke Greek and the "Hebrews" Aramaic.³¹ Aside from reference to the sound Greek names of the "seven," he makes an extended argument that most must have spoken Greek (for certain Stephen, Philip, and Nicolaus).³² But the argument quickly moves out from there when Esler reveals that underlying his treatment of the Hellenists is the premise that they were anti-temple while the Hebrews were pro-temple.³³ Indeed, Esler argues that it was the Hellenists who were first convinced to accept "God-fearers" (i.e., Gentiles) into the early Jerusalem community.³⁴ Esler's analysis

---

27. This is also Hill's position (*Hellenists and Hebrews*, 24), although he adds the geographical element: Greek-speaking Jew from the Diaspora. See also R. Murray, "Jews, Hebrews, and Christians: Some Needed Distinctions," *NovT* 24 (1982): 204. In his survey of the evidence, Brehm concludes that language is primarily in view, but that Christian use with reference to cultural associations does appear in later writings, especially from Eusebius onwards ("Meaning of Ἑλληνιστής," 298).

28. Geographical distinction may have some merit on the basis of the names mentioned in 6:5 related to the seven appointed deacons. The last one, Nicolaus, is identified as a proselyte from Antioch. Thus, we have the "origin" of one of the "seven" provided. Outside of the name "Philip," which does have a Palestinian provenance (M. H. Williams, "Palestinian Jewish Personal Names in Acts," in *Book of Acts* [ed. Bauckham], 98–99), the remaining names are more difficult to establish as Palestinian in origin (and Jewish, as is the case with "Stephen," which occurs rarely for Jews in the Diaspora and which lacks any attestation in Palestine. [111–12]). The names clearly mark the leaders of the "Hellenists" as being Greek, and may also reflect an intentional geographical shading as well. However, "Andrew," the name ascribed to one of the apostles, is also a rare Palestinian and Jewish appellation (97).

29. One must also take note in this context of the use of the phrase κρατήσας εὐθέως πρὸς τὸν Ἑλληνικὸν χαρακτῆρα in 2 Macc 4:10, as well as Ἑλληνισμός in 2 Macc 4:13 (cf. μεταλαβόντες Ἑλληνικοῦ βίου in 4 Macc 8:8). There is no denying that these phrases carry overt associations of more than just language; as they also imply in this context the adoption of perceived distinctive Greek customs. It is noteworthy, however, that this meaning has to be made explicit in the text by the use of verbs and qualifying nouns. It is difficult to make the argument that the use of these correlative words in the Maccabean texts should of necessity be used for interpreting the meaning of Ἑλληνιστής in Acts 6:1 (Luke betrays no hint of trying to make the same distinctions that one finds in 2 Macc 4:10, 13, although scholars frequently have the Maccabean usage in the back of their minds when reading Acts 6:1).

30. Esler, *Community and Gospel*, 135–63.

31. Ibid., 141–43.

32. Ibid., 141, 247 n. 35.

33. Ibid., 140.

34. Ibid., 158–59. Esler's approach is sociological. He argues that these "God-fearers" experienced marginalization because of their exclusion from the temple (154–58, 161). This position is basically a reformulation of the thesis that the Hellenists were the first to reach

is interesting precisely because he refers to his methodological step: "[W]hat actually happened to the Hellenists can be *deduced* from the text."[35] This move provides a window into the logic of the interpretation of 6:1–7. The narrative establishes that the Hebrews ignored the Hellenist widows in the daily distribution (presumably a doling out of food). No one disputes that this claim is explicitly made in the narrative. Many scholars, however, ask the obvious (to us) but textually unaddressed question, "Why were the Hellenist widows ignored?" Luke provides no answer for this,[36] although many scholars are convinced that the larger narrative of Acts 6:1–8:3 provides some rationale.[37]

As one analyzes the logic of an argument such as Esler's, the movement from assumption to assured result is surprising in this search for the real cause of the problem in the early Jerusalem community. The issues become even more complex as a result. The present Lukan narrative clearly describes a problem within the newly formed community; but the effort to get at the more basic issue not mentioned in the text requires one to argue that Luke has reworked a more primitive text/tradition. To get at the problem, one must sort out the tradition underlying, but not explicitly visible in, the text.[38] Luke thus deftly covers up the theological rift by leaving the motivation unspoken and rewriting other elements of the tradition. Luke's motivation

---

out to Gentiles and that this was the cause of the fissure between them and the Hebrews. The message of the gospel was liberating for these Gentiles in light of their experience of having been marginalized from the Jewish faith. The Hellenists, sympathetic with the proselytes (indeed, there was one in the Hellenist community, namely, Nicolaus), allowed them full access to their community.

35. Esler, *Community and Gospel,* 162 (emphasis added). See also Haenchen, *Acts of the Apostles,* 265: "As always, we must distinguish between what Luke himself wished to say and what may be inferred from his account."

36. A similar lack of motivation for conduct can be found in Acts 5:1–11: No reason is stated for why Ananias and Sapphira withheld money from the community. Indeed, even Peter's prophetic judgment does not specify the motivations (e.g., greed) behind the actions (5:4, 9). The only moral judgment made is that the husband and wife lied to God.

37. Hill supports the historical accuracy of this account (*Hellenists and Hebrews,* 25–27). He argues (following D. Seccombe, "Was There Organized Charity in Jerusalem before the Christians?" *JTS* 29 [1979]: 140–43; see also Bartchy, "Community of Goods," 315–18) that the daily distribution of food to widows in the community fits well with the picture of private charity in Jerusalem from this time period. Hill notes that Haenchen does not believe in the accuracy of the distribution account (27; citing Haenchen, *Acts of the Apostles,* 262), but he misreads Haenchen at this point. Haenchen's argument is that there must be more to the story than what we find in 6:1–7, not that the account is inaccurate in and of itself. He simply notes that the story in 6:1–7 assumes a point in time rather removed from the close association of synagogue and *ekklesia,* thus a period of time has elapsed and therefore any attempt to connect this feature with the earliest days of the nascent Christian movement may be questionable.

38. For instance, G. Lüdemann, *Early Christianity according to the Traditions in Acts: A Commentary* (trans. J. Bowden; Minneapolis: Fortress, 1989), 78, states, "[T]here was some conflict — if not over the care of widows (this is to be seen as a Lukan toning down of another conflict...) — between the two parties in Jerusalem." For Lüdemann, the historical "bedrock" of the tradition is the notice of the seven Greek names and the mention of a conflict in 6:1b (the rest can be counted as Lukan redaction, with a focus on toning down the "real" events; 77–78).

for doing so is usually framed as his "idealizing" tendency: Luke wants to portray the progenitors of the Christian movement in the best possible light.[39] Of course, since the "original" motivation is admittedly lacking, any construal is hypothetical and therefore impossible to disprove.

From this basic premise, numerous other problems arise for the interpretation of the narrative. Some scholars, attempting to integrate Luke's description more closely with the alleged larger tensions, suggest that the Hellenists were being neglected because they were violating purity regulations in their dietary practice.[40] Others argue that at the heart of this "division" lies a report about the formation of apostolic leadership in the Jerusalem community and subsequent rivalry.[41] Still others suggest that the real report behind 6:1–7 stems from a later period in Antioch, and has been placed in a different, and earlier, context by Luke.[42] Most recently, one scholar has suggested that a more egalitarian community tradition, with the original narrative detailing the whole community coming together to solve the problem of the widows, underlies Luke's attempt to delineate proper channels of authority in early Christianity.[43] Other scholars, attempting to avoid any underlying problems, simply follow the narrative as it now exists: There was

---

39. This aspect is often linked to Luke's apologetic interests: portraying the community as a harmonious entity that represents no threat to the authorities (Jewish and Roman). See R. Maddox, *The Purpose of Luke-Acts* (ed. J. Riches; Edinburgh: T & T Clark, 1982), 91–99. On Luke's idealizing tendency, see the comments by Haenchen, *Acts of the Apostles*, 98–103. Similar sentiments have been expressed more recently by F. S. Spencer, *The Portrait of Philip in Acts: A Study of Roles and Relations* (JSNTSup 67; Sheffield: Sheffield Academic Press, 1992), 195: Luke is aware of a "historic division" in the community, but downplays it by constructing a harmonious narrative. Tannehill suggests that the idealizing tendency has less to do with the avoiding of community problems and more to do with their quick resolution (*The Narrative Unity of Luke-Acts: A Literary Interpretation* [Philadelphia: Fortress, 1990], 2:81).

40. J. B. Tyson, *Images of Judaism in Luke-Acts* (Columbia: University of South Carolina Press, 1992), 112; and idem, "Acts 6:1–7 and Dietary Regulations," 145–61. This position allows Tyson to retain the substance of Luke's narrative, while still basing the problem in a deeper underlying issue.

41. G. Theissen, "Hellenisten und Hebräer (Apg 6,1–6). Gab es eine Spaltung der Urgemeinde?" in *Geschichte-Tradition-Reflexion: Festschrift für Martin Hengel zum 70. Geburtstag* (ed. H. Cancik et al.; Tübingen: Mohr Siebeck, 1996), 3:323–43. Theissen argues that underlying Luke's account is a report about the burgeoning movement in Jerusalem, when the Palestinian wandering missionaries began to stabilize their itinerancy in the city. As a result, different local leaderships were in competition. Although Theissen does not dispense with the theological differences either (see 332–36, 340), his main point is that there was not a "division" since there was not yet a unified entity to divide.

42. N. Walter, "Apostelgeschichte 6.1 und die Anfänge der Urgemeinde in Jerusalem," NTS 29 (1983): 370–93.

43. R. M. Price, *The Widow Traditions in Luke-Acts: A Feminist-Critical Scrutiny* (SBLDS 155; Atlanta: Scholars Press, 1997), 210–16. Price's treatment is overly simplistic and a little strange. His attempt to use Noth's character reversal principle (earlier major characters were replaced, in redaction, by other major characters, with the former being relegated to a minor status) as a tradition-critical axiom is highly questionable. Moreover, he fundamentally misconstrues the narrative: In no scholarly scenario have the widows been understood as a negative factor in the story ("a sarcastic put-down of the widows" [216]). The negative connotations surrounding "murmuring" (γογγυσμός), if there are any, refer to the Hellenists in general and not to the widows in particular (I see no way of construing the grammar so that the widows

a problem in food distribution (either within the community itself or within the larger daily distributions in Jerusalem), and the Hellenists were elected or brought in to deal with it (either for their own Hellenist group or for the entire newly formed community in Jerusalem).[44] Daube suggests that the incident is actually modeled on three Old Testament narratives: Exodus 18, Numbers 11, and Deuteronomy 1, all having to do with the establishment of overseers to govern specific groups or matters.[45] Despite these various suggestions, however, the narrative logic has been illuminated little as a result.

For instance, the narrative implicitly suggests that the Hebrews neglected the Hellenist widows (otherwise the complaints made by the Hellenists against the Hebrews would appear to be pointless).[46] Acts 6:2–4 thus represents the apostolic solution to the problem posed in 6:1. Although the language of 6:2 could be interpreted to mean that the apostles themselves had been waiting on tables and neglecting their preaching duties,[47] it is probably better understood to suggest that they should not give up their preaching ministry in order to serve tables or solve problems; hence the

---

become the subject of the participle). This revisionist reading would suggest that Luke has attempted to subvert stories about an egalitarian community (with the prominence of women in that structure), while completely ignoring the wealth of detail that suggests that Luke himself is interested in demonstrating the ideal nature of community formation. See T. K. Seim, *The Double Message: Patterns of Gender in Luke and Acts* (Edinburgh: T & T Clark, 1994), who argues that the Lukan perception of widows has "considerable distance from the confining treatment of widows in the Pastorals" (248).

44. Hyldahl, *History of Early Christianity*, 174–76; and Hill, *Hellenists and Hebrews*, 27–28.

45. D. Daube, "A Reform in Acts and Its Models," in *Jews, Greeks, and Christians: Religious Cultures in Late Antiquity; Essays in Honor of William David Davies* (ed. R. Hamerton-Kelly and R. Scroggs; SJLA 21; Leiden: Brill, 1976), 151–63. Earlier, Daube had suggested that the commissioning of Joshua in the Old Testament served as an exemplar for the Acts account (*New Testament and Rabbinic Judaism* [London: Athlone, 1956], 238–39). Daube, however, does not think that the Lukan account was invented from the Old Testament parallels, but rather that the presentation was shaped by them (159–60). For more on the Old Testament parallels, see Spencer, *Portrait of Philip*, 206–11.

46. The scribe of MS D appears to elaborate on 6:1 by indicating—through an epexegetical phrase—who was doing the "distributing": "...because their widows were being neglected in the daily service—the service of the Hebrews" (but Barrett is not sure what the scribe intended; *Acts of the Apostles*, 310). Noteworthy also is that D omits "of the Hellenists against the Hebrews" in the description of the "complaint."

47. Daube favors this reading ("Reform in Acts," 155). See also Johnson, *Literary Function of Possessions*, 212. The narrative in 4:32–37 depicts the community bringing the proceeds from the selling of the goods and laying them at the apostles' feet (cf. vv. 35, 37). As people had need, the proceeds were then distributed (v. 35). It is not clear that this is the same type of distribution going on in 6:1, however. The latter is a "daily" distribution, while the sense of 4:35 seems to be of a more occasional type. Moreover, that the apostles received the payment does not mean that they distributed it. In fact, the passive construction in 4:35 does not indicate who performed the distribution to the needy. Even if the two distributions are the same (and this is possible given that 6:1 does not specify that it is a distribution of food [ἐν τῇ διακονίᾳ τῇ καθημερινῇ]), it is not clear that Luke intends the reader to understand that in 4:32–37 the apostles were serving, but then wanted to abandon that duty later in 6:2. Rather, in both instances the narrative point seems to be thus: The apostles are the undisputed leaders and problem solvers of the Jerusalem community.

need for the appointment of the seven.[48] Therefore, the text implies the existence of two parallel ministries: the ministry of the word (6:4) and the daily ministry of food distribution (6:2).[49]

That the apostles themselves do not rectify the problem vis-à-vis the Hebrews (something akin to the type of solution and conference one finds in Acts 15) further increases the speculation that we are here catching a glimpse of the formation of a separate community in Jerusalem. The solution is not to resolve the dilemma with the Hebrews, and the consequent lapse in service to the Hellenist widows, but to appoint a group of Hellenists. Esler's interpretation of this process is standard: The Hellenists, due to their larger theological problems with the Hebrews, split from the Jerusalem community, establishing their own alms distribution system. Luke, both familiar with the split and embarrassed by it, attempts to cover it up by having the apostles endorse the ministry of the Hellenists. This latter detail is a Lukan redactional element, and the historical reality is that there was never any apostolic endorsement of the Hellenistic ministry; rather, it was a parallel mission, focusing on the God-fearing Gentiles in Jerusalem. As a result, it was only natural that Luke should leave aside the "waiting on tables" and move directly to the kerygmatic elements of the Hellenist narrative: the preaching of Stephen and Philip.[50] This view may represent the outer limits of the scenario in terms of modern scholarship, but it adequately reflects the positions of scholars such as Bultmann, Haenchen, and Lüdemann. For many of these interpreters, Acts 6:1–7 exists in Luke's work only because it functions as a pretense for the writer to introduce the Hellenist hero Stephen into the narrative.[51] The difficulties of refuting this angle of interpretation

---

48. See Seim, *Double Message*, 109–10.

49. Διακονία has a wide range of meanings, of which the more general and primary sense of "service" seems to be in view in 6:1. Moving from the more general sense, the word often carries with it the notion of religious function or duty (the sense evident most often in the New Testament; cf. Acts 6:4; 12:25; Rom 11:13; 12:7; 1 Cor 12:5), and gives rise to the terminology for the ecclesial office of "deacon" (although H. W. Beyer, "διακονέω, διακονία, διάκονος," *TDNT* 2:81–93, argues that it never loses its sense of "waiting on tables,"). It can, however, simply refer to menial tasks, especially those related to the preparation of meals (cf. Luke 10:40; Mark 1:31), and is used also to designate the giving of aid to those in need (as in Paul's collection for the poor of Jerusalem: cf. Rom 15:25, 31; 1 Cor 16:15; 2 Cor 8:4; 9:1, 12, 13). In Acts 11:29, διακονία is used to refer to the famine relief sent to the Jerusalem *ekklesia* by the community of Antioch. From the context in Acts 6:1–7, διακονία at first appears to refer to the daily distribution of food (esp. in light of 6:2: "to serve tables"; although this phrase may be used in the sense of "attending on people" [Collins, *Diakonia*, 231]). Yet one cannot limit the meaning to this sense (the type of ministry is "indeterminate"; ibid.). Indeed, if one reads 6:1–7 in light of the summary statement in 4:32–35, it may well refer to financial assistance. In the earlier narrative, Luke maintains that there was not a needy person in the community (4:34a) because of the selling of individual property (4:34b) and the subsequent distribution of the "price" (τιμή; i.e., that gained from the sale of the property) to those in need (4:35b; cf. 2:44–45). At any rate, διακονία in this context must remain relatively unspecific and certainly cannot easily be construed as referring to the origination of church "offices."

50. Esler, *Community and Gospel*, 145.

51. Haenchen, *Acts of the Apostles*, 265: "Luke wishes only to explain how Stephen (whose martyrdom he is planning to relate) came to occupy so prominent a position in the community."

is a testament to its lasting influence. Hill, who opposes any construction of 6:1–7 that presumes a split in the early Jerusalem community, nonetheless clearly struggles over the interpretation of many of the details in the text and leaves a precise construction of the "historical" aspects to one side. He is content to argue that there was a problem in the daily distribution to the Hellenist widows. Moreover, he seeks to combat the commonly held view that the seven Hellenists were in some ways precluded, according to the narrative logic, from preaching as well.[52] Yet Hill also admits the possibility that Luke seems to subordinate the seven to the Jerusalem apostles, although he does not want to speculate on the reasons for Luke's doing so.

From this brief discussion it is evident that numerous conjectures have been offered based on the sparse textual details and markers. While the vast majority of scholars is convinced that much of the present character of 6:1–7 is provided by the writer — although differing as to the exact redactional elements — there is also almost unanimous agreement that certain core historical details in this unit are beyond dispute. Richard's summary adequately represents the consensus on what is considered historical: the initial notice of the Hellenist-Hebrew conflict (6:1b), the list of the Greek names (6:5), and possibly the detail that there were seven of them (6:3a).[53] The elements of Lukan redaction, conversely, are often outlined as follows: the characterization of the role of the seven in a way that makes them appear subordinate to the twelve (6:2), their restriction to ministry of the table (6:3), the particular notion of ministry apparent in the narrative (6:2, 4), the act of commissioning (6:6), mention of the Spirit (and the remaining characteristics of the "seven men"; 6:3, 5), and possibly the number seven itself (6:3).[54] At the same time, Richard has forcefully demonstrated that the entire narrative of 6:1–7 is the composition of Luke and that it is impossible

---

See also Dibelius, "The Speeches in Acts and Ancient Historiography," in *Studies in the Acts of the Apostles* (ed. H. Greeven; London: SCM, 1956), 181.

52. Hill, *Hellenists and Hebrews*, 26–27 (cf. H. Räisänen, "Die 'Hellenisten' der Urgemeinde," *ANRW* 2.26.2 [1995]: 1476, who points out the weaknesses of Hill's argument: He cannot account for, and indeed overlooks, the way Luke intends the reader to understand Stephen and Phillip in the narrative). Johnson's work (*Literary Function of Possessions*, 212–23) on this section is important, as he recognizes the tension: The "seven" are appointed to oversee the distribution but in fact preach. His argument is that it is the Lukan theological and literary interest to use possessions in 6:1–7 as a means to represent the transfer of spiritual authority from the twelve apostles to the seven Hellenists (213). This is a significant observation, although the notion that Luke "forgets" the image of possessions and moves to spiritual power reveals Johnson's own difficulties with explaining how the narrative can completely leave to one side the original reason for the appointing of the seven (see also Johnson, *The Acts of the Apostles* [SP 5; Collegeville, Minn.: Liturgical Press, 1992], 111).

53. See also J. A. Fitzmyer, *The Acts of the Apostles* (AB 31; New York: Doubleday, 1998), 345; and J. T. Lienhard, "Acts 6:1–6: A Redactional View," *CBQ* 37 (1973): 236.

54. Richard, *Acts 6:1–8:4*, 273.

now to separate the traditional and redactional elements. Thus, while most scholars assert the traditional nature of key details in the passage — as few as there may seem to be — there is actually little evidence to support these conjectures.

In this way, scholars of Acts have been forced into a corner. Those interested in the history behind the narrative strip away everything that smacks of the Lukan theological program. In the similar manner, those scholars concerned with Lukan theological interests also frequently remove the elements that appear to reflect genuine historical details available from tradition. Both approaches must consequently seek explanations for Lukan additions and alterations to traditional materials. Once one has isolated Lukan tendencies with respect to the material, one can more readily disregard those elements that appear secondary. The overwhelming agreement in scholarship that Luke has subordinated the seven to the twelve in 6:6 provides a good example of this approach.[55] Since critics generally accept that the Jerusalem apostles hold a special place in the Lukan framework, they argue that anything that heightens their prominence in the text must be a result of Lukan redactional activity. The role of the apostles throughout 6:1–7 thus seems to mesh well with Luke's overall conception of these twelve characters.

There are certain details, however, that cannot easily be explained as a reflection of Lukan interest. For instance, the mention of the Hellenist widows remains rather undeveloped within the larger Lukan perspective in Acts, especially since such interest seems to be present in the Lukan gospel. The issue of "waiting on tables" or neglect in daily distribution resonates with Luke's emphasis on table fellowship, and internal division and external conflict are important elements in Acts 1–6. Yet one is left to ponder why Luke did not develop the problem in 6:1 in more detail as he did with the Ananias and Sapphira narrative (5:1–11). Luke provides few details of the conflict, and — even if he were relying on a limited tradition — this lack seems to go against his literary interests elsewhere in Acts.[56] While all of 6:3 is easy to relegate to Lukan concern regarding the character of those called to ministry, the number seven possibly and the specific names in 6:5 most certainly are more difficult to account for as particular Lukan inventions. If the number seven is possibly explained on the basis of Jewish

---

55. The subordination of the "seven" to the "twelve" as an element of Lukan redactional interest finds frequent support (see Walter, "Apostelgeschichte 6.1," 370, 372–73). However, some who argue for Lukan awareness and suppression of a "historic division" in the community do not think that it must automatically entail the Lukan subordination of the seven Hellenists to the twelve apostles (Spencer, *Portrait of Philip*, 195–99: The apostles and the seven Hellenists are *partners* in ministry).

56. Dibelius argued that the reason for this lack of emphasis was because the material did not have any specific kerygmatic value for the readers ("Speeches in Acts," 181).

models,⁵⁷ many would argue that certainly the Greek names cited in the text must reflect an element of tradition. As noted above, Richard, a scholar who has thoroughly and convincingly established Luke as the author of the entire episode, nonetheless cannot make sense of the names unless they are understood to be a reflection of an oral or, as is more probable in this case, a written tradition.⁵⁸

The list of names has greatly influenced interpretation of this text. Once one admits that the names themselves are a traditional non-Lukan element, then clearly many of the other aspects of the story coalesce around them. Aside from the obvious connections to the following story regarding Stephen (6:8–7:1; 7:54–8:2), the list of names also provides an air of reality and factuality to the narrative. The Greek names immediately resonate with the contrast between the "Hebrews" and "Hellenists" in 6:1, even though Luke does not explicitly state that the seven men came from the Hellenist community; they appear to represent the entire new community in the ministry of distribution (at least, this seems to be what Luke wants his readers to understand). Yet scholarship has largely maintained that the seven must come from the Hellenist group (and perhaps having their ministry limited to that group as well), and this largely on account of their Greek names.⁵⁹ As trivial a detail as the mention of the names in 6:5 may appear, it has proved to be a critical lynchpin in the reinforcement of the dominating interpretations of this passage.

From the preceding discussion, it is apparent that the issues in 6:1–7 are far from being resolved, irrespective of whether one takes a more radical reading (Baur, Haenchen, Hengel) or a more conservative one (Hill). Despite the quest for the historical realities underlying this narrative, there are numerous aspects of the structure of the text, its relation to antecedent and preceding narratives, and particular details that arise in the unit itself that move the interpreter forward toward a more sustained engagement of Lukan compositional dynamics.

---

57. Some scholars suggest that the number seven may be reflective of a common Jewish practice of appointing seven individuals for a particular task (see Barrett, *Acts of the Apostles*, 312, for ancient parallels).

58. This connection is one of the reasons for the perdurance of the Antiochian source theory behind the material in Acts 6:1–8:3. Once one admits the likelihood that the seven names are an element of tradition, one needs to account for the preservation of this tradition. Harnack's treatment is probably the most sustained. He argued that beginning in 6:1 Luke makes the move to a source that stems from Antioch (6:1–15:35, with the exception of the Caesarean "digressions" in 8:5–40; 9:29–11:18; and 12:1–14; A. von Harnack, *The Acts of the Apostles* [trans. J. R. Wilkinson; New York: Williams & Norgate, 1909], 169–75). His justification for regarding 6:1–6 as the beginning of the Antiochian source is that Nicolaus is described as a proselyte from Antioch (172). Harnack's premise, although not explicitly articulated, is that only a tradition connected with Antioch would "remember" the details of Nicolaus. See the similar approach and results in Barrett, *Acts of the Apostles*, 334, 340.

59. Hengel also suggests that their Greek names imply that they "came from abroad" (*Acts and the History of Earliest Christianity* [trans. J. Bowden; Philadelphia: Fortress, 1979], 71).

Textual Markers II:
Stephen in Narrative (6:8–7:1; 7:54–8:2)

In light of the previous observations regarding the larger context of 6:1–7, it is not surprising that the narrative in 6:8 now turns to the conflict between the newly formed community in Jerusalem — here expanded with the addition of priests, the identification of the seven men, and the presence of two groups, Hebrews and Hellenists — and external opponents. These opponents are also expanded in the process. Formerly the conflict with opponents had been limited to the Jewish authorities. Now "matching" opponents have arisen to counteract the "Greek" Stephen: the individuals identified as Hellenistic Jews in 6:9. At the same time, these new opponents work in tandem with the Jewish authorities identified as antagonists earlier in Acts (6:12, 15; 7:1; cf. 4:5–7; 5:17, 21, 27, 34, 41).

Stephen now surfaces as the main character of Lukan concern. The sudden shift away from the Jerusalem apostles suggests again to many scholars the presence (or continuance) of a source.[60] Paralleling the character description of the "seven" in 6:3, the characterization of Stephen in 6:5, and the portrayal of the apostles earlier in the narrative, Luke begins his story of Stephen by noting that he was "full [πλήρης; cf. 6:3, 5] of grace and power [cf. 4:33]" and "was performing great wonders and signs [cf. 5:12]."[61] Inevitably, as attested in Acts 2–6, once the author notes how well the *ekklesia* is doing, opposition immediately arises in the narrative. The opponents here in 6:9 are described as Jews who originate outside of Jerusalem. At the same time, it is difficult to delineate the precise interrelationships of these individuals/communities, since the grammar of the sentence might suggest that Luke has in view several synagogues, although this point is debatable.[62] The only one clearly identified is the "synagogue of the Libertines (i.e.,

---

60. Barrett, for instance, argues that 6:8 and 6:9 represent Luke's editorial activity as he attempts to link the Antiochian story of Stephen with the previous tradition of the "seven." Barrett's view is complicated, but essentially he believes that 6:1–7 rests on a tradition that Luke used (possibly oral, but probably written) and reworked considerably, while the Stephen narrative itself is probably better understood as a written source — actually two — that Luke takes over with little change (see Barrett, *Acts of the Apostles*, 322).

61. On the Stephen and apostle parallels, see S. Cunningham, *"Through Many Tribulations": Theology of Persecution in Luke-Acts* (JSNTSup 142; Sheffield: Sheffield Academic Press, 1997), 204–5.

62. The sentence runs thus: "...arose some of the ones from the synagogue [τινες τῶν ἐκ τῆς συναγωγῆς] of the Freedmen, and of the Cyrenians and of the Alexandrians and [some] of the ones [τῶν; presumably picking up on the τινες from the first line] from Cilicia and Asia." It is difficult to know exactly what is intended. Clearly, individuals from the synagogue of the Freedmen are in view. But "of the Cyrenians" and "of the Alexandrians" could either refer to specific individuals (modifying τινες) or to two additional synagogues (modifying συναγωγῆς). In either case, a switch seems to be made in the second part of the sentence to individuals (rather than synagogues) from Cilicia and Asia, referring to two regions in relative geographical proximity (likewise for "Cyrenians" and "Alexandrians"). Further complicating the reading is the possibility that Luke intends to identify the Cyrenian and Alexandrian elements as coming from the "synagogue of the Freedmen." It was these Cyrenians and Alexandrians who formed

Freedmen)."[63] The debate that is initiated by these individuals turns into a plot against Stephen, as the Jews from the synagogue are no match for Stephen's "wisdom and Spirit" (6:10, directly referencing 6:3; cf. 6:5).

The remaining narrative recounts their opposition to Stephen, the bringing of false charges against him, and his subsequent martyrdom. In 6:11 they "induce"[64] others by claiming that Stephen was speaking blasphemous words against Moses and God. In 6:12, paralleling 6:11, these same individuals "stir up" the people (including the elders and scribes; cf. 4:5). Paralleling the "arrest" of the apostles (4:3; 5:18), Stephen is taken before the council (cf. 5:21, 34) and false (ψευδής) witnesses bring charges against him. They claim that Stephen utters words continuously against "this holy place"[65] and the law, and that he has been overheard stating that Jesus will destroy "this place" and change the laws handed down by Moses. Acts 6:13 lays out the "false" charges (the charges are false by virtue of their being reported by "false witnesses"), which are then elaborated more precisely in 6:14. Thus, the accusation that Stephen attacks the temple and the law is substantiated by his claim that Jesus will destroy the former and alter the latter. This second set of charges (6:13–14) parallels, in a rough manner, the charges initially set out in 6:11. Acts 6:15 then presents the council waiting for Stephen's response to the charges.

This narrative provides a counterpoint to 6:1–7. In response to the word of the apostles, the community is pleased and responds positively (6:3–5). The seven are selected by the community and set before the apostles, who, in turn, lay hands upon them in order to commission them for ministry in the community (6:5–6). In contrast, the word of Stephen (6:10) is an affront to the Hellenistic Jewish community. They do not respond positively to the deeds and words of Stephen, but "stir up" the people and "seize" him, bringing him before the council. Moreover, as a mirror image of the

---

the predominant membership of the synagogue. This may be the more likely reading given that συναγωγῆς is here singular and not plural (cf. H. C. Kee, "Defining the First-Century C.E. Synagogue: Problems and Progress," in *Evolution of the Synagogue: Problems and Progress* [ed. H. C. Kee and L. H. Cohick; Harrisburg, Pa.: Trinity Press International, 1999], 17). If this construal is correct, then the complication arises when Luke adds the qualifier that identifies the name of the synagogue — "the one being called 'of the Libertines' " — as an aside (i.e., epexegetical phrase). The reading would then be as follows: " ... arose some of the ones from the synagogue both of the Cyrenians and Alexandrians — the one being called 'of the Libertines.' " If this reading is correct, it is also possible that Luke intended to identify the individuals coming from Asia and Cilicia as being part of this synagogue ("the synagogue of both the Cyrenians and the Alexandrians, as well as some [or, including some] from Cilicia and Asia").

63. Certain scholars have tried to identify this synagogue with the one mentioned in the Theodotus inscription (see R. Riesner, "Synagogues in Jerusalem," in *Book of Acts* [ed. Bauckham], 204–6; and Lüdemann, *Early Christianity,* 83). Although the latter provides an interesting historical reference, such a connection is impossible to substantiate.

64. The word here is ὑποβάλλω and it carries the notion of "prompting." The idea is that these individuals are the instigators of what is to follow (see *LSJ* v.).

65. This is a clear reference to the temple in Jerusalem. See Barrett, *Acts of the Apostles,* 327–38; Tannehill, *Narrative Unity,* 2:93; H. Köster, "τόπος," *TDNT* 8:196–205; and M. Hadas, *Aristeas to Philocrates (Letter of Aristeas)* (New York: KTAV, 1973), 122 n. 54.

apostles appointing the seven in 6:6, these opponents set up false witnesses as an extension of their own "ministry" of opposition.⁶⁶ Overall, then, we find in the Stephen narrative the classic form of the Jewish story of the righteous/wise man unjustly sentenced to death for crimes that he did not commit.⁶⁷

The artful play on the previous narrative seems deliberate, and the substantive analysis of Richard strongly suggests that Luke is fully responsible for the narrative as we now have it.⁶⁸ Yet modern scholarship has questioned numerous aspects of this account. The Baur/Hengel trajectory of interpretation has argued that Luke dilutes a more radical account of Stephen. For instance, while Hill observes that scholars often ignore Luke's explicit identification of the witnesses as "false," other interpreters suggest that Luke has turned originally accurate charges into false accusations (largely due to the more positive feelings Luke has toward the temple and law, as well as his desire to demonstrate that early Christianity is not a radical/threatening movement). As Lüdemann points out, "How remote Luke already is from the historical Stephen is evident from the fact that he presents the information about Stephen's criticism of the law as untrue."⁶⁹ But this is not the only problem that has arisen in interpretation. For example, numerous scholars maintain that there must be two different accounts combined in this narrative, especially in light of problematic historical and theoretical aspects. For instance, we appear to have two separate accounts of Stephen's trial: one in which there is an orderly trial (he stands before the council and delivers a speech) and one in which there is a rabid mob scene ending in his stoning. Some scholars argue that these two narrative strands can be held together (incited by words of Stephen, an orderly trial turns into a mob frenzy), but many other interpreters believe that Luke has combined two separate and irreconcilable accounts — a trial of Stephen and a mob murder⁷⁰ — with differing views as to which one is more historical and whether

---

66. Notice the use of ἔστησάν in 6:6 ("whom they set before the apostles") and again in 6:13 ("they established false witnesses").

67. On the formal elements, see G. W. E. Nickelsburg, *Resurrection, Immortality, and Eternal Life in Intertestamental Judaism* (HTS 26; Cambridge: Harvard University Press, 1972), esp. 170–71. Later developments include the actual death of the person unjustly accused and his exaltation to the heavenly realm at the time of death. Compare the elements of the Stephen narrative: wise/righteous individual (6:8); false accusers with charges related to legal violations (6:9–14); the trial scene (6:15); persecution and death of the righteous (7:54–55, 57–59a; 8:1); and the exaltation and vindication of the righteous individual (6:56, 59b–60).

68. Hill's position is even stronger: Luke composed the narrative, its conclusion, and the speech; we know very little about the historical Stephen (*Hellenists and Hebrews*, 101).

69. Lüdemann, *Early Christianity*, 85.

70. For the various breakdowns of the two narratives, see Barrett, *Acts of the Apostles*, 319–22, 380–81; Hill, *Hellenists and Hebrews*, 29–31; Haenchen, *Acts of the Apostles*, 273–74; and C. Burchard, *Der dreizehnte Zeuge: Traditions- und kompositions-geschichtliche Untersuchungen zu Lukas' Darstellung der Frühzeit des Paulus* (FRLANT 103; Göttingen: Vandenhoeck & Ruprecht, 1970), 28–31. Dibelius also observed that the trial scene in 6:12 seems to be followed by an orderly execution that is then intermixed with mob-like elements

both or only one belong to Lukan tradition. Moreover, there are historical questions regarding what kind of authority the Sanhedrin would have had vis-à-vis trying and convicting a Jewish-messianist missionary.[71] Therefore, many interpreters speculate that in fact there never was a trial, and that Luke has added that element simply to provide an occasion for the insertion of the speech (so Haenchen and Hengel).[72] Others maintain that the trial is original and Luke has attempted to make the Jews look bad by having them form a violent mob.[73] Still others, such as T. Seland, argue for the historical basis of the mob scene, placing it in the context of vigilante action against alleged blasphemers of Jewish law.[74] Barrett makes the more difficult argument that, although contradictory at points, these two different memories together bear witness to the historical event.[75]

From this larger issue related to the reality of the trial and/or mob scenes, scholars have debated which elements are traditional and which are Lukan. Thus, while most scholars argue that 6:8 is a Lukan addition and take 6:9 as an indication of a core historical fact about the existence of the synagogue and the opposing Hellenistic Jews,[76] others attempt to go beyond the narrative, arguing that Stephen comes from the synagogue out of which the opposition arises.[77] This latter scenario would then provide some form of motivation for the opposition, which is explicitly lacking in the narrative

---

(see "Paul in the Acts of the Apostles," in *Studies in the Acts of the Apostles*, 207–8). Regardless of where one makes the narrative break itself, the mention of Saul in 7:58b, 8:1, and 8:3 is frequently viewed as a Lukan insertion (Dibelius, "Paul in the Acts of the Apostles," 208; Hill, *Hellenists and Hebrews*, 29 n. 41, 35 n. 62; but not so Burchard, *Dreizehnte Zeuge*, 30). For a brief summary of the various positions on the trial narrative (with a view to its historical dating), see R. Riesner, *Paul's Early Period: Chronology, Mission Strategy, Theology* (trans. D. Stott; Grand Rapids: Eerdmans, 1998), 60–63. For a more detailed assessment, see H.-W. Neudorfer, *Der Stephanuskreis in der Forschungsgeschichte seit F. C. Baur* (Giessen, Germany: Brunnen, 1983), 183–218.

71. See Barrett, *Acts of the Apostles*, 381–82, who tries to reconcile the problems related to Jewish jurisdiction (cf. John 18:31). See also Riesner, *Paul's Early Period*, 60–61.

72. Dibelius made this argument as well ("Acts of the Apostles as an Historical Source," in *Studies in the Acts of the Apostles*, 106).

73. H. Conzelmann, *Acts of the Apostles* (ed. E. J. Epp and C. R. Matthews; trans. J. Limburg et al.; Hermeneia; Philadelphia: Fortress, 1987), 48.

74. T. Seland, *Establishment Violence in Philo and Luke: A Study of Non-Conformity to the Torah and Jewish Vigilante Reactions* (BibIntS 15; Leiden: Brill, 1995).

75. Barrett, *Acts of the Apostles*, 381. See also Fitzmyer, *Acts of the Apostles*, 355, who argues that Luke is using source material but has also "freely composed" the scene, thus accounting for the narrative difficulties.

76. As with the list of seven names in 6:5, this list of Hellenistic Jewish peoples connected with the synagogue seemingly provides real evidence of a historical conflict. Although less often noted than the list of seven names, the list in 6:9 is critical to theories of historical reconstruction of the Stephen narrative. Once again, scholars question the reason for Lukan invention of such a specific detail. Since no apparent motivation is evident, the simplest solution is to suggest a written source that contained the list. Theories that argue for Lukan composition of this narrative frequently falter on the details of 6:9 (see esp. Hill's treatment here, where he simply bypasses the issue altogether; *Hellenists and Hebrews*, 47–48).

77. See Lüdemann, *Early Christianity*, 84–85.

(cf. the similar problem with motivation regarding the lapse in distribution in 6:1). Moreover, the double list of accusations (6:11 and 6:13–14) is held to represent the charges stemming from two different sources,[78] now altered by Luke to downplay the real conflict. The "real conflict," of course, hinges on the previous identification of the Hellenists as anti-temple and anti-law (and the association of Stephen with this group).

Other elements of the narrative further complicate this picture. For instance, there seems to be some textual evidence that the account of Stephen was based on Old Testament parallels.[79] Moreover, the numerous points of correspondence between the account of Stephen here and the account of Jesus' trial and death in the Synoptics are striking.[80] Of these, most significant are the texts that occur in Mark (and the parallels in Matthew) but that Luke leaves out of his gospel account, yet apparently has allowed to shape his composition of the Stephen narrative (cf. the false witnesses of Mark 14:56–57; the saying regarding the destruction of the temple in Mark 14:58; and the charge of blasphemy in Mark 14:64).[81] As well, Stephen's vision in Acts 7:55–56, alongside its startling correspondence to the "Son of Man" saying in Mark 14:62 (and par.; based on Ps 110:1; Dan 7:13), similarly raises questions about the function of this material in the text and/or tradition.[82] Moreover, upon the death of Stephen, persecution breaks out against the *ekklesia* in Jerusalem and all but the apostles are forced out of Jerusalem (8:1b). The question naturally arises why the apostles are also not scattered. Either this feature is a Lukan narrative device to move the gospel out of Jerusalem, or it further reflects the tradition that the Hellenists — led here by Stephen — represented a wing of the larger newly formed community in Jerusalem that was more offensive and threatening than the apostles

---

78. These sources are often explicitly related to the two variants of the trial and mob narratives. See Barrett, *Acts of the Apostles*, 319.

79. This was also the case with 6:1–7. On this Old Testament connection, see T. L. Brodie, "The Accusing and Stoning of Naboth (1 Kgs 21:8–13) as One Component of the Stephen Text (Acts 6:9–14; 7:58a)," *CBQ* 45 (1983): 417–32.

80. On the parallels, see B. Witherington, *The Acts of the Apostles: A Socio-Rhetorical Commentary* (Grand Rapids: Eerdmans, 1998), 253; Hill, *Hellenists and Hebrews*, 59; G. W. Trompf, *The Idea of Historical Recurrence in Western Thought: From Antiquity to the Reformation* (Berkeley: University of California Press, 1979), 123; and esp. Kurz, "Narrative Models," 186–87.

81. It is difficult to know what to make of these parallels, especially since they become significant for interpretation precisely because we possess the account of Mark, which we cannot assume Luke's readers had before them (see the discussion in Cunningham, "*Through Many Tribulations*," 209–12, esp. his critique of Johnson [209 n. 78]). M. Sabbe, on the other hand, argues for the Lukan composition of the narrative portions of Acts 6:5–8:2 being based on the Synoptic parallels, creating a complementary passion story for Stephen ("The Son of Man Saying in Acts 7,56," in *Studia Neotestamentica: Collected Essays* [BETL 98; Leuven: Leuven University Press, 1991], 175).

82. On the details, see C. K. Barrett, "Stephen and the Son of Man," in *Apophoreta: Festschrift für Ernst Haenchen zu seinem 70. Geburtstag am 10. Dezember 1964* (ed. W. Eltester; BZNW 30; Berlin: Töpelmann, 1964), 32–38.

to both the religious authorities and Hellenistic Jews living in Jerusalem.[83] The latter, as noted above, further fuels the theories that the Hellenists had a more radical theological vision than the Hebrews.

Essentially, then, the interpretation of the Stephen narrative has involved two critical issues. The first is the role that Lukan models and exemplars play in the composition of the narrative. Here scholars are interested in both the motivations of some obvious Lukan elements (the Jesus-Stephen parallels, the use of Old Testament models, and the characterization of Stephen in light of both the account in 6:1–7 and the model of the apostles in Acts 1–5) and the overall function of these elements in the narrative. At the same time, many scholars are also concerned with the history behind the text. While most agree that Luke is responsible in some way for the whole account, there is also widespread agreement that an important moment in early Christian history exists beneath the narrative veneer. Some, such as Barrett, are content to leave the two alleged accounts as independent witnesses, attesting more to the enduring emotional effect of a circumstance than to the delineation of the exact nature of that incident. Others, however, are concerned to unravel the historical puzzle in the text. Perhaps it should not surprise us why this text is so important historically: The Stephen narrative relates the first death of a martyr in the Christian movement. This feature alone provides significant impetus for investigation. One need only look at Zeller's statement to underscore this point: "The death of Stephen is undoubtedly the clearest point in the history of Christianity before Paul. With this event we find ourselves on undeniable historical ground."[84] Once this powerful event is plugged into preexisting theories about the role of the Hellenist group in the formation of early Christianity, there is an inevitable snowball effect, as the larger supplied framework clarifies the obscure details of the narrative. Yet even those scholars who reject the Hellenist paradigm still find themselves focused on identifying specific realia from the narrative. Certainly, every indication from the account is that the story of Stephen was a turning point in the development of the new faith. The spread of the "good news" to the Gentiles has its origin in the subsequent events following the martyrdom (8:1b), as the fulfillment of the promise in 1:8 reaches its next stage. Critical questions, however, lie before us: Is the historicity of this event — as more or less described by Luke — conditioned and/or diminished by its place in Luke's historiographical work? What is one to make of the numerous parallels both inside the narrative and without? In what way does

---

83. See Haenchen, *Acts of the Apostles*, 103. S. G. Wilson, *The Gentiles and the Gentile Mission in Luke-Acts* (SNTSMS 23; Cambridge: Cambridge University Press, 1973), 142, identifies Acts 8:1 as the *crux interpretum* affecting the various attempts to reconstruct the "real" story behind Acts 6:1–8:3. Wilson aptly demonstrates through his own analysis (142–51) the way in which the theory builds and expands until the Hellenists have become theologically distinct from the Hebrews.

84. E. Zeller, *Die Apostelgeschichte nach ihrem Inhalt und Ursprung kritisch Untersucht* (Stuttgart: Mäcken, 1854), 146 (my translation).

this event serve Luke's historical purposes? What is the relationship, if any, between so-called Lukan redaction and the historical orientation of the narrative? Finally, is there a contradiction between Luke's intended purpose for this narrative and the inherent value of the material as historical referent? These are important matters, and the answers are bound up with both the preceding narrative in 6:1–7 and the speech that is situated in the middle of the Stephen account.

The Textual Character of Stephen's Defense (7:2–53)

Nature of the Speech

The shape and character of Stephen's speech is one of the vexing problems of New Testament study. The conjectures and theories related to the speech, its explicit and implicit content, and various other issues such as origin and use of tradition, are numerous and diverse. Perhaps the most important problem that almost all scholars point out is the perception that the speech does not fit well within its larger narrative context. P. Wendland's statement with respect to the placement of the speech and narrative is typical for its orientation:

> The speech of Stephen is hardly appropriate to the situation. The witnesses, who in 6:11ff accuse Stephen of blaspheming against Moses and God, the temple and law, are characterized as false. But Stephen does nothing to counter these charges. Rather, he appears to confirm them by rejecting the temple-building of Solomon in the second part of his speech, interrupted by lynch-justice.[85]

Modern reflection on this problem takes its cue from Dibelius's work. His view on this longest speech in Acts reflects a similar stance to Wendland's, albeit with even less commitment to the speech's connection to the charges.[86] Having stated that the accusation against the people that concludes the speech (7:51–53) has some grounding in the last portions of the oration (7:35–43 and 44–50) and admitting that there is some degree of connection to the charges regarding the "holy place" and "law" (6:13), Dibelius goes on to characterize the closing of the discourse as follows:

> With reference to the Temple, however, the speech is extremely reticent and seems to be very loosely connected with the charge — indeed, we ourselves shall probably be reading into it any significance that we may find. All this cannot alter the fact that the major part of the speech (7.2–34) shows no

---

85. P. Wendland, *Die hellenistisch-römische Kultur in ihren Beziehungen zu Judentum und Christentum* (HNT 1.2; Tübingen: Mohr Siebeck, 1912), 331 (author's translation). See also Fitzmyer, *Acts of the Apostles*, 365.

86. Dibelius, "Speeches in Acts," 167.

purpose whatever, but contains a unique, compressed reproduction of the story of the patriarchs and Moses.[87]

Dibelius here stresses several fundamentals that shaped the way in which subsequent scholarship would assess the speech. First, the speech does not address the charges laid out against Stephen in 6:13–14, even though the immediate formal trial scene that follows the accusations (6:15–7:1) raises the expectation for an *apologia* from the protagonist.[88] That Stephen's remarks largely seem unresponsive — or, as Dibelius phrased it, "irrelevant" — has been viewed as an indication that this speech was not originally given on the occasion of Stephen's martyrdom. This disjunction has led many scholars from Baur to Hengel to postulate that Luke has turned an original mob lynching into an orderly trial scene: "[The speech] has obviously been inserted by Luke into the story of the martyrdom of Stephen, which he already had at his disposal."[89] Second, Dibelius observes that there are some elements in the speech — especially the accusation of Israelite resistance to Moses and the apparent criticism of the temple ("whatever" the precise nature of the criticism may be, since Dibelius is reluctant to reconstruct it) — that do seem to connect back to the charges in 6:13–14, but then only loosely. Dibelius saw here some connection to the charges, particularly in the reversal of the accusations (it is the opponents, not Stephen, who have opposed Moses [law] and God [temple]). Yet again, while the opposition to Moses is clear, the nature of the temple polemic is not.

While Dibelius argued that the speech was inserted by Luke into a martyr scene, he was also interested in the character of the speech itself. Following his argument with respect to the speeches in general, Dibelius maintained that Luke has composed a speech that, at least in part, fits the occasion. While the speech does not answer the charges per se, it does represent the character of Stephen as a Hellenistic Jew responding to other Hellenistic Jews in the synagogue: "[I]n this case, a Christian is able to speak in the style characteristic of the synagogue, giving a recital of facts, and can in a

---

87. Ibid., 168.
88. Tyson, *Images of Judaism*, 113, correctly points out that elsewhere in Acts when characters confront charges (such as Peter in Acts 4 and 5, and Paul in the various speeches that are found at the end of Acts) there is always an engagement with the actual charges, albeit mixed with evangelistic motives. See also Hill, *Hellenists and Hebrews*, 53.
89. Dibelius, "Speeches in Acts," 168. Noteworthy is the twist M. Wilcox gives to this more common position as he concludes from the disjunction of narrative and speech in Acts 7 that Luke must have relied on older tradition for the speech and as a result was forced by the content of that tradition into creating a misfit between speech and context ("A Foreword to the Study of the Speeches in Acts," in *Christianity, Judaism, and Other Greco-Roman Cults: Studies for Morton Smith at Sixty* [ed. J. Neusner; SJLA 12; Leiden: Brill, 1975], 1:216–20. In Wilcox's view, if Luke had composed the speech *in toto*, then it would have fit better with the surrounding context. Wilcox then makes an unusual but interesting move, suggesting that it may actually be the narratives of Acts 1–7, rather than the speeches, that represent Lukan creations. In this hypothesis, Luke composed narrative settings, albeit somewhat awkwardly at times, in light of the traditional material reflected in the speeches.

unique way challenge the spirit of the synagogue."[90] This observation leads to Dibelius's assertion that the speech is Hellenistic Jewish in character. Perhaps this is simply a way of working backward to the earlier, and similar, conclusions of Baur: Stephen and the Hellenists are Hellenistic Jews and have used the patterns of Diaspora thought and practice to criticize conservative Palestinian Judaism. Here one can perceive the indebtedness to the *Religionsgeschichtliche Schule*'s understanding of Hellenistic Judaism as a more liberal, less law-bound religious expression of the Jewish faith. For Dibelius, then, Luke has taken an older text/tradition and reworked it into the recital now present in 7:2–34. The passages containing the polemic (7:35–50) were most likely Lukan compositions, tacked onto the larger recital of Israel's history. Dibelius understood the function of the speech to be Luke's means of preparing the way for the separation of the Christian church from Judaism and for its subsequent and consequent movement to the Gentiles.[91]

Scholarship on Acts 7 has more or less affirmed Dibelius's position: An original discourse reciting the history of Israel is worked over by Luke and then inserted into the context of a story relating Stephen's martyrdom. U. Wilckens, for instance, asserts that the "speech is doubtless not a work of Luke"[92] and that the speech "without a doubt belongs to the Hellenistic sphere of Diaspora Jewish-Christianity."[93] Evidently there is little doubt for many scholars both that Acts 7 is based on a preexisting (likely written) tradition and that its intellectual and cultural milieu is that of Diaspora Judaism.[94] Yet, while scholars generally assert that the speech existed prior to its placement in Acts, there is some debate over the precise historical and theological context and overall character of the former content. Hengel is surprisingly reserved on the matter:

> Stephen's speech can be used only with considerable qualifications as the main evidence for the "theology" of the Hellenists. Granted, it is not simply a literary composition from Luke's pen. He certainly made use of old and distinctive traditions in it. But it remains extremely dubious whether we should connect it directly with Stephen and the Hellenists. Even if we assume that Luke, as elsewhere, has carefully provided a theological characterization of his protagonist through his speech in the framework of what is known about him, we

---

90. Dibelius, "Speeches in Acts," 169.
91. Ibid., 169–70.
92. U. Wilckens, *Die Missionsreden der Apostelgeschichte: Form- und traditionsgeschichtliche Untersuchungen* (WMANT 5; 3d ed.; Neukirchen-Vluyn: Neukirchener Verlag, 1974), 208.
93. Ibid., 217. See also Seland, *Establishment Violence*, 225.
94. R. J. Dillon, *From Eye-Witnesses to Ministers of the Word: Tradition and Composition in Luke 24* (AnBib 82; Rome: Biblical Institute Press, 1978), delineates this view even further: "Stephen's speech, separable completely from the surrounding Acts narrative of his ill-fated ministry, contains a vision of sacred history and Old Testament exegesis that acquaint us with a distinctive Jewish-Christianity: hellenized but not Pauline, north-Palestinian, amply nourished by Samaritan tradition and expectation, therefore witness of the native culture and temperament of its recruited constituents" (256).

cannot infer more from the speech than what we also know from the accusations against Stephen. The speech simply accentuates these accusations. So we have to look above all at the accusation and the trial.[95]

Hengel is thus hesitant to trace much of the sermon back to Stephen and the Hellenists, although clearly he believes that the overall tenor of the discourse — with its Hellenistic Jewish emphases — represents Stephen's stance (although probably not as extremely as Stephen himself would have stated it). This viewpoint comes close to Baur's original position: Luke composed the speech, yet the basic thrust of it goes back to Stephen or, at the very least, to the/a Hellenist group.

Similar conclusions can be found in the most recent treatment of the speech by J. Jervell: The speech provides no reason for the attack on Stephen, it lacks any explicit kerygma with scriptural references (which is central to the other speeches that precede Acts 7), and it offers no challenge to repent (like the antecedent speeches). In short, it does not have the explicit missionary character of other important speeches in Acts. Moreover, Jervell, while acknowledging the presence of tradition behind the speech,[96] is reticent to designate precisely the nature of that tradition, although Jervell does follow Dibelius's suggestion that the polemical portions against the temple and the people come from Luke's hand. In contrast to Dibelius, however, Jervell is quick to maintain that Luke did not create *de novo* these polemical portions, but used tradition while "composing" the whole (he thereby distances Luke from the elements of condemnation and rejection). In the end, Jervell argues that the speech, despite all its Lukan features, is not an "ad hoc creation" but attests to a long history of theological reflection in the early church.[97]

This reluctance by certain scholars to trace explicit elements of the speech back to original traditions in fuller detail is countered by others who believe that more can be inferred on the matter. C. K. Barrett, for instance, is more willing to see here a sermon that can be attributed to the Hellenists: "Luke gives us, in outline, a 'Hellenist' sermon; the sort of sermon that might be preached in a 'Hellenist,' Diaspora, synagogue, and could easily be taken over and used when Hellenist Jews became Hellenist Jewish Christians."[98] Even here, however, Barrett believes the sermon bears witness to

---

95. Hengel, "Between Jesus and Paul," 19.
96. See his earlier statement on tradition in Acts as a whole (J. Jervell, "The Problem of Tradition in Acts," in *Luke and the People of God: A New Look at Luke-Acts* [Minneapolis: Augsburg, 1972], 19–39), where he affirms positively — over against Dibelius and Haenchen — the presence of important, detailed information about the nascent Christian movement.
97. J. Jervell, *Die Apostelgeschichte* (KEKNT 3; 17th ed; Göttingen: Vandenhoeck & Ruprecht, 1998), 248–50.
98. Barrett, *Acts of the Apostles*, 338. Barrett proffers that similar types of Hellenistic sermons underlie Acts 14 and 17. Further, Barrett maintains two points similar to Dibelius: (1) The speech could hardly have been given in the particular setting described by Luke (339); and (2) Luke inserted the "Hellenist" sermon into the existing martyrdom and trial scenes (340). See also Fitzmyer, *Acts of the Apostles*, 364–65 (who labels the speech "Antiochene");

the "sector of Judaism from which Stephen and his colleagues are said to have come" rather than to Stephen himself.[99] Once Luke's indebtedness to a source/tradition is admitted, a prior Jewish homily becomes the easiest explicable (and accessible) resource.[100] This connection of the review of Israelite history in the speech with a Hellenistic Jewish homily/sermon finds frequent support. Usually this view recognizes the Christian framing (prior to Luke or created by Luke) that places these Hellenistic Jewish themes and modes of argumentation in a specifically Hellenistic Jewish-Christian context.[101] Of course, various other backgrounds and trajectories of tradition

and Cullmann, "L'Opposition contre le Temple," 161–62. See further C. K. Barrett, "Old Testament History according to Stephen and Paul," in *Studien zum Text und Ethik des Neuen Testaments: Festschrift zum 80. Geburtstag von Heinrich Greeven* (ed. W. Schrage; BZNW 47; Berlin: de Gruyter, 1986), 57–69.

99. H.-W. Neudorfer takes a conservative line, arguing that there is no reason not to trace the threads of Acts 7 back to Stephen, who would have given a more expanded version of the discourse. Luke in turn has adapted the Stephen tradition to the present context ("The Speech of Stephen," in *Witness to the Gospel: The Theology of Acts* [ed. I. H. Marshall and D. Peterson; Grand Rapids: Eerdmans, 1998], 275–94). For a similar position, see M. Simon, *St. Stephen and the Hellenists in the Primitive Church* (London: Longmans, 1958), 39–40.

100. J. W. Bowker was one of the first to argue for the presence of Jewish homilies in the speeches of Acts; "Speeches in Acts: A Study in Proem and Yelamedenu Form," *NTS* 14 (1967/68): 96–111. On Acts 7 in particular, see G. Stemberger, "Die Stephanusrede (Apg 7) und die jüdische Tradition," in *Studien zum rabbinischen Judentum* (SBAB 10; Stuttgart: Katholisches Bibelwerk, 1990), 248–50; and H. Thyen, *Der Stil der jüdisch-hellenistischen Homilie* (FRLANT ns 47/65; Göttingen: Vandenhoeck & Ruprecht, 1955), 19–20. The connections of Acts 7 to Acts 13:16–41 (esp. vv. 16–22), where Paul offers a similar type of recitation of Israelite history, are important because of the similar associations of the latter with Hellenistic Jewish synagogue homilies. See L. M. Wills, "The Form of the Sermon in Hellenistic Judaism and Early Christianity," *HTR* 77 (1984): 278–80; and the summary of discussion in J. Pichler, *Paulusrezeption in der Apostelgeschichte: Untersuchungen zur Rede im pisidischen Antiochien* (ITS 50; Innsbruck: Tyrolia, 1997), 114–17. Against this view, see M. F.-J. Buss, *Die Missionspredigt des Apostels Paulus im pisidischen Antiochien* (FzB 38; Stuttgart: Katholisches Bibelwerk, 1980), 22–24. Although rarely discussed in the literature on Acts 7, the anonymous study (generally attributed to Walter Cassells), *Supernatural Religion: An Inquiry into the Reality of Divine Revelation* (London: Longmans, 1874; rev. ed., 1879; see the one-volume edition [London: Watts, 1902]), provides a strong argument for the Lukan creation of Acts 7 based on the parallels with the speeches of Paul (and Peter) elsewhere in Acts (659–72).

101. O. H. Steck, *Israel und das gewaltsame Geschick der Propheten: Untersuchungen zur Überlieferung des deuteronomistischen Geschichtsbild im Alten Testament, Spätjudentum, und Urchristentum* (WMANT 23; Neukirchen-Vluyn: Neukirchener Verlag, 1967), 265–69, argues that behind the speech of Stephen stands an early Hellenistic Jewish-Christian adaptation of the Deuteronomic prophetic and historical conceptions of Israelite history. Thus, there is both an indebtedness to the tradition of Deuteronomic preaching and also a uniquely Christian slant that grafts the history of Jesus and his disciples onto the fate of the Mosaic legacy. Wilckens helped disseminate this position in the third edition of his seminal work (*Missionsreden*), where he argued, similar to Steck, that Luke took over the Deuteronomic pattern from the Hellenistic sphere of the Christian movement. This adaptation then influenced the composition of the missionary speeches to the Jews overall in Acts (cf. M. L. Soards, *The Speeches in Acts: Their Content, Context, and Concerns* [Louisville: Westminster John Knox, 1994], 146–47). G. Schneider, "Stephanus, die Hellenisten und Samaria," in *Lukas, Theologe des Heilsgeschichte: Aufsätze zum lukanischen Doppelwerk* (BBB 59; Bonn: Hanstein, 1985), 246–47, combines a variety of these positions. For instance, he sees both Samaritan and Diaspora Hellenistic Jewish synagogue preaching in the text (especially the influence of a "heilsgeschichtliche Credo"). He argues that a speech can belong to Diaspora Judaism without necessarily

have been suggested for the speech, from an Aramaic source to a tradition preserved by the Christians in Antioch to a Samaritan background, the latter often being favored.[102] Yet the problems with the quest for the traditions in and behind Acts 7 are numerous and difficult. Aside from the fact that the speech in its present form is clearly a Lukan product, the various arguments used to support the diverse positions are relatively flimsy.[103]

From the issue of sources it is but a short step to another facet of the problem that Stephen's speech presents: The speech, in the only place it apparently does connect with the narrative context, does not support the narrator's presentation of Stephen. The alleged anti-temple portion of the oration seems to undermine Stephen's attempt at self-defense, supporting rather than negating the so-called false charges. If one grants a traditional basis for the speech, then the point at which themes in the speech coalesce with those in the narrative must represent that point which is nearest to tradition and furthest from Lukan compositional activity. While Dibelius

---

being viewed as originating from outside of Palestine (cf. G. Schneider, *Die Apostelgeschichte* [HTKNT 5; Freiburg: Herder, 1980], 1:101). See also the attempt by M. Klinghardt, *Gesetz und Volk Gottes: Das lukanische Verständnis des Gesetzes nach Herkunft, Funktion, und seinem Ort in der Geschichte des Urchristentums* (WUNT 2.32; Tübingen: Mohr Siebeck, 1988), 284–305, to ground the alleged temple critique both in the reception of a Hellenistic Jewish tradition as well as in the reform attempt by the circle of the Hellenists (cf. N. A. Dahl, "The Story of Abraham in Luke-Acts," in *Studies in Luke-Acts* [ed. L. E. Keck and J. L. Martyn; Nashville: Abingdon, 1966], 142).

102. See the review and brief assessment of the theories in Hill, *Hellenists and Hebrews*, 92–101.

103. For example, the Aramaic source theory overlooks the pervasive and evident influence of the Septuagint on the speech (see Dibelius, "Speeches in Acts," 169; cf. J. Dupont, "Apologetic Use of the Old Testament in the Speeches of Acts," in *The Salvation of the Gentiles: Studies in the Acts of the Apostles* [trans. J. Keating; New York: Paulist, 1979], 129–59, who argues for secondary "conscious literary activity" [151] in shaping Aramaic originals into the Greek speeches in Acts). The Antiochian theory, when the various arguments are peeled away, is essentially circular in nature: The material in Acts 6:1–8:3 deals with the Hellenists who founded the *ekklesia* in Antioch (a supposition) which therefore preserved the stories in Acts 6:1–8:3. The Samaritan source theory is a favorite among earlier scholars. It is based on a variety of Samaritan themes and traditions that allegedly correspond to the material in Acts 7. Most of what is referred to, however, is simply broad thematic parallels (e.g., rejection of the Jerusalem temple) that, if they do exist in the text at all, are present in other non-Samaritan groups as well (e.g., Qumran). Usually scholars invest a great deal of meaning in the "prophet like Moses" phrase in 7:37 and its associations with the Samaritan *Taheb*. A good example of this approach is found in R. Scroggs, "The Earliest Hellenistic Christianity," in *Religions in Antiquity: Essays in Memory of Erwin Ramsdell Goodenough* (ed. J. Neusner; SHR 14; Leiden: Brill, 1968), 176–206, who uses similarity of themes alongside explicit biblical citations, arguing that they are Samaritanisms and therefore from the Samaritan Pentateuch. One interesting case is the citation of Deut 18:15 in Acts 7:37 in the context of Exodus traditions, which Scroggs argues reflects the citation of Deut 18:18 after the Decalogue of Exod 20 in the SP (192). Scroggs suggests that since this combination (Exod 20 and Deut 18) is found nowhere else, there can be no coincidence regarding this same connection in Acts 7 (193). Yet, while Scroggs is correct that this combination is found in the SP, it is also found (exactly as in the SP) in two (pre-Samaritan?) texts from Qumran (4Q158 and 4Qtest; see E. Tov, *Textual Criticism of the Hebrew Bible* [Minneapolis: Fortress, 1992], 88, 99).

did not accept this conclusion,[104] the majority of scholars from Baur forward have tacitly ventured forward on this basis. Consequently, it is not by accident that the anti-temple ending of the speech has become the primary axis of investigation. The charges of 6:13–14 are interpreted in light of the tradition that allegedly exists in the speech. Hengel, who is more skeptical about tracing precise theological lines from the speech to the Hellenists, nonetheless is comfortable reading the speech in light of the alleged anti-temple and anti-law stance of the Hellenists (reconstructed from the charges in 6:13–14). In the final analysis, even if the speech is a Lukan composition, for Hengel and others it acknowledges the principles that were at work in the Hellenist movement or the sphere of its intellectual and cultural development.[105] This approach to the speech and charges is not as arbitrary as it might at first appear, as its impetus exists precisely because of the congruence of the charges and the anti-temple polemic in the speech. This association is what Hill correctly identified, seeking to undermine this construal by arguing that scholarship had misinterpreted the speech as being anti-temple and anti-law. The speech, according to Hill, does not support such a reading. In an interesting twist, Hill on the one hand undermines the Baur reading by reinterpreting the speech more positively, but on the other hand he also

---

104. Even Dibelius, however, was concerned to preserve some "traditional" elements in Acts 7. The subtle influence of form criticism in the discussion of Acts is evident here, although it has been expanded into the more general category of "tradition." Interestingly enough Dibelius, one of the individuals at the vanguard of form-critical inquiry into the New Testament, did not apply this methodology to Acts explicitly. He argued that Luke did not use the same methods in composition and did not have the same availability of sources as he did in the writing of his gospel. Haenchen took this approach even further, insisting that Luke's lack of sources led to a radical creative process in the writing of Acts. Yet in both Dibelius and Haenchen there is still an impulse toward retaining some "traditional" elements, and, as noted previously, for Haenchen at least the Acts 6:1–8:3 narrative and speech is one of those critical junctures where "tradition" must exist. Even those scholars who insist that Luke did not utilize an actual text cannot fathom how Acts 7 could be produced without a preexisting "preaching pattern" and/or "shaped/formed tradition" (see Schneider, *Apostelgeschichte*, 1:101–2). In conjunction, see also Lüdemann, *Early Christianity*, 86–89 (who is only interested in the redaction); J. Zmijewski, "Die Stephanusrede (Apg 7,2–53) — Literarisches und Theologisches," in *Das Neue Testament — Quelle christlicher Theologie und Glaubenspraxis* (Stuttgart: Katholisches Bibelwerk, 1986), 85–128; and K. Kliesch, *Das heilsgeschichtliche Credo in den Reden der Apostelgeschichte* (BBB 44; Bonn: Hanstein, 1975), 5–38, 155–59. Kliesch's work is foundational for research into the tradition behind the speeches in Acts 7 and 13, focusing on a preexistent formal tradition regarding the acts of God in the history of Israel (a credo) with reference to the life and death of Jesus. For Kliesch, the tradition Luke received was probably already formed and developed in the liturgy and worship of the early Christian movement (114).

105. Although rarely stated, this is also one of the reasons why scholars regard the Lukan description of the charges in 6:13–14 as "false" (an authorial "cover-up"). The speech — whether taken by Luke from a Hellenistic source or written by Luke — evidences Luke's knowledge of the "real" orientation of the Hellenistic message: It was anti-temple and anti-law (thus affirming the charges in 6:13–14 as fundamentally true). The fact that the ancient practice of composing speeches was based on articulating the "voice" of the speaker with content appropriate to the situation of the speech led Dibelius ("Speeches in Acts," 139–40) to suggest that Luke knew or at least thought that the characterization of Stephen by the antagonists was true even though he stated otherwise in the narrative.

subtly reinforces it. Luke rightly describes the charges as "false" and they, in this way, cohere with the true character of the speech as interpreted by Hill. Hill is beginning from the same premise, that the relationship between the charges and the speech is the axis of interpretation. It is, however, precisely this point that needs challenging. The relationship between speech and context is at once more complex and more nuanced than many scholars have recognized in the past.

In line with this approach to Acts 7, the apparent shift in more recent discussion of the speech is noteworthy. The primary subject of renewed scrutiny is whether or not the speech addresses the charges (i.e., relates to its context). As a result of the introduction of rhetorical analyses, several scholars have argued for viewing Acts 7 as a counteraccusation to the charges offered in the narrative of 6:13–14. Where past scholarship has failed to see a link between the charges and the speech, more recent scholarship is asserting that the speech does in fact respond directly to the charges, just not in the way one might expect.[106] By mapping out the rhetorical units of the speech, one can presumably better appreciate the role of the oration in its present context.[107] This observation certainly brings one closer to understanding how the speech functioned for the writer of Acts, although it still does not go far enough in appreciating the interrelationship between the narrative context and the speech itself.[108] In these approaches the relationship is structured formally between accusation and counteraccusation, and the speech is understood to reply to the charges leveled against Stephen in the narrative context as well as developing critical themes therein. This emphasis has brought about attempts to read the speech and narrative as a unified literary composition, which has been enhanced by studies that focus on the Lukan theme of the pattern and fate of the "prophet like Moses."[109] Thus,

---

106. See G. A. Kennedy, *New Testament Interpretation through Rhetorical Criticism* (Chapel Hill: University of North Carolina Press, 1984), 121–22, who argues that the speech is an *antengklema* (counteraccusation) that dwells on the stasis of jurisdiction (the tribunal's lack of right to place Stephen on trial). See also Soards, *Speeches in Acts,* 58; H. A. Brehm, "Vindicating the Rejected One: Stephen's Speech as a Critique of the Jewish Leaders," in *Early Christian Interpretation of the Scriptures of Israel: Investigations and Proposals* (ed. C. A. Evans and J. A. Sanders; JSNTSup 148; SSEJC 5; Sheffield: Sheffield Academic Press, 1997), 266–99; and R. G. Hall, *Revealed Histories: Techniques for Ancient Jewish and Christian Historiography* (JSPSup 6; Sheffield: Sheffield Academic Press, 1991), 195.

107. See the attempt by J. Dupont, "La structure oratoire du discours d'Étienne (Actes 7)," *Biblica* 66 (1985): 153–67. The problem with this approach, however, is that it is sometimes used as a way to make sense of the speech as given on the occasion cited in the text. If it is understandable rhetorically then there is a historical possibility/probability that it in fact was spoken by Stephen before the Sanhedrin, as Luke in fact suggests (so Witherington, *Acts of the Apostles,* 260).

108. This point lies behind my earlier treatment: T. Penner, "Narrative as Persuasion: Epideictic Rhetoric and Scribal Amplification in the Stephen Episode in Acts," *SBLSP* 35 (1996): 352–67.

109. See L. O'Reilly, *Word and Sign in the Acts of the Apostles: A Study in Lucan Theology* (AnG 243; Rome: Editrice Pontificia Università Gregoriana, 1987), 173–77.

a key element of the speech (7:37) reflects a larger theological theme and literary device apparent throughout the two-volume work. Consequently, the speech, when analyzed from the perspective of the whole book, takes on greater significance.[110]

Richard's groundbreaking study on Acts 6:1–8:4 has reinforced this particular direction of inquiry. His work on the sermon is especially important for its detailed examination of the style and method of Lukan composition. In particular, Richard compared Stephen's speech to the text of the Septuagint, demonstrating that, while Luke was dependent on the Greek Bible as a form of tradition, Acts 7 fundamentally represents an "independent composition."[111] Richard concludes that "the stylistic data listed in the corpus owe in large measure to the activity of the author. In spite of considerable and minute borrowing from the Old Testament, he has imposed his peculiar style upon the material."[112] Despite constant (and seemingly out of place) references to the "tradition" behind the Lukan redaction, it is clear that in the speech the primary "tradition" for Richard is Luke's familiarity with the Greek translation of the Hebrew Scriptures. Indeed, Richard admits that the "discourse is a creation of the author of Acts."[113] On the basis of establishing Acts 7 as a Lukan composition, Richard is able to demonstrate the same thematic and linguistic authorial hand in the surrounding narratives. Richard's analysis represents a building block for subsequent study on Acts 7, as he has demonstrated one clear point: The same hand that wrote 6:1–15 also composed the speech in Acts 7 (which is the same hand behind the rest of Acts). In other words, the separation of Lukan redaction from

---

110. This was one of Dibelius's main points; the speech interprets the larger Lukan narrative, not just the immediate account of Stephen's trial. Scholars have pursued this angle in various ways. Although not completely convincing, D. Wiens, *Stephen's Sermon and the Structure of Luke-Acts* (N. Richmond Hills, Tex.: BIBAL, 1995), argues that the sermon of Stephen is the critical link to understanding the entire theology and structure of Luke-Acts. Other scholars have suggested similar ideas (albeit with less complexity) regarding the role of this speech; see, e.g., Johnson, *Acts of the Apostles*, 137: "Stephen's speech...provides Luke's most explicit interpretation of his entire narrative, and shows us the logic of its two-fold structure." Also see D. P. Moessner, *Lord of the Banquet: The Literary and Theological Significance of the Lukan Travel Narrative* (Minneapolis: Fortress, 1989), esp. 298–307 (although his attempt to historicize the typology in terms of geographical areas related to the Stephen-Philip group is less convincing [318–19]).

111. Richard, *Acts 6:1–8:4*, 355.

112. Ibid., 214. See also J. Jeska, *Die Geschichte Israels in der Sicht des Lukas: Apg 7,2b–53 und 13,17–25 im Kontext antik-jüdischer Summarien der Geschichte Israels* (FRLANT 195; Göttingen: Vandenhoeck & Ruprecht, 2001), 119–42, who argues that any anomalies in the speech come about through the peculiarities of the "summaries of Israelite history" subgenre, which uses the literary techniques of "actualization," "solidarity," and "distancing" in its characterization of speaker and hearers (142–53).

113. Richard, *Acts 6:1–8:4*, 357. It is clear that Richard conceives of "tradition" in terms of discrete material ranging from the Septuagint to the Jesus story (see ch. 1, n. 66, in this volume). In other words, this conception amounts to a given: Luke is informed by Jewish (and Christian) traditions that shape his storytelling and his speech writing. Richard is clearly not attesting to the existence of prior written/oral traditions that Luke uses (such as an Antiochian source or a Jewish Hellenistic homily).

tradition — if tradition there be — is impossible. One may still presuppose the existence of the latter, but it is not possible to separate out a pre-Lukan *Grundschrift* that Luke uses for the composition of the speech.

When combined with the studies on the rhetorical, literary, and theological function of Acts 7 with respect to the surrounding narrative and Luke-Acts as a whole, Richard's study buttresses the point made earlier: Critical inquiry must move in a different direction than the Baur trajectory. Rather than focusing on an unidentifiable tradition in the discourse, one needs to explore more fully the relationship of the speech to its context. And this exploration must push beyond an attempt to make the speech fit a particular preconception of the trial scene, or vice versa. A more nuanced analysis is demanded, one that relates the function of the speech to the role it plays in the Hellenist and Stephen narratives. In this way, the so-called disjunction between speech and narrative and the suggested contradiction contained in the argument of the speech are not viewed as isolated phenomena pointing toward residual elements of the historical Hellenists or their environs, but as keys to unlocking the Lukan historiographical interest in this material.

Structure of the Speech

The structure of the speech is fairly evident even if the argument of the speech is less so. As many scholars have recognized, the speech revolves around the critical opening section detailing the history of Abraham, in particular the promise to Abraham in 7:6–7.[114] The promise of deliverance and worship is crucial to the flow of the narrative argument regarding the history of Israel that unfolds in the speech. Thus, beginning with Abraham (7:2–8), the narrative moves to Joseph (7:9–16), on to the Moses story (7:17–43), and finally to a brief Joshua-David-Solomon unit based on tabernacle and temple associations (7:44–50). The speech concludes with an invective against the leaders of the Jerusalem establishment and the opponents listening to Stephen's speech (7:51–53).[115] The Abraham and Joseph sections are the shorter portions of the historical review and are self-contained. The Abraham unit recounts the promise (and the context for it), while the Joseph unit accounts for the presence of Israel in Egypt (establishing the setting for the fulfillment of the promise to Abraham).

The Moses unit is by far the most important, and it is therefore not incidentally also the longest portion of the speech. It can be subdivided into

---

114. See Dahl, "Story of Abraham," 143–47; E. J. Via, "An Interpretation of Acts 7:35–37 from the Perspective of Major Themes in Luke-Acts," *SBLSP* 14.2 (1978): 211; Hall, *Revealed Histories*, 197; Penner, "Narrative as Persuasion," 361–62; and Tannehill, *Narrative Unity*, 2:88–90.

115. See the more detailed summaries/outlines of the speech in Soards, *Speeches in Acts*, 59; and Hall, *Revealed Histories*, 195–97.

four main sections: Moses' early years (7:17–22); his first attempt to deliver the Israelites from captivity (7:23–29); the second, successful attempt (7:30–36); and the rejection of the prophet Moses by the people and their subsequent punishment (7:37–43). It is only in the last of these subunits that the speech turns from its supposed "impartial" retelling of the events to a more harsh, denigrating tone. It is also in this latter unit that prophetic citations are first inserted in order to interpret the unfolding narrative (7:42–43; Amos 5:25–27). The Moses section revolves around the theme of deliverance/liberation and rejection, which led Steck to identify this material with the Deuteronomic pattern of the rejection of the prophet sent by God.[116] The dual attempt at deliverance is also an important feature, particularly since the "speaker" explicitly notes the first rejection in 7:35.[117] Moreover, the pattern is reentrenched in the narrative by the comment in 7:25 that Moses thought the people would understand that God was working through him to free the people.[118] From this structure of liberation and rejection the major argumentative axis of the speech arises, and the prophetic injunctions in 7:42–43 and 7:49–50 naturally flow from it, as does the conclusion to the speech proper (7:51–53). Although gaining momentum primarily from 7:37 onward, the crescendo effect is patent: The speech moves quickly to the main assertion that the audience represents, in their own actions toward Stephen, the ongoing opposition of the people to the prophets (be they Moses, Jesus, or Stephen).

Already in the earliest part of the speech — the promise to Abraham in 7:6 — the accent on deliverance is evident: God will deliver his people out of slavery. Thus, the major portion of the Moses section is anticipated in the first part of the promise. The second part of the promise — that the people will come out and worship God "in this place" — connects the theme of worship to the deliverance narrative, an element prevalent not only in the Moses story (7:33, 39–43), but also in the closing unit (7:44–50). The particular nature of rejection in the narrative takes on the form of worshiping other deities (a violation of the first command of the Decalogue). The tabernacle-temple discussion in the final section (7:44–50) revolves as well around the theme of the appropriate context for worship of God and, although the

---

116. Steck, *Israel und das gewaltsame Geschick*, 263–69. See also Tannehill, *Narrative Unity*, 2:87–88, 94–95.

117. On the dual liberation-rejection pattern, see Johnson, *Acts of the Apostles*, 136–37, who ties it in to the similar pattern evidenced in Jesus and the disciples (Jesus is rejected the first time and comes in the Spirit among his successors the second time).

118. This explicit reflection on Moses' attack on the Egyptian is missing in the Old Testament account (Exod 2:11–15). See J. M. G. Barclay, "Manipulating Moses: Exodus 2.10–15 in Egyptian Judaism and the New Testament," in *Text as Pretext: Essays in Honour of Robert Davidson* (ed. R. P. Carroll; JSOTSup 138; Sheffield: Sheffield Academic Press, 1992), 40–43, where he connects the changes in emphasis to Luke's christological program. See also Brehm, "Vindicating the Rejected One," 284–85.

argument is not entirely clear, the association with 7:39–43 seems evident from the context.[119]

In broad terms, then, there is a connection between the structure of the speech and its narrative context. The central section of 7:6–7 not only provides the axis for the logic of the speech, it also implicitly connects the themes of the speech to the preceding narrative context through the phrase "in this place." Through the combining of Exod 3:12 with Gen 15:14, the speech links the promise to Abraham with the promise to Moses. Moreover, the link to the charges in 6:13–14 is hardly coincidental: Stephen speaks against "this holy place" and threatens "this place" (the temple). The theme of "place" in relation to worship also occurs in 7:33 (the place that is holy = wilderness of Mount Sinai/place of the theophany) and in the citation from Isa 66:1 in Acts 7:49 (direct reference to the temple).[120] Thus, the reference in 7:6–7 undoubtedly is recalling the charges in 6:13–14, and quite possibly foreshadowing the later references (7:33, 49) as well.[121] An explicit connection between the speech and its narrative context is thus provided, demonstrating that whatever else may be going on in the text the issue of "temple"/"this place" supplies the focus for interpreting the relationship of speech to context. Similarly, the narrative that immediately follows (7:54–8:3) is also linked to the speech. In particular, the attack on Stephen is narrative confirmation of his invective in 7:51–53. The speech has predicated a pattern of behavior that is now exhibited by the audience. This manifestation confirms both the relevancy of Stephen's argument and its "persuasive" nature.

Not only is the speech a straightforward and well-structured piece (even if the precise nature of the argument is open to debate), the relationship of the speech to its narrative context is also apparent. That is not to say that there is necessarily a logical connection. Many scholars affirm that the speech does not respond to the charges and could not possibly, even if it

---

119. See Tannehill, *Narrative Unity,* 2:89–90.

120. It is more difficult to ascertain the referent of "this place" in 7:7, and likely the ambiguity is deliberate. For instance, many scholars argue that since "this place" in 6:14 refers to the temple, the temple must also be in view in 7:7. Tannehill, *Narrative Unity,* 2:92–93, perceives the implicit connection of "this place" in 7:7 to the "land" of 7:4, but argues that 6:13–14 determines the meaning in 7:7; thus, on the basis of the "continuity with the accusation...the promise in 7:7 anticipates a specific place of worship within the land, and that place will be the temple." Similarly, Barrett, *Acts of the Apostles,* 345; and K. Haacker, "Stephanus in der Geschichte des Urchristentums," *ANRW* 2.26.2 (1995): 1537. Yet, while it is quite clear that an association with 6:13–14 is intended, the coalescing of the promises to Abraham and Moses creates problems. In particular, the "place" of Abraham is land (7:4), while the "place" of Moses is the temple (or Mount Sinai, although in the Deuteronomic tradition these are associated). The argument that follows, especially regarding the tabernacle and temple, only makes sense if there is a dual association of land and temple in 7:7. In this reading, the latter is undermined by the primacy of the former (so the tabernacle in the land [7:45] represents the completion of the promise in 7:7). Thus, by bringing the two meanings of *topos* together, the speech moves between these two in order to make a specific argument about how God works/is working.

121. See Haacker, "Stephanus in der Geschichte," 1537–38.

were not irrelevant to the situation, be delivered in the manner and occasion Luke suggests. The logical connection is therefore still a matter for inquiry. However, the structural connection — the interweaving of the speech with the larger narrative framework — is evident and undoubtedly intentional. This brief analysis of the structure, then, confirms the conclusions drawn above: The speech in conjunction with the narrative points the critic toward the investigation of Lukan intention.

Argument of the Speech

Another challenge in the analysis of the speech has been the argument itself. Scholars have suggested that the anti-temple polemic apparent in the closing verses of the oration seems to undermine the portrayal of Stephen in the narrative (i.e., the charges against him are "false"), which, in turn, has fueled both a specific interpretation of the speech and the quest for the historical/traditional background of the "radical" elements. Thus, alongside the reappraisal of the interrelationship of the speech and narrative, a reassessment of the argument of the speech itself is necessary. In this final section I will touch on some of the main features, returning to them later in the last chapter.

Despite Dibelius's viewing the more negative elements as Lukan insertions into a preexisting unit, the brief structural outline given above indicates that the grounding of the speech in the promise to Abraham in 7:6–7 has implications for understanding the relationship of the whole. Alongside the critical function of 7:6–7 for structuring the argument, the unit also contains the deviations, contours, and accents that arise in the course of the retelling of Israel's salvation story. As with the combination of scriptural citations in 7:7, these particular features of the rehearsal provide clues to the intentions and motivations for the speech.

The pattern of deliverance and rejection is the theme that ties the various subunits of the oration together. Moreover, the relationship of deliverance and worship is a critical secondary element. Further, while the speech can only be understood in light of the larger literary and theological patterns at work in Luke-Acts, even a straightforward and simple reading of the text evinces the crescendoing effect of the argument as the various key elements unfold in the speech. The "response" of Stephen begins with what seems to be a fairly objective treatment of the Israelite story, but as it gains momentum it comes down harshly on the people, focusing on their rejection of Moses and, ultimately, their rejection of God. This much scholars agree on, as the ending of the speech (7:51–53) leaves little doubt of the intention here. The important concern, however, has been to identify those elements of the narrative that are intended to support the claim that the people are "stiff-necked," which represents more of a point of disagreement among scholars.

Acts 7:37–43 is fairly clear in its perspective on the people: They rejected Moses by building the golden calf; subsequently they were punished by exile. The speech also construes this action as a rejection — the second one (the first being their initial rejection of Moses as their deliverer in 6:27 and interpreted as such in 6:35) — of the "prophet" (hence the insertion of Deut 18:15 in 7:37). Aside from some of the implicit christological associations at work in this portion of the text, the argument is generally accessible. In 7:44–50, however, the case is different. Here there exists significant debate among critics over the precise meaning and function of the language. For instance, in a peculiar twist, the tabernacle quite unexpectedly enters the scene in 7:44–45. Alongside this sudden appearance, there is the problem in 7:46–47 with respect to David and Solomon. What distinction if any is being made between these two kings? This is a central problem in the speech, and, in many respects, understanding the speech as a whole rests in working out the details here at the end. Just when one expects a resounding indictment of the people, there arises this convoluted unit that one must assume is advancing the argument even if in ambiguous ways. The citation from Isa 66:1–2 in 7:49–50 suggests a critique of the temple, and the parallel prophetic citations in 7:42–43 would imply that the quotations are underscoring the writer's developing argument. Moreover, the general thrust of 7:44–50 seems to force the interpretation that the building of the temple was in some sense the last straw for this hard-hearted people. Indeed, the unmistakable association of the language in 7:41 (making idols "with their hands") with 7:48 (the temple made "with human hands") undermines the numerous attempts by scholars to avoid the serious (and seemingly un-Lukan) association of the temple with idolatry.[122] The difficulty lies precisely in the knowledge that this conclusion contradicts both the larger Old Testament story and the Deuteronomic theology undergirding the speech. But the former position, as seemingly difficult as it is, appears to be the best way to make sense of the last unit of the speech: The tabernacle in the land represents the fulfillment of the promise made to Abraham in 7:7 (worship in "this place" is in the land, not the temple). The building of the physical

---

122. See D. C. Harlow, *The Greek Apocalypse of Baruch (3 Baruch) in Hellenistic Judaism and Early Christianity* (SVTP 12; Leiden: Brill, 1996), 100–101; C. R. Koester, *The Dwelling of God: The Tabernacle in the Old Testament, Intertestamental Jewish Literature, and the New Testament* (CBQMS 22; Washington: Catholic Biblical Association, 1989), 80–83; and C. W. Stenschke, *Luke's Portrait of Gentiles prior to Their Coming to Faith* (WUNT 2.108; Tübingen: Mohr Siebeck, 1999), 64. It is unlikely that Luke would miss the unmistakable resonance of this language with the Septuagint vocabulary related to idolatry (see W. Beuken, "Does Trito-Isaiah Reject the Temple? An Intertextual Inquiry into Isa. 66.1–6," in *Intertextuality in Biblical Writings: Essays in Honour of Bas van Iersel* [ed. S. Draisma; Kampen, The Netherlands: Kok, 1989], 53; and J. J. Scott, "Stephen's Speech: A Possible Model for Luke's Historical Method?" *JETS* 17 [1974]: 94). Moreover, it is a theme found elsewhere, albeit in a more nuanced form, in Acts 17:24–25.

temple, however, appears to have been a further, and presumably negative, development from the perspective of the speech.[123]

There are underlying features of this section that need to be explored further in order to appreciate more fully the internal logic and coherence of the final argument regarding the tabernacle and temple. For instance, the connections between the speeches in Acts 7 and 15 are important, especially for the Lukan associations with the tabernacle.[124] As well, there is a play on the terms "house" and "place" in 7:46 (similar to 2 Sam 7), with underlying messianic overtones. Overall, however, scholarship is focused on the more obvious problem: Does this unit represent an anti-temple stance and, if so, whose position is it (Luke's or Stephen's)? Tannehill argues that Stephen stands against any restriction of God to the temple, an argument made, from Luke's perspective (and shared by his readers), with the knowledge that the temple has in fact been destroyed.[125] Therein lies a form of retrospective prophetic judgment, but one that mutes a more harsh statement against the temple. J. T. Sanders, conversely, applies a more thoroughgoing anti-temple stance to Luke himself: "[A]ll Christianity à la Luke oppose[s] the Temple and Mosaic custom."[126] In this view, the argument of the passage suggests that the building of the temple was the final act of disobedience toward God.[127] Others see a tension between Luke's positive portrayal of the temple elsewhere in Luke-Acts and the harsh sentiments expressed in Acts 7. Thus, J. B. Chance seeks to narrow the attack to the issue of the temple as God's resting place, a limitation of God's mobility that is counterbalanced by reference to the tabernacle.[128] Brehm, by contrast, argues that the real problem

---

123. Hall, *Revealed Histories*, 195.

124. These connections have been established by E. Richard, "The Divine Purpose: The Jews and the Gentile Mission (Acts 15)," in *Luke-Acts: New Perspectives from the Society of Biblical Literature* (ed. C. H. Talbert; New York: Crossroad, 1984), 195.

125. Tannehill, *Narrative Unity*, 2:93–95. See also N. Taylor, "Luke-Acts and the Temple," in *The Unity of Luke-Acts* (ed. J. Verheyden; BETL 142; Leuven: Leuven University Press, 1999), 709–21.

126. J. T. Sanders, *The Jews in Luke-Acts* (Philadelphia: Fortress, 1987), 248.

127. See Tyson, *Images of Judaism*, 114–15; Dahl, "Story of Abraham," 144; and H. Hübner, *Biblische Theologie des Neuen Testaments* (Göttingen: Vandenhoeck & Ruprecht, 1995), 3:150. C. K. Barrett, "Attitudes to the Temple in the Acts of the Apostles," in *Templum Amicitiae: Essays on the Second Temple Presented to Ernst Bammel* (ed. W. Horbury; JSNTSup 48; Sheffield: Sheffield Academic Press, 1991), 352, 363, 365–66, argues that Luke has used Hellenistic Jewish-Christian sources that reflect a real attack on the temple as the dwelling place of God. See also E. Trocmé, "'C'est le ciel qui est mon trône': La polémique contre le Temple et la théologie des Hellénistes," in *Le Trône de Dieu* (ed. M. Philonenko; WUNT 69; Tübingen: Mohr Siebeck, 1993), 195–203; Koester, *Dwelling of God*, 79–85, 98–99; and Cullmann, "L'Opposition contre le Temple," 161–62.

128. J. B. Chance, *Jerusalem, the Temple, and the New Age in Luke-Acts* (Macon, Ga.: Mercer University Press, 1988), 40–41. See also M. Bachmann, "Die Stephanusepisode (Apg 6,1–8,3): Ihre Bedeutung für die lukanische Sicht des jerusalemischen Tempels und des Judentums," in *Unity of Luke-Acts* (ed. Verheyden), 545–62, who perceives here a response to the misunderstanding of the proper place and function of the temple according to Jewish tradition. Similarly T. L. Donaldson, "Moses Typology and the Sectarian Nature of Early Christian Anti-Judaism: A Study in Acts 7," in *New Testament Backgrounds: A Sheffield Reader*

in this passage is not that the building of the temple is yet another act of disobedience, but that reference to the building represents rather a prophetic critique of an impure cultus. This emphasis takes the focus off the temple and places it on the Jewish people, or at least their religious representatives, who have made the temple an unholy sanctuary.[129] E. Larsson, nuancing the first option (Chance), views the temple section as Luke's way of expressing that the gospel has gone out to the Gentiles, in this manner avoiding any significant negative associations with the temple.[130]

In general, then, the tabernacle-temple section in the speech has become a critical juncture of disagreement among scholars, and much of the interpretation of the speech (and the Hellenists themselves) rests on the meaning therein. Unlike Hill, however, who downplays the negative aspects of the speech, I would claim that the way forward is to reassess the rhetorical strategy of the speech in terms of the Lukan historiographical purpose of the Hellenist narrative as a whole. In the past, it has been assumed that the speech reflects Luke's theology (Dibelius), that it denotes Luke's thoughts about what Stephen would have said (Cadbury), or that it actually reflects something about the theology of the real Stephen or the Hellenists more generally (Hengel). In each one of these possible scenarios there is an implied understanding of what it is that Luke is trying to accomplish with the

---

(ed. C. A. Evans and S. E. Porter; BS 43; Sheffield: Sheffield Academic Press, 1997), 230–52, who views here the use of "sectarian polemic" (like that evidenced at Qumran or among the Samaritans) against a Jerusalem-centered religion. H. Ganser-Kerperin, *Das Zeugnis des Tempels: Studien zur Bedeutung des Tempelsmotivs im lukanischen Doppelwerk* (NTAbh ns 36; Münster: Aschendorff, 2000), 240–62, tends to see in Acts 7 a relativization of the temple, especially in light of its destruction in 70 C.E., an event with which Luke and his readers would have been familiar.

129. Brehm, "Vindicating the Rejected One," 288–96. See also P. W. L. Walker, *Jesus and the Holy City: New Testament Perspectives on Jerusalem* (Grand Rapids: Eerdmans, 1996), 66–67, who suggests that, according to Stephen, the temple has become an objective idol in God's view because of the leadership's subjective idolatry (i.e., their attempt to preserve the temple against any form of criticism, leading to their rejection of Jesus). Similarly F. D. Weinert, "Luke, Stephen, and the Temple in Luke-Acts," *BTB* 17 (1987): 89–90; R. L. Brawley, "Abrahamic Covenant Traditions and the Characterization of God in Luke-Acts," in *Unity of Luke-Acts* (ed. Verheyden), 128; and W. Kraus, *Zwischen Jerusalem und Antiochia: Die "Hellenisten," Paulus, und die Aufnahme der Heiden in das endzeitliche Gottesvolk* (SBS 179; Stuttgart: Katholisches Bibelwerk, 1999), 44–55. M. Grossman observes that the framing narrative of the speech makes reference to "priests" entering the early Jerusalem community (6:7), and, coupled with the speech itself being a reply to the "high priest" (7:1–2; cf. the reference to Aaron in 7:40), she observes that the speech functions to undermine the "very things that make priests unique — service in the Temple, sacrificial offerings — stressing instead the value of the Holy Spirit, which is available to all people, not only the priests" ("Priesthood as Authority: Interpretive Competition in First-Century Judaism and Christianity," in *The Dead Sea Scrolls as Background to Postbiblical Judaism and Early Christianity: Papers from an International Conference at St. Andrews in 2001* [ed. J. R. Davila; STDJ 46; Leiden: Brill, 2003], 123).

130. E. Larsson, "Temple-Criticism and the Jewish Heritage: Some Reflexions on Acts 6–7," *NTS* 39 (1993): 379–95. See also G. E. Sterling, " 'Opening the Scriptures': The Legitimation of the Jewish Diaspora and the Early Christian Mission," in *Jesus and the Heritage of Israel: Luke's Narrative Claim upon Israel's Legacy* (ed. D. P. Moessner; Harrisburg, Pa.: Trinity Press International, 1999), 216–17.

speech. More to the point, in each one of these construals there is an assumption about the historiographical purpose of the material. In Dibelius's work this element is explicit, as he begins with the historical literature of antiquity before assessing Acts. But not all scholars have adequately reflected on the relationship of Acts to ancient historiography. Moreover, even Dibelius missed some key aspects in the comparison. The focus returns, then, to the point raised at the end of the first chapter: Are we asking the right questions of this text? Progress will rather be made in reassessing not the argument of the speech per se but the function of the speech in its narrative context. What is the speech meant to accomplish and in what way does it further the aims of Stephen's trial narrative? Here, then, we raise questions related to Lukan composition, organization, and intention.

Conclusion: Textualizing Interpretation

The above assessment of the important issues of interpretation in Acts 6:1–8:3 has highlighted some critical points of contention. First, most scholars agree that at one level or another, and despite Luke's own theological agenda that has admittedly shaped the narrative and speech, the history and theology of the early church breaks through in the narrative. They view the images and the dramatic scenes as witnessing to these historical realities lying beneath the surface of Luke's skillful presentation. In their interpretation of the narrative portions of Acts 6:1–8:3, many of these scholars use various historical paradigms and constructions to separate out tradition from redaction, moving from Lukan presentation to actual historical realities. As a result, the Lukan text becomes something of a veneer that, if appropriately sensitive to the ancient historical and literary context, one can peel back to reveal pristine elements of early Christian theology and practice. Scholarship disagrees as to the extent of historical detail one can recover (from a good amount [Barrett], to moderate [Hengel], to little [Hill]), but the approach is basically the same: One either adopts a more current literary approach to the text (Tannehill) or pursues one or both aspects of the twofold prong of the text—Lukan theological themes or the historical *Grundschrift* that surfaces despite or with the help of Luke's own efforts.

Second, if one were to isolate a single feature that contributes overwhelmingly to the general trends in the study of Acts 6:1–8:3, it might be the presence of the specific details in the narrative, such as the number seven, the list of Greek names, and the designation of specific synagogue(s). Since modern scholarship assumes historicity behind such details, critics have felt justified in working beyond the explicit narrative, attempting to recover the underlying basis in history. Moreover, speculation regarding who would have preserved such details (e.g., the community of Antioch) fuels tradition and source theories for this portion of Acts. The narrative function of the details—from specific names to the dramatic narrative sequences (e.g., daily distribution, trial and martyrdom) — has often been neglected in the discussion as a result of the focus on their historical character.

Third, while most scholars agree that the hand of Luke is evident in the speech of Stephen, differing only as to the degree, there is no unanimity on what role (if any) Luke had in formulating the narrative surrounding Acts 7. Few scholars have interacted extensively with Richard's assessment of the narrative and speech, which is surprising since he has raised some significant questions for more traditional approaches to the text. In particular, the position that there is a relatively seamless connection between the narrative and speech radically reorients analysis. It also makes any attempt to recover the historical core behind the text more difficult. Moreover, rather than viewing the speech as an abrupt insertion into the narrative of the first "Christian martyr," one must address the function of the speech for the larger Lukan account. As Dibelius had pointed out earlier, the speech helps identify the patterns and themes that are important to the writer, providing these with an overall framework of interpretation. Yet the very existence of those patterns and themes in the narrative portions of the text is provided first and foremost by the one who composes, organizes, and shapes the historical narrative. This connection means, then, that the speech and the narrative context form a symbiotic relationship: The speech and the narrative combine to provide implicit and explicit articulation of the writer's agenda.

The argument of the speech provides at least one more critical problem of investigation. The alleged abruptness of the speech has both heightened scholarly interest in traditional-historical analyses of its themes and alerted scholars to the problematic nature of the argument being made (i.e., it seems to undermine the claims of Stephen's innocence in the text). The question can be raised, then, whether or not another way of reading the speech exists that negotiates this situation any better. In particular, the relationship of the apparent anti-temple conclusion to the tenor of the rest of the speech and to the subtext provided by the narrative needs reassessment. A nuanced exposition of the speech in light of its function in the narrative setting and for the reader may well provide some possible headway in this respect.

Stemming from the analysis of Acts 6:1–8:3 in contemporary scholarship, it is my contention that the narrative and speech have largely been misunderstood, both in their own right as well as in their interrelationship. In part, there are significant textual markers that have created somewhat of a "chicken or the egg" problem in that the grand metanarratives related to the Hellenists are as much generated by the text as they are by modern scholarly agendas. Yet within these theories there are fissures and gaps that move us back to the text again, seeking to negotiate more adequately the terrain of interpretation. Furthermore, the problems evident in both specific interpretations and in the overall methodological approach point to more serious flaws in broader conception and application. On the one hand, those scholars intent on analyzing Acts 6:1–8:3 for its historical kernel have a view of Lukan *historia* that is both simplistic and arbitrary. On the other hand, scholars such as Dibelius, having attempted to move beyond the Baur school's commitment to historical paradigms and reconstructions, also construed the historical task of Luke in such a way as to undermine it. For instance, difficulties exist in moving between the dual roles of evangelist and historian, and scholarship in this vein has tended to deemphasize the historical character of the narrative and to focus on the speeches as an end in themselves (i.e., as the locus of Luke's historiographical and theological efforts). In both cases, therefore, scholars have concentrated on specific elements of the text, while sometimes losing sight of the larger question: How did the writer of Acts conceive of the writing of history, and how did he understand the character of the narrative he composed?

This situation, then, brings one back to the point raised by van Unnik at the beginning of this study. If one is going to assess Luke's work as a historical text, then it must be set in the context of the historical writings of antiquity. In particular, one needs to ask two critical questions: What is involved in writing history, and what should we be looking for? While Dibelius did advance the discussion in terms of comparing Luke to the ancient historians, his inquiry was narrowed to the speeches. Recent scholarship has made the turn more systematically, and as a result scholars such as G. E. Sterling and D. L. Balch have elucidated more clearly the nature of Luke's historical task. Yet there still exists a need for further exploration of Luke's particular historical and literary art. Past scholarship has tended to focus on specific historiographical genres or themes, while reflecting less on particular features of composition. I believe it is the latter, however, that will be most fruitful for understanding the Hellenist narrative in Acts 6:1–8:3.

III

Writing History in Antiquity
Identity, Rhetoric, and Compelling Narration

In a recent article entitled "In Defence of the Greek Historians," P. J. Rhodes frames the importance of studying ancient historical compositions in this way: "We must use all the means at our disposal to establish what the writers were trying to do, how they set about doing it, what material was available to them, what limitations they were subject to, what limitations we are subject to in studying them — and then if we are historians, we must make the best use of them that we can in investigating the questions which we want to investigate."[1] Rhodes goes on to point out, however, that although "Thucydides was not trained as a historian in a modern university; he was not impartial.... I still believe that he was not fundamentally dishonest, that it is a reasonable policy... to accept what he tells us."[2] Reflected in these statements is a significant ideological positioning related to the ancient and modern historiographical task. Rhodes is more balanced than some scholars in asserting a sufficient element of impartiality with respect to the ancient writers, although he also wants to maintain a high degree of reliability in terms of the accounts provided and is thus caught in the middle between the past and the present. At one level I subscribe to Rhodes's assessment that scholars need to understand more fully the context for ancient historical writing. Yet we may well need to rethink our own discursive cultural modes of historical practice and the values we assign to them in order to discover if and how these elements might be interfering with our construction of the past. In Rhodes's assessment, it appears that our own modern configurations still essentially frame the approach to ancient historiography and the discussion of its aims and methods. Despite seeing (or wanting to see) difference, there is still a tremendous pull to delineate sameness in terms of the basic aim of being a historian.

In the previous two chapters, I laid out the modern scholarly agenda on the Hellenists as well as the textual basis that elicited some of the critical moments of reconstruction in the history of scholarship. In this chapter, I

---

1. P. J. Rhodes, "In Defence of the Greek Historians," *GR* 2 (1994): 157.
2. Ibid., 166. Cf. S. Hornblower, "Narratology and Narrative Techniques in Thucydides," in *Greek Historiography* (ed. S. Hornblower; New York: Oxford University Press, 1994), 133.

intend to shift from the modern lens to the ancient, examining the social, cultural, and literary contexts that are essential for assessing Lukan narrative composition in Acts 6:1–8:3. To that end, this chapter focuses on a broadly contextualized approach to ancient historiography, attempting to lay out the rhetorical strategies and the sociocultural emphases that shaped the process and product of historical composition in antiquity. Along the way I challenge some of the fundamental modern conceptions of ancient historical composition, attempting to bracket for a moment our interests of investigation and to examine the ancient texts and writers on their own terms, to see what kind of (re)positioning of ancient historiography might result. To facilitate this broad discussion, then, this chapter has three major sections. After an introduction to some of the general issues in the study of ancient historiography, I first turn to an analysis of three contexts of historiographical composition: Greek, Roman, and Hellenistic. These contexts are more than just time periods; they represent interrelated matrices for and offer specific contributions to the development of the cultural discursive modes related to the composition of *historia* in antiquity. Drawing on the historiographical "spirit" developed in the first section, in the second I delineate various functional features related to the composition of *historia* in antiquity, seeking to intercalate ancient reflection on historiographical practice with sociocultural values, and clarifying the nature of the rhetorical and literary criticism of *historia* that is deceptively misleading for modern scholars. After establishing a larger literary, rhetorical, and sociocultural ethos for the composition of history in antiquity, I turn in the third section to delineating specific compositional features that arise from the larger framework established in the first two sections. These specific modes of composition are intended to aid in the fuller assessment and evaluation of the form, content, and function of the *narratio* of *historia*. Finally, I conclude by drawing some correlations with the book of Acts.

Thinking Historically about History

The *Protoevangelium of James* opens with the author noting that the narrative that follows represents a portion of the "Histories of the Twelve Tribes of Israel" (1.1). The *Protoevangelium* is usually classified as an "infancy gospel," because of its novelistic affinities, rather than a "history" proper, and clearly the majority of scholars would seriously question its connection to the great historical literature of Greek and Roman antiquity. Indeed, most scholars would categorize the *Protoevangelium* as a Christian novel that blends the gospel accounts with narratives of the Old Testament. J. L. Allen, however, has recently challenged this paradigm, suggesting that the writer of the *Protoevangelium* truly intended to have this narrative stand alongside a treatment such as Luke's: "[H]istory is understood as an allegorical-typological record preserved to communicate not primarily the 'what,' but the 'why' of past events."[3]

Whether or not one agrees with Allen's assessment of the *Protoevangelium*, one can ask to what degree the pool selected for comparison determines the results one finds. For instance, if one were to place the *Protoevangelium*, which smacks of the type of content Lucian was parodying in his *True Story*, alongside Acts, arguing that they both must be used in determining a definition of *historia*, it would be interesting to see what the end product might look like. Similarly, if one sets the *Peloponnesian War* of Thucydides alongside the *Historia Augusta* — a late Roman forgery in the style of Suetonius's *Lives of the Twelve Caesars* — the traditional meaning of *historia* as a narrative of inquiry and research becomes more problematic as a definition. One might readily object that, especially in the latter case, the time span separating the two literary products is well over six hundred years. Yet had Ctesias's *History of Persia* set the conditions for defining *historia* rather than Thucydides' history of the wars or Polybius's treatment of the rise of Roman dominion, the history of scholarship on this matter might indeed look very different.[4]

Historia (ἱστορία), in its traditional meaning, designates "inquiry," as classically used by Herodotus: "[W]hen I asked the priests whether the Greek accounts of the Trojan business were vain or true, they gave me the following answer, saying that they had inquired and knew what Menelaus himself had said" (2.118; cf. 2.113). This use of the term fulfills Herodotus's own designation of his work: "[W]hat Herodotus the Halicarnassian has learnt by inquiry (ἱστορίης) is set forth here" (1.1). Yet, as T. P. Wiseman reminds us, alongside the investigative and scientific nature of *historia* lay the other component of Herodotus's work: the setting forth in narrative form, as well as the publication and exposition, of the results of inquiry (ἀπόδειξις).[5] Thus, from the very "beginning of history" in Herodotus we find a dual and sometimes conflicting focus: inquiry and narration. It is precisely at this juncture that problems have arisen in Herodotean analysis, as scholars have questioned the way in which his goal of so-called inquiry conflicts with his narrative art.[6]

---

3. J. L. Allen, " 'The Protoevangelium of James' as an 'Historia': The Insufficiency of the 'Infancy Gospel' Category," *SBLSP* 30 (1991): 517. Allen argues for a perception of Christian *historia* as an "exegetical narrative" (508).

4. The fragmentary work of Ctesias (ca. fourth cent. B.C.E.), along with that of Iambulus (possibly third cent. B.C.E.), provides the impetus for Lucian's parody of historical writing (*Ver. hist.* 1.3); these were writers who, in Lucian's view, were bald-faced liars, recording fantastic events that could not have happened (1.4).

5. T. P. Wiseman, "Lying Historians: Seven Types of Mendacity," in *Lies and Fiction in the Ancient World* (ed. C. Gill and T. P. Wiseman; Austin: University of Texas Press, 1993), 136–37.

6. See D. Fehling, *Herodotus and His "Sources": Citation, Invention, and Narrative Art* (trans. J. G. Howie; Leeds: Cairns, 1989), who argues that the Herodotean concept of *historia* is wrapped up with the fictional and literary quality (including free invention of source citation) of his work. Thus, we find here a "pseudo-history" in the tradition of the *mythlogoi*, which is

It is in the former sense, however, that classicists have frequently and traditionally understood the meaning of the term: historical, scientific investigation and inquiry, producing in aim/intention verifiable and reliable results. As a consequence, one frequently finds assessments relating to either the reliability or unreliability of a particular ancient writer and the accuracy of his respective work. Resistance to the challenges of literary and postmodern types of criticisms for the reading of ancient texts is well grounded in classical studies and has been attributed by some to the conservative and traditional nature of the discipline itself.[7] Even when problem points in a particular narrative are made apparent, the defense that "one must remember that ancient historians were not doing modern historiography" is an apologetic (and sometimes rhetorical) statement too soon obscured in the ensuing course of analysis, often functioning to illustrate an exception to the rule that ancient historians, in most respects, were still interested in factual data. The renowned classicist Syme demonstrates this perspective well:

> It was a task to overpower any novice, and not to be managed by rhetoric or mere erudition. Tacitus came to the *Annales* with a proper equipment, mature experience, and well trained through having written about contemporary events. He is alert and vigilant, if ever an historian was. But he came against barriers and limits, those of his time and epoch in the development of human thought. Not to Tacitus was it permitted, or to anybody else, to defy, confute, and explode a century-old tradition supported by the consensus of reputable authorities. The method had not yet been invented.[8]

The recent work of scholars such as A. J. Woodman and T. P. Wiseman has challenged the more traditionalist notion of *historia,* arguing that ancient historians did not refrain from inventing actual narrative events.[9] As Woodman somewhat wryly observes,

---

where Aristotle, on the whole, placed Herodotus as well (J. Romm, *Herodotus* [New Haven: Yale University Press, 1998], 8–11), insofar as Herodotus bridged epic and historical writing (cf. S. Flory, *The Archaic Smile of Herodotus* [Detroit: Wayne State University Press, 1987], 54; and C. Calame, *The Craft of Poetic Speech in Ancient Greece* [trans. J. Orion; Ithaca: Cornell University Press, 1995], 90–91).

7. See the remarks by H. Y. McCullough, "The Historical Process and Theories of History in the 'Annals' and 'Histories' of Tacitus," *ANRW* 2.33.4 (1991): 2945–46.

8. R. Syme, *Tacitus* (London: Oxford University Press, 1958), 1:397. Surprisingly Syme defends Tacitus as a truly "modern" historian ("alert," "vigilant," "mature in experience"; cf. 378 where Syme asserts that "Tacitus does not need to be vindicated for accuracy. He consulted a variety of sources, and he was at pains to establish the truth") and then excuses him for accepting the *mythoi* of the Romans ("A Roman lacked the will for disbelief as well as the tools and the technique"). Contrast this statement with the more recent, and much less optimistic, assessment of Tacitus's "true quality as a historian" by C. L. Murison ("The Historical Value of Tacitus' 'Histories,'" *ANRW* 2.33.3 [1991]: 1712–13). Even here, however, there survives the notion that we should want or would be able to assess Tacitus against modern assumptions about the "reliable historical narrator."

9. See especially A. J. Woodman, *Rhetoric in Classical Historiography: Four Studies* (London: Croom & Helm, 1988), idem, *Tacitus Reviewed* (New York: Oxford University Press, 1998); Wiseman, "Lying Historians"; idem, *Clio's Cosmetics: Three Studies in Greco-Roman Literature* (Leicester: Leicester University Press, 1979), 2–53; idem, "Practice and Theory in

I believe that modern readers, misled by Thucydides' difficult style into thinking that his approach to historiography was the same as their own, have interpreted his narrative in anachronistically "scientific" terms which... it does not warrant. His ancient readers, blissfully unaware of the rise of "scientific historiography" in the nineteenth century, naturally made no such mistake.[10]

Scholars have generally asserted that in the Roman period there was an increasing rhetorical approach to the writing of history. Indeed, even a change in focus can account for some radical elaboration and invention; the movement from covering more recent events (e.g., Thucydides and Polybius) to more remote subjects (e.g., Livy's history of the origins of Rome) produces a significant gap in one's ability to inquire. Differing interests between modern and ancient historians have also long been recognized. As early as 1907, F. M. Cornford raised the provocative question: Why was Thucydides' introduction to his work so at variance with the modern person's desire to know the "real" causes of the outbreak of war (i.e., Why was Thucydides content with his first book, and why are we not content with it?)?[11] Yet to undercut the very reliability of Thucydides as Woodman has done — a writer who provides almost the sole data for Athenian history in the last half of the fifth century — is to move way beyond where previous scholarship has been willing to go. Despite the fact that scholars have recognized that Polybius and Thucydides may have been exceptions in antiquity rather than the norm,[12] there is still significant reticence to go much beyond referring to particular *Tendenzen* in ancient historical writers. More recent studies, however, have begun to explore further the literary and rhetorical dimensions of ancient histories, which has brought about a precipitated a perceptible shift in the kinds of questions asked of the material and the ways in which the enterprise of ancient historiography is being reconceived.

These issues in classical studies resonate with the various critical points surrounding the understanding of *historia* in Acts. Indeed, more often than not they represent a constituent part of the same fundamental issue: What can we know about the past and how firm are we in that knowledge? In a recent article on the speeches in Acts as viewed against the backdrop of

---

Roman Historiography," *History* 66 (1981): 375–93; and idem, "Origins of Roman Historiography," in *Historiography and Imagination* (Exeter: University of Exeter Press, 1994), 1–22. See also C. Pelling's brief assessment that Woodman's thesis on the role of *inventio* in ancient historical composition should be "taken as read," but with the proviso that there were limits ("Truth and Fiction in Plutarch's *Lives,*" in *Antonine Literature* [ed. D. A. Russell; New York: Oxford University Press, 1990], 51–52). Pelling promotes a middle-of-the-road position, arguing that while there was invention this does not imply that the material in Tacitus, for instance, was ahistorical (50).

10. Woodman, *Rhetoric in Classical Historiography*, 47.
11. F. M. Cornford, *Thucydides Mythistoricus* (London: Routledge & Kegan Paul, 1965), 52.
12. E. Gabba, "True History and False History in Classical Antiquity," *JRS* 71 (1981): 50–52.

Thucydides' discussion of his speech art (1.22.1), S. E. Porter concludes with this citation from M. Cogan: "If we claim that Thucydides has tampered with the facts of the historical circumstances in the case of the speeches, we must also be prepared to admit that he has tampered with the facts on other occasions as well.... To question the veracity of the speeches has the ultimate consequence of undermining — if not utterly destroying — the credibility of all of Thucydides' history."[13] At stake is precisely the same sort of logic that compels B. Witherington to make the argument that Luke should not be connected with his contemporaries (Livy and Josephus) in terms of the conception and scope of his history, but with the classical, more "reliable" writers (Polybius and Thucydides).[14] Aside from the seeming literary-historical improbability of this argument (Luke has clearly much more in common with Josephus than with Thucydides) and the reliance on the questionable truism — if Luke can be shown to be accurate in the portions of his narrative in which he can be checked he can be assumed to be reliable in the parts which cannot be verified — there is a more serious issue at stake regarding the relationship of the present to the past. The question should probably be asked with a different focus: Why does it matter to us whether Luke or Thucydides wrote historical narratives upon which we can rely? This framing represents a more challenging matter and, aside from the fact that in both cases these writers offer the most important information for the period and subject covered (fifth-century Athenian history; formation and development of the early Christian community), there is the nagging issue that without this material we might have to rethink in a substantive manner our relationship to the past.

These issues are of paramount importance for understanding the Hellenist episode in Acts 6:1–8:3. As noted earlier, the way forward is to reassess the understanding and context of *historia* in Luke's literary and cultural world. One aspect to be considered is the influence of rhetorical exercises such as declamation in the composition of historiography, which Witherington argues was practiced by those who "ignored traditional conventions and [who] cannot be ranked among serious historians."[15] This position, I would argue,

---

13. S. E. Porter, "Thucydides 1.22.1 and Speeches in Acts: Is There a Thucydidean View?" *NovT* 32 (1990), 141–42. See also A. E. Raubitschek, "The Speech of the Athenians at Sparta," in *The Speeches in Thucydides* (ed. P. A. Stadter; Chapel Hill: University of North Carolina Press, 1973), 47.

14. B. Witherington, "Editing the Good News: Some Synoptic Lessons for the Study of Acts," in *History, Literature, and Society in the Book of Acts* (ed. B. Witherington; Cambridge: Cambridge University Press, 1996), 324–47; and idem, "Finding Its Niche: The Historical and Rhetorical Species of Acts," *SBLSP* 35 (1996): 67–97. See also T. Callan, "The Preface of Luke-Acts and Historiography," *NTS* 31 (1985): 576–81; esp. his comment on 580: "[I]f this identification of the genre of Luke-Acts is correct, then Luke-Acts is one of the first examples of a new type of history which began to be written in the first century BCE, which de-emphasized the didactic function of history and returned to earlier classical models, especially Thucydides."

15. B. Witherington, "Addendum to W. J. Mccoy, 'In the Shadow of Thucydides,'" in *History, Literature, and Society* (ed. Witherington), 27. This same attitude is reflected in the

is a huge misstep, as the art of declamation was not practiced by just a small group of oratorical sophists in the empire, but was a fundamental part of identity formation and education in the Roman period (and Luke's educational pedigree is no exception in this respect).[16] Witherington does not deny the influence of rhetoric in composition and style, but argues that it neither involves the distortion or invention of events nor the completely fictitious rendering of speeches. On the latter, citing the conservative conclusions of the classicist C. W. Fornara, he argues that there was no "convention" of inventing speeches, "though some armchair and highly encomiastic historians, who did not bother to investigate their subject matter closely or inquire of the eyewitnesses what was said, did so."[17] Witherington reveals a common misconception of Polybius and Lucian at this point. Their critique of the "armchair" historians was not that they did not investigate their data per se, but that they did not have personal experience in the matters about which they wrote, a hallmark of serious historical writing in the ancient perception.[18] The significance and detail of this premise will be explored later in this chapter, but for now it is worth noting that Witherington has committed the common mistake of assuming an emphasis on veracity when verisimilitude was more frequently in view.[19] Moreover, the critique of encomiastic or eulogizing historiography is a much more nuanced discussion in Polybius and Lucian (and, for that matter, so is the positive discussion of it in Dionysius of Halicarnassus) than Witherington reflects in his assessment. At stake for these writers was obsequious flattery and verbose, distracting writing styles, both of which detracted from what, in their view, a history should achieve. At stake for Witherington, conversely, is the establishment of

---

influential study by C. W. Fornara, *The Nature of History in Ancient Greece and Rome* (Berkeley: University of California Press, 1983), who looks quite unfavorably upon those ancient writers who write rhetorical pieces "inimical to sober historiography" (103).

16. On the importance of declamation, see D. A. Russell, *Greek Declamation* (Cambridge: Cambridge University Press, 1983); R. A. Kaster, "Controlling Reason: Declamation in Rhetorical Education at Rome," in *Education in Greek and Roman Antiquity* (ed. Y. L. Too; Leiden: Brill, 2001), 317–37; and E. Gunderson, *Declamation, Paternity, and Roman Identity: Authority and the Rhetorical Self* (Cambridge: Cambridge University Press, 2003). For the possible influence of declamation on Acts, including further discussion of broad correlations between declamatory practice and the writing of ancient historiography, see T. Penner, "Civilizing Discourse: Acts, Declamation, and the Rhetoric of the *Polis*," in *Contextualizing Acts: Lukan Narrative and Greco-Roman Discourse* (ed. T. Penner and C. Vander Stichele; SBLSymS 20; Atlanta: Society of Biblical Literature, 2003), 65–104.

17. Witherington, "'Addendum' to W. J. Mccoy," 28. This emphasis by Fornara represents an understanding of rhetoric purely in terms of compositional style and adornment. For a critique and the suggestion of an alternative approach, see T. Penner, "Reconfiguring the Rhetorical Study of Acts: Reflections on the Method in and Learning of a Progymnastic Poetics," *PRSt* 30 (2003), 425–39.

18. See G. Avenarius, *Lukians Schrift zur Geschichtsschreibung* (Meisenheim, Germany: Hain, 1956), 30–40.

19. See the same misinterpretation in W. W. Gasque's discussion of Lucian's treatise on writing history (*A History of the Interpretation of the Acts of the Apostles* [Peabody, Mass.: Hendrickson, 1989], 226–27).

a canon of historiographical principles that one can then assume with confidence Luke used, which ultimately guarantees the veracity (i.e., historicity) of Luke's account.[20]

The meaning and function of *historia* is paramount, then, for interpreting a narrative such as one finds in Acts 6:1–8:3, as the entire discussion of this text from Baur to Hengel and beyond has largely been premised on the ability of scholars to delve beneath the surface of the narrative and to recover the core historical details of the era Luke is recording. Even if the majority of scholars concedes that the speech is essentially a Lukan creation, that still leaves the narrative intact — with its charges, trials, and conflicts — for the modern reconstruction of Christian origins. However, my contention in this study is that it is very difficult, if not impossible, to move beyond the framework, order, characterization, and style of the narrative to a concrete bedrock of assured reliable and verifiable data. The very understanding and practice of writing history in Luke's day would seem to bear this out. In this respect the Jewish historian Josephus provides a prime literary example for helping one understand the organic and dynamic nature of *historia* in the first century.

In the prologue to the *Jewish War,* Josephus goes to great lengths to affirm that the account he is about to transmit is truthful and accurate. Other accounts, according to Josephus, have either used inadequate evidence combined with a rhetorical style, or have as their basis Roman flattery (encomium) and/or Jewish hatred (invective; 1.1). Josephus's "outrage" spurs him on to record the "truth," an account that will correct the "flattering or fictitious narratives" of the Greeks and Romans (1.6). Josephus even goes as far as to make room for his own personal reflections on his country's downfall, while maintaining, at the same time, that he will not exaggerate the deeds of the Jews (1.9–11). History, for Josephus, is concerned with "veracity and laborious collection of the facts" (1.16), and his account of the Jewish war will be for "lovers of truth" (1.30). These are indeed high-minded claims, and one might wonder at first glance why it is that Witherington should wish to drive a wedge between this conception of history and Luke's own method.

The explanation, of course, is that Josephus's bold claims are not necessarily borne out by his narrative. In antiquity there existed a *topos* of claiming one's own account to be superior to preceding and alternate accounts, and the main goal of Josephus's introduction is to secure his own

---

20. Frequently the modern construction of the canon of conventions is conservative in nature, seeking to preserve and stabilize the historical reliability of the text. A. W. Mosley, "Historical Reporting in the Ancient World," *NTS* 12 (1965): 10–26. On the idea of "convention" being overly generalized for the ancient context, see the more recent assessment by J. Marincola, "Genre, Convention, and Innovation in Greco-Roman Historiography," in *The Limits of Historiography: Genre and Narrative in Ancient Historical Texts* (ed. C. Shuttleworth Kraus; MnSup 191; Leiden: Brill, 1999), 320–21.

authority as the "true" and "authentic" narrator of events.[21] While it is not my purpose at this juncture to explore the various problems with Josephus's account, it is worth noting that Josephus himself uses both encomium and invective throughout his narrative, and he is primarily interested in casting the Romans in a much better light than the Jewish "rebels."[22] Moreover, as J. S. McLaren has recently argued, the entire framework for the *Jewish War* (and the relevant sections of the *Antiquities*) — the prevailing situation of conflict and instability in Judea — may have been constructed by Josephus himself, and the narratives, then, have been shaped by him to support his interpretative framework.[23] Moreover, his account of the destruction of the temple and the utter chaotic state in the city of Jerusalem during the siege reveal the hand of a dramatic historian, seeking to blame certain Jewish groups for the disaster while exonerating the Romans of any wrongdoing.[24]

The situation with the *Antiquities* is little different. Josephus begins with similar assertions regarding the "truth" of his *historia* (*Ant.* 1.4, 17), yet the narrative itself belies this claim.[25] For instance, in an interesting parallel to Acts 7, Josephus, when "recounting" the story of Moses and the Israelites at Mount Sinai, conveniently leaves out the "small detail" about the building and worship of the golden calf (3.89–101). He leaves it out for exactly the opposite reason, as we shall see, that Luke includes it: Josephus is concerned to "praise" the Jewish people. Thus, in Josephus's account, Moses' first and

---

21. See further J. Marincola, *Authority and Tradition in Ancient Historiography* (Cambridge: Cambridge University Press, 1997), 34–43; and the brief comments by S. Mason, *Flavius Josephus on the Pharisees* (SPB 39; Leiden: Brill, 1991), 62–63.

22. L. H. Feldman, *Josephus's Interpretation of the Bible* (HCS 27; Berkeley: University of California Press, 1998), 11 n. 16.

23. J. S. McLaren, *Turbulent Times? Josephus and Scholarship on Judaea in the First Century CE* (JSPSup 29; Sheffield: Sheffield Academic Press, 1998), 122–26. See also K.-S. Krieger, *Geschichtsschreibung als Apologetik bei Flavius Josephus* (TANZ 9; Tübingen: Francke, 1994). On the effect of Josephus's excessive moralizing on his narrative, see H. W. Attridge, *The Interpretation of Biblical History in the Antiquitates Judaicae of Flavius Josephus* (HDR 7; Missoula, Mont.: Scholars Press, 1976), 109–44.

24. U. Rappaport is more conservative in assessing Josephus's accuracy in the *Jewish War*: "[A]s most scholars agree *War* is far from being Thucydidean and its veracity is often questionable. At least four kinds of considerations lead Josephus astray from the quest of truth: personal... political... national... and... the service he rendered to his Roman benefactors" ("Where Was Josephus Lying — In His *Life* or in the *War*"? in *Josephus and the History of the Greco-Roman Period* [ed. P. Parente and J. Sievers; SPB 41; Leiden: Brill, 1994], 282). Rappaport, despite offering grounds for Josephus's distortion of the truth, nevertheless tacitly affirms both that Josephus intended to offer a historically accurate narrative and that, despite the problems, one can still retrieve the reliable core.

25. The attempt to separate the literary activity of Josephus in the *Jewish War* and the *Antiquities* intends to show that in the former Josephus is more interested in objective political history and in the latter in antiquarian rhetorical history (see further Attridge, *Interpretation of Biblical History*, 43–57, who argues for this position based on his reading of the prologues). This view seems to go beyond the evidence, however, as Josephus is writing apologetic and rhetorical historiography in both cases (Feldman, *Josephus's Interpretation*, 9; and Mason, *Flavius Josephus*, 376–83).

second trip up the mountain are coalesced into one, with the result that the destruction of the initial code is omitted. While Josephus notes the fear of the people surrounding the fate of Moses due to his delay (Exod 32:1), he expands rather upon the various scenes of the people gathered at the base of Sinai. The omissions and expansions occur directly after Josephus notes that, should one be skeptical regarding the miraculous events surrounding Sinai, he is simply "constrained to relate [ἱστορεῖν] [the events] as they are recorded in the sacred books" (3.81).[26]

Josephus is brought in at this juncture to illustrate that the nature and meaning of *historia* in Luke's social and cultural milieu was certainly flexible. Josephus recounts events and rewrites texts that could have been checked by outsiders for accuracy in reporting. But this matter is precisely not Josephus's concern, despite his frequent claims to the contrary. Rather, at stake for Josephus is the construction of a narrative (either based on experiences to which he himself was an "eyewitness" or on the sacred and ancient histories of the Jews) that utilizes order, arrangement, and dramatic qualities to present a nuanced and tendentious portrayal of the subject and to effect emotion in the reader. It is precisely at this point that Josephus is to be set within the stream of ancient Greek and Roman historiography. Learning more about this stream may also help one to assess more adequately and accurately Luke's narrative in Acts 6:1–8:3 and, as well, to formulate how it functions as *historia* within Luke's two-volume work. However, it is difficult to formulate exact standards in the writing of ancient historiography, as the conception of the work varies so dramatically from writer to writer, from period to period.[27] Moreover, as the opening of the *Protoevangelium of James* illustrates, the issue of what is history and how we determine its boundaries and nature is of specific interest to modern scholars, but may be much more elusive in the ancient context. It is my aim, however, to focus on those aspects of ancient theory and practice that are fundamental for understanding Luke, Josephus, and the fragmentary Hellenistic Jewish historians, establishing the sociocultural, rhetorical, and ideological texture of their historiographical world, particularly with an emphasis on the elements related to their narrative art: the ordering, structuring, and characterization of their narrative events and personages. I will seek to demonstrate that not only can we see in these writings the essential influence of rhetorical practice in composition — emphasis on dramatic type-scenes, the elaboration of narratives, the characterization of individuals and groups, the composition of dual narratives for the purpose of implicit *synkrisis* (or comparison), the

---

26. Unless otherwise noted, translations of ancient Greek and Roman writers are taken from the Loeb Classical Library.

27. See the remarks of Fornara, *Nature of History*, 61: "To attempt to characterize Greek historiography, or even its separate varieties, as a whole would be to seek specious uniformity in a medium that more than most takes shape and character from the conditions of its political and cultural environment." See also Marincola, "Genre, Convention, and Innovation," 320–21.

construction of plausible narratives, and the import and meaning of *akribeia* ("accuracy") for the interpretative standpoint of the writer — but also that the discussion of the purposes of writing history in the Roman period take on an increasing moral and epideictic quality. Indeed, epideictic history, with an emphasis on praise and blame, became the history of choice in Luke's day, being aptly suited for the goals and aims of apologetic literature.

Contexts of Historical Composition in Greco-Roman Antiquity

Greek Context

Although the attempt to distinguish between what is a "true" history and what is not is a quandary posed by our modern post-Enlightenment historiographic commitments, it would not be too much to suggest that modern classical scholarship has posed the question in part because of the ancient precedent. Herodotus begins his *History* with precisely the same question modern readers might well ask: Whose account of the Persian war with the Greeks is more accurate? Herodotus points out the competing accounts of the cause of the "feud":

> Such is the Persian account of the matter: in their opinion, it was the taking of Troy which began their feud with the Greeks. But the Phoenicians do not tell the same story about Io as the Persians. They say that they did not carry her off to Egypt by force.... These are the stories of the Persians and the Phoenicians. For my own part, I will not say that this or that story is true. (1.5)

While Herodotus does not attempt to determine whose account is truthful, the framework, at the very least, is set for distinguishing and assessing true and false history.

Thucydides expresses a similar sentiment at the beginning of his historical work on the Peloponnesian wars. He refers to those Greeks who accept hearsay testimony without testing it adequately: They are "averse to taking pains...in the search for the truth...[turning] to what lies ready at hand" (1.20.2–3). Here Thucydides is not referring to competing accounts related to the subject matter of his history, but to various free-floating interpretations of particular facets of the war that he believes to be fallacious. He ends with the following assessment of his own work in relation to the descriptions of wars by his epic predecessors:

> Still, from the evidence that has been given, anyone would not err who should hold the view that the state of affairs in antiquity was pretty nearly such as I have described it, not giving greater credence to the accounts, on the one hand, which the poets have put into song, adorning and amplifying their theme, and, on the other hand, which the chroniclers have composed with a view rather of pleasing the ear than of telling the truth, since their [i.e., both the poets' and the chroniclers'] stories cannot be tested and most of them have from lapse

of time won their way into the region of the fabulous so as to be incredible. (1.21.1)

Thucydides argues that his method of recounting is superior to both the epic poets, who embellish their accounts, and the chroniclers/logographers (he probably includes Herodotus here), who simply relate stories that are entertaining but that frequently lack a basis in reality (i.e., myths) and who perhaps also invent events and characters.[28] Strabo clearly expresses disapprobation in his assessment of three major writers in this tradition:

> For seeing that those who were professedly writers of myths enjoyed repute, they thought that they too would make their writings pleasing if they told in the guise of history what they had never seen, nor even heard — or at least not from persons who knew the facts — with this object alone in view, to tell what afforded their hearers pleasure and amazement. One could more easily believe Hesiod and Homer than Ctesias, Herodotus, Hellanicus, and other writers of this kind. (2.6.3; cf. Lucian, *Philops.* 2)

Strabo lumps together Herodotus with a so-called tragic historian (Ctesias) and an ethnographer/chronicler (Hellanicus).[29] His critique is similar to the above comments of Thucydides in one important respect: The goal of pleasing the reader rather than offering purportedly accurate and reliable reporting is disparaged. In both cases the critique also centers on the blurring of the distinction between mythology and history.

From Thucydides' comments it is clear that he saw (or at least projected an image of) himself as writing an account that was based on real events. He also suggests that he was offering a version of reality that represented something more than the mythologies of the poets and the half-truths of the logographers. At the same time, there exists a tension: There are alternative ways of telling "history" alongside the tradition of historiography with which Thucydides aligned himself. By the time Polybius wrote his history of the ascendancy of Rome, it was clear that there was not simply a Thucydidean style of historical composition but that there existed other and, in Polybius's view, less appropriate forms of writing history as well. Frequently labeled as "tragic-historians," these writers seem to have valued what Thucydides and Strabo criticize, namely, writing events in a way that entertains and titillates the reader. Polybius's comment on Phylarchus (third cent. B.C.E.) aptly demonstrates the tenor of the criticisms:

---

28. Herodotus's predecessors were logographers, and the content of their work seems to have focused on ethnographic history, which relates myths, geography, customs, and some local history. See further G. E. Sterling, *Historiography and Self-definition: Josephos, Luke-Acts, and Apologetic Historiography* (NovTSup 64; Leiden: Brill, 1992), 22–33.

29. In a similar vein, Hermogenes categorizes Herodotus as the most "panegyric historian" writing in that tradition. Hermogenes, however, values Herodotus's work, while he has little use it seems for others (such as Theopompus and Hellanicus) in this same tradition (*On Types of Style* 408, 412).

> In his eagerness to arouse the pity and attention of his readers he treats us to a picture of clinging women with their hair disheveled and their breasts bare, or again of crowds of both sexes together with their children and aged parents weeping and lamenting as they are led away to slavery. This sort of thing he keeps up throughout his history, always trying to bring horrors vividly before our eyes. Leaving aside the ignoble and womanish character of such a treatment of his subject, let us consider how far it is proper or serviceable to history. A historical author should not try to thrill his readers by such exaggerated pictures, nor should he, like a tragic poet, try to imagine the probable utterances of his characters or reckon up all the consequences with which he deals, but simply record what really happened and what really was said, however commonplace. (2.56.7–10)

Polybius's designation of Phylarchus's style as evidencing the goals of tragic poetry gave rise to the term "tragic-historian." Indeed, it has become a general assumption among many classicists that there existed a tradition of tragic historical writing in antiquity that was distinct from the more scientific style that Thucydides followed. Despite his claims to the contrary, Polybius is also sometimes associated with this approach to historical composition,[30] as he himself was not beyond the manipulation of emotions and events.[31]

The differentiation that Polybius makes between tragic poetry and history is significant, and we will have cause to explore that connection later in this chapter. Polybius's distinction has some affinities with the classic formulation by Aristotle in his *Poetics:*

> The difference between the historian and the poet is...that one relates actual events, the other the kinds of things that might occur. Consequently poetry is more philosophical and more elevated than history, since poetry relates more of the universal, while history relates particulars. "Universal" means the kinds of things which it suits a certain kind of person to say or do, in terms of probability or necessity: poetry aims for this, even though attaching names to the agents. A "particular" means, say, what Alcibiades did or experienced. (1451b)

---

30. K. S. Sacks, *Polybius on the Writing of History* (Classical Studies 24; Berkeley: University of California Press, 1981), argues that Polybius opposed the excessive use of tragic elements (as in Phylarchus) but not the enterprise as a whole, which does find its way into Polybius's description of events and subject matter (166). See also P. Green, *Alexander to Actium: The Historical Evolution of the Hellenistic Age* (HCS 1; Berkeley: University of California Press, 1990), 284.

31. Green, *Alexander to Actium,* raises serious historical questions with respect to Polybius's portrayal of Callicrates and his relationship vis-à-vis Rome (275–76) and the consistent Scipioan (Polybius's patron) associations of the Roman speeches (277). He goes as far as to suggest that "despite his insistence on historical impartiality, his declared contempt for writers who inflate local or personal interests on their own behalf, one gets the constant nagging suspicion that Polybius's grandiose scheme of universal history conceals, at one level, an extended apologia for his own career and the aims of the Achaean League" (277–78). Also see D. Mendels, "Did Polybius Have 'Another' View of the Aetolian League?" in *Identity, Religion, and Historiography: Studies in Hellenistic History* (JSPSup 24; Sheffield: Sheffield Academic Press, 1998), 127–38.

Aristotle makes a crucial distinction, and its resonance with later Hellenistic historical writing is significant. Aristotle, while making a similar point as Polybius's, nonetheless favored poetry over historical writings because the former deals with what is universal. Whereas history relates only a banal sequence of events — Alcibiades did this or that[32] — poetry as a whole is mimetic; it functions to provide a unified presentation of universals and lays out aspects of higher signification.[33] Tragedy, most of all, is useful for this purpose because it plots the character, goals, and failures of human action.[34] Thus, Aristotle could claim that tragic poetry — with its historical emphasis arising from the use of the names of the mythological past, thereby relating not just plausible (as in comedy) but actual events (that which is possible) — can relate what is universal to the particular person so as to effect in that individual moral/philosophical virtue. In short, this is truth at its highest, since poetic invention is allowed to have the effect — a fictive and deceptive play — on the individual that is normally relegated to actual experience or philosophical speculation in its own right.[35] History does not have this effect for Aristotle, largely because it focuses on the particular, which cannot be applicable to all and hence cannot be truly mimetic (i.e., reflect a universal). This observation is true, of course, only up until the point someone is able to make the actions of Alcibiades universal and mimetic, or create a framework of interpretation in which doing (*ergon*) and saying (*logos*) can potentially and effectively evoke the imitation of virtue in the beholder.

While Aristotle may have intended a separation between history and poetry/tragedy, Polybius's remarks indicate that not all historians were so inclined.[36] Certain trajectories go back to Isocrates, who is often said to

---

32. On the possibility that Aristotle is here referring to Thucydides' work, see G. E. M. de Ste. Croix, "Aristotle on History and Poetry (*Poetics*, 9, 1451a36–b11)," in *Essays on Aristotle's Poetics* (ed. A. O. Rorty; Princeton: Princeton University Press, 1992), 24, 27–28. One should keep in mind, however, that Aristotle is using the historical genre as a foil for his discussion of poetry and tragedy. Thus, his comments on history are probably not to be read as a technical assessment of the genre per se (see C. Pelling, "Epilogue," in *Limits of Historiography* [ed. Shuttleworth Kraus], 331).

33. S. Halliwell, *Aristotle's Poetics* (2d ed.; London: Duckworth, 1998), 136–37.

34. See the important discussion in A. O. Rorty, "The Psychology of Aristotelian Tragedy," in *Essays on Aristotle's Poetics* (ed. Rorty), 4–6. See also Halliwell, *Aristotle's Poetics*, 236.

35. P. Woodruff, "Aristotle on Mimēsis," in *Essays on Aristotle's Poetics* (ed. Rorty), 91–92.

36. One might well characterize Hellenistic historiography as the attempt to merge history and poetics. The famous statement by Duris (*FGH* 76 F1), a student of Theophrastus in the Aristotelian school, is often taken as evidence for this attempt: "Ephorus and Theopompus [assumed "rhetorical" historians of the Isocratean tradition] were especially lacking in the events. For in the presentation (*phrasis*) they did not partake either of any representation of reality (*mimēsis*) or pleasure (*hedone*) at all, but were concerned only with the writing itself" (trans. Sacks, *Polybius on the Writing of History*, 146). This statement by a peripatetic is taken as evidence that Aristotle's students had altered some of his ideas (Halliwell, *Aristotle's Poetics*, 287–88) and were interested in unifying history and poetics. Even if one does not read here "theatrical" representation of reality but "imitation" of historical reality, one still

have initiated a more rhetorical and stylistic approach to historiography in contrast to the Aristotelian framework.[37] Yet the very existence of a school tradition of "tragic" or "dramatic" history, despite the frequent claims to the contrary,[38] is questionable. R. Doran has recently made the argument that the type of opposition one finds in Polybius to so-called tragic history is simply a *topos* for characterizing history one thinks is incorrect or inadequate.[39] Indeed, by caricaturing the work or account of a particular event by a previous historian, one is able to achieve a better hearing for one's own composition.

This framing raises an important issue, since if every historian who accuses another of being a dramatic and rhetorical historian is doing so to garner support for his or her own version of events, then the line dividing a Polybius from an Ephorus, Theopompus, Ctesias, or Phylarchus is much thinner than one might be led to believe from the initial comments. Indeed, it is for this reason that Polybius has been so problematic for modern historians: He condemns tragic history but then resorts to it himself. Evidently, the truth quality of historians' work was at stake in the very act of separating themselves from the work of their predecessors.[40] Josephus, for instance, states, "I wish my readers to know that we have said nothing more than what is true, and have not, by inserting into the history various plausible and seductive passages meant to deceive and entertain, attempted to evade critical inquiry, asking to be instantly believed" (*Ant.* 8.56). In Josephus's

---

achieves a sense that for Duris and others history produces an effect on the reader resulting in pleasure and/or profit (see further H. Cancik, *Mythische und historische Wahrheit* [SBS 48; Stuttgart: Katholisches Bibelwerk, 1970], 32–35; and Avenarius, *Lukians Schrift,* 135–40; cf. R. Doran, "2 Maccabees and 'Tragic History,'" *HUCA* 50 [1979]: 109, who argues that no particular poetic mode of historiography is attested in this comment by Duris). I would argue that this merger, such as it is, does not represent a conscious reliance on or the influence of Aristotle's *Poetics* as much as a cultural communicative environment in which one could readily move from the philosophical discussions in Aristotle to a more rhetorical and literary context in historiography (for a cultural focus rather than "school" orientation to this and related ancient historiographical phenomena, see F. W. Walbank, *Polybius* [Sather Classical Lectures 42; Berkeley: University of California Press, 1972], 38–39; and T. J. Luce, *The Greek Historians* [New York: Routledge, 1997], 119–22).

37. Feldman, *Josephus's Interpretation,* 3–7, provides a concise summary of the two traditions. On Isocrates and "rhetorical" historiographical tradition, see C. B. Welles, "Isocrates' View of History," in *The Classical Tradition: Literary and Historical Studies in Honor of Harry Caplan* (ed. L. Wallach; Ithaca: Cornell University Press, 1966), 3–25.

38. On this issue, see Sacks, *Polybius,* 144–70; Walbank, *Polybius,* 34–40; Doran, "2 Maccabees," 107–10; and idem, *Temple Propaganda: The Purpose and Character of 2 Maccabees* (CBQMS 12; Washington: Catholic Biblical Association, 1981), 84–97.

39. Doran, "2 Maccabees," 110.

40. On this common literary *topos,* see D. P. Moessner, "'Eyewitnesses,' 'Informed Contemporaries,' and 'Unknowing Inquirers': Josephus' Criteria for Authentic Historiography and the Meaning of ΠΑΡΑΚΟΛΟΥΘΕΩ," *NovT* 38 (1996): 121; and Marincola, *Authority and Tradition,* 217–36. Over a hundred years after Josephus, the Greek writer Herodian attests to the endurance of *topos*: "Many writers...have shown a contempt for the truth and a preoccupation with vocabulary and style, because they were confident that, even if they romanced a bit, they would reap advantages of the pleasure they gave to their public, without the accuracy of their research being investigated" (1.1).

last work, he attempts to undermine the "malicious" (*C. Ap.* 1.2) attacks on the Jewish people by Greek historians. He argues that many historians conjectured the facts (1.15) or relied on older incorrect accounts (1.20). The Greeks are thus not only overrated as historians, they frequently "rushed into writing... concerned not so much to discover the truth... as to display their literary ability" (1.24).[41] In both cases, Josephus garners a sympathetic hearing for his "true" and "accurate" description of events and persons by eliminating the work of predecessors. In these and similar statements (also found in Polybius) one must be careful not to presume that the account one is about to read will not be dramatic and rhetorical simply because the writer says it is not. Moreover, if what is actually at stake — despite Josephus's claims to the contrary — is not really or primarily the use of factually accurate data, then one must reassess exactly what is at issue when Josephus and Polybius refer in a derogatory manner to the use of dramatic episodes and the goal of pleasing the audience. That is, what does a tragic or overly tragic rendering of history do to a text that makes it so troublesome for these writers? This focus differs to a degree between Polybius and Josephus. For Polybius, in effect, this form of historiography takes away from the utility of the text because of its lack of historical realia, whereas for Josephus there is more clearly an interpretive issue at stake (i.e., "accuracy" and "truthfulness" refer to a particular line of interpretation with respect to historical events and persons).[42]

The treatment here is admittedly a brief survey of one fundamental issue in Greek history writing: how to tell true history from false, or, more precisely, how to tell good history from poor. The way this aspect is understood in modern scholarship varies, and there are still many scholars who insist that the quintessential quest for truth and accuracy is at the center of Greek historical writing. Yet the constant assault on the dramatic and tragic historians — as a mode of writing rather than a school tradition per se — raises the issue of just how widespread this type of history writing actually was in antiquity. At the very least, there was a segment of the enterprise in which exaggeration, elaboration, moralizing, rhetorical stylization, and more general historical and literary license were viewed as acceptable and indeed encouraged. Some scholars still attempt to hold Thucydides and Polybius

---

41. Cf. the telling comment by Sallust: "[B]ecause Athens produced writers of exceptional talent, the exploits of the men of Athens are heralded throughout the world as unsurpassed. Thus the merit of those who did the deeds is rated as high as brilliant minds have been able to exalt the deeds themselves by words of praise" (*Bell. Cat.* 8.4).

42. Moessner's article (" 'Eyewitnesses,' 'Informed Contemporaries' ") on Josephus's historical criteria is a significant piece in this regard, as he demonstrates the rhetorical function of the language of critical inquiry: Josephus is ultimately proffering himself not as a superior researcher, but as a superior interpreter of the events. See also Moessner, "The Lukan Prologues in the Light of Ancient Narrative Hermeneutics: ΠΑΡΗΚΟΛΟΥΘΗΚΟΤΙ and the Credentialed Author," in *The Unity of Luke-Acts* (ed. J. Verheyden; BETL 142; Leuven: Leuven University Press, 1999), 409–11.

above such tactics, and sometimes go as far as defending certain rhetorical historians as well,[43] but it is clear that there were numerous historical modes of writing that were concerned about something other than mere accuracy.[44]

Roman Context

While the modern debate about Greek historiography frequently centers on determining who were the reliable historians and who were not, a significant strain of classical scholarship agrees that the Roman period represents the bastardization of much that was glorious about Greek historical writing.[45] This extreme position juxtaposes a particular interpretation of Greek historiography over against a reading of Roman historical writing that views it as quite different from its Greek predecessor, as the poor imitation of a much superior original. M. von Albrecht, after characterizing the Greek tradition as committed to telling the truth and being impartial, goes on to state,

---

43. M. A. Flower, for instance, attempts to defend the historical accuracy of Theopompus, the Isocratean rhetorical historian (*Theopompus of Chios: History and Rhetoric in the Fourth Century BC* [New York: Oxford University Press, 1994], 184–210).

44. One must note in this context as well the interference run by our own cultural topics in the course of analysis, which make accuracy as a point of departure for modern investigation of ancient discussions and sources somewhat problematic. C. M. Thomas is correct, in my view, to move the discussion to ancient reception history and the perspectives of implied readers (and also writers) when it comes to the issue of fiction and fact in ancient composition (*The Acts of Peter, Gospel Literature, and the Ancient Novel: Rewriting the Past* [New York: Oxford University Press, 2003], 102). I would resist, however, her attempt to delineate (at least fully) between historical novels and history proper (although I do recognize her distinction between historical and erotic novels), which I regard as another modern classification still based not only on our own cultural topics but also on our limitations in being able to situate ourselves holistically within the gamut of ancient ideal and real reading audiences.

45. This position seems to represent the gist of the more conservative treatment by Fornara, in which the Greeks are the cultural and literary heroes: "Of the various principles laid down by the ancients, none is more fundamental than the honest and impartial presentation of the facts, and it is entirely consistent with their clarity of vision and intellectual emancipation that the Greeks gave it to the world" (*Nature of History*, 99). Engaging in a little epideictic rhetoric himself, Fornara goes on to state that if Ephorus (a so-called rhetorical historian) can be said to have had his narrative affected by his moralism, then this would mean an "early debasement of the genre" (109). Fornara defends Ephorus's historical integrity, leaving the "debasement of the genre" to the Romans. Thus, later Roman writers such as Fronto (ca. 95–166 C.E.) are portrayed quite differently: "The historian has degenerated into a professional rhetorician, whose chief purpose is to compile skillfully, to mould disparate material, all of it flattering, into a unitary historical narrative displaying the refinements of art... and devoted to the glorification of the emperor" (103). Likewise, he criticizes earlier Roman historians' emphasis on history as *exemplum*: "One negative result of placing a value on history for the examples it provided of men's virtue and vice... was a disinclination to engage in the kind of revisionist research that might have resulted in a closer approach to the historical truth" (117). One could cite numerous examples of this emphasis from Fornara's study, where the Greeks are viewed as much superior to the Romans in doing history proper. Fornara's framework of interpretation, however, severely distorts his conclusions, and the inherent assumptions contained therein reflect a metanarrative and mythology of the modern (i.e., liberal Enlightenment, but also particularly post–World War II) world, wherein nationalistic propaganda is perceived to distort the culturally superior, nonpartisan, more individualistic commitment to truth.

In Roman literature these demands are subject to noteworthy limitations. As a rule, Roman historical writing is patriotic and therefore not free from partisanship. It is moralizing and therefore not wholly concerned with the facts. For long stretches it follows "fabulous" traditions, which means that it falls short of the requirement for truthfulness. Moreover, its manner of presentation is influenced by drama in many ways, often replacing historical truth with literary probability.[46]

This extreme demarcation is not fully supported by the evidence, especially if one takes the existence of tragic modes of historical writing seriously (as Polybius at least does). It is much more likely that Roman historiography developed further what were latent, if not already more fully formed, elements of Greek historiographical practice. Writing in the second century C.E., Lucian continued the criticisms in the Polybian trajectory, likely representing a tradition of interpretation.[47] Of course, because of these similarities and his Eastern provenance, Lucian is easily linked with the great Greek historians of the past.[48] Lest anyone should attempt to separate Roman Latin histories from Greek histories written in the Roman period, however, one need only refer to the earlier Dionysius of Halicarnassus (first cent. B.C.E.), whose approach to history, as we shall see, took the dramatic/tragic style of the classical Greek model and developed it even further within an explicit rhetorical and literary-critical framework, which itself attests to broader patterns of rhetorical learning and display in both West and East during the Roman period.

Rhetorical training was a broad, multifaceted feature of education in the Roman period. The surviving handbooks used as school texts — the *progymnasmata* (principally those of Theon, Hermogenes, and Aphthonius) — demonstrate the essential elements of ancient education, developed in different but interrelated ways in both the Greek and Roman pedagogical systems.[49] Exercises described in these handbooks were intended to provide the necessary skills for oratory and thus focused on the recitation and composition of narratives and speeches. In the introduction to his work, Theon states, "[W]hat one should know and reasonably practice before the speech, I will try to convey.... I myself hope... to assist those who elect

---

46. M. von Albrecht, *A History of Roman Literature: From Livius Andronicus to Boethius* (rev. G. Schmeling; trans. F. and K. Newman; MnSup 165; Leiden: Brill, 1997), 1:360.
47. In his impressive study *Lukians Schrift*, Avenarius argues that there is a school tradition reflected in the continuity between Polybius and Lucian, and that Lucian's work on writing history should not be read as idiosyncratic, but as the end product of a long development of thinking on the issue.
48. A. Georgiadou and D. H. J. Larmour, "Lucian and Historiography: 'De Historia Conscribenda' and 'Verae Historiae,'" *ANRW* 2.34.2 (1993): 1450–53.
49. See S. Bonner, *Education in Ancient Rome: From the Elder Cato to the Younger Pliny* (Berkeley: University of California Press, 1977), 250–76, for a fuller treatment; also see the brief assessment in T. C. Burgess, "Epideictic Literature," *Studies in Classical Philology* 3 (1902): 108–9 n. 1.

to be speakers" (1.13–17).⁵⁰ Beginning with simple exercises related to the memorization and recitation of chreia, the exercises became increasingly more complex, moving from simple elaboration and amplification, to narrative reconfiguration, to the writing of speech-in-character, and finally to the composition of narratives themselves. While the exercises were intended to help shape the future orator and lawyer, it was also apparent that such exercises would be of immense value to those writing history.⁵¹ Thus, Theon states,

> That these exercises are certainly beneficial also to those who take up the rhetorical craft is in no way obscure. For the one who has recited a narrative and a fable correctly and in a variety of ways will correctly compose both a history (ἱστορία) and what in speeches is properly called a statement-of-the-facts proper. For a history is nothing other than a collection of narratives (διηγήσεως) (1.25–30).... The so-called commonplace (κοινὸς τόπος) and the description (ἔκφρασις) have a benefit that is most obvious everywhere, since among the ancients all the historians have used the description extensively, and the rhetoricians the commonplace. The speech-in-character (προσωποποιΐ) is also an exercise not only for history writing, but for rhetoric. (1.43–47)

It is evident from these brief comments that for Theon, at least, the exercises would be beneficial not only to potential orators, but also to all those using rhetorical skill in composition and speech. Historians, in his view, were prime examples of writers whose craft would be enriched by training in the rhetorical exercises. Indeed, what Theon states specifically with regard to "speech-in-character" (the practice of composing speeches and placing them in the "mouths" of characters in one's composition) one might more generally apply to all the exercises: "[E]ven in daily life and conversations it is very beneficial" (1.47–48). Theon even suggests that the exercises involving the use of chreia can produce "virtuous character" (1.40–42),

---

50. Translation of Theon is taken from J. R. Butts, "The Progymnasmata of Theon: A New Text with Translation and Commentary" (Ph.D. diss., Claremont Graduate School, 1986). See the new translation by G. A. Kennedy, trans. and ed., *Progymnasmata: Greek Textbooks of Prose Composition and Rhetoric* (SBLWGRW 10; Atlanta: Society of Biblical Literature, 2003).

51. On the *progymnasmata*, see Penner, "Civilizing Discourse"; idem, "Reconfiguring the Rhetorical Study"; M. C. Parsons, "Luke and the *Progymnasmata*: A Preliminary Investigation into the Preliminary Exercises," in *Contextualizing Acts* (ed. Penner and Vander Stichele), 43–63; R. F. Hock, "Homer in Greco-Roman Education," in *Mimesis and Intertextuality in Antiquity and Christianity* (ed. D. R. MacDonald; Harrisburg, Pa.: Trinity Press International, 2001), 70–76; and R. Webb, "The *Progymnasmata* as Practice," in *Education in Greek and Roman Antiquity* (ed. Too), 289–316. For broader but relevant discussions of the pedagogical ethos of the Hellenistic period, see R. Cribiore, *Gymnastics of the Mind: Greek Education in Hellenistic and Roman Egypt* (Princeton: Princeton University Press, 2001), 221–30; and T. Morgan, *Literate Education in the Hellenistic and Roman Worlds* (Cambridge Classical Studies; Cambridge: Cambridge University Press, 1998).

since they require one to dwell on the words of the wise. These claims by Theon, no doubt a little rhetorical in their formulation, demonstrate the overall importance, in the view of ancient writers, of this program of study.[52]

Perhaps the locus of the Roman tradition is best reflected in the Roman orator, statesman, and philosopher, Cicero. Cicero's discussion of historiography is particularly important, since it establishes the clear connections between rhetorical training for oratory and the writing of history in the Roman period. This element is frequently downplayed by classicists and biblical scholars alike, but the connection is, by and large, acknowledged as a given.[53] Rhetoric as a discipline had already played a formal part in earlier historiography. Polybius, for instance, was heavily indebted to rhetorical training for major facets of his composition.[54] While scholars show little reticence in acknowledging this element more generally, Woodman's *Rhetoric in Classical Historiography* pushes the matter beyond simply the adornment of a narrative with features derived from rhetorical training to the more substantive role rhetorical training performs in influencing the very substructure of what modern scholars refer to as "history." Indeed, Cicero understood, perhaps even better than Theon, just how closely history and rhetoric were connected: "[A]s history, which bears witness to the passing of the ages, sheds light upon reality, gives life to recollection and guidance to human existence, and brings tidings of ancient days, whose voice, but the orator's,

---

52. Such exercises generated particular approaches to narratives and shaped patterns of thinking and composing. This is essentially the point of V. K. Robbins's description of a "rhetorical" culture as one wherein speakers and writers compose "both orally and scribally in a rhetorical manner" ("Progymnastic Rhetorical Composition and Pre-Gospel Tradition: A New Approach," in *Synoptic Gospels: Source Criticism and the New Literary Criticism* [ed. C. Focant; BETL 110; Leuven: Leuven University Press, 1993], 110). See further V. K. Robbins, "Writing as a Rhetorical Act in Plutarch and the Gospels," in *Persuasive Artistry: Studies in New Testament Rhetoric in Honor of George A. Kennedy* (ed. D. F. Watson; JSNTSup 50; Sheffield: Sheffield Academic Press, 1991), 145–49; and B. L. Reardon, *The Form of the Greek Romance* (Princeton: Princeton University Press, 1991), 86–88. The study by B. L. Mack and V. K. Robbins, *Patterns of Persuasion in the Gospels* (Sonoma, Calif.: Polebridge, 1989), effectively demonstrates the broader implications of this methodological starting point (see esp. 195–208, where they detail the relationship between the oratorical emphasis on the elaboration of the complete argument and narrative compositional techniques in the gospels). For further discussion of the intersection of history and rhetoric in the Roman system, see R. G. Hall, "Josephus' *Contra Apionem* and Historical Inquiry in the Roman Rhetorical Schools," in *Josephus'* Contra Apionem: *Studies in Its Character and Context* (ed. L. H. Feldman and J. R. Levison; AGJU 34; Leiden: Brill, 1996), 231–40. Burgess, "Epideictic Literature," 199–202, argues that it was the *progymnasmata* that helped bring historical writing into such close connection with rhetoric, especially epideictic oratory.

53. See Pelling, "Truth and Fiction," 51–52.

54. T. Wiedemann, "Rhetoric in Polybius," in *Purposes of History: Studies in Greek Historiography from the 4th to the 2nd Centuries B.C.* (ed. H. Verdin et al.; SH 30; Leuven: Orientaliste, 1990), 289–300. Thucydides himself was indebted to the Sophists in Athens for both the content and style of his speeches, tracing the lines back to classical rhetoric rather than Herodotean historical inquiry (see J. de Romilly, *The Great Sophists in Periclean Athens* [trans. J. Lloyd; New York: Oxford University Press, 1992], 90–91).

can entrust her to immortality?" (*De or.* 2.36; cf. *Leg.* 1.2.5).⁵⁵ Cicero was concerned with two basic questions: first, to which branch of rhetoric — epideictic, judicial, or deliberative — did history belong; second, how was one to understand history as a compositional narrative art? His most famous comment on historiography, worth citing here at length, comes through the mouth of Antonius in *De oratore*:

> [W]hat class of orator, and how great a master of language is qualified...to write history?...For history began as a mere compilation of annals, on which account, and in order to preserve the general traditions...each High Priest used to commit to writing all the events of his year of office....[A] similar style of writing has been adopted by many who, without any rhetorical ornament, have left behind them bare records of dates, personalities, places and events.... [O]ur own Cato, Pictor and Piso, who do not understand the adornment of composition...and, so long as their narrative is understood, regard conciseness as the historian's single merit...now wonder...if this subject has never yet been brilliantly treated in our language. For not one of our own folk seeks after eloquence, save with an eye to its display at the Bar and in public speaking, whereas in Greece the most eloquent were strangers to forensic advocacy, and applied themselves...particularly to writing history....Do you see how great a responsibility the orator has in historical writing?...For who does not know history's first law to be that an author must not dare [say anything false]? And its second that he must make bold to tell the whole truth? That there must be no suggestion of partiality anywhere in his writings? Nor of malice? This groundwork [*fundamenta*] of course is familiar to every one; the completed structure [*exaedificatio*] however rests upon the story and the diction. The nature of the subject needs chronological arrangement and geographical representation: and since, in reading of important affairs worth recording, the plans of campaign, the executive actions and the results are successively looked for, it calls also, as regards such plans, for some intimation of what the writer approves, and in the narrative of achievement, not only for a statement of what was done or said, but also of the manner of doing or saying it; and, in the estimate of consequences, for an exposition of all contributory causes, whether originating in accident, discretion or foolhardiness; and, as for the individual actors, besides an account of their exploits, it demands particulars of the lives and characters of such as are outstanding in renown and dignity. (2.51–63)

In this extensive quotation, several essential elements surface in the understanding of the historical task.⁵⁶ First, Cicero distinguishes between two

---

55. For precisely this reason Quintilian would later view it as a natural move for an orator, upon retirement from public life, either to interpret law, to compose a treatise on oratory, or to "bequeath the history of his own times for the delight of after ages" (*Inst.* 12.11.4).

56. For a fuller discussion, see Woodman, *Rhetoric in Classical Historiography*, 78–95; R. Mellor, *The Roman Historians* (New York: Routledge, 1999), 24–28; A. D. Leeman, *Orationis Ratio: The Stylistic Theories and Practice of the Roman Orators, Historians, and Philosophers* (Amsterdam: Hakkert, 1963), 1:170–80; R. W. Cape, "Persuasive History: Roman Rhetoric and Historiography," in *Roman Eloquence: Rhetoric in Society and Literature*

different activities: the keeping of annals and the writing of history proper. Historical composition is not the recording of mere facts, places, and dates, but demands elaboration and amplification of *fundamenta* or "groundwork."[57] Second, Cicero believes that this elaboration of the bare details will involve chronological arrangement and geographical descriptions, the relation of actions to results (with full descriptions of causes), the inclusion of expressions of approbation and disapproval in narrative commentary, the depiction of the contexts for actions and speeches, and the articulation of praise for distinctive individuals of the history.[58] Cicero's argument arises precisely from his view that all these features of the superstructure are the foundation of an orator's training. R. W. Cape aptly summarizes this connection: "If Cicero insists that the orator is best qualified to write history, it is because of the necessary similarity of function, which requires similarity of style.... The style is thus determined by the style best suited to arousing people to action."[59] As we shall see later in this chapter, the distinction between the fundamentals and the superstructure is not to be seen as trivial, like the distinction between facts and descriptive, poetic license.[60] Cicero has in mind that historical narrative will, just like oratorical compositions, provide a persuasive argument, and thus must consist of credible and plausible narration. Cicero understands that the "duty" of an orator is "to arouse a listless nation, and to curb its unbridled impetuosity. By one and the same power of eloquence the deceitful among mankind are brought to destruction, and the righteous to deliverance" (*De or.* 2.35). Those writing history, as we shall see, partake of this same "duty," and thus narratives in historical composition must be as persuasive as oratory. Truth, in this view, is not quite the same as in modern historiography:

> Historians trained by the Roman rhetoricians in the art of narrative would seek to discover plausible arguments to form and support their interpretations of historical events. They would invent characters and motives for the agents

---

(ed. W. J. Dominik; New York: Routledge, 1997), 212–28; Wiseman, "Practice and Theory"; and the extended treatment in L. H. Feldman, "Cicero's Conception of Historiography" (Ph.D. diss., Harvard University, 1951).

57. See B. W. Frier, *Libri Annales Pontificum Maximorum: The Origins of the Annalistic Tradition* (Rome: American Academy, 1979), 71–79.

58. Dionysius of Halicarnassus reflects very similar sentiments in both his history and rhetorical writings. As we will see in the second part of this discussion, Dionysius is even more explicit on how to elaborate the *fundamenta* in terms of narrative amplification (cf. *Ant. rom.* 11.1–5; *Thuc.* 5. See also the similar comments by Sempronius Asellio [ca. first cent. B.C.E.] in Aulus Gellius, *Attic Nights* 5.18.8–9; cf. Cicero, *Fam.* 5.12.5–6). See further K. S. Sacks, "Historiography in the Rhetorical Works of Dionysius of Halicarnassus," *Athenaeum* 61 (1983): 67, 74–76. On Dionysius's relationship to Cicero in terms of his comments on the annalists, see Frier, *Libri Annales*, 77–78.

59. Cape, "Persuasive History," 224.

60. Indeed, Antonius's discussion of writing history corresponds directly with Cicero's discussions of rhetorical *inventio* of narratives for oratorical speeches (Woodman, *Rhetoric in Classical Historiography*, 85–87).

in the events they narrate: they would omit anything extraneous or implausible; they would order events chronologically or not as most contributed to a plausible narrative; they would carefully develop suspense, construct conversations, insert intriguing turns of plot and play on the emotions of the reader in order to increase the plausibility of their accounts.[61]

In the process, the cardinal virtue here as elsewhere is not being partial or biased in the presentation. As we shall see shortly, this is as much a *topos* as it is a substantive criterion (i.e., one historian's bias is another's impartiality), but the principle remains clear: In order for history to be instructive and persuasive it must be presented plausibly, while bias and impartiality can only lead to the distortion of this narrative aim. For the Romans, as with the Greeks, plausibility in historical writing had to be achieved at all costs. As soon as the narrative appeared to lose this component, the value of the history itself was thought to be undermined.

This point brings us to the third important feature: For Cicero, history is closest to the epideictic branch of oratory.[62] This connection was widespread in antiquity, and historians from Polybius to Lucian to Cicero made a similar association.[63] Cicero makes this link explicit elsewhere: "History is nearly related to this style [epideictic]. It involves a narrative in an ornate style, with here and there a description of a country or a battle. It has also occasional harangues and speeches of exhortation" (*Or.* 66; cf. 37, 207). In a famous and oft-cited letter to Lucceius, Cicero asks his friend to "eulogize" him in a historical treatise (*Fam.* 5.12.3), even if the "canons of history" have to be discarded (i.e., that Lucceius will be partial to Cicero and his achievements). Such a flattering history will be done, in Cicero's view, precisely according to the criteria for amplification and elaboration he set out in *De oratore* (*Fam.* 5.12.4). Similarly, Cicero can portray the orator's turning to write history as follows: "[I]t seems to me that you owe this duty not merely to the desires of those who take pleasure in literature, but also to your country, in order that the land which you have saved you may also glorify" (*Leg.* 1.5). This is a remarkable passage insofar as the orator who saves Rome

---

61. Hall, "Josephus' *Contra Apionem*," 236. On the nature of "truth" in this framework, see Mellor, *Roman Historians*, 26–27.

62. There is some debate on this explicit connection. Woodman argues that Cicero presents historiography in two ways: as judicial and epideictic (*Rhetoric in Classical Historiography*, 95–98), suggesting that the lines between all three types of oratory are blurred (but that in the passage cited above Antonius clearly links historical topics with forensic rhetoric [*De or.* 2.66–67]). Cape argues for consistency here (i.e., not judicial in the proper sense) with Cicero's comments elsewhere linking historiography to epideictic ("Persuasive History," 221, 226–27 n. 29).

63. Woodman, *Rhetoric in Classical Historiography*, 41–45. Quintilian (*Inst.* 3.8.63), referring to Aristotle's comments in his *Rhetoric* (3.12), states that the "the demonstrative type of oratory was the best suited for writing and that the next best was forensic oratory." Thus, from early on there was an association of epideictic with written texts. See also Burgess, "Epideictic Literature," 92, 199–214.

through speeches of deliberative and forensic rhetoric may now also write an epideictic history and complete the task in writing (cf. Quintilian *Inst.* 10.1.31).

It is no surprise, then, that many historians of the Roman period viewed the writing of history as teaching virtue and good policy by examples. Of course, one should be careful not simply to assume that all aspects of historical composition were epideictic in focus. The writing of history was acknowledged to be a complex process, and the lines between epideictic and deliberative rhetoric were not hard and fast. As Quintilian states, "[P]anegyric is akin to deliberative oratory inasmuch as the same things are usually praised in the former as are advised in the latter" (*Inst.* 3.7.28; cf. Aristotle, *Rhet.* 1.9.35). Thus, for historians of the Roman period there was a sense that epideictic and deliberative oratory usually went hand in hand. From a historiographical standpoint, Dionysius confirms this two-pronged aspect when referring to the reading of a finely composed historical treatise that covers all the circumstances accompanying particular events:

> [B]esides their pleasure, they have this advantage, that in difficult times they render great service to their countries as the result of the experience thus acquired [from reading the text] and lead them as willing followers to that which is to their advantage, through the power of persuasion. For men most easily recognize the policies which either benefit or injure them when they perceive these illustrated by many examples; and those who advise them to make use of these are credited by them with prudence and great wisdom. (*Ant. rom.* 11.1.4–5; cf. Diodorus 1.2.2–8)

In light of this broader rhetorical ethos for ancient historical composition reflected above, it would seem unfair to draw a sharp distinction between the Greek and Roman tradition of historiography. The Greeks accented the deliberative aspect of historical writing — offering the context for making civic decisions — but also realized that good choices required motivation for adoption. While works with an overly epideictic focus were often understood to detract from the deliberative emphasis (hence Polybius's sometimes contradictory tendencies), the Greeks also clearly provided the impetus for viewing history as a collection of *exempla*.[64] Roman period writers such as Dionysius, Cicero, Livy, and Tacitus were in part developing the inherent tendencies of Greek historical writing when they composed with a view to the didactic function of examples (cf. Livy 1.10; Tacitus, *Hist.* 1.3).[65]

---

64. C. Skidmore, *Practical Ethics for Roman Gentlemen: The Work of Valerius Maximus* (Exeter: University of Exter Press, 1996), 11–12. Also see R. B. Rutherford, *The* Meditations *of Marcus Aurelius: A Study* (Oxford: Clarendon, 1989), 55–59.

65. Roman literature was overtly concerned with culling historical characters for examples. Quintilian sets forth two distinct types of literary approaches in this regard: "It has sometimes proved the more effective course to trace a man's life and deeds in due chronological order, praising his natural gifts as a child, then his progress at school, and finally the whole course of his life, words as well as deeds. At times on the other hand it is well to divide our praises, dealing

Thus, through history, ancient readers had modeled for them the ideal character of state and individual. Here, then, we are reminded of Aristotle's remarks noted earlier, in which he emphasizes the mimetic quality of particular narratives. While one must appreciate the significant differences between Aristotelian philosophical mimesis and the more overt moral/*exemplum* form it takes in Roman historiography, history was nonetheless mimetic in the Roman perspective, and ancient historians made every attempt to elaborate and amplify their *fundamenta* with just this purpose in mind.[66] At the same time, however, from within a rhetorically saturated culture, only a plausible narrative had such value, and thus the historian was implored to refrain from extreme and overt panegyric — wherein the details were not "objective" but determined by the bias of the historian — as this detracted from the profitability of the narrative. With an emphasis on plausibility, then, one could affirm the overall epideictic accent of historical

---

separately with the various virtues, fortitude, justice, self-control and the rest of them and to assign to each virtue the deed performed under its influence" (*Inst.* 3.7.15; cf.12.2.29–30). One observes here the typology for significant literary developments in the Roman period (both East and West). In the first type, the emphasis is on biographies of great men, such as Arrian's *History of Alexander*, Philostratus's *Life of Apollonius of Tyana*, and Mark's Gospel. More importantly, the Roman period attests to the genre of collected lives, such as one finds in Plutarch, Cornelius Nepos, Diogenes Laertius, or even the short, anonymous catalogue of women, *Tractatus De Mulieribus Claris In Bello* (for similar catalogues in antiquity, see D. Gera, *Warrior Women: The Anonymous* Tractatus De Mulieribus [MnSup 162; Leiden: Brill, 1997], 40–56). In the second type, the stress is on collecting various deeds and words under specific headings. Stobaeus's anthology is late (ca. fifth cent. C.E.), but essentially replicates one trajectory with the focus on significant sayings, akin to the collection of chreia and the *apophthegmata* (such as Plutarch arranged under sayings of Romans, Spartans, Spartan Women, and Kings and Commanders; cf. Skidmore, *Practical Ethics*, 35–42, who also details the earlier Hellenistic precedents, such as book 2 of Pseudo-Aristotle's *Economics*). If the gospel sayings source Q does exist, it is probably to be understood within this moral context of the *chreia:* similarly providing words and deeds for emulation. One of the more significant collections of the first century is the *Memorable Deeds and Sayings* of Valerius Maximus. Notable for this study is the emphasis Valerius places on historical examples as precedents (cf. Quintilian *Inst.* 12.4.1–2) and the way in which the deeds, if presented properly, can forcefully and vividly make the past visible before the reader in the present (5.4. ext. 1 [Skidmore, *Practical Ethics*, 84–85]).

66. W. S. Kurz ("Narrative Models in Luke-Acts," in *Greeks, Romans, and Christians: Essays in Honor of Abraham J. Malherbe* [ed. D. L. Balch et al.; Minneapolis: Fortress, 1990], 176–85), demonstrates the pervasive pattern of offering models for imitation in Hellenistic historical works. Here we also see the nexus of particular literary features of ancient historiography: the imitation of literary patterns from past epic and history and the recurring patterns of behaviors and governments. G. W. Trompf, *The Idea of Historical Recurrence in Western Thought: From Antiquity to the Reformation* (Berkeley: University of California Press, 1979), has provided an extensive treatment of the reoccurrence motif in Polybius, Luke, and later historians. His summary with respect to Polybius illuminates the same emphasis one finds elsewhere: "While recognizing his interest in the considerable variety of human experiences, one must return again and again to his presuppositions about the general face of events, about types of dramatic situations, and about governing principles.... [Polybius] had a feeling for incidents possessing universal and paradigmatic qualities (and thus having affinities with the rhetorician's stock of pertinent examples). He did not write only to edify, but to affirm something of practical importance about the nature of history" (106).

composition while asserting that particular narratives in the treatise may require deliberative and forensic focus.[67]

Fundamentally, then, the Romans continued the Greek tradition of writing history with an intentional argumentative focus; history's purpose was beyond merely providing a succession of details, but was, more so, to establish an interpretive superstructure for the substrata of information. The Romans, moreover, deliberately melded rhetorical training and oratorical practice with the writing of history, something that the Greeks may have done implicitly but did not develop as systematically as one finds (at least theoretically articulated) in a writer like Cicero.[68] Furthermore, the Romans took the more subtle form of Greek panegyric and developed fuller and more expressive epideictic styles of historical composition, viewing praise and blame as contributing to the utility of narratives. Whether glorifying Rome or praising individual words and deeds, history as both a moral medium and a means of glorification and honor were emphasized. For the Romans, history was above all, about composing plausible and credible narratives that would persuade the reader, bolstering the utility of such compositions. This is precisely Polybius's concern as well, and thus Romans such as Cicero and Hellenistic writers such as Lucian and Dionysius were essentially perpetuating a long-standing historiographical ethos, which is best thought of as a broadly shared discursive practice based, at least in part, on patterns of *paideia* in the ancient world.

---

67. This is one of the reasons that Dionysius, a historian with clear epideictic emphases (D. L. Balch, "Two Apologetic Encomia: Dionysius on Rome and Josephus on the Jews," *JSJ* 13 [1982]: 107–14), nonetheless faults Thucydides for the use of demonstrative speeches (*Thuc.* 16–18). When a narrative becomes implausible, such as using the wrong type of speech (i.e., one not suited to the occasion or the person) in an assembly, then the history's function is undermined. Certain occasions naturally demand forensic and deliberative speeches, according to Dionysius, but this does not necessarily discourage the larger epideictic aims of history (contrary to K. S. Sacks, "Rhetoric and Speeches in Hellenistic Historiography," *Athenaeum* 64 [1986]: 390–93). Likewise, Diodorus warns against history becoming simply "an appendage of oratory," as is the case with many who look for every opportunity to wax their demonstrative skills (20.1.2). Diodorus is the most clear on this point: When history is no longer a simple narrative but overly wordy, it loses its main foci of being both pleasing and clear (as in providing a perceptible line of interpretive development; 20.1.5). Nevertheless, demonstrative speeches (when the situation requires a public address — "whoever does not boldly enter the contest of words would himself be blameworthy"; 20.2.2) can be included since "when the subject matter is great and glorious [one should not allow] the language to appear inferior to the deeds" (20.2.2).

68. In response to Woodman, D. S. Potter, *Literary Texts and the Roman Historian* (New York: Routledge, 1999), 138, seems correct in asserting that the *narratio* of oratory and the *narratio* of history were distinguishable for Cicero (although in rhetorical treatises the difference was attributed to length) and that Cicero, in principle at least, did make a distinction between the goals of rhetorical composition and history. History always aims at the truth (in agreement with Polybius, Dionysius, and Lucian), while oratory's aim may be truth or lies, depending on the needs of the situation (cf. Quintilian *Inst.* 2.17.19–20, 26–29; 3.8.63). Granting this framework, however, one must be careful to state that "truth" in history is something different to these writers than "historical fact" proper and that rhetoric and history were intricately linked together in practice.

Hellenistic Environment

Having detailed in the preceding section some of the broader cultural connections between the themes raised in Aristotle's *Poetics,* Greek historiography, and Roman historical writing, frequently perceived as the "degenerate" cousin to Greek practice, I now turn to the literary and rhetorical processes of the wider cultural milieu of the Hellenistic world. In this section I intentionally use a broadly conceived notion of "Hellenistic," focusing particularly on the syncretistic ethos perpetuated in that context. For a writer such as Luke, for instance, the compositional processes that influenced him were in some respects a result of various worlds and discourses already reconfigured in the Hellenistic sphere. Neither purely Greek nor Roman, these trajectories intermixed and intermingled in the environment created and sustained by Greek imperial expansion that persisted well after the Romans conquered the remnants of Alexander's empire. "Hellenistic" in this sense is a relative time period, but even more important it represents a conceptual and discursive environment that has ancillary roots beyond the exact chronological time frame traditionally designated.

Turning to this environment, then, one of the more important aspects that arises is the increasing interest in miracles and supernatural phenomena. Both Thucydides and Polybius (Lucian later articulates this tradition more clearly) eschew the addition of supernatural features to a narrative. Polybius does admit the alluring nature of "sensational" events, but argues that they are only appealing at first glance and certainly do not have an enduring influence (15.36.1–7). Rather, history should focus on that which is "natural or generally happen[s] in the world" (15.36.8). In an attack on dramatic accounts of Hannibal's crossing of the Alps, Polybius argues that those writers who utilize an epiphany to explain how Hannibal managed to find his way undermine the prudence and capability of this great leader (3.47.6–48.12). Polybius states that "they get into the same difficulties as tragic dramatists, all of whom, to bring their dramas to a close, require a *deus ex machina,* as the data they choose on which to found their plots are false and contrary to reasonable probability" (3.48.8–9).[69] Epic narratives contained such types of events, which was fine for epic,[70] but when these

---

69. By contrast, Polybius had been to the Alps himself (i.e., knows the lay of the land) and had inquired of the men with Hannibal during the crossing (i.e., talked with eyewitnesses), so that he knows that with proper planning and procedure, accompanied with the fact that there are villages existing in the Alps (i.e., it is not as remote as some historians would make it out to be), that the crossing, although difficult and admirable, is entirely possible by human effort (3.48.10–12).

70. Much of epic was viewed by ancient writers as historical, and there was in epic a stress on "realism" and historical chronology as a result. See F. Graf, *Greek Mythology: An Introduction* (trans. T. Marier; Baltimore: Johns Hopkins University Press, 1993), 140–41. Thus, Asclepiades, under the category of "true history," includes narratives about gods and heroes of the past, but excludes genealogical narratives (e.g., Hesiod), which are grouped under "false history" (Sextus Empiricus, *Adv. Gram.* 1.253). Similarly, Josephus will narrate miraculous events

elements entered the nondistant past they were often labeled as *plasmata* (fiction) precisely because they narrated episodes that stood contrary to general human experience. Roman writers could clearly call for dramatic elements and surprising turns in plot, but these are different from a tragic *deus ex machina* that interrupts the plot itself. Only those elements that contributed to a plausible narrative would support the persuasive aims of historical composition. This emphasis, however, would seem to leave in questionable status numerous narratives such as Luke-Acts, Philostratus's *Apollonius of Tyana*, and 2 Maccabees, which deal precisely with the intervention of transcendent elements in ordinary human affairs.[71]

From early on, paradoxography and history were intricately connected, as Herodotus's wide-ranging interests in geography and tales of distant lands and peoples frequently included details that more serious-minded historians rejected as incompatible with the true aims of historical composition. Strabo criticized Herodotus for including elements purely to "amaze" and to give "pleasure" to his readers (2.6.3), and, in objecting to the inclusion of epic and epic-like events (i.e., incredible events) in Herodotus's history, he delineates exactly what he has in mind by suggesting that Homer and Hesiod are more believable than Herodotus. Cicero provides a similar assessment of Herodotus: "[I]n history the standard by which everything is judged is the truth, while in poetry it is generally the pleasure one gives; however, in the works of Herodotus, the Father of History...one finds innumerable fabulous tales [*fabulae*]" (*Leg.* 1.1.5). Thus, one of the fundamental problems for historiography was the position one took vis-à-vis the inclusion of *fabulae*, a problem most pronounced in the empirical tradition of the skeptics.

In this empirical tradition, Sextus Empiricus records the views of Asclepiades (of Myrleia; ca. first cent. B.C.E.) on history. Asclepiades attempts to demonstrate that history as conceived by the older school of grammarians is not empirically verifiable and hence untrue, and that historical composition is not a technical art. Dividing the "subjects of history" into three categories (1.252) — true (factual narratives about real people in history), false (fictions, legends, myths), and as if true (comedy and mimes) — he especially attacks legends/myths *(mythos):* "[L]egend is the narrating of events which have never happened and are false [*pseudos*], like the story that the species of venomous spiders and snakes were born alive from the blood

---

so long as they are a part of biblical epic, but once he turns to the more recent (nonbiblical) period, the explicitly miraculous (although not always the incredible) is absent (similarly Livy).

71. L. C. A. Alexander, "Fact, Fiction, and the Genre of Acts," *NTS* 44 (1998): 380–99, aptly depicts the problem with respect to Acts. The miracles would certainly have been cause for its dismissal as overpleasing *plasmata* by a writer such as Lucian (indeed, his *True Story* makes fun of just such compositions). Yet, as Alexander maintains, Luke seems committed to the "broadly factual status of his narrative" (399).

of the Titans" (Sextus Empiricus, *Adv. Gram.* 1.263–64).[72] He goes on to suggest, with reference to the epic past, that in order to establish which historian is telling the truth with respect to variant narratives (e.g., the fate of Odysseus) one must investigate the facts, but this is difficult, since when "all relate what is improbable and false no opening is given for a technical criterion" (1.267–68).[73] Perhaps the harshest critic is Lucian, who, in *A True Story*, sets out to parody "histories" that include eyewitness accounts

---

72. Although often interpreted by scholars to exclude fiction wholesale from historical writings, the point rather seems to be similar to Cicero's above: "True" history has a basis in *fundamenta* (i.e., real people, places, and events), whereas comedy fabricates the *fundamenta*. Both have verisimilitude, but the latter has no basis in historical events at all (cf. 1.263–65). Quintilian (*Inst.* 2.4.2–3) uses a similar typology to break down the types of narratives (fictitious, realistic, and historical), demonstrating that there is a broader Greco-Roman convention being employed in these and similar discussions. In Quintilian, the fictitious deals with miraculous events and thus has no basis in reality (untrue) and correlates with the narratives of tragedy. The realistic is "like true" (i.e., has verisimilitude) but is based on fictitious *fundamenta* (as in comedy). The third, historical, is based on actual people and real deeds ("what Alcibiades said and did"). The latter does not necessarily exclude, however, the formulation of plausible as opposed to factual narratives, providing that the *fundamenta* are actual (cf. Cicero, *Inv.* 1.27; *fabula* [fictitious and no verisimilitude], *historia* [actual occurrences beyond the recollection of those in the present], and *argumentum* [fictitious but plausible]). Aristotle favors the "as if true" over the "true" because the former, he believes, has a greater mimetic value. Yet, as historiography developed, it became clear that "true" could have just as much value as "as if true" if, as Cicero states, a suitable superstructure were provided (but S. Byrskog, *Story as History — History as Story: The Gospel Tradition in the Context of Ancient Oral History* [WUNT 123; Tübingen: Mohr Siebeck, 2000], 205–13, argues against this position, although he does perceive the tension). See Wiseman, "Lying Historians," 129–30, who brings in the similar paradigms of Cicero (*Inv.* 1.27) and the *Rhetorica ad Herennium* (1.13). Wiseman designates the genre of the ancient novel as belonging to the category "as if true," so that the distinction between history and novel is based on whether the story is about real people, places, and events, or not (also see R. Reitzenstein, *Hellenistische Wundererzählungen* [2d ed.; Darmstadt: Wissenschaftliche Buchgesellschaft, 1963], 90–97; and Cancik, *Mythische und historische Wahrheit*, 28–32). In this sense, then, the *Protoevangelium* is a history (because it deals with a perceived "historical" personage, Mary), while the story about the star-crossed lovers Daphnis and Chloe is a novel because these characters are fictitious (see Thomas, *Acts of Peter*, 101–3). This positioning represents an extreme example, of course, but it is herein that the separation between history and novel becomes complicated and where distinctions, as much as we like them, may create artificial and unnecessary divisions. In antiquity we actually observe a wide range in perception of what is plausible, factual, and fictional.

73. Asclepiades' larger point with respect to the question of historical accuracy is interesting. He suggests that when one admits that historians record both legend (false) and fiction (as if true) with history (factually true), then it becomes impossible to separate out the true from the false. He here reflects the view of Cicero and Dionysius that the mere chronicling of data such as "Plato the philosopher was first called Aristocles and that, when a youth, he had an ear pierced and wore an earring" is "perfectly useless" (*Adv. Gram.* 1.258). Yet the elaboration of the bare details frequently results in fiction and competing versions of events. Asclepiades intends to undermine history as a *techne* of the grammarians, and therefore is overly "skeptical" of the discipline (so his rhetorical stance is critical to keep in mind in interpreting his comments). The empiricists (associated with ancient medical practice) placed a high value on *autopsia* (personal investigation) and promoted the thorough interrogation of "reports" (*historia*), with an emphasis on the general reliability of the source and its congruence with similar reports (R. J. Hankinson, *The Sceptics* [New York: Routledge, 1995], 227–28). Thus, *autopsia* and *historia*, two critical terms for historiography, are also grounded in ancient empiricist interests such as medicine (see R. Thomas, *Herodotus in Context: Ethnography, Science, and the Art of Persuasion* [Cambridge: Cambridge University Press, 2000], 161–212). While the roots

of marvelous tales, peoples, and sites: "I shall at least be truthful in saying that I am a liar.... [B]e it understood, then, that I am writing about things which I have neither seen, nor had to do with, nor learned from others — which, in fact, do not exist at all and, in the nature of things, cannot exist" (*Ver. hist.* 1.4).[74] For Lucian, then, there is a definite limit on what a history should include, and things that "cannot exist" are certainly to be excluded.

Despite these negative assessments of the use of fabulous and incredible mythic materials, in the Hellenistic period there was widespread interest in wonders, marvels, and miraculous tales. Early paradoxographers such as Callimachus (third cent. B.C.E.), the famous librarian of Alexandria, culled marvelous tales and curious details and facts from the wide array of literature available to him, publishing them as a compendium of curiosities.[75] These collections continued well into the later Roman period. Phlegon of Tralles's (second cent. C.E.) surviving *Book of Marvels* is a prime example, providing everything from longer tales of a dead girl who comes to life only to carry on an affair with a guest in her parents' home to shorter stories of men and homosexuals giving birth. There is also a significant emphasis on oracles, and several are quoted at length. Some of the stories are more credible than others (unearthing withered corpses as opposed to the capturing of Hippocentaurs), but the overall effect of pleasure and entertainment is evident throughout.[76] From this tradition of collecting curious and incredible stories, one finds literature that seeks to combine this interest with tales of "personal" journeys and/or geographical descriptions. In the case of the former, the later Roman period attests to numerous accounts of

---

in the Ionian scientific tradition may be the same, the development of the rhetorical and practical use of these terms is different in historiography and empiricism. At this juncture L. C. A. Alexander's work on the Lukan prefaces (*The Preface to Luke's Gospel: Literary Convention and Social Context in Luke 1.1–4 and Acts 1.1* [SNTSMS 78; Cambridge: Cambridge University Press, 1993]) should be challenged. Despite the similarity in language, the function of the language differs between historiography and the scientific manuals (see further Sterling, *Historiography and Self-definition*, 340–41; as well as D. E. Aune, "Luke 1:1–4: Historical or Scientific Prooimion?" in *Paul, Luke, and the Graeco-Roman World: Essays in Honour of Alexander J. M. Wedderburn* [ed. A. Christophersen et al.; JSNTSup 217; Sheffield: Sheffield Academic Press, 2003], 138–48; and Byrskog, *Story as History*, 48–65, who delineates the more traditional understanding of the role of inquiry in ancient historiographical theory).

74. On the complex levels of the parody, see M. Fusillo, "The Mirror of the Moon: Lucian's *A True Story* — From Satire to Utopia," in *Oxford Readings in the Greek Novel* (ed. S. Swain; New York: Oxford University Press, 1999), 351–81.

75. R. Blum, *Kallimachos: The Alexandrian Library and the Origins of Bibliography* (Madison: University of Wisconsin Press, 1991), 134–35. On the genre as a whole, see W. Hansen, *Phelgon of Tralles' Book of Marvels* (Exeter: University of Exeter Press, 1996), 2–11; and J. Romm, *The Edges of the Earth in Ancient Thought* (Princeton: Princeton University Press, 1992), 82–120.

76. Although of a very different sort, one might also include the inscription of the Lindos Chronicle, which lists a series of epiphanic events related to the city, temple, and island (Doran, *Temple Propaganda*, 103–4). Along these same lines, one might compare the various collections of miracle inscriptions, such as those found at Epidauros and Lebena (L. R. LiDonnici, *The Epidaurian Miracle Inscriptions: Text, Translation, and Commentary* [SBLTT 36; Atlanta: Scholars Press, 1995], 40–49).

fantastic personal excursions, the very kind that Lucian pokes fun at in *A True Story*.[77] In periegetic or travel texts like Pausanius's (second cent. C.E.) guide to Greece, one also finds description mixed with commentary from a wide array of sources — an intercalation of myth and history, etiological legend and fact. The first-century writer Pomponius of Mela offers a similar mixture of mythology and geography in his *Description of the World*.[78]

Overall, such texts — travelogues, itineraries, *periploi*/sea-voyage narratives — emphasized the benefit of knowledge and the pleasure of entertainment in remarkably similar ways to historical composition. Moreover, several significant developments emerged in the literary environment out of which these writings sprung. First, because many of these texts contained excerpted selections from histories and epics, hard and fast lines between genres began to fade as a result. New genres were created (travelogues, personal journeys) while, at the same time, older genres were transformed, blurring the lines between what could and could not exist. The book of Acts represents a prime example of the type of product created in this environment. While it has numerous explicit features of a history, it also has strong affinities with the novelistic tradition.[79] Sea voyages are combined with personal journeys and itineraries, which are conjoined with an emphasis on geography and description. The critical element, of course, is its miraculous and marvelous content. Acts does not occupy a peculiar place here, however, as it offers precisely the same kind of admixture of materials one finds in Philostratus's *Apollonius of Tyana*.[80] Second, attempts by writers like Lucian to keep *mythoi* out of serious works on history were undermined by the popular literature that combined interest in foreign lands and waters with tales of heroes and gods, marvels and wonders, and curious natural phenomena. Of course, all these elements go back to the "father of history" himself, Herodotus, and thus we should remember that whatever literary developments may have been reflected (and disdained) later existed *in nuce* from the beginning. Third, the increasing interest in the marvelous

---

77. See Romm, *Edges of the Earth*, 202–14; and J. J. Winkler, *Auctor and Actor: A Narratological Reading of Apuleius's* The Golden Ass (Berkeley: University of California Press, 1985), 257–73.

78. F. E. Romer, *Pomponius Mela's Description of the World* (Ann Arbor: University of Michigan Press, 1998), 22–24.

79. See R. I. Pervo, *Profit with Delight: The Literary Genre of the Acts of the Apostles* (Philadelphia: Fortress, 1987).

80. The biography of the famous prophet-sage Apollonius of Tyana provides an important parallel to Acts here, as it combines these various features even more explicitly: journey to a foreign land, description, quasi-travelogue elements, and wonders and marvels (G. Anderson, *Philostratus: Biography and Belles Lettres in the Third Century* A.D. [London: Croom & Helm, 1986], 199–26). All of these components are packaged in a purported historical-biographical framework, making the separation of fact and fiction difficult (see E. Koskenniemi, *Apollonios von Tyana in der neutestamentlichen Exegese* [WUNT 2.61; Tübingen: Mohr Siebeck, 1994], 188; G. Petzke, *Die Traditionen über Apollonius von Tyana und das Neue Testament* [SCHNT 1; Leiden: Brill, 1970], 156–57; and E. L. Bowie, "Apollonius of Tyana: Tradition and Reality," *ANRW* 2.16.2 [1978]: 1652–99).

and miraculous needs to be viewed as a combined social, cultural, and literary phenomenon. Too frequently scholars will analyze religious facets such as the divinization of the emperor, the development of *theios anēr* interests, wonder-working prophets, Christian and pagan miraculous accounts, the spread of cults and societies, and similar features apart from their larger literary and cultural milieu. Yet it is precisely this environment of intermingling that provides a context for the type of history that could elide so easily the distinction between fact and fiction. Further, despite the claims of certain intellectuals in antiquity, many ancient readers found the histories containing miraculous accounts quite credible.[81] Lastly, the line of literary development from Herodotus to the travelogue of Pausanius demonstrates the close relationship from the very beginning between what would become known as the "ancient novel" and history. This line also illustrates the lasting problem of genre classification for many ancient texts, especially as significant *topoi* and methods of composition cannot be relegated to specific types of literature.[82]

In short, then, one major feature of the Hellenistic and Roman period is the melding of literary types. Biography had increasingly focused attention on praising or denigrating particular individuals, often becoming, through the elaboration of historical details and the utilization of stock *topoi* of characterization, a tool of propaganda and polemic.[83] At the same time, the line between history, encomium, and biography was becoming difficult to establish firmly.[84] Thus, the particular interests, emphases, and rules of one

---

81. The nature of the intended audience is a problem. The gulf between popular religion and the intellectual elite in antiquity can sometimes support the negative view of wonder-literature frequently taken by modern scholars. Yet, as Acts itself suggests, the audience of such texts could vary considerably, suggesting increasing diversity in the reception of the text. See R. MacMullen, *Paganism in the Roman Empire* (New Haven: Yale University Press, 1981), 67–73.

82. See further Penner, "Reconfiguring the Rhetorical Study."

83. P. Cox, *Biography in Late Antiquity: A Quest for the Holy Man* (The Transformation of the Classical Heritage 5; Berkeley: University of California Press, 1983), 15–16; C. H. Talbert, "Biographies of Philosophers and Rulers as Instruments of Religious Propaganda in Mediterranean Antiquity," ANRW 2.16.2 (1978): 1619–51; T. Barton, "The *Inventio* of Nero: Suetonius," in *Reflections of Nero* (ed. J. Elsner and J. Masters; Chapel Hill: University of North Carolina Press, 1994), 48–63; and E. M. Jenkinson, "*Genus scripturae leve*: Cornelius Nepos and Biography at Rome," ANRW 1.3 (1973): 705–8.

84. Feldman, *Josephus's Interpretation*, 7. An excellent example of this phenomenon is Curtius Rufus's *History of Alexander the Great*, which scholars variously regard as biography or history (see J. E. Atkinson, "Q. Curtius Rufus' 'Historiae Alexandri Magni,'" ANRW 2.34.4 [1991]: 3456–57). This disagreement exists precisely because the work mixes the two genres. Also see Reardon, *Form of the Greek Romance*, 141–48. Some scholars point to Plutarch's famous line in *Alexander* (1.2) — "It is not Histories that I am writing, but Lives" — to demonstrate a conscious delineation between the various genres. Plutarch, however, makes it clear that his distinction is not between biography and history (indeed, elsewhere he refers to the *Lives* as "history" [cf. *Nicias* 1.5]), but between the narrative of individuals' deeds (history/biography) and the representation of their inner characters (which is Plutarch's explicit task in the *Lives*). See further A. Wardman, *Plutarch's Lives* (Berkeley: University of California Press, 1974), 2–10. On the complexity of separating these two genres in ancient writings, see Marincola, "Genre, Convention," 318–20; and esp. D. L. Balch, "ΜΕΤΑΒΟΛΗ ΠΟΛΙΤΕΙΩΝ. Jesus as

type of genre were easily adapted to another. History, for instance, became more encomiastic, apologetic, and polemical the more the lines between biography and history proper were difficult to draw. Xenophon is an early but interesting example here, as he wrote in a variety of literary genres. His *Hellenica* is intended as a continuation of Thucydides' great history, but with an even greater moralistic framework and dramatic style.[85] He also wrote the *Anabasis,* a historical work focusing on the rebellion of Cyrus against Athenian rule. In the latter, there are both overt apologetic and didactic interests combined with a dramatic style of writing. This fluid literary environment naturally provides the stimulus for Xenophon's biography of Cyrus the Great, the *Cyropaedia*. This text, sometimes considered to be a forerunner to the novel, is largely a fictional account based on historical personages, and yet it purports to be a historical narrative. For J. Tatum, it is precisely the "generic" flexibility of prose writing in the ancient world that allows Xenophon to move so easily between history and fiction.[86] Xenophon thus typifies the difficulty in discerning when the lines between history and novel have been crossed.

The complexity of the problem is especially clear with respect to the romance genre in antiquity. Generally speaking, modern scholars use the term "novel" to characterize narratives of fiction in the ancient world, "history" to designate narratives of fact. Yet it is evident from the foregoing discussion that such hard and fast distinctions are difficult to make. One must take into consideration that certain authors attempted to base their novels in historical events and construct rhetorically powerful yet plausible narratives. For instance, while most scholars have no difficulty viewing 1 Maccabees as a history in the Polybian and Thucydidean sense, 2 Maccabees has posed more of a problem. Often the terms "novelistic history" or "popular history" are used to describe a work such as 2 Maccabees, but L. M. Wills has recently argued that it, alongside 3 Maccabees, is better viewed as a historical novel.[87] Other scholars, such as Doran, rigorously defend its genre classification as "history," suggesting that the writer's use of the *topos* of epiphanic defense of a city by the patron deity cannot exclude it from consideration as a historical account.[88] For Wills, 2 Maccabees draws upon historical personages and events, but has an overarching fictive framework, while for Doran the treatise, while obviously involving some dramatic and

---

Founder of the Church in Luke-Acts: Form and Function," in *Contextualizing Acts* [ed. Penner and Vander Stichele], 139–88).

85. V. Gray, *The Character of Xenophon's* Hellenica (Baltimore: Johns Hopkins University Press, 1989), 154–75. Also see E. Lévy, "L'Art de la Déformation Historique dans les *Helléniques* de Xénophon," in *Purposes of History* (ed. Verdin et al.), 125–57.

86. J. Tatum, *Xenophon's Imperial Fiction: On the Education of Cyrus* (Princeton: Princeton University Press, 1989), 57; and Pelling, "Epilogue," 331.

87. L. Wills, *The Jewish Novel in the Ancient World* (Ithaca: Cornell University Press, 1995), 185, 193–201.

88. Doran, "2 Maccabees," 112–14; and idem, *Temple Propaganda,* 103–4.

tragically narrated events, is no less historical for all of that.[89] The writer of 2 Maccabees leaves no question as to the generic framework in which he intends the text to be read, as the prologue (2:19–32) to the work uses regular historiographical formulae and *topoi*. The work is an epitome of a longer, more detailed historical account that the writer of 2 Maccabees presents in an adorned and stylized manner for the benefit of the reader.[90]

This problem with the classification of 2 Maccabees persists throughout the modern attempts to categorize the literature of antiquity. Because of particular dramatic interests, Caesar's crossing of the Rubicon goes from barely notable in his own account to a full-blown epiphanic event in Suetonius, with various stages of dramatic development in between.[91] Here we have a relatively assured historical event that is elaborated and adorned in its reiteration. On the other hand, we also have a romance like Heliodorus's *Ethiopica*, a novel with a fictional setting and characters, yet undeniably associated with historical events.[92] Further, just as Xenophon had used a historical personage for his novelistic piece on Cyrus, so early fictional works such as the Ninus fragment and the *Alexander Romance* are based on historically famous individuals and events (cf. the accounts of Dictys and Dares on the fall of Troy).[93] The fact that the emphasis of rhetoric was on *narratio*, and since this was taken up by history, biography, romance, and all forms of prose writing, it meant that similar methods would be utilized in each. Thus, we find in both romance and history the use of plausible narration, geographical digression, and, most important, vivid description *(ekphrasis)*, combined in ways that make it often difficult and problematic to differentiate the genres in the Hellenistic and later Roman period.[94] While one

---

89. Doran, *Temple Propaganda*, 97.
90. On the critical nature of the prologue for determining the intended genre, see D. Earl, "Prologue-form in Ancient Historiography," *ANRW* 1.2 (1972): 842–56. Doran argues that the reference to "adornment" in 2:29 is not intended to signal elaboration of chronological details (*Temple Propaganda*, 81). The emphasis on "pleasing" the reader (2:25; 15:39) with the style of the story would suggest that the writer has not simply epitomized Jason of Cyrene's account but has in fact elaborated upon the narrative elements. It is tempting to view the adornment as consisting of the addition of both the dramatic and miraculous elements to the narrative. See Cancik, *Mythische und historische Wahrheit*, 110–26, esp. 125–26, where he compares what the writer of 2 Maccabees has done with the elaboration of the *fundamenta* to that notion put forth by Cicero.
91. T. P. Wiseman, "Crossing the Rubicon," in *Roman Drama and Roman History* (Exeter: University of Exeter Press, 1998), 60–63.
92. G. Anderson, *Ancient Fiction: The Novel in the Graeco-Roman World* (London: Croom & Helm, 1984), 88–105. See also the following treatments of Heliodorus and Chariton: J. R. Morgan, "History, Romance, and Realism in the *Aithiopika of Heliodoros*," *CA* 1 (1982): 221–65; R. Hunter, "History and Historicity in the Romance of Chariton," *ANRW* 2.34.2 (1993): 1055–86; and S. Swain, *Hellenism and Empire: Language, Classicism, and Power in the Greek World*, A.D. *50–250* (New York: Oxford University Press, 1996), 109–13.
93. This recognition gave impetus to M. Braun's theory, *History and Romance in Greco-Oriental Literature* (Oxford: Basil Blackwell, 1938), 89, that novels are descendents of "corrupt" forms of historiography (written by so-called romantic historians such as Ctesias).
94. Reardon, *Form of the Greek Romance*, 93–95, 141–48.

might be able to set Arrian apart from the tradition of the *Alexander Romance*, many ancient texts occupy a middle ground, problematizing precise classification as a result. And while compositions such as 2 Maccabees and Luke-Acts are intentionally classified as history by their authors, modern scholars have sometimes challenged this association based largely on the notion that generic differentiation between history and romance is possible based on content and function.[95] Yet romance as much as history was written for profit as well as for pleasure,[96] and both frequently have a historical *fundamentum*. The line between historical novel and novelistic history is much more porous than we might like to admit, and this recognition should give one pause when reflecting on appropriate methodologies for distinguishing various modes of prose writing in antiquity.

The problems with genre definition are amply illustrated by the category of "apologetic historiography" in the Hellenistic period. As a result of the melding of various forms of prose writing—history, novel, and biography—an environment was cultivated in which the writing and rewriting of traditions was not only fostered but also encouraged. Much has been written on the nativistic revivals that flooded the Near East and Asia Minor after the conquest of Alexander, and the subsequent resurgence of local interests and traditions. G. E. Sterling has contributed substantially to the discussion of apologetic historiography by analyzing the way in which it took shape on the basis of the Herodotean ethnological precedent.[97] Apologetic history, in the sense used by Sterling, consists of indigenous interpretations and rehabilitations of local histories, traditions, and cultures through tendentious narratives related to the given group.[98] Sterling defines the project as "the story of a subgroup of people in an extended prose narrative written by a member of the group who follows the group's own traditions but Hellenizes them in an effort to establish the identity of the group within the

---

95. Thus, while Witherington argues for the linking of Luke-Acts with the texts of Thucydides and Polybius, most classicists who would consider the latter reliable sources of historical data would not classify Luke-Acts in the same manner. Rather, in line with Polybius's denigration of fabulous tales, scholars such as G. W. Bowersock (*Fiction as History: Nero to Julian* [Sather Classical Lectures 58; Berkeley: University of California Press, 1994], 123) and Potter (*Literary Texts*, 144–45) argue that early Christian narratives such as Luke-Acts are fiction in the form of history with an emphasis on verisimilitude, but with little or no historical value.

96. Xenophon's *Cyropaideia*, for instance, is as much a manual of instruction as it is a novel about Cyrus the Great, and the *Alexander Romance* typifies the use of biography as *exemplum*. This lack of explicit boundary undermines the attempt to distinguish history and romance on the basis of purpose. Sterling, for instance, argues that the work of Artapanus is romantic national history rather than a romance proper, because of its overarching narrative aim (*Historiography and Self-definition*, 186). Artapanus's work is a history because it recasts biblical historical epic. The fact that it is done creatively and artfully does not, despite the claim of many scholars, lead to a classification as a novel. Notice also that the historical reliability of the antecedent narrative is of little consequence for differentiating "history" and "romance."

97. Sterling, *Historiography and Self-definition*, 20–102.

98. On the creative side of the enterprise, see D. Mendels, "'Creative History' in the Hellenistic Near East in the Third and Second Centuries BCE: The Jewish Case," in *Identity, Religion, and Historiography*, 357–64.

setting of the larger world."⁹⁹ The narrative consists of bolstering a claim to antiquity and greatness of culture in ways that will be appreciated and acknowledged by nonnative outsiders. By recasting the native traditions in ways the larger Greco-Roman audience could value, apologetic historians were creating their own identity and place/space within the larger Hellenistic social, cultural, literary, and political landscape. Such histories were, of course, overtly encomiastic, and not infrequently filled with narrative inventions and stock *topoi*, all of which further reflect the obfuscation of genre boundaries in the Hellenistic period and afterward. One thinks, for example, of the Egyptian high priest Manetho's *Aigyptiaka,* written in the third century B.C.E., wherein native traditions are recast in terms that Greek readers would esteem. The text seems to be an apologetic for indigenous Egyptian traditions in the time of the Ptolemies, valuing native culture and religion over against the syncretism of the Greeks. Given Manetho's own place in the Ptolemaic kingdom, one also finds the subtle importation of current political and religious phenomena back into his reconstruction of the past.[100]

The Jewish tradition of this practice is extensive, ranging from historical treatments in the Hellenistic Jewish historians such as Demetrius, Eupolemus, and Josephus, to writers such as Artapanus and compositions such as *Jubilees*. Some of these texts provide a challenge to Sterling's more narrow definition of apologetic historiography and at the same time expand our understanding of creative historical writing. The central emphasis in Sterling's definition is on the word "hellenize," so that apologetic is narrowed to those texts that seek to reframe native traditions with a view to Hellenistic themes and emphases. Josephus's *Antiquities,* as Feldman has demonstrated more thoroughly than anyone, is a prime example of this.[101] Sterling quite rightly includes the *Antiquities* as one of the premier examples of the Jewish rewriting of traditional narratives within a Hellenistic mode. Yet the *Antiquities* contains not only rewritten biblical texts but also a narration of more recent Jewish history. While the latter portion is equally full of apologetic concerns, it does not meet the generic definition that Sterling sets forth (i.e., being a rewriting of native traditions), which leads to the unusual problem that the last third of the *Antiquities* challenges the coherence of Sterling's own generic classification. Moreover, the *Jewish War* has a strong apologetic interest as well, and the commonality between the *Jewish War* and *Antiquities* cannot be overstated. For all of this, the *Jewish War* does not constitute an "apologetic historical" work according to Sterling's definition.

---

99. Sterling, *Historiography and Self-definition,* 17.
100. See D. Mendels, "The Polemical Character of Manetho's *Aegyptiaca,*" in *Identity, Religion, and Historiography,* 139–57; and Sterling, *Historiography and Self-definition,* 117–35. For the similar approach in Philo of Byblos, see R. A. Oden, "Philo of Byblos and Hellenistic Historiography," *PEQ* 110 (1978): 115–26.
101. See the collection of Feldman's various essays on the Hellenistic portrayal of biblical characters in *Josephus's Interpretation,* and *Studies in Josephus' Rewritten Bible* (JSJSup 58; Leiden: Brill, 1998). Also see Attridge, *Interpretation of Biblical History,* 109–44.

The problem becomes even greater when one looks at *Jubilees,* where a native tradition is also recast. While one is struck by just how similar the writer's purpose is to the rewriting of the biblical tradition that one finds in Josephus, there is no special emphasis in *Jubilees* on glorifying the traditions of Judaism for a Greco-Roman audience by using the *topoi* of the Hellenistic literary and cultural environment. Rather, there is a strong tendentious recasting of the narrative to further the particular moral, religious, and political aims of the writer.[102] Aside from the lack of the Hellenistic *Tendenz,* however, *Jubilees* evinces clear connections to the apologetic concern for rewriting past narratives.

Notwithstanding the caveats noted above, Sterling is quite right to isolate apologetic historiography as one of the central elements in Jewish historical composition of the Hellenistic period and later. Yet, by defining the particular genre so narrowly, he excludes a vast amount of narrative composition in this same time period that clearly ought to be aligned with this tradition, despite lacking some of the formal features he has detailed.[103] Moreover, Sterling's definition and elaboration of the Jewish tradition excludes the one work he desires to associate with this tradition: Luke-Acts. Josephus's rewriting of the biblical tradition is very different from what we find in Luke-Acts, which is much closer to what Josephus attempts to do in his treatment of "recent history" (i.e., the Jewish war). Luke has Hellenistic themes and emphases, but rather than rewriting native tradition, he places his narrative within the broad framework of biblical epic, utilizing *topoi* drawn from the tradition as a means to characterize persons and to elaborate, both explicitly and implicitly, the *fundamenta*. In sum, Luke is doing something very different than Josephus: Josephus hellenizes ancient history, whereas Luke biblicizes recent history. Sterling has, in essence, identified one particular strand of apologetic historiography: that which seeks to promote the reconfiguring of Jewish tradition and identity in terms that appeal to the larger values and outlook of the Hellenistic world. While he accounts for a significant trajectory of Jewish retelling of biblical narrative, his analysis needs to be refined in two ways. First, Sterling leaves the impression that it is simply the recasting of biblical narrative that lends itself to being apologetic in character. Yet Josephus's narrative of the Jewish war is every bit if not more apologetic than the repetition of the biblical text in the *Antiquities*.[104] Moreover, the reconfiguring of nativistic traditions is an important element

---

102. Mendels, "Creative History," 363–64.
103. In view here are two specific elements: (1) "hellenizing" (2) of "native traditions." Many times hellenization was the focus, but apologetic historiography could have a much broader goal (as Josephus himself demonstrates in his account of the Jewish war with Rome).
104. If apologetic historiography is understood more broadly, texts are brought into conjunction that might ordinarily be viewed in isolation. Thus, Esther, *Pseudo-Aristeas,* Daniel 1–6, *Jubilees,* the Hellenistic Jewish fragmentary historians, 3 and 4 Maccabees, and Josephus may all be read as narrating *historia* with similar purposes in view: praise and glorification of the Jewish people. The content and methodology may vary in these texts (Esther appears more

of apologetic historiography, but it is only one element. To limit apologetic historiography to this feature alone unduly narrows the focus, since much of what is *historia de novo* functions in the same way.

This observation leads to a second criticism of Sterling's analysis for his overly narrow demarcation of the boundaries of Jewish apologetic historiography to texts that exhibit a hellenizing *Tendenz*. There is no doubt that the positive portrayal of the Jewish tradition for the Hellenistic world is an integral feature of much of Hellenistic Jewish literature. Yet this is only one trajectory of Jewish apologetic in antiquity. We see, for instance, that 1 Maccabees, with its manifest Hasmonean bias, is as apologetic in function, tenor, and character as Josephus's work, but to a very different end. Luke-Acts uses numerous Hellenistic *topoi*, but its apologetic quality is evident on numerous fronts.[105] For some scholars, this will no doubt open up the category too far, allowing for just about anything to be included as "apologetic." I would argue that, while this broader understanding of apologetic historiography may make particular formal comparisons more difficult, it more accurately captures the ethos, spirit, and living context of ancient historiography.

Historical narrative, from the very beginning in Herodotus, but even more explicitly after Alexander, developed a tendentious focus that readily allowed for its use in either the denigration or praise of various peoples, cultures, and ideas. In this light, everything from the work of Dionysius of Halicarnassus, to Livy, to Ammianus Marcellinus can be seen as the attempt to shape and create narratives of identity. Specific individuals, from great rulers such as Alexander to prophets such as Jesus and Apollonius, could be praised and written large in life. Others, such as Alexander the "false" prophet, could be castigated and ridiculed by an adept writer like Lucian. Just as Livy and other early Roman writers could create a mytho-historical paradigm of Roman origins, Eusebius could do the same for Christianity. In both cases the emphasis on bringing the time of origins into line with the present of the writer (Livy or Eusebius) is paramount, demonstrating continuity between the past and the present.[106] The role of great men in this

---

novelistic in character, 4 Maccabees is closer to Sallust's presentation of history as a philosophical lesson, and Josephus is more faithful than Artapanus in his treatment of the antecedent biblical narrative); still, the writers' overarching aims appear remarkably similar.

105. It would be unrealistic in the case of Luke-Acts to limit the understanding of "apologetic" to one particular feature. Rather, like many ancient historical works, its function and aim is multifaceted. Luke-Acts reflects inner Christian polemics (e.g., stance on Paul), inter-Jewish conflict (defining Christianity in the stream of Jewish self-understanding), and dialogue with the values and concerns of the larger Greco-Roman world (see L. C. A. Alexander, "The Acts of the Apostles as an Apologetic Text," in *Apologetics in the Roman Empire: Pagans, Jews, and Christians* [ed. M. Edwards et al.; New York: Oxford University Press, 1999], 15–20, 42–44).

106. On the same in Jewish tradition, see, e.g., A. I. Baumgarten, "Invented Traditions of the Maccabean Era," in *Geschichte-Tradition-Reflexion: Festschrift für Martin Hengel zum 70. Geburtstag* (ed. H. Cancik, H. Lichtenberger, and P. Schäfer; Tübingen: Mohr Siebeck, 1996), 1:197–210.

paradigm is essential, as the history of a movement is based on the quality, substance, and character of the narrative representatives, a point not lost on Thucydides in his earlier work. Others, such as Plutarch, were more interested in retelling history so as to underscore particular features of virtue and character, implicitly praising moral ethos and creating not a mythology of origins as much as a demonstration of the enduring and successful patterns of the good life.[107] While in this instance the use of the past in the service of the present performs a more subtle epideictic function by redefining aspects of current identity in light of the past; in other cases, where polemic is involved, the stakes were even higher.

The above survey is sufficient to suggest that when one conceives of "apologetic" historiography one should think in much broader terms than is often done in practice. Moreover, it is clear that this "praise" and/or "blame" context lends itself to an array of literary activities: memorializing individuals, nations, cultures, and particular ideals; rewriting historical narratives and traditions; framing presentations in light of particular *Tendenzen;* overt polemicizing against perceived outside threats and hostilities; creating mythologies of the past; inventing and embellishing traditions and institutions; shaping identity in the present through narration; and historicizing current issues and concerns in the historical remembrance of the past.[108] Even though this tradition of "rewriting," "redaction," and "retrieval" is often seen as distinctive of Christian and Jewish discourse, in fact it was widespread in the broader Hellenistic environment, and Jewish and Christian methodologies were informed and molded in light of this larger literary and cultural ethos.

The root of this apologetic literary historiographical approach in antiquity is complex, but two features of that environment can be highlighted as crucial to the formation of this tradition. First, from the Hellenistic period onward the consistent and thorough upheaval in the Greek and then Roman worlds contributed to a climate of instability, culminating in a constant

---

107. See, e.g., Plutarch's stress on the interrelationship of education and moral development (S. Swain, "Hellenic Culture and the Roman Heroes of Plutarch," in *Essays on Plutarch's Lives* [ed. B. Scardigli; New York: Oxford University Press, 1995], 229–64). This use connects closely with the employment of history as *exemplum* in the Roman tradition, and most likely arises out of the rhetorical tradition wherein examples from history and myth were used to reinforce arguments about the present. Thus, even in ancient oratory the past tended to be reconfigured by present concerns (see S. Perlman, "The Historical Example: Its Use and Importance as Political Propaganda in the Attic Orators," *Scripta Hierosolymitana* 7 [1961]: 150–66).

108. M. Toher, "Augustus and the Evolution of Roman Historiography," in *Between Republic and Empire: Interpretations of Augustus and His Principate* (ed. K. A. Raaflaub and M. Toher; Berkeley: University of California Press, 1990), 146–50, argues for these facets in Roman historiography precisely because of its connection to the annalistic tradition that was concerned only with events that impinged on Roman interests. It is fair to suggest, however, that the Greeks and numerous other writers of different regions in the East were as tied to these methods as their Roman counterparts.

battle for control of political power and cultural definition.[109] The rise of Rome and the subsequent *imperium* in the East fueled the Hellenistic situation further. Although Roman imperial policy in the East was somewhat adaptable and sensitive to the political and cultural ethos of the newly conquered territories,[110] Roman power and control challenged the Greek structures and institutions, moving the flashpoint of interaction from political battles to cultural ones. The rise of the Second Sophistic (the cultural revival ca. 60–230 C.E.), for instance, was essentially an Eastern retrieval of the Greek past in response to the Roman cultural milieu.[111] In Judea, political and cultural issues were more closely intertwined, thanks to the legacy of heavy-handed Seleucid policies. As a result, Judean inhabitants developed a less than subtle response to Roman power. This environment lasted throughout late antiquity, giving impetus to the rewriting of identity and inventing of place in the context of imperial rule. Whether one was Jewish, Egyptian, Greek, or Roman, crafting historical narratives provided the chief medium through which individuals, nations, and cultures were able to garner interest, praise, and recognition within the ever shifting boundaries of empire.

The second feature that contributed to this cultural and literary environment was the social and political boundaries established by the patron-client framework, complexifying the value-laden matrices of Greco-Roman societies, which took on different shapes in differing places in empire and in society.[112] Yet the existence of this system within the larger political and

---

109. This point has been well documented in scholarship. Hengel's classic study (*Judaism and Hellenism: Studies in Their Encounter in Palestine during the Hellenistic Period* [trans. J. Bowden; Philadelphia: Fortress, 1974]) has done the most for explicating this context for Jewish and Christian studies. On the Near Eastern reaction more generally, the older study by S. K. Eddy, *The King Is Dead: Studies in the Near Eastern Resistance to Hellenism, 334–31 B.C.* (Lincoln: University of Nebraska Press, 1961), is still useful.

110. On this point, see the detailed assessment by E. S. Gruen, *The Hellenistic World and the Coming of Rome* (2 vols.; Berkeley: University of California Press, 1984).

111. See Swain, *Hellenism and Empire*, 65–100; idem., "Defending Hellenism: Philostratus, In Honour of Apollonius," in *Apologetics in the Roman Empire* (ed. Edwards et al.), 160–63; and E. L. Bowie, "Greeks and Their Past in the Second Sophistic," in *Studies in Ancient Society* (ed. M. I. Finley; London: Routledge, 1974), 166–209.

112. Frequently scholars refer more generally to "honor" and "shame" as binary conceptual categories to understand the social and cultural interaction in the period. For a summary of the issues as they relate to both dominant and minority cultural rhetoric, see D. A. deSilva, *Despising Shame: Honor Discourse and Community Maintenance in the Epistle to the Hebrews* (SBLDS 152; Atlanta: Scholars Press, 1995), 28–143; idem, "Investigating Honor Discourse: Guidelines from Classical Rhetoricians," *SBLSP* 36 (1997): 491–525; and J. H. Neyrey, *Honor and Shame in the Gospel of Matthew* (Louisville: Westminster John Knox, 1998), 83–88. But see the appropriate moderating comments by F. G. Downing, "Honor among Exegetes," *CBQ* 61 (1999): 53–73, who argues that the honor/shame matrix cannot always be viewed as the dominant and pervasive model for the ancient Mediterranean cultural system (cf. M. Sawicki, *Crossing Galilee: Architectures of Contact in the Occupied Land of Jesus* [Harrisburg, Pa.: Trinity Press International, 2000], 75–80, who offers a cogent critique of these categories as being based on our own binary polarities rather than the lens of the ancient world). The honor/shame framework represents a fairly conventional model of analysis, and, unless one

cultural sphere provided a social and personal context for writing oneself or one's nation into history. Regardless of whether the larger competitive value system was embraced, undermined, or subtly reversed, the very fact that it existed gave a sense of urgency to the literary enterprise outlined here. Moreover, that such values always loomed large demonstrates again the thin line between discrete literary forms and genres; a Polybius writing a so-called nonbiased account was as involved in this social matrix as was a writer such as Josephus. Thus, while it is one thing to suggest, as Hayden White does, that all histories are in fact literary fictions, it is another to appreciate the cultural and social climate of antiquity that makes this not so much an unsubconscious truism but a conscious and compulsory literary exercise every time an ancient writer sat down to write *historia*. For in each record of the past, writers from Herodotus to Ammianus Marcellinus were aware that their present was being shaped and molded as a result, and that at stake was one's perceived status within either the empire more generally or the local community more specifically.

Indeed, given the broader complexities of the Hellenistic environment, it is not surprising that the literary vehicles were many and varied as well. Within this ancient cultural context there emerged historiographical traditions that frequently blurred the lines between history, biography, and novel. It is precisely the legacy of this fluidity and hybridity in genre that allowed the writers of the ancient world to shape, create, and sustain narratives assigning praise and blame, honor and shame, to a wide array of characters. If the ancient context thus posed a problem, it also provided a solution. While there were explicit apologetic historians in antiquity, more generally there existed an apologetic ethos. Rather than thinking of this ethos in purely

---

analyzes specific texts, the particular content of this abstracted value system is fairly mutable (as deSilva admits [*Despising Shame*, 79]). I prefer, for this reason, to use the ancient rhetorical lenses of self-construction of character (*ethos*), masculine comportment, and establishment of *imperium* over others, which fundamentally shape the larger honor/shame discursive pattern in the Hellenistic and Roman periods with particular reference to societal gendered values. See J. Connolly, "Mastering Corruption: Constructions of Identity in Roman Oratory," in *Women and Slaves in Greco-Roman Culture* (ed. S. R. Joshel and S. Murnaghan; London: Routledge, 1998), 130–51; A. Richlin, "Gender and Rhetoric: Producing Manhood in the Schools," in *Roman Eloquence: Rhetoric in Society and Literature* (ed. W. J. Dominik; London: Routledge, 1997), 90–110; M. W. Gleason, *Making Men: Sophists and Self-Presentation in Ancient Rome* (Princeton: Princeton University Press, 1995); E. Gunderson, *Staging Masculinity: The Rhetoric of Performance in the Roman World* (Ann Arbor: University of Michigan Press, 2000); A. M. Keith, *Engendering Rome: Women in Latin Epic* (Roman Literature and Its Contexts; Cambridge: Cambridge University Press, 2000), 8–35; H. Moxnes, "Conventional Values in the Hellenistic World: Masculinity," in *Conventional Values of the Hellenistic Greeks* (ed. P. Bilde et al.; SHC 8; Aarhus: Aarhus University Press, 1997), 263–84; T. Penner, "*Res Gestae Divi Christi*: Miracles, Early Christian Heroes, and the Discourse of Power in Acts," in *The Role of Miracle Discourse in the Argumentation of the New Testament* (ed. D. F. Watson; SBLSymS; Atlanta: Society of Biblical Literature, forthcoming); and T. Penner and C. Vander Stichele, "Unveiling Paul: Gendering Ēthos in 1 Corinthians 11:2–16," in *Rhetoric, Ethic, and Moral Persuasion in Biblical Discourse* (ed. T. H. Olbricht and A. Eriksson; New York: T & T Clark, forthcoming).

reactive terms where authors attempted to defend themselves, their nation, or their traditions against false or even hostile perceptions, it is better to envision a more complex environment in which narratives were used to create or transform identities, or in which praise and blame could be meted out with the aim of underscoring individuals, values, or actions of lasting importance.

This recognition leads to two concluding observations. First, this present discussion has suggested that ancient historiography had an aim much different from our own post-Enlightenment concerns. As a result, our contemporary understanding of ancient historical writing may be too narrow and limited to account adequately for the complex data. Despite all the talk of Polybius and Thucydides being models of impartial critical-historical inquiry, it has to be acknowledged that when Polybius turns to illustrating his methodological interests, they almost never fit into the model that has been constructed for him. Indeed, his chief concern is to relate a history that will be of the most value to coming generations, and he has definite ideas on how this should be accomplished. Thus, whether one looks at the Greek, Roman, or Hellenistic context of historiography, in each case one finds a much more versatile and transformative genre than we are often led to believe by conventional treatments of ancient historiography.[113] By making the genre more malleable in this case, one is better able to appreciate the vast corpus of literature that neither looks nor reads like Polybius and Thucydides, yet claims, no less than these two great Greek writers, to represent *historia*.

A second observation arises out of this discussion: If the cultural and literary environment necessitated the approach to history outlined above, and the writing of *historia* was an explicit and conscious exercise in constructing identity, shaping values, and evaluating deeds and words in the complex social system (thereby revealing an epideictic motivation in narrating events and characters), then the connections between history and rhetoric are deeply rooted, revealing a complex substructure upon which the ancient historical enterprise is based. This observation does not necessarily mean, as Woodman has argued, that the *narratio* is consciously constructed on the pattern of oratorical composition, but it does suggest that we must take seriously the persuasive aim of writing *historia*. The ultimate end may not always be apparent or necessarily limited to one specific goal, yet underlying the task of writing history — indeed, necessitating the task — is the use of narratives to persuade readers. Thus, value-laden accounts are encoded through the use of stock characterization, type-scenes, and *topoi*, more effectively urging the readership in the chosen direction as a result.

---

113. Cf. Marincola, "Genre, Convention," 320: "[H]istoriographical genres of the Greeks and Romans were not static categories in which one writer merely followed all or most of the aspects of his predecessors, but rather... they were constantly dependent upon change and innovation."

Further, whether such persuasion is demonstrative, judicial, or epideictic in nature varies considerably depending on the time period and the writer, and determination of the "proper" category became one particular focus of ancient debate on historical composition. Yet even here we should notice that the debate was never whether history was to be persuasive — that was a given — but which method or aim was more appropriate to the genre of historiography and profitable for the reader. For ancient writers, then, the task of defining ancient historiography found itself squarely focused on the rhetorical methodologies conducive to persuasion. It is to these we now turn.[114]

Motivation and Pedagogy in Hellenistic *Historia*

This section will focus on some prominent features of ancient historical composition, particularly the reasons and methods that give shape to the preceding discussion. While there are obviously significant differences in style and method, one can gain a better understanding of the texture of historical composition in the first century C.E. by assessing particular features of the process. In particular, while the above discussion has attempted to lay out the larger literary and cultural context of historiography in Luke's time, in the following treatment I discuss more specifically the various strategies and concerns that reflect the environment just outlined. While recognizing the complexity of the nature and function of ancient *historia*,[115] I will highlight

---

114. In this chapter, three rather large, broad, and obvious streams of ancient historical writing have been identified. This type of designation can also create artificial boundaries for a much more integrated and interrelated literary history. There are naturally many more trajectories one could highlight as important aside from the Greco-Roman. For Luke-Acts, one would be remiss not to note the prominence of the biblical trajectory of historiography. Interesting for the argument developed here is the likelihood that biblical historical composition in the tradition of the Deuteronomist or the Chronicler attests to the pathetic, dramatic, and tragic qualities so despised by Polybius. The fact that biblical history is focused on creating and shaping identity in both original narratives (Deuteronomist) or rewritten biblical tradition (Chronicles and the whole enterprise of rewritten Bible that follows, from Pseudo-Philo to Josephus) already points us in this direction (see E. T. Mullen, *Narrative History and Ethnic Boundaries: The Deuteronomistic Historian and the Creation of Israelite National Identity* [SBLSemS; Atlanta: Scholars Press, 1993], and idem, *Ethnic Myths and Pentateuchal Foundations: A New Approach to the Formation of the Pentateuch* [SBLSemS; Atlanta: Scholars Press, 1997]). The style of the history, with its emphasis on the heavy moralizing, the presence of overt didacticism, and the predilection for the supernatural, indicates a tradition in the style of Ctesias and others, despite the latter's delimitation to a particular trajectory of Greek historiography. It is apparent that if one takes biblical historiography into account, one is then dealing with a much more widespread phenomenon in the ancient world. Indeed, one must ask whether the myopic view of some classicists has not obscured the possibility that the tragic flair in Greek historiography came not from the Aristotelian dramatic tradition but from much earlier Near Eastern influence (on such contact evidenced in Greek epic, see the important study by M. L. West, *The East Face of Helicon: West Asiatic Elements in Greek Poetry and Myth* [New York: Oxford University Press, 1997]).

115. W. C. van Unnik, "Luke's Second Book and the Rules of Hellenistic Historiography," in *Les Actes des Apôtres: Traditions, rédaction, théologie* (ed. J. Kremer; BETL 48; Leuven:

those features particularly pertinent to the subsequent analysis of Luke-Acts in the context of Jewish Hellenistic historiography. While cursory in nature, the following treatment nevertheless underscores the single most important feature of ancient historical composition: its thoroughly moral character.

At one level, there is little disagreement among scholars as to why ancient writers wrote historical narratives: They wrote to benefit the reader, adding in a certain degree of pleasure.[116] Yet, while there is consensus that most ancient historians understood their task as similar to that of Thucydides, there is debate with respect to the precise relationship between function and form in historical composition.[117] Thucydides' description of his task sets the stage — for contemporary scholars, at the very least — that subsequent historiographical reflection on method would follow:

> As to the facts of the occurrences of the war, I have thought it my duty to give them... only after investigating with the greatest possible accuracy each detail.... And it may well be that the absence of the fabulous from my narrative will seem less pleasing to the ear; but whoever shall wish to have a clear view both of the events which have happened and of those which will some day, in all human probability, happen again in the same or similar way — for those to adjudge my history profitable will be enough for me. And indeed, it has been composed, not as a prize-essay to be heard for the moment, but as a possession for all time. (1.22.2–4)[118]

Leuven University Press, 1979), 37–60, provides a useful outline of some of the main features. Also see the more detailed study by Avenarius, *Lukians Schrift*.

116. The literature on this particular subject is immense. For a selection with respect to some individual historians and time periods, see F. W. Walbank, "Profit or Amusement: Some Thoughts on the Motives of Hellenistic Historians," in *Purposes of History* (ed. Verdin et al.), 253–66; W. R. Connor, "Historical Writing in the Fourth Century B.C. and the Hellenistic Period," in *Cambridge History of Classical Literature* (ed. P. E. Easterling and B. M. Knox; vol. 1.3; Cambridge: Cambridge University Press, 1985), 46–59; Sacks, *Polybius;* idem, *Diodorus Siculus and the First Century* (Princeton: Princeton University Press, 1990); I. G. Kidd, "Posidonius as Philosopher-Historian," in *Philosophia Togata I: Essays on Philosophy and Roman Society* (ed. M. Griffin and J. Barnes; Oxford: Clarendon, 1989), 38–50; E. Gabba, *Dionysius and* The History of Archaic Rome (Berkeley: University of California Press, 1991), 60–90; P. G. Walsh, "Livy and the Aims of 'historia': An Analysis of the Third Decade," *ANRW* 2.30.2 (1982): 1058–74; V. I. Varneda, *The Historical Method of Flavius Josephus* (ALGHJ 19; Leiden: Brill, 1986), 242–79; and T. J. Luce, "Tacitus on 'History's Highest Function': *praecipuum munus annalium* (*Ann.* 3/65)," *ANRW* 2.33.4 (1991): 2904–27.

117. Particularly confusing in this respect is the repeated use of "truth" and "accuracy" in ancient historiographical reflection on method. It would seem a fairly easy task to take Polybius and Lucian at face value and suggest that good history writing in antiquity focused on reporting "truth" as accurately as possible (cf. Josephus, *C. Ap.* 1.23–27). The terms relating to "truth," "impartiality," "accuracy" and the like are, for instance, important components of Lucian's treatment of composition (*Hist.* 9, 39, 42, 43, 47, 63), and it is tempting to interpret Lucian to mean, as many scholars do, that history's main aim is to benefit future generations by focusing on "the tale as it happened" (39). After all, he says that "history has one task and one end — what is useful — and that comes from truth alone" (9; cf. Byrskog, *Story as History*, 180, who admits that Lucian "sounds almost Rankean" here).

118. This classic formulation by Thucydides is referred to by later writers as the proper model on which to style one's history: not for present glory and praise but so as to be profitable for

Thucydides believes that his tale of the Peloponnesian war — in his view the most important and greatest of all wars up until that time (1.21.2) — would provide future readers in similar situations with a useful tool because it displays the various sides of ethico-political issues, as well as the means and ends of civil action and discourse.[119] Indeed, Thucydides consciously acknowledges that the absence of the fabulous elements in his account, although decreasing the pleasurable effect of the narrative, would add to the greater utility of its content, as it would resonate with the everyday realities of all people everywhere rather than being associated with the work of the poets and chroniclers who attend to the "pleasing ear" of the reader rather than to the "truth" (1.21.1). This conception is not all that far off from Aristotle's understanding of the value of fictional narratives; they may differ in terms of the broader philosophical implications, but there is something fundamentally reminiscent in the articulation.

Aristotle rejects history as mimetic precisely because it relates the particular while poetry addresses the universal: "the kinds of things which it suits a certain kind of person to say or do, in terms of probability or necessity" (*Poet.* 1451b). The further problem of history is its inability to amplify and explore "single actions"; it focuses, rather, on particular periods of time, detailing various events and actions "without yielding a single goal" (*Poet.* 1459a). Thus, for Aristotle, historical composition lacks two key ingredients for mimetic narratives: It does not focus on the universal (that which happens to everyone everywhere), and it cannot, because of the random and frequently incoherent nature of particular events and people, examine complete actions with a view to the single goal that unites all elements of a dramatic plot; as a result, it has less potential impact.[120] In short, history is not fiction, and, whereas the former focuses on chronological relationships, the latter is able to detail logical relationships.[121] As K. Eden observes, "The spectator at an Aristotelian tragedy does not see a random sequence of events designed merely to excite his basest feelings. On the contrary, he sees a preeminently logical construct designed to increase his understanding and, with the aid of the proper emotional responses, enrich his judgement."[122] Fiction,

---

future generations. See Lucian, *Hist.* 5, 42 (in imitation of Thucydidean vocabulary in *Hist.* 61, 63).

119. On Thucydides' sense of his own methodology, especially with respect to the relationship between particular actions and universal truth and ideas, see L. Edmunds, *Chance and Intelligence in Thucydides* (Cambridge: Harvard University Press, 1975), 149–63, 205–9.

120. See Halliwell, *Aristotle's Poetics*, 106, 135–36, 200, 235–36. Halliwell rightly points out that for Aristotle the dramatic action of a poem actually exhibits a "higher level of intelligibility, particularly *causa* intelligibility, than is usually to be found in life.... [Moreover, the dramatic poem represents] a heightened notional pattern of possibility, and... [is] therefore more accessible to rational apprehension than are the events of ordinary experience" (135).

121. K. Eden, *Poetic and Legal Fiction in the Aristotelian Tradition* (Princeton: Princeton University Press, 1986), 33, 36–37, 49; and Halliwell, *Aristotle's Poetics*, 100–101.

122. Eden, *Poetic and Legal Fiction*, 61.

whether in the form of epic, tragedy, or comedy, is able to establish philosophical ideals, especially vice and virtue as exemplified in particular types of characters (cf. *Poet.* 1448a), and to demonstrate the necessary outcomes of particular actions, establishing the patterns of reversal and recognition, the aims of friendship, the tragedy of suffering, and the true ends of a virtuous life. Not only do such fictional accounts represent reality to the reader,[123] they also have the ability to persuade the reader to adopt and follow an exemplary kind of life.[124] Aristotelian narratives are thus mimetic not only because they imitate reality but because they also bring about imitation in the readership, or at least evoke reflection on the things being imitated in the audience as a result of the harmonization between emotion and reason brought on by *katharsis*.[125]

While Aristotle may reject *historia* as a mimetic narrative because it does not have the expositional qualities of fictional narrative, Thucydides, by contrast, repeatedly stresses the nonfictional nature of his account. He thinks that his narrative, because of its richness of detail, portrays reality in a way that would ensure that the events and personages described provide vivid, living lessons upon which future actions by cities and councils could and should be based. By leaving out the miraculous and fantastic in his account — things contrary to everyday experience — he thereby shows how his events and persons are based in the ordinary experience of his readers. In so doing he creates a type of universal — one not focused, however, on the respective ends of virtue and vice but on the various possibilities and potentials of human actions. Aristotle, by contrast, evinces less explicit concern about the fantastic and fabulous in narrative largely because the logical connections between characters, actions, and results are capable of illumination irrespective of whether a narrative is based in plausible, possible, or impossible circumstances.

There are, of course, significant and important differences between Aristotle's *Poetics* and Thucydides' *historia*, and I do not want to suggest that Thucydides is adopting the identical philosophical and psychological framework bolstering Aristotle's work. Yet there are important intersections with respect to the goals of the narrative (benefiting readers through the plot structure), which demonstrate a broader cultural poetics and literary ethos out of which both Aristotle and Thucydides articulate their respective narrative understandings/approaches. Thucydides is attempting to do something similar to Aristotle's tragic mimesis, yet his configuration is different. Whereas Aristotle understands that it is the function of narrative to reveal enduring patterns of character and actions (with consequent results) — an

---

123. But this should not be construed as merely or simply "reproduction." See Halliwell, *Aristotle's Poetics*, 136.
124. Ibid., 236.
125. Ibid., 200–201.

explicit philosophical and moral vision of the power of literary composition — Thucydides underscores the power of narrative to elucidate a variety of appropriate human responses to universal situations. In Aristotle character is universal; in Thucydides the events themselves are universal. Still, both writers converge in their main emphasis: Narratives are beneficial and serviceable to subsequent reading audiences precisely through presentation of actions and results. Of course, historical composition prior to and after Aristotle was focused on the characterization of individuals in the narrative according to types (in line with Aristotle's interest), and, as we shall see below, this shaped one aspect of the conception of "truth" in historical composition. But the debate would always exist among ancient historians between utilizing extreme characterization — either positive or negative — and a more nuanced, realistic portrayal of character (i.e., depicting both the good and negative aspects of individuals). Since Greeks valued moderation and were committed to representing reality as all people everywhere experienced it, they had to avoid both overt panegyric and outright slander.

This emphasis of ancient historiography becomes clearer when one seeks to understand the Thucydidean civic context of literary composition.[126] When Thucydides claims that his narrative will be a "possession for all time," it has much to do with the educative function of the history. By presenting the realia of civic politics both as a response to and the result of war, Thucydides offers future readers examples of political and military deliberation and decision, as well as a basis for making informed decisions in the future. From this starting point, the move toward overt didacticism, followed by the subsequent stress on the ethical and philosophical dimensions of historical narratives, was natural. Moreover, Thucydides' description of himself as someone who investigated the reports thoroughly, relied upon his own involvement, refrained from probable rather than actual constructions, and laboriously sifted through the biased accounts of various sides in the conflict (1.22.2–3) forms a critical component of the historian's task of presenting the options for political debate and decision. This theme surfaces in a variety of contexts in historiographical discussion, but the central tenet is clear: The historian is not there to choose sides and make the decisions himself, but rather to present the alternatives and their concomitant results openly and boldly. Thucydides' understanding of this narrative dynamic is also revealed in his treatment of speeches. Despite the attempt by numerous scholars to defend the historicity of the speeches[127] — emphasizing the

---

126. See further Penner, "Civilizing Discourse," 72–78.
127. See Porter, "Thucydides 1.22.1"; and S. Hornblower, *Thucydides* (London: Duckworth, 1987), 45–72. Cf. the slightly more nuanced positions of Byrskog, *Story as History,* 211–12; and C. Pelling, *Literary Texts and the Greek Historian* (New York: Routledge, 2000), 112–22. Since ancient speeches were seldom recorded in the first place (P. Green, "Clio Perennis: Aspects of Ancient History," in *Essays in Antiquity* [New York: World, 1960], 69), at best a historian could often only arrive at the gist of what was said.

phrase "I have adhered as closely as possible to the general sense of what was actually said (1.22.1)" — ancient writers such as Dionysius seemed to assume that Thucydides had invented not only the form of the speech but also its content (cf. *Thuc.* 37–42). "What was actually said" expresses the universals of human experience in the *polis* as they are understood by Thucydides. The line we might draw between "what someone would have done or said" and "what someone actually did or said" remains blurred. While this may not be as obvious in Thucydides' own statement, it becomes evident in later presentations of this ideal. Perhaps one better understands Thucydides' own approach to historical composition if it is viewed from the perspective of his "successors."

By clarifying what was implicit in Thucydides' understanding of the historical task, Polybius, for instance, unabashedly affirms the central function of history as being that which is useful and profitable for future readership:

> For all men are given to adapt themselves to the present and assume a character suited to the times, so that from their words and actions it is difficult to judge...the principles of each, and in many cases the truth is quite overcast. But men's past actions, bringing to bear the test of actual fact, indicate truly the principles and opinions of each, and show us where we may look for gratitude, kindness, help, and where for the reverse.... Therefore both writers and readers of history should not pay so much attention to the actual narrative of events, as to what precedes, what accompanies, and what follows each. For if we take from history the discussion of why, who, and wherefore each thing was done, and whether the result was what we should have reasonably expected, what is left is a clever essay but not a lesson, and while pleasing for the moment of no possible benefit for the future. (3.31.7–13)

In many respects Polybius here articulates a view similar to Aristotle's understanding of a complete action and a unified plot. The various logical (not purely chronological) relationships between events and people can benefit readers by establishing corroboration between present possibilities and past patterns of conduct. Ideal actions help clarify the present situation, but with less emphasis on virtue and greater stress on the role of the individual within social and political spheres of action. Elsewhere, Polybius argues that such a treatment "will be of great service to students and practical statesmen for forming or reforming other constitutions" (3.118.12). Thus, for Polybius, history also provides, as it does for Thucydides, practical models for future deliberation and decision (cf. Isocrates, *Nic.* 2.50–52).

The introduction to Polybius's work expands upon these themes more fully. Here Polybius acknowledges two explicit benefits of history: It has a "corrective" function enabling people in the present to learn from the past actions and consequences of others (1.1.1), as well as an explicit educative function: "Historians...have impressed upon us that the soundest education (παιδείαν) and training (γυμνασίαν) for a life of active politics is the study (μάθησιν) of history, and the surest and indeed the only method of learning (διδάσκαλον) how to bear bravely the vicissitudes of fortune, is to recall the calamities of others" (1.1.2). Striking is the use of several terms for the system of *paideia* in the ancient *polis*. It further becomes evident that Polybius is focused on Fortune (cf. 1.1.2–4), and believes that his systematic history will lay bare "the operations by which she has accomplished her general purpose" (1.4.2). Attributing the success of Roman imperialism to the guidance of Fortune (1.4.1, 4–6), Polybius further states that a successful general history must be able to do what an isolated, local history cannot do, namely, connect, on a grand scale, the various goals and ends of actions in history: "[I]t is only by study of the interconnection of all the particulars, their resemblances and differences, that we are enabled at least to make a general survey, and thus derive both benefit and pleasure from history" (1.4.11). Significant is the connection Polybius makes between the particular method and goal of history. He understands that his history provides benefit and pleasure precisely because of the attempt to connect the seemingly random actions of Fortune or *Tyche* in historical progress.[128] Unlike Aristotle, who viewed history as too localized and particular to provide the basis for his universal philosophical goals of tragedy,[129] Polybius believes history deals not with discrete and particular acts, but reveals various manifestations of a larger, universal guiding process, one which historical composition is able to uncover and lay bare. As G. Trompf aptly observes,

> While recognizing his interest in the considerable variety of human experiences, one must return again and again to his presuppositions about the general face of events, about types of dramatic situations, and about governing principles.... [Polybius] had a feeling for incidents possessing universal and paradigmatic qualities (and thus having affinities with the rhetorician's stock of pertinent examples). He did not write only to edify, but to affirm something of practical importance about the nature of history.[130]

Elsewhere, Polybius contrasts his task as historian with the work of the tragedian. Whereas dramatic historians such as Phylarchus, in his view, aim

---

128. The theme of Fortune is prevalent in ancient historiography (see E. Baynham, *Alexander the Great: The Unique History of Quintus Curtius* [Ann Arbor: University of Michigan Press, 1998], 101–31). Aristotle, however, excluded "chance" from a dramatic scenario because it undermines the cohesiveness of the plot and impedes generalized understanding (Halliwell, *Aristotle's Poetics*, 210, 231, 233). Part of this Aristotelian concern is addressed by the increasing centrality of Providence in Hellenistic historiography. On the latter, see J. T. Squires, *The Plan of God in Luke-Acts* (SNTSMS 76; Cambridge: Cambridge University Press, 1993), 15–36, 155–85; idem, "Fate and Free Will in Hellenistic Histories and Luke-Acts," in *Ancient History in a Modern University* (ed. T. W. Hillard et al.; Grand Rapids: Eerdmans, 1998), 2:131–37; O. W. Allen, *The Death of Herod: The Narrative and Theological Function of Retribution in Luke-Acts* (SBLDS 158; Atlanta: Scholars Press, 1997), 155–95; and Attridge, *Interpretation of Biblical History*, 71–107. For the same in Thucydides, see Edmunds, *Chance and Intelligence*, 174–89.
129. Halliwell, *Aristotle's Poetics*, 79, 234.
130. Trompf, *Idea of Historical Recurrence*, 106.

"to thrill" their readers, attempting to arouse pity and bringing the horrors of events "vividly before our eyes" (2.56.7–8), the historian such as Polybius seeks to "instruct" (διδάξαι) and "convince" (πεῖσαι) those "serious learners" (φιλομαθοῦντας), conferring on them "benefit" (2.56.11). Since Phylarchus's treatment does not deal with the causes of events and their true significance, his narrative fails to benefit the reader (2.56.14). Polybius's point is simple: Not only is his own method superior to that of Phylarchus because it is not focused on the immediate present, but it is also more effective in arousing pity because it focuses on the logical connections of events. For Polybius, knowledge of good and evil lies not in what is done, but in the underlying causes and ultimate effects of what is done (2.56.16). While it is easy to read Polybius's statements about "probability" and "verisimilitude" in Phylarchus as his effort to articulate an understanding of "historical truth" that is roughly correspondent with "brute facts," everything he says elsewhere seems to contradict this simplistic equation. He does accuse Phylarchus of creating "plausible utterances" rather than relating "what really happened" (2.56.10), but, when he goes on to discuss specific details related to the accusation, he objects mostly to the improper focus of and characterization in Phylarchus's narrative. For Polybius, Phylarchus's depiction of events may be "probable," but it is not necessarily a reflection of truth, which for him is a more important criterion than that of "probability."

One must be careful not to presume that Polybius is arguing against the use of probable narratives and verisimilitude in historical composition outright, for the historiographical tradition and/or the broader cultural poetic environment that comes after him clearly appreciates these as important elements of the literary process. Indeed, Polybius's interest is quite clear from the larger context. For instance, he objects to Phylarchus's depiction of the Mantineans because of commonly shared assumptions about Greek values and honor codes. The Mantineans, according to Polybius, were treacherous; they violated the social conditions of friendship, they undermined the cultural value of their obligation to the patron, and they violated the common laws of war (2.57.8–58.10). Yet Phylarchus attempts to arouse pity for these same individuals. According to Polybius they deserve the reader's loathing. In his view, Phylarchus has composed not only a series of falsehoods but also "improbable falsehoods" at that (2.58.13–14).

Two aspects are being challenged in this Polybius's discussion: Phylarchus's misplaced sympathy/empathy for violators of laws and customs, and the improbability of unwarranted and unnecessary aggression by a notable and honorable people such as the Achaeans.[131] The enthymematic

---

131. Polybius follows this example with another to emphasize the same flaws in Phylarchus. In this second case Phylarchus would have the reader feel pity/empathy for a "tyrant": "Aristomachus, if it is true that he was subjected to the most terrible punishment, as Phylarchus tells us, did not get his full deserts for the doings of one day" (2.59.7). Moreover, the possible suggestion that those torturing the "tyrant" may have acted criminally is also contrary to the

"truth" is that people get what they deserve and the Greeks are honorable in war. Since Greeks do not behave the way Phylarchus has characterized them, he not only lies but also does so unconvincingly. Phylarchus finds acts of shame and "sin" where there should be "praise and honourable mention of conduct noteworthy for its excellence" (2.61.5–6). Polybius praises the Megalopolitans by pointing out their honorable conduct in remaining loyal to their allies despite the bitter hardship they received as a result: "What more noble conduct has there ever been or could there be? To what could an author with more advantage call the attention of his readers, and how could he better stimulate them to loyalty to their engagements and to true and faithful comradeship [κοινωνίαν]?" (2.61.11). The issue in this debate between Polybius and Phylarchus is not the historicity of particular events, but how events and actors are portrayed.[132] When Polybius appeals to the "truth" of history, he means a particular kind of truth: the ability of historical narrative to explore and illuminate human action and conduct, both for education in the *polis* and for moral formation exemplified in honorable actions.[133] Throughout this debate both authors assume a shared value system regarding truth in history. For Polybius, historical truth cannot be understood apart from its role in benefiting the reader. It would be a stretch to suggest that Polybius precisely understands his account as "fiction" in the Aristotelian sense, but the function of his historical narrative is similar to that of Aristotle's notion of mimetic narratives: History is the presentation of people and events as they ought to be and generally should and do happen.

---

values and expectations of the Greek audience: what they had every right to do in war, they would also have been praised for doing during peace (2.60.2).

132. See 3.20.1–5, where Polybius actually addresses the issues of improbability in an account of a Roman debate after the fall of Saguntum:

> The Romans, when the news of the fall of Saguntum reached them, did not assuredly hold a debate on the question of the war, as some authors allege, even setting down the speeches made on both sides—a most absurd proceeding. For how could the Romans, who a year ago had announced to the Carthaginians that their entering the territory of Saguntum would be regarded as a *casus belli*, now when the city itself had been taken by assault, assemble to debate whether they should go to war or not? How is it that on the one hand these authors draw a wonderful picture of the gloomy aspect of the Senate and on the other tell us that fathers brought their sons from the age of twelve upwards to the Senate House, and that these boys attended the debate but divulged not a syllable even to any of their near relatives? Nothing in this is the least true or even probable, unless, indeed, Fortune has bestowed on the Romans among other gifts that of being wise from their cradles.... [These writers] rank in authority... not with history, but with the common gossip of a barber's shop.

Contrary to U. Scholz's assessment (*"Annales* or *Historiae,"* in *Ancient History* [ed. Hillard et al.], 2:208), Polybius's problem is not with the emotional nature of the speeches but with the improbability of the speeches and narrative context, as his analysis of the "logic" of the narrative suggests.

133. A. M. Eckstein, *Moral Vision in* The Histories *of Polybius* (HCS 16; Berkeley: University of California Press, 1995), has developed both of these elements in detail.

In this connection, Polybius's use of the term περιπέτεια in the introduction to his work is noteworthy. There he observes the "reversals" that frequently take place with *Tyche* as a guide (1.1.2).[134] Although Polybius is not the only ancient historian to express interest in the reversals of everyday life,[135] it is an element that surfaces throughout his narrative (cf. 1.13.11; 1.87.1; 9.12.6; 21.26.16; 32.8.4; 38.9.2). In fact, the entire history is essentially about one grand reversal: the rise of Rome and the fall of Greece. The theme of reversal is also prominent in Aristotle's *Poetics*, where it is one of the critical elements of mimetic narratives, alongside "recognition" and "suffering" (1452a–b). For Aristotle, reversal is a key component of the plot, and by carefully detailing the logical connections, one is able to demonstrate the causes — both probable and necessary (*Poet.* 1452a) — that bring about reversal. In line with Polybius, for Aristotle it is not enough simply to detail the event of reversal; one must illuminate the causal connections in order for the narrative of reversal to arouse the desired effect, namely, "fellow-feeling." Aristotle requires four elements in character portrayal: Characters should be good ("speech or action reveal the nature of a moral choice, and good character when the choice is good"; 1454a); characterization should be appropriate to classes and types of individuals ("it is inappropriate for a woman to be courageous"; 1454a); characters should be in the likeness of the reader (i.e., not morally extreme, but moderate in characterization);[136] and characterization should be consistent. With such an understanding of character portrayal in Aristotle's tragic fiction, it is easy to appreciate how the philosophical ethics of Aristotle could readily connect with the values of society and be mediated directly to the reader through the characters in the story who reaffirm, maintain, and inculcate the shared cultural and social system of the writer and audience.

Polybius's concern is consonant with Aristotle's: Characterization should be consistent with the values "everyone knows to be true." Thus, Polybius's attack on narratives that lack plausibility and verisimilitude impugn accounts such as Phylarchus's that may be theoretically possible (a brave woman, dishonorable Greeks) but not probable given the cultural and social value system shared by author and readers.[137] This premise should not surprise us, especially since Polybius makes a fairly overt reference to

---

134. On Polybius's interest in reversal, see Baynham, *Alexander the Great*, 120.

135. Diodorus Siculus, for instance, expresses this theme throughout his history (cf. 3.57.8; 4.43.2; 8.10.3; 13.33.2; 13.35.5; 14.112.1; 17.27.7; 17.46.6; 17.47.5; 17.86.3). Josephus also stresses this as an important aspect of biblical history (*Ant.* 1.13).

136. Halliwell provides a good discussion of "likeness" in this sense (*Aristotle's Poetics*, 217).

137. Elsewhere, Polybius gives some examples of what he understands the invention of "plausibilities" to include, and he specifically mentions the debates of the sophistic philosophers in Athens who questioned whether it was possible for people in Athens to smell eggs being cooked in Ephesus or whether a lecturer was really at home in bed dreaming about the lecture he was actually giving (12.26c.2–3). In this case, these inventions are possible, but they do not represent

the deliberative rhetorical function of history: instruction and persuasion (2.56.11). And, in line with standard oratorical procedure, one must argue persuasively from "commonplaces," that is, the values, propositions, and modes of argumentation a given society agrees upon.[138] Truth in history, then, is the truth of the *polis* as experienced in everyday life. Moreover, this kind of truth is not only beneficial but it is also pleasing.[139]

Polybius's famous attack on Timaeus in book 12 of his history must be understood in this same context. Polybius begins by criticizing Timaeus's description of Africa, noting that Timaeus did not investigate the reports of others thoroughly (12.4c.2–5) but simply handed down the false but ancient report that the land is "sandy, dry and unproductive" (12.3.2–3).[140] Accurate description of the context for historical actions is essential for Polybius. Turning from geographical issues to political ones, Polybius expends some effort detailing the contradictory explanations of Locrian political associations proffered by Timaeus and Aristotle. In the end, Polybius favors the tradition of Aristotle over that of Timaeus, as the latter, in Polybius's view, seeks to downplay some possible negative elements regarding the genesis of Locrian allegiances. In particular, Polybius attacks Timaeus's suggestion that it is "improbable" that the slaves of a particular people, when freed, would

---

common experience or reality. Thus, Polybius is more concerned about probability and plausibility than the merely possible: the common experience of everyone everywhere as opposed to the possible but not likely inventions of the philosophers.

138. Halliwell (*Aristotle's Poetics*, 101–2) points out two aspects of "probability" in persuasion of an audience: objective representation of the narrative plot (correspondences to "logic" of action) and subjective elements related to what an audience is likely to believe. Halliwell argues that Aristotle is more focused on the objective aspect of persuasion (although this may be debated based on the similarities between the *Poetics* and the *Rhetoric*). Polybius, by contrast, is much more concerned with the subjective element.

139. It is important to appreciate the kind of "pleasure" that Polybius is referring to in this context. Polybius's understanding comes closest here to Aristotle's discussion: "[S]ince learning and admiring are pleasant, all things connected with them must also be pleasant; for instance, a work of imitation, such as painting, sculpture, poetry, and all that is well imitated, even if the object of imitation is not pleasant; for it is not this that causes pleasure or the reverse, but the inference that the imitation and the object imitated are identical, so that the result is that we learn something. The same may be said of sudden changes [περιπέτειαι] and narrow escapes from danger; for all these things excite wonder" (1.11.23–25). By imitating an object accurately and clearly one is able to learn something, and this, for Aristotle, results in pleasure. It is in this way, then, that Polybius can understand history as both teaching and providing pleasure; the pleasure comes through the learning (this overcomes the problem posed by Walbank, "Profit or Amusement," 266, of how it is that readers could find Polybius's interest in causes pleasurable; cf. Maximus of Tyre, *Or.* 22.5; see also A. A. Long, *Hellenistic Philosophy: Stoics, Epicureans, Sceptics* [2d ed.; Berkeley: University of California Press, 1986], 69, where he makes similar comments with respect to Epicurius's association of virtue and pleasure). This emphasis on pleasure also helps one understand more fully Polybius's concerns about "tragic" elements in history. It is really the excessive and distorted use of those elements he despises. Polybius does not oppose vivid, dramatic scenes, but rather inappropriate, misguided, inconsistent, and implausible — in short, "false" — dramatic scenes.

140. Similarly, regarding the Roman custom of sacrificing a horse and Timaeus's suggestion that this is in commemoration of the destruction of Troy, Polybius finds this laughable and childish (12.4b.1–4c.1).

adopt the "friendly feelings of their masters for the friends of those masters" (12.6a.2–3). Polybius's logic is important, as he appeals to a shared cultural value assumption to undermine Timaeus's statement:

> Men, indeed, who have once been slaves when they meet with unexpected good fortune attempt to affect and reproduce not only the likings but the friendships and relationships of their masters, taking more pains to do so than those actually connected by blood, and hope to wipe out their former inferiority and disrepute by this very effort to appear rather as descendants than as freedmen of their late masters. (12.6a.3–4)

Polybius adequately reflects the values of the patron-freedman relationship, especially in the Roman tradition.[141] Polybius's criticism of this specific element of Timaeus's account thus focuses on the latter's failure to bring the narrative in line with the values of society.

Taking this line of thought one step further, Polybius arrives at the ultimate conclusion to his moral interpretation of history: Even if Timaeus's account were more probable, it should be dismissed because, "being darkened by prejudice" (12.7.2, 5–6), he attacks Aristotle. If history is ultimately an exercise in *paideia,* then the moral character of the historian is paramount.[142] Consequently, terms such as "flattery" and "malice" are ascribed to those would-be historians who so readily misplace their emphasis, misconstrue the value system of antiquity, and attack noted philosophers and statesmen such as Aristotle (12.8.1–2). Within this pedagogical framework, if one's goal is to teach, to instruct, and to persuade — as is the case with Polybius — then one's narrative will be construed in such a way as to accomplish these aims efficiently and effectively. If, however, one's composition aims at flattering or slandering particular individuals or nations, then one will construe the narrative to meet such ends. For this reason historians such as Polybius were able to bind up the character of the writer intricately with the ethos guiding the presentation of historical words and deeds, stressing that those who look to the future with the goal of instruction are morally superior to those who focus only on the present. With respect to the larger narrative, those accounts are more capable of instruction that more adequately represent the truer context (e.g., accurate geographical details, plausible descriptions of customs) of actions and the truer values of ancient society.

---

141. On the dynamics of obligation after manumission and the continued role in the *familias,* see K. R. Bradley, *Slaves and Masters in the Roman Empire: A Study in Social Control* (New York: Oxford University Press, 1984), 81; B. Rawson, "The Roman Family," in *The Family in Ancient Rome: New Perspectives* (ed. B. Rawson; Ithaca: Cornell University Press, 1986), 12–13; and esp. A. Kirschenbaum, *Sons, Slaves, and Freedmen in Roman Commerce* (Washington: Catholic University Press, 1987), 127–40. Noteworthy, then, is Polybius's appeal to the "likely" and "probable" nature of Aristotle's construal (12.6b.6–7; 12.7.4).

142. See Marincola, *Authority and Tradition,* 128–33.

Polybius is convinced that when you take away truth from history (12.12.2) you are left with an "unprofitable fable" or narrative (διήγημα; 12.12.3). He also believes that a narrative lacking truth can result from ignorance or maliciousness (12.12.4–5). Those who include miraculous events in their narratives may do so because of superstition and ignorance. But those who, like Timaeus, attack a notable figure such as the Greek orator Demochares, accusing him of "impurity," demonstrate a complete lack of civic duty and culture, evidencing less character than "inmates of a brothel" (12.13.1–3). Polybius "knows" that Timaeus is lying since Demochares, "as everyone knows," had good breeding: He was a nephew of Demosthenes and was accorded honor by the Athenians. Not only does noble and honorable background produce admirable character, but any attack on the person of Demochares amounts to an attack on the Athenians, who entrusted power and honor to him (12.13.4–6). Indeed, in every case in which Polybius assails Timaeus for being motivated by passions and jealousies (12.14.5; 12.25.5–7; 12.25c.1–5), Timaeus's baser side is understood to be reflected in the narrative and is portrayed as lacking the quintessential Greek quality: moderation in all things. By focusing, for instance, on the perverse nature of King Agathocles and failing to mention any positive qualities (which, Polybius insists, must exist by virtue of his being known as a king; cf. 12.15.7–9), Timaeus has failed to perform the proper function of history: depicting the positive and negative aspects of humanity and drawing out the significance and ends of each, which is conceptually close to Aristotle's emphasis on moderation in tragic characterization. Thus, when Polybius discusses problems in the narratives of others, the focus is always that they lack what, in his view, is necessary for educative and profitable narratives. Polybius criticizes excess in characterization, lack of moderation in commentary, indecent and disrespectful portrayal of famous men, failure to describe adequately the context for action, and the lack of consistent and plausible narration that undermines the utilitarian function of *historia*.[143]

---

143. Polybius's discussion of Callisthenes (12.17–22) yields similar results. Here Polybius illustrates numerous errors and implausibilities in terms of the descriptions of battle alignments. What Polybius disputes is the lack of military knowledge and experience on the part of Callisthenes, which is reflected in poorly conceived and inaccurate narratives (cf. his treatment of Ephorus in 12.25f1–7). If history is intended to educate in the art of warfare — providing a manual-like account of the practice — then such flaws are highly problematic (cf. similar sentiments regarding the lack of experience in Phylarchus; 2.62.2–3). Polybius's discussion of Hannibal's crossing of the Alps is also useful as an illustration (3.47.6–49.4). Here Polybius is most concerned to undercut any appeal to miraculous deliverance or exaggeration of the nature of the hardships. The reason is simple: Historians who do appeal to supernatural intervention turn a useful narrative of a capable and admirable general — who examined the lay of the land and executed a well-planned march through the mountains with "sound practical sense" (3.48.11) — into a pleasing narrative, appealing to the crass and vulgar sensibilities of the masses. The usefulness is bound up with the portrayal of Hannibal. If he were an "imprudent" and "incompetent" leader (3.48.1), then the ability of this narrative to demonstrate the critical qualities of leadership and the subtle praise of the vision of a great individual are undermined. It is no accident, then, that Polybius includes a manual on being an effective general in his own

When one turns to Polybius's discussion of speeches, it may be tempting to read his argument that Timaeus did not "set down the words spoken nor the sense of what was really said" (12.25a.5; cf. Thucydides 1.22.1) as an indication that Polybius is ultimately concerned with the historicity of speeches. He writes,

> The peculiar function of history is to discover, in the first place, the words actually spoken, whatever they were, and next to ascertain the reason why what was done or spoken led to failure or success. For the mere statement of a fact may interest us but is of no benefit to us: but when we add the cause of it, study of history becomes fruitful. For it is the mental transference of similar circumstances to our own times that gives us the means of forming presentiments of what is about to happen, and enables us at certain times to take precautions and at others by reproducing former conditions to face with more confidence the difficulties that menace us. But a writer who passes over in silence the speeches made and the causes of events and in their place introduces false rhetorical exercises and discursive speeches, destroys the peculiar virtue of history. (12.25b.1–4; cf. 12.25e.6–7; 12.25g.2–3; 12.25i.6)

Polybius's main emphasis, however, is clearly on proper arrangement of speeches in relationship to the narrative. The speeches should illuminate varying courses of action and state the various arguments for the different positions. This approach enables the historian to relate civic discourse to the realia of warfare. Timaeus, however, uses his speeches to break from the narrative and focus on entertaining the readers with rhetorical flourishes. Polybius, like all ancient historians, understands the invented nature of speeches, but nonetheless believes that invention has its limits. Historians should take their cue from the events that are being detailed and their own knowledge, that is, from tradition (e.g., a reading of Thucydides) and from experience (familiarity with or engagement in debates about these same issues), of the kind of arguments made in similar situations. In Polybius's view, speech that is unrelated to the narrative cannot be beneficial. "What was really said" in this case relates to the kinds of things that are typically said on such occasions or what is "appropriate" (τὸ πρέπον) to particular characters in specific situations. For Polybius and many other ancient historians this sense of "appropriateness" must derive from the historian's own personal experience of the various types of things the historian has described in the narrative.

For this reason, it is entirely necessary for historians to examine old memoirs (by which Polybius means former accounts of regions, battles, customs; cf. 12.25e.5), survey the geographical area of the activity, and investigate political activities (12.25e.1). These three tasks contribute to a writer's ability to the vivify the realia presented in the narrative, which, in turn, attract

---

treatment of Hannibal (9.12.1–21.1; see further Eckstein, *Moral Vision*, 177–92; for similar themes in Arrian, see P. A. Stadter, *Arrian of Nicomedia* [Chapel Hill: University of North Carolina Press, 1980], 89–103).

the interest of the reader (12.25h.1–6).[144] Thus, historians must have a diverse and wide array of experiences. Polybius realizes that it is impossible for one person to experience everything, but insists that historians should have "experience of the most important [events] and those of commonest occurrence" (12.25h.6). If they are able to draw upon this reservoir, they can be selective in their composition of the speeches. Whereas Timaeus does not know what to include or exclude because of his own lack of experience, a "true" historian can execute the task more adequately:

> ... the necessary thing being to choose on every occasion suitable and opportune arguments. But since the needs of the case vary, we have need of special practice and principle in judging how many and which of the possible arguments we should employ, that is if we mean to do good rather than harm to our readers. Now it is difficult to convey by precept what is opportune or not in all instances, but it is not impossible to be led to a notion of it by reasoning from our personal experience in the past. (12.25i.5–6)

The duty of the historian is to find the "necessary" and "opportune" arguments for specific situations, and they can do so best on the basis of their own experience of the past (i.e., the individual who has delivered a funeral oration in real life is better equipped to compose one for a history).[145] When Polybius turns immediately to argue that in composing speeches the historian must supply the situation (i.e., the motives and inclinations of the participants), report "what was actually said," and then detail the results and the logical connections, he has more in mind than simply the historicity of the event (12.25i.8). Indeed, in light of the above statement, "what

---

144. It should be emphasized, however, that for Polybius the reader is attracted by the reality of the narrative, not by the blatant and dramatic pleasurable elements other historians may add to lure their readers. This contention evidently reflects a pedagogical and cultural debate.

145. Polybius makes a similar point further on when he discusses "personal inquiry." Often associated with the "hard science" interpretation of ancient history, Polybius uses this phrase to refer to people who have gained experience in the matters they discuss: "Theopompus says that the man who has the best knowledge of war is he who has been present at the most battles, that the most capable speaker is he who has taken part in the greatest number of debates" (12.27.8–9). Polybius also uses "personal inquiry" to refer to the interrogation of witnesses or to one's own experience of the specific events, but even then, without prior personal experience, "even if present [one] is in a sense not present" (12.28a.10). Byrskog, *Story as History*, 182–84, 187–88, argues that "personal experience" for Polybius does not relate to plausible narration per se (i.e., the experienced historian will be able to relate events in a believable manner), but is required in order to be able to "inquire" properly (i.e., knowing what questions to ask of one's informants and how to gauge the information received). In 12.28a.8–10, it is indeed tempting to read Polybius in this latter sense. Polybius does refer to both general experience (12.28.6) and actual participation in the events being described (12.28a.6–7), but his overall point is that no matter which one chooses, Timaeus has neither. In other words, Timaeus is a coward (12.27.4–7; 28.7), and his personal character is bound up with his work as a whole. Consequently, one must pay attention to the rhetorical nuances of "experience" and "inquiry" in Polybius's polemic. In the end, his agreement with Theopompus on the significance of "personal inquiry" is noteworthy. If possible, presence at actual events will always be preferred since the historian then has the greatest resource for narrative composition and is less likely to enumerate implausible and contradictory elements (cf. 12.27.7; 28.5–6).

was actually said" could easily denote those arguments that one can intuit by reasoning from one's own experience. In this way, speeches can have a purpose in the historical work precisely because they illuminate the courses of action and thought (12.25i.9).[146]

Polybius's thoughts on the proper task of history and the aims of the historian are significant largely because they represent the articulation of an approach to history that was pervasive in the cultural and literary environment of the ancient world. There were, of course, trajectories of historiography that aimed to please the audience in much the same sense as Isocrates set out for King Nicocles:

> This much, however, is clear, that those who aim to write anything in verse or prose which will make a popular appeal should seek out, not the most profitable discourses, but those which most abound in fictions; for the ear delights in these just as the eye delights in games and contests.... [T]hose who desire to command the attention of their hearers must abstain from admonition and advice, and must say the kind of things which they see are most pleasing to the crowd. (*Nic.* 2.48–49)

Polybius, however, finds this approach problematic. Rather, a history should set forth events and explain their causes, contexts, and results. Speeches and actions should be appropriately conceived, then constructed out of the long tradition of antecedent texts as well as from the experience of the historian himself. Moreover, Polybius's *historia* imitates reality in categories authentic and integral to the ancient world, thereby gaining its power to instruct and to persuade readers through the subjective, rhetorical features embedded in this practice. Polybius is manifestly clear that the special value of history rests not in its ability to reveal historical minutiae — a stratum of real, brute *facta* — but in its capacity to parade characters in concrete, real-life situations before the reader, thereby inculcating within the reader the practical and moral foundation of *paideia*. Moreover, the presentation must be moderate in its depiction of its characters and appropriate in terms of ascribed speech and action. In other words, narratives should reflect the social, cultural, and moral commitments of the larger audience. While neither Polybius nor any other writer with historiographical interest made explicit reference to Aristotle's *Poetics,* it seems that at critical junctures the basic elements of the latter — particularly the understanding of plot and device — have important corollaries and intersections with the former, which attests less to explicit borrowing and more to a common Greco-Roman discursive

---

146. When Polybius goes on to analyze some of Timaeus's speeches, he is clear that the ultimate problem is that they lack probability in terms of situational appropriateness in relation to what the characters say. The speeches contain childish and petty themes, they are improbable, and they look like they have been composed by a schoolboy rather than a seasoned political advocate (12.25k.1–26a.4). In the end, Timaeus's speeches evince, for Polybius, the type of sophistic content that leads to frivolous explorations and paradoxes, exposing the characters and events to ridicule (12.26c.1–4).

practice that is localized and particularized by diverse writers. A brief look at the Polybian tradition of historiography illustrates this assertion further.

Various Greek and Roman writers continued the tradition of reflection and criticism of the historical task. Quintilian, for example, articulates the matter in almost identical terms to Polybius: "For history has a certain affinity to poetry and may be regarded as a kind of prose poem, while it is written for the purpose of narrative, not of proof, and designed from beginning to end not for immediate effect or the instant necessities of forensic strife, but to record events for the benefit of posterity and to win glory for its author" (*Inst.* 10.1.31). For Quintilian, the historian differs from the orator largely because the former's aim is the "truth" whereas the orator may deliberately shift truth and lie in order to make arguments for the moment (i.e., achieve the appropriate result by the best method of persuasion; cf. 2.17.19–20, 26–29; 3.8.63). Here again "truth" means precisely those types of arguments and depictions that will have long lasting value.[147]

When one turns to the historians who came after Polybius, one finds them working with similar themes and conceptual frameworks. In Dionysius of Halicarnassus, for instance, one discovers numerous incidental and programmatic statements on the proper function of history. One significant element he frequently underscores is the necessity of narrating a "complete" action: "...as my subject requires not only that a full account of the way the battle was fought should be given, but also that the subsequent tragic events, which resemble the sudden reversals of fortune seen upon the stage, should be related in no perfunctory manner. I shall endeavour...to give an accurate account of every incident" (*Ant. rom.* 3.18.1; cf. 1.5.2–4).[148] This

---

147. The theme of probability and the problem of myth and fable also occur frequently in the discussion of history. When Plutarch turns to his life of Theseus and Romulus, he argues that by "purifying Fable" he will be able to make "her submit to reason and take on the semblance of History" (*Thes.* 1.3). For Plutarch, the ancient period is full of marvelous stories and supernatural tales, many of which are inaccessible to "probable reasoning" (1.1). Yet even fables can be useful if they are reasoned through and rationalized. Strabo provides an interesting example of this overarching concern. In his discussion of the Amazon women, he observes that most cultures distinguish between myth, "the things that are ancient and false and monstrous," and history, which "wishes for the truth, whether ancient or recent, and contains no monstrous element, or else only rarely." He then elaborates upon this observation by dismissing the story of the Amazon women outright on the basis of its improbability: "[W]ho could believe that an army of women, or a city, or a tribe, could ever be organized without men, and not only be organized but make inroads upon the territory of other people, and not only overpower peoples near them...but even [to] send an expedition across the sea?" (11.5.3). One might smile at Strabo's dismissal of the "myth" based on a particular male cultural value, yet his argument is instructive: The story is a myth because although it is possible that such a thing could happen, it defies the basic experience and knowledge of the Greeks, and therefore is implausible. Truth here represents plausible narration; the benefit of which is associated with its coherence to a cultural masculine norm.

148. In his praise of Theopompus, Dionysius elaborates even further on the extent of establishing logical connections: The historian's task is "to examine the hidden reasons for actions and the motives of their agents, and the feelings in their hearts...and to reveal all the mysteries of apparent virtue and undetected vice" (*Pomp.* 6).

statement of purpose resonates strongly with the former Polybian themes. Yet two further elaborations should be noted. First, Dionysius, unlike Polybius, manifestly designates what his *historia* is imitating: tragedy on the stage. This statement quite naturally brings to mind Aristotle's *Poetics*. For Dionysius, history functions like poetry and tragedy, displaying human types and actions before the readership, drawing the individual into a moral and pedagogical process.

Second, the critical word "accuracy" (ἀκρίβεια) is brought into conjunction with the function of narrative. While frequently associated in the historiographical tradition with "scientific investigation,"[149] here it denotes a further nuance: It relates to the "exactitude" in depicting complete actions. For Dionysius, "accuracy" has an interpretive dimension and requires the historian to bring out the causes and effects of various actions and characters. The fuller and more logical the connections, the greater the accuracy of the account and the utility of the narrative. Indeed, it may not be going too far to suggest that the term ἀκρίβεια carries with it the nuance of "interpretation" in such contexts.[150] It connects more closely with Aristotle's deeper meaning

---

149. Alexander, *Preface to Luke's Gospel*, 131.

150. In this sense, then, ἀκρίβεια is closely related to παρακολουθέω (see Moessner, " 'Eyewitnesses,' 'Informed Contemporaries' "; idem, "The Appeal and Power of Poetics (Luke 1:1–4): Luke's Superior Credentials (παρηκολουθηκότι), Narrative Sequence (καθεξῆς), and Firmness of Understanding (ἠασφάλεια) for the Reader," in *Jesus and the Heritage of Israel: Luke's Narrative Claim upon Israel's Legacy* [ed. D. P. Moessner; Harrisburg, Pa.: Trinity Press International, 1999], 84–123; and idem, "Lukan Prologues," 412–13). J. H. Oliver, discussing the relationship between ἀκρίβεια and ἀλήθεια, suggests that the "truth" of something is "accurately" brought out by reflecting on "unseen causes and eternal truth" (*The Civilizing Power: A Study of the Panathenaic Discourse of Aelius Aristides against the Background of Literature and Cultural Conflict, with Text, Translation, and Commentary* [TAPS 58.1; Philadelphia: American Philosophical Society, 1968], 25–32). His conclusion is that, while Herodotus was the "father of history," Thucydides must be viewed as the "father of historical *akribeia*" (Oliver argues that in the former *akribeia* still carries the meaning of "scientific inquiry," but by the time Thucydides rearticulates the historical task the term comes to mean something more philosophical and ethical; cf. Wiseman, "Lying Historians," 143–44, who argues that Polybius and Thucydides cannot be grouped together with Dionysius in terms of how they understand *akribeia*). See also D. Schmidt, "Rhetorical Influences and Genre: Luke's Preface and the Rhetoric of Hellenistic Historiography," in *Jesus and the Heritage* (ed. Moessner), 44–46, who identifies *akribeia* with "sufficient detail" in the narrative or speech (similarly D. L. Balch, "ἀκριβῶς ... γράψαι [Luke 1:3]: To Write the Full History of God's Receiving All Nations," in *Jesus and the Heritage* [ed. Moessner], 232–39). Viewed in this light, fully detailing a subject — outlining all causes and effects — represents an interpretive principle: The meaning of the narrative comes to fulfillment in the details of the text. The meaning of *akribeia* changes slightly depending on the purposes of individual writers (sometimes, as Oliver states, it will mean [or lead to] philosophical and ethical truth [e.g., Sallust], but other times the details may relate more clearly to specific political and civic ends [e.g., Polybius]). But contrast Byrskog, *Story as History*, 182–83, who argues that *akribeia* reflects historical accuracy in the traditional sense (although his acceptance of Moessner's conclusions with respect to *akribeia* in Luke-Acts [231] would seem to contradict his assertion). In this context, then, the concept of *to saphes* connects with the same themes. In his assessment of Thucydides, Edmunds refers to the type of "clarity" in narrative composition that transcends the particulars of time and locale; the kind of precision in understanding acts and results that can only be comprehended at a distance (*Chance and Intelligence*, 175). This seems to be also what Polybius is getting at when he states that if

contained in poetry and tragedy — the "philosophical and more elevated" material (*Poet.* 1451b) — although in Dionysius it has a markedly stronger connotation of ethical and moral lessons than in Aristotle.[151] That Dionysius seeks a similar understanding of "truth" in this case is illustrated by the opening remarks to his treatise: "[T]hose who write histories, in which we have the right to assume that Truth, the source of both prudence and wisdom, is enshrined, ought first of all, to make choice of noble and lofty subjects and such as will be of great utility to their readers" (*Ant. rom.* 1.1.2; cf. Diodorus 1.2.2–2.8). Here one perceives a further elaboration of what is already implicit in Polybius.[152] It is perhaps true that Dionysius more so than Polybius views this focus in ethical rather than political terms (although the former is not lacking in Polybius either), but this is not a radical departure from the Polybian understanding as much as it is a natural progression. And even more so than for Polybius, the character of the writer is connected to their narrative composition, as "a man's words are the images of his mind" (cf. Dionysius, *Ant. rom.* 1.1.3; cf. Seneca, *Ep.* 114.2–3). In this way, reflection on poor moral characters or unworthy actions is an inappropriate subject for history, which should not only be educational but should also edify the reader by focusing on examples of virtue (*Ant. rom.* 1.5.3).

Consequently, Dionysius believes that both leaders in civic affairs as well as philosophers can learn from his history. The special value of *historia* is that by concentrating on the context of events, the necessities that brought about actions, the decisions that were reached and the reasons underlying them, the characters who persuaded others and the arguments they used, and the *exempla* being paraded in the narrative, one is able to move from mere words to the beholding of "fine actions" (*Ant. rom.* 11.1.1–5; cf. 1.8.2–4). This articulation may perhaps have been more crass than Aristotle's understanding of mimesis, but broadly speaking it may also have been more effective. Simply put, the beholding of such actions "before the eyes" leads to the imitation of these by the beholder. It is no surprise, then,

---

the historian relates the situation, motives, and inclinations of actors and reports "what was actually said," going on to provide the reasons for why the individuals succeeded or failed, then "we shall arrive at some true notion of the actual facts" (12.25i.8). In other words, the "actual facts" can only be perceived at the level of secondary reflection; the historian, rather than the original actors, is in the position to understand most accurately and truthfully (Edmunds, *Chance and Intelligence,* 155–57).

151. See Oliver, *Civilizing Power,* 29, where he suggests that σπουδαῖος means the "deeper more important" truth (i.e., the universals). Certainly in many instances it carries this sense in view of its more general meaning of "worthwhile," but, naturally, what is considered "excellent material" for repetition will vary from writer to writer.

152. See also Dionysius's statements in his treatise on Thucydides, where he states that the goal of philosophical studies "is the discovery of truth, by which the purpose of life itself is revealed" (*Thuc.* 3). Dionysius does not distinguish between the "truth of history" and the "truth of philosophy"; they are the same for him. When Dionysius comments on Thucydides' statement in 1.22, regarding the utility of history and the universal patterns of human experience, he states, "History is the High Priestess of Truth in our view, and Thucydides concerned himself above all with recording the truth" (*Thuc.* 8).

that this particular approach to historical composition can be summarized as "philosophy by examples."[153] Livy's sentiments summarize this tendency well: "What chiefly makes the study of history wholesome and profitable is this, that you behold the lessons of every kind of experience set forth as on a conspicuous moment; from these you may choose yourself and for your own state what to imitate, from these mark for avoidance what is shameful in the conception and shameful in the result" (*Preface* 9).

Herein one clearly observes the subsequent engagement of the emphasis on the practical and moral benefit of history. It is evident that the Romans became increasingly preoccupied with the moral benefit of history and tended to neglect the politically pragmatic elements. And while the pragmatic features of historical composition never completely faded, the increasing emphasis on the moral qualities of the narrative also gave way to an increasing epideictic focus in history, as opposed to the more overt deliberative emphasis one finds earlier in Polybius. Thus, Tacitus can state, "It is not my intention to dwell upon any senatorial motions save those either remarkable for their nobility or of memorable turpitude; in which case they fall within my conception of the first duty of history — to ensure that merit shall not lack its record and to hold before the vicious word and deed the terrors of posterity and infamy" (*Ann.* 3.65). The shift toward praise and blame was natural, yet it was also held in tension with the Polybian claim that the historian must be impartial in all matters, never one-sided in the characterization of historical figures (cf. *Ann.* 1.1; *Hist.* 1.1). Of course, these distinctions are also somewhat artificial, as the pragmatic and the moral are intricately bound together already in Polybius, and the shift from deliberative to demonstrative rhetoric was rather easily made in ancient oratory (cf. Quintilian, *Inst.* 3.7.28). Moreover, the practice of politics in the Roman imperial period was a thoroughly moral matter for writers such as Tacitus.

The logical consequence of this development is probably best reflected in the historiographical comments by Diodorus Siculus wherein history takes on the mantle of the teacher: "[H]istories... by offering a schooling... in what is advantageous... provide their readers... with a most excellent kind of experience" (1.1.1). The historian, in Diodorus's view, is a "minister of Divine Providence," who orders the material so as to understand the past and motivate imitation of that which is praiseworthy (1.1.3–4). History equips the reader for every possible situation in life, including endowing the young student with wisdom (1.1.5). History is the "prophetess of truth"

---

153. This famous citation from Pseudo-Dionysius's *Rhetoric* is often taken to be the low point in Roman historiography, yet it can be regarded as a natural outgrowth of the tradition from Polybius onward. It is also not surprising that in both of his historical works Sallust could turn the narratives into explicit reflection on ethical and philosophical themes such as excess and moderation. Earl notes that Sallust clearly articulates his task as philosophical rather than historical in the prologues to the two histories ("Prologue-form in Ancient Historiography," 856).

and the "mother-city of philosophy" (1.2.2), metaphors that deliberately underscore the ideological, religious, and moral power of historical narratives. Most important, history "contributes to the power of speech, and a nobler thing than that may not easily be found. For it is this that makes the Greeks superior to the barbarians, and the educated to the uneducated" (1.2.5–6). This particular function of history arises from its ability to unite fully word and deed in narrative form, "urging men to justice, denouncing those who are evil, lauding the good, laying up, in a word, for its readers a mighty store of experience" (1.2.7–8). In short, then, Diodorus boldly claims for history that quality so greatly prized by the philosopher in the late Hellenistic world — παρρησία: "[T]he frank language [παρρησία] of history should of set purpose be employed for the improvement of society" (31.15.1; cf. 15.1.1).[154] Here one finally arrives at the base of the superstructure that is created by the ancient historian. History's power rests in its ability to speak frankly and boldly to the actions and words of the past so as to persuade those in the present about particular courses of action and thought.[155]

This emphasis on the moral character of *historia* accounts for an oft-stated theme of ancient historiography: the standard of impartiality and the absence of malice, slander, and flattery.[156] One of the most important treatments of this subject in antiquity is Plutarch's *On the Malice of Herodotus*. In this work, which illuminates the "evil character" of Herodotus, Plutarch attacks "the father of history" on one fundamental point: his failure to characterize carefully and fairly individuals and people groups, thereby undermining the utility of his *historia*. Like Polybius and many other historians of antiquity, Plutarch was committed to the principle of moderation and balance in treating character and action (as Aristotle had also maintained in the *Poetics*). This position stemmed from the view that the individual is neither completely evil nor fully good. Rather, particular actions result from the conflict between reason and the passions. Moreover, since history is to model options and "speak frankly" to the reader in the present, it must

---

154. On παρρησία, see C. E. Glad, *Paul and Philodemus: Adaptability in Epicurean and Early Christian Psychagogy* (NovTSup 81; Leiden: Brill, 1995), 36–38, 107–24; idem, "Frank Speech, Flattery, and Friendship in Philodemus," in *Friendship, Flattery, and Frankness of Speech: Studies on Friendship in the New Testament World* (ed. J. T. Fitzgerald; NovTSup 82; Leiden: Brill, 1996), 30–44; S. B. Marrow, "Parrhesia and the New Testament," *CBQ* 44 (1982), esp. 431–39; D. Konstan, *Friendship in the Classical World* (Cambridge: Cambridge University Press, 1997), 103–5; and idem, "Friendship, Frankness, and Flattery," in *Friendship, Flattery, and Frankness* (ed. Fitzgerald), 7–19. For the construction of παρρησία in Acts, see S. C. Winter, "Παρρησία in Acts," in *Friendship, Flattery, and Frankness* (ed. Fitzgerald), 185–202; and esp. L. C. A. Alexander, " 'Foolishness to the Greeks': Jews and Christians in the Public Life of the Empire," in *Philosophy and Power in the Graeco-Roman World: Essays in Honour of Miriam Griffen* (ed. G. Clark and T. Rajak; New York: Oxford University Press, 2002), esp. 243–49.

155. Aelius Aristides (*Or.* 23) frames this discussion of frankness and flattery in terms of manliness (*andreia*) and cowardice (J. Connolly, "Like the Labors of Hercules: *Andreia* and *Paideia* in Greek Culture under Rome," in Andreia: *Studies in Manliness and Courage in Classical Antiquity* [ed. R. M. Rosen and I. Sluiter; MnSup 238; Leiden: Brill, 2003], 314–15).

156. See further Marincola, *Authority and Tradition*, 158–74.

reflect characters and actions that resonate with the value system shared by the reader, which brings the subjective rhetorical feature into play. In other words, the excesses of panegyric and invective do not adequately and faithfully represent the human condition in history. To use the words of Plutarch in another treatise, history's power comes from its being a friend not a flatterer (or slanderer, in the case of Herodotus):

> [A] friend, like a skilled musician, in effecting a transition to what is noble and beneficial, now relaxes and now tightens a string, and so is often pleasant and always profitable, but the flatterer, being accustomed to play his accompaniment of pleasantness and graciousness in one key only, knows nothing either of acts of resistance or of words that hurt, but is guided by the other's wish only, and makes every note and utterance to accord with him. (*Adul. amic.* 55; cf. Maximus of Tyre, *Or.* 14.5)

Elsewhere Plutarch equates the friend with a physician, who at times will prescribe bitter medicine but at other times will recommend a pleasing medication (*Adul. amic.* 55). For Plutarch, the flatterer and friend, with their respective roles, correspond to the two sides of the soul:

> [O]n the one side are truthfulness, love for what is honorable, and power to reason, and on the other side irrationality, love of falsehood, and the emotional element; the friend is always found on the better side as a counsel and advocate, trying after the manner of a physician, to foster the growth of what is sound and to preserve it; but the flatterer takes his place on the side of the emotional and irrational, and this he excites and tickles and wheedles, and tries to divorce from the reasoning powers by contriving for it divers low forms of pleasurable enjoyment. (*Adul. amic.* 61)

For Plutarch, the role of the historian takes its cue from these divergent roles. The flatterer titillates and serves the present moment; the friend looks to the future, attempting to encourage the noble and honorable in an individual and to give solid advice for future benefit.[157] Moreover, Plutarch's understanding of παρρησία is relevant in this context. For him, "frank speech" is the language of friendship, but slander is the ignoble speech of the flatterer: "[F]rankness is friendly and noble, but fault-finding is selfish and mean" (*Adul. amic.* 66). Frankness must also be balanced and moderate, avoiding excessive flourishes, inappropriate sentiments, and various vices of speech such as arrogance and ridicule (67).[158]

Turning again to Plutarch's analysis of Herodotus, one is struck by Plutarch's insistence that Herodotus has undermined the utility and benefit of

---

157. Konstan, *Friendship in the Classical World*, 98–103. See also Dionysius's contrast between those who flatter barbarians by providing inappropriate accounts of Rome's rise to power (*Ant. rom.* 1.4.3) and his own treatment that seeks truth and justice (1.6.5).

158. J. Connolly argues that Plutarch actually domesticates the Athenian political and civic side of παρρησία, taking it out of the realm of politics and into the private sphere. Connolly situates this move within Plutarch's Roman imperial context ("Problems of the Past in Imperial Greek Education," in *Education in Greek and Roman Antiquity* [ed. Too], 362–63).

history by the manner in which he makes comments, establishes connections, and draws insinuations about particular characters and peoples: "flattering some people in the basest possible manner, while he slanders and maligns others" (*Her. mal.* 854F). While it is easy to construe the debate that Plutarch creates as nothing more than disagreement about the interpretation of events, it is in effect much more: It is at every point an issue of values and cultural codes. If for Plutarch the writer of *historia* is to be a "friend" and is to "speak frankly," historical narratives must be composed in line with appropriate and accepted norms. Moreover, while the historian is allowed to criticize particular actions, the overall tenor of the account should be impartial and fair-minded, teasing out nuances and allowing readers to make their own judgments. Above all, narratives that undermine generally respected standards, long-held traditions, and cultural assumptions threaten the very frankness that history is supposed to engender. So, in criticizing Herodotus, Plutarch accuses him of using extreme language when moderation should have sufficed; of including elements that discredit character but are unrelated to the narrative (i.e., inappropriate to the moment; cf. *Adul. amic.* 68); of omitting worthy elements of character when they are appropriate to the narrative; and of seizing upon less suitable versions of events (*Her. mal.* 855B–F).

This last point is significant because it is frequently construed as an argument for the historian's ability to sift out the truer account through critical inquiry. But this is not necessarily what Plutarch has in mind. For instance, when Plutarch refers to a situation when two or more accounts of an event are current, he notes that the historian, "if he is to be fair, declares as true what he knows to be the case and, when the facts are not clear, says that the more creditable [account] appears to be the true account rather than the less creditable [account]" (*Her. mal.* 855E–F). Plutarch does not mean that the historian knows "for a fact" which account has the greatest claim to historicity. Rather, various accounts are more or less "creditable" based on other considerations, and the historian has the obligation to choose more edifying narratives over those that are less so. Choosing a baser narrative reveals the sordid nature of the historian himself.[159] "What is known to be the case" is precisely the narrative that best reflects the honorable and notable values of the society. Thus, in Plutarch's own example, if a historian suggests that success in a particular venture was the result of money not valor, or that success came easily rather than through hard work or as a result of good fortune rather than intelligence (*Her. mal.* 856B–C), that historian has chosen the less honorable and less noble motivation, thereby producing an ineffectual narrative and consequently inviting a charge of malice.

---

159. Ethos argumentation — the establishment of the "character" of the writer — is fundamentally in view here. See further Penner and Vander Stichele, "Unveiling Paul."

As a result, Plutarch can dismiss whole sections of Herodotus's narrative on the basis of one single principle: Herodotus was "pro-barbarian" (*Her. mal.* 857A–858F). Here it is clear that the inappropriate nature of this slant on narrative composition is founded on what is deemed honorable and noble from a Greek point of view.[160] On numerous occasions Herodotus makes statements that are unflattering to the Greeks. He suggests, for instance, that the Delphic prophetess might be persuaded to give a false oracle (860D), undermining the integrity of Greek prophecy. Elsewhere he detracts from the victory of war by suggesting that the Athenians broke an oath (862B–C) or were treacherous in battle (867C–D). Occasionally Plutarch will challenge a particular fact of Herodotus's account based on other information (cf. 863B), but more often than not he focuses on the unconvincing nature of Herodotus's narrative and the ignoble and unworthy charges he makes about the Greeks: "Herodotus knows the truth, while everybody else, everyone who has ever heard of the Greeks, has been deceived by the tradition which represents these events as magnificent achievements? ... We must not be tricked into accepting unworthy and false notions about the greatest and best cities and men of Greece" (*Her. mal.* 874A–C). In many respects, one could take the cynical position that from Plutarch's perspective Herodotus is a malicious liar precisely because he frequently comes too close to the truth of the "real world" (e.g., Greeks are capable of great wrongs, and barbarians of performing praiseworthy deeds), but any "truth" that undermines the larger cultural value system is by definition a "lie" and a "fiction."

Plutarch's treatise thus fits comfortably within the historiographical ethos being outlined here. If history does not reflect the values of the Greeks and exhibit balanced and moderate assessments of human actions in the past, the historian is no longer a friend but a flatterer, looking to please readers in the present by detracting from the ability of history to lead readers down the path of reason and control of the passions. While it might be tempting to suggest that Herodotus has developed his own type of frank speech, from the Greek perspective any form of speech that undermines rather than bolsters the cultural and social norms is slander and flattery.[161] Attacking the best of the Greek tradition is not παρρησία but "baseness and stupidity" (*Her. mal.* 859D). Frankness in historical presentation produces nuanced descriptions

---

160. The discursive nature of this language and discourse shifts depending on who the writer is and where he is situated: Much in the same way that the Greeks could feminize the "barbarian," the Romans could in turn feminize the Greeks (P. Briant, "History and Ideology: The Greeks and 'Persian Decadence,'" in *Greeks and Barbarians* [ed. T. Harrison; New York: Routledge, 2002], 193–210). See further C. Connors, "Field and Forum: Culture and Agriculture in Roman Rhetoric," in *Roman Eloquence: Rhetoric in Society and Literature* (ed. W. J. Dominik; New York: Routledge, 1997), 75, 84–88; and C. Edwards, *The Politics of Immorality in Ancient Rome* (Cambridge: Cambridge University Press, 1993), 92–97. On the shifting nature of such and similar characterizations even within particular localized contexts, see Gleason, *Making Men*.

161. Glad, *Paul and Philodemus*, 33–36.

of character and action that honors what is worthy in Greek culture. It also focuses attention on those aspects of virtue that lead to a better life and avoids anything that smacks of pleasure for its own sake, excess, slander, bitterness, bad taste, or base desire (cf. Josephus, *Ant.* 1.30: "[M]y work is written for lovers of truth and not to gratify my readers").

It is fitting that we should now come full circle back to Lucian, because he correlates well with the historiographical ethos outlined above. As noted at the outset of this discussion, it is tempting to read Lucian as an exponent of fact-based historiography. He notes in several places his commitment to "what really happened": "The historian's sole task is to tell the tale as it happened.... [O]nly to Truth must sacrifice be made" (*Hist.* 39–40). He goes on to praise Thucydides for his fidelity to "what happened," his avoidance of fiction, and the utility of his narrative for future readers (42). He even offers advice on the methodology of historical composition, detailing the need for jotting down notes and arranging them prior to moving on to literary embellishment (47–48). In line with the above discussion, he argues that the historian must refrain from flattery, being "fearless, incorruptible, free, a friend of free expression and truth, intent... on calling a fig a fig... giving nothing to hatred or friendship, sparing no one, showing neither pity nor shame nor obsequiousness, an impartial judge, well disposed to all men... not reckoning what this or that man will think, but stating the facts" (41). It is no wonder, in light of such statements, that scholars such as W. W. Gasque can claim, "A careful study of this document will make it clear... that [Lucian's] standards for writing history differ little from that of a modern historian who has any literary ambitions."[162]

A surface reading of Lucian's text would perhaps confirm such an assessment, yet there is much in Lucian's famous study on *How to Write History* that suggests otherwise. To begin with, Lucian forswears flattery in the process of historical composition. By this he means to exclude explicit panegyric as an appropriate form of narration, since the "encomiast's sole concern is to praise and please in any way he can the one he praises, and if he can achieve his aim by lying, little will he care" (*Hist.* 7; cf. 10–14, 17). He is careful to distinguish between the aims appropriate to history and those proper to poetry (8). Yet with this distinction Lucian clarifies his understanding of how "fact" and history are interrelated. Poetry's embellishments — consisting of "myth and eulogy and the exaggeration of both" — should not enter history.[163] So far, then, this much is evident: "What happens" for Lucian cannot belong to the realms of the supernatural (mythology) or of extreme panegyric, because in both instances everyday human experience

---

162. Gasque, *History of the Interpretation*, 227. See also Byrskog, *Story as History*, 180 (for his similar sentiments on Lucian), and 182–83 (for his articulation of this emphasis with respect to Polybius's comments in 12.12.3).

163. Lucian actually allows room for mild encomium in history, but it should be appropriate and nuanced (*Hist.* 9).

and values are circumvented. He argues, rather, that "history has one task and one end—what is useful—and that comes from truth alone" (*Hist.* 9; cf. 42). Unlike poetry, which gives pleasure but has no utilitarian value for Lucian, history aims at presenting reality in order to benefit the future reader without explicit focus on pleasure at least as an end in itself. As with Polybius and Dionysius, history in this view is true if it is useful—a conception of "truth" that is much more complex and nuanced than simply equating it with "historicity" as some modern scholars such as Gasque (quoted earlier) do. Lucian illustrates this basic understanding frequently in his ensuing discussion.

Given Lucian's understanding of historical truth, it is no surprise that he should quickly turn to criticizing those historians who overuse description *(ekphrasis)* in composition, as they sidetrack the reader's focus from the significant elements of the narrative (*Hist.* 20). Moreover, improbable events—people dying because of a wounded toe or starving to death in three days (even though "everyone knows" it should take at least a week; 20–21)—also detract from the utility of the narrative by bringing in marvelous, improbable, and imaginary fictions. Further, in line with the historiographical cultural and literary context outlined above, Lucian lays stress on accuracy in the details of the setting for actions and events (24). But even more critical for Lucian is the belief that history must focus on appropriate subjects and reflect the "real world" of the reader of the text.

Two examples are interesting in this regard. First, Lucian takes issue with a particular historian's description of the death of a certain Severianus. The historian, interested solely in dramatic effect, had Severianus take his own life with the shards of a drinking glass he happened to break. Lucian finds this particular scenario absurd. Reminiscent of Plutarch's criticism of Herodotus, however, it is evident that Lucian does not in fact know the actual cause of Severianus's death any more than the historian he is criticizing does. Rather, he makes an argument from cultural values and norms with respect to the suicide scene: "as if there were no dagger, no javelin to be found to bring him a manly and heroic death!" (*Hist.* 25). In other words, the problem with the narrative is related to the concern for "truth" and "facts," but in a different way than we might expect: If one fails to depict the manner of death in less than a "manly" or "virtuous" way, one has offered a narrative of little value outside of providing fodder for ridicule. The utilitarian function of the narrative—its lasting benefit for the state/city—has given way to pleasure in the present (i.e., titillation from a pathetic death). Thus, for Lucian, dramatic flair and embellishment detract from the function of the historical composition. In the same way, then, when in imitation of Thucydides' famous funeral oration by Pericles, this same criticized historian has a centurion deliver a rather innocuous speech (but one for which the crowd wildly praises him), following upon which the centurion slays himself over Severianus's tomb (26), the narrative and speech have failed the single most important criterion of history: There is no lasting value in this dramatic and immoderate exercise.

The second example also focuses on the principle of appropriate narration. Here Lucian refers to a historian who, while setting out to cover the Battle of Europus, instead passes over it in seven lines, choosing instead to dwell on incidental and banal matters, such as the story of a Moor wandering through the hill country looking for something to drink (*Hist.* 28). Lucian concludes with this indictment: "[O]ur famous historian forgot the great killings, charges, imposed truces, guards, and counter-guards at Europus" (28). Thus, that which is most important about history — its presentation of situations and actions of greatest interest to the state — has been replaced by a completely irrelevant story about a lost horseman. Notice, also, that while Lucian may in fact have some idea of the actual facts surrounding the battle, in actuality his real concern is that those inevitable aspects of all battles everywhere — charges, killings, well-laid plans and strategies, truces, impositions, and the like — need to be brought to the forefront of the historical narrative, since it is precisely these elements and the nature of their unfolding in the narrative that inform the citizen and *polis* in future situations.

For Lucian, then, history must consist of two critical elements: It should have an appropriate subject matter (of interest to the state), and it must be a believable and consistent narrative. For all of Lucian's rhetoric of "truth in history" and "what actually happened," there is no substantive case in which Lucian challenges the account of a historian by proffering an alternative, more reliable tradition.[164] In most cases, Lucian simply challenges the probability and plausibility of the action and speech, demonstrating its inappropriate and inconsistent nature. He is clearly interested in narratives that both have the appearance of truth and reflect the values and larger interests of Greco-Roman society. Lucian, for instance, ridicules another historian who, while claiming to be recording what he has seen and heard, narrates that an advancing Parthian army is preceded by an enormous living serpent. Lucian recognizes that this writer has confused the symbol of a serpent on a Parthian banner for an actual living creature. Lucian avers that this individual has neither seen a real battle nor even viewed a picture of one painted on a wall (*Hist.* 29). In other words, in Lucian's sardonic phrasing, had this historian observed even a painting of a real battle, he should have been able to provide a more realistic portrayal of the Parthian army than he does now, lapsing into mythology and superstition.

The outcome of this line of argument in Lucian is obvious: The person who undertakes the writing of history must be able to understand the needs

---

164. Debate surrounds whether Lucian did not in fact fictionalize all, or at least some, of his repertoire of negative examples. If this is the case, then we have here an insight into Lucian's actual practice: invention for the sake of making a useful argument. See G. Anderson, "Lucian: Tradition versus Reality," *ANRW* 2.34.2 (1993): 1433–34.

of the state and be able to present the material in a convincing manner. It is no surprise, then, that Lucian argues that the two supreme qualifications for the historian are "political understanding and power of expression" (*Hist.* 34). Therefore, the historian will be

> a man with the mind of a soldier combined with that of a good citizen, and a knowledge of generalship; yes, and one who has at some time been in a camp and has seen soldiers exercising or drilling and knows of arms and engines; again, let him know what "in column," what "in line" mean, how the companies of infantry, how the calvary, are manoeuvred, the origin and meaning of "lead out" and "lead around," in short not a stay-at-home or one who must rely on what people tell him. (*Hist.* 37)

The historian is portrayed as one who knows the rules of war and the norms and values of citizenship, and is able to construct narratives that reflect the realia of actual situations. This focus stands in direct line with the emphases from Polybius onward, that true historians are those who have actual experience and knowledge of the kinds of things they relate. Ideally they should have firsthand knowledge of the specific or at least type of event being recorded (47–49). Most importantly, however, Lucian is overtly concerned that the historian be able to arrange the material and provide exposition of its content (50). The historian is to "give a fine arrangement to events and illuminate them as vividly as possible" (51). In line with Cicero's notion of elaboration and Dionysius's emphasis on demonstrating the sequence and connection of events, Lucian also understands that arrangement of material is intricately interwined with to the utility of the narrative: The better the lines of connection between discrete events are traced and underscored, the more value the larger composition will have for instructing future generations of readers.

The last element in the development of the Lucianic historian is the inculcation of free speech and frankness: "[L]et his mind be free, let him fear no one and expect nothing, or he will be like a bad judge who sells his verdict to curry favor or gratify hatred" (*Hist.* 38; cf. 41, 61). Here again, the emphasis is on the ability of the historian to speak to the moment, not faltering in the presentation of the details that adequately — even if harshly — address the quintessential aspects relevant to the reader. Those historians who flatter rulers or malign individuals without just cause render their history useless. Historical narrative should depict the events and personages of history boldly and freely, without muting its voice for fear of censure or for the desire of praise. The word παρρησία in this context harks back to its original meaning in the *polis*: the freedom of the citizen to speak what needs to be said on a given occasion.[165] The historian, in effect, exercises

---

165. The connection of παρρησία with the rights and language of citizenship is underscored by Marrow, "Parrhesia and the New Testament," 439; and H. Schlier, "Παρρησία, παρρησιάζομαι," *TDNT* 5:872.

civic rights and responsibilities in the composition of historical narratives. Just as citizens are expected to voice their opinions in the *demos* of the *polis*, so in writing history, historians are expected to speak the things necessary for the health and welfare of the state. The Thucydidean comment in Pericles' famous funeral oration perhaps best summarizes this interconnection of political duty and reflection on events:

> For we alone regard the man who takes no part in public affairs, not as one who minds his own business, but as good for nothing; and we Athenians decide public questions for ourselves or at least endeavour to arrive at a sound understanding of them, in the belief that it is not debate that is a hindrance to action, but rather not to be instructed by debate before the time comes for action. For in truth we have this point also of superiority over other men, to be most daring in action and yet at the same time most given to reflection upon the ventures we mean to undertake. (2.40.3)

In some respects, then, it is not going too far to consider historical composition in antiquity a civic duty, especially as it provides explicit reflection on actions and fodder for debate. And, as a corollary, it is no accident that Lucian believes only citizens are truly capable of writing effective *historia*, since they perceive most clearly the nature of the political state and its norms.[166]

From this brief survey on the motivation for historical composition in antiquity, some overarching principles emerge that should help clarify the place of Luke-Acts within this larger framework. First, there was a pervasive understanding that works of history ought to be useful to and beneficial for the reader. The particular form of utility might vary from writer to writer — from the ethnographical framework of Herodotus, to the psychological view of history in Posidonius, to the moral emphasis of Sallust, to the political focus of Thucydides and Polybius — but the underlying motivation is consistent. The emphasis on the future rather than the present is clear throughout, revealing the conviction of these historians that particular actions are not limited in scope, but, if clearly articulated and carefully reflected upon, have lasting and universal value. History, in this view, reveals principles and establishes paradigms that can instruct those who find themselves in similar situations in the future. In short, historical composition, in the trajectory outlined above, has a close connection to *paideia;* it educates the reader in the strategies, actions, and morals that transcend limited locales and time periods. Of course, for history to take its place in the order of *paideia* it was necessary that it be written correctly, appropriately, and with the right motives. Only those histories most truly and effectively representing their genre — in the opinion of a Lucian at least — would provide the surest

---

166. In this connection, compare Arius Didymus's summary of the activities of the "wise man": "[He] takes part in politics...[and] he makes laws and educates his fellow men; furthermore, it is fitting for the worthwhile to write down what is able to benefit those who happen upon their writings" (11b; A. J. Pomeroy, ed. and trans., *Arius Didymus: Epitome of Stoic Ethics* [SBLTT 44; Atlanta: Scholars Press, 1999]).

ground of instruction. As Maximus of Tyre aptly states, "[H]istorical narratives delight the uninitiated with the pleasures they offer, but also offer the initiate a most attractive reminder of what he already knows" (*Or.* 22.5).[167]

Second, we must contend seriously with the culture wars of antiquity in our assessment of historiography. As is evident from writers such as Plutarch, Polybius, and Lucian, there were historians who were characterized as not living up to the ideal of the so-called Thucydidean tradition. The first section of this chapter touched upon this debate. One of the problems is that it is difficult to recover fully the nature and extent of the ancient discussion and the precise dividing lines between good/true and bad/false history. Lucian condemns explicit eulogizing in history, including invention of deeds and pure flattery in speech (*Hist.* 12–13, 17, 61). At the same time, the demarcations were always much grayer in practice. Part of the debate reflects not so much the use of flattery versus bold speech in historical composition, but differences of opinion over the utility and benefit of the narratives. Lucian, Thucydides, and Polybius represent a particular configuration of historiography that stresses the deliberative function of the *historia*: It persuades the readers toward particular courses of action (or provides the raw material for deliberation). Others, Plutarch (possibly), Sallust, and Dionysius tend toward the epideictic function, focusing on the power of history to model examples for the reader. The difference in method is really of degree, as the moral qualities in the narratives of Thucydides and Polybius are as pronounced as the political elements in the accounts of Sallust and Dionysius.[168]

While it is tempting to create a division such as Lucian would have us envision — between history with a deliberative focus and history with an epideictic one — we should rather distinguish between history as pure panegyric and history that seeks to benefit its readers, in a variety of forms and manners, through narrative presentation. Moreover, we cannot overlook the feature of culture and value conflict, especially as it relates to specific writers

---

167. Translation from M. B. Trapp, ed. and trans., *Maximus of Tyre: The Philosophical Orations* (New York: Oxford University Press, 1997). Maximus goes on, however, to clarify that history is inferior to philosophy precisely because it does not have the power to change individuals: "What advantage did the Athenians gain from the great Athenian *History?* ... [T]he greater part of history is taken up with greedy tyrants and unjust wars and undeserved successes and wicked deeds and cruel disasters and tragic situations. Such things are dangerous to imitate and harmful to remember" (22.6).

168. This shift to the demonstrative function of history is partially the result of the successful Augustan program of wedding history and mythology (P. Zanker, *The Power of Images in the Age of Augustus* [trans. A. Shapiro; Ann Arbor: University of Michigan Press, 1983], 210, 215; on the broad moralizing substructure, which also fuels the demonstrative focus, see Edwards, *Politics of Immorality*, 58–59). On the other hand, the connection of historical composition to the Athenian tradition of the funeral oration — explicitly epideictic in function — is reflected quite clearly in Thucydides' work, despite his own attempt to offer an alternative to the mythology of the *epitaphoi* (N. Loraux, *The Invention of Athens: The Funeral Oration in the Classical City* [trans. A. Sheridan; Cambridge: Harvard University Press, 1986], 287–91, detects this tension).

and audiences. Finally, one would be remiss not to point out that beyond the theoretical aspects embedded in the discussion of historiography in antiquity lies the competitive and combatant environment, which ultimately defines the larger discursive language game. The attempt to separate the work of others from one's own in this context has everything to do with raising the status of some individuals over others.[169]

Third, evident from the foregoing discussion is the moral emphasis of ancient historiographical theory and practice. This feature cannot be overstated. The ancient world understood historical composition to be as much a moral as a political act. Thus, we see the repeated emphasis on malice and flattery as representing bad character, not simply the reflection of poor writing skills. The ancient contrast between the flatterer and the friend in moral terms adequately sums up the historiographical concern. Ideological and rhetorical commitments aside for the moment, Lucian clearly understands the task of the historian as one of friendship: to aim for the truth, for fairness, and for future benefit. Furthermore, in the realm of deliberative forms of historiography, the mark of good citizenship is displayed in the act of writing appropriate history, especially in the practice of bold and frank speech — freely addressing the issues of utmost import for the state. Historians also had the express duty to uncover truth in the concrete actions they detailed. This focus brought on, in effect, a call to trace the universal in the particular events. That Sallust should have written a philosophical treatise in historical guise simply reflects the logical outcome of this emphasis.

Not unexpectedly, one also finds here the source for other historiographical principles. So, for instance, the insistence that history be "useful" is not simply political pragmatics, but arises out of the Greek belief that that which is useful is also good.[170] Moreover, the insistence by historians such as Polybius (4.11) and Dionysius (11.1.4–5) that history should also provide pleasure for the reader is also grounded in Greek ethical understanding.[171] Furthermore, the numerous comments of the historians on what is or is not appropriate in historical narrative reflects not only a sense of good style but, even more importantly, a conviction that the historian should model the virtues in literary art.[172] Alongside bold and frank speech, one is also called

---

169. See further Penner, "*Res Gestae Divi Christi.*"
170. This point is frequently missed by those scholars who categorize Thucydides and Polybius as "pragmatic" historians. On "usefulness" in Greek ethical theory, see J. M. Rist, *Human Value: A Study in Ancient Philosophical Ethics* (PA 40; Leiden: Brill, 1982), 11–15; and K. J. Dover, *Greek Popular Morality in the Time of Plato and Aristotle* (Indianapolis: Hackett, 1994), 296–99.
171. Cf. n. 139.
172. Cf. Cicero, *Off.* 1.94, where he identifies "appropriateness" with that which is morally right; and 1.142, which details the related concepts of "orderliness of conduct" and "seasonableness of occasions."

upon, above all, to reflect moderation, proportion, and appropriateness in narrative composition. Polybius, as we saw above, found excess in other historians particularly troubling. Rather, in line with traditional Greek values, he insists on the Aristotelian mean: avoiding the extremes in both positive and negative directions. The virtue of *sophrosyne,* is thus prominent, reflecting the value of self-control and moderation in all circumstances.[173] Perhaps the most significant development following out of this focus on self-control is the emphasis on moderation in narrative composition: eschewing excess and promoting proportion and the mean.[174] Consequently, the act of writing history was also a moral enterprise, wherein individual historians exercised the qualities of good citizenship and virtue. This emphasis is one of the reasons why the discourse on virtue and historical writing is so intricately bound up with the criticism of "inferior" predecessors.[175] Although the following are evident rhetorical tropes, charges of maliciousness, inaccuracy, excess, and bad character naturally flow out of the understanding of historical practice as a moral and civic responsibility. Further, the emphasis on the act of writing history then naturally spills over into discussions of the content itself. There are particular cultural values and norms that need to be upheld in historical composition. These values and norms are not incidental to the task, but are at the very heart of ancient historiography. One ought to construct narratives that represent reality and that reinforce rather than undermine the political, social, and moral basis of the *polis.*

Fourth, from the three previous points the following becomes clear: The essential feature of ancient historiography is the narrative itself. The relationship of historical composition to historicity is a complex and multifaceted phenomenon in antiquity, historical composition itself being a self-declared act of interpretation, one in which the accurate tracing of events and consequences is carried out in order to illuminate more fully the particular in relationship to the universal. Lucian's description of the historian as "Homer's Zeus" is completely apropos in this respect: The historian discerns the universal and necessary patterns that escape the actor caught in the particularity of the historical moment (*Hist.* 49; cf. Aristotle, *Poet.* 1454b: "[W]e ascribe to the gods the capacity to see all things"). While it is evident that in the minds of ancient historians there had to be raw data of some sort from which to draw out interpretation and analysis, the narrative, in

---

173. H. North, *Sophrosyne: Self-Knowledge and Self-Restraint in Greek Literature* (Ithaca: Cornell University Press, 1966), 258.

174. On the mean *(moderatio)* in Greek and Roman ethical understanding, see North, *Sophrosyne,* 304–7; and J. Annas, *The Morality of Happiness* (New York: Oxford University Press, 1993), 59–61, 312–13. Cf. Dionysius, *Thuc.* 51: "[E]xcess is an abomination even in quite pleasant things, whereas moderation is everywhere desirable"; and Lucian, *Hist.* 49: Everything "should be in moderation, avoiding excess."

175. Marincola, *Authority and Tradition,* 128–33.

a sense, is an intentional symbolic construction.[176] The narrative thread is not incidental to *historia;* it is precisely that which makes the history "a possession for all time." When Cicero and Dionysius therefore clarify the importance of tracing connections between actors, events, and outcomes — moving from the *fundamenta* to historical composition proper — these critics are explicitly identifying the locus of *historia*. It is distinguished from the chronicle by its essential concern for interpretation, exposition, and understanding of discrete and particular events. In this way *historia* comes to be presented as mimetic just like poetry; history does not deal with indiscriminate and incoherent series of events, but should ideally, like tragedy, create believable and necessary lines of plot development.[177]

In light of the reflection on historiographical method outlined above, it is apparent that the aim and goal of ancient *historia* is not simply to provide the bare facts of an event, but to produce a narrative framework for relating and interpreting events. Thus, in view of this intent, the reader of such texts has the primary responsibility to comprehend the larger interpretive framework into which the *fundamentum* has been set. The attempt to determine the historicity of particular narrative accounts may be a legitimate modern concern, but this is not the primary preoccupation in ancient historical composition. Once one perceives history as a literary enterprise, the gulf that is often established between a Thucydides and a Livy narrows. The methodology itself leaves open a wide variety of approaches for executing narrative composition, from those accounts that tend toward more precise chronicling to those that invent whole sequences of events. The main payoff comes in understanding that in this literary and cultural environment questions of factual truth are largely subordinate and subservient to the higher truth of philosophy and politics.[178] Whatever we may desire to do with respect to the historical core of the narrative, the ancient historian's main

---

176. Calame, *Craft of Poetic Speech*, 94–96.

177. See further E. S. Belfiore, *Tragic Pleasures: Aristotle on Plot and Emotion* (Princeton: Princeton University Press, 1992), 113, 119–22, 248. On the convergence of tragedy and history in Hellenistic and Roman historiography, see A. Feldherr, *Spectacle and Society in Livy's History* (Berkeley: University of California Press, 1998), 7, 166–68.

178. We are dealing here with a fundamentally different understanding of truth than our modern conceptions. Truth is not necessarily the opposite of falsity in this environment. Arius Didymus, for instance, aptly sums up the Stoic conception in this way: "It is said that the wise man does not lie, but tells the truth in all cases. For lying does not occur in telling a falsehood, but in telling the falsehood in a false way and for the deception of one's neighbours. However they believe that he will sometimes avail himself of the falsehood in numerous ways without assent: in accord with generalship against the opponents, and in accord with his foresight of what is useful, and in accord with many other types of management of life" (11m; Pomeroy). Here one can state a falsehood in the strict sense without lying if one does not intend to deceive one's neighbors (presumably to their detriment) or if it is useful to do so (i.e., achieves a greater good/end). The latter sense stands very close to the understanding of truth in the rhetorical tradition. For a different but also correlative take on historical truth in relationship to *imperium* in Roman historiography, see Feldherr, *Spectacle and Society,* 74–78.

aim rests in the story taken as a whole. As Cicero clearly states in his comments on historiographical method, the narrative is the primary vehicle by which the historian clarifies the "booming, buzzing confusion" of discrete particulars.

I conclude this section with three final points: First, ancient historians understood the narrative framework to be an intentional literary creation that would interpret the actions and events being described. This element is what brings *historia* to life in the ancient world. Second, some historians like Thucydides may have attempted to reflect actual occurrences and personages to a higher degree than other writers such as Josephus or Livy. This distinction is not in dispute. What is in dispute, however, is how one properly understands the delimitation of the genre of *historia* in antiquity, and whether it is fair to characterize Roman historiography as a devolution of the ideal Greek form. Since every historian had a different conception of what proper narration was and how it might be most effective (hence the existence of both a Polybius and a Phylarchus), one must either take Polybius's and Lucian's comments as normative or attempt to uncover the more fundamental shared methodological presuppositions of most if not all ancient historians. Third, and most important, historical compositions should not be evaluated as worthwhile or useful on the basis of our modern understanding. Completely fabricated accounts may in fact be better *historia*, according to ancient standards, than narratives that display accurate detail in the narration of events and people. This type of understanding in many cases will blur the lines between our categories of "history" and "fiction," but will ultimately provide us with a better means for assessing not the historicity of historical works, but their raison d'être.

Features of Historical Composition

Given the primacy of the narrative in ancient historiography, it is essential to gain an appreciation for the literary quality and art of narrative composition in historical works. While treatment of compositional techniques and narrative art in ancient historiography is obviously a multifaceted and complex phenomenon, what follows is a brief and somewhat tendentious presentation. In particular, I am interested in pulling together some of the more prominent features of historical narrative writing that will prove fruitful, in the last chapter, for understanding Luke's composition of the Hellenist episode in Acts 6:1–8:3. To narrow the focus at present, I will briefly flesh out the following elements: plot development and interpretation; description and vivid detail; *topoi*, type-scenes, characterization, double narratives, and comparison; and the use of speeches. In the course of this discussion the correlation and intersection of rhetorical composition in oratory and in historical works become evident. It is clear that ancient writers did not make the distinction between oratory and history that we are wont to do.

We mistake Lucian's comments on the gap between history and oratory as a statement about the relationship of rhetorical training and history, when in fact Lucian was commenting on one particular trajectory of oratory, namely, panegyric (*Hist.* 8; cf. Diodorus 20.1). Indeed, the ancient orators, especially those in the Roman period, frequently used history to illustrate rhetorical method.[179] From this perspective, historical composition was viewed as a natural offspring of ancient rhetorical training. It is thus not surprising that there are so many convergences between the rhetorical handbooks and those treatises detailing historiographical reflection. The *progymnasmata* were one critical component that fostered this kind of interaction, and from Aristotle's *Poetics* to Polybius's history and beyond there is ample attestation to the broader cultural and literary patterns that were also inculcated in pedagogical processes and products.[180] This point of confluence also helps us understand the reason why the art of narrative composition is so important to the ancient historians: It was the legacy of their primary education.

The Persuasive Narrative: Arrangement, Illumination, and Plot

At the heart of ancient historical composition lies the concept of a "complete narrative." Cicero's extended comment in *De oratore*, which illustrates this principle well, bears repeating in part:

> This groundwork [*fundamenta*] of course is familiar to every one; the completed structure [*exaedificatio*] however rests upon the story and the diction. The nature of the subject needs chronological arrangement and geographical representation: and since, in reading of important affairs worth recording, the plans of campaign, the executive actions and the results are successively looked for, it calls also, as regards such plans, for some intimation of what the writer approves, and in the narrative of achievement, not only for a statement of what was done or said, but also of the manner of doing or saying it; and,

---

179. In Theon's *Progymnasmata*, for instance, one observes the intriguing use of a Thucydidean narrative to illustrate probable narration in oratory (5.195–225). When referring to style in oratory, Quintilian uses both Sallust and Livy to illustrate styles to be avoided by the orator (*Inst.* 10.1.32; cf. 4.2.45). Elsewhere Quintilian refers to Sallust's imitation of the *exordium* of demonstrative oratory (3.8.9). Dionysius analyzes Thucydides' introduction on the basis of the rhetorical handbooks (*Thuc.* 19), and elsewhere in the same treatise he studies Thucydides' content and style on the basis of acceptable rhetorical form, finding that in the second element, style, he "frequently falls short of requirements" (34). In Dionysius and Quintilian, then, one discerns a rhetorical form of literary criticism: applying the canons of oratory to literary analysis (see G. M. A. Grube, *The Greek and Roman Critics* [Toronto: University of Toronto Press, 1965], 229).

180. See van Unnik, "Luke's Second Book," 46–47; and Penner, "Reconfiguring the Rhetorical Study." It is not by accident that the epideictic focus of historiography coincides with the prominence of the *progymnasmata* in the Roman era. Unlike the rhetorical handbooks in which demonstrative rhetoric played a peripheral role (Connolly, "Like the Labors," 305–6), the training exercises centered on epideictic discourse (D. A. Russell, "The Panegyrists and Their Teachers," in *The Propaganda of Power: The Role of Panegyric in Late Antiquity* [ed. M. Whitby; MnSup 183; Leiden: Brill, 1998], 49). For the influence of the *progymnasmata* on historical composition, see Burgess, "Epideictic Literature," 200–201.

in the estimate of consequences, for an exposition of all contributory causes, whether originating in accident, discretion or foolhardiness; and, as for the individual actors, besides an account of their exploits, it demands particulars of the lives and characters of such as are outstanding in renown and dignity. (*De or.* 2.63)

This formulation represents Cicero's most explicit statement on historical narrative composition. Elsewhere, in detailing *narratio* in oratory, his discussion seems almost identical: "The *narrative [narratio]* is an exposition of events that have occurred or are supposed to have occurred" (*Inv.* 1.27). Such a narrative will be clear if events flow naturally from one to another (1.29) and will be plausible

> if it seems to embody characteristics which are accustomed to appear in real life; if the proper qualities of the character are maintained, if the reasons for their actions are plain, if there seems to have been ability to do the deed; if it can be shown that the time was opportune, the space sufficient and the place suitable for the events to be narrated; if the story fits in with the nature of the actors in it, the habits of ordinary people and the beliefs of the audience. (1.29; cf. *Rhet. Her.* 1.16)

Here Cicero makes an explicit connection between plausibility and verisimilitude in the *narratio*. Its success rests in its appropriateness to the occasion and actors (the origin of its persuasiveness) and in its ability to demonstrate the interrelationship of actors and events (the origin of its utility). For Cicero, then, one of the most important elements in historical and oratorical composition is the capacity of the writer to develop complete narratives of action and consequences. This particular theme comes to dominate ancient discussion on historiography.

In Pseudo-Plutarch's *Essay on the Life and Poetry of Homer,* we find a similar understanding of narratives in ancient oratory and history: "The historical is that which contains the narration of past events. The subjects of all narratives are character, place, cause, instrument, deed, impact, and manner, and no narrative contains within it any element beyond these" (74).[181] The writer is referring to the poetic/epic text of Homer as a historical narrative and ascribing to it an accepted pattern for narrative composition. Just as important is the resonance of this description of narrative to that found in the *progymnasmata*. For instance, in Theon one finds a similar presentation of the narrative (διήγημα):

> A narrative is an explanatory account of matters which have occurred or as if they have occurred. Elements of the narrative are six: 1) the character can be either one or many; 2) the act done by the character; 3) the place in which the activity was done; 4) the time during which the activity was done; 5) the manner of the activity and 6) the reason for these things. Since these are the

---

181. Translation from J. J. Keaney and R. Lamberton, eds., *[Plutarch] Essay on the Life and Poetry of Homer* (ACS 40; Atlanta: Scholars Press, 1996).

main elements of which the complete narrative is comprised, it is composed from all of them plus what is related to them. The narrative which lacks one of these elements is incomplete. (5.1–11)

Theon goes on to elaborate on each of these six elements of a complete narrative. In discussing the "act done by the character," for example, he states that one must delineate whether it "is important or unimportant, dangerous or not dangerous, possible or impossible, easy or difficult, necessary or not necessary, advantageous or disadvantageous, just or unjust, honorable or dishonorable" (5.15–18). Moreover, Theon also lists the stylistic qualities of a proper narrative, which consist of clarity, conciseness, and plausibility (5.40ff.).[182] Noteworthy also is Theon's description of the set of commonplace arguments used to analyze narrative (5.449ff.). The way in which one criticizes other narratives exhibits a particular pattern and order. Thus, the critic can seize on the following: narrative obscurity, the recounting of an impossible (it is unnatural or there is inconsistency in the presentation) or implausible event, a particular lack in the narrative in terms of appropriate narrative elements, excessive description, contradictions in the narrative, failure to properly order and arrange the material, and the inclusion of inappropriate and disadvantageous material (i.e., some events and actions "ought not to have been done, and it is advantageous to be silent about those done previously"; 5.471–73).[183] This delineation represents an important list of the argumentative resources for the critic of *historia,* since one finds in Polybius, Dionysius, and Lucian each of these various arguments used in criticizing inadequate and improper historical narratives. When Polybius offers a critique of Timaeus's narrative or Dionysius analyzes Thucydides', they are in effect running through the repertoire of appropriate criticisms of narrative reflected in Theon's *Progymnasmata.*

When one turns to Polybius it is evident that his understanding of narration is consonant with what one finds in Cicero and Theon. In history, Polybius argues, mere facts may interest us, but they are useless unless one illuminates the causes of events (12.25b.1–3). For Polybius this means precisely what Cicero and Theon intend by the "complete narrative": tracing out the interconnecting threads of events and clarifying as fully as possible the context of action. Polybius's stress on the three facets of historical investigation — study of memoirs, geographical survey, and review of political

---

182. The rhetorical context of these three qualities is patently clear when one examines the *narratio* or "statement of facts" in the rhetorical handbooks (cf. *Rhet. Her.* 1.14–16, where the order is brevity, clarity, and plausibility). In his *Letter to Gnaeus Pompeius* (3), Dionysius follows the first two — clarity and conciseness — but also adds vividness (ἐνάργεια) and imitation (μίμησις).

183. Similar to this emphasis is Demetrius's assertion that persuasion comes through clarity and familiarity, the latter referring to the use of words and concepts that the audience will recognize and with which it will sympathize (*Eloc.* 221).

events (12.25e.1–2)—aims at establishing the character, action, and the political and geographical setting of the narrative. Elsewhere Polybius denotes the beneficial nature of complete narratives:

> [B]oth writers and readers of history should not pay so much attention to the actual narrative of events, as to what precedes, what accompanies, and what follows each. For if we take from history the discussion of why, how, and wherefore each thing was done, and whether the result was what we should have reasonably expected, what is left is a clever essay but not a lesson, and while pleasing for the moment of no possible benefit for the future. (3.31.11–13)

The utility of historical narratives derives from their ability to provide secondary and universal reflection on particular and discrete events: "making clear to us the reasons why the speakers [in the narrative] either succeeded or failed" (12.25i.8). This aspect then culminates in the analysis of all the components of an action that are necessary, in the historian's view, for examining, explaining, and elucidating historical events and characters.

Moreover, Polybius also favors a high degree of appropriateness in composition, arguing for the use of suitable and fitting arguments (12.25i.5). For Polybius, the ability to choose the proper type and volume of arguments in the narrative is the mark of a seasoned historian. Excess detracts from the power of the narrative to draw clear and distinct lines of connection. Polybius's commitment to plausibility in narrative composition is in line with this emphasis. While he does in places eschew misstatements given in plausible guise (3.33.17), he argues on several occasions for the value of his narrative on the basis of plausibility (3.47.6–48.12; 12.4b.1–12.7.6). But there is one important difference with respect to plausibility and verisimilitude in historical narrative as opposed to oratory: In the latter, plausibility has its basis in general human experience and internal narrative consistency (cf. Cicero, *Inv.* 1.31); in the former, plausibility is inherently connected to the experience and character of the historian. Since *historia* is intended to be persuasive, the plausibility of the narrative must reflect the geographical, political, and social realities known to the reader. In some sense, then, the standard of plausibility in history is more exact and higher than in oratory, and this is why so much attention is given to establishing the various boundaries for the setting of an event. In other words, failure to describe accurately a geographical region or battle formation would greatly undermine the plausibility of the narrative for those with a more accurate knowledge of the situation. When plausibility breaks down, the entire structural goal of the narrative—drawing the various particular threads into a universal whole—follows suit.

Perhaps more so than any other historian in antiquity, Dionysius of Halicarnassus gives detailed attention to narratives in historical composition. Critiquing one aspect of composition in Thucydides' history, he reiterates the importance of arrangement, which all writings, whether philosophical or rhetorical, require. According to Dionysius, arrangement, as in rhetorical method, more generally consists of division, order, and development. History should be presented as "an uninterrupted sequence of events" (*Thuc.* 9). In Dionysius's view, Thucydides' haphazard arrangement results in a disorderly narrative that makes it difficult for the reader to perceive the relationship of events.[184] This critique concerns "order" (τάξις) or arrangement, which in ancient historiography considered one of the primary compositional elements, alongside the choice of an appropriate subject matter and the designation of a clear line of development (i.e., a beginning, middle, and end of the narrative; *Thuc.* 12; cf. Aristotle, *Rhet.* 3.12.6). In line with this criterion exists also the expectation that the historian will develop and/or downplay particular episodes, depending on their contribution to the larger structure of the narrative (13; cf. the same with respect to the composition of historical speeches [17–19]). In his critique of a rather unseemly scene in Herodotus, Dionysius states that "the incident was not only undignified and unsuitable for artistic embellishment, but also insignificant and hazardous, and closer to ugliness than to beauty" (*Comp.* 3). Therefore, certain episodes could and should be suppressed based on the fact that they detract from the larger aims of the narrative. Naturally, this stress also demands for a measure of good taste and appropriateness in narrative selection, as these qualities most naturally produce pleasure in the reader (*Comp.* 12, 20; *Pomp.* 3).[185]

The choice of subject matter also receives attention in Dionysius's literary treatises. For Dionysius, Herodotus has chosen a more noble and honorable subject — wonderful deeds — as opposed to Thucydides, who has elected to dwell on a Greek disaster (*Pomp.* 3).[186] More important is his assertion that Herodotus has done a better job of ordering his narrative in terms of beginning, middle, and end. Whereas Herodotus has demonstrated a logical progression from initial actions and motivations to the consequences (punishment and retribution), Thucydides, by contrast, fails to exploit the potential impact of his narrative due to the lack of proper arrangement. At

---

184. This criticism of Thucydides' narrative was common in antiquity (cf. Theon 5.62–71). At the same time, Thucydides also shares this ideal of "order" and "arrangement." Precisely this emphasis motivated Thucydides to combine several independent wars into a holistic portrayal of the Peloponnesian war for his readers, creating a fiction of war on a grand scale (see further B. S. Strauss, "The Problem of Periodization: The Case of the Peloponnesian War," in *Inventing Ancient Culture: Historicism, Periodization, and the Ancient World* [ed. M. Golden and P. Toohey; New York: Routledge, 1997], 165–75).

185. The theme of suitability and appropriateness extends to all aspects of narrative composition, from the selection and presentation of the narrative to the vocabulary and literary style utilized. On the latter, Dionysius states, "The most important of all literary qualities is propriety (τὸ πρέπον)." This theme also comes to the fore in the discussions of the appropriateness of speech to character (cf. Cicero, *Off.* 1.142–44), detailed below.

186. Here one observes Dionysius's shift from the deliberative emphasis of Thucydides to the more epideictic focus of Roman historiography. Dionysius also goes on to praise Herodotus for taking pleasure in good deeds and displaying displeasure over the bad, another clear feature of the subtle shift in historiographical perception.

the very least, in Dionysius's view, Thucydides should have concluded his narrative with a great triumph: the return of the exiles and the city's initial recovery of freedom. Here Dionysius reveals a more elaborate sense of plot and narrative development; the goal of narrative is to move through a variety of stages of conflict and resolution, achieving a climactic and dramatic end. The historian, not the events themselves, establishes this structure: "Herodotus has chosen a number of subjects which are in no way alike and had made them into one harmonious whole" (*Pomp.* 3). In his own history, Dionysius claims that, in addition to describing the battles in great detail, he will also depict the "subsequent tragic events, which resemble the sudden reversals of fortune upon the stage" (*Ant. rom.* 3.17.1). His point is simple: He will illustrate, through plot development, the consequences of particular actions. Thus, elaborate, detailed, and embellished narratives are critical components for the understanding of historical connections. It is precisely in this context that Dionysius uses the term "accuracy" (ἀκρίβεια). The most accurate narrative is the one that most fully expounds all the causes, motivations, and results of particular actions, with a view to illustrating the logical progression of the plot. In referring to his detailed discussion of a particular Roman civic controversy, including the various speeches on the different sides of the debate, Dionysius claims that he chose to make his "narration accurate rather than brief" (7.66.5). In other words, detailed narratives that elucidate cause and effect, character and action, event and moral consequence represent accurate portrayals of history precisely because of the overt interpretive structure placed on the material (cf. Lucian, *Hist.* 50–51).

The primary role of the narrative in ancient historiography is evident even from this brief discussion. In fact, it is the presence of narrative — as understood by these historians — that separates history from the annalistic tradition. The famous comments by Asellio, recorded in Aulus Gellius's *Attic Nights*, support this interpretation:

> [B]etween those ... who have desired to leave us annals, and those who have tried to write the history of the Roman people, there was this essential difference. The books of annals merely made known what happened and in what year it happened, which is like writing a diary.... For my part, I realize that it is not enough to make known what has been done, but that one should also show with what purpose and for what reason things were done.... For annals cannot in any way make men more eager to defend their country, or more reluctant to do wrong. Furthermore, to write over and over again in whose consulship a war was begun and ended, and who in consequence entered the city in a triumph, and in that book not to state what happened in the course of the war, what decrees the senate made during that time, or what law or bill was passed, and with what motives these things were done — that is to tell stories to children, not to write history. (5.18.8–9)

On the one hand, despite the clear literary character of this activity, it is easy to appreciate how it can also be traced back to the scientific tradition in antiquity; explanation of phenomena and events lies at the heart of each. By tracing all the various threads — motivations, actions, results — one is able to understand most fully human actions in history, thereby setting a pattern for the future. The historiographical tradition, in all of its manifestations, is thus never that far from the virtues and methods of ancient scientific classification, especially in the Aristotelian tradition. At the same time, where history took on a life of its own is precisely in the complexity that lies behind human actors and events in history. The ability to ascribe motivation, assess consequences, and judge results is a convoluted and multifaceted task in the realm of real human experience. It is therefore subject to the particular philosophical, psychological, and political predilections, commitments, and assumptions of individual historians. Since precisely the tracing of the threads distinguishes the historical task, literary and rhetorical artistry could not help but emerge as prominent features of historical composition, as the aims of ancient rational, scientific classification and analysis (here signaling a distinctive mode of argumentation rather than an objectivist approach to reality) could be achieved therein.[187]

In view of this emphasis on the central role of the narrative in historical composition, the correlation with Aristotle's notion of plot in tragedy is striking. Aristotle was attached to tragedy precisely because the actor and events were inextricably bound together in order to illustrate actions and their results. By contrast, history, in his view, was disjunctive, containing innumerable unrelated events and actions with no single goal (*Poet.* 1459a). Yet, as the discussion laid out here has shown, ancient historians did not necessarily share this view, seeking rather to gain the "view of the gods" with respect to discrete actions in history. In his *Poetics,* Aristotle outlines three important features that would resurface in a more significant role in ancient historiography: "I use 'plot' to denote the construction of events, 'character' to mean that in virtue of which we ascribe certain qualities to the agents,

---

187. The legacy of the classical scientific tradition is pervasive in nearly all features of historical composition. The impact of vivid/dramatic narratives on the reader stems from Aristotelian psychological theory (see S. Halliwell, "Pleasure, Understanding, and Emotion in Aristotle's *Poetics,*" in *Essays on Aristotle's Poetics* [ed. Rorty], 241–60). The *topoi* of characterization arise out of the scientific principle that certain types of individuals can be described in, and will act by, particular rules of character (see, e.g., Theophrastus's *Characters;* on the scientific background, see S. Trenkner, *The Greek Novella in the Classical Period* [Cambridge: Cambridge University Press, 1958], 147–54). Indeed, the impulse toward classification of all categories of human understanding and learning is rooted in classical science. Thus, for instance, the classification of rhetoric itself — and all its various divisions — as *techne* represents a science of rhetoric with the intention of distancing the discipline from the marvelous and superstitious (J. de Romilly, *Magic and Rhetoric in Ancient Greece* [Cambridge: Harvard University Press, 1975], 47–48, 59–61, 64–65). Consequently, the grounding of historical narrative composition in rhetoric did not undermine the ancient scientific basis of history but rather affirmed similar values and assumptions.

and 'thought' to cover the parts in which, through speech, they demonstrate something or declare their view" (1450a). Aristotle here gives priority to plot: "[T]he events and the plot are the goal of tragedy, and the goal is the most important thing of all" (1450a), which itself must be "complete, whole, and of magnitude" (1450b). As with Dionysius's criticism of Thucydides, Aristotle notes that good plots cannot end at an arbitrary place, but must further the aims of the narrative: the elucidation of action and consequence. In line with this, Aristotle argues that the writer must carefully include only material that will advance the "complete action": a unified congruence of events that can be linked by "necessary or probable connections" (1451a) as opposed to "episodic" plots that lack these connections (1451b). In epic poetry, Homer best demonstrates the effectiveness of a complete, single, unitary action (1459a), with the appropriate beginning, middle, and end.[188] Moreover, the three major elements of a tragic plot — whether in tragedy or epic — include reversal, recognition, and suffering (1452a–52b). The plot, then, links events together in such a way so that these three crucial elements are explicated and the hearers of the tragedy come to understand the relationship between certain actions and results. Aristotle's comments on plot pertain particularly to tragedy and epic. Yet, when Dionysius comes to criticize the *historia* of Thucydides, he especially highlights the latter's failure in presenting an appropriately unified narrative that begins and ends in the proper place. As noted above, in Dionysius's view Thucydides did not properly plot out the narrative so as to achieve the illumination of all the events. In short, for Dionysius, Thucydides' narrative lacked an appropriate plot and clear development of the narrative so as to elucidate the climaxes of reversal, suffering, or similar appropriate and typical denouements.

In his *Poetics*, Aristotle is preoccupied with the appropriate order and arrangement of narratives so that they will most effectively bring about their aim; in this case mimesis of an action producing imitation in the hearer, or at least provoking audience reflection on the elements being plotted. While constructing such a narrative was a philosophical and moral exercise in part, it was also based on a scientific premise: Proper plot construction would naturally lead to certain assumed results in the audience. Because tragedy and epic poetry were so malleable — resulting from their fictitious nature —

---

188. The fact that most epic poets, in Aristotle's view, tend to compose narrative like historians rather than following Homer's example achieves, for the latter, the special designation of "inspired" (θεσπέσιος; *Poet*. 1459a). Homer's particular virtue is his ability to separate out one section of the Trojan War, using various other elements as episodes that support the overarching goal of his narrative. Thus, the cataloguing of ships, for instance, now "diversifies the composition" rather than being in itself a significant focus of the plot. In this particular instance Aristotle's understanding is very close to Lucian's: "You need especial discretion in descriptions of mountains, fortifications, and rivers, to avoid the appearance of a tasteless display of your word-power and of indulging your own interests at the expense of the history; you will touch on them lightly for the sake of expediency or clarity, then change the subject...as you see Homer doing in his greatness of mind" (*Hist*. 57).

Aristotle viewed these genres to be the primary vehicles of mimetic effect. At the heart of his framework was the well-plotted narrative coupled with the complete action: unifying the actors and events so as to produce necessary and probable connections. The audience would then recognize itself in the narrative and receive both pleasure and benefit. Despite Aristotle's own dismissal of history as mimetic — based on its lack of a unified plot — it is apparent that the historians' own conception of what they were doing in the process of composition resonates with the theory in Aristotle's *Poetics*. Historians such as Thucydides, Polybius, Dionysius, Josephus, and Lucian were committed to the "true aim" of history: arranging and ordering material so as to bring the events into a logical connection, thereby elucidating actions in history. The historian and Aristotle's tragedian/epic poet consequently have a similar task before them: focusing on the appropriate subject matter, constructing a single and unitary plot (even if it has subordinating episodes), and drawing the various threads together so as to offer a necessary and probable interpretation of the data for the audience. Most important, the result of this well-plotted narrative will be the audience's pleasure and benefit, as individuals recognize from the events of the past patterns for themselves in the present. The goal of Aristotle's tragedian and poet is similar to the historian's in at least this focus: They intend to provide benefit to the reader through the complete narrative. To reiterate my earlier assertion, I do not suggest that the *Poetics* forms the basis for or the direct source of these later historiographical analogies, but that together the two point to a broader common discursive practice in the Greco-Roman world. I do affirm, however, that comparisons with Aristotle's formulations in the *Poetics* can inform our understanding, appreciation, and assessment of the socio-rhetorical context of writing historiography in this environment.[189]

---

189. Although Hayden White's work on historiography is decidedly postmodern in its orientation, many of his conclusions are consonant with the suggestions in this study, especially related to the issue of interpretive frameworks and the fictionalization of history. See H. White, "The Fictions of Factual Representation," in *Tropics of Discourse: Essays in Cultural Criticism* (Baltimore: Johns Hopkins University Press, 1978), 121–34; and idem, "The Value of Narrativity in the Representation of Reality," in *The Content of the Form: Narrative Discourse and Historical Representation* (Baltimore: Johns Hopkins University Press, 1987), 1–25. See also F. Watson, *Text and Truth: Redefining Biblical Theology* (Grand Rapids: Eerdmans, 1997), 54–63, who makes the connection with P. Ricoeur's work on the Aristotelian understanding of plot in tragedy and its relevance for plot in historiography (*Time and Narrative* [3 vols.; trans. K. McLaughlin/Blamey and D. Pellauer; Chicago: University of Chicago Press, 1984–88], esp. 1:175–225). Ricoeur's following comment is apropos: "My thesis is that historical events do not differ from the events framed by a plot. The indirect derivation of the structures of history starting from the basic structures of narrative... allows us to think that it is possible... to extend to the notion of historical event the reformulation of the concepts of singularity, contingency, and absolute deviation imposed by the notion of emplotted event" (1:208). Ricoeur, however, is referring to an unintentional process whereas the argument here has been for the very intentionality of this process in the cultural environment of antiquity. M. Sternberg, although eschewing the use of the term "fiction" in this connection, adds to this discussion by distinguishing between historical truth and history writing, as well as between historical reliability and "historiographic force" (*The Poetics of Biblical Narrative: Ideological Literature*

This observation leads, lastly, to the implicit element in Aristotle's understanding of plot: A well-constructed plot is ultimately the most persuasive. At the center of this understanding of plot construction lies the implied rhetorical character of narratives. Narratives, if properly executed, will persuade readers in a particular direction (to adopt a course of action, to avoid or to model certain behavior, to re/consider a complex political phenomenon, to change or to entrench their opinion about a particular individual). In the historical narrative, as in tragedy, the writer convinces the reader of the case being established and elucidated through their own literary activity and skill. Ultimately, then, it is the goal of creating a persuasive narrative (as reflected in the Aristotelian understanding of plot) that links historical composition to rhetorical training and ultimately to *paideia*. The congruence between the *narratio* of the historian and the *narratio* of the orator is thus not accidental. As one rhetorical handbook suggests with respect to the *narratio* in speech:

> A narration becomes persuasive if (the speaker) tries to make everything he says resemble the truth. This would be the case...if we do not set out bare facts but add the "parts" by which the narration is filled out. The "parts" of a narration are person, thing, place, manner, time, and cause; in addition, if the things said agree with each other and are not dissonant or contradictory; moreover, if we do not simply present the parts but narrate each in detail...One should add reason for all the (actions described); (stating the reason) is most inducive of persuasion. The ethos and pathos of the speaker also create persuasiveness. (Anon. Seguerianus, *On Narrations* 89–94)[190]

This text relates to the composition of the *narratio* in an oration. Yet almost every element also surfaces in the treatment of the historians with respect to the aims and goals of historical composition. Indeed, Cicero's famous citation on writing *historia* given above corresponds almost exactly with the pattern laid out in the rhetorical handbooks for composing the *narratio* in speeches (cf. *Rhet. Her.* 1.9.15–16). That this coherence exists should not surprise us, especially in light of the argument being made in this chapter that the *narratio* of history is, for all intents and purposes, identical to the function of the *narratio* of speech.[191] This feature persuades

---

and the Drama of Reading [Bloomington: Indiana University Press, 1985], 23–35, esp. 26, 33). See also Byrskog, *Story as History,* 213, who tries to hold the brute factual aspect of history in balance with the interpretive narrative framework, without subordinating the former to the latter.

190. Translation from M. R. Dilts and G. A. Kennedy, eds., *Two Greek Rhetorical Treatises from the Roman Empire* (MnSup 168; Leiden: Brill, 1997).

191. When the rhetorical handbooks do make a distinction between the two, it generally comes down to length. For instance, Aphthonius states, "Narrative [*diegema*]...differs from narration [*diegesis*] as does a poem from an entire poetical work" (*Prog.* 2; P. P. Matsen et al., eds., *Readings from Classical Rhetoric* [Carbondale: Southern Illinois University Press, 1990]). In other words, the *diegema* is simply a shorter, self-contained unit of a longer narrative work, which itself combines a series of episodes. See also the comment by Lucian: "For all the body

the reader — by virtue of its arrangement, order, and power of expression — of a particular interpretation of the raw data of historical personages and events. Finally, then, the goals of history can best be achieved by the well-plotted narrative, because it is exactly in the arrangement and order of the material that the power of persuasion and conviction rests.

The Vivid Narrative: Profit through Pleasure

If narrative composition is the key to understanding the program of historiography in antiquity, then it is not surprising to find that one of the most important elements of narration, aside from supplying all the necessary elements of a connected and persuasive narrative thread, is the presentation of the material in such a way that it immediately attracts the interest of, and creates an impact on, the reader. In his *Poetics*, Aristotle uses the term "spectacle" (ὄψις) to designate such episodes. This term literally means "appearance," "a thing seen," or "vision," but in the Aristotelian understanding it denotes the sense of a dramatic narrative that vividly displays the actual events and characters so as to affect the physical senses of the reader. The quality of ὄψις is one of the six elements of tragedy (*Poet.* 1450a), and is perhaps, alongside properly structuring events, one of the most significant means to create a mimetic narrative, as both aim at arousing pity and/or fear in the audience (cf. 1449b). Aristotle explains the goal as follows:

> For the plot should be so constructed that, even without seeing it performed, the person who hears the events that occur experiences horror and pity at what comes about.... To create this effect through spectacle has little to do with the poet's art, and requires material resources. Those who use spectacle to create an effect not of the fearful but only of the sensational have nothing at all in common with tragedy, as it is not every pleasure one should seek from tragedy, but the appropriate kind. And since the poet should create the pleasure which comes from pity and fear through mimesis, obviously this should be built into the events. (1453b)

Aristotle understands that in order for tragedy to impact the audience it must contain depictions of events that themselves bear such inherent emotional weight that they have an immediate and natural effect on the hearer. For Aristotle this aspect produces pleasure in the audience. Since the play or prose piece represents reality at a distance, it is important that it produces events that transport the reader to the inner nature of the event that is being reproduced, so as to have lasting philosophical impact. One of the examples that Aristotle uses, and which I will come back to in the discussion of the Hellenist narrative, is the breakdown of "fellow-feeling" (φιλανθρωπία). Alongside the production of fear and pity in the audience, Aristotle argues

---

of the history is simply a long narrative [*diegesis*]. So let it be adorned with the virtues proper to narrative" (*Hist.* 55). See Byrskog, *Story as History,* 203, for a similar position.

that "fellow-feeling" should be the positive outcome of tragic narration (1452b, 56a).[192] Consequently, its disintegration brings about feelings of pity and fear. Aristotle views such pity and fear being aroused "within relationships, such as brother and brother, son and father, mother and son, son and mother — when the one kills (or is about to kill) the other, or commits some other such deed" (1453b).[193] The breakdown of "fellow-feeling" in these intimate social and familial relationships is precisely what generates the deepest levels of human fear and pity.[194] When tragedy displays such episodes, it brings events before the reader that are experienced as if they were real, and in doing so generates pleasure. This aspect results in the creation of an immediacy between the reader and the event being described.

Closely related to this feature is Aristotle's use of the term "vividness" (ἐνάργεια) with respect to narration. For Aristotle this term is related to diction and has to do with narrating events in the right words so as to produce the same effect as "spectacle,"[195] namely, bringing the narrated events palpably and visibly before the mind of the audience, which is enabled to partake vicariously in the events being portrayed. As Aristotle states, "In this way, by seeing things most vividly [ἐναργέστατα], as if present at the actual events, one will discover what is appropriate and not miss contradictions" (1455a). The writer is able to make the audience aware of particular characters and actions through the use of language and tropes that help visualize the narrative content. In his *Rhetoric*, Aristotle similarly clarifies that bringing something "before the eyes" means to "signify actuality" (3.11.1–3). Aristotle regards Homer as providing an excellent example of this phenomenon because the latter can bring even inanimate objects to life by the use of animating metaphors (e.g., "the ruthless stone," "the spear-point sped eagerly through his breast"). Although here Aristotle has in view the use of diction and choice of metaphor in particular, the same point is stressed: the importance of animating a description in order to attract the interest and raise the pleasure of the audience.

The use of vivid imagery and language, combined with evocative scenes, were critical elements of Aristotle's presentation of tragedy. As with his understanding of plot, there is also significant correlation with ancient historiographical practice. Taken from the rhetorical education of the young orator, the exercise of description (ἔκφρασις) represents an important

---

192. On the concept and its importance in Aristotle's thought, see Belfiore, *Tragic Pleasures*, 70–81.

193. As illustrated by Aristotle's scenario, one of the most important designations of *philia* is the family, and thus its breakdown is most tragic. See M. W. Blundell, *Helping Friends and Harming Enemies: A Study in Sophocles and Greek Ethics* (Cambridge: Cambridge University Press, 1989), 39–43; and Belfiore, *Murder among Friends: Violation of* Philia *in Greek Tragedy* (New York: Oxford University Press, 2000), 3–20.

194. Belfiore, *Tragic Pleasures*, 235.

195. The two concepts are essentially identical and are sometimes used interchangeably. On their connection, see Feldherr, *Spectacle and Society*, 4–12.

component of the repertoire of the historian.[196] The description is one of the exercises in Theon's *Progymnasmata,* and involves "an informative account which brings vividly [ὄψιν] into view what is being set forth" (7.1–2). This exercise is just that: a detailed accounting of an event, thing, custom, and so forth. The most important qualities of the description are "clarity and vividness [ἐνάργεια], in order that what is being reported is virtually visible" (7.53–54; cf. 6.88–89). Here the task is to report events in such a way so as to bring them to life for the reader/hearer. Quintilian aptly defines this feature: "[E]nargeia...makes us seem not so much to narrate as to exhibit the actual scene, while our emotions will be no less actively stirred than if we were present at the actual occurrence" (*Inst.* 6.2.32; 8.3.61–70).[197] For Quintilian this vivifying ability is not only important for the audience but also for the speaker who is to be empathetic with the subject of the speech ("[W]hat will the orator do whose duty it is to picture to himself the facts and who has it in his power to feel the same emotion as his client whose interests are at stake?"; 6.2.35). The vivid narrative, then, whether in the form of a description of an object or a narration of an event/character, requires that the orator/writer have a complete grasp of all facets of the thing being "brought before the eyes." It is not surprising that this should connect so clearly with historical composition: A full understanding of the logic of the plotted actions and events allows the writer to "get inside" the events themselves, filling out (embellishing, in the proper rhetorical sense) the details that enliven the episode. This focus leads, finally to the power of imagination itself: "There are certain experiences which the Greeks call *phantasiai,* and the Romans *visions,* whereby things absent are presented to our imagination with such extreme vividness that they seem actually to be before our very eyes. It is the man who is really sensitive to such impressions who will have the greatest power over the emotions" (Quintilian, *Inst.* 6.2.29–30). Herein self-mastery leads to mastery over one's audience in both rhetoric and historical composition.

---

196. On ἔκφρασις in ancient literature, see S. Bartsch, *Decoding the Ancient Novel: The Reader and the Role of Description in Heliodorus and Achilles Tatius* (Princeton: Princeton University Press, 1989), 7–39; G. N. Sandy, "Apuleius' 'Metamorphoses' and the Ancient Novel," *ANRW* 2.34.2 (1993): 1565–69; G. Anderson, *The Second Sophistic: A Cultural Phenomenon in the Roman Empire* (New York: Routledge, 1993), 144–55; J. R. Morgan, "Make-Believe and Make Believe: The Fictionality of the Greek Novels," in *Lies and Fiction* (ed. Gill and Wiseman), 211–14; A. Wilson, "Reflections on Ekphrasis in Ausonius and Prudentius," in *Ethics and Rhetoric: Classical Essays for Donald Russell on His Seventy-Fifth Birthday* (ed. D. Innes, H. Hines, and C. Pelling; New York: Oxford University Press, 1995), 149–59; J. B. Burton, *Theocritus's Urban Mimes: Mobility, Gender, and Patronage* (HCS 19; Berkeley: University of California Press, 1995), 93–122; and M. M. Mitchell, *The Heavenly Trumpet: John Chrysostom and the Art of Pauline Interpretation* (Louisville: Westminster John Knox, 2002), 100–104. For historiography more specifically, see Varneda, *Historical Method,* 169–80; and Avenarius, *Lukians Schrift,* 142–49.

197. See further R. Webb, "Imagination and the Arousal of the Emotions in Greco-Roman Rhetoric," in *The Passions in Roman Thought and Literature* (ed. S. M. Braund and C. Gill; Cambridge: Cambridge University Press, 1997), 118–19.

From the above rhetorical and educational background, the device of *enargeia* finds its way quite naturally into the composition of historical narrative.[198] Polybius, in his treatment of Timaeus's account, criticizes the latter's frequent misstatements and errors that result from Timaeus's own admission that he has "no experience of active service in war or any personal acquaintance with places" (12.25h.1). According to Polybius, Timaeus's narrative drastically suffers as a result. The holes in logic and the errors in describing places and events (i.e., the lack of verisimilitude to the real-life experience of the readers) results in a portrayal that lacks in "vividness [ἐμφάσεως] and animation [ἐνεργείας] of the real figures."[199] Similar to Aristotle's understanding, a vivid narrative must have the appropriate detail — being clear and logical (i.e., no contradictions) — in order to bring the events to life for the audience. As Polybius states,

> We miss in them [i.e., historians such as Timaeus] the vividness [ἔμφασις] of facts, as this impression can only be produced by the personal experience of the author. Those, therefore, who have not been through the events themselves do not succeed in arousing the interest of their readers. Hence our predecessors considered that historical memoirs should possess such vividness [ἔμφασις] as to make one exclaim when the author deals with political affairs that he necessarily had taken part in politics and had experience of what is wont to happen in the political world, when he deals with war that he had been in the field and risked his life, and when he deals with private life that he had reared children and lived with a wife, and so regarding the other parts of life... it is necessary to have had experience of the most important and those of commonest occurrence. (12.25h.4–6)

Polybius associates several important narrative elements in this comment: The historian can only create a persuasive and convincing narrative if it both reflects the reality of life and experience (i.e., demonstrates the kind of consistency that can only come from someone personally acquainted with the types of elements being described) and contains the complete and logically connected actions combined with a fully established setting for the same. In other words, both the method of the historian (experience and knowledge reflected in composition) and the aim of the historian (connecting the threads in order to provide a useful narrative) coalesce in the practice of creating vivid narratives that are both dramatic and logically consistent. Consequently, when Polybius attacks Phylarcus for "trying to bring horrors vividly before the eyes," which results in creating exaggerated

---

198. See van Unnik, "Luke's Second Book," 55–57; and Avenarius, *Lukians Schrift,* 130–40.
199. The translator of the Loeb edition has used "vividness" to render ἔμφασις, although normally it is used to translate ἐνάργεια. The two terms are related and could be used as synonyms in terms of narrative composition, as they both designate the attempt to bring out the full meaning and significance of an event. In particular, ἔμφασις connotes the proper presentation/representation of events so as to be a *reflection* of those events, while ἐνάργεια means to bring about *clarity* in perception.

images, "probable utterances," and establishing incidental consequences of actions (2.56.9–10), he is not undermining the basic premises that give rise to so-called tragic history, but only its precise method of execution. Polybius affirms the importance of vivid images, but insists that they must relate to the events themselves and not draw undue attention to insignificant or ignoble narrative elements; they ought rather to be attached to what, in his view, are the important events of history.[200] Vividness in and of itself does not detract from the goal of *historia;* rather, it clarifies the meaning and significance of human actions. When narratives are enlivened through the experience of the writer, the audience is more likely to experience profit through pleasure.

Dionysius of Halicarnassus is another writer who gives significant attention to ἐνάργεια in historical composition, making an implicit connection with the rhetorical tradition.[201] For instance, when Dionysius turns to criticism of the historian/orator Hegesias, he is particularly appalled by the latter's use of improper rhythms to describe the "visual horror" of the suffering of the commander of Gaza at the hands of Alexander (*Comp.* 18). Dionysius goes on to provide Hegesias's version of the account and then compares it with a similar account in Homer (Hector's treatment by Achilles). The result is that Homer's account is found to be superior because the poetic flavor of its rhythms and metaphors both treat the subject (the commander) with dignity and bring the pathos of the suffering to life more vividly for the reader. For Dionysius, then, "vivid" narratives — the Aristotelian ὄψις — are achieved by elaborating upon the details of the context and nature of action.[202] In his own historical composition, Dionysius states clearly that "all men take delight in being conducted through words to deeds and not only in hearing what is related but also in beholding what is done" (*Ant. rom.* 11.1.3). For Dionysius precisely the composition of a detailed and full account accomplishes this goal.

---

200. Similarly, D. S. Levene, "Pity, Fear, and the Historical Audience," in *Passions in Roman Thought* (ed. Braund and Gill), 134–36.

201. For instance, Dionysius praises the orator Lysias for his use of ἐνάργεια:

[He has] a certain power ... of conveying the things he is describing to the senses of his audience, and it arises out of his grasp of circumstantial detail. Nobody who applies his mind to the speeches of Lysias ... will not feel that he can see the actions which are being described going on and that he is meeting face-to-face the characters in the orator's story. And he will require no further evidence of the likely actions, feelings, thoughts or words of the different persons. He was the best of all the orators at observing human nature and ascribing to each type of person the appropriate emotions, moral qualities and actions. (*Lys.* 7)

Here Dionysius links ἐνάργεια with the ability to compose realistic descriptions, as well as to detail in full the states and motivations of the actors. Thus, both fullness of detail and appropriate description are critical for achieving vividness in representation.

202. Cf. Dionysius's discussion of the "vividness" of Odysseus's description of the torments of Sisyphus (*Comp.* 20).

Consonant with the tradition that recognizes the importance of ἐνάργεια in historical composition, Lucian describes the task of the historian as arranging the material and illuminating events as "vividly as possible" so that when a person "who has heard... [the historian] thinks thereafter that he is actually seeing what is being described" (*Hist.* 51). It is precisely through the arrangement of the data that the historian gives life to the *fundamenta* of *historia*. The role of the historian as "Homer's Zeus" allows the writer to make the kind of narrative connections that will bring the events and actors to life, literally parading the past before the eyes of the present audience. Writing some time earlier, Demetrius makes a similar point in his treatise *On Style:* "[V]ividness [ἐνάργεια]... comes first from the use of precise detail [ἀκριβολογίας] and from omitting and excluding nothing" (209). Here the other important literary quality, accuracy (ἀκρίβεια), is linked with vivifying narrative. For a literary critic such as Demetrius, as for the historians, this association provides the ability to illuminate all the accompanying details necessary for interpreting and understanding the event. Demetrius also notes that alongside precise detail, one can also use repetition, circumstantial description, and harsh sounds to bring about *enargeia* in the narrative (211, 217, 219). Using the so-called tragic historian Ctesias as a positive example, Demetrius argues that this historian is successful in having the reader share the emotions of the characters in the narrative (216). Thus, while *enargeia* comes about through proper arrangement and fully detailed accounts, making completely visible what is not necessarily apparent in the events themselves,[203] its aim is to arouse emotion and pleasure in readers so as to engage them directly in the thing palpably made visible and present (214; cf. Quintilian, *Inst.* 8.3.67–68).[204] Ultimately, then, the utility of historical narratives is achieved through the vividness of the composition itself; the more vivid the narrative, the greater is the potential benefit to the reader.

One should also not miss the other important, yet unspoken, element in this emphasis on *enargeia*: Vivid narratives are also truthful and trustworthy.[205] This stress is implicit in Aristotle's argument in the *Poetics,* and is

---

203. In describing the images of Philostratus the Elder, which represent the exercise of vividly and artfully describing various objects, Bartsch notes the importance of temporal and rhetorical connections in animating an account: "[I]nterpretation for Philostratus entails seeing — and describing — more than what could be immediately visible. In his highly rhetorical accounts, the painted characters are given thoughts, motives, and emotions; they are often made to pass through a whole sequence of actions and states; and their stories are extrapolated into the period before and after the moment captured on the picture" (*Decoding the Ancient Novel,* 17).

204. Levene, "Pity, Fear," 131–33.

205. This premise holds within the larger framework of ἐνάργεια; the vivid narrative must be consistent, logical, and coherent with the reality of the world as perceived by the audience. Narratives that relate the superstitious and marvelous (tales of gods) or that contain errors of fact with respect to everyday experience (battle formations, nature of warfare) or knowledge (culture of a people, geography of a country) cannot, by definition, be vivid narratives because they do not represent the reality of the world as experienced by the audience. They can arouse

hinted at repeatedly in the historiographical theorists. It stems from the belief that apprehensible presentations are the best criterion of truth. In other words, by creating vivid narratives — bringing them "before the eyes" of the audience — the historian/poet/dramatist is, in effect, providing the most verifiable narrative account. As J. Annas observes, "Apprehensible presentations are the criterion of truth because they can be guaranteed to put us in touch with the way the world really is. They do not reveal everything about it, but what they do reveal can be utterly trusted."[206] Thus, by "seeing" the narrative and having the events and actors animated, rather than merely hearing words, the audience is ensured of receiving the truest and most trustworthy account. Most important, the information contained in this depiction — the elaboration of the significance and meaning of the elements described — will be firmly grounded in the real, trustworthy world of sense perception. For this reason it is so important for the historian to be acquainted experientially with the contexts and types of events being described. The truth quality of the narrative is inextricably bound up with the ability of the author to present the details "as they actually happened." If the representation fails to be consistent, logical, or reflective of the real world, it will consequently also fail in its power of vivid apprehensible presentation, which is, ultimately, its failure to be true.

Characters and Commonplaces: The Function of Comparison

From the above discussion it is evident that two features of historical composition are paramount for ancient historiography. Just as the writer is to connect the various threads unifying the events being described, so also the characters have to be woven into this narrative thread. By character, Aristotle means "that in virtue of which we ascribe certain qualities to the agents" (*Poet.* 1450a). In ancient narrative composition this literary interest encompasses a diversity of strategies. In particular, one should be aware of characterization, the use of *topoi* and type-scenes, and the role of comparison.

In his discussion of *ethos* in the *Poetics*, Aristotle further defines the task of "characterization" as taking place when "speech or action reveals the nature of a moral choice" (1454a). The compositional technique of characterization itself involves four specific elements: the presentation of good characters, appropriateness, likeness (i.e., representative of the human class), and consistency of character. Aristotle conceives of character in purely moral

---

the passions of the audience through titillating details or pathetic horrors, but such narratives cannot make visible those things known to be true or that will be recognized as such by the readers.

206. J. Annas, "Truth and Knowledge," in *Doubt and Dogmatism: Studies in Hellenistic Epistemology* (ed. M. Schofield et al.; Oxford: Clarendon, 1980), 85. This emphasis relates to the ancient dictum of Heraclitus that "the eyes are more accurate witnesses than the ears" (Polybius 12.27.1). See also Byrskog, *Story as History,* 49–53, 64–65.

terms,[207] and understands that the narrative itself will reveal the character of the actor through the presentation of the choices made. In particular, Aristotle is interested in the revelation of choices that reveal an actor's basic motivations, assumptions, and aims.[208] It is easy to appreciate how this links up with Aristotle's understanding of the "complete action": Characters make choices that are borne out in narrative form, and the basic elements of choice — motivation, intention, deliberation — are part of the larger thread that connects events and consequences. While *ethos* is critical for the orator in order to gain credence from the audience (cf. *Rhet.* 1.2.4), in tragedy it is important so that the audience can see clearly the philosophical/moral lines linking events and actors. Critical to the achievement of this end is the attempt of the writer to "paint" characters with the intention of "enhancing [their] beauty" (*Poet.* 1454b). The writer should avoid excess in characterization, attempting to make even those who are "irascible and indolent" appear to be "decent." While there are admittedly "bad" characters, even these must reflect positive aspects so that their moderate depiction will bring about the edification of the audience.

Characterization was one of the most important features of narrative composition in antiquity. While Aristotle reveals a preference for positive characterization or measured and moderate character portrayal for mimetic purposes in his *Poetics,* overall ancient writers assumed that both good and bad characters could be typified in particular ways. The *ethos* of characters revealed their moral nature through choice in action and speech, but there also emerged particular patterns of action that could be classified and categorized according to types. In the *Rhetoric,* Aristotle thus categorizes individuals according to their emotions, habits, ages, and place in life (2.12–17). According to Aristotle, older men, for instance, tend to be malicious and small-minded, lacking in generosity (2.13). The middle-aged, by contrast, reflect the mean between the old and the young:

> At this age, men are neither over-confident...nor too fearful...neither trusting nor distrusting all, but judging rather in accordance with the facts. Their rule of conduct is neither the noble nor the useful alone, but both at once. They are neither parsimonious nor prodigal, but preserve the due mean. It is the same in regard to passion and desire. Their self-control is combined with courage and their courage with self-control.... Speaking generally, all the advantages that youth and old age possess separately, those in the prime of life possess combined; and all cases of excess or defect in the other two are replaced by due moderation and fitness. (2.14)

---

207. S. Halliwell, *The Poetics of Aristotle: Translation and Commentary* (Chapel Hill: University of North Carolina Press, 1987), 140.
208. See Belfiore, *Tragic Pleasures,* 94–95; and N. Sherman, *The Fabric of Character: Aristotle's Theory of Virtue* (Oxford: Clarendon, 1989), 79–83.

Here Aristotle has stereotyped the middle-aged male, demonstrating, in contrast to youth and old age, how the active citizen reflects all the basic values and virtues of Greek society. Most important, Aristotle has created a typified image that can be translated into any narrative context; if one is a middle-aged male (and citizen), then these are the qualities that can be expected of him. If, however, one were instead interested in a wealthy character, Aristotle also provides a character sketch of people with money: They "are insolent and arrogant, being mentally affected by the acquisition of wealth.... [T]hey are luxurious and swaggerers.... [I]n a word, the character of the rich man is that of a fool favored by fortune.... [T]heir unjust acts are not due to malice, but partly to insolence, partly to incontinence, which tends to make them commit assault and battery and adultery" (*Rhet.* 2.16). In this example, Aristotle not only lays out the motivations and character of wealthy individuals, he also classifies the kinds of negative actions they are likely to commit. In contrast to the wealthy, those with power are more "manly in character," as well as more energetic and dignified. Moreover, when those with power commit unjust acts, in contrast to the wealthy, their actions "are never petty, but great" (2.17). Aristotle has thus created a stereotypical image of the powerful that reinforces the Greek perception of the superiority of rulers over the ruled.[209] Naturally, when a writer comes to narrate the actions of a "great man" this pattern would be in view, and the resultant portrayal would doubtless reflect the prevailing assumption.

With such clear images and traits assigned to particular types of people, one can readily see how ancient historians interested in motivations and dispositions of their characters would turn instinctively to typified patterns as a resource for narrative composition. Consequently, in his work *Characters*, Theophrastus could compile the various types, providing descriptions of characters given to flattery, superstition, mistrust, bad taste, arrogance, slander, and the like. A somewhat more refined treatment can be found in the Pseudo-Aristotelian treatise *On Virtues and Vices*, in which the writer defines key virtues such as "righteousness" in terms of the types of moral character exhibited:

> To righteousness it belongs to be ready to distribute according to desert, and to preserve ancestral customs and institutions and the established laws, and to tell the truth when interest is at stake, and to keep agreements. First among the claims of righteousness are our duties to the gods, then our duties to the spirits, then those to country and parents, then those to the departed; and among these claims is piety.... Righteousness is also accompanied by holiness and truth and loyalty and hatred of wickedness. (5.2–3)

---

209. See C. A. Williams, *Roman Homosexuality: Ideologies of Masculinity in Classical Antiquity* (New York: Oxford University Press, 1999), 125–42, for an application of this predominant stereotype to masculinity as perceived by the Romans.

Here the writer has typified the character of the righteous individual, in whom there emerges a particular moral pattern of conduct that can be expected of any one labeled a δίκαιος. While at one level there may be a certain degree of critical observation or speculation in such a statement, it also takes on the force of a prescription in depiction of characters: If one is to portray a righteous individual, there are certain elements that readers will expect in the narrative.

In Aristotle's *Eudemian Ethics,* the principle of suitability (τὸ πρέπον) is similarly used, denoting certain actions and attributes that naturally apply to particular individuals depending on their social standing. While Aristotle is not referring to *ethos* in particular, it is apparent that the emphasis on suitability of certain actions and gestures to specific individuals based on social rank fits in quite well with this current discussion. For instance, there are certain actions that correspond to the weddings of slaves and others to those of "favorites," and conduct appropriate to one situation is not necessarily suitable for the other (3.6.4). Aristotle is here thinking of the goal of action: One should aim for suitable and fitting actions, and evaluation of these is to a degree relative. Yet it is not difficult to see how this preoccupation could expand into a prescription:. When portraying characters there are certain expected patterns that emerge and, correspondingly, characters must be depicted in these suitable and fitting ways.

In a similar vein, the discussion on commonplaces/topics or *konoi topoi*[210] relates closely to this paradigmatic cultural system of evaluation. The commonplace generally deals with vice (although it could include virtuous acts), and it rests on a given premise that is assumed to have had prior substantiation and agreement and therefore will be accepted by the audience without argument (cf. Cicero, *De or.* 2.206-8; Quintilian, *Inst.* 2.4.22).[211] In his *Progymnasmata,* Theon describes the *topos* as an

> amplifying speech about a commonly accepted subject, either about a wrong or a brave act. For the commonplace is double: 1) one commonplace is against those having acted wickedly; for example, a tyrant, a traitor, a murderer, a profligate; whereas 2) another one is on behalf of those who have accomplished something virtuous; for example, in behalf of a tyrant-slayer, a person of valour, a law-giver.... [I]t is called a "commonplace" because by starting

---

210. One must distinguish here between two different uses of this terminology in ancient rhetoric. Aristotle uses *konoi topoi* to refer to a list of twenty-eight specific types of amplifications for enthymemes (*Rhet.* 2.23). Alongside this usage of the phrase, one also finds it used to refer to the presupposed cultural characterizations discussed earlier (on the distinction, see Butts, "*Progymnasmata* of Theon," 403 n. 1). Frequently, the two uses could be fused together. For instance, in Theon's *Progymnasmata* (6), he begins with the culturally shared assumption (enthymemic in nature), and then proceeds to amplify the themes inherent in the subject. In this way, the two different uses of *konoi topoi* depend, in part, on which end of the process one analyzes (i.e., form or content).

211. Bonner, *Education in Ancient Rome,* 263-64.

out from it, as from a familiar place, we readily argue against those who are widely regarded as acting unjustly. (6.1–5, 11–13)

As Theon goes on, it is evident that the elaboration of the assumed *topoi* (e.g., that a tyrant is evil) is carried out through a narrative that combines a series of arguments addressing everything from motives for to results of typical tyrannical deeds (6.40ff.). Yet even in the pattern of elaboration there are certain "givens" that can be relied upon in terms of persuading the audience: When one discusses wrongdoing one should note with respect to "the intention of the culprit, that it is wicked... in terms of the subject which the injustice concerns, that it belongs to the most necessary matters... in terms of what the injustice encompasses, that on the surface the injustice is singular, but in reality it encompasses in itself many injustices" (6.46–56). On the one hand, these elements are simply part of elaborating the original theme of evil action. On the other, the elaboration frequently depends on other commonplaces, such as the belief that ignoble action springs from evil motives, that truly wicked deeds will involve the necessary things of life, and that each wrongdoing can be broken down even further into other violations. When Theon comes around to explicit characterization, then, it is simply the culmination of what has been the inherent goal of the progymnastic exercises all along:

> Next we will argue in terms of the events prior to our main subject; for example: that against the temple-robber, that prior to sacrileges against the gods, it is likely that the temple-robber has perpetuated many injustices against the people and against the dead; had neglected many things that have customarily been done in honor of the gods, such as festivals, sacrifices, prayers; and has also often sworn falsely, and similar things. (6.71–76)

Theon here establishes the basis for the very thing Aristotle had achieved with respect to *ethos* in describing particular characters.[212] Once one has been characterized as a temple-robber, this "fact" naturally brings into view other types of activities one has "likely" and "in all probability" committed. This characterization is not an impartial attempt to uncover the actual deeds of the temple-robber, but to portray the said individual in terms of a larger pattern of ascribed behavior. Finally, Theon turns to the use of *enargeia* in this process of expanding the *topoi*. With the use of "vividness," one is able to bring the unjust action "before the eyes" of the audience, demonstrating the suffering of an individual at the hand of the unjust, and also the various elements of the evil actor's crime: all the "gory details" and dramatic components that will cause the audience to adopt the view of the narrator of

---

212. On the evident connection between *ethos* and *topoi*, see T. Barton, *Power and Knowledge: Astrology, Physiognomics, and Medicine under the Roman Empire* (Ann Arbor: University of Michigan Press, 1994), 110–11.

the events (6.88–97). Thus, in terms of function, these threads of the narrative become something akin to type-scenes that have the power to evoke particular responses in the reader.[213]

It is not difficult to identify the ways in which understandings of characterization and *topoi* could and did influence historiography. While historians were to avoid the extreme elements of characterization in oratory (in theory at least), the method repeatedly found its way into the literary texts of antiquity and was usually coupled with an emphasis on particular virtues and vices.[214] Whether it provides a resource for establishing motive or fleshing out characters, becomes a means of polemic, or simply furnishes the elemental details for vivid narration or the classification necessary for elaboration, characterization is an essential feature of narrative composition across the spectrum. Some writers, such as Polybius, seem to link up with the Aristotelian view that even negative characters should be portrayed as decent and all should be depicted in moderation. Others, such as Josephus, paint their villains and heroes overtly, enacting in the narrative all the assumed features of a given *topos*. The use of *ethos* and *topoi* depends in part, then, on the function of the historical writing itself. All writers, however, could probably agree with the writer of the *Rhetoric to Alexander* that "narratives mirror [men's] characters and manners" (1441b).

The ancient world, then, tended to classify individuals in terms of specific types of behavior, motivations, geographical origins, gender, and physical features,[215] which resulted in the evolution of a vast array of *topoi* that could conveniently be culled to characterize particular individuals or groups. The

---

213. Aristotle's use of plot type-scenes such as reversal, recognition, and suffering in the *Poetics* is somewhat related. There are admittedly certain patterns of actions (not just actors) that have the power to evoke specific responses in the audience.
214. Rutherford, Mediations *of Marcus Aurelius*, 55–56.
215. *Topoi* were wide ranging, and the fact that physiognomics was an important aspect of characterization demonstrates just how pervasive and thorough the enterprise became (Barton, *Power and Knowledge*, 115–28; and Gleason, *Making Men*, 33–36). See, e.g., the combination of elements in Ammianus Marcellinus's characterization of the Persians:

> Among these many men of differing tongues there are varieties of persons, as well as of places. But, to describe their bodily characteristics and their customs in general, they are almost all slender, somewhat dark ... eyebrows joined and curved in the form of a half-circle, not uncomely beards, and long shaggy hair. All of them without exception, even at banquets and on festal days, appear girt with swords.... Most of them are extravagantly given to venery, and are hardly contented with a multitude of concubines.... They avoid luxurious banquets, and especially, excessive drinking.... They are immensely moderate and cautious.... Besides this, one seldom sees a Persian stop to pass water or step aside in response to a call of nature; so scrupulously do they avoid these and other unseemly actions. On the other hand, they are so free and easy, and stroll about with such a loose and unsteady gait, that one might think them effeminate; but in fact they are most gallant warriors; though rather crafty than courageous, and to be feared only at long range. They are given to empty words, and talk madly and extravagantly. They are boastful, harsh and offensive, threatening in adversity and prosperity alike, crafty, haughty, cruel, claiming the power of life and death over slaves and commons. (23.6.75–80)

heart of this enterprise rests on two fundamentals. First, moral character is primarily in view (whether one is focusing on physical features or skills such as generalship). Second, the principal point of characterization is that it aids in the understanding of narrated actions, thereby creating greater impact on the audience. Since the primary purpose of narration is, as we have seen, the ability to connect the threads of characters, thought, and actions so as to make a coherent, logical, and consistent plot, a historian has to be capable of generating known characters whose relationship to narrated actions and thought is manifest and unambiguous. Given this understanding of the larger context for ancient historiography, it would have been difficult to accomplish the task of elucidation and explanation of events without the freedom to use the commonplaces wherever appropriate. Effective narratives require the threads to be connected, and only by classifying patterns of behaviors and motivations is one able to relate actors clearly, palpably, and vividly to specific consequences. Thus, what we are given in the narrative with respect to character and motivation is, for all intents and purposes, all that "historically" exists.[216] It should not therefore surprise us that the historians both implicitly and explicitly reinforced this use of characterization in their narratives.[217] As L. Pearson explains,

> In addition to the "raw material" of history there are the conventional current ideas which cannot be ignored unless the writer is willing to startle and offend his readers. There is the pious convention that the gods saved Greece; there is the democratic convention that a free people proved its superiority; and there is the nationalist Greek convention that the Barbarian (especially the barbarian king) has none of the Greek virtues.... The conventional character

---

216. This element is one of the significant features that distinguishes modern and ancient historiography. Modern interpreters conceive of motivation and character on multiple and complex levels, and never (at least not usually) in purely moral terms. In antiquity, the view of character was much simpler, surface-level, and predominately moral in nature. As M. M. Bakhtin states, "[C]haracter is predetermined and may be disclosed in a singled defined direction. Historical reality itself... serves merely as a means for the disclosure... but historical reality is deprived of any determining influence on character as such, it does not shape or create it, it merely manifests it. Historical reality is an arena for the disclosing and unfolding of human characters" (*The Dialogic Imagination: Four Essays* [ed. M. Holquist; trans. C. Emerson and M. Holquist; Austin: University of Texas Press, 1981], 141). While it is tempting to define the concept of personality reflected here in the terms B. J. Malina has set — "they were anti-introspective, not psychologically minded, and thought in terms of stereotypes" ("Understanding New Testament Persons," in *The Social Sciences and New Testament Interpretation* [ed. R. L. Rohrbaugh; Peabody, Mass.: Hendrickson, 1996], 53) — in actuality in the process of narrative composition there is a deliberate and conscious attempt at rhetorical construction of character and identity that goes way beyond mere stereotyping.

217. In her earlier work on Tacitus, B. Walker draws attention to this phenomenon in ancient historiography (*The* Annals *of Tacitus: A Study in the Writing of History* [Manchester: Manchester University Press, 1952], 204–34). See also H. D. Westlake, "Individuals in Xenophon's *Hellenica*," in *Essays on the Greek Historians and Greek History* (Manchester: Manchester University Press, 1969), 206–7, who argues that Xenophon has constructed a consistent characterization of the ideal military commander used throughout the *Hellenica*.

of the tyrant was firmly implanted in the popular mind — unbalanced, ruthless, infatuated.[218]

Such fundamental convictions and values proved essential for establishing a convincing narrative.

Moreover, the emphasis on particular patterns of action combined with the stress on appropriate types of characterization frequently led to the generation of type-scenes.[219] That is, alongside particular patterns of motivation and behavior, specific narrative models for describing certain types of events formed part of the repertoire for composition and argumentation. W. O. Allen, for instance, has demonstrated the influence of a type-scene related to the demise of a tyrant in which there is a prevailing formula for narrating the scene of conflict, punishment, and death.[220] In the Jewish tradition, one can point to the prevalence of the narrative pattern of the pious Jew defying the sacrilegious orders of a tyrant, combining suffering and martyrdom with emphases on resurrection and retribution.[221] This link between appropriate characterization and the development of narrative patterns is a natural one. Consequently, type-scenes are essentially cultural phenomena that, like the establishment of *ethos* and use of *topoi*, aid in the clarification and exposition of historical events. At the same time, particular characters of the past (frequently from epic) can typify these patterns in a unique and perhaps even ultimate way. That is, either the character or the pattern of events enacted by an individual becomes a flashpoint for typifying characterization and *topoi*. If, as argued here, classification is fundamental to the construction of *ethos* and the use of *topoi*, then it is not difficult to understand how ancient writers could focus on particular individuals who stood out "in their class." In the Jewish tradition, for instance, Antiochus IV Epiphanes is not simply one tyrant among many, but represents that type in an ultimate sense. Or, conversely, Moses crystallizes the virtues of "lawgiver" and "prophet." In such cases, particular events or virtues in the figures themselves may be drawn upon in the same sense as the typologies of character one finds in Aristotle. In Aristotelian terms, by acting like a notable figure from the past one is, in effect, acting like one of that group (of which the notable figure is the outstanding type).

Related to this discussion, and stemming from the emphasis on moral characterization, is the feature of comparison (*synkrisis*) in narrative composition, which is also a natural development of the construction of *ethos* and the use of *topoi*. Aristotle already makes this explicit move in the passage

---

218. L. Pearson, "Real and Conventional Personalities in Greek History," in *Selected Papers of Lionel Pearson* (ed. D. Lateiner and S. A. Stephens; Chico, Calif.: Scholars Press, 1983), 114.
219. For a general discussion of ancient type-scenes, see Allen, *Death of Herod*, 30–35.
220. Ibid., 35–66. Also see J. A. Darr, *Herod the Fox: Audience Criticism and Lukan Characterization* (JSNTSup 163; Sheffield: Sheffield Academic Press, 1998), 92–136.
221. See further G. W. E. Nickelsburg, *Resurrection, Immortality, and Eternal Life in Intertestamental Judaism* (HTS 26; Cambridge: Harvard University Press, 1972), 93–111.

from the *Rhetoric* cited above. There he not only delineates the characters of the old and the young, but also goes on to discuss the mean evidenced in the middle-aged individual. Further, his discussion of the character of those with power is done in correlation with an analysis of the character of the wealthy, using this comparison to highlight major facets of the powerful. In his treatment of the enthymemic *topos* of comparison in his *Topica*, Aristotle defines the argumentative strategy and its goal as follows: Synkrisis "is concerned with things that are closely related and about which we discuss which we ought preferably to support.... [I]f one or more points of superiority can be shown, the mind will agree that whichever of the two alternatives is actually superior is the more worthy of choice" (3.1). While Aristotle has in view a discussion related to the relative merits of two entities, such as wealth and happiness, set in comparison, it is evident that this same emphasis could quite easily be adapted to narration. Thus, accounts could be composed that demonstrate in narrative the relative merits of one choice, virtue, or character over another, or, at the very least, bring two "closely related" actions or people into association for purposes of comparison.

Synkrisis in historiography takes its cue from its place of prominence in Greco-Roman rhetorical education. In Theon's *Progymnasmata*, *synkrisis* is defined as a "speech which shows what is better or what is worse" (10.1). Theon states that such comparisons are made on the basis of what is similar and in dispute, rather than between disparate objects or characters lacking any real basis of similarity. In comparison of characters, then, one "will first set side by side their noble birth, their education, their children, their public offices, their reputation, their bodily health" (10.13–15), which is then followed by setting their respective actions side by side. Moreover, Theon states that by comparing the head of one class of people or characters to the head of another (e.g., the most courageous man with the most courageous woman) one can make a determination not just about the superiority of the individuals but also of the classes they represent.[222] Theon is here referring to speeches that deliberately set out to argue for the superiority of one character or virtue over another. Plutarch's *Lives* are representative of this particular method and aim, demonstrating that comparison is not limited to the *prooimion* and *synkrisis*, which are the explicit and formal units of the exercise. Rather, the narrative structure of the parallel lives *in toto* is critical to the formal comparisons that Plutarch intends to make.[223] In other words,

---

222. As Theon demonstrates, the outcome of such comparison is wholly dependent upon the representative characters selected. For instance, Theon provides two different sets of characters for comparison depending on whether one wants to prove that males are more courageous than females or the reverse (10.56–65).

223. D. H. J. Larmour, "Making Parallels: *Synkrisis* and Plutarch's 'Themistocles and Camillus,'" *ANRW* 2.33.6 (1992): 4159, 4200. See also Balch, "ΜΕΤΑΒΟΛΗ ΠΟΛΙΤΕΙΩΝ"; Wardman, *Plutarch's Lives*, 18–26; C. Pelling, "Synkrisis in Plutarch's Lives," in *Plutarch and History* (London; Duchwork, 2002), 349–63; and esp. T. E. Duff, *Plutarch's Lives: Exploring Virtue and Vice* (New York: Oxford University Press, 1999), 243–86.

synkrisis is not simply a discrete evaluative exercise, but represents, in effect, the real goal of narration taken as a whole. This observation becomes more clear when one turns to the use of *synkrisis* in the ancient historians.

For Polybius, *synkrisis* does not take on the overt epideictic features of some Roman historiography, but reflects the more reasoned deliberative approach to historiography wherein the reader is to weigh different actions and consequences. In his criticism of Timaeus's narrative composition, Polybius states, "[O]wing to this excessive addiction to paradox, he does not induce us to consider and compare [σύγκρισις], but exposes to ridicule the men and the actions he is championing" (12.26c.1). Polybius envisions writing narratives and speeches that set relatively equal entities side by side, allowing for the audience to judge the relative merits of one course of action over another.[224] When Polybius himself uses the technique, he compares Scipio to Lycurgus, the famous Spartan legislator from the past (10.2.8–13). Here the comparison enhances the image of Scipio by demonstrating that he meets the standards set forth by a former exemplar.[225] Thucydides, by contrast, offers a more negative form of *synkrisis* when he sets the characters of Pericles and Nicias side by side. In this instance, Thucydides narrates the two very different courses of action, personalities, and motivations of the respective leaders, with a definite personal predilection for the public and rational Pericles over the more superstitious and private Nicias.[226] As Rawlings points out in his study of the parallels, Pericles is presented as the popular favorite while Nicias is portrayed as having little public support. These images are directly antithetical, and Thucydides' intention is to demonstrate in narrative the superiority of Pericles over Nicias through his own selective and creative composition.[227]

In Josephus's *Antiquities* there is an excellent example of implicit *synkrisis* in the double narratives of Paulina (the Roman follower of Isis) and Fulvia (a Jewish proselyte), both of whom fall prey to corrupting male influences (18.65–84). In this comparison Josephus parallels the respective harsh treatment of the Jews en masse by Tiberius in the second narrative, with the more moderate and justifiable actions of Tiberius with respect to the priests of Isis in the first, the obvious suggestion being that the first narrative reflects a superior form of justice (where only those actually involved

---

224. Here the deliberative, agonistic side of historiography emerges, particularly in the speeches, where various views on a subject are contrasted and evaluated (Sacks, "Rhetoric and Speeches," 390–91).

225. W. W. Batstone, "The Antithesis of Virtue: Sallust's *Synkrisis* and the Crisis of the Late Republic," *CA* 7 (1988): 3 n. 9. Also see C. Becker, "Sallust," *ANRW* 1.3 (1973): 731–42. For a similar phenomenon in Tacitus, see M. G. Morgan, "The Unity of Tacitus, *Histories* 1,12–20," *Athenaeum* 81 (1993): 572–77.

226. H. R. Rawlings, *The Structure of Thucydides' History* (Princeton: Princeton University Press, 1981), 138. See also Hornblower, *Thucydides*, 168; and Luce, *Greek Historians*, 72–73.

227. Rawlings, *Structure of Thucydides' History*, 139. In Sallust, the aim of the comparisons between Cato and Caesar is more difficult to pin down, as Sallust allows for significant ambiguity in his use of *synkrisis* (Batstone, "Antithesis of Virtue," 3–4, 6).

in the plot are punished). By thus paralleling two similar characters and events, Josephus makes a statement not just about the specific characters, but even more so about the Roman government's repeated mistreatment of the Jews (which becomes clear by seeing the two different types of response side by side).[228] Josephus provides another example of such *synkrisis* in his *Contra Apionem*, where he compares the Jewish law with the laws and institutions of the Greeks (especially working with Plato and his followers), demonstrating the superiority of the Jewish constitution.[229] These few examples are suggestive of more wide-ranging manifestations of *synkrisis* in ancient historical composition. In sum, the purposes served are varied. For those such as Polybius, comparisons can legitimate a certain character. For Thucydides, comparisons create oppositions, setting off a superior from an inferior character.[230] Similarly, in Josephus one account can be understood to reflect superior treatment and actions, although there is also a larger statement being made with respect to the overall narrative, demonstrating that *synkrisis* operates at the macrolevel as well. Lastly, in the case of Sallust, he undertakes comparison that does not necessarily place stock in either side in particular, but results in a mediating position, one offsetting the other.

In conclusion, then, one cannot ignore the wide-ranging and pervasive impact of characterization in ancient historiography. Too frequently the discussion of this particular facet of composition leads to the simplistic understanding of the phenomenon as stereotyping or type-casting and is dismissed accordingly.[231] The construction of *ethos* and the use of *topoi*, however, are much more varied and complex than might appear at first glance. Moreover, when historians in antiquity use these compositional techniques, these features converge quite well with the emphases of historiography observed elsewhere. Only by demonstrating aspects of character, motivation, and thought is the historian able to portray with accuracy the connections necessary to bring profit and pleasure to the reader. This resource for narrative composition arises from the ancient literary and rhetorical environment that placed great stock in characterization and the

---

228. On this episode and the use of the "double narrative," see B. Justus, "Zur Erzählkunst des Flavius Josephus," in *Theokratia: Jahrbuch des Institutum Judaicum Delitzschian (1970–72)* (Leiden: Brill, 1973), 2:113–22, esp. 118–19.

229. See further C. Gerber, *Ein Bild des Judentums für Nichtjuden von Flavius Josephus: Untersuchungen zu seiner Schrift* Contra Apionem (AGJU 40; Leiden: Brill, 1997), 204–18.

230. In Thucydides one observes the tendency to include encomium alongside invective, creating sharply contrasting antithetical portraits (cf. Aphthonius, *Prog.* 10).

231. Hornblower, *Thucydides*, 57–59, for instance, rejects any serious influence of characterization under the premise that Thucydides' portrayal of individuals is more complex than the process of typification might suggest (cf. C. Pelling, "Conclusion," in *Characterization and Individuality in Greek Literature* [ed. C. Pelling; Oxford: Clarendon, 1990], 259–60). Hornblower deliberately adopts a narrow view of characterization, failing to recognize the more complex interplay between differing *topoi* (e.g., a "general" who also happens to be a "barbarian") or even variations within the same type (M. W. Blundell, "*Ēthos* and *Dianoia* Reconsidered," in *Essays on Aristotle's Poetics* [ed. Rorty], 165).

use of commonplaces to describe people in terms of broad and intersecting patterns of behavior. While the overarching framework is primarily moral, the specific context determines whether the focus will be on social, political, and/or economic status; morality; ethnicity; physiognomy; or any combination of these and other broader categories.

Rather than being viewed as only a rhetorical or literary process and product, the emphasis here is on classification with the aim of increasing understanding. Thus, the primary assumption is that because people act according to the certain rules of their class, one is able to describe, predict, and recreate the relationship of character and action that would otherwise be impossible without the employment of such typification. Therefore, one should not be surprised to find that historians repeatedly refer to the necessity of suitability in the description of actions and speech. In his criticism of one of Thucydides' speeches, for instance, Dionysius of Halicarnassus states, "[T]hese would have been suitable words for barbarian kings to address to Greeks, but no Athenian should have spoken thus to Greeks whom they had liberated from the Persians" (*Thuc.* 39). Dionysius maintains that certain patterns of speech are related to a particular class of people — barbarian or Greek — and should not be confused. Similarly, Lucian criticizes the unnamed historian for the story about Severianus, who killed himself with shards from a drinking bowl, "as if there were no dagger, no javelin to be found to bring him a manly and heroic death" (*Hist.* 25). For Lucian, warriors have a particular quality of courage that necessarily evinces itself in heroic patterns of death. The need for a suitable mode of death results in a type-scene in this instance: Warriors and generals die by the sword. Therefore, when the historians refer to appropriate description, likeness of characters, and consistency in representation, they can be viewed as working out of the model of characterization: Certain expected patterns of behavior and action should emerge in the composition of the narrative.

When charges of malice arise, it is usually with respect to issues of characterization. When characters are inappropriately portrayed, ancient literary critics assumed that the description is deliberate, done explicitly to undermine the historical figures. Plutarch, for instance, in describing the malice of Herodotus, states,

> In the fifth book [Herodotus] says that Cleisthenes, a member of one of the leading noble families in Athens, persuaded the Delphic prophetess to deliver counterfeit responses, when she continually told the Spartans to free Athens from its tyrants. Thus he attaches the charge of grave impiety and fraud to a noble upright action and he denies all credit to the god of a noble and honourable response, worthy of Themis who is said to have a part in these responses. (*Her. mal.* 860D)

Plutarch criticizes Herodotus on the basis of the latter's use of *topoi*: Deposing tyrants is a good and noble act; oracles are from the gods and should be believed; noble families do not act impiously and fraudulently. Herodotus is malicious, in this instance, because he contravenes the accepted commonplaces of description. Consequently, as one might well expect from the holistic practice of historiography, the character of the historian — his own *ethos* — is dependent on his usage of characterization and commonplaces in the narrative. This feature reinforces the moral dimension that already undergirds the task of the historian. At the same time, it reveals that, for historiography in particular, Aristotle's emphasis on the decency of characters also rings true. Vilification and panegyric, while employed by some historians, is perceived by others to undermine the task of historical composition. One should aim instead at a moderate representation of individuals, so as to portray best the likeness of the characters to the reader and to achieve greater profit through moderation in narration.

Thought, Word, and Deed: The Role of Speeches

The final element in Aristotle's tripartite formula for narration given above is "thought" *(dianoia)*, by which is meant "the parts in which, through speech, [actors] demonstrate something or declare their view" (*Poet.* 1450a). Alongside plot and character, then *dianoia* fills out the complete narrative. Moreover, it is a natural development of the previous discussion of *ethos* and *topoi* with respect to the emphasis on the need for congruence between action and speech. In particular, while the construction of *ethos* in Aristotelian tragedy results from the choices made in action, *dianoia* represents the reasoning processes upon which the former is based, making the two conceptions only logically distinguishable.[232] For Aristotle, *dianoia* establishes the means by which the characters lay out their deliberative, judicial, and/or demonstrative reasoning for particular actions ("the parts in which [characters] demonstrate that something is or is not so, or declare a general view"; 1450b). This feature represents the clearest and most explicit connection of narration to the theory and practice of rhetoric (1256a). As Aristotle states,

> "Thought" covers all effects which need to be created by speech: their elements are proof, refutation, the conveying of emotions (pity, fear, anger, etc.), as well as enhancement and belittlement. It is clear that the same principles should also be used in the handling of events, when one needs to create impressions of what is pitiable, terrible, important, or probable — with this difference, that the latter effects must be evident without direct statement, while the former must be conveyed by the speaker in and through speech. For what would be the point of the speaker, if the required effects were evident even without speech? (1256b)

Aristotle herein makes several critical assertions. First, *dianoia* is revealed in the speech of the character and this "thought" adopts rhetorical tropes

---

232. Blundell, "*Ethos* and *Dianoia*," 170–71; and Halliwell, *Poetics of Aristotle*, 155–56.

and methods in order to clarify the nature of action. Second, narrative arrangement of both events and speech accomplishes the same aim, namely, evoking the desired response from the audience to the events being treated. The vivid narrative achieves this goal by portraying narrative elements dramatically before the audience. The speech, then, in some senses does the same; it is the vivid *logos* that brings the preceding action before the eyes of the audience. Yet there is a distinction: The speech clarifies and vivifies the preceding action in a way that is not completely apparent from the narration itself. Third, and perhaps most important, there is an inherent connection between *dianoia, ethos,* and plot. The speech not only reveals the underlying rationale behind the choices of the character, it also explicitly ties together the threads of the plot, giving a reasoned assessment and explanation for the unfolding events. Speechs thus elucidate in some way the narrative context.[233]

In line with the other elements of Aristotelian poetics, it is not surprising to find similar themes surfacing in the rhetorical handbooks. Theon has an exercise that, although not coalescing fully with Aristotle's term *dianoia,* nonetheless represents one manifestation of *dianoia* in narrative: "speech-in-character" or *prosopopoiia*.[234] According to Theon, "a speech-in-character is the introduction of a character which sets forth in a non-controversial way words suitable to both the character himself and to the subject" (8.1–3). For instance, as Theon goes on to point out, husbands about to start out on a journey say certain things to their wives, as do generals who are about to send their soldiers into battle. In this exercise, then, one must first assess the particular character-type *(ethos)* of the speaker:

> The same words do not fit an older and a younger man, but the speech of the younger man will be in our eyes a mixture of simplicity and self-control, whereas the speech of the older man will be one of sagacity and experience. Because of gender, different words would be appropriate to a woman and a man. Because of status, different words would be appropriate to a slave and a freeman. Because of vocation, different words would be appropriate to a soldier and a farmer. On account of disposition, different words would be appropriate to one in love and one showing self-control. On account of nationality, some words are characteristic of the Laconian: few and lucid ones; some words are characteristic of the Attic man: fluent. And we say that Herodotus often made speeches in a non-Greek fashion, even though he wrote them in Greek, because he was imitating the speech of non-Greek people. (8.16–25)

---

233. Of the three elements of tragedy, Aristotle tends to value *dianoia* in composition least, largely because the character and single plot are frequently clear on their own (Halliwell, *Poetics of Aristotle,* 156). It should be noted, however, that Aristotle's understanding of *dianoia* is not always clear and thus becomes the most difficult of his categories to clarify.

234. For a discussion of the theory and practice of *prosopopoiia,* see S. K. Stowers, "Romans 7.7–25 as a Speech-in-Character (προσωποποιία)," in *Paul in His Hellenistic Context* (ed. T. Engberg-Pedersen; Minneapolis: Fortress, 1995), 180–91.

Theon emphasizes the correlation between *ethos* and *prosopopoiia*. Yet alongside the congruence of the words with the character of the speaker, the writer must also assess the appropriate occasion and nature of the subject. For instance, as Theon observes, what one says in an army camp on the verge of war is different from what one would say in a public assembly in a time of peace. Moreover, each subject dictates the nature, degree, and progression of argument in the speech. A speech of consolation has a different tone and arrangement than a speech of exhortation.

In Aphthonius's *Progymnasmata,* we find greater precision in the terminology for the exercise. Composing speech and placing it in the mouth of a known living person, thereby inventing that person's *ethos,* is referred to as *ethopoeia;* the similar in the mouth of a dead person is *eidolopeia;* and when both the *ethos* and actual person are invented, it is known as *prosopopoiia* (11). Although essentially the same in terms of Theon's configuration, here there are three different designations depending on whether the character is invented or real. Further, the speech models in words the actor's character, either actual or invented. While *prosopopoiia* does not represent the full extent of *dianoia* in narrative, it is its most evident expression in literary composition. Since logical consistency lies at the heart of the conceptions of plot and character, creating speeches that present *dianoia* necessitates the ability to shape the content in terms of the character of the speaker, the occasion of the speech, and the nature and strategy of the subject being articulated.

The movement to historiography in this respect is fairly simple: Ancient historians created speech-in-character for the individuals in their narrative compositions, attempting to demonstrate *dianoia* from the perspective of the characters with respect to the action ongoing in the narrative.[235] Frequently, of course, the *dianoia* expressed derives from the historian himself. At the same time, however, the specific uses of speeches in ancient historical composition are varied and complex. Dibelius lists several possible functions of speeches in ancient histories: to provide (1) insight into the complete situation (often times utilizing several speeches to provide different standpoints on an event); (2) clarification of the meaning of the historical moment; (3) a viewpoint on the character of the speaker; and (4) understanding of general

---

235. Thucydides' promise to record faithfully "what was actually said," while often leading modern scholars to affirm the ancient commitment to historical accuracy (e.g., A. B. Bosworth, *From Arrian to Alexander: Studies in Historical Interpretation* [New York: Oxford University Press, 1988], 94–96; Fornara, *Nature of History,* 142–68; Porter, "Thucydides 1.22.1"; and Hornblower, *Thucydides,* 71; for a mediating position, see Pelling, *Literary Texts,* 112–22), can also be read as an attempt to reflect faithfully the character, situation, and subject of discussion (i.e., *prosopopoiia*) rather than a slavish rendering of actual words spoken (indeed, the concept of "truth" in the famous statement seems to be subordinated to "suitability," as Byrskog notes [*Story as History,* 211]).

ideas that explain the situation but may only be loosely related.[236] Within the framework of historical composition outlined above, the role of speech as the medium for revealing thought should be self-evident. It is the place wherein the historian, using the voice of the narrative characters, lays out the patterns of thought that ground the narrative. Yet the historian's own commitment to the content of the speech must be determined on a case by case basis. The relationship of plot, *ethos*, and *dianoia* is more complicated in historiography largely because history, unlike ideal Aristotelian tragedy, does not have a single line of plot development, but is episodic in nature. Therefore, the use of speeches will vary depending on the function of the speech in a given context. Sometimes historians use a speech to reveal their own perspective on the historical moment, but at other times they may use a speech to demonstrate the *ethos* of a particular character.[237] In this latter case, the relationship of the historian to the content of the speech is determined in large part by the writer's portrayal of the character in the historical narrative (i.e., whether the writer is sympathetic to the character or not). In other cases, however, one finds speeches placed in dialogue with one another, with various viewpoints being proffered with respect to particular courses of action. The speeches in Thucydides, for instance, frequently detail general views on specific courses of action, thereby re-creating the types of debates on political events taking place in the *polis*. The function of these speeches is clearly related to the narrative, but in a different sense: They establish various responses to the course of action in the account, providing the audience with different perspectives (representing the closest parallel to Aristotle's precise use of *dianoia*).[238]

The situation becomes more complicated because of the actual practice of writing speech-in-character. A good historian — from the perspective of the ideal in historiography — should be able to provide narrative *dianoia* that represents and imitates the character developed in the narrative. Consequently, the speeches should be deliberately varied in style, content, and function, making it all the more difficult to separate out the historian's artistry from something resembling the historian's beliefs. Even in speeches where the content seems to coalesce with the writer's own implied perspective on events, it is difficult to make a wholesale association of the content with the historian's own position, since the goal of *prosopopoiia* is in fact

---

236. M. Dibelius, "The Speeches in Acts and Ancient Historiography," in *Studies in the Acts of the Apostles* (ed. H. Greeven; London: SCM, 1956), 139–40. See also W. J. Dominik, *Speech and Rhetoric in Statius' Thebaid* (ATS 27; Hildesheim, Germany: Olms-Weidmann, 1994), 68–69.

237. Livy frequently uses speeches in this way (Walsh, "Livy and the Aims," 1068–69). See also Westlake, "Individuals in Xenophon's *Hellenica*," 205–6.

238. In assessing the complexity of Thucydides' own commitment to the content of the various speeches, H.-P. Stahl ("Speeches and Course of Events in Books Six and Seven of Thucydides," in *Speeches in Thucydides* [ed. Stadter], 60–62) focuses on the dramatic setting of the speeches as the key to Thucydides' own interpretation.

to compose in the character of someone else.²³⁹ Speeches in ancient historiography, then, are highly significant but also ambiguous, and must be analyzed with care in their respective contexts. If the approach taken to historiography in this chapter is correct, however, then speeches in some sense represent *dianoia* in the narrative. Whether these simply present one trajectory of choice, offer the reasoning for a particular character's actions, or illuminate more broadly the events of the narrative, the one constant is that speeches are intricately connected to the narrative in some manner.²⁴⁰ In one way or another, then, speech advances the complete plot of the historical composition, and thus by necessity promotes a reasoning process underlying characters and their actions.²⁴¹ Finally, it is also fair to suggest that, as a result, there exists a relationship between the larger goals of a particular historical work and the roles of the speeches contained therein. The function of a historical composition determines to a large degree the nature and shape of the speeches that the writer chooses to compose and insert. Consequently, from section to section of particular historical treatises, the interpreter should assume the integration of speech and narrative, despite occasional difficulties in determining the precise relationship.²⁴²

Polybius is particularly helpful in this respect since, in his attack on Timaeus's work, he makes the explicit association between speeches and the purpose of historical composition:

> [T]he peculiar function of history is to discover, in the first place, the words actually spoken...and next to ascertain the reason why what was done or spoken led to failure or success...but a writer who passes over in silence the speeches made and the causes of events and in their place introduces false rhetorical exercises and discursive speeches, destroys the peculiar virtue of history. (12.25b.1–4)

Polybius directly criticizes the inclusion of speeches that demonstrate the rhetorical prowess of the writer but fail to relate to the events and characters. For Polybius, there is a direct correlation between action in the narrative, its results, and the reflection contained in the speeches. Even though Polybius has particular forms of political discourse in view, the effect is similar to that which one finds in Aristotle: Speeches reveal the *dianoia*—good, bad,

---

239. Potter, *Literary Texts*, 132.

240. Dibelius does not always recognize this connection, suggesting that at times speeches are only loosely connected to their contexts ("Speeches in Acts," 140, 144; but see the comments and criticisms by M. L. Soards, *The Speeches in Acts: Their Content, Context, and Concerns* [Louisville: Westminster John Knox, 1994], 136, 142; although Soards does hold that many of the speeches in Acts are "loosely fitted").

241. Hornblower, *Thucydides*, 66–69.

242. For a particularly fine study of integration in Tacitus, see E. Keitel, "Speech and Narrative in *Histories* 4," in *Tacitus and the Tacitean Tradition* (ed. T. J. Luce and A. J. Woodman; Princeton: Princeton University Press, 1993), 39–58. Cf. Dominik, *Speech and Rhetoric*, 69; and D. S. Levene, "Tacitus' *Histories* and the Theory of Deliberative Oratory," in *Limits of Historiography* (ed. Shuttleworth Kraus), 197–98.

or neutral—behind (in the case of Polybius) political courses of action. The widely attested motif in ancient historiographical theory that there were certain historians who used speeches to show off their own rhetorical sophistry affirms in the negative this core commitment. As Polybius states again, "But, I fear, it is difficult to assign causes, and very easy to invent phrases by the aid of books, and while it is given only to a few to say a few words at the right time it is a common accomplishment and open to anyone to compose long speeches to no purpose" (12.25i.9). In his critique of Timaeus it is apparent that Polybius has a particular problem with speeches that are not closely related to the causes of events. Thus, Polybius has a narrow view on the use of speeches in historiography: They must serve (in the presentation of what is said) the end of making the larger narrative politically beneficial for the *polis*.

Dionysius of Halicarnassus establishes the same connection between causes and speeches in his own history:

> For everyone, upon hearing of extraordinary events, desires to know the cause that produced them and considers that alone as a test of their credibility.... And since they did not make this change in their government by using compulsion upon one another... but by the persuasion of words, I thought it necessary above all things to report the speeches which the heads of both parties made upon that occasion. I might express my surprise that some historians, though they think themselves obliged to give an exact account of military actions and sometimes expend a great many words over a single battle... yet when they come to give an account of civil commotions and seditions, do not consider it necessary to report the speeches by which the extraordinary and remarkable events were brought to pass. (*Ant. rom.* 7.66.1–3)

Dionysius, like Polybius, views speeches as providing the *dianoia* behind the narrative events, which, in tandem with the delineation of the causes and outcomes, connect the threads of character and action.[243] In one sense, then, speeches provide a "dynamic, motivating function" for the narrative.[244] In his treatise *On Thucydides,* moreover, Dionysius places significant stress on the suitability and appropriateness of the speeches. In one striking comment, Dionysius essentially combines the presentation of *prosopopoiia* in the rhetorical handbooks with Thucydides' comments on his speeches: "It now remains to consider whether he has composed the dialogue in such a way that it is consistent with the facts and fits the character of the delegates to the meeting, 'adhering as closely as possible to the general sense of

---

243. See the excellent examples of the speech of Vindex in Cassius Dio's history (63.22.3–6) in relation to the narrative argument of Nero's depravity (cf. A. M. Gowing, "Cassius Dio on the Reign of Nero," *ANRW* 2.34.3 [1997]: 2584–86); and the speech of Catiline in Sallust's history of the war (*Bell. Cat.* 20; cf. A. M. Stone, "Was Sallust a Liar? A Problem in Modern History," in *Ancient History* [ed. Hillard], 2:242).

244. E. Hilgert, "Speeches in Acts and Hellenistic Canons of Historiography and Rhetoric," in *Good News in History: Essays in Honor of Bo Reicke* (ed. E. L. Miller; Atlanta: Scholars Press, 1993), 90.

what was actually said,' as he said he would do in his introduction" (*Thuc.* 41).²⁴⁵ Dionysius holds that Thucydides was biased in his presentation of the exchange between the Athenians and the Melians (37–42). Dionysius finds the entire exchange implausible and therefore assesses that Thucydides must have distorted the truth because of his own treatment at the hands of the Athenians, which led to personal resentment (41). The issue is not whether the exchange really happened or not (because Dionysius assumes from the outset that Thucydides never had a clue what was really said on the occasion), but whether Athenian generals would speak this way in actuality (i.e., they make the argument that justice is the imposition of the will of the stronger on the weaker; a morally offensive argument since Athens is the mother city of just laws and principles, according to Dionysius).²⁴⁶ Dionysius argues that the exchange is implausible, and thus Thucydides' partiality has resulted in a flawed and unconvincing narrative. In other words, Dionysius understands that appropriate and fitting speeches — ones that relate to the character of the person speaking and the situation and context of the address — are not only speeches-in-character, but also represent "what was actually said" on that occasion. Given the understanding of *ethos* explored in the previous section, a logical formulation results: If the speech reflects the character of the speaker and the facts of the situation, then it will also be a "general sense of what was actually said."²⁴⁷

It is not difficult to appreciate how the speech relates to the composition of the complete narrative, precisely because, as Diodorus Siculus states, in historical narration "word [*logos*] and fact/deed [*ergon*] are in perfect agreement" (1.2.7). In other words, what is done in action is buttressed and elucidated by speech, and vice versa. Elsewhere in his history Diodorus criticizes the excessive use of speeches by some writers, which detracts from the continuity and coherence of the narrative and distracts the reader. Yet he also acknowledges the utility and indeed, at certain points, necessity of including speeches:

> [T]he genius of history is simple and self-consistent and as a whole is like a living organism. If it is mangled [by excessive use of speeches], it is stripped of its living charm; but if it retains its necessary unity, it is duly preserved and, by the harmony of the whole composition, renders the reading pleasant and clear.... [S]ince history needs to be adorned with variety, in certain places it is necessary to call to our aid even such passages [i.e., rhetorical speeches]... so that, whenever the situation requires either a public address from an ambassador or a statesman, or some such thing from the other characters, whoever

---

245. See the similar comments by Lucian: "If a person has to be introduced to make a speech, above all let his language suit his person and his subject, and next let these also be as clear as possible. It is then, however, that you can play the orator and show your eloquence" (*Hist.* 58). See also Hilgert, "Speeches in Acts," 88.
246. Potter, *Literary Texts,* 133.
247. See further Hilgert, "Speeches in Acts," 85–86; Attridge, *Interpretation of Biblical History,* 54–55; and K. S. Sacks, "Rhetoric and Speeches," 383–95.

does not enter the contest of words would himself be blameworthy. For one would find no small number of reasons for which on many occasions the aid of rhetoric will necessarily be enlisted; for when many things have been said well and to the point, one should not in contempt pass over what is worthy of memory and possesses a utility not alien to history, nor when the subject matter is great and glorious should one allow the language to appear inferior to the deeds; and there are times when, an event turning out contrary to expectation, we shall be forced to use words suitable to the subject in order to explain the seeming paradox. (20.1.5–20.2.2)

This comment provides significant insight into the use of speeches in ancient historiography because it combines reflection on the use of speeches with Diodorus's perception of the function and method of history. First, in continuity with his predecessors Diodorus observes that a proper history needs to be focused, complete, and unitary. The threads of events must be tied together and nothing (including speeches) should interfere with that aim. Second, Diodorus argues that while some writers both overuse speeches and make them overly (and so inappropriately) rhetorical and polished in style, speeches can be necessitated by the situations represented in the narratives. Third, Diodorus suggests that regardless of whether the speech is inserted by the writer to clarify the narrative or simply to reflect in words the grandeur that is indicated in deeds, speeches themselves "possess a utility not alien to history." In short, speeches aim at accomplishing the goals of "harmony" and "necessary unity" in the representation of historical events. When necessary, then, speeches advance the unitary conception of character, action, and consequence that is at the heart of ancient historical composition. Diodorus's presentation of the use of speeches in history thus correlates well with Aristotle's understanding of *dianoia* outlined earlier, except that Diodorus has expanded the concept of "reason for action expressed in thought" to include a greater diversity of function (from Aristotle's more narrow focus on reason to the writer's commentary on the narrative to epideictic elaboration of narrative themes). In the final analysis, however, the aim of speech-in-character is to further the larger goals of the historical composition, bringing the various and diverse threads evident in the narrative into a tightly focused point, achieving profit and pleasure as a result.

Ancient *Historia* and Acts: Reading the Hellenist Narrative in Context

In the above discussion several features of ancient historiography have received repeated attention. In the first main section of this chapter, I argued that traditional notions of history and historical composition are often limited in their scope and frequently incapable of accounting for the vast array of texts that are represented as historical in nature and yet from the perspective of modern analysis do not appear to adhere to the standards of the classic historians such as Thucydides or Polybius. However, these modern categories need to be either abandoned or considerably expanded in order to account for the ancient literary data. If classification is to provide a heuristic tool for interpreting and understanding ancient literature, then it is paramount that we carefully scrutinize the use of our terminology and the applicability and utility of the conceptions contained therein. Narrow definitions of a literary genre — be it history or a subgenre of history (such as universal or political history) — run into the problem of identifying a clearly perceivable core while regularly failing to capture the broader and more fluctuating literary categories that often lie outside of the classifications constructed by modern scholarship.

In short, if a work claims to be *historia*, then for all intents and purposes it is (and conversely, even if it does not make such a claim, it still may be). Rather than assessing the merits of this claim based on our assessment of the presence of historical facts contained within the work, perhaps the focus should be on, to borrow a phrase from M. Sternberg, the "historiographic force" of a particular historical composition.[248] Scholars have tended to conceive of ancient historiography in terms of a fact-based enterprise. For instance, C. J. Hemer claims that ancient history entails

> 1) the existence of a distinctive and rigorous theory of historiography; 2) the stress on eyewitness participation; 3) the importance of interviewing eyewitnesses; 4) the limitation of coverage to material where the writer has privileged access to evidence of guaranteed quality; 5) the stress on travel to the scene of events; 6) the prospect then (and for us) of checking details with contemporary documents; 7) the occasional insistence on the use of sources for speeches; and 8) the vigour of the concept of "truth" in history "as it actually happened."[249]

By contrast, in this chapter I have argued for viewing ancient historiography as a particular methodological approach to the presentation of reality, factual and otherwise. While searching for historicity behind historical narrative may be a legitimate exercise in its own right — at least from the perspective of modern historical interests — it is another matter altogether whether or not ancient readers of *historia* approached their texts in this manner. If the argument made in the second section is persuasive, then in all likelihood ancient readers and certainly writers approached historical composition with different expectations, interests, and concerns than modern scholars do. While there may not have been uniformity in reader reception

---

248. Sternberg, *Poetics of Biblical Narrative*, 26.
249. C. J. Hemer, *The Book of Acts in the Setting of Hellenistic History* (ed. C. H. Gempf; WUNT 49; Tübingen: Mohr Siebeck, 1989), 100. See the recent attempt by Byrskog, *Story as History*, 179–90, to formulate a more nuanced position for New Testament studies, wherein investigation and brutal facts are simultaneously conjoined with interpretation in the process of transmission. See also his most recent treatment of the role of orality in this process: "History or Story in Acts — A Middle Way? The "We" Passages, Historical Intertexture, and Oral History," in *Contextualizing Acts* (ed. Penner and Vander Stichele), 257–83.

and perception in the ancient world, with its emphasis on understanding and explanation, the holistic methodology employed by ancient writers differs categorically from the canons of modern historical inquiry. Indeed, as noted in the preceding discussion, while many ancient historians were concerned about the factual nature of their enterprise, they placed their emphasis less on the *fundamenta* and more on the plausibility of their representation.

This conclusion represents the major premise underlying the second section of this chapter. Ancient historians were concerned ultimately with the narrative depiction of the events they described. While some emphasize the role of inquiry and the status of eyewitnesses, these features are, as Lucian notes, simply the first stage of historical composition. The real historiographical task rests in the arrangement of the narrative and the amplification of the historical themes. As Lucian so aptly describes, the historian is "Homer's Zeus," looking down on discrete particulars and innately understanding/creating the relationship between actor, actions, and consequences. It is the ability to reflect clarity or accuracy in narration that separates the historian from the annalist in terms of the ideal image created by the ancient writers themselves. Precisely for this reason, then, *historia* is understood to possess a lasting value, rather than being limited to the present. The focus on the utility of historical narratives — and this aspect as the test of their ultimate truthfulness — stems from this framework for historiography: History aims at benefiting future audiences by representing explanatory accounts of unfolding human action in space and time, tying the narrative threads together so as to make history meaningful for subsequent members of the *polis*. Malice must be eschewed, as well as rhetorical display and sophistry of various kinds, as these vices detract from the utilitarian function of the narrative. This observation leads to another important conclusion regarding ancient historiography: It is the attributed motivation (as perceived from within various cultural and rhetorical contexts), rather than the content per se, that leads to negative and positive evaluations of the literary text. While it is true that certain types of content are discouraged in some writers (e.g., the use of miraculous and superstitious elements), overall the motivation for writing is determinative for the lasting value of the historical composition.

If the goal of historical composition is profit and pleasure — or, more precisely, profit through pleasure — then there are certain general rules that follow. Since the narrative lies at the center of the historian's task, it is natural that narration should figure so prominently in historiographical discussion. As outlined above, the ancient historians were keenly interested in executing a composition that reflected a complete, focused, and unified depiction of a particular event or series of events. In this approach, the duty of the historian is to assess the various facets of an event, attempting to tie in all the narrative elements. The historian not only arranges the material to this end but also renders an accurate portrayal of the complete action as a result:

an interpretation of the logical and sequential relationships between actor, action, and consequence. This particular methodological program bears striking resemblance to Aristotle's understanding of the complete action in tragic drama. Indeed, I have already pointed out numerous correlations between Aristotle's discussion in his *Poetics* and the theoretical comments of the ancient historians. Although there is no direct dependence per se and there are some significant differences resulting from variant ideological contexts, one can account for these commonalities based on the prevalence of particular patterns of literary composition and emphases that surface across a variety of genres in antiquity.[250] In particular, the various elements that make up Aristotle's presentation of the complete action — plot *(mythos)*, character *(ethos)*, and thought *(dianoia)* — all find parallels in the principal exercises of the *progymnasmata*, the rhetorical and educational training manuals of Greek and Roman youth. This broad cultural ethos accounts for some of the similarity between Aristotle's *Poetics,* the practice of Roman oratory, and the composition of Greco-Roman *historia.* Moreover, while the writers on historiographical theory never express indebtedness to the sources of their literary art, almost all ancient historians were concerned to represent the triad of plot, character, and thought that also underlies the *Poetics*. It is precisely these Aristotelian affinities that separate the historical task from that of the chronicler (at least as articulated from the perspective of ancient historiographical reflection on the matter). This association represents the legacy of the educational training of ancient historians, which involved being steeped in the various methods for composing the complete and persuasive narrative, which was fundamentally a rhetorical, literary, and ideological process.

Viewed in this light, historical composition, like the art of the tragic dramatist, becomes a matter of connecting the various facets of an event in order to create a plot. One particularly important element in this presentation is the use of vivid description, which is the ability to describe the events and personages in such dramatic light that the audience nearly visually perceives the development and movement of the plot. This emphasis is then followed by appropriate characterization, using both *topoi* and *ethos* construction to correlate the character of the historical actor with the direction of the plot. Finally, there is *dianoia*, which relates to speech-in-character that clarifies, in one way or another, the movement of the plot. In this manner, the writer of *historia* creates an accurate and useful account that will benefit and enrich readers in the present and future.

I have thus argued for broad patterns of cultural communicative strategies surfacing in a wide array of literature in the ancient Mediterranean world. I do not suggest a static nature to this phenomenon either synchronically or

---

250. Levene ("Pity, Fear," 130) refers to this as a "part of a general cultural complex that is emerging separately in Aristotle and the Roman *historia*" (cf. 148–49).

diachronically, but argue rather for a base structure of communication and persuasion, which could and did take on differing manifestations of form and expression depending on individual factors related to social, political, and ideological contexts situated in divergent locales and time periods. A more pervasive literary and cultural environment thus emerges for interpreting Acts 6:1–8:3. Consequently, in turning to the study of Luke-Acts in terms of its ancient historiographical context, several significant features come to the fore. First, there is considerable recent debate concerning the literary genre of Luke-Acts. The discussion focuses on whether Acts is a novel or a historical work in terms of the ancient understandings of those respective genres. It is difficult at times to separate fully these two genres in antiquity, and Luke-Acts may prove to be a *prima facie* case in this regard. What appear to be novelistic affinities may in fact be features of narrative composition shared by the novelistic and historical traditions. Determinative for the question of genre is rather Luke's self-understanding of his task, content, and presentation as reflected in Luke-Acts. The essential task, then, is to trace the Lukan narrative features that correlate with the historiographical tradition outlined earlier.

The preface to Luke-Acts goes far in substantiating that Luke's intent was to compose *historia*.

> As many have undertaken to compile narratives [διήγησις] concerning the things having taken place among us — these being handed down to us from the beginning by eye-witnesses and servants of the word — it also seemed good to me, having gone over everything thoroughly, to write [about the events] accurately [ἀκριβῶς] and in order [καθεξῆς] for you, most noble Theophilus, so that you might know the certainty about the words which you were taught. (Luke 1:1–4; author's trans.)

Despite the brevity of this opening preface in comparison to others in historical works, it is clear that Luke intends what follows to be read in light of the historical model. While L. C. A. Alexander insists that this opening does not suggest any affinity with the Greco-Roman tradition of historiography,[251] there are several points of overlap in terms of the stated purpose of the composition. First, Luke begins with a quasi-comparative statement with respect to the preceding narratives that have been written, an important *topos* of the historiographical tradition.[252] Luke offers not just any narrative, but one that is accurate and orderly, an implied contrast with

---

251. Alexander, *Preface to Luke's Gospel*, 200–201.
252. See Josephus's preface to the *Jewish War*, where he maintains that his account of the war with Rome will be superior to the "other" records of the event (1.1). See further Marincola, *Authority and Tradition*, 221, who notes the importance of acknowledging predecessors, but usually in a polemical context, where the historian argues for the supremacy of his own account. While Luke acknowledges predecessors, his preface lacks overt polemic (most scholars argue it is completely absent: e.g., Byrskog, *Story as History*, 230; and V. K. Robbins, "The Claims of the Prologues and Greco-Roman Rhetoric: The Prefaces to Luke and Acts in Light of Greco-Roman Rhetorical Strategies," in *Jesus and the Heritage* [ed. Moessner], 71–75) although the presence of such a feature should not be dismissed outright.

the former treatises.²⁵³ Second, Luke notes that he has "gone over everything thoroughly," a concept that entails a deliberate interpretive reading of the data. In line with this, the use of ἀκριβῶς, in the sense of offering an accurate or detailed rendering of events, further reinforces the notion that Luke is interested in the historiographic *to saphes*: the clarity and precision in understanding that can only be achieved from the perspective of "the gods/God." The use of καθεξῆς is also noteworthy in this regard, as Luke identifies the critical function of the historian's task: arrangement and ordering of the events as the key to creating a complete narrative.²⁵⁴ This does not necessarily imply "chronological order,"²⁵⁵ but, in line with the rest of the terminology, represents the means by which Luke will achieve an "accurate" narrative portrayal of the events, which, ultimately, means a "convincing" account.²⁵⁶ It is through the arrangement and ordering of the discrete events, tying them together so as to demonstrate a logical and necessary connection between actors, actions, and consequences, that Luke achieves *akribeia* and demonstrates his thorough personal understanding of the events. Hence, Luke consciously aligns his work with the tradition of ancient historiography, emphasizing the task of creating a unitary, focused, well-plotted, and persuasive narrative.

Third, and finally, the preface also reveals one of the most important features of the historiographical task: a purposeful treatment of the events. For Luke, the goal of historical composition is to produce "certainty" or "assurance" (ἀσφάλεια) in Theophilus with respect to the gospel in which he has been instructed.²⁵⁷ This stated purpose, while reflecting Luke's own ancient intellectual, rhetorical, and cultural contexts, nonetheless coalesces fully with the emphasis on utility and benefit in ancient historiographical theory. There is little doubt that Luke intends this narrative to be useful and beneficial to Theophilus and that the well-ordered narrative will itself be the

---

253. See F. Ó Fearghail, *The Introduction to Luke-Acts: A Study of the Role of Lk 1,1–4,44 in the Composition of Luke's Two-Volume Work* (AnBib 126; Rome: Pontifical Biblical Institute, 1991), 114; D. L. Dungan, *A History of the Synoptic Problem: The Canon, the Text, the Composition, and the Interpretation of the Gospels* (ABRL; New York: Doubleday, 1999), 14; Moessner, "Appeal and Power of Poetics," 113; and L. T. Johnson, *The Acts of the Apostles* (SP 5; Collegeville, Minn.: Liturgical Press, 1991), 30.

254. If read in light of the historiographical emphasis on arrangement and presentation of the complete narrative, the ambiguities surrounding καθεξῆς disappear. On the debate in past scholarship, see J. A. Fitzmyer, *The Gospel according to Luke I–IX* (AB 28; New York: Doubleday, 1981), 298–99; I. H. Marshall, *Commentary on Luke* (NIGTC; Grand Rapids: Eerdmans, 1978), 43; G. Schneider, "Zur Bedeutung von καθεξῆς im lukanischen Doppelwerk," ZNW 68 (1977): 128–31; and F. Mussner, "Καθεξῆς im Lukasprolog," in *Jesus und Paulus: Festschrift für Werner Georg Kümmel zum 70. Geburtstag* (ed. E. E. Ellis and E. Gräßer; Göttingen: Vandenhoeck & Ruprecht, 1975), 253–55.

255. Ó Fearghail, *Introduction to Luke-Acts*, 108.

256. Parsons, "Luke and the *Progymnasmata*," 51–53.

257. Similarly W. C. van Unnik, "Remarks on the Purpose of Luke's Historical Writing (Luke I 1–4)," in *Sparsa Collecta: Part One; Evangelia, Paulina, Acta* (NovTSup 29; Leiden: Brill, 1973), 13–14.

means to achieve this certainty in knowledge. While Theophilus appears to be a living individual, thus making this a narrative for the present, there is no reason to suggest that the intention is also not to produce a lasting composition that aims to produce similar results in future readers.[258] Overall, Luke's approach is consistent with that of the ancient historians detailed above. Where Luke parts ways to a degree is in not adopting the common deliberative paradigm of Polybius and Lucian.[259] Rather, with the emphasis on producing "assurance" of the things taught, Luke has explicitly identified his historiographical accent as epideictic in nature.[260] This feature is fully at home in the tradition explored above, and, as we will see in the next chapter, is most suitable for a first-century Jewish/Christian writer narrating historical events with a view to explicit apologetic concerns. Luke's preface, then, raises the expectation that he will be attempting to execute a historical narrative in the format of, and using the aims consonant with, the larger historiographical environment of antiquity.

Following upon Luke's comments in the preface to Luke-Acts, one can actually go further in anticipating some important compositional features of his narrative based upon the discussion in the latter part of this chapter. Luke clarifies that he will be providing an "accurate" and "orderly" narrative so as to produce "assurance" in Theophilus. Already in the opening statement, then, we find reference to one of the most notable features of historical composition: the well-plotted, unified, and complete narrative presentation. The ancient historians are adamant that only such a narrative can produce the results of utility and future benefit. Consequently, when viewing Acts 6:1–8:3, one must inquire how the various threads of the events in the episode are tied together into a focused plot, how the preceding and

---

258. F. G. Downing, "Theophilus's First Reading of Luke-Acts," in *Luke's Literary Achievement: Collected Essays* (ed. C. M. Tuckett; JSNTSup 116; Sheffield: Sheffield Academic Press, 1995), 91, offers a brief assessment of the options with respect to Theophilus's status vis-à-vis Luke.

259. Political emphases and themes, however, are not lacking in Acts; see Penner, "Civilizing Discourse," 89–98.

260. G. A. Kennedy (*New Testament Interpretation through Rhetorical Criticism* [Chapel Hill: University of North Carolina Press, 1984], 74) defines the epideictic genre as having as its goal "the strengthening of audience adherence to some value, as the basis for a general policy of action." This identification of the demonstrative focus of Luke-Acts should not be taken to mean, however, that everything that takes place in the narrative will have this sole focus. One of the central elements of ancient historiographical theory outlined above is appropriateness. As Dionysius maintains, one does not "address a jury, a political assembly and a festival audience in the same style" (*Lys.* 9). Thus, when Paul stands before his various accusers at the end of Acts, one expects not an epideictic speech praising Christianity, but suitable judicial responses (as J. H. Neyrey has shown; "The Forensic Defense Speech and Paul's Trial Speeches in Acts 22–26: Form and Function," in *Luke-Acts: New Perspectives from the Society of Biblical Literature* [ed. C. H. Talbert; New York: Crossroad, 1984], 210–24). A proper *historia* will combine diverse forms according to the varied situations that arise (cf. Dionysius, who claims that his history will combine forensic, speculative, and narrative so as to provide something for everyone [i.e., political debate, philosophical discussion, and purely entertaining accounts]; *Ant. rom.* 1.8.3).

following episodes are related, and, finally, how the overarching unity of narrative composition situates Stephen and the Hellenists. The second feature that one can expect to find is the use of vivid narration in order to bring the events "before the eyes" of the reader. As demonstrated above, this feature is an important element in the historian's literary repertoire, involving not only a well-ordered plot but also dramatic representation of the events.[261] The third feature that can be anticipated is the use of characterization with respect to the actors in the narrative, including the use of *topoi*.[262] But most important for Acts 6:1–8:3, the writer makes extensive use of the related phenomenon of *synkrisis* for comparing two or more distinct groups in terms of their respective responses and actions.[263] Finally, in line with the preceding assessment, when one finds a speech such as that contained in Acts 7, it is paramount to investigate in what ways it contributes to the construction of character and the *dianoia* of the narrator/narrative. Thus, one must inquire about the relationship between Stephen and the speech-in-character, as well as the possible connections between the speech and the surrounding narrative context.

Given the central aspects of ancient historiographical expectations and practices I have outlined in this chapter the narrative in Acts 6:1–8:3 should come more clearly into focus. A sense of how to read the text will yield a greater appreciation for the methodology and purpose behind the Lukan composition. Yet, while this chapter has focused on ancient historiography more broadly, left unexplored is a significant element of the Lukan literary context left unexplored: apologetic historiography. It remains to be seen how this specific trajectory of ancient *historia* might further illuminate the understanding of Luke-Acts generally and the Hellenist narrative specifically.

---

261. E. Plümacher, *Lukas als hellenistischer Schriftsteller: Studien zur Apostelgeschichte* (SUNT 9; Göttingen: Vandenhoeck & Ruprecht, 1972), 80–111, has analyzed the presence of the "dramatische Episodenstil" in Acts at length. W. Braun, *Feasting and Social Rhetoric in Luke 14* (SNTSMS 85; Cambridge: Cambridge University Press, 1995), 11–13, connects the presence of these scenes in Luke to the tradition of tragic-pathetic historiography (cf. C.-J. Thornton, *Der Zeuge des Zeugen: Lukas als Historiker der Paulusreisen* [WUNT 56; Tübingen: Mohr Siebeck, 1991], 355–60). Aside from the vivid scenes, Braun lays stress on the lack of narrative continuity in this mode of historical composition. Writers such as Polybius and Lucian, however, make clear that vivid narration is not only required for all histories but that it is precisely continuity and unity in narrative presentation that best accomplishes vividness in historical presentation.

262. For some general comments on characterization in Luke-Acts, as well as special attention to the use of stereotypes in Acts 17, see J. H. Neyrey, "Acts 17, Epicureans, and Theodicy: A Study in Stereotypes," in *Greeks, Romans, and Christians* (ed. Balch et al.), 118–34, esp. 121, 129–33.

263. On *synkrisis* in Acts, see A. Smith, "'Full of Spirit and Wisdom': Luke's Portrait of Stephen (Acts 6:1–8:1a) as a Man of Self-Mastery," in *Asceticism and the New Testament* (ed. L. E. Vaage and V. L. Wimbush; New York: Routledge, 1999), 97–114, esp. 101–2; J. C. Lentz, *Luke's Portrait of Paul* (SNTSMS 77; Cambridge: Cambridge University Press, 1993), 91–101; D. Marguerat, "Luc-Actes: Une Unité à Construire," in *Unity of Luke-Acts* (ed. Verheyden), esp. 70–74; and esp. A. C. Clark, *Parallel Lives: The Relation of Paul to the Apostles in the Lucan Perspective* (Carlisle, England: Paternoster, 2001).

IV

Jewish Apologetic Historiography
Cultural Identity and Rewriting the Past

In the previous chapter I explored the larger literary and cultural context of ancient historiographical theory and practice. This examination will prove to be important insofar as the story of Stephen and the Hellenists can be elucidated as part of Luke's larger historiographic practice. Yet, as noted in the last chapter, the ancient world attests to a wide variety of historiographical works, and to appreciate fully a particular writer or treatise one must explore not only the wider patterns of historical composition in antiquity but also particular kinds of historical compositions. In this chapter, I focus on Jewish apologetic historiography and provide a fuller contouring of Luke's ancient historiographical context. This shift to the Jewish historiographical literary environment will prove fruitful for the analysis of Acts 6:1–8:3 to follow, not only for understanding certain aspects of Stephen's retelling of biblical history in Acts 7 but also the larger narrative framework of the speech. While I do not argue here that this tradition of historiography provides some sort of direct literary model for Luke (although that does remain a possibility), I do suggest that examining Acts in the context of this particular mode of cultural communication will reinforce some of the broader literary patterns outlined in the previous chapter.

Jewish Apologetic Historiography

There is a fair degree of debate surrounding the nature and extent of Jewish apologetic interests in antiquity, as well as the larger Greco-Roman context that gave rise to the Jewish literary phenomenon labeled "apologetic." The standard modern formulation of the issue is thus: Jews in the ancient world often found themselves in hostile environments, where they were required to defend their religious commitments and heritage. This interpretation — the defensive stance vis-à-vis Jewish religious and cultural life — hinges on the belief that there was widespread antagonism to Judaism in antiquity.[1]

---

1. J. N. Sevenster's study, *The Roots of Pagan Anti-Semitism in the Ancient World* (NovTSup 41; Leiden: Brill, 1975), provides one of the more important articulations of this position of widespread antipathy toward the Jews in antiquity. He argues that the Jewish

Viewed in this larger framework, most of the literature of Judaism in the Second Temple period could be viewed, from one angle or another, as apologetic in nature.[2] Indeed, in his classic study of Jewish apologetic literature, M. Friedländer casts almost all the literature of Jewish antiquity in this way, from the *Testaments of the Twelve Patriarchs* to Sirach, from Daniel to Josephus and Philo.[3] Moreover, Friedländer identifies the Diaspora — the primary environment of the Jewish encounter with Hellenism — as the birthplace of apologetic literature, an identification that has persisted in scholarship.[4]

From this interpretative matrix for Jewish apologetic, scholars soon added a further development: the presence of a supposed propagandistic aspect to the tradition. In this view not only is this literature defensive in its posture — addressing charges and responding to calumnious and malicious characterizations by outsiders — it also seeks to missionize the Greco-Roman world by demonstrating the superiority of its own tradition to that of the Greeks.[5] This further assessment results in a more complex rhetorical classification of Jewish apologetic literature. On the one hand, defense is clearly in view, and this stance may be defined as the judicial side of apologetics. On the other hand, the effort to build bridges with other cultures while arguing for the superiority of one's own tradition results in making certain claims for one's past, culture, and individual as well as collective identity. Thus, there is also a degree of deliberative emphasis in this literature: persuasion toward accepting the Jewish religion as the superior tradition and perhaps even to elicit conversion. Speaking of the translation of the Hebrew Bible into Greek, Friedländer states, "A beginning was made with the monumental work, which for the propagation of Mosaic religion

---

emphasis on separation from the larger Gentile population provoked reaction from representatives of Greco-Roman culture. See the more recent study by P. Schäfer, *Judeophobia: Attitudes towards the Jews in the Ancient World* (Cambridge: Harvard University Press, 1997), who narrows the strongest hostility to Egypt (169). See also the recent discussion by K. Berthelot, *Philanthrôpia judaica: Le débat autour de la "misanthropie" des lois juives dans l'Antiquité* (JSJSup 76; Leiden: Brill, 2003).

2. See A. Kasher, "Polemic and Apologetic Methods of Writing in *Contra Apionem*," in *Josephus' Contra Apionem: Studies in Its Character and Context* (ed. L. H. Feldman and J. R. Levison; AGJU 34; Leiden: Brill, 1996), 144; and H. D. Betz, "In Defense of the Spirit: Paul's Letter to the Galatians as a Document of Early Christian Apologetics," in *Aspects of Religious Propaganda in Judaism and Early Christianity* (ed. E. Schüssler Fiorenza; Notre Dame, Ind.: University of Notre Dame Press, 1976), 99–101.

3. M. Friedländer, *Geschichte der jüdischen Apologetik* (Amsterdam: Philo, 1973).

4. Ibid., 22–25. See also E. Schürer, *The History of the Jewish People in the Age of Jesus Christ (175 B.C.–A.D. 135)* (rev. and ed. G. Vermes et al.; Edinburgh: T & T Clark, 1986), 3.1:594; H. Conzelmann, *Gentiles, Jews, Christians: Polemics and Apologetics in the Greco-Roman World* (trans. M. E. Boring; Minneapolis: Fortress, 1992), 140–44; G. Hata, "The Story of Moses Interpreted within the Context of Anti-Semitism," in *Josephus, Judaism, and Christianity* (ed. L. H. Feldman and G. Hata; Detroit: Wayne State University Press, 1987), 180–97; and Kasher, "Polemic and Apologetic Methods," 146–47.

5. Kasher, "Polemic and Apologetic Methods," 145.

in the pagan world would have an unpredictable import: the translation of the Bible into Greek in order to bring the spiritual treasure of Judaism nearer to the Greeks."[6] Given substantive formulation by P. Dalbert,[7] this approach stresses the missionary nature of Jewish propaganda arising out of the apologetic tradition. With its emphasis on the common ethic of Judaism, an overtly defensive compositions such as Josephus's *Contra Apionem* could therefore be construed as missionary propaganda for Gentile conversion.[8]

The above view on Jewish apologetic literature was standard for most of the twentieth century. It has, however, been more closely scrutinized in recent times, and some of the long-standing assumptions have been challenged as a result. For instance, despite the long-held belief that there was an active missionary agenda among Jews in the Diaspora,[9] scholars such as S. McKnight have recently argued that the missionary impulse was not that strong in Second Temple Judaism (particularly before the second century C.E.).[10] There is perhaps some evidence suggesting Gentile attachment to

---

6. Friedländer, *Geschichte der jüdische Apologetik*, 26 (my translation).
7. P. Dalbert, *Die Theologie der hellenistisch-jüdischen Missions-Literatur unter Ausschluss von Philo und Josephus* (TF 4; Hamburg: Reich, 1954). See further H. G. Meecham, *The Oldest Version of the Bible: 'Aristeas' on Its Traditional Origin. A Study in Early Apologetic* (London: Holborn, 1932), 110–14. N. Walter suggests a gradual development from the more polemical earlier Jewish literature (e.g., Aristobulus) to a more overt propagandizing stance in *Aristeas*, Josephus, and Philo (*Der Thoraausleger Aristobulos: Untersuchungen zu seinen Fragmenten zu pseudepigraphischen Resten der jüdisch-hellenistischen Literatur* [TU 86; Berlin: Akademie, 1964], 49–51). See also D. Georgi, *The Opponents of Paul in Second Corinthians* (Philadelphia: Fortress, 1986), 83–151, whose discussion of Judaism of the Hellenistic and Roman periods as a missionary religion is the *locus classicus* for more contemporary discussion (see the most recent support of this position in S. Matthews, *First Converts: Rich Pagan Women and the Rhetoric of Mission in Early Judaism and Christianity* [Contraversions; Stanford: Stanford University Press, 2001], 1–4, 11–16).
8. See G. Klein, *Der älteste christliche Katechismus und die jüdische Propaganda-Literatur* (Berlin: Reimer, 1909), 92–94 (on Josephus, *C. Ap.* 2.190–210). S. Mason has recently designated *Contra Apionem* as a *logos protreptikos*, a classic form of deliberative rhetoric that seeks to attract converts to a particular philosophic or religious tradition ("*Contra Apionem* in Social and Literary Context: An Invitation to Judean Philosophy," in *Josephus' Contra Apionem* [ed. Feldman and Levison], 217–19, 222–24). Mason, however, does not connect this feature with the apologetic tradition per se (207). See also P. Bilde, *Flavius Josephus between Jerusalem and Rome* (JSPSup 2; Sheffield: Sheffield Academic Press, 1988), 120; and F. Siegert, "Protreptik und Polemik bei Josephus: Eine Einleitung in sein *Contra Apionem*," in *Persuasion and Dissuasion in Early Christianity* (ed. P. W. van der Horst et al.; CBET 33; Leuven: Peeters, 2003), 64–85.
9. See M. Simon, *Verus Israel: A Study of the Relations between Christians and Jews in the Roman Empire (A.D. 135–425)* (trans. H. McKeating; Oxford: Oxford University Press, 1986), 271–305; and L. H. Feldman, *Jew and Gentile in the Ancient World: Attitudes and Interactions from Alexander to Justinian* (Princeton: Princeton University Press, 1993), 288–341, 383–415.
10. See S. McKnight, *A Light among the Gentiles: Jewish Missionary Activity in the Second Temple Period* (Minneapolis: Fortress, 1991); A. T. Kraabel, "Immigrants, Exiles, Expatriates, and Missionaries," in *Religious Propaganda and Missionary Competition in the New Testament World: Essays Honoring Dieter Georgi* (ed. L. Bormann, K. Del Tredici, and A. Standhartinger; NovTSup 74; Leiden: Brill, 1994), 76–81, 84–85; and esp. M. Goodman, *Mission and Conversion: Proselytizing in the Religious History of the Roman Empire* (Oxford: Oxford University Press, 1994).

Judaism in the ancient world,[11] but this phenonmenon is not quite the same as the existence of an extensive missionary effort to a non-Jewish audience. Moreover, the assumption of widespread Greco-Roman antipathy toward Judaism — the bedrock of the traditional understanding of apologetic — has likewise been challenged in recent scholarship.[12] Aside from a few severe critics such as Apion,[13] most Greeks and Romans seem to have tolerated Judaism fairly well, and only had serious problems when members of their own communities adopted beliefs and practices of Jewish culture and religion.[14]

---

11. One thinks here primarily of the "God-fearer"/proselyte issue. On the evidence, see I. Levinskaya, *The Book of Acts in Its Diaspora Setting* (BAFCS 5; Grand Rapids: Eerdmans, 1996), 19–126. But see A. T. Kraabel, "The Disappearance of the God-fearers," in *Diaspora Jews and Judaism* (ed. J. A. Overman and R. S. MacLennan; SFSHJ 41; Atlanta: Scholars Press, 1992), 119–30, who argues that there is scant evidence for this category of "believer." The category of θεοσεβής is notoriously difficult to delineate. It is debatable whether or not the term was ever a widely recognized technical designation of a Gentile "hanger-on," and much of the evidence is difficult to date (see Levinskaya, *The Book of Acts in Its Diaspora Setting*, 25). The word may refer to Jews, proselytes, nonconverted Gentiles, or, at one time or another, to all three groups (which is more likely the case). Given the syncretistic environment of late antiquity, it is ultimately futile to make an argument one way or another on the basis of whether the name of a person identified as a God-fearer is Greek or Jewish. Moreover, given the possibility that Jewish synagogues modeled themselves on Greco-Roman *collegia* (see P. Richardson, "Early Synagogues as Collegia in the Diaspora and Palestine," in *Voluntary Associations in the Graeco-Roman World* [ed. J. S. Kloppenborg and S. G. Wilson; New York: Routledge, 1996], 90–109), the possibility exists that some if not many of the God-fearer inscriptions, if they do refer to Gentiles, are references to patrons of Jewish associations, which does not necessarily imply anything about the religio-philosophical commitments of these same individuals. This debate aside, there is some evidence of Gentiles in Jewish communities (cf. Epictetus, *Diatr.* 2.9.19ff.), but the extent is difficult to determine, as is the type of commitment and the exact role the Jews themselves played in such conversions.

12. See L. H. Feldman, "Reading between the Lines: Appreciation of Judaism in Anti-Jewish Writers Cited in *Contra Apionem*," in *Josephus' Contra Apionem* (ed. Feldman and Levison), 250–70; and E. S. Gruen, *Heritage and Hellenism: The Reinvention of Jewish Tradition* (HCS 30; Berkeley: University of California Press, 1998), 49–72. Also see Feldman's various essays detailing this position further: "Pro-Jewish Intimations in Anti-Jewish Remarks Cited in Josephus' *Against Apion*," "Pro-Jewish Intimations in Tacitus' Account of Jewish Origins," and "The Jews as Viewed by Plutarch," in *Studies in Hellenistic Judaism* (AGJU 30; Leiden: Brill, 1996), 177–236, 377–407, 529–52.

13. Apion's calumnious account of Jewish practice and belief seems to have origins in some deep-seated dislike of the Jews. One might be tempted to generalize this sentiment, but precisely here we should be cautious. The reason for this assertion is that Apion's work is explicitly connected with Alexandria, where, as the extant fragments of the *Acts of the Pagan Martyrs* attest, there seemed to exist a strong anti-Jewish sentiment. The various Jewish uprisings in Alexandria attest to a long tradition of Jewish and Greek conflict in the city, and evidently the Greek population and the Jews had a mutual distrust of and dislike for one another. The papyrus containing Claudius's edict to the Alexandrians (*CPJ* 153) reflects such a context. The comments by the Alexandrian Apion, therefore, cannot be taken as indicative of general Greco-Roman views of Judaism in antiquity. See further Schäfer, *Judeophobia*, 136–60. On the likelihood that Apion evinces a more positive, albeit somewhat distorted, Egyptian representation of Judaism, see Gruen, *Heritage and Hellenism*, 67–68; and idem, *Diaspora: Jews amidst Greeks and Romans* (Cambridge: Harvard University Press, 2002), 219–20, in which he argues that a text such as 3 Maccabees actually portrays more concord than dispute between Jews and Greeks in Alexandria.

14. Strongest censure is reserved not for Jews per se but for those Greeks and Romans who would abandon their own customs and practices in order to adopt the ways of an "inferior"

These more recent reflections on the relationship of Judaism to its Greco-Roman environment have complicated the picture of apologetic literature. On the one hand, scholars still affirm that Jews could be fiercely combative in confronting a hostile environment. The literary remains of Artapanus, the second-century B.C.E. Jewish writer, is sometimes referred to as "competitive historiography" because of the way in which he creatively reformulates biblical tradition and develops a highly praiseworthy account of Judaism to contrast with more negative portrayals such as one finds in Manetho.[15] Similarly, Josephus's *Antiquities* is frequently interpreted as an explicitly apologetic work that represents the Jews in a positive light in an environment that is perceived, by Josephus at least, to be negatively positioned vis-à-vis Judaism.[16]

On the other hand, recent scholarship has pushed the understanding of apologetic literature further. G. E. Sterling's work on apologetic historiography has clarified, in part, some of the issues surrounding the understanding of apologetic as a defensive posture. As we saw in the previous chapter, Sterling defines this literary enterprise in the ancient world as one in which writers follow their own native traditions, but hellenize the material in order to establish a particular group's identity in the larger context.[17] Following the Greek model of ethnographic composition, writers would relate their own native traditions of culture and religion in such a way as to advance their own standing in the Greco-Roman cultural world. The practice became

---

ethnos. In this context, the castigation of Jews for proselytizing is noticeable (cf. Valerius Maximus 1.3.3, where the Jews are described as "infecting" the Romans). It should be emphasized, however, that this position does not represent a particular hostility to Judaism per se, but reflects a general disregard for that which is not Greek/Roman. This point especially holds true for those practices that violated basic Greek sensibilities, such as circumcision and strict dietary regulations (cf. Tacitus, *Hist.* 5.5.1). The observance of the Sabbath, on the other hand, was not as serious an issue, and in fact Suetonius records that Augustus himself bragged that in his keeping of a particular fast he was even more fastidious than the Jews observing their Sabbath fasts (*Aug.* 76.2), indicating the generally favorable impression of this Jewish practice. The sharp reaction to Gentile conversion to Judaism apparent among Greco-Roman writers may well reflect the increasing incidents of this phenomenon toward the end of the first century and into the second (cf. Strabo 16.2.34–46; Horace, *Sermones* 1.4.139–143; Martial 7.82, 11.94; Juvenal 14.96–106).

15. See J. J. Collins, *Between Athens and Jerusalem: Jewish Identity in the Hellenistic Diaspora* (New York: Crossroad, 1982), 33–34. Collins refers to Manetho's account as "hostile," although the evidence may suggest a more neutral stance (see Feldman, "Reading between the Lines," 267).

16. See H. W. Attridge, *The Interpretation of Biblical History in the Antiquitates Judaicae of Flavius Josephus* (HDR 7; Missoula, Mont.: Scholars Press, 1976), 60–62; Collins, *Between Athens and Jerusalem*, 49–50; J. M. G. Barclay, *Jews in the Mediterranean Diaspora: From Alexander to Trajan (323 B.C.E.–117 C.E.)* (Edinburgh: T & T Clark, 1996), 358, 361–62; P. Spilsbury, "*Contra Apionem* and *Antiquitates Judaicae*: Points of Contact," in *Josephus' Contra Apionem* (ed. Feldman and Levison), 352–62; L. H. Feldman, "Josephus as an Apologist to the Greco-Roman World: His Portrait of Solomon," in *Aspects of Religious Propaganda* (ed. Schüssler Fiorenza), 69–98; and idem, *Josephus's Interpretation of the Bible* (HCS 27; Berkeley: University of California Press, 1998), 132–62.

17. G. E. Sterling, *Historiography and Self-definition: Josephos, Luke-Acts, and Apologetic Historiography* (NovTSup 64; Leiden: Brill, 1992), 17.

widespread following the conquests of Alexander and helped to foster a literature of protest against foreign invasion that also adopted Greco-Roman values, assumptions, and modes of argumentation in order to establish the validity of the suppressed tradition.[18] Sterling has provided a significant shift in the traditional understanding of apologetic texts, however, by maintaining that insider identity is just as important as outsider perceptions in this literature. His summary of the aims of Josephus's *Antiquities* brings the various strands together:

> [T]he *Antiquities* offers a self-definition of Judaism in historical terms. It presented Judaism to the Greek world in a bid to overturn misconceptions and to establish a more favorable image. It presented Judaism to the Roman world with the hope that the favorable status Judaism had enjoyed would continue unabated. Finally, it presented Judaism to the Jews themselves in the form Josephos thought would best serve as the basis for a reconstructed Judaism.[19]

Sterling has retained the older sense of apologetic as responding to outsiders' negative perceptions of Judaism. Yet Sterling also adds a significant supplementary aim: Apologetic work edifies the Jewish audience by presenting a particular Hellenistic-Jewish fusion that situates Jewish identity in the midst of the larger value system of the Greco-Roman world. The recasting of the native tradition thus creates, maintains, and reinforces the self-understanding of a particular minority group. In his classic article, V. Tcherikover articulated a similar understanding of Jewish apologetic literature: The vast corpus of traditionally designated apologetic texts was aimed inward at the Jewish audience, not outward at the Greeks.[20]

This line of interpretation has two important aspects. First, it recognizes that in presenting one's tradition to outsiders, one must consistently and pervasively articulate that tradition not in traditional insider categories but in terms the outsider will understand and appreciate. Among other things, this emphasis requires a restructuring of one's own tradition in light of dominant cultural values, defining oneself over and against but also within the larger

---

18. Sterling's monograph details the development of this genre with great precision. Also see the earlier comments by E. J. Bickerman, "The Jewish Historian Demetrios," in *Christianity, Judaism, and Other Greco-Roman Cults: Studies for Morton Smith at Sixty* (ed. J. Neusner; SJLA 12; Leiden: Brill, 1975), 3:76–77; and S. K. Eddy, *The King Is Dead: Studies in the Near Eastern Resistance to Hellenism, 334–31 B.C.* (Lincoln: University of Nebraska Press, 1961), 272–76.

19. Sterling, *Historiography and Self-definition*, 308. See also L. T. Johnson, *The Writings of the New Testament: An Interpretation* (Minneapolis: Fortress, 1986), 74. Attridge, *Interpretation of Biblical History*, 56, reflects elements of this definition when he asserts that, alongside the defensive posture, Josephus also envisions that his works will have a moral pedagogical effect on the reader.

20. V. Tcherikover, "Jewish Apologetic Literature Reconsidered," *Eos* 48 (1956): 171–83. Tcherikover admits that some literature represents a self-defensive posture, but limits it to a few select texts at the beginning of the Roman period (182).

sociocultural environment.[21] As Sterling points out, in the case of Judaism this phenomenon involves above all the hellenization of Jewish history and theology. Second, it recognizes the importance of shaping insider identity. Rather than being aimed (solely) at an outsider audience, apologetic literature helps to fashion and maintain a particular group's self-understanding in its portrayal of a specific historical, cultural, and religious heritage. In short, rather than simply constructing identity as a defensive measure over against the dominant culture, Jewish apologetic literature reflects a robust self-consciousness that continues to bolster the group's perceptions of its heritage and self-identity.[22]

In one sense, then, the motivation underlying many Hellenistic Jewish texts is quite simple: In line with Roman historiography more generally, there exists a tendency to articulate one's history — national, communal, ethnic, or personal — in terms of epideictic modes of historiography, presenting one's tradition in a praiseworthy manner and, on occasion, presenting other competing traditions in a derogatory way. Thus, along with judicial and possibly some deliberative emphases, apologetic literature also reveals a significant demonstrative component. Those Jewish works that appear to be offering a description of Judaism as being on par with or superior to Greco-Roman traditions perhaps should be reread in this light.[23] Species of rhetorical designation are best viewed as heuristic tools, not as definitive categories. Thus, an important question is what difference reading the material through an epideictic lens might make more generally. If one moves from a judicial analysis of the texts to an epideictic one, are there significant changes in the perception of the literature? Or, how does an epideictic reading of the literature help one understand the discourse of apologetic literature? A more detailed analysis of epideictic discourse itself will aid in exploring these issues further.

Epideictic Composition

Aristotle gave classic formulation to the category of demonstrative/epideictic discourse. He defines epideictic as that species of rhetoric that focuses on

---

21. See A. Momigliano, "An Apology of Judaism: The *Against Apion* by Flavius Josephus," in *Essays on Ancient and Modern Judaism* (ed. S. Berti; trans. M. Masella-Gayley; Chicago: University of Chicago Press, 1994), 58–59.

22. This is a major emphasis throughout Gruen, *Heritage and Hellenism,* focusing on Jewish literary activity in the Hellenistic period (cf. 188; see also Gruen, *Diaspora,* 147–48, 170, 181).

23. In some sense, rhetorical species classification of ancient apologetic literature will constantly run into problems when the analysis becomes more formalistic, since texts and purposes for writing are not linear in orientation; there is complexity, hybridity, ambiguity, and multivalency deeply embedded in the persuasive strategies adopted. Although providing more of a formal analysis J. W. van Henten and R. Abusch acknowledge that in combining judicial and epideictic in *Contra Apionem* Josephus "was blurring distinct rhetorical categories" ("The Jews as Tryphonians and Josephus' Strategy of Refutation in *Contra Apionem,*" in *Josephus' Contra Apionem* [ed. Feldman and Levison], 303).

praise and blame, with a view to the present. Epideictic stands in contrast to the emphasis on the future in deliberative rhetoric and the past in judicial. Its mode of discourse, according to Aristotle, focuses on the honorable and shameful, bringing in various related aspects that correspond to these two major qualities (*Rhet.* 1.3.3–5). First and foremost for Aristotle, this mode of argumentation involves an appreciation of the good (*kalon*), which includes virtue, and more specifically things such as justice, courage, self-control, magnificence, generosity, gentleness, prudence, and wisdom (1.9.3–13).[24] In this framework, the goal of a composition that praises an individual would be to highlight the various virtues, demonstrating that the person in view is honorable in word and deed.[25] As Aristotle states, "[S]ince praise is founded on actions, and acting according to moral purpose is characteristic of the worthy man, we must endeavor to show that a man is acting in that manner, and it is useful that it should appear that he has done so on several occasions" (1.9.32). The depiction of an individual's general virtue or specific deeds thus accents the habitual nature of goodness in his or her character. In light of Aristotle's views regarding *ethos* delineated in the former chapter, it is not surprising that he could conclude that "achievements ... are signs of moral habit; for we should praise even a man who had not achieved anything, if we felt confident that he was likely to do so" (1.9.33). In this way, praise of individuals is intricately bound up with their character-type, and their deeds that are outwardly manifested reflect their inner disposition. For Aristotle, particular types of characters can be expected to act in an admirable manner and thus be honored before the fact.[26] The opposite, of course, is also true.

While Aristotle's delineation of epideictic focuses squarely on praise and blame of either virtue or deeds,[27] the larger picture is more complex.[28] Any

---

24. This list represents the classic virtues of the ancient world. On the history and development of the list, see H. F. North, "Canons and Hierarchies of the Cardinal Virtues in Greek and Latin Literature," in *The Classical Tradition: Literary and Historical Studies in Honor of Harry Caplan* (ed. L. Wallach; Ithaca: Cornell University Press, 1966), 165–83.

25. It is sometimes suggested that epideictic discourse originally had an edge of social and cultural challenge that Aristotle seeks to domesticate. In this reading, Aristotle's emphasis on the present and the common *topoi* undermines the earlier transformative role of demonstrative rhetoric (see further E. Schiappa, *The Beginnings of Rhetorical Theory in Classical Greece* [New Haven: Yale University Press, 1999], 184–206).

26. See J. H. Neyrey, *Honor and Shame in the Gospel of Matthew* (Louisville: Westminster John Knox, 1998), 71–78; and P. L. Shuler, *A Genre for the Gospels: The Biographical Character of Matthew* (Philadelphia: Fortress, 1982), 49–50.

27. In the case of praise of deeds, Aristotle designates this instance as an encomium, in contrast with epideictic proper, which focuses on character (i.e., virtue; cf. *Rhet.* 1.9.33). T. Burgess, "Epideictic Literature," *Studies in Classical Philology* 3 (1902): 113, points out the sometimes imprecise use of epideictic terminology in ancient discussion.

28. See the outline of ancient commentary on demonstrative discourse in Burgess, "Epideictic Literature," 102–13. D. A. Russell, "The Panegyrists and Their Teachers," in *The Propaganda of Power: The Role of Panegyric in Late Antiquity* (ed. M. Whitby; MnSup 183; Leiden: Brill, 1998), 49, observes that epideictic was never a major focus of the ancient rhetorical handbooks. It was especially in the *progymnasmata* that demonstrative oratory took on greater importance.

speech or composition that does not attempt to persuade a hearer or reader to take a particular course of action (deliberative), or that does not respond to specific charges or proffer counteraccusations (judicial), is considered epideictic. This framework obviously lumps together in the category of epideictic a wide variety of forms of speech and composition. As G. A. Kennedy states,

> Aristotle's view of epideictic, based on his observation of public address in Greece, is too narrow for a general theory. Epideictic is perhaps best regarded as including any discourse, oral or written, that does not aim at a specific action or decision but seeks to enhance knowledge, understanding, or belief, often through praise or blame, whether of persons, things, or values. It is thus an important feature of cultural or group cohesion.[29]

Yet, while epideictic literature in the Aristotelian framework is quite broadly conceived, there are some distinguishing characteristics, especially, as Aristotle himself notes, the stress on praise and blame or honor and shame, the focus on the present, and the accent on values. This last element is particularly important since, as Kennedy argues, epideictic literature encourages group cohesion as a natural function of its value-laden underpinnings. In this sense, then, epideictic discourse can be seen as functioning similarly as epic and tragedy, as those are conceived by Aristotle in his *Poetics*.[30] It is also easy to appreciate how, with this particular function of the literature in view, the later Hellenistic and early Roman writers could subsume all forms of composition, including history, under the category of epideictic.[31]

It is not surprising, then, that there are some significant elements in Aristotle's theory of epideictic that overlap with the understanding of historiography outlined in the previous chapter. First, emphasis is placed on attendant matters in order to elucidate fully the particular thing being praised. For instance, in praise of an individual one should list things such as good birth and education (*Rhet.* 1.9.33). As we shall see later, this stress became particularly important in epideictic theory in the Roman period, corresponding to the historiographical emphasis on the complete narrative whereby persuasion is achieved through tying together various disparate threads under a common interpretive strategy. Second, similar to Lucian's

---

29. G. A. Kennedy, "The Genres of Rhetoric," in *Handbook of Classical Rhetoric in the Hellenistic Period 300 B.C.–A.D. 400* (ed. S. E. Porter; Leiden: Brill, 1997), 45. Also see his treatment in *New Testament Interpretation through Rhetorical Criticism* (Chapel Hill: University of North Carolina Press, 1984), 73–85.

30. G. A. Kennedy, *The Art of Persuasion in Greece* (Princeton: Princeton University Press, 1963), 153.

31. Kennedy, "Genres of Rhetoric," 45; and Burgess, "Epideictic Literature," 92.

understanding of history (*Hist.* 51), we find that "amplification is most suitable for epideictic speakers, whose subject is actions which are not disputed, so that all that remains to be done is to attribute beauty and importance to them" (*Rhet.* 1.9.40). Thus, epideictic concerns itself with elaboration and embellishment of the *fundamenta* in a manner similar to Cicero's understanding of the aims of *historia*.[32] Third, *synkrisis* is an integral element of epideictic in terms of contrasting the character and actions of one person with another, demonstrating the superiority of the person being praised over the inferior narrative foil (1.9.38).[33]

Quintilian's treatment of epideictic literature more fully details some of the specifics outlined above. He observes at the outset that the goal of panegyric *(laudis)* is to amplify and embellish its appropriate themes (3.7.6). Epideictic rhetoric focuses primarily on the praise of gods and humans, elaborating the themes appropriate to each category. With respect to individuals, Quintilian delineates a variety of antecedent elements that the orator should include in praising (or denouncing) virtues and actions. The topics related to the main theme highlight the grandeur and honor of an individual by making reference to praiseworthy features of his history and character:

> With regard to things preceding a man's birth, there are his country, his parents and his ancestors, a theme which may be handled in two ways. For either it will be creditable to the objects of our praise not to have fallen short of the fair fame of their country and of their sires or to have ennobled a humble origin by the glory of their achievements. Other topics to be drawn from the period preceding their birth will have reference to omens or prophecies foretelling their future greatness.... [T]he praise of the individual himself will be based on his character, his physical endowments and external circumstances. (3.7.10–12)

Herein one finds two critical components of epideictic composition: (1) the presentation of antecedent detail that serves to enhance the portrayal of the thing or person being praised, and (2) the focus on the worthy features of character, physical appearance, and outward circumstances such as wealth and power used honorably by the individual (3.7.14). In the latter case, appearance, character, and actions provide the outward manifestation of one's inner virtue and goodness. Aside from the presentation of antecedent detail and the personal comportment of the individual, there is also an emphasis on personal deeds. Actions are what finally convince the reader/hearer of the worthiness of the individual being praised. As Quintilian states, "[W]hat most pleases an audience is the celebration of deeds which our hero was the first or only man or at any rate one of the

---

32. See Shuler, *Genre for the Gospels*, 50.
33. Ibid., 50–51; D. L. Clark, *Rhetoric in Greco-Roman Education* (New York: Columbia University Press, 1957), 198–99; and Burgess, "Epideictic Literature," 125–26.

very few to perform: and to these we must add any other achievements which surpassed hope or expectation, emphasizing what was done for the sake of others rather than what he performed on his own behalf" (*Inst.* 3.7.16).

Theon develops some of these main themes in his *Progymnasmata*. In particular, he highlights the specific categories of praise related to character, body, and external qualities (cf. *Rhet. Her.* 3.10). With respect to virtue and character, Theon underscores the key values of the Greco-Roman world: prudence, self-control, courage, justice, piety, freedom, and magnanimity (9.21–24). He identifies external qualities as follows: "1)... good breeding, and that in two senses: the good breeding of city, race, and good government, and the good breeding of parents and other relatives; then, 2) education, 3) friendship, 4) reputation, 5) public office, 6) wealth, 7) the blessing of children, 8) and easy death" (9.15–19). The list includes precisely those qualities that would be expected of the good citizen. Moreover, with respect to the body, one should praise "health, strength, beauty, quick sensibility" (9.20). Noble actions, the quintessential manifestation of good character, are those "applauded after death" (9.25) and done for the sake of others, with a view to what is noble as opposed to acting for one's own advantage or pleasure (9.28–30). For Theon, the complete narrative of the encomium would include a description of noble actions combined with the delineation of the good character and external qualities that led to such action. The logic behind the encomium thus rests on amplifying the various facets of good character and action. It is not enough to say that the person praised is healthy, wealthy, and wise, but one must demonstrate the way in which these circumstances and characteristics contribute to the praise of the individual. For instance, the writer of the *Rhetorica ad Herennium* observes that if one is praising a person on the basis of descent, it should be demonstrated that the person in view is equal or superior to his illustrious ancestors (3.13). If the person is of lowly origin, then one must demonstrate how the individual relied upon his own merit to achieve a better station in life. In terms of physical features, one would observe that "if by nature he has impressiveness and beauty, these have served him to his credit, and not, as in the case of others, to his detriment and shame; if he has exceptional strength and agility, we shall point out that these were acquired by worthy and diligent exercise; if he has continual good health, that was acquired by care and by control over his passions" (*Rhet. Her.* 3.14).

Epideictic composition, then, represents a species of literature that praises or blames particular individuals in terms of culturally accepted values, inverting the positive quality and logic when focusing on censure (cf. *Rhet. Her.* 3.10). More importantly, it follows a specific model of elaboration and amplification that intersects both antecedent and attendant contextual data with the character of the individual, thereby producing something akin to the complete plot outlined in the previous chapter (e.g., personal character and actions are interconnected with good birth, breeding, and education).[34] Given this emphasis on praise, we should expect that the major issue in terms of stasis theory would be quality, as Quintilian affirms (*Inst.* 3.7.28). In essence, this means that the argumentative strategies of demonstrative discourse will focus on the following questions: Is a particular action just? Is it good? Is it honorable? Is it noble? (*Inst.* 3.6.32, 80; cf. Hermogenes, *On Issues* 37). Therefore, compositions in this mode will not only amplify particular actions and characters but will also attempt to persuade readers that specific actions are right and honorable.

Epideictic discourse is thus not focused on deeds and characters for their own sake, but on the way in which deeds and characters are exemplary. This utilitarian emphasis is accomplished through the amplification of the themes appropriate to the particular subject. In his treatise on epideictic types of speeches, Menander Rhetor notes with respect to "the talk" *(lalia)* that, in praising a provincial governor, one should use examples and parallels to illustrate various points of the talk "so as not to appear to be dealing in bare facts, in which there is no charm" (2.4).[35] As in historiographical theory, one finds the same stress on elaborating and amplifying the subject so as not to rest on the *fundamenta* alone but to bring the material to life. The natural affinity between epideictic and biography,[36] as well as with historical composition more generally, is therefore not surprising.[37] Furthermore, given the value-laden nature of this mode of discourse, the moral aspects of this branch of oratorical composition are noteworthy. The assumption is that the audience will share the values underpinning the composition, and, as a result, the entire moral system is reaffirmed. As Quintilian states, "[M]uch depends on the character of the audience and the generally received opinion, if they are to believe that the virtues of which they approve are preeminently characteristic of the person praised and the vices which they hate of the person denounced" (*Inst.* 3.7.23). On the one hand, epideictic rhetoric reinforces and maintains the shared value system of the audience. On the other hand, such compositions may also challenge the social and cultural sphere, subtly yet perceptibly shaping the perspective of the audience rather than merely legitimating cultural patterns.[38] Finally, as noted earlier, Kennedy argues that this mode of cultural discourse moves one into the

---

34. See J. H. Neyrey, "Josephus' *Vita* and the Encomium: A Native Model of Personality," *JSJ* 25 (1994): 178–88; and idem, *Honor and Shame*, 78–83, where he details the patterns of elaboration and amplification more fully. See also Burgess, "Epideictic Literature," 120–26.

35. Translation from D. A. Russell and N. G. Wilson, eds., *Menander Rhetor* (Oxford: Oxford University Press, 1981).

36. Shuler, *Genre for the Gospels*, 56; and Burgess, "Epideictic Literature," 117–18. See further T. Hägg and P. Rousseau, "Introduction: Biography and Panegyric," in *Greek Biography and Panegyric in Late Antiquity* (ed. T. Hägg and P. Rousseau; The Transformation of the Classical Heritage 31; Berkeley: University of California Press, 2000), 1–28.

37. Neyrey, "Josephus' *Vita*," 203.

38. See the fine discussion by T. Poulakos, "Towards a Cultural Understanding of Classical Epideictic Oratory," *PreText* 9 (1988): 153–61.

realm of establishing group cohesion,[39] which is a critical element in the use of epideictic rhetoric for social formation and control.

Hellenistic Jewish Literature: Presenting the Past, Praising the People

Given the understanding of epideictic composition delineated in the previous discussion, one can appreciate how such emphases could find their way into historiographical composition. Ancient historians readily adapted narration for the purpose of praise and blame. As a result, *historia* shifted from the more deliberative stance of Thucydides to the more epideictic focus of Livy, Dionysius, and Tacitus. While writers such as Lucian praise the "classical" model of Thucydides — one that focuses on the deliberative strategies of the *polis* — and distance outright panegyric (with its known penchant for excessive elaboration) from history proper, it is evident that the vast majority of historical literature from the Roman period has a sharp epideictic accent. Part of this shift in focus may be explained on the basis of the political environment that existed particularly from the early principate onward,[40] but the literary legacy of the Hellenistic age also helped nurture literature with both explicit and implicit epideictic features. Not only were individuals frequently praised as *exempla*, but particular groups of people were lauded as well. For instance, D. L. Balch argues that Dionysius composed an explicit encomium for Rome at the outset of his history (*Ant. rom.* 1.9–2.29), using the pattern for the elaboration of praising a city.[41] While particular units of historical narrative can be analyzed in terms of epideictic amplification, it is also apparent that works such as Josephus's *Antiquities* represent large-scale epideictic efforts praising a particular subject, in this case the Jewish people as an *ethnos*. Given the importance of ethnic identity and cohesion in the ancient world, it is not surprising that epideictic composition would wed itself

---

39. Kennedy, "Genres of Rhetoric," 45. See further M. Moreland, "The Jerusalem Community in Acts: Mythmaking and the Socio-Rhetorical Functions of a Lukan Setting," in *Contextualizing Acts: Lukan Narrative and Greco-Roman Discourse* (ed. T. Penner and C. Vander Stichele; SBLSymS 20; Atlanta: Society of Biblical Literature, 2003), 285–310.

40. The transfer from the republic to the empire had a tremendous impact on the formation and development of Roman literature. T. H. Habinek notes that this brought with it two significant developments: "the transformation of Rome from a city-state to a traditional aristocratic empire and the crisis of identity provoked in Rome's rulers by that very transformation" (*The Politics of Latin Literature: Writing, Identity, and Empire in Ancient Rome* [Princeton: Princeton University Press, 1998], 35; see also 103–21). See further G. Williams, *Change and Decline: Roman Literature in the Early Empire* (Berkeley: University of California Press, 1978), 154–71, 297–303; E. Fantham, *Roman Literary Culture: From Cicero to Apuleius* (Baltimore: Johns Hopkins University Press, 1996), 67–84, 126–52; and esp. J. P. Sullivan, *Literature and Politics in the Age of Nero* (Ithaca: Cornell University Press, 1985), 19–73.

41. D. L. Balch, "Two Apologetic Encomia: Dionysius on Rome and Josephus on the Jews," *JSJ* 13 (1982): 107–14. Livy's history can also be read as an encomium for Rome.

to the ethnological roots of historiography, creating a form of ethnographic historiography praising (or possibly denouncing) specific people and groups.

Sterling's definition of Hellenistic apologetic literature is relevant in light of the comments made here. He defines the genre as "the story of a subgroup of people in an extended prose narrative written by a member of the group who follows the group's own traditions but hellenizes them in an effort to establish the identity of the group within the setting of the larger world."[42] If one takes this definition as an appropriate model for understanding Jewish apologetic historiography, then one is working from an explicit epideictic model. Writers in this tradition take their own native tradition, rewrite it so as to incorporate the cultural and social values of the larger world, and in turn seek to mediate the native group's indigenous identity to the dominant culture. As I observed at the outset of this chapter, one could interpret this move as one of defense — *apologia* in its classic sense. Yet, while not denying defensive posturing in and of itself, it may be better and more helpful to view apologetic literature in its macro framework as epideictic compositions that seek to praise a particular people or group. This feature is achieved by demonstrating coherence with the values of the dominant culture and legitimating peculiar tendencies of the group (the outward focus), as well as realigning the values and commitments of the native group itself, thereby creating group cohesion and reinforcing and maintaining identity within the larger environment (the inward focus). As C. R. Holladay aptly observes, it is undoubtedly "an exercise in ethnic promotion as well as ethnic self-preservation."[43]

The *Letter of Aristeas* represents an important example of a literary composition in this mode of discourse. Purportedly a letter to a certain Philocrates, the text details the attempt by Ptolemy II of Egypt (285–247 B.C.E.) to have his librarian Demetrius collect all the known books in the world. Demetrius decides that the "lawbooks of the Jews" are worthy of inclusion, but they need to be translated into Greek first. The story that follows reports the various stages in the production of the "Septuagint." The writer — adopting a Gentile persona — makes clear at the outset that this narrative relates his own eyewitness testimony of the visit to Eleazar, the high priest of Jerusalem. Writing as an ostensible outsider, the author sets out various elements of the Jewish faith that are commendable from a Gentile perspective, and, while the translation of the Jewish Bible into Greek is the main subject of the narrative, the underlying premise throughout is that Jewish culture and religion represent a highly valued, respected, and venerable tradition that can take its rightful place alongside the universal ethic of the Greeks. While it has been argued that the focus on the law is intended at

---

42. Sterling, *Historiography and Self-definition*, 17.
43. C. R. Holladay, "Jewish Responses to Hellenistic Culture in Early Ptolemaic Egypt," in *Ethnicity in Hellenistic Egypt* (ed. P. Bilde et al.; SHC 3; Aarhus: Aarhus University Press, 1992), 144; cf. M. Hadas, *Aristeas to Philocrates (Letter of Aristeas)* (New York: KTAV, 1973), 60.

the very least for Diaspora Jews who were having trouble appreciating the significance of the finer points of Judaism (and practicing them),[44] there is nothing overtly polemical in this text. Rather, the main emphasis is on the praise of the Jewish temple and law.

The narrative begins with the release of Jewish captives under the premise that the Jews worship the same deity as the Greeks:

> [T]he same God who has given them their law guides your kingdom also, as I have learned in my researches. God, the overseer and creator of all things, whom they worship, is He whom all men worship, and we too. Your Majesty, though we address Him differently, as Zeus and Dis; by these names men of old not unsuitably signified that He through whom all creatures receive life and come into being is the guide and lord of all. (15–16; cf. Paul in Athens; Acts 17)[45]

At the very beginning of the story, then, the tone for what follows is set: The God of the Jews is to be identified with the Greek deity, which demonstrates that both Jews and Greeks have common ground in a quasi-monotheistic system of belief. While the particular argument is that the Jews in captivity should be released because "they are just like us," in reality we observe here a description of Judaism in a praiseworthy manner, exhibiting the best qualities of the Hellenistic philosophical world. The epideictic accent of this material is implicit, reflected in the unfolding of the narrative rather than in outright statements of praise. For instance, when the entourage returns from Jerusalem with the seventy-two translators, the king, in dramatic fashion, demonstrates the greatness of the Jewish tradition (if not its superiority) as he bows before the Torah scrolls:

> When they had uncovered the rolls and had unrolled the parchments the king paused for a considerable space, and after bowing deeply some seven times said, "I thank you, good sirs, and him that sent you even more, but most of all I thank God whose holy words these are." And when all with one accord...exclaimed in a single voice, "Excellent, Your Majesty!" he was moved to tears out of the fullness of his joy.... "It was right, my God-fearing friends, first to pay homage to those treasures for whose sake I summoned you, and thereafter to extend the right hand to you.... This day upon which you have come I regard as a great day, and each year through all the length of my life it shall be held in high esteem." (177–80)

In a type-scene reminiscent of ones found in Esther, Daniel 1–6, and 3 Maccabees (including traces of the ancient Near Eastern images of subjugated dignitaries paying homage to the vanquishing power), the foreign

---

44. Hadas, *Aristeas to Philocrates*, 65–66. See also G. W. E. Nickelsburg, "Stories of Biblical and Early Post-Biblical Times," in *Jewish Writings of the Second Temple Period* (ed. M. E. Stone; CRINT 2.2; Philadelphia: Fortress, 1984), 78–79.

45. This translation of *Aristeas* and those that follow are taken from Hadas, *Aristeas to Philocrates*.

king — the one subjecting the Jews to captivity — acknowledges the sanctity of the Jewish law, the highest form of praise. While it is the king who praises the Jewish law scrolls in *Aristeas,* it is clear that the narrator intends to honor and adulate the Jewish tradition as a whole.

In a similar vein, the dinner scene, structured on the time-honored Platonic symposium/banquet,[46] represents the Jewish sages/translators in dialogue with the king over a period of seven days. The Jewish responses evidence a careful blending of biblical tradition and Greek philosophy, to the increasing pleasure and delight of Ptolemy. The narrator addresses his readers at the end of the sequence in the following way:

> If I have been tedious in this account... forgive me. I admired beyond measure the way in which the men on the spur of the moment framed responses which required long meditation; since their interrogator had carefully pondered each question while the respondents replied to the queries one after the other, they seemed admirable to me, and also to the others present, but especially to the philosophers. I suppose that everyone likely to get hold of this account will find it incredible. (295-96)

Here again one finds explicit praise of Judaism by a purported outsider intermingled with an account that glorifies the Jewish ability to respond to the most significant questions of Greek philosophy. One would also include within this larger rubric the statements related to the law given by the high priest Eleazar to the visitors in Jerusalem. In this section he begins by reiterating the Jewish teaching on monotheism (132), followed by a denunciation of polytheism (134-38). Eleazar continues with a speech in praise of the Jewish law:

> When therefore our lawgiver, equipped by God for insight into all things, had surveyed each particular, he fenced us about with impregnable palisades and with walls of iron, to the end that we should mingle in no way with any of the other nations, remaining pure in body and in spirit, emancipated from vain opinions, revering the one and mighty God above the whole creation. (139)

Such statements can be read as quasi-apologetic or polemical in nature, addressing either Greco-Roman negative assessments of Jewish law or inner-Jewish failure to apply, from the writer's perspective, the full extent of Jewish practice.[47] Whatever broader awareness may be indicated vis-à-vis charges by outsiders (these may well be reflected in the text taken at face value),[48] the passage ultimately reaffirms the divine purpose and human utility of the

---

46. See O. Murray, "Aristeas and Ptolemaic Kingship," *JTS* 8 (1967): 346-47.
47. In view may be Jews who, because of their excessive allegorization, have abandoned (or found little use for) the literal practice of the tradition (i.e., the type of Alexandrian Jews whom Philo has in mind in *Migr. Abr.* 89-93 and who are sometimes associated with these statements in *Aristeas*).
48. See further Berthelot, *Philanthrôpia judaica,* 192-203.

Jewish law, in effect offering an honorable description of Jewish law and life that would find support from both Jewish and Greek traditions. Similarly, when Eleazar explains that even the laws detailing the minutiae of practice have a purpose, the same premise is reinforced: "Do not accept the exploded idea that it was out of regard for 'mice' and the 'weasel' and other such creatures that Moses ordained these laws with such scrupulous care; not so, these laws have all been solemnly drawn up for the sake of justice, to promote holy contemplation and the perfecting of character" (144). While the writer does proffer a negative — "Do not accept the exploded idea..." — that is then refuted, the overall theme of the larger unit is that the law has as its purpose the inculcation of the best of Greek moral expectation in the adherent of the Jewish law.[49] Whatever the negative assertion at the beginning may indicate about Jewish awareness of and response to Greek criticism of their legal practices, in *Aristeas* the so-called judicial element generates the epideictic discursive patterns that burst to the forefront throughout the text. Rather than fixating solely, merely, or even at all on refutation, the traditions of the Jews are shown not to be peripheral to the concerns of the Greco-Roman world, but are linked with the same philosophical, religious, and cultural values.[50] At one level, this focus on similarity would obviously resonate with a Greek reader. On the other, a Jewish reader is left with the impression that the Jewish law is equal or superior to Greek philosophical and religious traditions. Indeed, the comparison *(synkrisis)* between Jewish belief in one God and the Greek/Egyptian affirmation of many deities earlier in this text (132, 134, 138) leaves one with the distinct impression that the writer is asserting the superiority of the Jewish tradition, following the pattern of epideictic elaboration on the theme of law.

Added to this treatment of Jewish legal, moral, and philosophical themes, the writer also includes two virtual paeans: one on the Jewish temple, the other on the gift sent by Ptolemy II to Eleazar in Jerusalem. The narrator first describes the magnificent gifts, praising the craftsmanship and symbolism of their construction:

> [The works of art] were wrought with extraordinary artistry, for the king made generous grants and supervised the craftsmen at every step [51].... [A]s for diversity in artistic ingenuity, [the king] ordered that it be applied in lavish measure.... Where there was no prescription in Scripture he ordered the construction to follow principles of beauty [56].... [A]ll the parts [of the table of shew-bread] were carefully made and fitted, the ingenious art corresponding to truth to such a superlative degree that if a breath of wind blew the leaves stirred

---

49. Or, the view is that the Torah promotes harmony between Jewish and Greek principles and society (so Gruen, *Diaspora*, 219). On this ethical emphasis in the Torah in *Aristeas*, see G. Schimanowski, "Der *Aristeasbrief* zwischen Abgrenzung und Selbstdarstellung," in *Persuasion and Dissuasion* (ed. van der Horst), esp. 55–59.

50. See N. Walter, "Jüdisch-hellenistische Literatur vor Philon von Alexandrien (unter Ausschluss der Historiker)," *ANRW* 2.20.1 (1987): 83–85.

in their place; so closely was every detail modeled on reality [70]... inimitable in its art and superlative in its beauty [72].... When they were finished and the vessels were placed one after the other... the character of the spectacle was altogether indescribable, and those who came to view it could not tear themselves from it, so dazzling and entrancing was the sight [77].

The writer points out that such a description of the works of art is essential for the reader (83). Presumably, along with the goodwill demonstrated in the release of the Jewish captives in Egypt, we are to see here a further expression—in extreme form—of the magnanimity of the Hellenistic king toward the people of Jerusalem. While there is some praise of the architect of the gift (56), the overall point is to extol the elaborate nature of the gifts themselves, showing the great lengths a great ruler goes to in order to display friendship toward the Jews (and to attain a translation of their laws). From the writer's perspective, these ornate gifts raise the status of the Jewish people in the text; honor of the sort reserved for kings is bestowed upon the Jerusalemite priesthood and temple. Thus, the function of the description is not so much to praise the gifts as to reflect the superior position of those who are in a place to receive such gifts as these. The lavishing of the king's attention on the donations functions to highlight the character of the Jews, their temple, the priesthood, and Jerusalem.

Following upon the description of the gifts, the narrator focuses on the temple:

> Upon [Jerusalem's] crest stood the Temple in its splendor... built with a lavishness and sumptuousness beyond all precedent [84].... The style of the curtain corresponded in every respect to the door [86].... The altar was built in keeping with the size for the place.... The ascent was gradual, from a proper regard for decency, and the ministering priests were swathed in "coats of fine linen" [87].... The water supply is inexhaustible... and there are furthermore marvelous underground reservoirs passing description [89].... In its exhibition of strength and in its orderly and silent performance the ministration of the priests could in no way be surpassed [92].... The total effect of the whole arouses awe and emotional excitement, so that one would think he had passed to some other sphere outside the world. I venture to affirm positively that any man who witnesses the spectacle I have recounted will experience amazement and astonishment indescribable, and his mind will be deeply moved at the sanctity attaching to every detail [99].

The writer offers a suitable amplification of the epideictic theme of praise for a temple. In detailing the various subjects that one might use for such epideictic elaboration, Quintilian mentions temples in particular: "Praise too may be awarded to public works, in connexion with which their magnificence, utility, beauty and the architect or artist must be given due consideration. Temples for instance will be praised for their magnificence, walls for their utility, and both for their beauty or the skill of the architect" (*Inst.* 3.7.27). The writer of *Aristeas* observes most of these elements: the striking and beauteous nature of the temple's structure, the magnificence of the walls, the serviceability and appropriateness ("proper regard") of the form and function of various features of the temple (from the water supply to the system of reservoirs to the curtains and doors), and the utility and grandeur of the priests. While the architect/artist is praised for designing the works of art (56), there is no explicit praise for the architect of the temple. The general pattern, however, is striking. The ornate character of the king's gifts is fully paralleled in the resplendency of the Jerusalem sanctuary, truly a temple worthy of the gifts bestowed upon it by the king. Rather than being out of place in this letter describing the translation of the Jewish law into Greek, the praise of the temple conforms well to the writer's overall purpose: Alongside the Jewish law, the temple represents one of the fundamental themes for epideictic amplification in the Jewish tradition. In a similar way to the gifts, the temple also represents the people/community/city with which it is identified. Thus, the praiseworthy character of the temple reflects and embodies, again, the *ethos* of the Jewish tradition.

Traditionally the *Letter of Aristeas* has either been viewed as apologetic in the traditional sense (developing a congenial understanding of Judaism for the Greco-Roman world) or as a piece of polemic (promoting a newer and better translation of the Hebrew Bible, a more culturally appropriate perception of Judaism, or some variation of these positions). There are definitely overtones of both of these elements in this text, yet the overarching feature seems to be an extended narrative praising Judaism, which develops and elaborates the pivotal themes of temple and law against the foil of the commissioning of the Greek translation of the Jewish law. The story of the translation, which frames the main body of the text and which provides the overriding theme of the significance of the Jewish law for the Greco-Roman world, is ultimately not the real focus of the narrative. Rather, the writer uses this framework in order to delve into the key themes of Jewish pride and honor in the ancient world. Through a purported eyewitness account, these themes are developed and amplified not so much as an attempt to convince others of their truth, but as a source of cultural and religious affirmation. By reading this encomiastic piece on Jewish tradition and values, the Jewish reader in the Diaspora learns what is of cultural and religious importance and has essential indicators of Jewish identity solidified.

The Jewish literature of the Hellenistic period abounds with similar examples of such epideictic treatments of Jewish history and tradition. In Esther and Daniel 1–6 (including the LXX narrative additions) one finds a corresponding framework: stories that demonstrate the superiority of the Jewish tradition and religious outlook by comparing the life of the pious Jew with those of non-Jews. The image is always the same: The dedicated and righteous Jew wins out over competitors, and Jewish law and practice are praised by outsiders for their remarkable and superior nature. Such narratives evidence a particular pattern of confrontation, wherein the praiseworthy qualities of Judaism in a foreign environment are demonstrated through implicit comparison.

Jewish epic of the period reveals similar tendencies. Among the preserved fragments of Philo, the Epic Poet, there exists this paean for Abraham and his progeny:

> A thousand times have I heard in the ancient laws how once (when you achieved something) marvelous with the bonds knot, O far-famed Abraham, resplendently did your God-beloved prayers abound in wondrous counsels. For when you left the beauteous garden of dread plants, the praiseworthy thunderer quenched the pyre and made his promise immortal. From that time forth the offspring of that awesome born one have won far-hymned praise. (frg. 1; cf. frg. 3, for a similar treatment of Joseph)[51]

While this text is only a fragment of a presumably much larger work, it appears that Philo intended to retell the biblical story heaping praise on the exemplary characters of the past. In philosophy one finds similar themes brought to the fore. Thus, Aristobulus tries to connect various elements of Jewish tradition with the larger values and philosophical commitments of the Greeks. In the process, there is explicit and implicit praise for the Jewish tradition in contradistinction to the Greek. For instance, Aristobulus states that "our lawgiver Moses proclaims arrangements of nature and preparation for great events by expressing that which he wishes to say in many ways, by using words that refer to other matters (I mean matters relating to outward appearances). Therefore, those who are able to think well marvel at his wisdom and at the divine spirit in accordance with which he has been proclaimed as a prophet also" (frg. 2). In a classic statement of Hellenistic Jewish apologetic, Aristobulus argues for the dependence of the Greeks on the Jewish law: "[I]t is evident that Plato imitated our legislation and that he had investigated thoroughly each of the elements in it.... Pythagoras [also] ... transferred many of our doctrines and integrated them into his own system" (frg. 3; cf. frg. 4). Such statements function to depict the Jewish law and tradition in an honorable light. They represent explicit affirmation of the superiority (because of its antiquity) of Jewish thought and practice, as well as the cultural correspondence of the Jewish faith with the Greek heritage.

In a similar manner Eupolemus praises Moses: "[He] was the first wise man.... [H]e first taught the alphabet to the Jews, and the Phoenicians received it from the Jews, and the Greeks received it from the Phoenicians, and ... Moses first wrote laws for the Jews" (frg. 1; cf. Pseudo-Eupolemus 8–9; Artapanus frg. 3.3–6). Also in Eupolemus's fragmentary remains one

---

51. This translation and those of the fragments of the Jewish Hellenistic authors that follow are taken from J. H. Charlesworth, ed., *The Old Testament Pseudepigrapha* (2 vols.; Garden City, N.Y.: Doubleday, 1983, 1985).

finds the fictitious correspondence between Solomon and both Vaphres of Egypt and Souron of Tyre, demonstrating the grandeur of the Davidic-Solomonic empire, an image of the past used to characterize the Jewish people in the present (cf. Josephus, *Ant.* 8.50–56; *C. Ap.* 1.110–27). As Souron states in his letter to Solomon: "Praise be the God, who created heaven and earth and who chose a noble person, the son of a noble man" (frg 2.34.1). In Eupolemus reference is also made to Solomon's lavish temple, which, while lacking the explicit evocative features found in *Aristeas,* nevertheless clearly has as its goal the demonstration of the beauty and majesty of the Jerusalem temple. Finally, in the fragments of Artapanus one finds numerous statements reflecting the superiority of Jewish heroes: the superior wisdom, skill, and knowledge of Joseph (frg. 2.1–3), as well as the innovations of Moses, including the organization of Egyptian religion (frg. 3.4–6). Even his enemies, the Ethiopians, "loved Moses so much that they learned the circumcision of genital organs from him, and not only they, but also all the priests" (frg. 3.10).

Since these various texts are all fragmentary in nature, it is difficult to reconstruct fully the orientation of the underlying narrative argument. Yet in almost all cases the remains do permit a glimpse into the spirit of the Jewish heritage being promoted: It is a tradition that elevates itself and, in nearly every aspect, matches if not exceeds the cultural and philosophical values of the Greek world. Moreover, while some of the praiseworthy elements are attested in the biblical tradition, the developments and elaborations attest to a vibrant Jewish literary-rhetorical self-characterization in antiquity, which fits well within the broader literary and cultural currents of the Hellenistic and Roman periods. Furthermore, the larger narrative contexts, as much as can be determined from the limited material, reinforce and bolster in narrative form the explicit praises rendered by the writers, sometimes with a corresponding and more subtle denigration of non-Jews in the process.

These same themes also surface in other Hellenistic Jewish texts. The Jewish *Sibylline Oracles* contain numerous encomia on the Jews, with some occasional denunciations as well (based on the biblical Deuteronomic pattern). For instance, the third oracle includes the following unit of praise of the Jewish people:

> There is a city...in the land of Ur of the Chaldeans, whence comes a race of most righteous men. They are always concerned with good counsel and noble works for they do not worry about the cyclic course of the sun or the moon or monstrous things under the earth.... [T]hey care for righteousness and virtue and not love of money.... They have just measurements in fields and cities and they do not carry out robberies at night against each other...nor does a very rich man grieve a lesser man nor oppress widows in any respect, but rather helps them. (3.18–45)[52]

---

52. Translation from Charlesworth, ed., *Old Testament Pseudepigrapha.*

Elsewhere the writer composes a similar piece on the future establishment of "a sacred race of pious men who attend to the counsels and intention of the Most High, who fully honor the temple of the great God...sharing in the righteousness of the law of the Most High...for to them alone did God give wise counsel and faith and excellent understanding" (573–85). Here again, one finds the theme of the superiority of the Jewish people over non-Jews, connected especially with the temple and law.

Several treatises of Philo of Alexandria are illustrative of this point, as they offer some of the most thoroughgoing and explicit examples of epideictic composition among Jews in the Hellenistic period. His book *On Abraham*, for instance, is a work in praise for the first patriarch of the Jewish people. In his recalling of the major incidents in Abraham's life, Philo repeatedly notes his surpassing virtue: "[F]illed with zeal for piety, the highest and greatest of virtues, [Abraham] was eager to follow God and to be obedient to His commands; understanding by commands not only those conveyed in speech and writing but also those made manifest by nature with clearer signs, and apprehended by the senses which is the most truthful of all" (*Abr.* 60). Elsewhere Philo undertakes a lengthy treatment of Abraham's willingness to sacrifice Isaac, comparing it to non-Jewish rites of child sacrifice (178–99). In this unit Philo's aim is to demonstrate the superiority of Abraham's action because of his lack of compulsion and due to the fact that it was not a Jewish custom.[53] That Philo intends to extol Abraham for his deed (183) is made evident at the outset and, following the use of *synkrisis* in epideictic composition (cf. Aristotle, *Rhet.* 1.9.38), he sets forth Abraham's sacrifice as the most praiseworthy feature in the portrayal. His conclusion is that Abraham's action "really deserves our praise and love" (*Abr.* 191) and that all good people will be "overwhelmed with admiration for his extraordinary piety" (199). In fact, Philo goes on to designate the literal sense of the story of Lot and Abraham dividing up the land as a narrative "encomium" for Abraham (217), while the allegorical reading of the text underscores the best of Greek virtues.[54] Further on in the text, in an explicit delineation of Abraham's character, Philo states that "the man of worth was not merely peaceable and a lover of justice but courageous and warlike, not for the sake of warring, for he was not quarrelsome or cantankerous, but to secure

---

53. Philo's argument is that if child sacrifice is part of one's cultural practice, then it is "equal to nature" and requires little real reflection by the one performing the act (*Abr.* 185; see S. Sandmel, *Philo's Place in Judaism: A Study of Conceptions of Abraham in Jewish Literature* [Cincinnati: Hebrew Union College, 1956], 128–30). Due to Philo's comment that certain critics have undermined the significance of Abraham's intended sacrifice of Isaac because of the prominence of these rites in other cultures (*Migr. Abr.* 179), Sandmel, recognizing the usual designation of this unit as apologetic as traditionally conceived, reads it instead as polemical: Philo attacks the views of assimilationist Alexandrian Jews (128). Philo's comment, however, is better read as setting up the comparison he will make between Abraham's action and similar ones in other cultures. His major concern is to demonstrate the superiority of Abraham, not the refutation of charges (real or fictionalized).

54. Sandmel, *Philo's Place in Judaism*, 131–32.

peace for the future" (225).⁵⁵ Philo thus uses the Jewish patriarch's actions as a basis for elaborating the virtues he exhibited in life.

Probably the most interesting feature of Philo's treatise on Abraham, however, is the reversal of several primary elements of the epideictic pattern. In Quintilian, the pattern is laid out so that one proceeds chronologically from birth, to childhood, to education, and finally to deeds and accomplishments in adult life. One is also to include physical endowments and external circumstances such as the possession and then employment of wealth and power (*Inst.* 3.7.10–11, 15).⁵⁶ When Philo comes to the discussion of Abraham's education and external circumstances, however, he questions the pattern itself, setting out why he finds such forms of elaboration problematic. Philo acknowledges that Moses (as the writer of the Pentateuch) "praised" Abraham for his trust in God (*Abr.* 262). According to Philo, this is the greatest achievement of any individual, since wealth, power, and good birth cannot be counted on to attest to good character, as even impious individuals have these qualities (263–65). Further, physical endowment cannot set an individual apart, as the baser animals have the upper hand in this category (266). In this way, Philo deliberately turns the various themes of individual encomia on their head, arguing that Abraham as a man who "trusted in God" (indeed, the "friend of God") surpasses the ordinary, recognized categories of individual praise for humans (268).⁵⁷ This statement reflects an extraordinary Jewish counterargument, demonstrating not only that Abraham is superior to other non-Jewish cultural heroes, but that in fact the very categories of comparison traditionally used in encomia are not applicable to the foremost Jewish patriarch. Embedded herein is an ideological and cultural stance of Judaism in Alexandria and elsewhere, which on the one hand reveals an acceptance of cultural discursive modes of self-praise, but on the other also manifests a form of resistance, signaling the uniqueness of Judaism over and against the dominant cultural discourse. In any case, while the understanding of this Philonic argument has often been framed within the context of Abraham as the prototypical proselyte in Philo,⁵⁸ it is more probable that Philo is offering a commendable account of Jewish origins. Moreover, his interest in allegorical interpretation of various incidents in Abraham's life should also be viewed in light of epideictic amplification: Not only does a literal reading support a commendable account of

---

55. Ibid., 132–35.
56. See Neyrey, *Honor and Shame*, 79.
57. See Philo's more explicit statement in this respect in *On the Virtues*, 187–89: "Those who hymn nobility of birth as the greatest of good gifts and the source too of other great gifts deserve no moderate censure" (187).
58. Elsewhere Philo explicitly labels Abraham as such: "He is the standard of nobility for all proselytes, who, abandoning the ignobility of strange laws and monstrous customs...have come to settle in a better land" (*Virt.* 219). See M. Philonenko, *Joseph et Aséneth: Introduction, Texte Critique, Traduction et Notes* (SPB 13; Leiden: Brill, 1968), 55.

the patriarch's life, but allegorical interpretation also attests that the underlying meaning reflects well on Judaism, containing as it does the absolute realization of Greek values and virtues in these Jewish stories. There is thus in Philo evidence of a fairly well-entrenched pattern of epideictic elaboration of common themes related to either major biblical heroes or to long-standing Jewish institutions.[59]

One should also situate the work of Josephus in a similar context, as it represents in extended prose form the most substantive epideictic composition on Judaism in antiquity. In the *Antiquities,* Josephus not only retells the story of Israel up until his own time, but he also rewrites that story so as to reflect the recognized values of the Hellenistic world, including extensive efforts to reconfigure biblical characters in order to correspond to the main categories delineated in Greek praise of individual virtue.[60] Moreover, in Josephus's work there is the recognition that Judaism is split into camps, between good, pious, law-abiding Jews and those who oppose the traditions of Moses. This stance reflects the Deuteronomic position embedded in the biblical text, but it is also heightened by Josephus.[61] This framework also becomes one of the major themes of his *Jewish War.* In both the *Antiquities* and the *Jewish War,* however, there exists an express framework of praise for the Jews and their tradition. Josephus distances the malignant factions from "true tradition" and overtly praises the history and beliefs of the latter, carrying out the epideictic pattern most fully: praise of the Jews and denunciation of others. Even his *Contra Apionem* carries a distinctive epideictic edge, despite the obvious judicial features of Josephus's response to

---

59. One might also add here Philo's treatise *On Joseph,* where he undertakes a similar assessment of the life of this patriarch. In this treatise he maintains that the biblical text "has ... set before us three characteristics of the statesman, his shepherd-craft, his household-management, his self-control" (*Ios.* 54). Philo's narrative then bolsters the overarching theme of Joseph as the ideal statesman. In his two books that make up *On the Life of Moses,* Philo also sets out to demonstrate the superiority of the Jewish lawgiver: "I hope to bring the story of this greatest and most perfect of men to the knowledge of such as deserve not to remain in ignorance of it" (*Mos.* 1.1). Overall, Philo aims to demonstrate that Moses not only embodies the Platonic ideal — states prosper most fully when the kings are philosophers and the philosophers are kings — but also the Jewish superior rendition of the Greek formulation: the ruler as philosopher, *as well as* lawgiver, high priest, and prophet (2.2). The pattern of comparison evidenced in his account of Abraham is continued more vigorously here: "That Moses himself was the best of all law-givers in all countries, better in fact than any that have ever arisen among either the Greeks or the barbarians, and that his laws are most excellent and truly come from God ... is shewn most clearly" (2.12). Philo's *On the Virtues* is also interesting in this respect. This text amounts to both an encomium for the lawgiver as well as for the law itself. This emphasis readily connects with Quintilian's discussion of epideictic composition: "[L]aws [reflect glory] on those who made them" (*Inst.* 3.7.18). *On the Virtues,* then, represents a panegyric piece on the law, demonstrating how the key virtues of value to the Greeks are substantiated in the legal texts of Judaism.

60. See L. H. Feldman, *Studies in Josephus' Rewritten Bible* (JSJSup 58; Leiden: Brill, 1998), 546–51.

61. See P. Spilsbury, *The Image of the Jew in Flavius Josephus' Paraphrase of the Bible* (TSAJ 69; Tübingen: Mohr Siebeck, 1998), 145–46.

non-Jewish criticisms.[62] Not only does he refute the charges in the text, he also uses them as a foil to demonstrate (albeit more subtly) the superiority of Jewish culture and religion.

This brief survey of some important texts of Hellenistic Judaism demonstrates that the material functions at a variety of levels. Overall, there is a distinctive and pervasive epideictic pattern in composition, the aim of which is to adulate Jewish tradition and culture, demonstrating its superiority over the dominant Greco-Roman environment. This material represents apologetic in the sense that it not only offers a defense of Judaism, but it also provides arguments for the excellence and exceptional standing of the Jewish heritage. While there is occasional response to "critics," except in cases such as Josephus's *Contra Apionem* these do not find extensive formulation. Rather, one observes the main aim of epideictic composition surfacing throughout: elaborating and amplifying the themes relative to the demonstration of the meritorious character of the subject in question. I would argue that epideictic patterns predominate in much of this material, driving the specific elaboration of themes (even undergirding judicial and deliberative elements on occasion) and motivating the discursive practice of praise and blame. For Judaism of the Hellenistic and Roman periods this focus manifests itself not only in the adulation of biblical heroes but also of the law (with some significant attention paid to the temple as well). This emphasis does not suggest that Jews in antiquity did not defend their tradition against outside attack, but that the overarching framework for Diaspora Jewish literature is much more internally focused than the forensic category allows. The literature of Hellenistic Judaism points inward: praising Judaism and occasionally denouncing outsiders, which should be taken as both a reflection and a reentrenchment of Jewish self-perception and identity in the larger sociocultural and political contexts. One of the main vehicles for this emphasis in Jewish literature, as we have seen in the work of Philo and Josephus, is the rewriting of the biblical narrative (i.e., native tradition) so as to underscore the core elements of identity.

Rewriting the Past: The Exodus Tradition

The exodus narrative is perhaps the most pivotal story in the Jewish account of origins. For Hellenistic Jewish writers, it was an essential narrative not only for ethnic but also for political and constitutional identity as well, which accounts for its prominence in elaboration and reconfiguration in Jewish discursive practice. Thus, examination of the Hellenistic Jewish rewriting of their past is helpful to illustrate the broader historiographical ethos outlined earlier. Moreover, the Hellenistic Jewish pattern that seems to surface across a broad spectrum of retellings is quintessential for understanding Stephen's

---

62. van Henten and Abusch, "Jews as Tryphonians," 297.

speech in Acts 7, the argument of which not only hinges on the exodus narrative as developed in that context but also seems deeply indebted to the broader Hellenistic Jewish pattern that emerges in other texts.

The rewriting of traditions in the ancient world was a pervasive and multifaceted phenomenon. The preliminary exercises of Greco-Roman education readily reinforced this practice. For instance, in his *Progymnasmata* Theon details the various exercises with respect to the fable: "1) we recite the fable, 2) we inflect it, 3) we combine it with a narrative, and 4) we expand and condense it. And 5) it is also possible to add some saying to it, or after some saying has been put forth, to fashion a fable appropriate to it. Then, in addition to these exercises, 6) we refute and confirm the fable" (4.37–43). These same exercises also apply to narratives (5.235–37), with a particular emphasis on reversing the order of narrated events (5.238). These various exercises aim at developing argumentative strategies in the student, stressing skill in amplification and expansion and naturally leading to the practice of paraphrasing texts. The younger Pliny offers a reflection on the end result:

> [W]hen you have read a passage sufficiently to remember the subject-matter and line of thought, there is no harm in your trying to compete with it; then compare your efforts with the original and consider carefully where your version is better or worse.... You may also choose a passage you know well and try to improve on it.... You can also revise the speeches you have put aside, retaining much of the original, but leaving out still more and making other additions and alterations. (*Ep.* 7.9.3–5)[63]

The practice of the rhetorical paraphrase, as opposed to the stricter grammatical paraphrase, stresses the use of stylistic improvements in the text with some degree of poetic interpretation,[64] although the goal is generally to retain the sense and the structure of the original. Alongside these more limited paraphrases one also finds literary ones, which are more radical in their departure from the original text, generally with a view to interpreting and exegeting the original.[65] As Pliny notes, the aim of this literary enterprise is "to graft new limbs...on a finished trunk without disturbing the balance of the original" (*Ep.* 7.9.6). As an outgrowth of this educational and literary interest in rewriting existing texts and traditions, ancient writers also frequently imitate the writing style and specific stories of their predecessors. In history, Tacitus could borrow from Livy, and the latter himself from writers such as Homer, Herodotus, and Thucydides.[66] The Homeric poems,

---

63. On the view that this passage refers to paraphrasing as opposed to translating, see M. Roberts, *Biblical Epic and Rhetorical Paraphrase in Late Antiquity* (Liverpool: Cairns, 1985), 19–20.
64. Ibid., 47.
65. Ibid., 54–57.
66. T.[A. J.] Woodman, "Self-Imitation and the Substance of History: Tacitus, *Annals* 1.61–5 and *Histories* 2.70, 5.14–15," in *Creative Imitation and Latin Literature* (ed. D. West and T. Woodman; Cambridge: Cambridge University Press, 1979), 153. For a similar relationship

given their classic status in antiquity,[67] were also a mainstay for imitation among ancient writers.[68] Mediterranean antiquity thus reveals a pervasive environment of literary borrowing, imitating, and rewriting.[69]

The Second Temple period amply attests to this broader phenomenon, offering a diverse array of literary rewritings of Israelite and Jewish texts and traditions, including major works such as *Jubilees, Pseudo-Philo,* and Josephus's *Antiquities*. So-called rewritten biblical narratives formed a significant element of apologetic historiography, as the Hebrew biblical stories were retold, paraphrased, amplified, and elaborated upon with a view to emphasizing Jewish themes and concerns. Not only the method of apologetic historiography but also its themes frequently derive from these reconfigurations of the biblical narrative. Underlying this form of narration is the explicit argumentative goal of establishing the admirable and exemplary nature of Jewish practice, belief, and history. Naturally, those seeking to denigrate the tradition could use these same themes, but in a derogatory manner. For this reason, the motifs of the exodus story, as they are elaborated and amplified in Jewish retellings, are fundamental for understanding Luke's own subtle reconfiguring of that tradition. Helpful also in this connection is an analysis of several non-Jewish uses of the exodus themes and pattern, as these confirm the *topoi* prevalent in the Jewish tradition itself.

The exodus story — especially in connection with the exploits and character of Moses — received repeated attention by those Jews articulating the biblical tradition for the ancient Greek world. In Alexandria, both Philo and the writer of the Wisdom of Solomon give detailed attention to the nature of the event and its importance for Jewish religious life. The themes that surface in Philo's work surrounding the figure of Moses are particularly noteworthy in terms of the development of the *topoi* that become associated with the exodus story in the Hellenistic and later Roman period. One of the common themes found in Philo's account relates to the superior intellect, training, and wisdom of Moses. Not only was Moses more intelligent than

---

between Thucydides and Herodotus, see the assessment by T. Rood, "Thucydides' Persian Wars," in *The Limits of Historiography: Genre and Narrative in Ancient Historical Texts* (ed. C. Shuttleworth Kraus; MnSup 191; Leiden: Brill, 1999), 152–59.

67. See F. Siegert, "Early Jewish Interpretation in a Hellenistic Style," in *Hebrew Bible/Old Testament; The History of Its Interpretation:* vol. 1, pt. 1, *Antiquity* (ed. M. Sæbø; Göttingen: Vandenhoeck & Ruprecht, 1996), 130–31.

68. On Apollonius's *Argonautica* as an example, see J. J. Clauss, *The Best of the Argonauts: The Redefinition of the Epic Hero in Book 1 of Apollonius's* Argonautica (HCS 10; Berkeley: University of California Press, 1993), 5–8; and M. Palmer Bonz, *The Past as Legacy: Luke-Acts and Ancient Epic* (Minneapolis: Fortress, 2000), 102–3. See also A. B. Bosworth, *Alexander the Great and the East: The Tragedy of Triumph* (Oxford: Clarendon, 1996), 45–46; and S. Hinds, *Allusion and Intertext: Dynamics of Appropriation in Roman Poetry* (Roman Literature and Its Contexts; Cambridge: Cambridge University Press, 1998).

69. See further T. Penner, "Reconfiguring the Rhetorical Study of Acts: Reflections on the Method in and Learning of a Progymnastic Poetics," *PRSt* 30 (2003): 425–39.

any of his teachers (*Mos.* 1.21), he also reaches the heights of human prosperity in the royal court of Pharaoh (1.32). Moreover, his character was above reproach, as he manifested in both word and deed all the superior values of the Greek world (1.48, 63, 148–54). According to Philo, Moses was the ideal king and "world citizen" (1.157), "for he was named god and king of the whole nation, and entered...into the darkness where God was, that is into the unseen, invisible, incorporeal and archetypal essence of existing things" (1.158). This portrayal contains essential elements that Philo will later develop in book 2—Moses as legislator and high priest (1.334), which achieve importance largely because the exodus event becomes intricately connected to the founding of a city-state (law) and the establishment of worship (temple) through the person of Moses.

Philo also plays up the connection of Moses to the conquering of the promised land, leaving the reader with the impression that Moses is more closely associated with this event than the biblical narrative itself indicates. For instance, in the second year after their departure from Egypt, Moses decides to inspect the land (*Mos.* 1.220). This event functionally becomes the beginning of the conquest narrative. Passing over the thirty-eight years of wandering in the wilderness in a few short lines (1.237–38), Philo immediately returns to the people poised to enter the land (1.239, 251). The first book ends with the following description of the conquest of the Transjordan: "All these wars were fought and won without crossing the river of the land, the Jordan, against the inhabitants of the rich and deep-soiled country on the outer side" (1.319). For Philo, the victories in the Transjordan are already key elements of the larger conquest of the land. This emphasis on the continuity of the action functions to connect Moses more closely with the activity that takes place in the land proper: A perspective that receives further support in Philo's text. For instance, Philo's first book ends with the story in Num 32, where Moses urges the two tribes desiring to stay in the Transjordan to aid in the conquest of the land. This final note of Philo's story depicts Moses as the warrior-king, inspiring his people to go forward into battle. Indeed, since Philo does not mention the giving of the law in the first book (in its biblical "chronological" place) and since he only briefly notes the forty-year wandering, one is left with the distinct impression from the narrative that the exodus event is immediately connected to the possession of the land and the establishment of the Jewish *politeia*.

This emphasis is confirmed in the second book. Here Philo begins with a discussion of Moses as the ideal lawgiver: "Moses himself was the best of all law-givers in all countries, better in fact than any that have ever arisen among either the Greeks or the barbarians.... [H]is laws are most excellent and truly come from God, since they omit nothing that is needful" (*Mos.* 2.12). For Philo, the superiority of Moses' law is proved in that all those who seek virtue have "grown in holiness as to honour our laws" (2.17). In Philo's presentation, Greeks, taking an unprecedented step (2.18–19), have come to recognize the greatness of the Jewish law. Most striking, however, is Philo's explicit claim that Moses' true aim was to establish the laws so as to guide the *oikoumene*. Moses did not write the constitution of a narrowly defined city-state, but for the "world city":

> [Moses] considered that to begin his writings with the foundation of a man-made city was below the dignity of the laws, and, surveying the greatness and beauty of the whole code with the accurate discernment of his mind's eye, and thinking it too good and godlike to be confined within any earthly walls, he inserted the story of the genesis of the "Great City," holding that the laws were the most faithful picture of the world-polity. Thus whoever will carefully examine the nature of the particular enactments will find that they seek to attain to the harmony of the universe and are in agreement with the principles of eternal nature. (*Mos.* 2.51–52)

This statement makes the following evident: First, Moses' main achievement as lawgiver is to articulate a constitution that, while observed by the Jews, is intended for all humans. Philo depicts in no uncertain terms the superiority of the Jewish law, using this feature as a foil to glorify the lawgiver. Second, in the process, Moses is portrayed not merely as the founder of the religious law but of the civic and political constitution of the Jewish people. The Jewish law is herein characterized as the constitution for the Jewish *politeia*. To further this portrayal Philo separates out the explicit religious elements of the legislation and treats these independently under the theme of Moses' high priestly office. Third, the aim of Philo's depiction — separating Moses' function as leader from that as lawgiver — is to give the impression that the conquering of the land under Moses directly leads to the founding of the Jewish *politeia* under his leadership.

The last significant feature of the portrayal in Philo's praise of the Jewish hero is his treatment of Moses as high priest. Here Philo is particularly interested in depicting Moses as the founder of the Jewish cultus, with a stress on the tabernacle as functioning as a quasi-temple. While biblical tradition assigns the building of the temple to a later period in Jewish history, Philo, picking up the hints already contained in Deuteronomy that implicitly connect Moses with the legitimate "place" of sacrifice (Deut 12:5, 11, 13–14, 18, 21, 26), equates the building of the temple with the institution of the tabernacle under Moses. With respect to Moses' priestly duties, Philo says that first and foremost he was charged with the establishment of the sanctuary (ἱερόν). Philo goes on to detail his understanding of the function of Moses' action: "Now, if they had already occupied the land into which they were removing [lit. "into which they were migrating"], they would necessarily have had to erect a magnificent temple on the most open and conspicuous site, with costly stones for its material, and build great walls around it, with plenty of houses for the attendants, and call the place the holy city" (*Mos.* 2.72). Instead, however, Moses institutes a "portable sanctuary" because they were wandering in the desert (2.73). Further on in his discussion Philo again makes the same connection: "The tabernacle (σκηνή)... was constructed to resemble a sacred temple (νεώς ἅγιος)" (2.89).[70] Furthermore, alongside instituting the Aaronic priesthood, Moses appoints "temple attendants" (νεωκόροι), who assist in the sacrifices (2.159). This detail colors Philo's interpretation of the conflict reflected in the stories in Num 16–18: He portrays the Levites as "temple attendants" attempting to gain advantage over the priests.[71] Consequently, Philo creates an image in which Moses, as high priest, founds the central institutions of Jewish worship, with the tabernacle becoming a surrogate temple in the wilderness. Lest there be any doubt of the resultant portrait, in his discussion of the tabernacle being a copy of the "immaterial forms of the material objects" that are constructed from "patterns conceived in the mind" (2.74), Philo affirms unequivocally that "it was fitting that the construction of the sanctuary should be committed to him who was truly high priest (ἀληθῶς ἀρχιερεῖ), in order that his performance of the rites belonging to his sacred office might be in more than full accordance and harmony with the fabric" (2.75).

In Philo's treatment of the life of Moses, then, the central event of liberation from Egyptian oppression is linked directly with both the founding of the constitutional laws of the Jewish *politeia* and the establishment of the temple cult. Moses is shown to be superior in every respect, and is praised as an excellent leader, king, and high priest. Central to this scheme is the association of law and temple with the exodus and its larger narrative context, which might legitimately be isolated as *topoi* in the Philonic elaboration and amplification of the biblical story. Philo evidently intends to praise Moses through this paraphrasing and reorganizing of the biblical material, with the result that particular epideictic patterns emerge, connecting Moses with the two central facets of Jewish life: law and temple.

Josephus's portrait of the similar event bears some significant resemblance to Philo's treatment. Like Philo, in his *Antiquities* Josephus begins with the outstanding events connected with the character and birth of Moses. Josephus particularly stresses Moses' beauty of appearance, the surpassing nature of his intellect (*Ant.* 2.230–31), and his early prophetic abilities

---

70. It is worth noting that Philo also changes the Greek terms in Exod 26:17–27 from the common biblical word στῦλος to the nonbiblical κίων. Although both words can denote "pillar," this move may reflect an attempt to bring the language more clearly in line with (in Philo's mind) a more immediately recognizable Greek designation for "pillar," and hence enhance the image of the tabernacle-as-temple being established in his narrative.

71. In the biblical narrative the conflict is more complex but seems to involve a similar structure: The lower stationed Levites challenge the higher positioned priesthood. Philo does not change the nature of the conflict but frames it more explicitly in light of the temple hierarchy: An internal Levite debate becomes a more explicit temple conflict between attendants and priests (the term "Levite" disappears altogether from his account). Cf. Josephus's rendition (*Ant.* 4.14–66), where the Levite factor does play a role.

(2.232–35).⁷² In a rare nonbiblical addition, Moses is depicted as the grand general (στρατηγός) of the Egyptian army who leads a successful campaign against the Ethiopians (2.238–53; cf. Artapanus, frg. 3.7–11). For Josephus, this theme functions as a main feature of his narrative portrait of Moses as a capable military and political leader (cf. *C. Ap.* 2.157–59).⁷³ It is thus no coincidence that Josephus, upon narrating the parting of the Red Sea, should find a parallel from the exploits of another great general, Alexander the Great (*Ant.* 2.347–48; cf. Arrian, *Anab.* 1.26.1–2). Josephus then turns his attention to the character of the Sinai revelation, where Moses is portrayed as the religious and political founder of the Jewish people.

Josephus first pays attention to the founding of the tabernacle and the cultic rituals, reordering the account of Exodus by placing this material prior to the discussion of the legal code. This significant change is in that religious origins precede constitutional foundations in Josephus's narrative. That both aspects are of critical importance for Josephus is indicated by his description of Moses' first words upon descending from the mountain: Moses told the people that God "had during these days shown him that manner of government which would promote their happiness, and that He desired that a tabernacle should be made for Him" (*Ant.* 3.99). After his extensive discussion of the origin of the tabernacle and its various artifacts, Josephus goes on to defend the elaborate details of the Jewish cultus by arguing that they are representational in nature, symbolically bringing the universe to mind (3.179–80). Thus, the Jewish cultus is not bound to minute details as an end in themselves, but, in line with the apologetic of *Aristeas*, the tabernacle, like the food laws, is a symbolic representation of greater realities.

In Josephus's portrait, unlike Philo's, Moses is never explicitly referred to as a priest. Rather, Aaron is deemed the only one righteous enough to don the mantle of the high priest of the cultus. Nevertheless, Josephus does have Moses make a final reference to himself in this connection: "For my part, had the weighing of this matter been entrusted to me [i.e., office of the priest], I should have adjudged myself worthy of the dignity.... But now God has judged Aaron worthy of this honour" (*Ant.* 3.190). The implication is that Moses would have considered himself a capable high priest, viewing this as just another self-giving act for his people. Thus, while on the one hand Josephus creates some distance between Moses and the high priestly office, based largely, one would surmise, on Josephus's more faithful adherence to the biblical text of Leviticus, at the same time he makes implicit

---

72. On Moses' moral superiority in Josephus, see Attridge, *Interpretation of Biblical History*, 143–44; and Feldman, *Josephus's Interpretation*, 397–425. See also C. Gerber, *Ein Bild des Judentums für Nichtjuden von Flavius Josephus: Untersuchungen zu seiner Schrift* Contra Apionem (AGJU 40; Leiden: Brill, 1997), 258–68.

73. Feldman has detailed this emphasis in several studies (see most recently, *Josephus's Interpretation*, 386–97).

suggestions in the other direction, having Moses state his own qualifications for the office, with the only catch being that God chose Aaron over him.[74] Aside from this small caveat, however, it is abundantly clear that Josephus intends to associate the founding of the Jewish cultus as the first Mosaic act at Sinai.

The second aspect of the presentation focuses on Moses as the legislator of the Jewish law. Depicted as the reception of oracles from God (*Ant.* 3.212), the laws of Moses form the next major section of Josephus's treatment. For Josephus, the law is not religious per se, but is rather the constitution and law of the Hebrews (3.213; cf. 4.196–98). It represents the founding of a civic and political entity — the *politeia* of the Jews. Moreover, while some laws are relevant to the "narrative time" of Moses, clearly others only make sense from the viewpoint of the established cult in Jerusalem. Recognizing this, Josephus maintains that Moses devised some laws in advance, which were intended to be practiced once they conquered Canaan (3.280–81). For Josephus, the entire *politeia* of the Jews thus finds its source in Moses' legislation. Indeed, for Josephus the constitution of the Jews was founded by God through the person of Moses, and this theocracy (cf. *C. Ap.* 2.163) is far superior to anything the Greek world has to offer (*Ant.* 3.322).[75] Consequently, then, although it is more oblique in Josephus's text, there is still a clear line of connection between the exodus from Egypt and Moses' establishment of the religious and political foundations of the Jewish people.

The presentation of the exodus event as leading to the formation of two distinct aspects of Jewish life (establishment of religion and the Jewish *politeia*), which one finds in the renditions of the Moses story in Philo and Josephus, likewise surfaces in non-Jewish accounts of the exodus tradition. This connection might at first seem surprising, as one would initially wonder why non-Jews would expend the effort to retell Jewish nativistic traditions. The ethnographical tradition of the Greeks can partly explain this phenomenon, as it encouraged Greek writers to examine the roots and stories of other peoples so as to classify the known world. Even more importantly, however, the Jewish motivation to rewrite biblical tradition was a reflection of a larger ethos of creating identity through competitive literary composition. This epideictic focus included not only writing about one's own people or group, but also telling the stories of others, thereby shaping a particular portrayal of the other. At times this emphasis would take on a particularly

---

74. It is tempting to read the notice in *Ant.* 3.212 as another implicit connection between Moses and the priesthood. Immediately after noting that Aaron could not grieve at the loss of his two sons because he was already high priest and thus had to fulfill religious duties to God, Josephus remarks, "Moses, for his part, having declined every honour which he saw that the people were ready to confer on him, devoted himself solely to the service of God [i.e., legislation]." See Spilsbury, *Image of the Jew,* 104–5.

75. See further Gerber, *Bild des Judentums,* 215–17; and Gruen, *Diaspora,* 216.

negative focus, as writers would seize upon the opportunity to denounce and deride particular traditions and groups by construing their traditions in negative ways. At least for a time in Alexandria, this approach became one way non-Jews would utilize the exodus tradition (e.g., Manetho).[76] At the same time, however, there are more positive retellings of the exodus event by non-Jews, where the topics that seemed important to Jews in the epideictic elaboration of the biblical narrative appear to have influenced the Greco-Roman perspective on Judaism as well.

The pattern of Moses as founder of a religion and legislator of a political constitution is present, for instance, in the famous account by Hecataeus of Abdera related by Diodorus Siculus (40.3.1–8). When native Egyptians cast out aliens from Egypt because of a pestilence that arose, a great number of these found their way to Judea. Here Moses, "outstanding both for his wisdom and for his courage" (40.3.3), founds the city of Jerusalem and its temple, as well as institutes the religious rituals and the Jewish laws and political institutions (πολιτεία). Moses also appoints the chief priests to govern the temple (40.3.4). Further, as a result of the Jewish experience in Egypt, Moses initiates laws that set the people apart from other nations, which, from Hecataeus's perspective, promote an "unsocial and intolerant mode of life" (40.3.4). Various other facets of Jewish religious and cultural practice are also highlighted in the fragment (sacrifices, lack of images, nature of the priesthood, military organization, distribution of land, and laws relative to family life). Moses' military prowess is also commented upon (40.3.6–7). The fragment from Hecataeus in Diodorus is significant for this discussion because it coheres so closely with the framing of the same tradition by Philo and Josephus.[77] The citation from Hecataeus is generally held to be authentic,[78] reflecting a Greek ethnological description of Jewish life and

---

76. For a helpful summary of Manetho's tradition of interpretation, see C. Aziza, "L'utilisation polémique du récit de l'Exode chez les écrivains alexandrins (IVème siècle av. J.-C.–Ier siècle ap. J.-C.)," *ANRW* 2.20.1 (1987): 41–65; as well as J. G. Gager, *Moses in Greco-Roman Paganism* (SBLMS 16; Nashville: Abingdon, 1972), 113–33; P. Schäfer, "The Exodus Tradition in Pagan Greco-Roman Literature," in *The Jews in the Hellenistic-Roman World* (ed. I. M. Gafni et al.; Jerusalem: Zalman Shazar Center for Jewish History, 1996), 9–38; idem, *Judeophobia*, 15–33; and J. J. Collins, "Reinventing Exodus: Exegesis and Legend in Hellenistic Egypt," in *For a Later Generation: The Transformation of Tradition in Israel, Early Judaism, and Early Christianity* (ed. R. A. Argall, B. A. Bow, and R. A. Werline; Harrisburg, Pa.: Trinity Press International, 2000), 56–62.

77. A. J. Droge, "Josephus between Greeks and Barbarians," in *Josephus' Contra Apionem* (ed. Feldman and Levison), 136–37, similarly argues that so-called anti-Jewish accounts such as one finds in Apion or Manetho were reliant on the preexistent model in Hecataeus, thus emphasizing, albeit in a negative way, the role of Moses as founder-figure.

78. So R. Doran, "Pseudo-Hecataeus, Introduction," in *Old Testament Pseudepigrapha* (ed. Charlesworth), 2:905; B. Bar-Kochva, *Pseudo-Hecataeus, "On the Jews": Legitimizing the Jewish Diaspora* (HCS 21; Berkeley: University of California Press, 1996), 18–43; and Gager, *Moses in Greco-Roman Paganism*, 26–37. See also F. H. Diamond, "Hecataeus of Abdera and the Mosaic Constitution," in *Essays in Ancient History and Historiography in Honor of T. S. Brown* (ed. S. M. Burstein and L. A. Orkin; Lawrence: Coronado, 1980), 77–95.

practice. Moreover, scholars recognize that Hecataeus's account is a Greek interpretation of the founding of the Jewish *politeia* based on the *topos* of the founding of a Greek colony.[79] This association accounts for the presentation of Moses in a thinly veiled Greek guise, as well as the commonly used device of telescoping events so as to bring future developments into line with the founder-leader figure.[80] There is also general agreement that the particular interpretation of Moses in this fragment has its roots in Jewish interpretations, whether in dialogue with the Jews of Alexandria[81] or in connection with priestly traditions stemming from Judea.[82] While the charge that Moses' law was unsocial (ἀπάνθρωπος) and hateful toward strangers (μισόξενος) may be more difficult to explain as a Jewish interpretation,[83] the rest of the text is fully consonant with the manner in which Moses is characterized by both Philo and Josephus.[84] Particularly, one finds here the same

---

79. D. Mendels, "Hecataeus of Abdera and a Jewish *Patrios Politeia*," in *Identity, Religion, and Historiography: Studies in Hellenistic History* (JSPSup 24; Sheffield: Sheffield Academic Press, 1998), 338; and Bar-Kochva, *Pseudo-Hecataeus*, 26. See also the broader discussion of this theme by W. T. Wilson, "Urban Legends: Acts 10:1–11:18 and the Strategies of Greco-Roman Foundation Narratives," *JBL* 120 (2001): 77–99.
80. Bar-Kochva, *Pseudo-Hecataeus*, 26.
81. Gager, *Moses in Greco-Roman Paganism*, 37; and Bar-Kochva, *Pseudo-Hecataeus*, 28. See also Attridge, *Interpretation of Biblical History*, 170–71, who ascribes the view more generally to "Jewish propaganda or apologetic" or possibly (in the case of the Strabo fragment) to the work of an anti-Hasmonean Jewish writer.
82. See Mendels, "Hecataeus of Abdera," 350, who connects it with Ezra-Nehemiah traditions.
83. However, there exists in the text a sympathetic understanding of the basis for the Mosaic law: It rests on the Israelites' own experience of having been aliens expelled as "strangers" from a foreign land (cf. the similar type of reasoning stated by Pompeius Trogus; Justin, *Epitome*, 36.2.15). Moreover, one must keep in mind that it is difficult to know if and/or at what points Diodorus may have altered Hecataeus's account so as to bring it in line with his own view (cf. Bar-Kochva, *Pseudo-Hecataeus*, 24). The possibility that the charges were added to Hecataeus's account by Diodorus is strengthened by his own comments on Judaism in his earlier description of Antiochus's entrance into the temple: "Moses, the founder of Jerusalem and organizer of the nation, the man, moreover, who had ordained for the Jews their misanthropic [μισάνθρωπος] and lawless [παρανομος] customs" (35.1.3). While it has been argued that the charges become associated with the exodus narrative in Greco-Roman tradition as a result of strong anti-Jewish sentiment (Schäfer, "Exodus Tradition"; and idem, *Judeophobia*, 15–33), in the Hellenistic and Roman periods (perhaps manifested for somewhat different reasons by Greeks and Romans) there existed a strong reaction toward groups who were perceived to be exclusionary in their cultural and social practices. Thus, the tendency observed in some of these so-called anti-Jewish writings may have less to do with the Jews per se and more with broader sociocultural concerns of the period.
84. Problematic is the suggestion that certain features such as the provisions for military training and the note that the high priests were appointed according to merit cannot be Jewish since they lack clear Jewish parallels (see Bar-Kochva, *Pseudo-Hecataeus*, 29). Yet the provision of military training is consonant with the portrayal of Moses as the ideal general and leader elsewhere in Jewish texts, and Josephus explicitly states that Aaron was selected high priest because of his merit (Aaron is the "most deserving among us" [*Ant.* 3.191]). Moreover, the whole point behind apologetic literature as understood here is that changes in the antecedent narrative denote an attempt to bring one's tradition in line with Greco-Roman values and expectations. Thus, the lack of Jewish precedent means very little one way or the other with respect to whether these elements could have originated in Jewish circles.

topics with respect to the exodus narrative: Moses becomes the religious and political founder of the Jewish people, establishing the law, Jerusalem, and the temple as foci of Jewish piety and life.

Similar themes surface in Strabo's account of Moses, where Moses is exhibited as leaving Egypt because of his distaste for Egyptian worship, especially the extensive Egyptian use of images for the divinity. He brings the people to the place where Jerusalem now stands, and organizes the religious and political structures of Jewish life: "Moses... [was] resolved to seek a seat of worship for Him and promis[ed] to deliver to the people a kind of worship and a kind of ritual which would not oppress those who adopted them either with expenses or with divine obsessions or with other absurd troubles. Now Moses enjoyed fair repute with these people, and organized no ordinary kind of government" (Strabo 16.2.36). One of the unique features added to the basic outline is that after Moses left the scene others arose who were at first superstitious and later tyrannical, and it was these who distorted the Mosaic legislation, adding food laws and circumcision (16.2.37). Thus, the time of holy beginnings devolves after the life of the founder.

Tacitus similarly describes the exodus of the people under Moses as resulting in the founding of a city and the dedication of a temple (*Hist.* 5.3.2). He also maintains a similar pattern of devolution in Jewish practice: "Whatever their origin, these rites [i.e., rest on the seventh day, abstaining from pork, frequent fasting, animal sacrifices] are maintained by their antiquity: the other customs [e.g., circumcision] of the Jews are base and abominable and owe their persistence to their depravity" (5.5.1). Here Tacitus makes a distinction between Mosaic legislation and the types of customs and laws that appear to have developed after Moses (cf. Tacitus's description of the later development of the sabbatical year; 5.4.3). Consequently, in both Tacitus and Strabo, the rudimentary outline of the exodus narrative links Moses with the founding of the political constitution and city of the Jews, as well as their unique religious laws and customs, at least the ones perceived to be original (and less barbaric) over against so-called later developments.[85]

---

85. Schäfer, *Judeophobia*, 24–26, 31–33, views both Strabo and Tacitus as perpetuating the basic anti-Jewish interpretation of the exodus tradition (although Strabo [25] to a lesser degree than Tacitus [32]). His comments on Strabo are particularly interesting: "[W]hether it is the result of Strabo's deliberate revision of an antecedent or whether he just quotes a source we do not have...it does not lead us back to the 'true' story of the Exodus tradition" (26). However, both Philo and Josephus are closer to the portrayal of Moses one finds in Strabo and Tacitus — in terms of the structure of the story — than they are to the biblical tradition itself. The Jewish exodus story was being (re)told by Greeks and Romans in precisely the same way Philo and Josephus (and presumably other Hellenistic Jewish writers) were recasting it, albeit in the latter case without the negative comments inserted into the narrative by writers such as Tacitus.

These three non-Jewish writers reveal a representation of the exodus tradition fairly consistent with that found in Philo and Josephus. Hecataeus, Strabo, and Tacitus are frequently portrayed as reflecting an anti-Jewish bias in their interpretations, and it is evident that for some, especially Tacitus, there is some strong distaste for Jewish practices, which in the case of the latter probably needs to be situated in the context of his general dislike and distrust of anything non-Roman (i.e., non-Italian). Overall, however, the basic structure of the exodus tradition is familiar: The exodus leads to the foundation of the city of Jerusalem and the Jewish *politeia* by Moses. Strabo and to a lesser degree Tacitus also make the further argument that the bastardization of the tradition occurs only after the death of Moses, thereby preserving the time of beginnings as a more pure and sacrosanct period.[86] While dependence of one writer on another is one way of explaining the continuity between these diverse texts, more likely is the explanation that Hellenistic Jews such as Philo and Josephus self-consciously promoted this understanding of the exodus narrative. Thus, non-Jewish tradition may in fact attest to the effect that Hellenistic apologetic historiography may have had on outsiders.

In conclusion, several important aspects of the preceding discussion should be highlighted. Hellenistic Jews such as Philo and Josephus were concerned to rewrite their native traditions in light of Greek values and perspectives. The tradition of the exodus affords a brief glimpse into the literary environment of some Jewish writers in antiquity. Both Philo and Josephus were interested in recasting the Moses narrative so as to articulate more clearly the founding of the Jewish *politeia* in terms appropriate and acceptable to the Greek world. Indeed, not only is Moses depicted as the founder of the holy city of Jerusalem, the political constitution of the Jews, and the religious laws, as well as being brought into close association with the temple, but also in all of these instances Moses' unsurpassed greatness is repeatedly highlighted. In two respects, then, we perceive epideictic emphases: (1) the portrayal of the origins of Jewish territory and practice in

---

86. It is by no means clear that this particular addition to the Hellenistic Jewish pattern is by definition a non-Jewish one. There may well have existed Jewish traditions that deliberately tried to dissociate the constitution of Moses and the more "unseemly" (from a Greek point of view) aspects of Jewish tradition. Presumably Philo's allegorizing Jews would have been possible candidates for this approach. On the theme of decay of Jewish institutions in these Greco-Roman writers, see M. Klinghardt, *Gesetz und Volk Gottes: Das lukanische Verständnis des Gesetzes nach Herkunft, Funktion, und seinum Ort in der Geschichte des Urchristentums* (WUNT 2.32; Tübingen: Mohr Siebeck, 1988), 296–97; D. L. Balch, "Comments on the Genre and a Political Theme of Luke-Acts: A Preliminary Comparison of Two Hellenistic Historians," *SBLSP* 28 (1989): 348–49; idem, "ΜΕΤΑΒΟΛΗ ΠΟΛΙΤΕΙΩΝ. Jesus as Founder of the Church in Luke-Acts: Form and Function," in *Contextualizing Acts* (ed. Penner and Vander Stichele), 139–88; and Attridge, *Interpretation of Biblical History*, 170–75, who also elaborates the theme more generally in terms of Greek historiography (on the theme of decay in Josephus's account, see 126–40). Finally, since the Deuteronomistic History contains the same pattern as its framing narrative, the emphasis on decay may justifiably also be considered a biblical pattern.

terms consonant with the Greek tradition of the origin of city-states; and (2) the presentation of the praiseworthy features of the Mosaic narrative, stressing the superior nature of the Jewish tradition.

The accounts of Philo and Josephus can be considered apologetic historiography, as they rewrite their native tradition in light of dominant cultural values and perceptions. In both cases, the accent is less on defense and more squarely on praising the origins of the Jewish *politeia* as not only measuring up to Greek standards but surpassing them as well. In the process, the identity of the Hellenistic Jewish reader is shaped. The recreation of the biblical narrative reinforces Jewish values and perceptions, instilling a sense of pride in the story of origins and the heroes of the Jewish faith. It also firmly entrenches Jewish self-understanding in terms of the larger dominant culture's values, thereby refracting Jewish identity through a particular Greek lens. Furthermore, Hecataeus, Strabo, and Tacitus may reveal that outsiders were also acquainted with Jewish retellings such as Philo and Josephus present. In this case it seems that some Greco-Roman writers adopted the basic scheme of Hellenistic Jewish self-presentation. This pattern was repeated in non-Jewish literature less in an explicitly epideictic formulation and more as a straightforward description *(ekphrasis)*, albeit with occasional negative developments/additions on the part of the non-Jewish writers. Yet the very fact that this pattern surfaces outside of Jewish literature affirms that the line between the construction of identity within the community and self-promotion without cannot be drawn too firmly.

There is thus a broad *ethos* argument being established throughout with respect to law, temple, and forefathers (particularly the interconnection of the three) in Jewish tradition, and this greatness of the past and the founding of the Jewish institutions are associated with the people in the present; the glorious beginnings and the splendid heritage yield an implied characterization of the current Jewish *politeia*. The founding of the group is particularly important in this discursive mode, precisely because derivative features are bypassed in order to highlight the inner essence of the tradition, thereby characterizing those associated with that tradition in the writer's own time. In this manner, epideictic themes come readily to the forefront in Jewish apologetic literature, and even simple descriptive narratives have a fundamentally rich and complex underlying argumentative core, which plays into the elements of praise and blame in self and group imag(in)ing.

Finally, there is an important feature in these exodus accounts that further promotes the epideictic emphasis being underscored in this chapter. In her extensive study of the ancient use of sanctuary discourse as a discursive mode of creating community identity through the delineation of sanctuary space as cosmic representation, J. Økland delineates the manner in which Josephus portrays sanctuary space in his *Contra Apionem* (2.77), wherein the rituals enacted in the temple have a universal efficacy, representing the *philanthropia* of the Jews toward all humanity.[87] In light of the preceding argument, it is not surprising to observe the temple functioning in a similar way throughout the stories of Moses in the Jewish tradition, where the temple and law are not ends in themselves, but in fact characterize the Jews and their culture and traditions more generally.

Luke-Acts and Jewish Apologetic Literature

The thesis advocated in this study promotes Luke-Acts as a premiere example of early Christian historiography written in the tradition of Jewish apologetic literature. As a result, there are certain features of Jewish apologetic historiography one might anticipate showing up in the Lukan composition. The most important one, in light of the argument made in this chapter, is the predominance of epideictic patterns of argumentation and elaboration. In particular, we must examine the way in which Luke's narrative in Acts 6:1–8:3 seeks to demonstrate the laudable qualities of the early Christian community and its heroes. In line with Philo and Josephus, Luke is concerned to present the origins of the new community or *politeia* in continuity with its Jewish heritage and in a manner consonant with Greco-Roman values and perspectives. Moreover, if the larger narrative of Acts is viewed as a piece of demonstrative rhetoric, one may anticipate not only explicit praise but also a degree of blame as well. Blame in epideictic composition is an integral part of *synkrisis,* whereby one establishes the superiority of one's own group by contrasting it with a rival. This feature is more muted in Hellenistic Jewish apologetic texts, but becomes more prominent in competitive environments such as that out of which Christianity originated, wherein the historian has alternative ways of construing the relationship of Christianity vis-à-vis its Jewish heritage.

Furthermore, while all complex compositions will contain all three species of rhetoric in varying degrees and narrative settings, the presence of judicial and deliberative emphases in a work of apologetic such as Luke-Acts may be subordinate to the larger epideictic focus. This observation is critical when it comes to analyzing the function of Stephen's speech in its larger narrative context. Rather than simply seeking the way in which Stephen provides a judicial response to the charges brought against him in the narrative, one must also attempt to place this speech within the larger epideictic framework of Luke's apologetic historiography, determining the way in which praise and blame are established in and through the speech. Lastly, if the key *topoi* of Jewish epideictic elaboration are such entities as the city of Jerusalem, the law, the temple, and the fathers of the faith, then one should address what role, if any, these components play in Luke's work. The speech of Acts 7 is

---

87. J. Økland, "Women in Their Place: Paul and the Corinthian Discourse of Gender and Sanctuary Space" (Ph.D. diss., University of Oslo, 2000), 255.

especially important in this regard, since Luke here evinces an indebtedness to both the Jewish and Greco-Roman interpretations of the founding of the Jewish *politeia* by Moses. Further, Luke demonstrates in this speech what is perhaps the hallmark of Jewish apologetic historiography: the rewriting of the biblical tradition so as to construct a particular identity within the community and to promote it without. This feature functions in tandem with the larger epideictic aim motivating the Stephen and Hellenist narrative, which is to produce assurance in the readers of Luke-Acts.

V

In Praise of Origins

The Hellenists, Stephen, and the Christian Foundation Narrative

In this final chapter, I return to the narrative of Stephen and the Hellenists in Acts 6:1–8:3, using the framework set up in the previous chapters to advance the understanding of Luke's historiographical method of composition. In chapter 2, I suggested that the first seven chapters of Acts are important insofar as they map out, from Luke's perspective, the complexities involved in the growing community in Jerusalem. In chapter 3, I established the importance of the *narratio* in historical composition. The complete plot — that which unites the various discrete elements of the narrative — is critical for understanding the Lukan perspective of interpretation and forms the basis of the analysis in this chapter. In the study that follows, I will supplement this emphasis with reference to the other components of historiographical composition discussed in chapter 3. In chapter 4, I dealt more specifically with Jewish apologetic historiography, which is particularly relevant for understanding both the speech of Acts 7 and the larger function of the Lukan narrative in terms of the use of the *topoi* of epideictic persuasion and the methods for their elaboration. The reading of the Hellenist unit that follows is offered not only as an alternative to the interpretation of the Hellenists reviewed in chapter 1, but also, finally, as a model that reflects a different use of Lukan *historia* in Acts.

Praising the Founding: *Philia/Philanthropia* in the Jerusalem Community (Acts 6:1–7)

The pattern of conflict within and without the early Jerusalem community[1] forms the main plot device of this larger unit: founding of the community

---

1. It is difficult to establish precise designations for the various groups Luke weaves into the Christian foundation narrative. It is not until Acts 11:26 and then only once more in 26:28 that the designation χριστιανός is used, and in these cases it seems to be used by outsiders. Luke uses the term Ἰουδαῖος in a nonpreferential way (the context determines whether the term "Jews" is used oppositionally or descriptively [cf. 2:5, 14; 26:4, where Ἰουδαῖος carries no negative connotation], although admittedly most often the term occurs in contexts that are

(1:1–2:44); summary statement (2:43–47); conflict with outsiders (4:1–31); summary statement (4:32–35); conflict with insiders (5:1–11); summary statement (5:12–16); conflict with outsiders (5:17–41); summary statement (5:42); conflict with insiders (6:1–6); summary statement (6:7). Already one catches a glimpse here of Luke's interest in offsetting inner-community conflict with the friction that arises between the Jerusalem religious establishment and the apostles of the newly formed assembly. Whereas the inner life of the community continually resolves the critical issues that threaten its survival, the strife between the establishment and the community increasingly escalates as the narrative progresses.

The escalation of conflict between the religious leaders and the newly formed community is an intentional reflection and continuation of the same feature in the ministry of Jesus in Luke's first volume, focused especially in the travel narrative of Luke's central section in his gospel (9:51–19:44).[2] Throughout that narrative, as Jesus moves toward Jerusalem and his impending death, there is increasing conflict between Jesus and the Pharisees/scribes.[3] D. P. Moessner has argued that not only is there growing hostility between the two, ultimately culminating in Jesus' death at the hands of the Jerusalem establishment, but at the same time Jesus himself is progressively revealed as the "Lord-Host of the Heavenly Banquet which is now dynamically being fulfilled in his *journeying* to Jerusalem."[4] Whatever the intended nature of that revelation is, it does seem that there is a deliberate contrast between the "house" of the leaders of the Jews and the "house" of Jesus. The images of eating, for instance, resonate with the theme of the

---

negatively structured; cf. 9:23; 13:45, 50; 14:2, 19; 17:5, 13; 18:12, 14; 21:11, 27; 23:12, 20; 24:9, 19; 25:7; 26:21). The picture is further complicated in Acts 16:20, where Paul and Silas are themselves called "Jews" by their accusers. It is clear that Luke's use of the term Ἰουδαῖος increases once he moves to the narratives of Paul, and that an oppositional quality between Paul and Jewish opponents exists that is linguistically marked in a way that the earlier conflict between the apostles and the Jerusalem leaders is not. Further, from a metanarrative standpoint the entire account relates the foundation of the group that comes to be designated "Christian" in Acts 11:26. Thus, from Luke's perspective, although the portrayal of the Jerusalem apostles is in terms of their affinities with Judaism, they are, finally, the progenitors of the χριστιανός movement. Designation of specific groups in the narrative, then, is a complex phenomenon. It is evident that categorizing the groups in Jerusalem as "Jewish" versus "Christian" goes against Luke's narrative grain — that distinction does not exist yet in the narrative — and one inevitably creates distinctions (already well-embedded in Christian history and discourse) that actually create polarity and opposition (particularly of a theological or even religious variety) where there is more complexity, nuance, and tension in Luke's own construction. At the same time, one also needs to represent the structures of conflict that occur throughout all portions of the narrative, including the opening chapters. In what follows, I seek to signify (hopefully) the oppositional discursive patterns that are patently evident in the narrative without capitulating to a broader theological/ideological polarization that pits Christianity against Judaism.

2. J. B. Tyson, *The Death of Jesus in Luke-Acts* (Columbia: University of South Carolina Press, 1986), 77; and B. R. Grangaard, *Conflict and Authority in Luke 19:47 to 21:4* (StBL 8; New York: Peter Lang, 1999), 195–97.

3. D. P. Moessner, *Lord of the Banquet: The Literary and Theological Significance of the Lukan Travel Narrative* (Minneapolis: Fortress, 1989), 197–207.

4. Ibid., 174.

household in Luke, and it is in the travel section that the bulk of the Jesus material related to household concerns is situated.[5]

The material in Acts 1–7 appears to function in a similar manner. The contrast between the household of the new community and the temple of the Jewish leadership is explicit and prominent in this section.[6] Moreover, the increasing conflict between the two groups results in the death of Stephen. The pattern of the central section of the Lukan gospel is likewise present in Acts. As in the travel section of the gospel, the portrayal of the respective groups provides the narrative reason for the death of key community figures and the motivation for the consequent break with the Jewish establishment, while the contrastive features of their narrative depictions establishes a basis for comparison or *synkrisis*. In this way, the growing strife provides the opportunity for the reader to observe the nature and character of the respective groups based on their responses to the situations created unfolding in the narrative. In both cases *philia*, or friendship, is at stake. Aristotle argues that the breakdown of fellow-feeling *(philanthropia)*[7] is the quintessential element that produces pity and fear in the audience. Indeed, this disintegration is particularly poignant when it occurs "within relationships, such as brother and brother, son and father, mother and son, son and mother — when the one kills (or is about to kill) the other, or commits some other such deed" (*Poet.* 1453b).

In the beginning of Acts we see this developed in two ways. First, within the Jerusalem community there exists the potential for the dissolution of *philia*. The threat of internal divisions provides some significant tension, escalating until the apostolic conference of Acts 15 and perhaps even after that.[8] The other major tension is the erosion of *philia* between the Jewish religious establishment and the leadership of the newly formed community, providing a combination of threat from within and without. This tension is akin to Aristotle's sense of the dissolution of fraternal bonds, which, from the Aristotelian perspective, is one of the major plot devices that creates the kinds of dramatic tension necessary to evoke responses in the reader. Finally, the entire narrative framework sets the two entities side by side, initiating a comparison of the respective groups based on their responses to

---

5. J. H. Elliott, "Temple versus Household in Luke-Acts: A Contrast in Social Institutions," in *The Social World of Luke-Acts* (ed. J. H. Neyrey; Peabody, Mass.: Hendrickson, 1991), 227–28.

6. Ibid., 215–17.

7. I use the specific term and theme of *philanthropia* as developed in chapter 3 of this study. While the term *philadelphia* may reflect the notion of kinship ties evoked in the Lukan narrative, *philanthropia* represents the specific ancient virtue of hospitality or fellow-feeling. It is also a word that Luke himself uses elsewhere in Acts (28:2; cf. 27:3).

8. See further A. Rakotoharintsifa, "Luke and the Internal Divisions in the Early Church," in *Luke's Literary Achievement: Collected Essays* (ed. C. M. Tuckett; JSNTSup 116; Sheffield: Sheffield Academic Press, 1995), 165–77. We saw the similar stress on dramatic tension and intracommunity conflict in Josephus's treatment of Moses (*Ant.* 4) in the previous chapter.

the narrative tensions: One will escalate the breakdown of *philanthropia*, while the other will attempt to resolve it.[9]

Community Resolution of Stasis

The opening scene of Acts 6:1–8:3, which is important for the development of Luke's larger plot in chapters 1–7, begins with a deceptively simple line: "Now during those days, when the disciples were increasing in number, the Hellenists complained against the Hebrews because their widows were being neglected in the daily distribution of food" (6:1). As we saw in chapter 2, scholarship has frequently attempted to move beyond the explicit statement given in this narrative in order to establish the "real" nature of the conflict. Rather than going beyond what is explicitly given, however, I suggest that one first examine what the narrative itself reveals.

The first important detail is the mention of widows (χῆραι), something easily overlooked in the haste to move beneath the "veneer" of the text. In Luke-Acts, widows are highly significant, having a heightened role in this work in comparison to the other gospels. Indeed, out of all the references to χῆρα in the gospels and Acts, all but three (Mark 12:40, 42, 43) are found in Luke-Acts (Luke 2:37; 4:25, 26; 7:12; 18:3, 5; 20:47; 21:2, 3; Acts 6:1; 9:39, 41). For Luke, the response of a person or group to widows characterizes them either positively or negatively in the narrative.[10] The Greek word χῆρα, used throughout the Septuagint, occurs with special frequency in Deuteronomy (10:18; 14:29; 16:11, 14; 24:17, 19, 20, 21; 26:12, 13; 27:19). If one follows Moessner's argument that Luke has gone to great lengths to cast Jesus and his disciples in the mode of the prophet like Moses of Deut 18:15,[11] then it is not difficult to perceive how this pattern fits in with the emphasis on widows in Luke's narrative. The prophet and his people take the same proactive stance toward the outcast (especially widows, orphans, and aliens) that prominently defines the righteous individual/community throughout Deuteronomy. The response to the widows provides a foil for developing the positive characteristics of the newly established Jerusalem community in Acts 1–7.[12]

---

9. For a discussion of the narrative comparison, see R. P. Thompson, "Believers and Religious Leaders in Jerusalem: Contrasting Portraits of Jews in Acts 1–7," in *Literary Studies in Luke-Acts: Essays in Honor of Joseph B. Tyson* (ed. R. P. Thompson and T. E. Phillips; Macon, Ga.: Mercer University Press, 1998), 327–44.

10. For fuller discussion, see F. S. Spencer, "Neglected Widows in Acts 6:1–7," *CBQ* 56 (1994): 715–33.

11. Moessner, *Lord of the Banquet*, 259–88. See also L. T. Johnson, *The Literary Function of Possessions in Luke-Acts* (SBLDS 39; Missoula, Mont.: Scholars Press, 1977), 60–76.

12. This suggestion is similar to Johnson's (*Literary Function*, 220), regarding the symbolic nature of possession language in Acts: Treatment of possessions affirms those characters who positively model the *ethos* of the prophet like Moses and who form the new authority of the prophetic community as a result.

Luke's narrative focuses on the widows precisely because the response to this "crisis" will reveal something about the character of the first adherents to the nascent Christian movement and their community. Added to this point is the further observation, made initially by D. Daube, that Luke has deliberately modeled the scene of the community's response to the widows on Hebrew Bible parallels. In particular, Daube has identified Exod 18, Num 11, and Deut 1 as important exemplars.[13] These narratives are significant because in all three cases Moses appoints helpers to assist him in his tasks of governing the people. Exodus 18:13–26 provides a good example, since a potential crisis in the early Israelite community is averted because Moses, following the advice of his father-in-law, establishes an organizational structure of support by selecting outstanding men from the community. In the passage from Num 11, an additional feature appears: God transfers some of the "spirit" of Moses over to the seventy elders he has appointed to help him with the "burdens" of the people (11:17). Moreover, in this same text the initial problem arises because of the "complaining" of the people (ὁ λαὸς γογγύζων; 11:1 LXX). This feature parallels the "complaining" that arises in the Jerusalem community (ἐγένετο γογγυσμός; Acts 6:1). Even more striking are the verbal parallels between Acts 6 and Deut 1:

Deut 1:13 (cf. 1:15) LXX	Acts 6:3
δότε ἑαυτοῖς ἄνδρας σοφοὺς καὶ Ἐπιστήμονας καὶ συνετοὺς εἰς τὰς φυλὰς ὑμῶν καὶ καταστήσω ἐφ' ὑμῶν ἡγουμένους ὑμῶν	Ἐπισκέψασθε δέ, ἀδελφοί, ἄνδρας ἐξ ὑμῶν μαρτυρουμένους ἑπτά, πλήρεις πνεύματος καὶ σοφίας, οὓς καταστήσομεν ἐπὶ τῆς χρείας

Here those being "appointed" are "wise men" in the community. In Deut 1:13 they are also "discerning" and "understanding," while in Acts 6:3 the other characteristics are "reputable" and "full of the spirit." These parallels are important largely for the reason that Luke portrays the leaders of the Jerusalem community as confronting and then responding to the same kind of problem evidenced in the community under Moses. The typological correlation is probably less significant than the straightforward emphasis on the response to crisis resulting in the establishment of community organization; just as the Israelites under Moses were in need of organized leadership during their formative period, so the assembly under the apostles also requires a similar structure. One should observe also that this formative period in the Hebrew Bible account is the post-exodus founding of the Jewish *politeia* under the governance of Moses. In a similar way to the Hellenistic Jewish retellings of the exodus event (cf. Josephus, *Ant.* 4) explored in the previous chapter, Luke's portrayal of the origin of the Christian movement evidences,

---

13. D. Daube, "A Reform in Acts and Its Models," in *Jews, Greeks, and Christians: Religious Cultures in Late Antiquity; Essays in Honor of William David Davies* (ed. R. Hamerton-Kelly and R. Scroggs; SJLA 21; Leiden: Brill, 1976), 151–63.

in the founding of the community, a reenactment of the patterns of formation of the *politeia* in the biblical account, demonstrating points of contact between the people of the prophet Jesus and the people of Moses.

In Acts 6:1–7 Luke is thus depicting a critical juncture in the foundation narrative: When internal conflict arises, the apostles respond by appointing a group to "wait on tables." The exact nature of the appointment has been problematic for modern scholars precisely because the newly appointed group never actually waits on tables or deals with the daily distribution in the narrative. Rather, the next time we meet one of the seven, it is in Stephen's role as prophet and teacher (6:8). L. T. Johnson has attempted to overcome this problem by suggesting that the actual "job description" is symbolic; it is Luke's way of bestowing power on the seven, demonstrating in the narrative the transfer of authority to the Hellenistic missionaries by showing their power over possessions in the community.[14] Johnson has rightly pushed beyond the traditional arguments highlighted in chapter 2 that suggest that in this disjunction lies the hint of real historical problems between Hellenists and Hebrews, further evidenced by Luke's attempt to subordinate the seven Hellenists to the twelve apostles. For Johnson, the story must rather be understood in light of its function in the larger narrative, and this means interpreting it symbolically. At the very least, this shift in focus eliminates the problem of the lack of consistency, as it is not Luke's concern to portray the seven and their specific duties in the *ekklesia* in entirely consistent terms.

This particular explanation makes sense insofar as it emphasizes the theme of the transfer of power through appropriate channels. Luke seems concerned to demonstrate not only the adequate response of the *ekklesia* to a critical community situation but also to provide an account of the origin and development of the structures that demonstrates the praiseworthy features of that early community in light of the values and expectations of Luke's readers. If Luke is composing a piece in praise of the early Christian assembly, then his portrayal of the Jerusalem community must be deliberately nuanced and multilayered. He is not simply trying to accomplish one aim with this narrative, but is tying together various plot threads in 6:1–7; more specifically, the following general components of Acts 1–7 resurface in 6:1–7: the careful transfer of authority (particularly from the story of Matthias in 1:12–26), the special role of the Twelve in the Jerusalem *ekklesia* (especially the central role of Peter), the sharing of common property and fellowship (2:42–47; 4:32–37), and the use of discipline (5:1–11). Viewed in the light of the larger themes of the opening chapters of Acts, the Hellenist episode evidences in addition one of the critical functions of ancient historiography: shaping the narrative in light of current values and ideals so as to praise the subject being delineated and to establish a convincing,

---

14. Johnson, *Literary Function*, 213.

plausible, and edifying narrative. In this portrayal of the Jerusalem community, Luke's primary purpose is not to focus on any one detail in particular, but to project an overarching image of the early community of believers. In this portrayal, the development of structures of authority and ministry are important, as they ground the experience of Luke's readers in his narrative of the founding of the Christian movement.[15]

Viewed in this light, the appointment of the seven (6:3, 5) may also be interpreted from the perspective of similar Lukan interests. Just as there is the decision to "appoint" Matthias as the successor to Judas in 1:24 (ἀνάδειξον ὃν ἐξελέξω ἐκ τούτων) so also there is an "appointment" of leaders in the community (καὶ ἐξελέξαντο Στέφανον; 6:5), who are placed in charge of "waiting on tables."[16] One of the important insights of the older redaction-critical method has been the suggestion that Luke is here reading into the narrative the role of deacons in his own day. In a classic article, B. S. Easton wrote, "Acts 6 as it stands at least shows Luke's conception of the function of deacons in his own age: that it was their primary duty to care for the poor."[17] There is much to commend this view, coupled with the insight that Luke makes a consistent effort to distinguish the authority of the apostles from those of the subordinated seven.[18] Some have taken these insights further,

---

15. Luke's use of baptism and breaking of bread in the early chapters of Acts provides a good example of this phenomenon. These two early Christian rites appear out of nowhere among the practices of the newly formed community in Jerusalem. In fact, unlike in Matthew (28:19; assuming this to be a likely reference to water baptism), in Luke-Acts baptism by water is not directly associated with Jesus (the "baptism" Jesus refers to in Acts 1:5 is "Spirit baptism"). It should be noted that Luke simply assumes the existence of the practice of baptism in Acts as if it were always present in the community. We can presume, then, that the portrayal of the early church baptizing new converts such as we find in 2:38, 41 would have seemed natural to Luke's readers. An explanation is necessary neither for its presence (although there is some reflection on John's baptism in relation to Jesus' Spirit-baptism; cf. 1:5; 10:37; 11:16; 13:24; 18:25; 19:3, 4; see F. Avemarie, *Die Tauferzählungen der Apostelgeschichte: Theologie und Geschichte* [WUNT 139; Tübingen: Mohr Siebeck, 2001], 196–213, who attempts to trace the pre-Lukan elements) nor for the explicit connection between being "filled with the Spirit" and water baptism proper (although the Lukan pattern of Jesus' own baptism by John in Luke 3:21–22 appears to be a model).

Similarly, the breaking of bread (2:46; cf. 2:42; 20:7, 11; 27:35) in the narrative presumably represents a practice well known to Luke's readers. Luke does not offer a direct explanation for this practice in the early church (unlike Paul; cf. 1 Cor 11:23–26), but simply presents the rite as if it had always been present in the community. Thus, with two important early Christian rites, the early church simply begins with the practice of the Christian cultic features that had become established by Luke's day. There is no sense of development or a need for a rationale. Rather, there is only implicit legitimation of these practices through their being grounded in the story of the earliest community. See further L. Hartman, *"Into the Name of the Lord Jesus": Baptism in the Early Church* (Edinburgh: T & T Clark, 1997), 127–28; and J. Bihler, *Die Stephanusgeschichte im Zusammenhang der Apostelgeschichte* (MTS 1.16; Munich: Hueber, 1963), 200–201.

16. The correspondences between the two appointment narratives in Acts are numerous (Bihler, *Stephanusgeschichte*, 192–94).

17. B. S. Easton, "The Purpose of Acts," in *Early Christianity: The Purpose of Acts and Other Papers* (ed. F. C. Grant; Greenwich, Conn.: Seabury, 1954), 79.

18. Bihler, *Stephanusgeschichte*, 195–216.

suggesting a close relationship between the Pastoral Epistles and Luke.[19] Clearly the apostolic act of the laying on of hands (6:6) resonates with the commissioning practice mentioned in the Pastorals (cf. 1 Tim 4:14; 5:22; 2 Tim 1:6). Yet beyond the actual act of commissioning, there is nothing in the narrative to suggest that Luke is here providing the reader with an intentional account of the origin of the office of deacon.[20] The fact that even in the Pastorals *diakonos* does not seem to be a technical term should also give one pause in seeing here the Lukan etiology of a church office.[21]

There does, however, seem to be a way in which the seven serve a critical function in Luke's conception of the *ekklesia*. It is noteworthy that throughout Acts, the centrality of the apostles/Jerusalem leadership is of primary importance.[22] While some scholars have suggested that Acts lacks a concept of apostolic succession,[23] a seemingly important succession in the narrative is that of the Holy Spirit manifested in signs and wonders, empowering the *ekklesia* and moving it forward (esp. 1:5, 8; 2:4; 4:8; 8:15-17; 10:44-46; 13:2-4, 9; 15:8, 28; 19:1-6), thus also establishing a bridge between the Lukan gospel and Acts. The apostles are clearly central in all of this, forming the core component of the original group that receives the baptism of the Holy Spirit in Acts 2:1-4. As Luke's historical narrative progresses from this point, not only does the geography move outward in concentric circles but so does the transfer of power.[24] The commissioning of the seven for service (ἐπέθηκαν αὐτοῖς τὰς χεῖρας; 6:6), for instance, is followed by the commissioning of Paul and Barnabas by the community of Antioch in 13:1-3 (καὶ ἐπιθέντες τὰς χεῖρας αὐτοῖς). Luke is thus linking certain events together, demonstrating the transfer of the Spirit in the act of commissioning that ultimately stems from the twelve apostles in Jerusalem. All the major characters in Acts who have the function of missionizing or church ministry are affirmed/confirmed in this manner. Indeed, we see that as soon as the ministry of the apostles is about to fade into the background, the Hellenists are commissioned for service, occupying the central stage in Acts 6-8. A break right in the middle of Acts interjects the critical issue of the conversion of the Gentiles (chs. 10-11), which segues then to the narrative entrance of the missionary to the Gentiles, that is, Paul (chs. 13-14). In this conjunction, Luke is careful to correlate the creation of the *ekklesia* at Antioch with the Jerusalem community. In a small aside (11:19-21) Luke mentions that the

---

19. See S. G. Wilson, *Luke and the Pastoral Epistles* (London: SPCK, 1979), 53-68.
20. See S. G. Wilson, *The Gentiles and the Gentile Mission in Luke-Acts* (SNTSMS 23; Cambridge: Cambridge University Press, 1973), 130.
21. Wilson, *Luke and the Pastoral Epistles*, 56.
22. C. C. Hill, *Hellenists and Hebrews: Reappraising Division within the Earliest Church* (Minneapolis: Fortress, 1992), 28; and J. T. Squires, "The Function of Acts 8.4-12.25," *NTS* 44 (1998): 616.
23. Wilson, *Luke and the Pastoral Epistles*, 62-63.
24. S. E. Porter, *The Paul of Acts: Essays in Literary Criticism, Rhetoric, and Theology* (WUNT 115; Tübingen: Mohr Siebeck, 1999), 172-73.

Antiochian community was founded "by those scattered because of the persecution that took place over Stephen" (11:19). Luke is cautious to connect here the founding of the community at Antioch with the leaders in Jerusalem, and this association is then confirmed with the coming of Barnabas to inspect the situation (11:22).

Admittedly, as in 8:4, we are not given the full details in 11:19 regarding "those who were scattered." Scholars have often noted the rather artificial nature of the scattering in 8:1–2, where all but the apostles have to flee for their lives. It seems quite possible that Luke has simply created a plot device whereby the gospel can move outward from Jerusalem to the "ends of the earth."[25] While this may be the case, we should note that Luke is overtly concentrating on the links back to Jerusalem in 11:19. With the Antiochian *ekklesia* thus brought under the auspices of the Jerusalem community, the commissioning of Paul and Barnabas in 13:1–3 demonstrates further the way in which the power of the Spirit brings these two new figures into line with the original power manifested in Acts 2. Moreover, the function of the oddly placed chapter 12 (relating Peter's imprisonment and the death of James) focuses the narrative back on the Jerusalem *ekklesia* immediately following the founding of the community at Antioch. Chapter 15 dovetails the first missionary journey of Paul and Barnabas with Jerusalem concerns once more before the longer unit of Acts 16–21 focuses on Paul's missionary journeys. At the conclusion of Acts, Luke once again brings the Jerusalem *ekklesia* back into the picture (22:16–26). While the mediatory function of this intercalation of Pauline and Jerusalem narratives has long been noted,[26] more essential for the current analysis is the clear evidence that Luke is bringing together the threads of the discrete narrative events. In this context, the account in Acts 6:1–6 plays a central role. It provides the initial link in the transfer of authority from the apostles to other significant narrative figures. As those scattered at the death of Stephen move outward, so does this locus of power. Thus, the founding of the *ekklesia* in Antioch is undertaken by people from Jerusalem, and this community, in turn, similarly commissions Paul and Barnabas for ministry. Therefore, while it is true to say that Luke demonstrates no sense of apostolic succession, there is the succession of apostolic power and authority emanating outward from Jerusalem through the power of the Spirit. In fact, it might not be too far a stretch to suggest that for Luke the Spirit becomes the means whereby the historian can link together the events being narrated.

In one sense, then, these seven men appointed by the community and commissioned by the apostles do form a bridge between Jerusalem and Paul; they

---

25. See Hill, *Hellenists and Hebrews*, 32–39; and Wilson, *Gentiles and the Gentile Mission*, 142–43.

26. See A. J. Mattill, "The Purpose of Acts: Schneckenburger Reconsidered," in *Apostolic History and the Gospel: Biblical and Historical Essays Presented to F. F. Bruce on His 60th Birthday* (ed. W. W. Gasque and R. P. Martin; Grand Rapids: Eerdmans, 1970), 111–12.

are the first in the movement of power outward from the early community's center. The interconnection of the various mission activities of the *ekklesia* in Acts is of critical importance for the image Luke seeks to project: the existence from the beginning of an authoritative community presence, bolstered by supernatural powers, ensuring the purity of the faith as it spreads throughout the empire.[27] Indeed, even the strange event in Ephesus with Apollos (19:1–7) demonstrates the power of unification present in the laying on of hands (19:6). As the *ekklesia* progresses toward Rome, then, it also continually has its authoritative structures reaffirmed. Thus, the Hellenist narrative in 6:1–6 forms a critical component in the movement of the gospel and in the initiation and affirmation of the narrative structures Luke is creating. Moreover, once one perceives the multiform way in which Luke is using this unit, one is no longer puzzled by what has generally been treated in past scholarship as a problematic disjunction in the account: Although the Hellenists are appointed for taking care of the widows in 6:1, the next unit details instead their preaching prowess.

Scholarship has frequently fixated on the detail that the Hellenists are commissioned for "ministry of the table" so as to relieve the apostles of that duty, freeing the latter up for the "ministry of the word." The two activities are deliberately contrasted in the narrative. Yet the fact that the Hellenists also participate in the "ministry of the word" has led many, as we saw earlier, to speculate that Luke has attempted to subordinate an originally independent group to the twelve apostles. In one sense this observation is true. There is no evidence to suggest, however, that one is herein dealing with an originally independent group in Jerusalem. Rather, the narrative functions to demonstrate the superiority of the Jerusalem community's response to problems developing internally. Johnson aptly sums up the problem and the particular solution:

> [T]here seems to be no connection at all between the purported role of the Seven and their actual role. They were supposed to be placed over the possessions, but they actually are ministers of the Word. Not only that, there seems to be only the most tenuous connection between the account of their placement over the community possessions and the account of their actual ministry. The discrepancy disappears when we are aware that Luke uses authority over possessions as a symbol of spiritual authority.[28]

Thus, the problem of the widows and the community response is intended to affirm and to legitimate the Hellenist ministry in the proceeding narratives. In one sense, this argument is similar to the point I have been

---

27. See further T. Penner, "*Res Gestae Divi Christi*: Miracles, Early Christian Heroes, and the Discourse of Power in Acts," in *The Role of Miracle Discourse in the Argumentation of the New Testament* (ed. D. F. Watson; SBLSymS; Atlanta: Society of Biblical Literature, forthcoming).

28. Johnson, *Literary Function*, 213.

arguing here, except that the actual problem and even the community itself seemingly becomes less important (from Luke's perspective) than the seven narrative characters themselves.

The alleged discrepancy and disjunction in the narrative role of the seven is thus essentially a modern creation. We observe an apparent inconsistency and therefore are led to postulate an alternative story that lies behind the present narrative. This underlying account then comes to stand for the event as it "really happened," while the Lukan narrative represents an attempt to "hide the truth" (i.e., it becomes necessary to explain why it is that Luke seems to reflect a different version of the other and presumably more original story). Yet it is unlikely that from a historiographical standpoint one can really approach the narrative in this manner. To address the problem of 6:1, the community selects a group of men who will take responsibility for the dilemma. After establishing the narrative fact that the seven are appointed for this task, Luke goes on to have both Stephen and then Philip preach. Does this mean the widows suffered as a result? If Luke's intention is to focus on the plight of the widows throughout Acts, perhaps this would be a legitimate question. As with all his minor characters, however, as soon as he has the opportunity he abandons them to move on to other praiseworthy features of the early Christian movement.[29] From Luke's perspective the problem has been solved and the new characters take on a life of their own, with the widows having (we are to assume) no further need and Luke showing no further interest in them. For Luke, the Jerusalem community is defined by its response to crisis/need. At each stage of development outward, not only does one observe the emphasis on commissioning and the central role of Jerusalem and the Spirit, but also each respective stage brings with it a response to the community's need. The early Jerusalem *ekklesia* under the Twelve in fact is preemptive of a possible crisis: The community of goods ensures that there "were no needy people among them" (4:34; cf. 2:45). The major challenge to the Jerusalem community under the Twelve comes when certain characters undermine the practice, such as in the case of Ananias and Sapphira. When the Hellenists come on the scene, however, they are part of the Jerusalem community's response to the situation of need among the widows. Similarly, the community at Antioch, the next major step forward in the expansion of the Christian movement, begins with the description of its response to famine in Judea (11:27–30). In this way Luke continually characterizes the *ekklesia* as a brotherhood of believers seeking to help those in need. The community thus becomes defined by its actions toward its poor.

---

29. Even focusing on the possible negative response of the apostles to the situation of 6:1, as Spencer ("Neglected Widows," 730) does, seems to read against the grain of the Lukan text. By Lukan standards, the apostles have not responded improperly to the situation of the widows by refusing to abandon their "ministry of the word" for the care of the poor. Luke views this as a praiseworthy effort of community administration, despite how it may look to our modern perspective.

As Cicero observes, "[I]f one defends a man who is poor but honest and upright, all the lowly who are not dishonest... look upon such an advocate as a tower of defense raised up for them" (*Off.* 2.70; cf. 1.185).

Taken as a whole, 6:1–7 reveals something about Luke's understanding of the newly established Christian community *(ekklesia)*, namely, its fundamental *ethos* constructed in Christian narrative. The primary function of this account is to depict the community as a whole coming together in order to address a need either among its own people or in the city of Jerusalem as a whole. Luke's aim, as with the other scenes in Acts, is to portray the assembly of believers as superior in every respect, but the idealizing tendency so frequently discussed does not entail the absence of conflict or problems in the *ekklesia*.[30] Indeed, problems and their resolution are significant features of any *politeia* or civic body (δῆμος).[31] As we saw in the third chapter, one of the key elements of traditional Greek historiography is the modeling of various types of situations one might encounter in the *polis*, combined with a variety of responses to them. In this way, *historia* could be viewed as being of benefit and profit for future readers. In the epideictic mode of historiography the emphasis might shift to specific types of responses that were known to be appropriate and ideal for certain described situations. If one follows this model — that Luke is narrating the founding of a Christian *dēmos* or *politeia* — then the issue of distribution and civic conflict (στάσις) forms an essential component of the portayal.

D. L. Balch has demonstrated that in Dionysius's history one critical feature is the historian's attempt to mediate the Roman strife between rich and poor through an emphasis on concord.[32] Balch concludes by summarizing

---

30. Thompson, for example, is surprised that Luke undermines his own idealizing attempts with the narratives of Acts 5 and 6 ("Believers and Religious Leaders," 334–37).

31. Some scholars, such as S. C. Winter, have argued that Luke is anti-democratic and therefore deliberately refrains from presenting the adherents to the new faith as forming their own δῆμος. Luke, in this view, does not emphasize this feature because of his post-Jewish uprising (and Roman) context, which persuades him to adopt the position that Judean democracy/love for freedom leads to "mob rule" (see S. C. Winter, "Παρρησία in Acts," in *Friendship, Flattery, and Frankness of Speech: Studies on Friendship in the New Testament World* [ed. J. T. Fitzgerald; NovTSup 82; Leiden; Brill, 1996], 201–2). Certain features of Acts, however, particularly the Jerusalem assembly in chapter 15, would seem to speak against this view. Indeed, there appears to be a distinct comparison between the Jewish δῆμος and the δῆμος of the newly founded community as contrasting types, one which leads to mob rule and the other which leads to order (largely assured by the centrality of Jerusalem and the apostles). On *dēmotikos* as a virtue in the imperial period, see A. Wallace-Hadrill, "*Civilis Princeps:* Between Citizen and King," *JRS* 72 (1982): 44.

32. D. L. Balch, "Rich and Poor, Proud and Humble in Luke-Acts," in *The Social World of the First Christians: Essays in Honor of Wayne Meeks* (ed. L. M. White and O. L. Yarbrough; Minneapolis: Fortress, 1995), 221–26; and idem, "ΜΕΤΑΒΟΛΗ ΠΟΛΙΤΕΙΩΝ. Jesus as Founder of the Church in Luke-Acts: Form and Function," in *Contextualizing Acts: Lukan Narrative and Greco-Roman Discourse* (ed. T. Penner and C. Vander Stichele; SBLSymS 20; Atlanta: Society of Biblical Literature, 2003), 159–60. For Josephus's treatment of the *stasis topos* in *Ant.* 4 (i.e., Zambrias's challenge to Moses' leadership), see Balch, ΜΕΤΑΒΟΛΗ ΠΟΛΙΤΕΙΩΝ, 146–47. For a more detailed assessment of Josephus's general use of the *topos*, as well as

Dionysius's perspective as follows: "One of the major themes of Greco-Roman historiography, as exemplified by Dionysius, is that this tension does not lead to chaos; rather the Roman rich listen to speeches of the poor and work out an accommodation, so that there is *koinōnia* and concord" (cf. Dionysius, *Ant. rom.* 1.8.2; 7.65.3, 5).[33] Thus, the proper response to the civil strife that arises in the conflict between rich and poor includes the rich making concessions to the poor in order to maintain harmony and fellowship in the Roman city. If such represents the ideal response to *stasis* in the ancient world, then it would seem Luke has modeled the best form of behavior in his presentation of the community.[34]

Using Hebrew Bible patterns that deal with the appointment of overseers in the early stages of community formation, Luke deliberately casts the Jerusalem community as a type of civic body or *politeia*, responding to *stasis* in the community (cf. 6:1). The following citation from Diodorus Siculus is instructive in this respect:

> Since a great spirit of contention now threatened the state, the most respectable citizens, foreseeing the greatness of the danger, acted as ambassadors between both parties to reach an agreement and begged them with great earnestness to cease from the civil discord (τῆς στάσεως) and not plunge the fatherland into such serious distress. In the end all were won over and a mutual agreement was reached as follows: that ten tribunes should be elected. (12.25.1–2)

Acts 6:1–6 follows this pattern closely: Discord in the community leads to the settlement of the dispute through the election of certain individuals. This civic conflict arises because of the neglect of the widows, similar to the "murmuring" that necessitates the Mosaic response in the Hebrew Bible parallels noted earlier. The response is to appoint a group to oversee this distribution, thereby ensuring resolution of the problem and resultant community *koinōnia* and concord. The summary statement in 6:7 confirms that in fact the response by the community results in continuing growth. The immediate apostolic reaction in 6:2 demonstrates that they listened to the group in question. It is this ideal civic response that Luke holds up before the reader, demonstrating in narrative form the praiseworthy nature

---

his reliance on Thucydides' pattern, see G. Mader, *Josephus and the Politics of Historiography: Apologetic and Impression Management in the* Bellum Judaicum (MnSup 205; Leiden: Brill, 2000), 55–103. On the theme of concord/harmony in Josephus, see C. Gerber, *Ein Bild des Judentums für Nichtjuden von Flavius Josephus: Untersuchungen zu seiner Schrift* Contra Apionem (AGJU 40; Leiden: Brill, 1997), 360–66.

33. Balch, "Rich and Poor," 232. See also E. Plümacher, "The Mission Speeches in Acts and Dionysius of Halicarnassus," in *Jesus and the Heritage of Israel: Luke's Narrative Claim upon Israel's Legacy* (ed. D. P. Moessner; Harrisburg, Pa.: Trinity Press International, 1999), 263–66.

34. For this theme in ancient literature, see A. Fuks, *Social Conflict in Ancient Greece* (ed. M. Stern and M. Amit; Leiden: Brill, 1984), 66–72, 120–22, 136–37, 172–71, 177–79, 186–89.

of this new group in Jerusalem, which models the best of Greek civic and personal virtue.[35] This accentuation coheres nicely with Luke's emphasis on the ethics of the biblical tradition, demonstrating continuity between the Deuteronomic emphasis on care for the widows and the Greek stress on maintaining *koinōnia, philanthropia,* and charity.[36]

Finally, in his description of the founding of the *ekklesia* Luke is doing what a historian of antiquity ought to do: He is painting in broad strokes the image of the community he wishes to project, making a narrative argument for the manifestation of the best Greek and Roman virtues in this new and emerging *politeia*. When scholarship emphasizes the "problem" that immediately after their appointment certain Hellenists are seen preaching rather than ministering to the widows, the point is missed. After demonstrating the assembly's adequate response to the situation of crisis, Luke's need for the widows and the situation immediately disappears; they are a narrative foil to aid in the construction of the *ethos* of the new community. The narrative moves on rather to contrast the opposition that the new group — the Hellenists — meets in their own communities, just like the Jerusalem apostles have met in the temple establishment. Moreover, one must also be cautious about the attempt by some, such as Hill, to focus on the historical reliability of the events described.[37] The narrative's primary (and perhaps sole) function is to demonstrate the praiseworthy response of the community to a crisis

---

35. One might also observe here the importance of distributions in the *polis*. G. M. Rogers's study of the foundation myths of Ephesus demonstrates the civic necessity of monetary distributions in terms of maintaining and solidifying civic hierarchy in the city. Thus, depending on rank and station, people would receive various amounts of distribution from the funds provided by civic donors (*The Sacred Identity of Ephesos: Foundation Myths of a Roman City* [New York: Routledge, 1991], esp. 39–41, 66–72). This particular connection is enhanced when one stresses, as does R. I. Pervo, that equity in food proportionment at civic distributions and *symposia* is a critical theme with respect to friendship and the obligations of the wealthy toward the poor ("*Panta Koina*: The Feeding Stories in the Light of Economic Data and Social Practice," in *Religious Propaganda and Missionary Competition in the New Testament World: Essays Honoring Dieter Georgi* [ed. L. Bormann, K. Del Tredicii, and A. Standhartinger; NovTSup 74; Leiden: Brill, 1994], 188–89). There may well be resonances of these themes in Acts 6:1–6, as the community there seeks to establish equity in their own distributions. On distribution to the poor more specifically, see Fuks, *Social Conflict,* 179–81.

36. Balch points out that Luke is here not introducing new values to the Greco-Roman world, but redefining and reaffirming well-established ones for his audience ("Rich and Poor," 232–33). Readers should also take note of the emphasis on friendship. As Cicero describes, "[O]f all the bonds of fellowship, there is none more noble, none more powerful than when good men of congenial character are joined in intimate friendship" (*Off.* 1.55). Indeed, in Acts, as in Cicero, friendship is based on mutual attraction on the basis of virtues, the highest of which are justice and generosity (*Off.* 1.56), which finally produces love. See further A. C. Mitchell, "'Greet the Friends by Name': New Testament Evidence for the Greco-Roman *Topos* on Friendship," in *Greco-Roman Perspectives on Friendship* (ed. J. T. Fitzgerald; SBLRBS 34; Atlanta: Scholars Press, 1997), esp. 236–57; idem, "The Social Function of Friendship in Acts 2:44–47 and 4:32–37," *JBL* 111 (1992): 255–72; and T. Penner, "Civilizing Discourse: Acts, Declamation, and the Rhetoric of the *Polis,*" in *Contextualizing Acts* (ed. Penner and Vander Stichele), esp. 89–98.

37. Hill, *Hellenists and Hebrews,* 25–26.

situation. As we saw earlier, Luke uses widows to represent symbolically the proper response of the people of the prophet Jesus to the poor and the outcast, and the whole situation has been contoured in terms of civic strife. Further, the narrative itself has been modeled on Hebrew Bible parallels. While this does not mean that the events have no basis in historical reality,[38] there are serious difficulties in attempting to reconstruct any type of original situation; the primary stress on the functionality of the narrative obscures, if not prevents, any reasonable assessment of its historicity. One may attempt to intuit the likelihood of the event having happened based, for instance, on Jewish precedents in Jerusalem,[39] but in the final analysis the persuasive quality of this narrative rests in its plausibility not its actuality. It must resonate with historical realia in order for the narrative to achieve its intended function, making it quite difficult to establish the historical reliability of the events described.

Progressive Openness to Foreigners

Based on the scholarship discussed in the first two chapters, one objection to the line of interpretation developed so far may well be that the mere mention of the Hellenists — viewed as Greek-speaking Jews — "clearly" points to an underlying historical reality. One might argue that, given this datum, there is ample justification for the modern historian to reconstruct the original situation of the Hellenists in Jerusalem. As we have seen, this move usually develops into a full-fledged assessment of the reason why the Hellenist widows were excluded, which frequently comes down to differences of theology, culture, or society, setting these Hellenists in opposition to other more conservative Jews (insiders to the newly formed community and/or outsiders). The entire trajectory of this interpretation, however, is premised on one significant assumption: The Hellenists in 6:1 could not have been a Lukan invention or a reflection of authorial interest. Indeed, most scholars

---

38. Hill affirms this point (ibid., 25), although at the same time he argues that this does not mean the event is necessarily unhistorical. Similarly Daube, "Reform in Acts," 159.

39. See further S. S. Bartchy, "Community of Goods in Acts: Idealization or Social Reality?" in *The Future of Early Christianity: Essays in Honor of Helmut Koester* (ed. B. A. Pearson; Minneapolis: Fortress, 1991), 315–18; B. Capper, "The Palestinian Cultural Context of Earliest Christian Community of Goods," in *The Book of Acts in Its Palestinian Setting* (ed R. Bauckham; BAFCS 4; Grand Rapids: Eerdmans, 1995), esp. 350–55; A. Lindemann, "The Beginnings of Christian Life in Jerusalem according to the Summaries in the Acts of the Apostles (Acts 2:42–47; 4:32–37; 5:12–16)," in *Common Life in the Early Church: Essays Honoring Graydon F. Snyder* (ed. J. V. Hills et al.; Harrisburg, Pa.: Trinity Press International, 1998), 202–18; J. Taylor, "The Community of Goods among the First Christians and among the Essenes," in *Historical Perspectives: From the Hasmoneans to Bar Kokhba in Light of the Dead Sea Scrolls. Proceedings of the Fourth International Symposium of the Orion Center for the Study of the Dead Sea Scrolls and Associated Literature, 27–31 January 1999* (ed. D. Goodblatt, A. Pinnick, and D. R. Schwartz; STDJ 37; Leiden: Brill, 2000), 147–61; and G. Theissen, "Urchristlicher Liebeskommunismus: Zum 'Sitz im Leben' des Topos ἅπαντα κοινά," in *Texts and Contexts: Biblical Texts and Their Textual and Situational Contexts: Essays in Honor of Lars Hartman* (ed. T. Fornberg and D. Hellholm; Oslo: Scandinavian University Press, 1995), 689–712.

have generally argued that Luke has toned down the roles of these figures, who were allegedly more dynamic and charismatic in the original tradition.

Since scholars have been so preoccupied with assessing the historical elements that lay beneath and behind Lukan redaction, little work has been done to establish the relationship of the Hellenists to the larger framework of Acts. Some critics have noted that in Lukan *historia* the separation between the newly formed community and the Jewish leaders and institutions takes place in terms of successive development.[40] The impetus for the movement has usually been articulated in this way: The Jerusalem community is depicted by Luke as being opposed to the inclusion of Gentiles, but it happens in any case under the divine will and plan of God, given impetus by further Jewish opposition to and rejection of the prophet and his people.[41] This developmental view seems correct on one level, but it is also oversimplified in many respects. A closer examination of Luke's narrative in Acts demonstrates a more careful and nuanced scheme for the expansion of the newly created people and the role the Hellenists within this broader framework.

Acts 2:5–12 performs a critical function for Luke's larger narrative framework. At the very moment that the new people of the prophet are formed under the power of the Spirit, the known world is present *in nuce* to perceive God at work.[42] From the outset only Jews are in view (2:5). Thus, the Jewish people from around the world ("every nation"; 2:5), gathered in Jerusalem, become witnesses to the reconstitution of God's people in the Spirit, a clear eschatological event from Luke's perspective.[43] Luke has carefully

---

40. G. Theissen, *The Religion of the Earliest Churches: Creating a Symbolic World* (trans. J. Bowden; Minneapolis: Fortress, 1999), 181–82, points out the following movement: the announcement of the extension of Israel in the infancy narratives, Jesus' preaching ministry and ultimate rejection by the Jerusalem establishment, the post-Easter apostolic ministry in Jerusalem, the renewing of the people through the Spirit, and, finally, the mission to the Gentiles that results from Jewish rejection (cf. Acts 13:46–47; 18:5–6; 28:27–28).

41. On the rejection theme, see Johnson, *Literary Function*, 76; and idem, *The Acts of the Apostles* (SP 5; Collegeville, Minn.: Liturgical Press, 1992), 136–38.

42. D. R. Edwards, *Religion and Power: Pagans, Jews, and Christians in the Greek East* (New York: Oxford University Press, 1996), 88, argues that the regions mentioned represent the principal directions. Others, such as J. M. Scott, have suggested that the groups mentioned in 2:9–11 are grounded in the biblical Table of Nations tradition ("Luke's Geographical Horizon," in *The Book of Acts in Its Graeco-Roman Setting* [ed. D. W. J. Gill and C. Gempf; BAFCS 2; Grand Rapids: Eerdmans, 1994], esp. 527–30). Scott goes on to suggest (530–41) that the structure of Acts can be understood as the progression of the gospel from Shem (2:1–8:25), to Ham (8:26–40), to Japheth (9:1–28:31). On the imperial aspirations reflected in this geographic emphasis and its connections to Roman imperial propaganda, see G. Gilbert, "The List of Nations in Acts 2: Roman Propaganda and the Lukan Response," *JBL* 121 (2002): 497–529; and idem, "Roman Propaganda and Christian Identity in the Worldview of Luke-Acts," in *Contextualizing Acts* (ed. Penner and Vander Stichele), 233–56.

43. Cf. the citation of Joel 2:28–32 in Acts 2:17–21, which provides the midrashic interpretation of the narrative event in Acts 2:1–13 (see further C. A. Evans, "The Prophetic Setting of the Pentecost Sermon," *ZNW* 74 [1983]: 148–50).

constructed this unit to ensure that world Jewry is represented, including the mention that there were Jews from Judea present on the occasion as well. Some scholars have viewed this latter detail as an odd addition to the account, given that Luke is here delineating the presence of Diaspora Jewry in Jerusalem.[44] Luke, however, states that there were Jews "from every nation under heaven" living in Jerusalem at the time of the events in Acts 2. Naturally, then, this group would also include Judean Jews. It would thus seem that Luke is concerned not to present just Diaspora Jews but all Jews as witnesses to this miraculous event.

The rest of Acts must be understood within this framework. Luke takes great pains as a historian to demonstrate the constant interrelationship of the new community with its broader Jewish context. This feature is a consistent aspect of Luke's narration. Not only do the apostolic or other community leaders sanction each successive stage of the progression of the message, but also, and more importantly, at every stage Jews are both positively and negatively involved. Thus, the Antiochian *ekklesia* is founded by Jews from Jerusalem (11:19–21) and is validated in like manner (11:22). The Lukan Paul, moreover, is consistently portrayed as merging the worlds of Diaspora and Palestinian Judaism: He was born in Tarsus (9:11; 21:39; 22:3) but was thoroughly conservative in his attitudes toward the law (21:24), having studied in Jerusalem under Gamaliel (22:3). Luke deliberately juxtaposes these two Pauline locations—Tarsus and Jerusalem—to demonstrate that Paul embodies the meeting place of Diaspora and Palestinian Jew.[45] In connection with this emphasis, it is critical to Luke's overall framework not only that the Gentile mission results from Jewish rejection, but even more so that there is Jewish rejection at each successive stage in Paul's ministry to the Gentiles (9:29; 13:5, 14–47; 14:1–7, 19–20; 16:1–3; 17:1–9, 10–14, 17; 18:4–8, 12–17, 19, 26–28; 19:8–10, 33; 20:3, 18–21). In 21:27, with Paul back in Jerusalem, the "Jews from Asia" are the first to seize Paul and initiate what will become a long process of opposition to Paul in that city. Of course, the theme of Jewish rejection forms only one aspect of the Lukan scenario, since at almost every step of the way Jews also convert to and support the new movement (13:43; 14:1; 17:4, 11–12; 18:8, 19–21; 19:10–18; 28:17–24). Thus, the adherents of the newly formed community established by Jesus divide Israel (i.e., those Jews living in Jerusalem and in the Diaspora) much like Jesus the prophet did in the Lukan gospel. No doubt part of this complex interweaving of rejection and acceptance lies in Luke's characterization of Christian missionaries (especially Paul): They

---

44. Hence the attempt by some ancient and modern commentators to change Ἰουδαίαν to some other non-Judean country (see B. M. Metzger, "Ancient Astrological Geography and Acts 2:9–11," in *Apostolic History* [ed. Gasque and Martin], 133).

45. See further J. C. Lentz, *Luke's Portrait of Paul* (SNTSMS 77; Cambridge: Cambridge University Press, 1993), 23–61.

are not responsible for the reaction of the Jews toward them (i.e., they are innocent).⁴⁶

And reaction there is. The end of Acts is saturated with references to Jewish opposition to Paul (21:11, 20, 27, 30; 23:12, 20–21, 27; 24:5–9, 19–20; 25:2–3, 7–10, 15; 26:2–7, 21; 28:17–19), providing insight into the larger framework of Acts. While some scholars have argued that the evidence suggests a Lukan attempt to portray the gradual institutional separation of Jewish leaders and the newly formed *ekklesia*, with the emphasis on rejection by Jews becoming increasingly prominent,⁴⁷ L. C. A. Alexander is likely correct in her assertion that Luke seems most concerned in the closing chapters, as well as earlier, to deal with Jewish issues for a Jewish audience.⁴⁸ Leaving aside the precise historical and cultural context for the moment, it appears that Luke shows great interest in demonstrating Jewish interconnections with the nascent Christian movement at every step of the latter's development. Moreover, Diaspora Jews perform a critical role right from the beginning, as Acts 2:5–11 demonstrates. It thus comes as no surprise that Diaspora Jews are the ones to accuse Paul in the temple of Jerusalem (Jews from Asia in 21:27; cf. 6:9). Lastly, Acts concludes with Paul in dialogue with Diaspora Jews in Rome (28:17). This focus is a critical theme for Luke, and it is my contention that the Hellenists fit into this larger picture.

When the Hellenists appear on the scene in 6:1, the reader is in some sense prepped for the entrance right from the beginning of the book. In 2:36 Peter addresses the audience of 2:5–11 by the title "all the house of Israel." When in 2:37–42 one reads that many repent, are baptized, and join the Jerusalem community, one is led to believe that the group of 2:9–11 is in view here, only a portion of which is from Judea. Thus, it is implied from the start that there are Jews from the Diaspora in the newly formed community. If one takes "Hellenist" in the sense in which I argued for in chapter 2 — that is, "Greek-speakers" — then in 6:1 certain of these individuals "complain...against the Hebrews." Luke from the very beginning wants the reader to understand that the Jerusalem community consists of Palestinian and non-Palestinian Jews. Indeed, one of the first problems in the *ekklesia* arises between/among the groups. It is difficult to determine if Luke intends Ἑλληνιστής to represent the entire range of people in 2:9–11 (which

---

46. This observation comes close to the classic Roman apologetic argument that the Christian movement is not a threat and is not guilty of possible outsider accusations against the movement (see R. Maddox, *The Purpose of Luke-Acts* [ed. J. Riches; Edinburgh: T & T Clark, 1982], 93–96). L. C. A. Alexander, "The Acts of the Apostles as an Apologetic Text," in *Apologetics in the Roman Empire: Pagans, Jews, and Christians* (ed. M. Edwards et al.; New York: Oxford University Press, 1999), 34–38, raises some challenges to this classic argument, based largely on the narrative ineffectiveness of this approach in Luke's hands. In the end the theme may have more to do with characterization and epideictic elaboration of *topoi* than apologetic concerns in the classic sense (i.e., defense of the early Christian movement).

47. Maddox, *Purpose of Luke-Acts*, 42–46, 93.

48. Alexander, "Acts of the Apostles," 43.

means that Parthian Jews are being lumped together with Egyptian and Cappadocian Jews as Greek-speakers) or whether this is the Greek-speaking group that is affected as one alongside several other distinct language groups in the community. Given that Luke will later accentuate the role of Jews of the Asian Diaspora in the Pauline mission (i.e., explicit differentiation occurs subsequently in the narrative) and that Greek was the lingua franca of Luke's world, it is possible that Luke is here lumping all Diaspora Jews mentioned in 2:9–11 under the rubric of "Hellenists."

Although scholarship at this point has frequently sought out the reason for the division between the two groups, Luke in fact does make it evident why there is a problem: The Greek-speaking widows are being neglected (6:1). To seek a fuller or different underlying historical basis is to miss Luke's more fundamental point: The community consisted of Palestinian and Diaspora Jews at its initial stages, and this situation itself has resulted in conflict. There is a direct line of development from Jesus to the apostles and followers of Jesus to the reconstituted community in Jerusalem containing Jews from around the world. Luke intends to illustrate two features: (1) the *ekklesia* of Jesus the Messiah reconstitutes Israel in its eschatological sense (the ingathering of the people from dispersion);[49] and (2) this newly established community begins with embracing a diversity of Jews from around the world, and will soon expand, rather rapidly, to include Gentiles based on the same symmetric pattern: to the Jews first and then to the Gentiles (Acts 26:23; cf. Rom 1:16). This latter point is important, since aside from the so-called eschatological motivation, the combination of Palestinian Jews with Diaspora Jews provides the paradigm for the way in which the community will grow, gradually moving in concentric circles until Gentiles are included alongside Jews. It is therefore tempting to read the Hebrew/Hellenist grouping in Acts 6:1 as the prototype for the community's Jew/Gentile composition that results from the Jerusalem conference in Acts 15. If this is the case, then the Hellenists — or Diaspora Jews more generally — form the Lukan *literary* connection between the mission of the Twelve in Jerusalem and the mission of Paul to the Gentiles.

Along these lines, the list of the seven names in 6:5 helps further the narrative argument. These names are obviously Greek-sounding, and although

---

49. Joel 2:28–32 (cited in Acts 2:17–21) is immediately followed by the expectation of Israel's ingathering in Joel 3:1–3: "Then, in those days and at that time, when I restore the fortunes of Judah and Jerusalem, I will gather all the nations and bring them down to the valley of Jehoshaphat, and I will enter into judgment with them there." This passage deals with both the ingathering of the dispersed Jews and the gathering of the Gentiles for judgment. Despite the latter emphasis on judgment and punishment, given Joel's prominence at the beginning of Acts it may not be a stretch to suggest that this larger context could have provided the scriptural basis for Luke's narrative logic: Jews gathered first, followed by the Gentiles/nations (for salvation, however, not judgment). On the ingathering motif, see further *Pss. Sol.* 8:28; 11:2–6; 17:26–28; Bar 4:4–5:9; and Tob 14:4b–7, as well as M. Palmer Bonz, *The Past as Legacy: Luke-Acts and Ancient Epic* (Minneapolis: Fortress, 2000), 106, 124–25.

Luke does not state that these seven came from the Hellenists, it is likely that he intends for the reader to infer that they did. Thus, the seven Diaspora Jews are appointed to "wait on tables" presumably for the whole community. More important at present is the last name provided in the list: "Nicolaus, a proselyte from Antioch." It is significant that Nicolaus's religious status vis-à-vis Judaism and his locale are given in the list. The Jerusalem community now contains an explicit connection to the *ekklesia* soon to be formed at Antioch. From Luke's account it seems that the Antiochian community is deliberately portrayed as a crucial stage in the development of the Christian movement in Acts and, from what we can glean from Galatians (2:11–14), it seems to have been an important center in early Christian history as well. For Luke, then, already in the earliest community in Jerusalem there is an Antiochian presence. But far more essential is that Nicolaus is a proselyte. For Luke, this means that in the reconstituted Israel there are not only Palestinian and Diaspora Jews but also proselytes, advancing the narrative argument that "all Israel" is present at the formative moment of the *ekklesia*.[50] Already in Acts 2:5 Luke notes that Jews and proselytes were present to hear Peter's sermon, and so one is to conclude that some of the latter converted at that time as well (2:37–42). Moreover, having a proselyte in the *ekklesia* offers a primary point of origin for the gradual inclusion of the Gentiles, moving from synagogues (with proselytes) to God-fearers (quasi-proselytes) to those fully Gentile (with no prior Jewish association). We should remember, however, that these features connect well with Luke's literary-historical framework that he has cast for the well-ordered and well-plotted narrative and do not necessarily reflect the underlying historical realities that existed in the early community.

Already in 6:5 a hint of what is to come is provided in the narrative: The reconstituted Israel in Jerusalem will expand even further, incorporating every Lukan category of religious adherent. For this reason, the oft-noted feature of the Lukan Pauline mission—that Paul goes first to Jews and then to God-fearers[51]—is fundamental to Luke's larger historiographical argument. Helpful in this connection is A. T. Kraabel's extensive work suggesting that Luke has used the category of "God-fearer" associated with the synagogue as a construct to promote a particular image of the growth of the

---

50. This growth and mixing also brings priests into the community in 6:7, demonstrating that progressive inclusion also brings with it diversification in social function and status from the larger community in Jerusalem.

51. In Acts it is probably best not to view "God-fearer" as a technical category. It is frequently understood this way in modern scholarship, but the occurrences of "fearing God" in Acts seem to connote a more general disposition toward the deity (cf. esp. 10:2, 22, 35). In all cases, "fearing God" is coupled with a qualifying characteristic such as "piety," "righteous," or "doing righteous works." The use of σέβομαι is equally problematic as a technical term. Nothing in the text suggests that the characterization of someone as a "devout person" or "worshipper of God" is in any way a technical designation (cf. 13:43, 50; 16:14; 17:4, 17; 18:17). M. Wilcox, "The 'God-fearers' in Acts: A Reconsideration," *JSNT* 13 (1981): 102–22, argues that the language may in fact not even refer to Gentiles at all.

ekklesia.[52] Kraabel's specific conclusions, however, are more problematic: "Luke uses the God-fearers as a device to show how Christianity had legitimately become a gentile religion, without losing its roots in the traditions of Israel. The Jewish mission to the gentiles represented by the Godfearers [*sic*] was intended to be ample precedent for Christianity's far more extensive mission to the gentiles."[53] There probably is a sense in which Luke here is legitimating the inclusion of Gentiles in the new community, but Kraabel's articulation assumes that Luke is a Gentile writing to Gentiles and this position is less convincing.[54] Rather, Luke seems to use the "God-fearers" as he does the proselytes and the Diaspora Jews: as a means for gradually expanding the *ekklesia* in an interconnected manner, grafting each successive addition into the former. Beginning with Judaism at the center, the new people move outward, gradually embracing more and more of the Greco-Roman world. Ultimately, then, Luke appears less interested to justify the mission to the Gentiles (after all, the narratives of Acts 10–11, 15 already provide sufficient theological justification) and more concerned to demonstrate in a plausible way the manner in which the community established by Jesus incorporates ever increasing diversity in this new δῆμος or *politeia*.

The reader is left, then, with the possibility that the movement toward Gentile inclusion in the "full people of Israel" is to be read as a praiseworthy feature of Luke's historical presentation precisely because of the emphasis on full participation rather than exclusion at the time of origin. Balch's work on ancient political historiography is useful in this respect. On the basis of his study of Dionysius of Halicarnassus, Balch argues that there are two important values reflected in Dionysius's political history of Rome: "1) valid customs and laws must be ancient, and 2) one of these ancient Roman customs is the reception of foreign nations into the body politic."[55] Balch proceeds to demonstrate the differing viewpoints on these themes in ancient Rome, showing how in his history Dionysius grafts the openness to foreigners and outsiders into the very foundation of the Roman

---

52. A. T. Kraabel labels this phenomenon a "theological" and "literary" construct. It might be better to consider it historiographical in nature (helping unite the diverse threads of narrated events). See his "The Disappearance of the God-fearers," in *Diaspora Jews and Judaism* (ed. J. A. Overman and R. S. MacLennan; SFSHJ 41; Atlanta: Scholars Press, 1992), 119–30; and idem, "*Synagoga Caeca*: Distortion in Gentile Interpretations of Evidence for Judaism in the Early Christian Period," in *Diaspora Jews* (ed. Overman and MacLennan), esp. 41–46.

53. Kraabel, "Disappearance of the God-fearers," 140.

54. Some scholarship is challenging the traditional designation of Luke as a Gentile writing for a predominantly Gentile audience. Alexander's recent study provides some support for the view that Luke wrote for a Diaspora Jewish audience ("Acts of the Apostles," 43). G. E. Sterling has argued that Luke was himself a Diaspora Jew ("'Opening the Scriptures': The Legitimization of the Jewish Diaspora and the Early Christian Mission," in *Jesus and the Heritage* [ed. Moessner], 217). See also the recent comments by J. Jervell, who, in line with his past work, suggests that Luke was a Jewish Christian steeped in the Jewish tradition (*Die Apostelgeschichte* [KEKNT 3; 17th ed.; Göttingen: Vandenhoeck & Ruprecht, 1998], 50–51).

55. D. L. Balch, "Comments on the Genre and a Political Theme of Luke-Acts: A Preliminary Comparison of Two Hellenistic Historians," *SBLSP* 28 (1989): 354.

constitution.⁵⁶ Luke's narrative could be viewed in the same light, at once demonstrating that the *ekklesia* is not violating the ancient customs of the Jews (and Romans)⁵⁷ and that the intermixing of peoples in this movement represents the hallmark of the openness of this new people toward outsiders.⁵⁸ The importance of this Roman value for Luke is evidenced by the fact that the entire narrative of Acts demonstrates the increasing intermixing of *ethnoi* as the story progresses. Moreover, that Luke, as I suggested earlier, places emphasis on the intermixing of Palestinian and Diaspora Jews (including also proselytes) at the moment of the inception of the community commends the view that this scheme provides a paradigm for the increasing mixing of all peoples in the nascent Christian movement. Indeed, in the ongoing Lukan comparison of the newly founded community with the Jewish establishment, one of the features that sets the Jerusalem believers apart from their Jewish compatriots is that they are more open to outsiders than the latter. From the beginning the community is mixed, with the eschatological restoration theme thus being transformed into a historiographical principle in Lukan composition. Luke does not view this mixing as a recent religious innovation and departure from the Jewish heritage, but something that was inherent in the tradition "received" in the Christian movement (as the citation of Amos 9:11–12 in Acts 15:15–17 establishes). At the same time, Luke is cautious to demonstrate the gradual nature of the mixing and also its providential impetus by God (as the story of Peter in Acts 10 affirms). Furthermore, Luke maintains, as the Romans also did, that each group that intermixes is expected to live according to its own laws and

---

56. Ibid., 354–60. Also see his discussion of 2 Maccabees and other Hellenistic Jewish writers in light of this same theme; Balch, "ἀκριβῶς... γράψαι [Luke 1:3]: To Write the Full History of God's Receiving All Nations," in *Jesus and the Heritage* (ed. Moessner), 229–50.

57. If customs were changed or challenged, it was God who initiated this shift (i.e., the apologetic of divine providence; see further J. T. Squires, *The Plan of God in Luke-Acts* [SNTSMS 76; Cambridge: Cambridge University Press, 1993], 60–61; and Balch, "ΜΕΤΑΒΟΛΗ ΠΟΛΙΤΕΙΩΝ," 182–83).

58. See Balch, "Comments on the Genre," 360–61, as well as V. K. Robbins, "Luke-Acts: A Mixed Population Seeks a Home in the Roman Empire," in *Images of Empire* (ed. L. C. A. Alexander; JSOTSup 122; Sheffield: JSOT Press, 1991), 218–19. In this connection, alongside the Deuteronomic emphasis on not oppressing the widow, there is also similar stress on the alien in that tradition (Deut 24:17–21; 27:19; cf. Lev 19:10, 33–34; 23:22). For a similar argument in Josephus's *Contra Apionem*, see M. Goodman, "Josephus' Treatise *Against Apion*," in *Apologetics in the Roman Empire* (ed. Edwards et al.), 54–55. See also the more detailed treatment of *philanthropia* in Josephus by Gerber, *Bild des Judentums*, 367–79; and in Philo and Josephus by K. Berthelot, *Philanthrôpia judaica: Le débat autour de la "misanthropie" des lois juives dans l'Antiquité* (JSJSup 76; Leiden: Brill, 2003), esp. 265–87 (Philo), 324–49 (Josephus). On the Lukan parallels with Roman rather than Greek social emphases with respect to the theme of inclusion, see the fine study by D. L. Balch, "The Cultural Origin of 'Receiving All Nations' in Luke-Acts: Alexander the Great or Roman Social Policy," in *Early Christianity and Classical Culture: Comparative Studies in Honor of Abraham J. Malherbe* (ed. J. T. Fitzgerald, T. H. Olbricht, and L. M. White; NovTSup 110; Leiden: Brill, 2003), 483–500. See also Balch, "ΜΕΤΑΒΟΛΗ ΠΟΛΙΤΕΙΩΝ," 167–70, where he details how mixing brings about growth.

customs.⁵⁹ Consequently, there is intermixing but with the maintenance of traditional identities.

For Luke, then, the Hellenists represent a stage in the intermixing of diverse peoples in the newly founded community, which itself relates to the *philia* and *philanthropia* of the new movement. Just as the community's response to the problem of the widows attests to the virtue of the newly formed *politeia*, so also the Hellenists represent the first stage in a progressive argument that the intermixing of peoples in the earliest stages of the Christian movement is also, finally, a demonstration of this community's "love of humanity."⁶⁰ The first book of Dionysius's history offers an instructive parallel, demonstrating the type of framework out of which Luke may have been operating:

> Hence, from now on let the reader forever renounce the views of those who make Rome a retreat of barbarians, fugitives and vagabonds, and let him confidently affirm it to be a Greek city, — which will be easy when he shows that it is at once the most hospitable and friendly of all cities (μὲν κοινοτάτην τε πόλεων καὶ φιλανθρωποτάτην), and when he bears in mind that the Aborigines were Oenotrians, and these in turn Arcadians... and, last of all, those who left the Troad... were intermixed with the earlier settlers. For one will find no nation that is more ancient or more Greek than these. But the admixtures of the barbarians with the Romans, by which the city forgot many of its ancient institutions, happened at a later time. And it may well seem a cause of wonder to many who reflect on the natural course of events that Rome did not become entirely barbarized after receiving the Opicans, the Marsians, the Samnites, the Tyrrhenians, the Bruttians... and Gauls, besides innumerable other nations, some of whom came from Italy itself and some from other regions and differed from one another both in their language and habits; for their very ways of life, diverse as they were and thrown into turmoil by such dissonance, might have been expected to cause many innovations in the ancient order of the city. (*Ant. rom.* 1.89.1–3)

In this summary of his main argument in the first book, Dionysius argues that the foundation of the city of Rome was Greek, and that Greek values and customs remained constant throughout its history. Moreover, even when barbarians were allowed to settle in Rome, there was preservation of the fundamental Greek values and customs, although he does admit that there was some barbarization of culture and language (although not as much as most other cultures that had been absorbed by the barbarians; 1.89.4). Indeed, Dionysius goes on to state that in reality it was only the language of Rome that suffered (i.e., it is not pure Greek), and that "all other indications

---

59. See further S. G. Wilson, *Luke and the Law* (SNTSMS 50; Cambridge: Cambridge University Press, 1983), 103–6. On the Roman context, see D. L. Balch, "'...you teach all the Jews...to forsake Moses, telling them not to...observe the customs' (Acts 21:21; cf. 6:14)," *SBLSP* 32 (1993): 374.

60. A point demonstrated by Balch, "'...you teach all the Jews,'" 379–81. See also Penner, "Civilizing Discourse," 91–92.

of a Greek origin they preserve beyond any other colonists" (1.90.1). Dionysius's pattern is strikingly similar to Luke's: Greeks first — all types of Greeks (i.e., in their totality) — followed by the addition of non-Greeks/barbarians, which has little serious effect on the Greek values instituted at the founding of the movement. Moreover, a sign of this constancy amid mixing is that Rome represents *koinōnia* and *philanthropia,* and its openness to all Greeks as well as barbarians demonstrates these two central Greco-Roman virtues. As argued here, Luke follows the same pattern: Jews first — all Jews (i.e., in their totality) — followed by Gentiles ("barbarians" from the Jewish perspective). It is this nature of the newly founded *politeia* that Luke highlights as praiseworthy, epitomized in the movement's *koinōnia* and *philanthropia.* Thus, Luke's articulation of these themes in the narrative represents his epideictic elaboration of historiographical *topoi* in order not only to praise the characters and community responsible for the origins of the *ekklesia* but also to argue for its superiority over its narrative counterpart embodied in the Jewish leaders and adversaries in Jerusalem, who oppose this mixing and growing community at every step, while failing to exhibit the virtues themselves (as the impending Stephen narrative and speech make clear).

To reiterate in conclusion, traditionally there are two aspects scholarship has insisted are critical for any "true" understanding of Acts 6:1–8:3: the widows and the Hellenists.[61] As Haenchen argues, "Luke's attempt to reduce

---

61. The actual listing of the names of the seven men elected in 6:5, often viewed as the bedrock tradition of 6:1–7, is left out of the above discussion. No matter where one comes down on the historicity of the names mentioned in 6:5, that assessment makes little difference for the argument developed here.

From the literary-historical perspective developed in this chapter, however, one should bear in mind the following: (1) It is a near axiom of oral traditional studies that while historical names are persistent in the tradition, the characterization and details associated with those names could evidence a significant degree of elasticity (see further C. M. Thomas, *The Acts of Peter, Gospel Literature, and the Ancient Novel: Rewriting the Past* [New York: Oxford University Press, 2003], 40–71, who emphasizes this same phenomenon in written texts, particularly with respect to secondary characters). (2) The number seven is a traditional referent in Jewish and early Christian tradition. For people, see Matt 22:25, 26, 28; Acts 19:14; Tob 3:8, 15; 6:14; 7:11; 2 Macc 7:1 (and the frequent references in 4 Maccabees to the "seven brothers/sons"); for inanimate or inhuman subjects, see Matt 12:45; 15:34, 36, 37; 16:10; 18:22; Mark 16:9; Luke 2:36; Acts 13:19; 20:6; 21:4, 27; 28:14; Rev 1:4, 11, 12, 16, 20; 4:5; 5:1, 6; 10:3; 12:3; 15:1, 7; 17:9, 11; Tob 12:15; 1 Macc 13:28; Sir 37:14; Zech 3:9; 4:2, 10. The Hebrew Bible is replete with the number; there are nearly fifty references in Genesis alone. (3) The designation "seven" is also the traditional unit for the Jewish "local board" overseeing community matters. The "seven men of the city"/"seven outstanding men of the city" thus becomes a traditional means of designating a group in authority or in charge (so *Str-B* 2:641). Compare the references to the "seven wise men" in Diodorus 9.1.2; 9.3.3; 9.7.1; 9.28.1; 10.10.1; also see Plutarch's *Dinner of the Seven Wise Men,* or the story of the "seven Persians" who revolted against the Magus in Herodotus 3.70–3.84. The tradition of "seven wise men" is ancient and pervasive (see further, R. P. Martin, "The Seven Sages as Performers of Wisdom," in *Cultural Poetics in Archaic Greece: Cult, Performance, Politics* [ed. C. Dougherty and L. Kurke; New York: Oxford University Press, 1998], 108–28). (4) There is a parallel in 20:4 to the seven of 6:3 and (cf. 21:8). Here, at the end of Acts, Paul is depicted as being in the company of seven men: Sopater (cf. Sosipater, Rom 16:21), Aristarchus (Acts 19:29; 27:2; Col 4:10; Phlm 1:24), Secundus, Gaius (Acts 19:29; Rom 16:23; 1 Cor. 1:14), Timothy (Acts 16:1; 17:14; 18:5; Rom

the tension between 'Hellenists' and 'Hebrews' to the minimal issue of the widows has not succeeded."[62] In other words, according to Haenchen, the widow problem is viewed as the Lukan cover-up of the real issues involved in the strife between the Hellenists and the Hebrews, but Luke has not been successful in his attempt to "hide" the real problem, as the historically astute modern scholar knows better. As I argued above, however, Luke may not have hidden anything from the reader's purview, as both the widows and the Hellenists perform a critical role at the level of historical narrative composition. In his portrayal of the formation and development of the Christian movement, Luke is composing a piece in praise of its founding. This Lukan configuration is not so much an attempt to idealize the early history of the movement and hence tone down real, historical conflict. Rather, Luke wants to demonstrate two things. First, by combining Hebrew Bible ethical mandates (particularly Deuteronomic) with the virtues of the Greco-Roman *dēmos*, Luke depicts the Jerusalem community as modeling the best of both traditions. The leaders of the emergent *politeia* in Jerusalem display the necessary response to a situation of civic strife, resulting in a *koinōnia* and concord dependent on the *philanthropia* exhibited by the main characters. If anything, this feature is the Lukan *Tendenz* rather than, as often thought, the avoidance of conflict. In one sense, Luke maintains not only continuity with the Hebrew and Greek traditions on this point but also presents a community that fulfills those ideals even better than the Greeks and Jews do, as the unfolding narrative shows.[63]

Second, as part of this framework demonstrating the community's *philanthropia*, Luke uses the Hellenists as a core component of a larger narrative argument detailing the increasing openness of this newly formed *politeia* to non-Jews. Read in this way, the Hellenists form a narrative bridge between the early Jerusalem community and the imminent influx of Gentile adherents to the new faith. Luke uses the Hellenists both to illustrate the continuity with Jewish custom and law and to demonstrate that openness to outsiders (here represented by Greek-speaking Diaspora Jews) forms one component of the former. The Hellenists, together with Palestinian Jews and proselytes, make up all Israel united in the new people of the prophet Jesus. Luke, however, seems less interested in the eschatological ingathering motif (although this is present in a rudimentary form) and more concerned to

---

16:21; 1 Cor 16:10; 2 Cor 1:1; Phil 1:1; Col 1:1; 1 Thess 1:1; 2 Thess 1:1; Phlm 1), Tychius (Eph 6:21; Col 4:7; 2 Tim 4:12; Titus 3:12), and Trophimus (Acts 21:29; 2 Tim 4:20), all of whom, with the exception of Secundus, are traveling companions of Paul known from his letters. Therefore, just as the Jerusalem apostles have their seven, so Paul also has his. Further, while the seven in Acts 6 close off the Jerusalem unit, the seven in Acts 20 open up Paul's Jerusalem narrative.

62. E. Haenchen, *The Acts of the Apostles: A Commentary* (trans. R. Mcl. Wilson et al.; Philadelphia: Westminster, 1971), 103.

63. In terms of the theme of rich and poor, Dionysius also sets out to demonstrate that the Romans are better Greeks than the Greeks themselves were (see Balch, "Rich and Poor," 221).

use this already mixed group as the pattern and justification for the further intermixing of the nations in God's new people,[64] an emphasis contoured in light of the themes of concord in the community and continuity with the past. The Hellenists, when analyzed with Acts 6:1–7 viewed in isolation from the larger Lukan narrative, do then seem like an oddity. When they are perceived within the wider context, however, their pivotal role is more readily apparent. Luke seem interested in neither the widows nor the Hellenists as ends in themselves. Rather, he wants to demonstrate through these narrative characters the praiseworthy *ethos* of the *ekklesia*. Indeed, this community, when contrasted with the reactions of the Jewish establishment (and ultimately the Greeks and Romans themselves), is proven to be superior in every respect. The guiding principle of *philanthropia* in Acts 6:1–7 finds continual reinforcement throughout Acts, but in its immediate context receives even greater emphasis by being contrasted with the *misanthropia* of the narrative opponents in the textual unit that directly follows (6:8–15 and 7:54–8:1).

Breakdown of Fellow-Feeling: *Misanthropia* and Opposition (6:8–15; 7:54–8:3)

The two textual units of 6:8–15 and 7:54–8:3 provide a significant clue to the larger purpose of Acts 6:1–8:3 in Lukan composition, establishing not only the context for Stephen's speech but also furnishing a continuation of the narrative argument situated in 6:1–7. As I argued in chapter 2, scholars have speculated that Luke has combined two accounts of Stephen's untimely demise: an orderly trial before a Jewish court and a mob-instigated lynching. Scholars have repeatedly emphasized the inconsistent and fragmented character of this text (esp. 6:8–15), suggesting that Luke not only wove together several accounts but went even further by inserting a speech (whether connected to the original Hellenists or representing a type of Hellenistic Jewish sermon) into the narrative context. The theory that the speech was a later insertion explains for many scholars why it is that Stephen does not appear to answer the charges brought against him in the narrative.

The argument I develop here is that past scholarship has misread the Lukan use of the Stephen narrative and speech. Following the analysis of 6:1–7, where one witnesses the culminating acts involved in the formation

---

64. In several signal essays, J. Jervell has emphasized Luke's deliberate portrayal of a mixed community ("The History of Early Christianity and the Acts of the Apostles," in *The Unknown Paul* [Minneapolis: Augsburg, 1984], 21–22; and idem, "The Church of Jews and Godfearers," in *Luke-Acts and the Jewish People: Eight Critical Perspectives* [ed. J. B. Tyson; Minneapolis: Augsburg, 1988], 11–20). While it is true that for Jervell this entails the depiction of law-observant and more liberal-minded Jews (i.e., as interpreted in the Baur tradition), the accent nevertheless is placed on diversity in the community as a model for the reader of Luke-Acts. Jervell, however, tends to view this as the real, historical core of early Christian history ("This is not so much a part of Luke's concept but is inherent in the material which he treats in a faithful manner" ["History of Early Christianity," 21]).

of the *ekklesia* in Jerusalem, it is now the function of 6:8–15 and 7:54–8:3 to articulate the conflict between this emerging community and the Jewish *politeia* embodied in its leaders. Luke's work is a form of epideictic historiography: His goal is to write in praise of Christian origins. At the same time, as we have seen in previous chapters, an important part of both epideictic elaboration and historiography proper is the use of *synkrisis*, the comparison of two similar entities, which in some cases can be used to demonstrate the superiority of one class in contrast to a like subject. In the process, in order to achieve adulation one frequently will also ascribe its opposite — that is, blame — to the narrative foil. Thus, epideictic composition tends toward polarization. It is not surprising, then, that in the Stephen narrative and speech epideictic themes predominate, while explicit and extensive polarization is created between Stephen (as representative of the *ekklesia*) and the Jewish establishment. Understandably this polarization has also caused discomfort among contemporary scholars and theologians.

Luke consciously and consistently characterizes Stephen as the praiseworthy figure in the narrative. When we first encounter Stephen in 6:5, we already know that he is an individual "full of faith and the Holy Spirit," which deepens the praiseworthy features already generalized for the entire group in 6:3 ("of approved character," "full of the Spirit," "full of wisdom"; cf. 6:10). As Stephen comes into his own in 6:8, we are alerted, again, that he is "full of grace and power," "doing great wonders and signs." The latter part of the description is a fundamental element of Lukan characterization. The proof of God's blessing on this new movement is the fact that the main characters perform divinely empowered acts ("wonders and signs"; 2:43; 4:30; 5:12; 14:3; 15:12; cf. 8:6, 13). That this emphasis places the main characters (the Jerusalem apostles, Stephen, Philip, and Paul) in line with the Mosaic paradigm is evident from Stephen's speech, in which Stephen describes Moses as similarly performing "wonders and signs" (7:36; cf. Exod 10:1; 11:9, 10; Deut 6:22; 7:19; 11:3; 28:46; 29:2; Ps 77:43 LXX; Ps 134:9 LXX; Jer 39:20 LXX). This correlation is significant, since the signs and wonders of Moses in Egypt are an important feature of the biblical characterization of this divinely appointed leader, substantiating that God is working in and through him.[65] While it might be tempting to interpret this narrative in light of a classic judicial sense of apologetic, and while such elements may not be entirely absent, it is more likely that these images of the main characters are more broadly intended to elevate their status based on the biblical comparison.[66] The parallels between the formation of the exodus

---

65. The mention of Stephen's wisdom and the reference to the Spirit draws further associations with Moses (cf. Acts 7:10, 22; Exod 28:3; Num 11:17, 25; Deut 34:9).

66. In order for epideictic composition to be effective it must reflect the shared value system of the hearer/reader (cf. Quintilian, *Inst.* 3.7.23), not attempt (in its primary sense) to persuade one to adopt that value system (= deliberative). One can make a case that Luke's entire argument in terms of the characterization of the narrative figures is predicated on the assumption that

community under Moses and Acts 6:1–7 noted above reinforce this comparison, as the Jerusalem community and its leaders perform analogous words and deeds to their earlier biblical counterparts. The parallels with Moses, furthermore, are significant for epideictic composition since they provide an established and well-known exemplar as the basis of positive comparison for Stephen. Thus, Stephen is both contrasted with his opponents and compared to Moses.[67] Since there would be broad affirmation of Moses as the ideal exemplar, it follows that not only is Stephen viewed as praiseworthy as a result of his associations with Moses (including the nature of his imminent demise, flowing, as it does, out of the rejection of Moses by the people in the speech and leading to the narrative rejection of the "prophet like Moses" by Stephen's opponents), but this correspondence also becomes a narrative affirmation that Stephen could not have violated the laws and customs of Moses (6:11, 13–14). In this way the explicit epideictic themes give way to implicit judicial ones.

The major feature of *synkrisis* in the narrative, however, is clearly the comparison of Stephen with the character of his adversaries, which is blatantly obvious from the way in which the narratives of 6:8–15 and 7:54–60 are juxtaposed yet also interwoven.[68] One should take note of several

---

Jewish and Gentile readers would share Luke's cultural *topoi* (e.g., God is at work in those who evidence signs and wonders). This feature explains, in part, why Luke is careful to control the presentation and thereby to circumscribe the power of Simon the Magician in 8:9–25 and Bar-Jesus/Elymas in 13:6–12 (cf. 16:16–24; 19:11–20).

67. While not a major part of the treatment here, one should note that alongside the Moses parallels one finds extensive correspondences between Stephen and Jesus, which would heighten the characterization of Stephen in this narrative for the reader of Acts. See D. P. Moessner, "'The Christ Must Suffer': New Light on the Jesus-Peter, Stephen, Paul Parallels in Luke-Acts," in *The Composition of Luke's Gospel* (ed. D. E. Orton; Leiden: Brill, 1999), 117–53; and idem, *Lord of the Banquet*, 54–55, 300–307.

68. As with the seven individuals in the earlier narrative, I leave to one side the historical issues related to the synagogues of Stephen's adversaries. The problem with the discussion of the possibility of the existence of Jerusalem synagogues in the early first century is the same that one encounters with reference to the presence of God-fearers: There is much at stake both historically (in terms of the reliability of Acts) and theologically (in terms of how one conceives of Second Temple Judaism and its relationship with Christianity) in this debate. Our knowledge is obviously limited, but the evidence for pre-70 C.E. synagogues in Jerusalem is ambiguous at best (but cf. K. Atkinson, "On Further Defining the First-Century CE Synagogue: Fact or Fiction?" *NTS* 43 [1997]: 491–502, who, arguing that Qumran and other Palestinian sites preserve pre-70 C.E. buildings for worship, infers the same for Jerusalem), and almost all positions come down to the dating of the famous Theodotus inscription. While some maintain that the evidence for a date prior to 70 C.E. is clear (R. Riesner, "Synagogues in Jerusalem," in *Book of Acts in Its Palestinian Setting*, 192–200), H. C. Kee is probably correct to state that the date is impossible to determine with any certainty ("Defining the First-Century C.E. Synagogue: Problems and Progress," in *Evolution of the Synagogue: Problems and Progress* [ed. H. C. Kee and L. H. Cohick; Harrisburg, Pa.: Trinity Press International, 1999], 7–10). Further, while some have attempted to identify the synagogue of the Theodotus inscription with the synagogue of 6:9 (Riesner, "Synagogues in Jerusalem," 204–6), it seems more likely that the Theodotus synagogue was used by local Jerusalem Jews, having the ability to house visitors to Jerusalem if the need should arise (P. Richardson, "Early Synagogues as Collegia in the Diaspora and Palestine," in *Voluntary Associations in the Graeco-Roman World* [ed. J. S.

features in this regard. First, the two scenes, although separated by the speech, are linked through the adverbial expression "full of" (6:8, "full of grace and power"; 7:55, "full of the Holy Spirit"; cf. 6:3, 5). Luke thus adeptly weaves together the narrative of Stephen and his conflict with both the previous narrative of the appointment of the Hellenists (6:3, 5) and the subsequent narrative of his martyrdom (7:55). Second, one should note that Luke has paralleled the various actions of Stephen and his opponents so as to highlight the respective quality of character of each (see the table on the following page).

The moral contrast between Stephen and his opponents is obvious. Stephen is superior to his adversaries, and, if one reads here an argument from the respective *ethoi* of the characters, good character produces good works (a death modeled on the death of Jesus in Luke; cf. esp. Acts 7:59/Luke 23:46 and Acts 7:60/Luke 23:34),[69] and the appalling acts of the opponents likewise attest to their bad moral character. There can be little debate that (at the very least) the leaders are being portrayed in highly negative terms.

We can also see that there is a reversal of speaking characters from 6:8–15 to 7:54–60. In the first part, Stephen does not speak directly, but his opponents do (6:11, 13). In the concluding narrative, Stephen does speak

---

Kloppenborg and S. G. Wilson; New York: Routledge, 1996], 99). This point attests to one of the fundamental problems in this discussion: Scholars are reading assumptions regarding the historical value of 6:9 into the articulation of the issues themselves. Thus, Riesner readily affirms that the synagogue of the Theodotus inscription is for Hellenistic Jews, despite no clear evidence to support this assertion. If the reliability of 6:9 is in question, it cannot, of course, be used for support in the argument over whether synagogues existed in pre-70 C.E. Jerusalem.

Moreover, the debate is further complicated since the meaning of "synagogue" (συναγωγή) is contested as well. There is some evidence to suggest that it does not refer to a building in 6:9 or most places in Acts, but merely to an "assembly" (R. A. Horsley, "Synagogues in Galilee and the Gospels," in *Evolution of the Synagogue* [ed. Kee and Cohick], 53). Scholars who argue that Luke must have had knowledge of particular synagogues given the specificity of detail in the reference (e.g., D. D. Binder, *Into the Temple Courts: The Place of the Synagogues in the Second Temple Period* [SBLDS 169; Atlanta: Society of Biblical Literature, 1999], 158) miss the point of plausible narration in ancient composition: The reader is supposed to assume exactly that the writer did not invent the details.

Although the reliability of the information provided is impossible to prove one way or the other, the following considerations deserve further reflection. First, the reference in 2:9–11 provides Luke with characters who not only reappear in 6:5, but who also serve as a basis for the adversaries in 6:9. As argued earlier, Luke brings various groups into conflict with their like kind, and so it is not surprising that the (Jewish) Greeks of 6:5 find their initial opposition from Hellenistic synagogues. This connection is part of Luke's architectonic style of composition. The listing of the places of origin for the Jews in 2:9–11 provides Luke with the locales upon which to base the references to the Cyrenians, Alexandrians, and Asia in 6:9. Second, the reference in 6:9 refers to two large regions: Asia Minor (Asia and Cilicia) and North Africa (Cyrene and Alexandria). From archaeological evidence, the most predominant evidence for pre-70 C.E. synagogues comes from Egypt and the Mediterranean Diaspora (Richardson, "Early Synagogues," 90, 97, 99). It is thus possible that Luke transposed the information from his own period into his depiction of the early Christian movement.

69. In favor of this text's originality to the Lukan gospel, see D. Crump, *Jesus the Intercessor: Prayer and Christology in Luke-Acts* (Grand Rapids: Baker, 1999), 79–85.

Stephen	*Opponents*
Stephen "full of grace and power" (6:8)	Opponents stand up and argue with Stephen (6:9)
Stephen is eloquent and persuasive, "speaking with wisdom and the Spirit" (6:10)	Opponents cannot withstand Stephen's eloquence and persuasive power (6:10)
Stephen passive	Opponents instigate men to accuse Stephen (6:11)
Stephen passive	Opponents stir up the people and seize Stephen (6:13)
Stephen passive	Opponents set forth "false witnesses" (6:13–14)
Stephen's face shines like an angel's (6:15)	Council looks intently (6:15)
Stephen "filled with Holy Spirit," gazes into heavens and sees "glory of God and Jesus standing at the right hand of God" (7:55)	Council becomes enraged (7:54)
Stephen announces the vision (7:56)	Council is further enraged (7:57)
Stephen cries out to God and asks for the pardon of his adversaries (7:60a)	Council drags Stephen out to stone him (7:58)
Stephen dies (7:60b)	Saul, who is present, approves of Stephen's killing (8:1)

directly, while his opponents do not (7:56, 59–60). Thus, Stephen has the final word, so to speak. And his words, as we would expect from historical narration, are made consonant with his character elucidated in 6:8–15. Not only is he forgiving toward those who are killing him (manifesting the prized virtue of *clementia*),[70] but the vision of Jesus in the midst of the mob lynching confirms that Stephen is indeed one chosen by God. Much has been

---

70. On the significance of *clementia*, see A. Wallace-Hadrill, "The Emperor and His Virtues," *Historia* 30 (1981): 302; and H. F. North, "Canons and Hierarchies of the Cardinal Virtues in Greek and Latin Literature," in *The Classical Tradition: Literary and Historical Studies in Honor of Harry Caplan* (ed. L. Wallach; Ithaca: Cornell University Press, 1966), 178. Cf. the following comments by Diodorus: "[T]he spirits of civilized men are gripped...most perhaps by mercy, because of the sympathy which nature has planted in us" (13.24.2).

made of this visionary scene in modern scholarship,[71] but at the narrative level Luke is clearly using this visionary experience to entrench further the positive characterization of Stephen. The dying wise and spirit-filled individual is thereby revealed to be a prophetic seer in his final moments. In the end, then, the vision is not about Jesus per se, but about the characterization of Stephen as someone who sees visions and whose actions and words are thereby given sanction by the heavenly court, which implicitly proclaims/confirms his innocence. As we saw in the last chapter, epideictic composition is primarily concerned about the good *(kalon)*, which, according to Aristotle *(Rhet.,* 1.9.3–13), covers such virtues as justice, courage, self-control, magnificence, generosity, liberality, gentleness, prudence, and wisdom (cf. Theon 9.20–24). Given this framework, Luke's depiction of Stephen represents an embodiment of the cardinal values that Aristotle outlines as being fundamental to the Greeks, particularly Stephen's piety and wisdom.[72] Wisdom is a predominant feature of Stephen's characterization, while *pietas* is split between the description of Stephen as one "full of the Holy Spirit" and in his being a just and righteous individual. In Stephen's death one perceives both courage (cf. Cicero, *Off.* 1.67) and self-control *(Off.* 1.93–94).[73] Diogenes Laertius provides the following apt summary of the virtues one finds in a narrative such as this: "Of the beautiful there are...four species, namely, what is just, courageous, orderly, and wise; for it is under these forms that fair deeds are accomplished....[T]he beautiful is that which lends new grace to anything, as when we say of the wise man that he alone is good and beautiful" (7.100). Further, Stephen dies on behalf of what is noble and honorable rather than for what is advantageous or pleasant (cf. Theon 9.28–31) and thus receives even greater praise.[74]

Moreover, at the core of this extended narrative lie the charges in Acts 6:11, 13–14. These elements are essential for understanding the larger epideictic

---

71. For a summary of positions, see Crump, *Jesus the Intercessor,* 178–90.

72. On these two classic virtues, see North, "Canons and Hierarchies," 177–78; and Wallace-Hadrill, "Emperor and His Virtues," 302.

73. See further A. Smith, " 'Full of Spirit and Wisdom': Luke's Portrait of Stephen (Acts 6:1–8:1a) as a Man of Self-Mastery," in *Asceticism and the New Testament* (ed. L. E. Vaage and V. L. Wimbush; New York: Routledge, 1999), 97–114; and T. Penner and C. Vander Stichele, "The Tyranny of the Martyr: Violence and Victimisation in Martyrdom Discourse and the Movies of Lars von Trier," in *Sanctified Aggression: Vocabularies of Violence in Bibles and Cultures* (ed. Y. Sherwood and J. Bekkenkamp; New York: T & T Clark, forthcoming). Theon's comments on composing encomia are also informative in this respect: "When detailing his achievements (for example, that he was self-controlled; ὅτι ἦν σώφρων) it is necessary to state and to cite immediately what self-controlled deed he has done; likewise in the case of the other virtues" (9.78–81).

74. For some further connections in this regard, see O. Glombitza, "Zur Charakterisierung des Stephanus in Act 6 und 7," *ZNW* 53 (1962): 238–44. See also D. Mendels's discussion of the civic and cultural contributions of the culture-heroes of Luke's narrative ("Pagan or Jewish? The Presentation of Paul's Mission in the Book of Acts," in *Identity, Religion, and Historiography: Studies in Hellenistic History* [JSPSup 24; Sheffield: Sheffield Academic Press, 1998], 407–11).

framework of this unit, largely because they raise the particular *topoi* that, as we saw in the previous chapter, were prominent for Hellenistic Jewish writers: law and temple. One should begin by observing the pattern of repetition in the charges themselves:

6:11 Charge: blasphemy against Moses (A)   Blasphemy against God (B)

6:13 Charge: speaks against this holy place (A′)   Speaks against the law (B′)

6:14 Elaboration: says Jesus will destroy this place (A′+ B?) and change the customs of Moses (A + B′)

One might well make the argument that these cultural *topoi* form the centerpiece not just of the Stephen narrative and speech but of the whole of Acts. The speech addresses explicitly that aspect of the charge dealing with "God" and "this place," whereas the Stephen narrative and speech in combination deal implicitly with the elements of "law" and "custom" associated with Moses. It is not difficult to perceive what Luke has done: He has brought in *topoi* that will provide and ultimately arbitrate the perception of justice in this presentation. Stephen is falsely charged with breaking the law, but it is the adversaries who are condemned for rushing to judgment against a righteous man (7:51–53). Here we see the way in which the end of Stephen's speech confirms what is about to happen in the subsequent narrative. Unlike Stephen, who is explicitly said to be "filled with the Holy Spirit" (7:55), the accusers oppose the Holy Spirit (7:51), they are about to persecute Stephen, they will kill him as "they" did the prophets and Jesus (7:52); finally, this type of action is amplified in terms of violation (7:53), where it is said that while the people received the law from angels (a good thing), they have not kept it. From this it is clear that by killing Stephen the adversaries are the ones who have broken the law of God. In terms of the narrative *synkrisis* in this text, while Stephen is alleged to have broken the law and blasphemed God, it is Stephen's opponents who are actually portrayed as doing so. They thereby become the mirror image of Stephen in the story, manifesting vice in their unjust killing of a blameless man.

Within this framework, the opponents demonstrate several inappropriate modes of behavior: They lack *civilis* (to respect law and tradition in that they produce false testimony and kill a righteous man)[75] and moderation. With respect to the latter, Cicero's comments on punishment are noteworthy: It should not issue forth out of anger, malice, or be controlled by the passions; otherwise it will result in injustice (*Off.* 1.89). Further, orderly decorum ought to be maintained in all aspects of life (1.142). Excess and disorder

---

75. Wallace-Hadrill, "*Civilis Princeps,*" 42–43.

thus go hand in hand in the Stephen narrative. Just as Stephen fulfills the sequence of cardinal virtues, the opponents similarly achieve the cardinal vices, of which, Diogenes Laertius notes, "there are four species of the base or ugly, namely, what is unjust, cowardly, disorderly and unwise" (7.100). Aside from these features, the contrast of respective behavior between 8:1, 3 and 8:2 is also apparent. While the Jerusalem *ekklesia* demonstrates appropriate acts of *pietas* toward its dead martyr (8:2),[76] the opponents (here including Paul) seek to persecute its adherents (8:1, 3). This characterization represents a development of the theme of excess. Diodorus states that if one wreaks vengeance on the vanquished, one is guilty of an offense against human weakness (13.24.4–5). Diodorus articulates an argument for compassion, leniency, and mercy toward one's foes, virtues completely lacking among Stephen's accusers, who now also turn to murder.[77] One should recall in this context the widespread Greek and Roman affirmation that fair practice and administration of law was a supreme value — indeed, the manifestation of the highest virtue, wisdom (Cicero, *Off.* 1.153–59). Cicero writes that "the citizen... will not expose anyone to hatred or disrepute by groundless charges, but he will surely cleave to justice and honour" (*Off.* 1.86). Diodorus similarly argues that the Athenians' fair-minded application of their just laws to the outsider represented the pinnacle of their *philanthropia* (13.25.2–3). One notices as well that the concept of justice in Exod 23:1–9 is reversed in this portrayal of Stephen's opponents: They spread false reports and join hands with the wicked (Exod 23:1); they follow the majority in injustice in their giving of false testimony and in the perversion of justice (Exod 23:2); and they do not refrain from false charges, but kill the innocent (Exod 23:7; cf. Lev 19:11–17; Deut 16:18–20). Scripture is here used implicitly to characterize the narrative antagonists.

Alongside the accusations, another significant component of Luke's narrative composition is that Stephen does not address the charges outright in his speech. This feature, as we saw in the first two chapters, has resulted in endless speculation. Some scholars have taken this as evidence that Luke has inserted and/or created a speech for Stephen, others that Luke is attempting to cover up the truth of the charges by concealing the real nature of the Hellenist mission (which, contrary to the narrative, did engage in the activities of which Stephen is accused). Further exploration suggests, however, that there may be a simple explanation for why Luke does not have Stephen address the charges directly: To do so would change the speech from an epideictic composition to a judicial one. Theon is helpful at this juncture. In his treatment of encomic composition, Theon states,

---

76. Cf. Josephus's treatment of this theme of piety and law in his *Contra Apionem* (see Gerber, *Bild des Judentums*, 285–99).

77. On the importance of the theme of *clementia* for Josephus's understanding of *philanthropia*, see Berthelot, *Philanthrôpia judaica*, 337–40.

One should either not mention false accusations [διαβολάς] at all (since memory attaches itself to misdeeds [ἁμαρτημάτων]) or as occasion allows mention them imperceptibly and unobtrusively, lest we inadvertently compose a defense [ἀπολογίαν] instead of encomia. For it is proper to give a defense [ἀπολογεῖσθαι] concerning those who are charged with wrongdoing [τῶν ἀδικεῖν αἰτίαν ἐχόντων], whereas it is proper to praise [ἐπαινεῖν] those who excel in some good quality. (9.82–86; cf. 10.27–30)[78]

There is much here that is useful for understanding Luke's narrative. Most importantly, Theon expressly cites the utilization of "false accusation" in encomia. His argument is that if one mentions false charges or dwells on them at length, these indictments will predominate in the hearer's mind ("since memory attaches itself to misdeeds"), thereby undermining the function of a narrative of praise. Bad thoughts rather than good thoughts will be the lasting effect of the composition, even if the charges are in fact false. Thus, if the point of the narrative is to demonstrate a praiseworthy response under duress, then to focus on responding to the charges skews the intended aim (cf. Isocrates, *Hel. enc.* 14–15).

Theon argues that if one must mention the false charges against the main character, one should do so only in passing. In this way, the narrative can implicitly refute the false accusations without drawing undue attention to them. In being preoccupied with the charges, scholars have frequently overlooked as a result the encomiastic features of Luke's composition. Some might argue that for the length of the narrative, Luke's notation in 6:11, 13–14 is already too obtrusive and long. This assessment may be a fair criticism in line with Theon's argument, although one must keep in mind that Luke includes these elements largely to characterize Stephen's opponents as unjust and scurrilous and to provide the themes that are important for his epideictic elaboration. In the final analysis, then, Stephen's alleged failure to respond to the charges is in fact not a failure at all. If Stephen's speech were to address the accusations, the speech and narrative would move from epideictic to more overtly judicial *(apologia)* in focus, as Theon affirms. Thus, the fact that Luke does not include an explicit response strongly suggests that the speech and the larger narrative are being composed on the encomiastic model rather than as apologetic traditionally understood.

It is worth noting in this context that Luke is drawing upon a traditional motif, one which is used throughout Acts and which R. C. Tannehill has identified as a "public accusation" type-scene. Tannehill isolates four episodes in the Pauline narratives that exhibit this form: the narratives set in Philippi (16:19–24), Thessalonica (17:5–9), Corinth (18:12–17), and

---

78. See further T. C. Burgess, "Epideictic Literature," *Studies in Classical Philology* 3 (1902): 118.

Ephesus (19:23–40).⁷⁹ He focuses on the Greek-Christian conflict scenes, but one could also add the three major Jewish conflict scenes as well: the apostles and the Jerusalem council (4:1–22; 5:17–42), Stephen and the Greek opponents/Jerusalem council (6:8–15; 7:54–8:1), and Paul and his various trials in Jerusalem/Caesarea (21:27–23:11; 24:1–21; 25:1–12; 26:1–32, all of which flow out of the original accusation scene in 21:27–31). There is some evidence that the Stephen and Pauline accusation/trial scenes are strategic for Luke's narrative, as is suggested by the striking correspondences between the two accounts (see the table on the following page).

While some of these associations are perhaps stock elements of Luke's vivid narrative style, this outline suggests that at least several of these correspondences are deliberate and are intended to draw the two accusations/trials of Paul and Stephen together. While for all intents and purposes Paul's accusation/trial scene covers a significant portion of the remaining chapters of Acts, the length of it should not cause one to lose sight of Luke's historiographical interest in associating the characters of Stephen and Paul.⁸⁰ Both of these figures, like the Jerusalem apostles, encounter the same forms of opposition that Jesus did.⁸¹ More important, the three major groups represented by the apostles, the Hellenists, and Paul receive attention not only with respect to how they fit into the origins and expansion of the Christian movement but also with respect to the opposition to each from within their corresponding spheres of operation. Noteworthy, in this regard, is that both Stephen and Paul are originally accused by Hellenistic Jews living in Jerusalem, and only subsequently bring down on themselves the wrath of the council/people. Furthermore, the combination of mob violence with orderly court appearances occurs in both instances. Whereas in the Pauline section Luke has given ample space to couple these contrasting venues consistently, in the Stephen account he simply has the council scene turn into a mob lynching.⁸² Lastly, the contrast in the Stephen section between the

---

79. R. C. Tannehill, "Paul outside the Christian Ghetto: Stories of Intercultural Conflict and Cooperation in Acts," in *Text and Logos: The Humanistic Interpretation of the New Testament* (ed. T. W. Jennings; Atlanta: Scholars Press, 1990), esp. 248–55.

80. The association is initiated already in the Stephen narrative, as Luke has Paul present at the stoning, giving his approval (8:1). The fact that Paul will soon undergo a very similar trial of his own demonstrates a reversal in the character of Paul: from accuser at Stephen's death to one who is willing to stand trial on the same accusations and in the same manner (cf. Acts 22:20). On the parallels between Paul and Stephen and their connection to Jesus and Moses, see Moessner, *Lord of the Banquet*, 297–307. Paul's explicit reference to his role in Stephen's death (22:20; cf. 8:1) in his speech before his "brothers and fathers" in 22:1–21 not only serves to characterize Paul's past life (and highlight the transformation he undergoes, which seems to be the essential reason for Luke to have him present in 8:1), but also reminds the reader of Paul's narrative exemplar.

81. The charges are similar as well (Moessner, *Lord of the Banquet*, 299, 301).

82. The so-called problem of the combination of two types of scenes in Acts 6:8–8:3 should not be as troublesome as it is frequently construed, given that a very similar combination occurs in 23:1–10. In the middle of Paul's speech, the council is thrown into an uproar (23:9), including the rise of civic *stasis* (23:10; Πολλῆς δὲ γινομένης στάσεως), and the tribune is afraid

Stephen	*Paul*
Opposed by Hellenistic Jews (some from Asia; 6:9–13)	Opposed by Jews from Asia (21:27)
Opponents stir up the people: συνεκίνησάν τε τὸν λαόν (6:12)	Opponents stir up the people: συνέχεον πάντα τὸν ὄχλον (21:27; cf. 21:30)
Opponents seize Stephen: καὶ ἐπιστάντες συνήρπασαν αὐτόν (6:12); cf. καὶ ἐκβαλόντες (7:58)	Opponents seize Paul: καὶ ἐπέβαλον ἐπ' αὐτὸν τὰς χεῖρας (21:27); cf. ἐπιλαβόμενοι τοῦ Παύλου (21:30)
Stephen is falsely accused (6:11, 13)	Paul is falsely accused (implied) (21:29)
Stephen is charged with violating law and temple ("this holy place"; 6:11–14)	Paul is charged with violating law and temple ("this place," "this holy place"; 21:28)
Stephen brought before council/Sanhedrin (6:12) Stephen's speech does not respond to charges.	Paul brought before council/Sanhedrin (22:30) Despite Paul's speech being called an *apologia* (22:1), he does not respond to actual charges.
Opponents "rush" at Stephen, drag him outside, and kill him (7:57–8:1)	Opponents "rush" at Paul, drag him outside, and try to kill him (21:30–31)
Opponents lay their coats down (7:58)	Opponents throw off their coats (22:23)
Opponents react to conclusion of Stephen's speech and are whipped into frenzy (7:54)	Opponents react to conclusion of Paul's speech and are whipped into frenzy (22:22; cf. 22:23)
Opponents (7:57) and Stephen cry out (7:60)	Opponents cry out (21:28; 22:23)
Council looks intently at Stephen: καὶ ἀτενίσαντες εἰς αὐτὸν πάντες οἱ καθεζόμενοι ἐν τῷ συνεδρίῳ (6:15)	Paul looks intently at the council: ἀτενίσας δὲ τῷ συνεδρίῳ ὁ Παῦλος (23:1)
Opening address to council: ἄνδρες ἀδελφοὶ καὶ πατέρες, ἀκούσατε (7:2)	Opening address to accusers: ἄνδρες ἀδελφοὶ καὶ πατέρες, ἀκούσατέ μου (22:1) + 23:1: council
Stephen has (7:55) and recounts (7:56) a vision of the risen Lord	Paul recounts two visions of the risen Lord (22:6–10, 17–21)

hero and the antagonists is similarly present in the Pauline account, and together these accusation/trial scenes are further enhanced by the tradition upon which they draw: the unjust accusation and death of the righteous individual.

One of the type-scenes that appears to be underlying the account of Stephen is that of the persecution of the righteous individual by the unrighteous.[83] The *locus classicus* of this framework comes from the Wisdom of Solomon (2:10–21; 3:1–11), which is significant in this discussion largely because it provides the *topoi* and framing narrative that helps one understand Jewish martyrdom accounts. Herein one observes the following main features: The righteous one is castigated by the unrighteous because his status confounds and convicts them ("the very sight of him is a burden to us, because his manner of life is unlike ours"; 2:15). Especially noteworthy in this conjunction is that the righteous is said to accuse the wicked of breaking the law ("he reproaches us for sins against the law"; 2:12). The unrighteous then go on to torture and finally kill the righteous individual ("a shameful death"; 2:20). From the larger perspective, however, the righteous have not really been placed out of the picture ("in the eyes of the foolish they seemed to have died"; 3:2), since they will appear again resurrected ("in the time of their visitation they will shine forth...they will govern nations and rule over peoples"; 3:7–8) to judge those who persecuted them ("the ungodly will be punished as their reasoning deserves"; 3:10).

This framework is important for understanding the agonistic settings in which Jewish martyrs face down the unrighteous tyrant. The book of 4 Maccabees is particularly significant for its extensive use of this typescene, wherein pious Jews refuse to acquiesce to the demands of the foreign king. Rather than relinquishing their Jewish way of life, the righteous submit to torture and eventual martyrdom for Jewish law and practice. The confrontation between Eleazar and Antiochus in 4 Macc 5:1–6:35 provides a good example. Eleazar's resistance to eating pork results in his death, but the ultimate winner in the contest between the wicked tyrant Antiochus and the pious, law-abiding Jew Eleazar is the latter, since his faithfulness results in blessing: "[T]hey now stand before the divine throne and live the life of eternal blessedness" (4 Macc 17:17).[84] In this light, the writer of 4 Maccabees

---

they will tear Paul to pieces (23:10). It is part of Luke's intention to contrast orderly and self-controlled behavior in the *ekklesia* (cf. assembly in Acts 15) with the inability of the Jerusalem leaders and opponents to maintain order, self-control, and rationality (cf. 19:28–41). This component represents the interplay of praise and blame with respect to core values that is apparent throughout Acts.

83. See G. W. E. Nickelsburg, *Resurrection, Immortality, and Eternal Life in Intertestamental Judaism* (HTS 26; Cambridge: Harvard University Press, 1972), 170–71.

84. On the dynamics of the face-off between the Maccabean martyrs and Antiochus, especially on the interplay of the masculinity of the former and the feminization of the latter, see S. D. Moore and J. Capel Anderson, "Taking It like a Man: Masculinity in 4 Maccabees," *JBL* 117 (1998): 249–73.

takes the opportunity afforded by the narrative to offer a Greek-influenced reflection on the role of reason in the control of the passions (6:31–35). Eleazar both receives reward as the righteous sufferer and models the proper function of reason in the life of the individual. In closing off the section on Eleazar, the writer launches into a panegyric on the martyred figure (7:1–22), who "though buffeted by the stormings of the tyrant...in no way did he turn the rudder of religion until he sailed into the haven of immortal victory" (7:2–3). Thus, the account of the martyrdom ends in an encomium for the righteous sufferer who uses reason to control the passions.

The Stephen narrative is dependent on this type-scene, wherein the righteous individual is persecuted by the unrighteous, suffering humiliation and death. In this connection, not only does Stephen explicitly challenge his adversaries on their adherence to the law (7:51–53), but he also suffers an ignoble death by stoning (7:58–59). This adheres closely to the paradigm in the Wisdom of Solomon. Moreover, the vision of Jesus at the "right hand of God" (7:55–56) may well function as the theme of resurrection does in the Wisdom of Solomon: The righteous sufferer is vindicated and affirmed as "righteous" by the presence of Jesus/God. Thus, the reader (and apparently even the adversaries; cf. 7:56–57) knows that Stephen's death is an unrighteous act perpetuated by the wicked and that he will be welcomed into heaven as the first martyr of the early Christian movement. There is thus notable overlap between the Jewish martyrdom tradition and the Stephen narrative.[85] Indeed, the agonistic motif that one finds in 4 Maccabees is important precisely for epideictic forms of composition,[86] setting apart those who are truly law-abiding from those who break the law. Thus, the focus on conflict is essential to the scheme insofar as it clearly depicts the respective characterization of the narrative figures. Not only has Luke drawn parallels between Stephen and Moses (and Stephen and Jesus) in this narrative, but he also draws on specific cultural and literary *topoi* and type-scenes, thereby establishing in a culturally formulated and accepted manner the respective natures of the righteous and the wicked in the account of Stephen's martyrdom.[87] In the end, then, this scene does not represent a defense of Stephen, just as Eleazar, the seven brothers, and their mother are not defended in

---

85. See esp. H.-W. Surkau, *Martyrien in jüdischer und frühchristlicher Zeit* (FRLANT ns 36/56; Göttingen: Vandenhoeck & Ruprecht, 1938), 105–19. One obvious aspect is the name of the main character himself: *Stephanos*. Not only is this a personal name, but it also denotes "crown," which is a major symbol in Jewish, Greco-Roman, and Christian understandings of reward for martyrdom (see further T. Penner, *The Epistle of James and Eschatology: Rereading an Ancient Christian Letter* [JSNTSup 121; Sheffield: Sheffield Academic Press, 1996], 186 n. 3).

86. For 4 Maccabees, see B. Dehandschutter, "Martyrium und Agon: Über die Wurzeln der Vorstellung vom ΑΓΩΝ im Vierten Makkabäerbuch," in *Die Entstehung der jüdischen Martyrologie* (ed. J. W. van Henten et al.; SPB 38; Leiden: Brill, 1989), 215–19.

87. I would include here Hebrew Bible parallels that demonstrate the same pattern, such as the death of the righteous Naboth by the hand of the tyrant Ahab. This text may also have been influential in the composition of the Stephen narrative (see T. L. Brodie, "The Accusing

4 Maccabees. Rather, the story highlights the praiseworthy features of these righteous individuals who are willing to die for their loyalty to the law. In a remarkable shift, then, while Stephen's opponents accuse him of violating the law (6:11, 13–14), Stephen's own death in line with the rejected prophets demonstrates the law-breaking character of his narrative adversaries.

In summary, then, the narrative of Stephen's conflict and eventual death functions at several levels, just like the story of the widow problem in 6:1–7 is similarly multifaceted. On the one hand, it is used to further Luke's literary efforts to tie together the various narrative threads. The Paul/Stephen parallels are important in this respect, as Luke has brought these two narratives together through structural and linguistic connections. These parallels attest to the architectural features of Luke's narrative noted earlier in the discussion of 6:1–7. The apostles' conflict with the Jerusalem leaders spreads to the Hellenist conflict with Hellenistic Jews and the Jerusalem leadership and this then to the culmination in Paul's final trial sequence, which includes Hellenistic Jews, Jerusalem leaders, and Gentiles. Just as the *ekklesia* in Jerusalem increases gradually and in an orderly fashion, so the ensuing conflict spreads out gradually, becoming more inclusive, fierce, and disorderly as the narrative advances in Acts. Luke's architectonic structuring of these narrative parallels demonstrates fine historiographical control, as he is able to use these connections to illustrate continuity and enduring patterns in his account of the formation, development, and expansion of the *ekklesia*.

Further, aside from advancing the plot connections and adding to the complete narrative, Luke also uses the Stephen account to elaborate and amplify the epideictic themes of his composition. In particular, Luke utilizes the compositional technique of *synkrisis* to draw the newly formed *politeia* founded by Jesus into comparison with the Jewish *politeia,* used as a foil to enhance the praiseworthy features of the nascent Christian movement attested in 6:1–7. Thus, Stephen is contrasted with his adversaries, and the conclusion is that the former is truly law-abiding and righteous while the latter are depicted as his mirror opposites. Alongside these comparisons, the associations of Stephen with Moses and Jesus further heighten the glorification of the early Christian martyr. Of course, the narrative in 6:8–15 and 7:54–8:3 is not as much about Stephen as it is about Stephen as representative of the community. Thus, the encomium for Stephen in turn reflects more generally on the *ethos* of the *ekklesia* depicted in Acts 1–7.[88]

The aspect of *synkrisis* perhaps comes into sharper focus if one bears in mind the suggestion made above that Luke is here tapping into the larger literary and cultural theme of *philanthropia* and potential threats to its

---

and Stoning of Naboth [1 Kgs 21:8–13] as One Component of the Stephen Text [Acts 6:9–14; 7:58a]," *CBQ* 45 [1983]: 417–32).

88. This point has been developed further by G. E. Sterling, "'Athletes of Virtue': An Analysis of the Summaries in Acts (2:41–47; 4:32–35; 5:12–16)," *JBL* 113 (1994): 679–96.

disintegration. On the one hand, 6:1–7 deals with the potential for the breakdown of *philanthropia* in the newly formed assembly, but ends in resolution rather than dissolution. In the narrative immediately following, however, one observes the breakdown in *philanthropia* of another kind: between members of the Jerusalem *ekklesia* and their brothers-turned-opponents in the broader Jewish community. The Stephen narrative thus juxtaposes the nature of the respective communities in Jerusalem. In the latter scenario, the opponents of Stephen demonstrate the dissolution of the fraternal bonds between Jews of different religious commitments. This is one of the reasons why Luke portrays the initial conflict as arising from within Jewish Hellenistic communities in Jerusalem: Stephen encounters opposition from among "his own brothers and fathers."

Indeed, Luke consistently and consciously reminds the reader of the fraternal bonds that exist between the newly formed assembly of believers and the larger Jewish community in which it is embedded. For instance, when Stephen addresses the council he does so as "brothers and fathers" (7:2), using the possessive pronoun "our" repeatedly throughout the speech (7:2, 11, 12, 15, 19, 38, 39, 44, 45). In fact, numerous times in the speeches in Acts Luke uses "brother" to refer to the Jewish audience (1:16; 2:29; 3:17; 13:26, 38; 22:1; 23:1; 23:6; 28:17), but never of non-Jews in the narrative. It is evident from this that Luke consciously underscores the fraternal relationship of the various members of the early Christian movement in Acts — the apostles, Stephen, and Paul — with the larger Jewish narrative audience. This association is vital for understanding the way in which the relationship is portrayed on a macronarrative level. We have seen that for Aristotle the breakdown of *philanthropia* between family members is a particularly potent theme for creating dramatic tension. In this Aristotelian perspective, this type of breakdown would typically also lead to the murder of a family member, which is precisely what happens in the Stephen episode; the breakdown of fellow-feeling between Stephen and his opponents ends in the stoning of the protagonist. But more than the creation of a dramatic mimetic narrative, the juxtaposition of 6:1–7 and 6:8–15/7:54–8:1 develops the Lukan comparison between the respective communities: In one the threat to *philia* and *philanthropia* results in resolution to conflict; in the second the threat to *philanthropia* issues forth in the dissolution of the relationship, leading not only to the death of Stephen but also to the persecution of the entire Jerusalem *ekklesia*. In this way, the notice of 8:1 is not simply a literary strategy for having the gospel move beyond the environs of Jerusalem. The more important function of the notice is to demonstrate the degree to which *philanthropia* has eroded, to the point that there is an irreparable and irrevocable break between the two communities. In the process, the narrative reversals so important for Aristotle's concept of plot in tragedy are also apparent in Acts 6:1–8:3: The righteous Stephen is murdered, his accusers now stand accused themselves, and the community of 6:1–7 that just established internal harmony now finds itself persecuted in 8:1 because of a lack of *koinōnia* with its "outside" brothers. Luke's account thus contains several levels of narrative reversals.[89] Ultimately, the point of these is to draw the reader into the story, affirming the truth of the account: The newly formed community founded by Jesus and led by his apostles is superior to its narrative counterpart, as the latter exhibits behavior that could be categorized as *misanthropia* over and against the predominance of harmony, justice, and generosity evidenced in the nascent Christian movement here being extolled by Luke.

Furthermore, these resultant reversals draw out from the reader a significant emotional reaction, which is achieved through Luke's use of vivid description. In fact, the Stephen narrative is perhaps one of the most dramatic and vivid accounts in the whole of Acts. Luke repeatedly uses descriptive verbs, which vivify the narrative for the reader.[90] This vivid narrative style with respect to the depiction of murder receives some emphasis in the literature examined in chapter 3. For instance, referring to vivid composition, Theon states,

> [W]e will do vivid description whenever we report the unjust action just as it is carried out and the suffering of the one treated unjustly; for example, against a murderer: for we will sketch in detail 1) what sort of person the one committing the murder is as he cruelly and mercilessly becomes a murderer of a human being, even though he is human; 2) as he draws his sword; 3) as he lands a blow; and 4) if the blow is perhaps not mortal, as he strikes blow after blow; and 5) as he is defiled by the blood of the one being murdered; and 6) what screams the latter lets out: first, begging the murderer, second, calling upon as helpers now men, now the gods; and other things as these. (6.88–97; cf. Quintilian, *Inst.* 6.2.31–32)

This text provides a framework for understanding the account of Stephen in Acts. Not only does Luke report a clear "unjust action," but he also details

---

89. A notable feature of the Roman foundation myth was the dissolution of the fraternal bonds between Romulus and Remus. Traditional notions of brotherly *pietas* (the combination of affection and devotion to the fraternal figure) become blended with civic identity and strife in the Roman Republic. Thus, while fraternal *pietas* ought to lead toward the resolution of conflict and establishment of harmony, it frequently develops into brotherly disharmony and ultimately fratricide. The ideal values of the private sphere thereby become reversed in the account of the breakdown of fraternal *pietas* in the civic realm (see further C. J. Bannon, *The Brothers of Romulus: Fraternal Pietas in Roman Law, Literature, and Society* [Princeton: Princeton University Press, 1997], 4–9, 149–73). The similar combination of civic and fraternal aspects in Luke's foundation narrative is therefore not surprising.

90. See esp. the following: ἀνέστησαν, συζητοῦντες (6:9); ἴσχυον ἀντιστῆναι (6:10); ὑπέβαλον, λέγοντας (6:11); συνεκίνησάν, ἐπιστάντες, συνήρπασαν, ἤγαγον (6:12); ἔστησάν, λέγοντας (6:13); ἀκηκόαμεν, λέγοντος, καταλύσει, ἀλλάξει (6:14); ἀτενίσαντες, καθεζόμενοι, εἶδον (6:15); ἀκούοντες, διεπρίοντο, ἔβρυχον (7:54); ὑπάρχων, ἀτενίσας, εἶδεν, ἑστῶτα (7:55); εἶπεν, διηνοιγμένους, ἑστὼ (7:56); κράξαντες, συνέσχον, ὥρμησαν (7:57); ἐκβαλόντες, ἐλιθοβόλουν, ἀπέθεντο (7:58); ἐλιθοβόλουν, λέγοντα, δέξαι (7:59); θεὶς, ἔκραξεν, στήσῃς, εἰπὼν, ἐκοιμήθη (7:60).

the "suffering of the one treated unjustly." Moreover, the speech (7:51–53) and the narrative both define the character (i.e., "what sort of person") of the one committing the crime, with the participles providing a vivid image of the various elements of action involved in the trial and death of Stephen. Further, in light of early Christian tradition, Luke provides a reconfiguration of the last element in Theon's list: the cries of the victim. In Stephen's case, there is a call to the murderers (not "begging" for mercy but to "see" the vision) and there is also an address to the "gods" (not for "aid" but to take "mercy" on the murderers and to "receive" the spirit of the victim). At the very least, it is apparent that Luke's narrative resonates with the type of vivid description to which Theon attests. The purpose of such dramatic style is to transport events "before the eyes" of the hearer/reader, so as to have a lasting effect on their emotions (arousing pity and fear). In this manner the reader of Luke's text is engaged palpably in the events being described. Since the goal of vivid narration is to advance the larger historical purposes of a text, it follows that for Luke these dramatic scenes affirm the broader demonstrative features of his narrative, highlighting the relative merits of this newly formed community over and against its narrative fraternal counterpart in which it is embedded.

Stephen's Speech: Epideictic Themes and Invective (Acts 7:1–53)

Drawing on the preceding discussion of Stephen and the Hellenists, it seems that the proper way to interpret the speech of Acts 7 is within the framework provided by the surrounding narrative. Given the suggestion detailed above that Luke is developing epideictic themes in this portion of Acts, I would argue that the speech must similarly be understood in terms of demonstrative rhetorical strategies. Read in this light, Stephen's speech represents an invective against the narrative opponents. The judicial context of the speech — Stephen standing before the Jewish council — has always been the primary focus for interpretation of the speech. Yet, as outlined in chapter 2, this emphasis has caused endless difficulties and speculation regarding the disjunction between speech and narrative, as Stephen in his speech does not address — at least not directly — the charges brought forth in the narrative. Thus, scholarship has traditionally argued that Luke inserted a sermon — perhaps akin to something the Hellenists did or might have preached — into a historical recollection regarding Stephen. Based on my earlier analysis, however, I would suggest that Luke has carefully crafted a speech to further the epideictic themes of the narrative portions of Acts 6:1–8:3, focusing on both *ethos* and *dianoia* and further establishing in *logos* a complement of the *ergon* of the main character, as well as expanding on and contributing to narrative development.

In line with Theon's comments on false charges quoted earlier, Luke seems uninterested in having Stephen respond to the accusations made in the narrative. Rather, the charges are meant to supply the themes of the speech, and, while Luke does have something to say about the charges in the speech (amounting to a counteraccusation), in the narrative they function to shape the character of the opponents rather than that of the protagonist. One of the main features of epideictic discourse is its polarizing nature and, given that the surrounding narrative details a comparison between the community established by Jesus (here represented by Stephen) and the Jewish *politeia*, it is not surprising that the contrast should continue into the speech itself. In this way, the speech has both features of praise and blame. There is praise for Jewish ancestry, insofar as figures of the nascent Christian movement are embedded in that lineage, but there is also blame for the negative features of Jewish ancestry associated with Stephen's narrative opponents. Therefore, on the one hand, Stephen's *ethos* is further established both by the Moses/Stephen parallels and the conclusion to the speech (7:54, 57), which affirms the statement of 6:10 to be true; the opponents could not withstand Stephen's power of persuasion and conviction. On the other hand, the *dianoia* of the narrative *synkrisis* is articulated in terms of an intentional retelling of the biblical story. Indeed, as we shall see shortly, here Luke taps into the tradition of Jewish apologetic retellings of the exodus story (the Jewish foundation narrative), which praises the founder and founding of the *politeia* under Moses. Luke is thus using the patterns and themes of Jewish apologetic literature to support his own effort to praise the founding of the Christian movement.

This epideictic nature of Acts 7 has previously been noted by Balch, who has argued that it represents Lukan invective.[91] His comparison with the encomia of Dionysius on Roman origins is helpful, as is his emphasis on the role of genealogies in a speech of censure. Balch cites the *Rhetoric to Alexander* at this point, and it is worth exploring some of the themes presented there for the light shed on Acts 7. When the writer of this rhetorical text turns to speeches of praise and blame, he delineates genealogy as one of the topics useful for composing such speeches. The writer thus states,

> The proper way to employ genealogy is this. If the ancestors are men of merit, you must enumerate them all from the beginning down to the person you are eulogizing, and at each of the ancestors summarily mention something to his credit. If the first ones are men of merit but the rest do not happen to have done anything remarkable, you must go through the first ones in the same way but omit the inferior ones. (*Rhet. Alex.* 1440b)

If the person being praised has no ancestry of which to speak, the orator not only should downplay the importance of ancestry but should also

---

91. Balch, "Comments on the Genre," 346–49.

"rebuke all the other people who praise their ancestors by saying that many who have had distinguished ancestors have been unworthy of them" (*Rhet. Alex.* 1441a). The writer also declares that in "vituperation use must be made of genealogy in a case of bad ancestry" (i.e., bad people should be shown to have bad ancestors; 1441a). These various features related to the genealogy of a group/person are important for understanding how Luke develops the particular Jewish themes in the speech. Genealogy is the central concern and, while there is a careful attempt to portray the ancestors positively, his adversaries are depicted as both being "unworthy" of the lineage of the heroes of the Jewish past as well as having had "bad ancestry." Luke thus combines several separate elements of the scheme also reflected in the *Rhetoric to Alexander*.

Even more striking for understanding the speech are these comments by the writer:

> We must not scoff at the person we are vituperating, but recount his career; for narratives carry more conviction with the hearers than scoffs ... [because] narratives mirror their characters and manners. Be careful not to denigrate even his base actions by base names, in order that you may not traduce his character, but to indicate such matters allusively, and to reveal the fact by using words that denote something else. In vituperations also you should employ irony, and ridicule your opponent for the things on which he prides himself. (*Rhet. Alex.* 1441b)

There are several important features here that help illuminate certain parts of both the narrative and speech in Acts. First, what the writer states for vituperation also applies to eulogy: One should be subtle in the presentation since narratives make obvious the respective characters and manners of individuals. This formulation means that Luke does not have to have explicit denunciation or praise in order for his narrative and speech to achieve its intended aim, since carefully crafted narratives will "naturally" have the desired effect on the audience. Further, name calling is to be abandoned for more allusive references. Thus, deprecating comments about character are less effective than making allusions to known *topoi* or, in Luke's case, Scriptures, that clearly set forth the nature of the behavior being depicted. While the closing of the oration is clearly vituperative in nature (7:51–53; "ridiculing" the opponents for those things in which they pride themselves [i.e., observance of the law]), the remaining portions are more implicit in terms of their function.

In light of this association with the *Rhetoric to Alexander*, the entire speech from beginning to end can be viewed as an invective against the adversaries introduced in the narrative framework. As the speech progresses, one can perceive a continuing division in Israel between the main heroic individuals and those that reject them. In this way, the respective characters of Stephen and his adversaries are now grafted onto a Deuteronomic reading of the history of Israel that establishes, in a retelling of the past, the type of conflict current in the present. Furthermore, given the narrative context, the speech displays less interest in articulating the division as a means of explanation than in denigrating the opponents themselves: The division in the speech underscores the polarity already manifested in the narrative framework. Read in this light, the closing unit on the temple must be interpreted as forming one element in the argument against the character elicited by Stephen's opponents. A clear anti-temple polemic can thus be seen. Yet as is evident from the *Rhetoric to Alexander,* the *topoi* are most effectively used to the advancement of one's argument, which means that the temple section is important in terms of characterizing Stephen's adversaries rather than necessarily revealing the Lukan perspective on the temple per se.

Structure of the Speech

I have already outlined in chapter 2 the importance of the charges levied against Stephen (6:11, 13–14) for understanding the speech. These charges raise topics of cultural significance that form the basis for amplification in the speech: Moses/God (6:11); this holy place/law (6:13); this place/customs of Moses (6:14). Although articulated in a threefold pattern, the charges can be narrowed to two fundamental themes: the temple in Jerusalem ("this place") and the laws of Moses. Moreover, the two main characters of Acts 7 — God and Moses — are also introduced through the repetition in the accusations.

As far as the structure of the speech is concerned, there are several noteworthy features related to the opening unit (7:2–8). First, the reference to "ancestors" throughout is essential for the reversal that is achieved in the speech. Stephen's reference to "our ancestor Abraham" (7:2) resonates with the opening line of the speech in which Stephen addresses his audience as "brothers and fathers," but this connection with his adversarial audience also highlights (probably with some irony) the dissolving fellow-feeling/fraternal bonds of kinship between Stephen and the other Hellenistic Jews. While references to "our ancestor(s)" occur frequently in the speech (7:11, 12, 15, 19, 38, 39, 44, 45), by the end — at the point where Stephen turns to overt use of invective — the pronoun is changed to "*your* ancestors" (7:51, 52), establishing a disjunction between the opponents and Stephen. One other place, prior to the conclusion, where Stephen differentiates himself from his opponents is in his reference to "their" occupation of the land to which God brought Abraham ("the land in which you are now living"; 7:4).

Second, and more important, the opening section of the speech structures the rest of the oration. It accomplishes this structuring in two ways. First, the promises to Abraham in 7:6–7 provide the overarching framework to the narrative, as the remaining story unfolds in a promise-fulfillment scheme.⁹² God promised that the people will be resident aliens in a foreign land, that they will be enslaved, that God will deliver them, and, finally, that they will come out and worship God "in this place." The scheme of slavery-deliverance-worship is fulfilled respectively in 7:9–29; 7:30–43; and 7:44–46.⁹³ The second aspect is that key words of this opening appear elsewhere in the speech, underscoring the significance of the introductory unit for structuring the whole: ὤφθη (7:2; cf. 7:26, 30); κατοικέω (7:2, 4; cf. 7:48); δοῦναι (7:5; cf. 7:38); κατάσχεσις (7:5; cf. 7:45); θεός (7:2, 6, 7; cf. 7:9, 17, 20, 25, 32, 35, 37, 42, 43, 45, 46, 55, 56); ἐπηγγείλατο (7:5; cf. τῆς ἐπαγγελίας, 7:17); πάροικος (7:6; cf. 7:29); κακόω (7:6; cf. 7:19; τὴν κάκωσιν, 7:34); τόπος (7:7; cf. 7:33, 49). Some of these connections are more significant than others, but overall they attest to what appears to be a conscious use of the opening unit for providing the central themes and words that dominate the rest of the speech. Alongside these linguistic connections, there are also several important elements in 7:2–8 that are reversed in the course of the oration: "settled" (μετῴκισεν in 7:4 and μετοικιῶ in 7:43); "worshiping" (λατρεύσουσίν in 7:7 and λατρεύειν in 7:42); and "circumcision" (διαθήκην περιτομῆς in 7:8 and ἀπερίτμητοι καρδίαις καὶ τοῖς ὠσίν in 7:51).⁹⁴ This aspect of reversal is critical to the function of the speech in characterizing Stephen's opponents. Thus, just as Abraham "settled" in the land of Israel (7:4), so the ancestors were "settled" in Babylon (7:43);⁹⁵ just as the goal of the exodus is to worship the God of Israel, the ancestors worshiped "the host of heaven" (i.e., idolatry; 7:42); and just as God gave to Abraham's descendants a covenant of circumcision, the ancestors have become "uncircumcised in their hearts and ears" (7:51). These elements form a significant component of the epideictic speech, since they demonstrate in their

---

92. This element is discussed by N. A. Dahl, "The Story of Abraham in Luke-Acts," in *Studies in Luke-Acts* (ed. L. E. Keck and J. L. Martyn; Nashville: Abingdon, 1966), 143–45, 147 (cf. R. G. Hall, *Revealed Histories: Techniques for Ancient Jewish and Christian Historiography* [JSPSup 6; Sheffield Academic Press, 1991], 197; and J. Dupont, "La structure oratoire du discours d'Étienne [Actes 7]," *Biblica* 66 [1985]: 153–67). The primacy of the Abrahamic covenant and promises is a consistent feature of Luke's narrative emphases (see further R. L. Brawley, "Abrahamic Covenant Traditions and the Characterization of God in Luke-Acts," in *The Unity of Luke-Acts* [ed. J. Verheyden; BETL 142; Leuven: Leuven University Press, 1999], 109–32; and R. C. Tannehill, "The Story of Israel within the Lukan Narrative," in *Jesus and the Heritage of Israel* [ed. Moessner], 327–28).

93. The remaining portion of the speech (7:44–53) is loosely structured on the themes arising in 7:35–43. The themes provided here include the coming prophet (7:37), the law (7:38), and idolatry (7:39–43), which are picked up, in reverse order, in 7:44–50 (the temple-idolatry connection), 7:52 (prophet killed), and 7:53 (law not kept). This phenomenon is known as "ring composition" and is common in ancient historical speeches (see I. Worthington, "History and Oratorical Exploitation," in *Persuasion: Greek Rhetoric in Action* [ed. I. Worthington; New York: Routledge, 1994], 115).

94. See further R. C. Tannehill, *The Narrative Unity of Luke-Acts: A Literary Interpretation* (Minneapolis: Fortress, 1990), 2:90.

95. See E. Richard, "The Creative Use of Amos by the Author of Acts," *NovT* 24 (1982): 42, who further notes the structural importance of the Jewish people beginning (7:4) and ending (7:43) in Babylon.

initial reference in the opening unit the ideals that the descendants will fail to emulate in the ensuing narrative, thereby supplying the main features of denunciation and reproach for shameful behavior.

The Topos *of* Topos: *The Place of 7:7 in the Invective*

I discussed the importance of the promise in 7:7 in the second chapter, but it bears outlining again. The context of 7:7 is established in 7:5, where the promise consists of land that is to be given to Abraham's seed. This verse represents a paraphrase of the promises set forth by God in Gen 15:1–11 (cf. Gen 17:8). The explicit references to Gen 15:13–14 in Stephen's speech have their immediate Hebrew Bible context in between explicit promises of land to Abraham (Gen 15:7–11 and 15:17–19). Genesis 15:13–14 is part of God's covenant promise to Abraham linking the people to the land, as the Israelites will be delivered from slavery to possess it. Luke makes this same connection by having 7:5 precede the promises in 7:6–7; the promises are therefore grounded in the possession of "the land." Acts 7:6 goes on to predict the suffering of Israel in Egypt (Gen 15:13). Acts 7:7 then follows with a direct recitation of the Septuagint: God will judge the nation enslaving the Israelites, and they will leave that country (7:7; cf. Gen 15:14). A significant change occurs in the text at this point, however. Rather than following the biblical text and reading "and they will come out with great possessions" (the reading of the MT and LXX: μετὰ ἀποσκευῆς πολλῆς), Acts 7:7 reads, "[T]hey shall come out and worship me in this place" (καὶ λατρεύσουσίν μοι ἐν τῷ τόπῳ τούτῳ). The narrator has thus deftly elided words from Exod 3:12 with the recitation of Gen 15:14: "[W]hen you have brought the people out of Egypt you shall worship God on this mountain" (καὶ λατρεύσετε τῷ θεῷ ἐν τῷ ὄρει τούτῳ).[96] Luke has not only coalesced the texts of Gen 15:14 and Exod 3:12, he has also made an important change to the latter, altering the reference from "this mountain" to "this place." The modification is small, but it has tremendous ramifications for the meaning of Acts 7, as the only antecedent for "this place" in Acts 7:7 is "the land" of 7:4 (cf. 7:5). Thus, the "place" as the mountain changes to the "place" as the land in Stephen's speech.

The further implications of this shift are evident when one examines the charges in 6:13–14, where Stephen is accused of uttering blasphemies against "this place." As we have already seen, here the reference is unambiguously to the temple. The former use of "this holy place" to refer to the temple in 6:13–14 allows Luke to make a play on τόπος in 7:7.[97] The

---

96. This point has been frequently observed by scholars (e.g., Dahl, "Story of Abraham," 143; and J. S. Siker, *Disinheriting the Jews: Abraham in Early Christian Controversy* [Louisville: Westminster John Knox, 1991], 122–23).

97. The identification of τόπος with "temple" is a well-entrenched Hebrew Bible/Jewish practice. In Deut 12 the term occurs several times in reference to the temple (Deut 12:5, 11, 13–14, 18, 21, 26). There are also Targumic readings, which identify the mountain of Exodus

promise to Moses in Exod 3:12 has a long Jewish tradition of association with the temple: "This mountain" is the place of the temple. But Luke intentionally reconfigures the promise so that the mountain/temple associations are subordinated to "the land."[98] By telescoping the narrative, Luke has heightened the connection between deliverance and land to the exclusion of Mount Sinai (cf. Josephus, *Ant.* 2.269).

In this way, the place of Moses becomes the place of Abraham in Acts 7:7.[99] In the speech, reference is also made in 7:33 to the τόπος of Moses in the "wilderness of Mount Sinai" (7:30). Moreover, the citation from Isa 66:1-2 in 7:49 also refers to the temple (οἶκος) as "the place" (ἢ τίς τόπος). Thus, we find both Mount Sinai and the temple being referred to as τόπος in the speech. The framework of the speech has been cast in 7:7, however, and here the τόπος of Abraham — the land — is what God promises to Abraham's descendants upon their deliverance from Egypt. This association provides the *crux interpretum* of the passage because this reading would mean that the

---

with the sanctuary or "House of the Shekhinah" (e.g., *Targum Neofiti* to Exod 15:17). Further, Targumic traditions also connect the promises to, and covenants with, the patriarchs to this same motif: Worship at the temple forms the fundamental locus of God's promises, and the land is symbolic of this more primary emphasis (see R. Hayward, *Divine Name and Presence: The Memra* [Oxford Center for Postgraduate Hebrew Studies; Totowa, N.J.: Allanheld, Osmun & Co., 1981], 71–98; the presence of this same tradition in Philo and Josephus was highlighted in the last chapter). Already in the "Song of Moses" one finds a reference to this theme: "You brought them in and planted them on the mountain of your own possession, the place [MT = מכון; LXX = εἰς ἕτοιμον κατοικητήριόν), O Lord, that you made your abode, the sanctuary, O Lord, that your hands have established (ὃ ἡτοίμασαν αἱ χεῖρές σου)" (Exod 15:17). This passage also has clear textual connections to the language in Acts 7:48 and 50 (cf. 17:14), where Stephen negatively characterizes the temple as a dwelling "made by hands." Furthermore, the reference to *topos* in Acts 7:33, while a recitation attributed to God, also draws upon this same complex of associations, especially the connection between "the place" on the mountain and the sanctuary of God, a coalescing of Mount Horeb/Sinai with Mount Zion.

98. Given the importance of the phrase "this place" with reference to the temple in Deuteronomy, it is noteworthy that in the Septuagint text of Jeremiah it seems to carry a different connotation, referring instead to the land (cf. 7:3, 6, 7, 20; 14:13; 16:2, 3; 19:3, 4, 12; 22:3; 24:5; 28:62; 29:10; 32:30; 33:10; 35:3, 6; 36:10; 39:37; 40:2; 42:18). Jeremiah 7:6–7 reads, "[I]f you do not oppress the alien, the orphan, and the widow, or shed innocent blood *in this place* (ἐν τῷ τόπῳ τούτῳ), and if you do not go after other gods to your own hurt, then I will dwell with you *in this place* (ἐν τῷ τόπῳ τούτῳ), in the land (ἐν γῇ) that I gave of old to your ancestors forever and ever." This text is significant for two reasons: It resonates closely with the language of Acts 7:7 and in a similar way reinterprets "this place" of Deuteronomy (= the temple) as the land promised to the ancestors. This reinterpretation is made explicit in Jer 7:3–4, where "this place" (as land; cf. Jer 7:6–7) is juxtaposed with the "deceptive words" that proclaim "this is the temple."

99. Tannehill, *Narrative Unity*, 2:92–93, recognizes that τόπος in 7:7 is related back to the land of 7:4. Yet his conclusion that 7:7 "anticipates a specific place of worship within the land, and that place will be the temple" fails to appreciate the various nuances of τόπος in Acts 7. Similarly, J. Kilgallen, *The Stephen Speech: A Literary and Redactional Study of Acts 7,2–53* (AnBib 67; Rome: Biblical Institute Press, 1976), 33–35; and K. Haacker, "Stephanus in der Geschichte des Urchristentums," *ANRW* 2.26.2 (1995): 1537. Siker, *Disinheriting the Jews*, 123–25, emphasizes the shift to the land in 7:7, but focuses on the act of worship itself, thereby downplaying the explicit Lukan connection to the land and avoiding problems with any anti-temple nuances as a result.

fulfillment of the promise of 7:7 occurs when the "tent of testimony" enters the land with Joshua in 7:45. At this point, two features of the Abrahamic opening unit are fulfilled: the promise of possession in 7:5 and the promise of "worship in this place" in 7:7. Acts 7:45 does not explicitly state that worship is going on in the land, but given the prominence of the tabernacle in 7:44, we should probably assume that once it enters the land the promise of true worship has been fulfilled. In this vein, the narrator's statement that the tent of testimony remained in the land "until the time of David" is a brief but important temporal clause. It means that there is, in the writer's mind, a shift occurring in 7:46, as the temple under Solomon replaces the tabernacle. This transition to the temple as "the place" then initiates the explicit invective/ridicule that issues forth in 7:48–53. In order to make sense of the conclusion to the speech, there is no other possibility but to take the disjunction between 7:46 and 7:47 as an indication that there was a problem with the building of the temple.[100]

Thus, we arrive at the major interpretive problem in modern scholarship: the alleged anti-temple stance of 7:47–50. Focusing on the end of the speech, apart from what has been accomplished in the larger retelling of the exodus narrative up until this point, is to start at the wrong place. The conclusion of the speech strikes the modern reader as most blatant and obvious, but scholarship has frequently missed the more subtle and allusive aspects that are intended to lead the reader to the particular inferences of the conclusion. As discussed in the previous chapter, the retelling of the exodus narrative was one major component of Jewish rewritings of biblical tradition. In the process of recasting this biblical story, Jewish writers tended to play up the connection between the exodus from Egypt and the establishment of the Mosaic *politeia* in the land. Moreover, there was an attempt to bring Moses into close association with Jerusalem and the temple. But we have seen what happened when others, drawing upon this Jewish tradition, retold the same exodus story but to different ends. For instance, Greco-Roman writers such as Hecataeus, Strabo, and Tacitus reveal the tendency to idealize the Mosaic foundation and organization of the Jewish *politeia* but also (in the cases of Strabo and Tacitus) to see a decline and dissolution under subsequent Jewish leadership. I would suggest that Luke is tapping into this tradition of retelling the exodus narrative, tailoring the presentation in Acts 7 so as to imply something similar to what one observes in these other non-Jewish rewritings of Jewish history.[101]

---

100. On this disjunction, see also Haacker, "Stephanus in der Geschichte," 1536–37; and S. Arai, "Zum 'Tempelwort' Jesus in Apostelgeschichte 6.14," *NTS* 34 (1988): 408.

101. This connection is also suggested by Balch, "Comments on the Genre," 348–49. Balch affirms a linguistic link between Acts 7:45 (διαδεξάμενοι οἱ πατέρες ἡμῶν) and Strabo 16.2.37 (οἱ διαδεξάμενοι). Balch is correct to point out that in both instances there is express concern regarding the "successors" of Moses. M. Klinghardt, *Gesetz und Volk Gottes: Das lukanische*

In Stephen's speech, then, the implication is that the promises to Abraham were fulfilled when Joshua entered the land with the tent of testimony. Thus, while David himself still found favor with God, the building of the temple by Solomon represents a dissolution of the practices sanctioned by Moses (and enacted by his prophetic heirs; cf. Deut 34:9; Acts 7:45). For this reason the tabernacle plays such an important role in Acts 7; it is a form of worship associated with Moses that is different from the temple constructed under Solomon. It is noteworthy that Stephen here makes reference not only to the "tent of testimony" (cf. Exod 33:7) but also to the fact that this "tent" was made according to the pattern Moses "had seen" (7:45; cf. Exod 25:9). Although a small detail, this description characterizes the "tent" of Moses as being modeled on heavenly realities. In the context of Stephen's speech, of course, the implication seems to be that while the tent of testimony was based on the heavenly pattern, the temple, by contrast, "was made by human hands" (7:48). This distinction might explain in part the contrast between the tent and temple in the closing unit of the speech. If so, the note in 7:46 confirms that the religious practice instituted under Moses was divinely sanctioned, instituted, and shaped, further shoring up the argument that once the tent has entered the land "worship in this place" is fulfilled. Moreover, this confirmation bolsters the argument that it was only after Moses that the heavenly modeled religious practice was abandoned for a human distortion.[102] The point here is to contrast the respective forms of worship, thereby implying that the later development was not in line with the Mosaic constitution and founding of the *politeia* in the land of Abraham. Read in this way, the progression of the speech becomes clear: At each stage, there is fulfillment of the promises given to Abraham in 7:6–7, with the final promise coming to fulfillment in 7:45 when the "ancestors" and "Joshua"[103] bring the tent of testimony into the land and "dispossess

---

Verständnis des Gesetzes nach Herkunft, Funktion, und seinem Ort in der Geschichte des Urchristentums (WUNT 2.32; Tübingen: Mohr Siebeck, 1988), 295–303, has similarly paralleled Acts 7 with Strabo.

102. The focus on the tabernacle may have further implications, given postbiblical Jewish speculation. Philo and Josephus, for instance, both offer cosmological interpretations of the tabernacle and its contents, based on the premise that Moses "copied the paradigm" of heaven (Philo *Mos.* 2.74; *QE* 2.52–53, 76; Josephus, *Ant.* 3.123; cf. Wis 9:6; Sir 24:8–12). See further C. R. Koester, *The Dwelling of God: The Tabernacle in the Old Testament, Intertestamental Jewish Literature, and the New Testament* (CBQMS 22; Washington: Catholic Biblical Association, 1989), 59–63; and C. R. Holladay, *Theios Aner in Hellenistic Judaism: A Critique of the Use of This Category in New Testament Christology* (SBLDS 40; Missoula, Mont: Scholars Press, 1977), 82–86.

103. While a fair rendering of the biblical tradition at this point, one cannot ignore the way this passage reads in the Greek: ἣν καὶ εἰσήγαγον διαδεξάμενοι οἱ πατέρες ἡμῶν μετὰ Ἰησοῦ ἐν τῇ κατασχέσει τῶν ἐθνῶν. Although it is difficult to ascertain what Luke's readers would have made of the expression "with Jesus," it certainly is noteworthy that at the very point that the promises to Abraham in 7:6–7 are fulfilled (and the κατάσχεσις of 7:5 is repeated) one finds the mention of Joshua/Jesus in the text (the deliberate play on the names here in Acts 7:45 is suggested by A. T. Hanson, *Jesus Christ in the Old Testament* [London: SPCK, 1965], 167; and

the nations." But the story does not end there, and the disobedience already surfacing in the earlier parts of the speech now culminates in further acts that separate the "ancestors" from the promises given to Abraham. There is, therefore, a natural progression toward the explicit denunciations of the opponents in 7:51–53.

There are two important considerations that lend credence to this interpretation of the speech. First, Luke, unlike Josephus, makes sure to include the account of the construction of the golden calf at Mount Sinai. This element is part of his effort to characterize the ancestors of the Jewish leaders and opponents (7:37–41) as disobedient, which is evident throughout the retelling of the narrative. After mentioning the event, a citation from Amos 5:25–27 (LXX) is used to characterize the violators. In Luke's rendition, the violators are the "ancestors" (7:39), and the punishment for this act of disobedience is that they are given over to the worship of foreign gods and finally exiled to Babylon.[104] Luke achieves this interpretation by bringing the citation from Amos into association with the golden calf incident. Moreover, 7:41 states that they "offered a sacrifice to it [the calf] and reveled in the works of their hands." The phrase "works of their hands" (ἐν τοῖς ἔργοις τῶν χειρῶν αὐτῶν; cf. 7:48) is a reformulation of the identification of the golden calf as an idol. The phrase itself is frequently associated with idol worship in the Septuagint (cf. Deut 4:28; 27:15; 31:29; Isa 2:8; 17:8; 37:19; Jer 1:16; 25:6; 51:8). Thus, Luke amplifies the idolatrous nature of the Israelite disobedience at Mount Sinai, interpreting the later exile to Babylon as a form of punishment for the violation under Moses.

Second, and following from the first point, it is interesting that this citation from Amos should be used at this juncture, for it has two striking parallels to the unit of the speech that follows. In 7:43 there is a reference to both the "tent [τὴν σκηνήν] of Moloch" and the "images" that are made for worship (τοὺς τύπους οὓς ἐποιήσατε προσκυνεῖν; cf. Amos 5:26). These motifs are noteworthy since in the following verse (7:44) there is a seemingly deliberate contrast with "the tent of testimony" (ἡ σκηνὴ τοῦ μαρτυρίου) and the construction of the tent by Moses according the "image" that he saw (ἣ ποιῆσαι αὐτὴν κατὰ τὸν τύπον ὃν ἑωράκει).[105] The "tent of Moloch" (the sign of the ancestors' disobedience) is thus contrasted with the "tent of

---

R. P. C. Hanson, "Studies in Texts [Acts 6.13–14]," *Theology* 51 [1947]: 142). The promises to worship God "in this place" thus seem to find their fulfillment "with Jesus" in 7:45, providing a more nuanced context for reading Stephen's comments about regarding the temple.

104. H. van de Sandt notes the importance of 7:42, where the initial punishment for the golden calf incident is that God replaces the Mosaic cult with the worship of foreign deities ("Why Is Amos 5,25–27 Quoted in Acts 7,42f.?" *ZNW* 81 [1991]: 86–87).

105. The idea of the tabernacle as the Mosaic representation of the cosmos, highlighting the universal nature or at least implication of the Jewish customs associated with the sacred tent (cf. Josephus, *Ant.* 3.179–87), may be the theme lying behind the Lukan configuration in the speech.

testimony" (the sign of Moses' obedience), and the images/idols that the ancestors made to worship are similarly paralleled with the divine pattern for the tabernacle.[106] There is without a doubt a deliberate polarity and *synkrisis* being established in this text between the rebellious ancestors and Moses. Moreover, following this line of interpretation, the implication seems to be that the disobedient ancestors' misplaced worship led to their missing the significance of the real image and tent under Moses.

It is precisely in this context that one must interpret the temple unit at the end of the speech, as it represents a continuation of the rebellious ancestors' rejection of the Mosaic constitution and form of worship. Despite attempts by some scholars to downplay the negative elements of the closing of the speech (outlined in chapter 2), it becomes difficult to read the closing unit other than in a calumnious manner. One of the chief indications of this tone is the transition between David in 7:46 and Solomon in 7:47. With respect to David, he is said to have "found favor with God" as well as having had the desire to find a "dwelling place" (σκήνωμα) for the "house of Jacob."[107] The similarity between σκήνωμα (7:46) and σκηνή (7:44) would appear intentional. Moreover, it seems probable that in the argument being developed the σκήνωμα in 7:46 means "tabernacle" or "tent" rather than "temple."[108] The word σκήνωμα can carry both meanings,[109] but given the argument, here, that David and Solomon are being distinguished in some way, it makes the most sense to view the point of separation as being that David continued in line with the tent worship established by Moses, while Solomon shifted emphases by building the temple (cf. the adversative use of δέ in 7:47). Of course, like most retellings of the Bible in the Second Temple period, Luke is taking liberties with the text, including and excluding features of the biblical narrative in order to establish his main line of argument. Thus, while it is true that David sought to build a temple for God (but was not allowed to), there also exists the narrative in 2 Samuel where David establishes a "tent" to house the ark (2 Sam 2:6; cf. 1 Kgs 2:28, where σκήνωμα is used for this same "tent"). Further, in response to David's desire to build a house

---

106. See further Richard, "Creative Use of Amos," 43–44.

107. The variant "God of Jacob" would seem to make more sense here, although οἶκος in "house of Jacob" provides a better play in terms of what is going on in the text (esp. the use of 2 Sam. 7:1–7). Yet οἰκοδόμησεν αὐτῷ οἶκον in 7:47 should have an antecedent, which "God of Jacob" would provide (see further A. F. J. Klijn, "Stephen's Speech — Acts VII.2–53," NTS 4 [1957]: 29–30). Since σκήνωμα can mean either "tent" or "house"/"sanctuary," a copyist may have been seeking to clarify the logic of Stephen's argument. The parallel to Ps 131:5 (LXX; ἕως οὗ εὕρω τόπον τῷ κυρίῳ σκήνωμα τῷ θεῷ Ἰακωβ) would appear to provide supporting evidence, in this case, that "God of Jacob" is probably the original reading.

108. So also C. K. Barrett, "Old Testament History according to Stephen and Paul," in *Studien zum Text und Ethik des Neuen Testaments: Festschrift zum 80. Geburtstag von Heinrich Greeven* (ed. W. Schrage; BZNW 47; Berlin: de Gruyter, 1986), 67. Cf. D. D. Sylva, "The Meaning and Function of Acts 7:46–50," JBL 106 (1987): 264, 266–67.

109. For its use as "tabernacle," see esp. Ps 77:60 (LXX) and 1 Kgs 2:28 (possibly also Lam 2:6; Ps 131:5 [LXX]; Jdt 9:8).

for God in 2 Sam 7:2, it is indicated that not only does the deity not need a house, but that the pattern of the tabernacle has been sufficient up until David's time (2 Sam 7:6).[110] If this passage is in view in Acts 7, and it seems likely it is, then the logic of the argument becomes clearer: David continued in the tradition of Moses, but Solomon built the temple, which represents a departure and devolution from the Mosaic pattern. It must be stated that it does not matter that the Hebrew Bible text, viewed in its entirety, may negate such a picture. The function of the retelling is precisely to highlight the details that serve the function of the present narration. Luke has accomplished this aim by taking up the theme of the exodus and providing an account that emphasizes the disintegration of the pure tradition after the time of David.[111]

Added to this developing picture is the unambiguous association of the "house" *(oikos)* of Solomon with idolatry.[112] At this point many scholars attempt to circumvent the problem of the harsh connection by arguing that neither in the Hebrew Bible nor in Luke's larger work is such a view attested and, hence, Luke cannot be proffering or reporting such a view in Acts 7.[113] But this position assumes that there must be a literary precedent

---

110. The parallels between 2 Sam 7:6 and Acts 7 are significant: ὅτι οὐ κατῴκηκα (Acts 7:48 [κατοικεῖεν οἴκῳ]; cf. Acts 7:47 [οἶκον], 49 [ποῖον οἶκον]) ἀφ᾽ ἧς ἡμέρας ἀνήγαγον ἐξ Αἰγύπτου τοὺς υἱοὺς Ἰσραηλ ἕως τῆς ἡμέρας ταύτης (cf. Acts 7:45: ἕως τῶν ἡμερῶν Δαυίδ καὶ ἤμην ἐμπεριπατῶν ἐν καταλύματι καὶ ἐν σκηνῇ. As a whole, the 2 Sam 7:1–17 narrative is a central text for both Zion and Davidic messianic traditions, which are reflected in Luke-Acts. It is this narrative that seems to underlie the text of Acts 7:46–47 and indeed may have provided the impetus for the wordplay on σκήνωμα and οἶκος in the speech (cf. 2 Sam 7:6–7). In 2 Sam 7:10 God promises to establish a "place" that will be a safe haven for the people of Israel (καὶ θήσομαι τόπον τῷ λαῷ μου τῷ Ἰσραηλ). The reference to τόπος here could either be to the temple or to the land; it is not entirely clear from the context. The climax comes in 2 Sam 7:11, where God declares that instead of David building an οἶκος for him, God will establish an οἶκος for David (οἶκον οἰκοδομήσεις αὐτῷ), referring, of course, to a dynasty. In 2 Sam. 7:13 this descendant of David will build a "house" for God, and God in turn will establish his "house" (τὸν θρόνον αὐτοῦ) for all eternity, providing an obvious play on οἶκος.

111. In Acts 15:16, the "dwelling" that David sought in Acts 7:46 (cf. Ps 131:5) finds an intriguing parallel. During the apostolic conference, James recites Amos 9:11–12 as evidence that Gentiles should be permitted to enter the new community, an event that was in fact prophesied from ancient times (Acts 15:16–17). In this recitation, God promises to restore the fallen "dwelling place of David" (τὴν σκηνὴν Δαυίδ; cf. Koester, *Dwelling of God*, 85–87). The promise in Amos 9:15 is particularly interesting since it corresponds to the promise to David in 2 Sam 7:10 that God would "plant" the people in "the place" (καὶ θήσομαι τόπον τῷ λαῷ μου τῷ Ἰσραηλ καὶ καταφυτεύσω αὐτόν). In Acts 15 the Amos text is used as a witness to the present restoration of God's people in the newly formed assembly of believers, with ἡ σκηνή Δαυίδ understood to be the *ekklesia* composed of both Jews and Gentiles. While the theme of restoration is significant throughout all of Luke-Acts, the restoration in Acts 15 has particularly close association with the promise of restoration and deliverance given to Abraham in Acts 7:7, as the promise to be delivered and to worship "in this place" (cf. the use of the same themes in the Benedictus [Luke 1:68–75]; see further Dahl, "Story of Abraham," 146–47).

112. Similarly, F. S. Spencer, *Acts* (Sheffield: Sheffield Academic Press, 1997), 78; and S. Légasse, *Stephanos: Histoire et Discours D'Étienne dans les Actes des Apôtres* (LD 147; Paris: Cerf, 1992), 64–66.

113. Cf. F. F. Bruce, "Stephen's Apologia," in *Scripture: Meaning and Method; Essays Presented to Anthony Tyrell Hanson for His Seventieth Birthday* (ed. B. P. Thompson; Hull: Hull

for the speech or that Luke's more positive portrayal of the temple elsewhere in Luke-Acts demands that he cannot use the *topos* of temple negatively in Stephen's invective. The problem with this position is that ancient writers, especially when it comes to epideictic composition, were not constrained by the need for consistency in their use of a particular *topos*. The focus is generally on maximizing the effectiveness of the argument in order to persuade the reader, and this is done frequently by focusing on function over content (i.e., the role of the speech in the narrative setting is sometimes more significant than what is explicitly stated in the speech itself). In the section of the *Rhetoric to Alexander* outlined above, for instance, the writer is clear that when genealogy is helpful for establishing an argument one pursues it, but when it is not one can and should disparage its usefulness. The desired effect determines how one uses the *topos*. It is therefore fallacious to conclude from Stephen's speech that "all Christianity *à la Luke* oppose[s] the Temple and Mosaic custom,"[114] not only because the larger narrative of Luke-Acts does not in any way confirm this assertion (and does much to negate it), but also because it equates, rather simplistically, material that serves to characterize Stephen's Jewish opponents with the theological viewpoint of the writer of Acts.

Equally problematic are those readings that recognize but then attempt to downplay the idolatry connections, suggesting that the temple is not portrayed as the real problem in Stephen's speech, but rather the conception that the temple *is* the "house of God,"[115] with the real issue surfacing in the conclusion of the discourse: a failure to appreciate God's transcendence[116] or the misplaced localization of the Jerusalem cult.[117] These reservations expressed by modern scholars are understandable (even commendable), but any attempt to diminish the harshness at the end of the speech mitigates against the intended effect: The conclusion must enhance the developing accusations of the rewritten text in order to justify the condemnation of 7:51–53. If one reads the speech as Luke's justification for the Gentile mission, then perhaps one can interpret the ending in a less harsh light.[118] Yet, as I have suggested in this chapter, the entire narrative framework is one

---

University Press, 1987), 47, who argues that this "outburst of invective [is] not specifically related to the central argument of the apologia."

114. J. T. Sanders, *The Jews in Luke-Acts* (Philadelphia: Fortress, 1987), 248.

115. So J. J. Kilgallen, "The Function of Stephen's Speech (Acts 7,2–53)," *Biblica* 70 (1989): 177–81.

116. So Sylva, "Meaning and Function," 268–74.

117. So T. L. Donaldson, "Moses Typology and the Sectarian Nature of Early Christian Anti-Judaism: A Study in Acts 7," in *New Testament Backgrounds: A Sheffield Reader* (ed. C. A. Evans and S. E. Porter; BS 43; Sheffield: Sheffield Academic Press, 1997), 236.

118. This view represents a common interpretation of the speech. Sterling, "Opening the Scriptures," 199–217, offers one of the more compelling readings of the speech in this light, demonstrating how Acts 7 aims to legitimate the early Christian mission to the Gentiles just as the Hellenistic Jewish historians attempted to legitimate the Jewish Diaspora.

of comparison, with the speech serving to further characterize the narrative agents. Read as an invective from the beginning, the speech's role in characterizing the opponents becomes clear. Therefore, the argument that the building of the temple was an act (perhaps final act) of disobedience,[119] further misconstruing God's purposes manifested under the leadership of Moses, deserves further investigation.

That the building of the temple for all intents and purposes is referred to as an act of idolatry seems fairly evident from the context, as the comments related to the temple are set within a larger framework established by the reference to idolatry in 7:39–42. The ancestors made an idol, preferring this image to the tent of Moses. The passage from Amos (5:25–27) further clarifies the nature of the action in 7:39–42. The reference in 7:41 to the "works of their hands" (ἐν τοῖς ἔργοις τῶν χειρῶν αὐτῶν) is then significant, as it supplies the interpretive context for the language in the temple unit (7:47–50). After 7:47 declares that Solomon built the "house" for God, the next verse states, "Yet the Most High does not dwell in houses made with human hands [ἐν χειροποιήτοις]." Few ancient readers would have missed this clear association between the golden calf incident in 7:39–42 and the building of the temple in 7:47–48.[120] Just as the ancestors worshiped idols made with their hands, so the temple as the place of worship is also made with human hands. The citation from Isa 66:1–2 in 7:49–50 provides the rationale for why God does not need a temple: "His hands" have made everything, and "his temple" is therefore the heavens and the earth. The suggestion that here one is presented with evidence that Israel had an overly restrictive view of the deity misses the point, as the prophetic passage serves to justify the narrative judgment of 7:48 that the building of the temple was an act of idolatry.[121] The function of the citation from Isaiah, like the

---

119. So Klijn, "Stephen's Speech," 29–31; Bruce, "Stephen's Apologia," 46–47; and Barrett, "Old Testament History," 67–68.

120. Similarly, Koester, *Dwelling of God,* 83.

121. The underlying influence of Ps 131 may be one way of accounting for some of these emphases toward the end of the speech. For instance, Acts 7:46 states that David sought to "find a dwelling place for the God of Jacob." This text provides a clear reference to Ps 131:5 (LXX): I will not sleep (131:4) "until I will find a place for the Lord, a tent for the God of Jacob" (ἕως οὗ εὕρω τόπον τῷ κυρίῳ σκήνωμα τῷ θεῷ Ἰακώβ; cf. 7:46 [following textual variant]: εὑρεῖν σκήνωμα τῷ Θεῷ Ἰακώβ). In light of the larger context of this psalm, it is evident that the σκήνωμα is not the temple. It is, rather, the "tent" that David set up in Jerusalem to house the ark of the covenant (2 Sam 6.17; made more clear in Ps 131:8: ἀνάστηθι κύριε εἰς τὴν ἀνάπαυσίν σου [cf. Acts 7:49: τῆς καταπαύσεώς μου] σὺ καὶ ἡ κιβωτὸς τοῦ ἁγιάσματός σου). Also, the τόπος of Ps 131:5 is the σκήνωμα, which is the "tent" of David (cf. Ps 131:7: εἰσελευσόμεθα εἰς τὰ σκηνώματα αὐτοῦ προσκυνήσομεν εἰς τὸν τόπον). Thus, the logic underlying the argument in Acts 7:46–50 — that it was Solomon who built the temple in contrast to David, who found favor with God — may be affirmed by reference to Ps 131. Further support for this contention may lie in the extensive parallels between Acts 7:48–49 (which includes part of the citation from Isa 66) and Ps 131: Acts 7:48–49: ἀλλ' οὐχ ὁ ὕψιστος ἐν χειροποιήτοις κατοικει ... Ὁ οὐρανός μοι θρόνος, ἡ δὲ γῆ ὑποπόδιον τῶν ποδῶν μου; ποῖον οἶκον οἰκοδομήσετέ μοι, λέγει κύριος, ἢ τίς τόπος τῆς καταπαύσεώς μου ... ; Ps 131: 7, 14: εἰσελευσόμεθα εἰς τὰ σκηνώματα αὐτοῦ [cf. Acts 7:46] προσκυνήσομεν εἰς τὸν τόπον οὗ ἔστησαν οἱ πόδες αὐτοῦ ... αὕτη ἡ κατάπαυσίς μου εἰς αἰῶνα αἰῶνος ὧδε κατοικήσω.

similar one from Amos in 7:42–43, is intended to provide authoritative and unambiguous support for the argument being formulated in the speech. Aside from the context of 7:39–48, which situates the act of Solomon in 7:47 within the setting of disobedience through idolatry, and aside from the resonance of "made with hands" (χειροποιήτοις) in 7:48 with "made with hands" (ἐν τοῖς ἔργοις τῶν χειρῶν αὐτῶν) in 7:41, there is, finally, the substantive point that the Greek word "made with hands" (χειροποίητος) is one of the words used to translate "idol" in the Septuagint (Lev 26:1, 30; Isa 2:18; 10:11; 19:1; 21:9; 31:7; 46:6; Dan 5:4, 23; 6:28 [LXX expansion]; Jdt 8:18; and esp. Deut 4:8 and 31:29 [cf. Acts 7:41]). In this conjunction there is also the notable reference in Isa 16:12, where the description of Moab's sanctuary is "that made with hands" (τὰ χειροποίητα αὐτῆς), linking "made with hands" (χειροποίητος) there with a pagan temple (cf. Acts 17:24: κύριος οὐκ ἐν χειροποιήτοις ναοῖς κατοικεῖ). It seems unlikely that Luke or his readers would have missed the nuances of the language used in 7:48.[122] Up to this point Luke has been allusive and more subtle in his presentation, but now at the end he is verging on ridicule, assaulting the heart of the cherished beliefs of Stephen's opponents: that the temple is sacrosanct. The writer has effectively developed the theme of rebelliousness and disobedience, ultimately connecting it to the practice of idolatry (cf. Deut 31:27–29, where disobedience is explicitly linked with idolatry; also Deut 4:25–28; 30:17–19). As the story continues, the building of the temple is also interpreted as an act of disobedience and, as a result, not surprisingly linked to idolatry as a "thing made by human hands."[123] This attribution clearly results in a harsh assessment of the temple, which now represents the culminating act of impiety in this particular retelling of the biblical narrative.[124]

In the end, then, Stephen's opponents stand condemned alongside their ancestors as unrighteous, disobedient idolaters, failing to grasp the work of God among them. The factuality of this account for Luke is beside the

---

122. See further Richard, "Creative Use of Amos," 43–44.
123. Similarly, C. H. Talbert, *Reading Acts: A Literary and Theological Commentary on the Acts of the Apostles* (New York: Crossroad, 1997), 78.
124. There are similar anti-temple sentiments expressed elsewhere in Luke-Acts with respect to "pagan" sanctuaries. In Acts 14:13–18, Paul and Barnabas decry the pagan practices of the people of Lystra, especially the sacrifices of the priest "of the temple of Zeus" (14:13, 18). The famous speech of Paul on the Areopagus establishes the same point found in Stephen's oration: God neither dwells in temples made by human hands nor is worshiped by human hands (17:24–25). The pagan anti-temple/anti-ritual stance of Luke is usually taken as given (C. W. Stenschke, *Luke's Portrait of Gentiles prior to Their Coming to Faith* [WUNT 2.108; Tübingen: Mohr Siebeck, 1999], 64; and Jervell, "Church of Jews," 17–19). Luke's own position vis-à-vis pagan temples may be less easy to equate with his view of the temple in Jerusalem, because the latter is reverenced as the place where the "name" of the God of heaven and earth dwells (Deut 12:11; 1 Kgs 8:27, 43). Therefore, the anti-temple sections of Stephen's speech (7:47–50), combined with the Jerusalem apostles' (4:1–22; 5:17–42) and Paul's (21:27–36) conflict in and around the temple, should not necessarily be linked with the sentiments expressed elsewhere in Acts.

point, as he has here used stock Jewish/biblical *topoi* to characterize the virtuous and wicked characters of the surrounding narrative. The promise to Abraham in 7:7 involves worship in "this place" — that is, the land. This promise was fulfilled when Joshua entered the land with the "tent of testimony." The building of the other "place" fundamentally misconstrued the promises (according to the recitation of these in Acts 7:6–7). The purity of the *politeia* thus dissolves after the death of the founder, in particular when the temple is established under Solomon. Therefore, the accusations against Stephen in 6:11, 13–14 are not only false, but the accusers themselves are shown to be the real violators of the laws of Moses and "this holy place." The narrative reversal suggested earlier is thus predicated, in part, on the reversal achieved in the speech itself, in which the insiders are written out of their own tradition.

Characterizing Stephen's Opponents: The Topos of Disobedience

If Stephen's speech is intended to characterize the narrative opponents as belonging to a long line of disobedient ancestors, the task remains to flesh out briefly how this aim is achieved. As an epideictic composition, the speech achieves polarity in terms of its characterization: The heroes of Israel (Abraham, Joseph, and Moses) are separated out from the anonymous fathers or ancestors who reappear throughout the discourse. This polarity is significant in terms of the way in which the speech relates to its narrative context, both bringing Stephen into line with the heroes of the Jewish past and identifying his adversaries with a particular trajectory of opposition within biblical history. The speech attests to the enduring Deuteronomic biblical contrast between the prophets that God raises up for Israel and the rejection of those same prophets by the people.[125] The narrative focus on idolatry also connects well with this larger framework, as the rejection of the prophet frequently can be distilled down to a more fundamental rejection of God through idolatry.

The unit detailing the origins of the people of Israel in 7:2–8 provides the structure for the rest of the speech. There are no negative features in this section, since its function is to lay out the nature of God's promises of enslavement, deliverance, and land that will find progressive fulfillment in the course of the speech. God, who is the main character and agent of Stephen's discourse, tells Abraham that, after deliverance from Egypt, the people are to come to "this place" and worship him (7:7). The focus on "this place"

---

125. On these connections in Acts 7, see O. H. Steck, *Israel und das gewaltsame Geschick der Propheten: Untersuchungen zur Überlieferung des deuteronomistischen Geschichtsbild im Alten Testament, Spätjudentum, und Urchristentum* (WMANT 23; Neukirchen-Vluyn: Neukirchener Verlag, 1967), 265–69; and T. Römer and J.-D. Macchi, "Luke, Disciple of the Deuteronomistic School," in *Luke's Literary Achievement: Collected Essays* (ed. C. M. Tuckett; JSNTSup 116; Sheffield: Sheffield Academic Press, 1995), 182–84.

as "land" is the key for understanding the polemic in the closing portions of the speech. The opening unit thus serves to provide both the structural features of the speech and the overarching themes used to characterize the heroes and ancestors in the ensuing story.

The unit on Joseph initiates the first negative element in the speech: His brothers were "jealous" (ζηλώσαντες, 7:9; cf. the other negative use of this term in 17:5). While this is the only explicit negative reference in the Joseph unit (7:9–16), the biblical tradition upon which it draws is more strongly negative toward the brothers of Joseph. In Luke's case, there may be a sense in which "the patriarchs" (οἱ πατριάρχαι) are being given special dispensation in terms of their characterization due to their biblical status as the eponymous ancestors of the twelve tribes. Yet, in 7:11–13, 15, the phrase οἱ πατέρες ἡμῶν is used in connection with the brothers of Joseph. Given the overtly negative way this phrase is developed in the speech, the patriarchs seem to be painted with the same broad brushstrokes as the rest of the ancestors in Acts 7.

While the Joseph unit is often neglected in treatments of Acts 7, there is much to suggest that the larger themes of the discourse are already present here.[126] Indeed, one point frequently overlooked is that Stephen supplies the explicit motivation (jealousy) for selling Joseph into slavery, which is lacking in the Genesis account.[127] Moreover, the opposition in this narrative is represented by Joseph's "brothers" (7:13), which connects these characters back to the opening line of Stephen's speech in 7:2, where he addresses his own "brothers." Thus, just as the "brothers" in the Joseph narrative were jealous with respect to Joseph, we may be meant to infer that the adversaries of Stephen—his brothers (7:2)—were also jealous and therefore oppressed him (i.e., they cannot withstand his wisdom and spirit and so secretly conspire against him; 6:10–11]). The Joseph narrative may therefore aid in substantiating the larger narrative framework regarding the breakdown of *philia/philanthropia* within the Jewish family.

Moreover, the positive characterization of Joseph in the narrative creates a polarity in the text that further highlights the implied negative connections between Stephen's narrative audience and the ancestors in the Joseph unit. One observes first that the pattern of slavery and deliverance noted in 7:6–7 is already foreshadowed in God's rescue of Joseph from his affliction (7:10), and at the end of 7:9 the speaker notes that "God was with him." Therefore, Joseph is affirmed as one of the righteous characters in the narrative. Further confirmation occurs when Stephen asserts that God gave Joseph grace and wisdom in the eyes of Pharaoh (7:10). Moreover, while the rest of the unit (7:11–15) explains how Israel ended up in Egypt, it also

---

126. E. Richard, "The Polemical Character of the Joseph Episode in Acts 7," *JBL* 98 (1979): 255–67, stresses this feature of the unit.
127. Ibid., 258.

further characterizes Joseph as merciful, because he reached out to those who had persecuted him (7:13–14). The resonance with Stephen should not be missed: Stephen is likewise blessed with "grace" (6:9) and "wisdom" (6:10), and he demonstrates mercy toward those who persecute him (7:60). Thus, given the polarization in the narrative and the clear parallels between Stephen and Joseph, it is likely that the reader is intended to draw similar associations between the brothers/patriarchs and the opponents.

After the unit on Joseph and his brothers comes to a close with their burial in Shechem (7:16), the reader is immediately pointed back to the structuring element of the speech: "But as the time drew near for the fulfillment of the promise that God had made to Abraham..." (7:17a). Stephen then briefly recalls the circumstances leading to the slavery of the people (7:17b–19). Once established, Stephen introduces Moses with praiseworthy features similar to those found in the presentation of Joseph: He is "beautiful before God" (7:20; cf. Heb. 11:23; Josephus, *Ant.* 2.231). Moreover, after being abandoned by his family and being adopted by Pharaoh's daughter (7:21), Stephen notes that Moses was "instructed in all the wisdom of the Egyptians" (7:22; cf. Philo, *Mos.* 1.21, 32; Josephus, *Ant.* 2.230) and that he was "powerful in his words and deeds" (7:22). Aside from Luke characterizing Moses in a fashion akin to the representation of the law-giver in Josephus and Philo, he also draws explicit lines to Stephen as well, who is presented as similarly powerful in word (6:10) and deed (6:8).

The next unit (7:23–29) is critical for the argumentative aims of the discourse. Stephen recounts the story in Exod 2:11–12, in which Moses saves an Israelite from the harsh treatment of an Egyptian taskmaster, killing the latter (7:23–24). In a significant addition to the story, however, the action of Moses is interpreted as a self-conscious attempt on the part of Moses to deliver the people (7:25). The people, however, do not understand. This misunderstanding is developed further when, on the very next day, Moses reproaches some fellow Israelites for fighting among themselves (7:26; cf. Exod 2:13). In almost an exact quotation from Exod 2:14, Moses is rejected as "ruler and judge" over the people by the "unrighteous" individual in the conflict (7:27). Several details are critical at this juncture. First, the narrative in Acts 7 plays up the role of injustice. While the word occurs once in the Exodus narrative in relation to the Israelite perpetrator in the conflict (Exod 2:13), in Acts 7 it occurs three times, once to characterize the action of the Egyptian beating the Israelite (7:24), once to describe the people in the conflict (7:26), and lastly to single out the Israelite perpetrator who rejects Moses (7:27). Moreover, the alignment of the action of the Hebrew with that of the Egyptian is based on the moral quality (injustice) of that action rather than on its specific outward nature as it is in the biblical account (cf. Exod 2:11, 13, where the parallel is limited to the fact that both characters "strike"). Second, the attempt by Moses to reconcile or make peace (7:26) is lacking in the Exodus account. Third, in Acts 7:26b the response of Moses to the quarreling Hebrews is presented in an expanded form (cf. Exod 2:13) with what may appear on the surface to be rather innocuous words: "men," "brothers." These referents are significant because they draw the reader's attention back to the opening address of Stephen in 7:2. It seems that in the Moses narrative (as in the previous Joseph account) there is a similar breakdown of *philia*. In light of the possible allusion to 7:2, one is perhaps to see here again a paradigm for what is happening between Stephen and his opponents. Fourth, unlike in the Exodus account, where Moses flees to Midian because Pharaoh seeks to kill him (2:15), in the account given by Stephen it is suggested that Moses flees because of the words of rejection uttered by the unrighteous Israelite. In this way, the rejection by the "brother" directly leads to Moses' own "exile" (πάροικος) in a foreign land, just as the Israelites are themselves resident aliens in Egypt (πάροικον ἐν γῇ ἀλλοτρίᾳ; 7:6). In a telescoped retelling of the biblical story such as one finds in Acts 7, there is by necessity significant selection in the elements retained. This means that one should pay particularly close attention to narratives that are expanded, such as 7:23–29, which is actually slightly longer in Stephen's speech than in the Exodus account. The various additions and alterations heighten the feature of the rejection of Moses, but more importantly elevate the breakdown of *philia/philanthropia* among the sons of Israel in Egypt, leading to the exile of Moses by the people he seeks to save.

Acts 7:30–34 represents a lull in the speech, insofar as this material supplies a relatively non-oppositional account of Moses' call to save Israel in Egypt. In 7:34 God states that the time has come to fulfill the promises to Abraham in 7:6–7. As in other Jewish retellings of Moses' call narrative, his reluctance to perform the task is completely left out of the treatment. Although the narrative is once again telescoped, one should also bear in mind that the speech is implicitly creating polarity by highlighting the praiseworthy features of the hero. There is thus good reason to leave to one side anything that might mitigate against the desired effect of creating a glorified image of Moses.

The polarity in the remaining portion of the speech now evolves exponentially. The notice of the people's full-scale rejection looks back to the first rejection in 7:25–29: "It was this Moses whom they rejected when they said, 'Who made you a ruler and a judge?' (cf. 7:27) and whom God now sent as both ruler and liberator through the angel who appeared to him in the bush" (7:35). One sees immediately not only the narrator's acceptance of the legitimacy of the first attempt at rescue but also that the singular respondent of 7:27–28 is now pluralized; the Israelites as a whole now seem to be implicated in the first rejection of Moses. Moreover, 7:35 also provides an answer to the question posed in 7:27: It was indeed God who had sent Moses, just as Moses had thought in 7:26. The text then goes on to list the praiseworthy acts Moses did for the people in the second attempt at deliverance. Moses leads the people out, he performs "wonders and signs" (7:36;

cf. Stephen in 6:8), he prophesies that God would raise up a prophet (7:37), and he receives "living oracles" from the angel on Mount Sinai (7:38). The major achievements of Moses are thus placed before the reader, and the explicit judgment is clear: These are all praiseworthy and honorable deeds. Moreover, all of these actions ultimately relate back to God: the fulfillment of God's promise of deliverance (7:7), God as the one who will raise up the prophet (7:37), and the reception of the "living oracles" that are God's law (7:38). Thus, it is no surprise that, in the end, the act of rejecting Moses is in fact portrayed as a rejection of God (7:39–42; cf. 1 Sam 8).

For the second time, then, the people reject Moses, and, even more fundamentally, God. The ancestors who were "in the wilderness with the angel" — the same one who gave the people "living oracles" — rejected the one whom God had raised up for them. They had seen the "wonders and signs" but chose idols "made with hands" over the God of Sinai. For this rejection, they were punished with exile (7:42–43). But the text also foreshadows the inevitable long-term implications of the rejection of Moses: If the people reject the prophet whom God raised up for their deliverance from Egypt (7:34), they will no doubt also reject the prophet like Moses (7:37) whom God will also raise up for the future deliverance of the people (7:52).[128] Here, then, the mention of God and Moses in the charges of 6:11–14 is played out in the speech — but is now reversed: The people, not Stephen, are shown to "speak blasphemous words against Moses and God."

As we saw earlier, the last part of the speech continues to develop the theme of rejection that goes on in spite of the fulfillment of the promises in 7:6–7. The ancestors had the tent of testimony in the wilderness — the one made according to the divine pattern (7:44) — and when it entered the land under Joshua, the promise of "worshiping in this place" (7:7) was fulfilled (7:45). Indeed, David, who like Joseph (and Stephen) also "found favor" (7:46), sought a σκήνωμα for the "God of Jacob." Although mentioned only briefly in the text, David thus joins the list of praiseworthy heroes of the Jewish past. As the speech continues, however, Solomon is depicted as building an οἶκος for God — a temple "made with hands," giving evidence to the fact that even once the people are in the land, they still, according to the speech, fail to grasp the true plan of God. The citation from Isa 66:1–2 demonstrates that God does not live in earthly temples whatever else can be said about the temple in the speech. God does not dwell in the οἶκος that Solomon built. The inability to appreciate Moses' tent of testimony now

---

128. These Mosaic themes have a prominent place in Luke's composition. In a similar way the exile motif is also significant. Just as Moses is exiled to Midian because of rejection (7:29), so also will Stephen suffer death (as the righteous one of 7:52), and the Jerusalem community will be driven out of Jerusalem and scattered (8:1). Thus, the Mosaic pattern established in Stephen's speech is formative for the surrounding narratives. One might also argue that the exile theme related to the disobedient Israelites (7:43) finds a parallel in the Pauline statements in Acts that the gospel is going to the Gentiles because of Jewish rejection (cf. 22:18–21; 28:25–28). See also Sterling, "Opening the Scriptures."

leads to this culminating act of disobedience.[129] The final strike has thus been landed: The temple and the law that form the basis for the accusations against Stephen in 6:11, 13–14, are now viewed in the opposite light.

The rehearsal of Israel's history results in the portrayal of a checkered past that includes the rejection of God's prophets, the violation of the commandment against idolatry, the display of envy, the murder of a prophet, and, finally, a misplaced understanding of God's desire for an οἶκος. The closing of the speech makes these implied charges more explicit: The people are "stiff-necked" and disobedient; they inherited a covenant of circumcision (7:8) but are uncircumcised in their hearts (7:51); they oppose the Holy Spirit (7:51), despite the presence of wonders and signs in their midst (cf. 6:8, 10; 7:36); their ancestors persecuted the prophets and killed those who prophesied about the coming of the Messiah, despite having heard from Moses himself that such a one would be raised up (7:37); the opponents of Stephen have, in turn, also betrayed and murdered this prophesied "Righteous One"; and, lastly, they received the law (ordained by angels, no less; 7:38), but failed to keep it. The harsh tone in ending of the speech (7:51–53) is thus not an afterthought, but is substantiated by the retelling of the biblical narrative that forms the body of the discourse. The explicit invective is the final result of the implicit characterization that has been increasingly impressed on the reader throughout the speech. Moreover, the heroes of the Jewish past are exhibited opposite the disobedient ancestors. These heroes are those whom God has favored and blessed and who represent God's agency in various periods of history. These are the righteous whose own character stands as a witness to the degenerate behavior of the ancestors in this speech and now also Stephen's opponents.

Conclusion

Stephen's speech forms a critical component of the Hellenist/Stephen narrative in Acts 6:1–8:3 and achieves several goals vis-à-vis the larger surrounding unit as a result. First, it characterizes Stephen as someone who speaks with wisdom and whose words "cannot be withstood" (6:10).[130] The speech both culminates in accusations that strike to the heart of the Lukan perspective on Stephen's opponents and also leads to the lynch-mob

---

129. There may be some resonances between this closing of the speech and the pericope on the destruction of Jerusalem in Luke 21:20–24. In 21:22 the express statement is made that the destruction may be both punishment by God and fulfillment of Scripture. While one must keep in mind the situational and "in character" nature of the speech, the main features of Acts 7 would support that Lukan interpretation. The disobedience of the people brought punishment upon them. The citation of Amos 5:25–27 (Acts 7:42–43), then, could have a dual function, pointing to the discipline for the building of the golden calf and creating an expectation for punishment as a consequence for the second "idol": the temple. At the same time, it must be emphasized again that Luke has a multifaceted perspective on the temple, which is determined largely by the narrative context.

130. Tannehill, *Narrative Unity*, 2:83.

scene at the end. The vicious response depicted in the narrative confirms the convictions of the speech: The people continue to reject the prophets and to treat each other with injustice (cf. 7:26–27). Moreover, the language that characterizes Stephen repeatedly occurs in the context of the heroes of the Jewish tradition, placing him in line with Abraham, Joseph, Moses, and David.

Second, the speech retells a story from the past that is in fact happening in the narrative present. The characters find themselves in the midst of a conflict between the God-appointed prophets of the newly formed community and the people outside. There is an apparent breakdown in *philia/philanthropia* among the people, with various members turning against each other. In the case of Stephen, this break will lead to the dramatic reversal evident in his death, where his "brothers and fathers" (7:2) turn on their "brother and son" and in an act of great injustice transgress the law by killing a righteous individual. This fundamental breakdown in *philanthropia* is predicated on a long line of rejection and conflict in the Jewish community as depicted in the speech, and this established paradigm helps the reader appreciate how Stephen, being above reproach in every respect, can suffer the degradation of stoning. From Jewish tradition (esp. Wis 2:12, 14–16) we have seen that the impious are portrayed as lashing out at those who accuse them of violating the law, just as Stephen does in 7:53. And yet the wicked "will see the end of the wise, and will not understand what the Lord purposed for them" (Wis 4:17). So it is with the wise Stephen; although he dies, he is bound for greater things, as the narrative vision of the resurrected Lord reveals (7:55–56). At the same time, while Stephen receives his "crown" for remaining steadfast, the tale of the brothers in the narrative and speech is intended to effect pity and fear in the reader. The speech serves this end in part by creating an environment of rejection and conflict, thereby providing an interpretive framework for what takes place in the narrative setting of the speech. Furthermore, the speech reveals the great biblical reversal: Although God reversed the situation of the Hebrews in Egypt and fulfilled his promise of land to Abraham, the ancestors rejected God, failed to perceive the proper fulfillment of the promises, and ultimately killed his prophets. The speech, then, demonstrates this reversal precisely in the breakdown of *philia* with God, which then plays itself out in further narrative reversals elsewhere in Luke's account, with the ultimate result being that the place of Israel in the biblical story is slowly taken over by the newly founded and expanding *ekklesia* established by Jesus and empowered by his Spirit.

Third, the speech serves to create polarity, with the strongest focus being on Stephen's opponents, who are characterized as disobedient and hardhearted through comparison with their ancestors. Stephen's adversaries come from a long line of the same. The speech thus provides a biblical precedent for viewing these adversaries as impious and unrighteous, confirming that which is already more or less stated in the narrative context.

The rehearsal of Israel's past in Acts 7 is tailored for just this purpose, and taps into a tradition of retelling the exodus event and the founding of the Jewish *politeia* under Moses. While Jewish interpretations, as seen in chapter 4, frequently focused on the praiseworthy elements of this story, in Acts 7 one observes the pattern of the dissolution of law and religion after the time of Moses.[131] Already during Moses' time there is opposition, but the building of the temple in Acts 7 represents a fundamental shift from the time of holy beginnings. This is not, finally, a pro-tabernacle or anti-temple argument in its own right, but a means by which the opponents in the narrative can be characterized as disobedient. Thus, while the *topos* of disintegration of religion under tyrants is reflected in Luke's presentation of the building of the temple, the heart of Acts 7 is not invested here but rather in the explicit invective in 7:51–53. The building of the temple reveals to the reader something significant about Stephen's adversaries, and thus the function of the temple unit rather than its specific content is the most important contribution for Acts 6:1–8:3 as a whole.

Fourth, the speech of Stephen does not address the charges in the narrative and is intentionally so constructed. It is not a judicial speech, despite the judicial narrative setting. It is, rather, an invective against Stephen's opponents. It is an epideictic speech that elaborates the well-established *topoi* of law and temple, utilizing well-entrenched strategies for tendentious and praiseworthy retellings of the biblical narrative. In this case, it uses these elements to proffer not an anti-Jewish stance, but a particular slant on the story that is predicated on the belief that this newly founded *ekklesia* represents the "restored tent" of David (Acts 15:16–17). As is the case in Philo and Josephus, the rewriting of the history of Israel in Acts 7 reveals corresponding values, ideals, and commitments. Further, like the use of genealogies in the *Rhetoric to Alexander*, such retellings of past ancestry highlight either the praiseworthy or blameworthy characters of those in the present. Most importantly, though, the speech explains the action that is taking place in the larger narrative setting, with a focus on Stephen first, but also on the respective treatment of the other heroes of the early Christian movement in Acts. Thus, in line with speeches in ancient historiography more generally, this discourse explains the opposition to the emerging communities depicted in the narrative. Further, just as the narrative portion of Acts 6:1–8:3 emphasizes the praiseworthy features of the newly formed Jerusalem community, so also the speech ultimately provides a counterpart: its mirror opposite in the "outsider" leaders and opponents. In this way, condemnatory features of the shared tradition are highlighted, demonstrating divergence in the

---

131. Cf. the accounts of Strabo and Tacitus delineated in the previous chapter. The parallel in the *Clementine Recognitions* is also noteworthy (1.38.5–39.1), where there is a similar connection between the move to the temple and the transfer from king to tyrant, which, it should be added, also finds associations in the biblical tradition itself (1 Sam 8:9–18; 1 Kgs 5:13; 9:15; 2 Kgs 12:4, 14). See further Klinghardt, *Gesetz und Volk Gottes*, 297–98, 300–302.

people of Israel from its very inception, thereby establishing both a righteous heroic trajectory that ends in the early community of Jerusalem and a disobedient tradent that leads directly to Stephen's accusers. In the process, the speech confirms the narrative elements being developed, subsequently providing amplification of the implicit results of the narrative *synkrisis* already achieved.

Fifth, Stephen's discourse represents speech-in-character, which means that Luke has composed a speech that sounds like the kind Luke thought would have been spoken by such a one as Stephen on this type of occasion. While there are clear connections to other actions and speeches of characters in Luke-Acts, the voice in the text is Stephen's as best articulated and approximated by Luke, which is not to suggest that this voice can necessarily be identified with a historical Stephen. The way Stephen speaks is not the way Peter or Paul do, and although there is a consistent "resonating voice" behind these various speeches, the voice of Luke the historian is consciously submerged. It is thus difficult to ascertain whether Luke himself was committed to the harsh anti-temple statements that surface at the end of the speech. These *logoi* characterize primarily Stephen, not Luke. Moreover, while one can seek specific christological or messianic justifications for the argumentative logic of the speech, ultimately Luke does not have to have any such motivation or reason for composing the speech. On the occasion of being brought up on false charges of blaspheming against the law, Moses, God, and the temple, such a speech as this one that creates reversal by turning the accusers into the accused — by whatever means possible — would seem to be fitting and appropriate to both the character of Stephen as developed by Luke and the specific setting in which the speech is placed. Furthermore, one must also bear in mind that the speech, despite its expansive sweep of Jewish history and its broader implications for the Lukan narrative, fundamentally characterizes the adversaries gathered to render judgment on Stephen. As speech-in-character, this is its primary function. The focus is thus not on Judaism or all Jews in Luke's narrative but on those who are about to stone the prophet. Again, this does not mean it does not have broader implications for other narratives and for the presentation of Jewish characters as a whole in Luke-Acts, but as an effective composition to fit the occasion it must primarily be localized to its immediate narrative setting. That Luke elsewhere portrays the temple as a worthy institution or that many Jews throughout Acts join the new movement are not features that in themselves undermine or conflict with the orientation of the speech. A good ancient historian such as Luke will naturally develop a multifaceted and complex picture of his subject, not allowing a situational speech such as Acts 7 to control in a mechanical way the larger historiographical aims of Luke-Acts. This conclusion should not be taken as a suggestion that serious engagement and criticism of Lukan discursive practices are inappropriate or unnecessary. Rather, the elements of power and violence embedded in this text need to be understood and assessed against a complex backdrop of sociocultural modes of literary production that should nuance the ways interpreters perceive these elements unfolding.

Framing the Hellenists: Luke's Historiographical Aims

In the above analysis of Acts 6:1–8:3, I have argued that the whole unit, including the ordination of the seven as a response to a community crisis in 6:1–7, forms a critical component of the Lukan narrative. Not only is this account situated at a crucial turning point in Acts, but it also draws on some larger themes of Lukan *historia*. Moreover, this unit is also interesting for the window it opens onto the compositional world of Luke. By analyzing the account of the Hellenists and Stephen in detail, one is able to gain a greater appreciation for Luke's literary artistry and historiographical achievement.

The narrative itself details the founding, rise, and development of the newly formed community established by the prophet Jesus through the Spirit among the apostles and followers in Jerusalem. This new *politeia* is embedded in the broader Jewish community of Jerusalem, and Luke intentionally brings the two into comparison throughout Acts. I suggested that in 6:1–7 Luke has drawn on biblical narratives relating to the establishment of the Israelite nation under Moses. I also observed in chapter 4 that the exodus story — representing the movement from Egypt to the founding of the Jewish *politeia* — was an important theme of Jewish retellings of biblical history. It is thus no surprise that Luke uses a particular feature of that tradition — the selection and ordination of elders to help Moses in running community affairs — in his own retelling of the founding of the community in Jerusalem. Here we saw that leaders of this new community respond to the crisis of neglect of the widows by selecting individuals to serve alongside the apostles. Under the leadership of the Twelve, the community in Jerusalem demonstrates not only solid biblical and Greco-Roman virtues, but also, in its constitution of a diversity of Jews from around the world, an openness to foreigners and intermixing that was much prized in Roman sociocultural ideology of the period.

The story of Stephen and his conflict with Hellenistic Jews of the Jerusalem synagogues and the Jerusalem council further draws upon these same themes. Having just seen how the Jerusalem community responds to crisis within its own ranks and receiving affirmation of its *philanthropia* in the process, the reader now observes Luke bringing the Jewish *politeia* into direct comparison with the newly founded entity in 6:1–7. But in this context the results are different. Not only do the opponents evidence the opposite of the virtues and characteristics of Stephen, but the end product is the breakdown of *philia/philanthropia* between two fraternal communities, resulting in the shocking murder of Stephen by his "brothers and fathers." In the Aristotelian sense, this event represents tragedy, with the vivid and dramatic narrative style arousing pity and fear in the reader. By bringing the event before the eyes of the reader, the deep division evidenced in the Jewish people is laid bare. Moreover, the superiority of the newly founded community is manifested not just in its demonstration of the best of Greco-Roman values but also in the narrative implication that it is this movement that is most loyal to God's covenant and law. Concern for the widows and halting of potential civic *stasis* or discord is contrasted with the violation of Mosaic legislation by Stephen's opponents. The literary *synkrisis* results in the negative characterization of the outsiders and the positive depiction of Stephen, who, as one of the heroic martyrs remembered in Acts, embodies, in some respects, the nascent Christian movement as a whole.

Stephen's speech further advances the themes of the narrative. I suggested that the speech, despite its explicit judicial context, is in fact a conscious piece of epideictic invective, which evokes implicit praise for the newly formed community as well. It draws on the *topoi* of land and law, using the exodus theme of the founding of the Jewish *politeia* to polarize the prophets and the people in the development of Jewish history. Figures such as Abraham, Joseph, Moses, and David represent the wise and chosen leadership of the Jewish people, while the people themselves demonstrate throughout a consistent pattern of opposition to and rejection of God's leadership through human representatives. Thus, the speech creates polarity and characterizes each respective group accordingly. Stephen's speech, on the one hand, does not respond to the charges because that is not the interest of the writer of the epideictic composition. On the other hand, it in fact does respond to the charges — at least implicitly — as it evinces a clear and deliberate reversal of the main characters; the accusers end up being the accused and vice versa. The (purported) righteous in word end up illustrating their unrighteousness in deed, whereas Stephen is shown to have a unity of both *logos* and *ergon*.

Further, the basic argument of the speech appears to draw on the theme of the dissolution of religious practice and belief after the time of Moses, although the Deuteronomic pattern of rejection in the Mosaic period contributes to the speech as well. The promises to Abraham therefore are utilized to frame the account so as to illustrate that the ancestors/fathers fundamentally misconstrued the nature of "worshiping in this place" by worshiping other gods and by building the temple. This rejection of God was also present in the rejection of Joseph by his brothers and the rejection of Moses by the Israelites in Egypt during the time of Moses' initial attempt to liberate his people. The rehearsal of Israel's history in Acts 7, like most other retelling in Second Temple Judaism, seeks to make a particular argument vis-à-vis the material being recast. In Acts 7 that point is simple: Stephen and the community he represents manifest wise and chosen leadership, which the people continue to reject in their own time. This rejection is confirmed in the narrative when Stephen is stoned and massive persecution breaks out against his fellow believers in Jerusalem. Lastly, the speech of Stephen ultimately characterizes the speaker as the wise, Spirit-filled individual he is purported to be, demonstrating further the superiority of the *politeia* founded by Jesus and emerging in the early chapters of Acts over and against the narrative foil of Jewish leadership in Jerusalem.

I should make two last points at this juncture. First, throughout Acts 6:1–8:3 Luke evinces the main features of historiographical composition highlighted in chapter 3. In particular, Luke demonstrates interest in tying together the various threads of the historical narrative, joining the apostles with the Hellenists and then these together with Paul. Luke manifests a clear concern to show the way in which the community and the leadership follow a particular line of development, gradually growing and expanding, becoming increasingly intermixed under the direction of the Spirit. Moreover, the city of Jerusalem is the center from which everything moves outward in concentric circles, and it seems to be important for Luke that already at the inception of the community in the city there is Jewish representation from around the known world present *in nuce*. The Hellenists of Acts 6:1–8:3 thus provide a crucial link in Luke's larger narrative, as they are the Diaspora component that exists from the beginning in the Jerusalem community alongside the Hebrew adherents. The designations "Hellenist" and "Hebrew," so important to modern scholars, can quite readily be viewed as Lukan tropes that demonstrate lines of continuity and expansion. These referents are artificial historiographical structures that enable the historian to make a particular argument with respect to the progress of events and characters. For Luke that interest seems to be focused on God as the initiator of both this new *politeia* and its eventual inclusion of Gentiles, which is already prefigured in the openness to foreigners in the earlier section of Acts. Regardless of their actual importance or even existence in the real nascent Christian community of Jerusalem, it is evident that for Luke the Hellenists form the bridge between the apostles of Jerusalem and the Pauline mission among the Gentiles. That link rests not so much on their being the founders of the Antiochian community, but more on their being representative of the expansion of the community beyond the Jewish followers of Jesus in Judea and Galilee, demonstrating intermixing, inclusion, and consequently opening the way for the Gentiles. There is nothing to suggest, however, that the way is opened because they are more liberal in their attitudes toward the law. Rather, the openness comes about precisely because they, as Diaspora Jews living in Jerusalem and present at the inception of the newly founded community, exemplify that God's new work in the Jerusalem apostolic community has not only restored "all Israel," bringing in those dispersed among the nations, but also has established a model of inclusiveness that will soon move out to the next logical step of Gentile incorporation.

Second, in the composition of Acts 6:1–8:3 Luke has exhibited affinities with the Jewish apologetic tradition. In particular, as I argued in the last chapter, this tradition deemphasizes explicit rebuttal and focuses rather on amplification of epideictic themes praising characters and events in light of accepted Greco-Roman values and social norms. This retelling of the tradition in light of cultural dominant values provides a basis for a group's own self-assertion and affirmation in an environment of competitive self-representation. Luke reflects these similar emphases. Acts 6:1–8:3 is not an apologetic piece in terms of providing a judicial response to charges, but is, rather, an epideictic amplification of accepted themes that demonstrate the superiority of the nascent Christian movement. Luke's main interest in the Hellenists and Stephen, then, is the way in which they serve to highlight the praiseworthy features of the newly founded community in its origins and early development. Even the sections of *synkrisis* and invective (Acts 7) form part of this larger literary strategy. They affirm, by negative depiction of the comparative counterpart, the superiority of the offshoot. In the literary environment of competitive historiography, the arguments articulated by Luke look more like intracommunal conflict over self-identity than outright rejection or anti-Jewish sentiment. Luke appears similar here to the Paul of Romans: There is a concerted effort to flex the muscles of a new movement's identity with respect to the larger religious and cultural ethos out of which it emerges, including the distortion and narrative suppression of alternative and competing perspectives.

The rhetorical emphasis, then, is not on adopting a particular set of values or on defending the new movement against hostile attacks, but to affirm the readers in their knowledge that the Christian movement represents the true line of development from Abraham-Joseph-Moses-David to the time of the apostles and Paul, to promote the view that the early Jerusalem community manifests the best of Greek, Roman, and biblical values, and to confirm that this movement is, as attested by the narrative, God-ordained and -instituted. In this way, Luke's story of Stephen and the Hellenists produces assurance regarding the events about which the readers have been instructed. Like Livy's history of Rome or Josephus's history of the Jewish people, the *historia* is a means whereby the writer grounds the values and ideals of his own day in the past story of the people. In the case of Luke, the community of his own time is encouraged to base its self-identity in the story of the foundation and formation of the community in Jerusalem. It is thus a past created for the present.

Epilogue

Historiography, History, and the Academy

The Hellenists as a Lukan Bridge

In the first chapter of this study I set out to situate the Hellenists in modern New Testament scholarship and historiography. I demonstrated the central role this group has played in constructions of the early church's development and theology. With respect to the questions and problems posed in that first chapter, the conclusion of this study should be apparent: the importance attributed to the Hellenists in modern scholarship is a product of its own theological and historical commitments, and may have very little to do with the actual realities of life in the early church. I close here with several concomitant points.

The question of the historicity of the Hellenist episode is both difficult to answer and ultimately irrelevant for understanding Acts as a sociocultural and sociohistorical product. The speech of Acts 7 is most likely a Lukan creation *de novo,* as were many speeches in ancient historiography. The persistence in the history of scholarship to view here a remnant of tradition attests to the entrenchment of scholarly tradition, but ultimately fails to convince for lack of persuasive evidence. If by "tradition" one means that Stephen's speech draws heavily on the characters and text of the Septuagint, then it is indeed a speech that has deep roots in tradition. But according to this standard any speech in an ancient historical work will be traditional in that sense (and not much has been said as a result). Speeches were to resonate with the character of their speakers and be appropriate to their situations, so therefore any effective speech should appear traditional. But there is nothing in Acts 7 to suggest that there lies behind it anything but an adept ancient writer, someone extremely well-versed in Jewish traditions and styles of rewriting the biblical story.

The narrative portions of Acts 6:1–8:3 leave one with the same impression. Could the narratives be historically accurate and true? Absolutely. Could they be completely fabricated? Absolutely. Could the truth rest somewhere in between? Absolutely. The problem, of course, is that it is impossible to prove any of these premises. Attempts by Hengel and others to intuit their way behind the stories aside, the unit is too tightly knit to allow one to go beyond what is given in the narrative itself. If the dominant view in Acts scholarship is that one can separate out the core historical events from the Lukan redaction, this study argues for the futility of such attempts. The charges against Stephen function perfectly well in the narrative context, playing an important role in setting up the speech. The combination of mob scene and court hearing functions to characterize Stephen's opponents (moving from order to disorder in the story), as well as to further the vivid and dramatic qualities of the account, creating a plausible setting and impacting the reader. The community problem reflected in 6:1–7 may mirror real community problems in the early church (or in Luke's own day), but as with the story of Ananias and Sapphira, it also fits well into Luke's larger historiographical aims and patterns. The fact that it does fit does not make it unhistorical, just as the realia surrounding the problem do not preclude it from being viewed as anything but Lukan invention. This scenario, of course, leaves one at an impasse. But perhaps that is the best place to be, since in the overall scheme of Acts the historicity (or lack thereof) of these episodes does not mitigate against the historiographic force of the narrative itself.

What can be affirmed, at present, is that the line of tradition from Baur to Hengel seems to have had much more invested in the Hellenists than may be justified by the place given to them in the Lukan narrative. By attempting to construct a theological history behind a narrative that is, in my perception, impenetrable beyond its current (con)textual setting, this trajectory of scholarship has created a house of cards. The main concern of this focus on the Hellenists can be understood as an attempt to draw a line of development from Jesus to Paul, in order to explain the rise of dissent over Jewish law in the early church. Although such lines may be established elsewhere from New Testament and early Christian evidence, the Hellenist narrative contributes little to this discussion. The attempt to move from one improbable connection to another based on intuition and speculation is a creative exercise, but it will not provide modern critics with any hidden window into the theological and practical life of the early church.

The argument set forth in this monograph is that it is in and through the narrative itself that the historiographic quality is manifested. Luke qua historian has created an account from the viewpoint of "Homer's Zeus" (or, "Moses' Yahweh"), and this feature ultimately makes the narrative impenetrable in terms of the search for bare facts. Luke has produced links, tied events together, drawn connections, constructed the *ethos* of his characters, composed speeches, energized the narrative with vivid and dramatic representations, and fabricated plausible scenarios, all of which further the literary-historiographical aims of his work. Almost all scholars recognize this fundamental framework, despite their repeated attempts to go behind the narrative Luke has constructed. Yet the very admission of this feature of the Lukan project should give one serious pause. The entirety of Luke-Acts is composed in just this manner, and it is highly problematic from a literary standpoint to suggest that one can go through and deftly separate out the Lukan elements from those that are non-Lukan.

Indeed, herein lies one of the possible misconstruals of modern scholarship: the distinction between Luke the historian and Luke the theologian. This dichotomy has proved useful in an attempt to delve beneath the Lukan narrative because at any point that Lukan redactional-theological interest could be detected, the assumption could be made that that part of the narrative or speech is most probably unhistorical. Yet there are two problems with this approach. First, the dichotomy between historian and theologian is largely a modern distinction. The entire Lukan project—including the most pious-sounding "Christianized" phrases—reflect Luke's historical interests. Elements we may choose to label "redactional" could just as easily be construed as obvious Lukan narrative links and plot devices. But there may be many more that we do not perceive because they appear "less theological." Ultimately, from an ancient historiographical perspective, there is significant justification for fusing the historical-critical paradigm with narrative-critical approaches, resulting in a new historical-critical poetics that intersects literary representation with ancient sociocultural reconfiguration. The nature of the genre itself would seem to indicate the appropriateness of this move. If this is the correct approach, then the way in which Acts is understood to be history probably needs to shift from a modern to an ancient notion of *historia*. In terms of the ancient perspective established in this study, *historia* is the narrative taken as a whole and each part viewed in relationship to that whole. One might well make the case that if one studies a text such as Acts solely for what it can yield about the real historical Hellenists, irrespective of the narrative, that text has, from the perspective of Luke, ceased to function as *historia*.

Lastly, it is imperative to restate here the thesis of chapter 5: The entire episode of Acts 6:1–8:3 fits perfectly well into the larger narrative framework created by the writer of Acts. This conclusion means that everything from the community response to the widows, mention of the Hellenists, the ordination of the seven, the account of the accusations against Stephen, his death, his speech, and the persecution of the Jerusalem church all support the larger historiographical interests apparent elsewhere in Acts. There is nothing distinctive in Acts 6:1–8:3 that would somehow set it apart as the one sure point of historicity in the work. The Hellenists are of importance to Luke precisely as Greek-speaking Jews from the Diaspora. Indeed, within the larger framework, it seems fair to suggest that the Hellenists do form a bridge between the apostles and Paul, understanding this bridge to be, in the end, a Lukan historiographic creation. The alleged link that has so often been trumpeted as a reflection of a Lukan cover-up may thus well be a Lukan invention. As noted above, the Hellenists function in a variety of different ways for Luke, but all elements of Acts 6:1–8:3 do eventually tie in with the rest of the Lukan narrative. Luke intends his readers to see a central role for the Hellenists and Stephen, not just in terms of contributing to the diversity of the early Jerusalem community but also, as Hengel has rightly noted, as a link in the expansion of the gospel outward from the apostles and Jerusalem to Paul and the Gentiles. Where Hengel went wrong, however, was in suggesting that this represents a factual, reliable historical link existing in the development of the Christian movement. My own assessment is that Luke probably did not know enough about the early church and its development to be in a position to judge one way or the other.[1] This appraisal, however, is inconsequential for Luke's *historia* — and an effective *historia* it is. The very tenacity evidenced by scholars such as Hengel in holding to the Hellenists as the historical bridge between Jesus and Paul demonstrates the success of Luke's literary achievement, ranking him as a premiere first-century historian. After all, while Luke may have created the bridge, it is a testament to his historiographical imagination and rhetorical prowess that we should so firmly hold to a version of Christian origins that cannot dispense with it.

Concluding Post-Critical Reflections

In the preface I conclude with the observation that one of the suggestions of this study is that there is an explicit interrelation between the ideology of the text and that of subsequent interpreters with respect to the Lukan Hellenist narrative. There exists a connection between Lukan literary artistry and rhetorical sophistication in the composition of the narrative and its consequent power in shaping perspectives of modern scholars. More important and in need of further reflection, however, are the implications of this observation for the history of interpretation, as the interplay between the ideology of the text and interpreter has also resulted in the reproduction of the text's ideology in the modern world — sometimes with devastating consequences.[2] This point also represents the basis for justifying a more thorough analysis of the ideology embedded in the Lukan narrative. It is not enough to argue, as I have done in chapter 5, that Luke's rhetorical stance is representative of more extended patterns of socially and culturally contextualized modes of argumentation. Indeed, since interpreters of this text have frequently reproduced the oppositional qualities of the discourse embedded in the text,

---

1. This position was articulated earlier by M. Dibelius, "The Acts of the Apostles as an Historical Source," in *Studies in the Acts of the Apostles* (ed. H. Greeven; London: SCM, 1956), 103. Cf. M. Palmer Bonz, who argues that "had Luke decided to do so, he certainly could have written an informed history of Christian Origins" (*The Past as Legacy: Luke-Acts and Ancient Epic* [Minneapolis: Fortress, 2000], 188). This assertion is not at all clear and certain.

2. I have traced this point in somewhat more detail in T. Penner, "Early Christian Heroes and Lukan Narrative: Stephen and the Hellenists in Ancient Historiographical Perspective," in *Persuasion and Performance: Rhetoric and Reality in Early Christian Discourse* (ed. W. Braun; SCJ; Waterloo, Ont.: Wilfrid Laurier Press, forthcoming).

it will never be enough to remain at the level of merely examining the modern interpretation of the text. Rather, the original text is bound up with the effective history of interpretation.

Thus, while I have not entered into that engagement of the Hellenist narrative in this study, I consider that to be the next logical and very necessary step. However understandable the representation of Jewish characters may be in the Lukan narrative, it is, finally, a sociocultural representation in which the voice of those characters is not given a chance to be heard on its own terms, and in which the subaltern other is made into the violator of the victim(s) in the narrative. This reversal makes perfect sense within the epideictic framework outlined in chapters 3 and 4, but "making sense" is different from "making meaning," and it is in the latter that the effective power of the story resides. The fact that Jewish representations of the other in the same relative time period reflect similar discursive practices and agendas only serves to heighten the need for postcolonial challenges to oppositional rhetoric in any form, but perhaps especially so in texts that ground the legitimization of such rhetoric in ultimate and final topics of social and cultural discourse.

Finally, and in line with some of the broader observations in this study, I should reflect briefly on two features that will no doubt raise some objections by scholars: the view of *historia* that is touted as the "ancient understanding" and the nature of Lukan narrative as fundamentally epideictic in orientation. I have laid out my reasonings and arguments throughout this study. I will not repeat those here. I do realize, naturally, that my own personal and cultural topics are very much involved in my construal and reconfiguration of the ancient historiographical discussion reflected in chapter 3. To deny that would be futile; although I maintain the viewpoints articulated herein, I am also aware that others with different "final topics" and different positionings within the modern world will view and interpret the evidence differently. Further, with respect to the role of epideictic rhetoric in historical composition, and particularly with respect to Acts, I must admit my frustration that I did not have the space in this study to detail that with respect to the entire book of Acts. No doubt, the persuasiveness of the argument made in chapter 5 would be more robust had I developed an entire reading of Acts in this light. I am currently working on such a project in larger and smaller ways.[3] Further elaboration on this theme will be necessary to convince the more skeptical.

---

3. The larger project is a socio-rhetorical commentary on Acts for the Rhetoric of Religious Antiquity Series (ed. D. F. Watson; DEO Press, forthcoming). For smaller excursions, see T. Penner, "Civilizing Discourse: Acts, Declamation, and the Rhetoric of the *Polis*," in *Contextualizing Acts: Lukan Narrative and Greco-Roman Discourse* (ed. T. Penner and C. Vander Stichele; SBLSymS 20; Atlanta: Society of Biblical Literature, 2003), 65–104; idem, "*Res Gestae Divi Christi*: Miracles, Early Christian Heroes, and the Discourse of Power in Acts," in *The Role of Miracle Discourse in the Argumentation of the New Testament* (ed. D. F. Watson; SBLSymS; Atlanta: Society of Biblical Literature, forthcoming); and T. Penner and C. Vander Stichele, "Gendering Violence: Patterns of Power and Constructs of Masculinity in the Acts of

Aside from these more general points, however, I believe that there is inevitably some degree of correlation between the epideictic emphasis and the nature of *historia* argued for in this study. On the one hand, I can imagine some readers of this monograph will resist the historical implications of my understanding of *historia*, given the difficulty that results for reconstructing earliest/earlier/early Christianity. As far as that goes, I am not convinced that we are in a much better position to reconstruct the "Lukan community" either. Hence, aside from broader correlations with ancient modes of discourse and the embedded sociocultural topics, a "history of Christianity" from within this framework looks and is quite different. Without denying the importance of material remains, it is, ultimately, a textual and discursive history. On the other hand, my choice to highlight the epideictic discursive practices of Lukan narrative may strike some as equally problematic. No doubt the argument at one level will be that I have overlooked or, at the very least, deemphasized the judicial and deliberative features of the discourse. Perhaps this is the case. But I wonder if there is not more to this scenario than might at first be apparent.

A strong and pervasive commitment in the history of modern scholarship, particularly in post–World War II criticism, encourages the construction of trajectories of what I would label "safe" or "comfortable" spheres from which to describe and assess the discursive practices and products of early Christianity. For example, there has been repeated emphasis on the Hebrew biblical tradition ("according to the scriptures") for understanding Lukan narrative dynamics.[4] This emphasis is not incorrect per se, but nonetheless reflects broader ideological and theological (alongside cultural) commitments of scholarship that should at the very least be noted and examined more fully. To what degree and in what ways, then, are the conventional modes of analysis also protecting our texts? In the context of this study, I would suggest that negative reaction to emphasis on epideictic is caught up, at least in part, in these larger issues. No doubt an aspect of this phenomenon is the frequent affiliation of epideictic composition with fictionalizing and fictive literature, an association that conflicts with modern understandings of ancient *historia* as being factually true. Thus, I think the issues related to one not inconsequentially spill over into the other. More than this, at the conclusion of this study I have come to wonder more generally about the nature of Aristotle's famous tripartite classification of oratory into deliberative, forensic, and demonstrative, with the subsequent muting of the epideictic/demonstrative tradent. Given the nexus of the ancient *polis*, particularly the power politics at stake/play in deliberative and judicial oratory,

---

the Apostles," in *Feminist Companion to Acts* (ed. A.-J. Levine and M. Blickenstaff; FCNT; New York: Continuum, forthcoming).

4. For further discussion along these lines, see my "Contextualizing Acts," in *Contextualizing Acts* (ed. Penner and Vander Stichele), 1–21; and "Madness in the Method? The Acts of the Apostles in Current Study," *CurBR* 2 (2004): 224–95.

it is necessary to question the guild's overwhelming emphasis on both of these categories at the expense of epideictic, particularly with respect to the canonical Christian writings.[5] Is there something here about our own guildish ethos being inscribed on the writings of the past? Do we have a need to assert the civic (religious?) importance of our writings in a way that the category "epideictic" just does not do in our own frames of reference? Ultimately, it seems there may be more at stake in our classifications of ancient literature than we realize or admit. Indeed, one may go as far as to suggest that similar to our ancient counterparts, we not only interpret and construct the present through the past, but we also reconfigure and construct the past through our present values and ideologies. Aristotlean mimesis ends up being a river that flows in both directions.

The challenge of this study perhaps lies most clearly at this juncture: How carefully and fully have we considered and thought through our historiographical and historical frameworks? If there is a connection between the ideology of the Lukan narrative of the Hellenists and modern scholarly interpretation, is there also then a relative social, political, and cultural similarity? To what degree are our own serious, high-minded scholarly convictions and conventions also about our own identity formation? Are there losers in this process? If so, who are they? The power of the guild and its traditions holds a significant (sometimes spellbinding) sway over our viewing, and there may be much at stake in terms of power alignments and configurations should dominant paradigms change. Nonetheless, this study suggests that wherever we end up on the issues related to Acts, history, *historia,* and the sociocultural world of antiquity, the questions raised are at least worth considering. In the end, perhaps further reflection on the nature of learning and evolution of knowledge in the academy may finally help us move one step closer to understanding Luke and his world. Despite all our differences, we may, in the end, be more similar than we realize.

---

5. For similar observations with respect to the genre of Acts, see C. Vander Stichele, "Gender and Genre: Acts in/of Interpretation," in *Contextualizing Acts* (ed. Penner and Vander Stichele), 311–29; and T. Penner, "Reconfiguring the Rhetorical Study of Acts: Reflections on the Method in and Learning of a Progymnastic Poetics," *PRSt* 30 (2003): 425–39.

Bibliography

This bibliography contains a list of works cited. Most translations of ancient authors were taken from the Loeb Classical Library. Those translations that were not can be found here as well.

Albrect, M. von. *A History of Roman Literature: From Livius Andronicus to Boethius.* 2 vols. Revised by G. Schmeling. Translated by F. and K. Newman. MnSup 165. Leiden: Brill, 1997.

Alexander, L. C. A. "The Acts of the Apostles as an Apologetic Text." Pages 15–44 in *Apologetics in the Roman Empire: Pagans, Jews, and Christians.* Edited by M. Edwards et al. New York: Oxford University Press, 1999.

———. "Fact, Fiction, and the Genre of Acts." *NTS* 44 (1998): 380–99.

———. " 'Foolishness to the Greeks': Jews and Christians in the Public Life of the Empire." Pages 229–49 in *Philosophy and Power in the Graeco-Roman World: Essays in Honour of Miriam Griffen.* Edited by G. Clark and T. Rajak. New York: Oxford University Press, 2002.

———. "The Preface to Acts and the Historians." Pages 73–103 in *History, Literature, and Society in the Book of Acts.* Edited by B. Witherington. Cambridge: Cambridge University Press, 1996.

———. *The Preface to Luke's Gospel: Literary Convention and Social Context in Luke 1.1–4 and Acts 1.1.* SNTSMS 78. Cambridge: Cambridge University Press, 1993.

Allen, J. L. " 'The Protoevangelium of James' as an 'Historia': The Insufficiency of the 'Infancy Gospel' Category." *SBLSP* 30 (1991): 508–17.

Allen, O. W. *The Death of Herod: The Narrative and Theological Function of Retribution in Luke-Acts.* SBLDS 158. Atlanta: Scholars Press, 1997.

Anderson, G. *Ancient Fiction: The Novel in the Graeco-Roman World.* London: Croom & Helm, 1984.

———. "Lucian: Tradition versus Reality." *ANRW* 2.34.2 (1993): 1422–47.

———. *Philostratus: Biography and Belles Lettres in the Third Century* A.D. London: Croom & Helm, 1986.

———. *The Second Sophistic: A Cultural Phenomenon in the Roman Empire.* New York: Routledge, 1993.

Annas, J. *The Morality of Happiness.* New York: Oxford University Press, 1993.

———. "Truth and Knowledge." Pages 84–104 in *Doubt and Dogmatism: Studies in Hellenistic Epistemology.* Edited by M. Schofield et al. Oxford: Clarendon, 1980.

Arai, S. "Zum 'Tempelwort' Jesus in Apostelgeschichte 6.14." *NTS* 34 (1988): 397–410.

Atkinson, J. E. "Q. Curtius Rufus' 'Historiae Alexandri Magni.' " *ANRW* 2.34.4 (1991): 3447–83.

Atkinson, K. "On Further Defining the First-Century CE Synagogue: Fact or Fiction?" *NTS* 43 (1997): 491–502.

Attridge, H. W. *The Interpretation of Biblical History in the Antiquitates Judaicae of Flavius Josephus.* HDR 7. Missoula, Mont.: Scholars Press, 1976.

Aune, D. E. "Luke 1:1–4: Historical or Scientific Prooimion?" Pages 138–48 in *Paul, Luke, and the Graeco-Roman World: Essays in Honour of Alexander J. M. Wedderburn.* Edited by A. Christophersen et al. JSNTSup 217. Sheffield: Sheffield Academic Press, 2003.

Avemarie, F. *Die Tauferzählungen der Apostelgeschichte: Theologie und Geschichte.* WUNT 139. Tübingen: Mohr Siebeck, 2001.

Avenarius, G. *Lukians Schrift zur Geschichtsschreibung.* Meisenheim, Germany: Hain, 1956.

Aziza, C. "L'utilisation polémique du récit de l'Exode chez les écrivains alexandrins (IVème siècle av. J.-C.–Ier siècle ap. J.-C.)" *ANRW* 2.20.1 (1987): 41–65.

Bachmann, M. "Die Stephanusepisode (Apg 6,1–8,3): Ihre Bedeutung für die Lukanische Sicht des jerusalemischen Tempels und des Judentums." In *The Unity of Luke-Acts.* Edited by J. Verheyden. BETL 142. Leuven: Leuven University Press, 1999: 545–62.

Bacon, B. W. *The Gospel of the Hellenists.* Edited by C. H. Kraeling. New York: Henry Holt, 1933.

Bakhtin, M. M. *The Dialogic Imagination: Four Essays.* Edited by M. Holquist. Translated by C. Emerson and M. Holquist. Austin: University of Texas Press, 1981.

Balch, D. L. "ἀκριβῶς... γράψαι [Luke 1:3]: To Write the Full History of God's Receiving All Nations." Pages 229–50 in *Jesus and the Heritage of Israel: Luke's Narrative Claim upon Israel's Legacy.* Edited by D. P. Moessner. Harrisburg, Pa.: Trinity Press International, 1999.

———. "Comments on the Genre and a Political Theme of Luke-Acts: A Preliminary Comparison of Two Hellenistic Historians." *SBLSP* 28 (1989): 343–61.

———. "The Cultural Origin of 'Receiving All Nations' in Luke-Acts: Alexander the Great or Roman Social Policy." Pages 483–500 in *Early Christianity and Classical Culture: Comparative Studies in Honor of Abraham J. Malherbe.* Edited by J. T. Fitzgerald, T. H. Olbricht, and L. M. White. NovTSup 110. Leiden: Brill, 2003.

———. "ΜΕΤΑΒΟΛΗ ΠΟΛΙΤΕΙΩΝ. Jesus as Founder of the Church in Luke-Acts: Form and Function." Pages 139–88 in *Contextualizing Acts: Lukan Narrative and Greco-Roman Discourse.* Edited by T. Penner and C. Vander Stichele. SBLSymS 20. Atlanta: Society of Biblical Literature, 2003.

———. "Rich and Poor, Proud and Humble in Luke-Acts." Pages 214–33 in *The Social World of the First Christians: Essays in Honor of Wayne Meeks.* Edited by L. M. White and O. L. Yarbrough. Minneapolis: Fortress, 1995.

———. "Two Apologetic Encomia: Dionysius on Rome and Josephus on the Jews." *JSJ* 13 (1982): 102–22.

———. "'...you teach all the Jews...to forsake Moses, telling them not to... observe the customs' (Acts 21:21; cf. 6:14)." *SBLSP* 32 (1993): 369–83.

Bannon, C. J. *The Brothers of Romulus: Fraternal Pietas in Roman Law, Literature, and Society.* Princeton: Princeton University Press, 1997.

Barclay, J. M. G. *Jews in the Mediterranean Diaspora: From Alexander to Trajan (323 B.C.E.–117 C.E.).* Edinburgh: T & T Clark, 1996.

———. "Manipulating Moses: Exodus 2.10–15 in Egyptian Judaism and the New Testament." Pages 28–46 in *Text as Pretext: Essays in Honour of Robert Davidson.* Edited by R. P. Carroll. JSOTSup 138. Sheffield: Sheffield Academic Press, 1992.

Bar-Kochva, B. *Pseudo-Hecataeus, "On the Jews": Legitimizing the Jewish Diaspora.* HCS 21. Berkeley: University of California Press, 1996.

Barr, D. L., and J. L. Wentling. "The Conventions of Classical Biography and the Genre of Luke-Acts: A Preliminary Study." Pages 63–88 in *Luke-Acts: New Perspectives from the Society of Biblical Literature Seminar.* Edited by C. H. Talbert. New York: Crossroad, 1984.

Barrett, C. K. "Attitudes to the Temple in the Acts of the Apostles." Pages 345–67 in *Templum Amicitiae: Essays on the Second Temple Presented to Ernst Bammel.* Edited by W. Horbury. JSNTSup 48. Sheffield: Sheffield Academic Press, 1991.

———. *A Critical and Exegetical Commentary on the Acts of the Apostles.* 2 vols. ICC. Edinburgh: T & T Clark, 1994, 1998.

———. "Old Testament History according to Stephen and Paul." Pages 57–69 in *Studien zum Text und Ethik des Neuen Testaments: Festschrift zum 80. Geburtstag von Heinrich Greeven.* Edited by W. Schrage. BZNW 47. Berlin: de Gruyter, 1986.

———. "Stephen and the Son of Man." Pages 32–38 in *Apophoreta: Festschrift für Ernst Haenchen zu seinem 70. Geburtstag am 10. Dezember 1964.* Edited by W. Eltester. BZNW 30. Berlin: Töpelmann, 1964.

Bartchy, S. S. "Community of Goods in Acts: Idealization or Social Reality?" Pages 309–18 in *The Future of Early Christianity: Essays in Honor of Helmut Koester.* Edited by B. A. Pearson. Minneapolis: Fortress, 1991.

Barton, T. "The *Inventio* of Nero: Suetonius." Pages 48–63 in *Reflections of Nero.* Edited by J. Elsner and J. Masters. Chapel Hill: University of North Carolina Press, 1994.

———. *Power and Knowledge: Astrology, Physiognomics, and Medicine under the Roman Empire.* Ann Arbor: University of Michigan Press, 1994.

Bartsch, S. *Decoding the Ancient Novel: The Reader and the Role of Description in Heliodorus and Achilles Tatius.* Princeton: Princeton University Press, 1989.

Batstone, W. W. "The Antithesis of Virtue: Sallust's *Synkrisis* and the Crisis of the Late Republic." *CA* 7 (1988): 1–29.

Baumgarten, A. I. "Invented Traditions of the Maccabean Era." Pages 197–210 in *Geschichte-Tradition-Reflexion: Festschrift für Martin Hengel zum 70. Geburtstag*. Edited by H. Cancik, H. Lichtenberger, and P. Schäfer. Vol. 1. Tübingen: Mohr Siebeck, 1996.

Baur, F. C. "Die Christuspartei in der korinthischen Gemeinde, der Gegensatz des petrinischen und paulinischen Christentums in der ältesten Kirche, der Apostel Petrus in Rom." *TZTh* 4 (1831): 61–206.

———. "De orationis habitae a Stephano Act. Cap. VII. Consilio, et de Protomartyris hujus in christianae rei primordiis momento." *Festum Christi Natalitium* (Tübingen) (1829): 1–40.

———. *Paul the Apostle of Jesus Christ, His Life and Works, His Epistles and Teachings; A Contribution to a Critical History of Primitive Christianity*. Edited by E. Zeller. 2 vols. 2d ed. London: Williams & Norgate, 1873, 1875. Reprint, Peabody, Mass.: Hendrickson, 2003.

Baynham, E. *Alexander the Great: The Unique History of Quintus Curtius*. Ann Arbor: University of Michigan Press, 1998.

Becker, C. "Sallust." *ANRW* 1.3 (1973): 720–54.

Belfiore, E. S. *Murder among Friends: Violation of* Philia *in Greek Tragedy*. New York: Oxford University Press, 2000.

———. *Tragic Pleasures: Aristotle on Plot and Emotion*. Princeton: Princeton University Press, 1992.

Berger, K. *Exegese und Philosophie*. SBS 123/124. Stuttgart: Katholisches Bibelwerk, 1986.

———. *Theologiegeschichte des Urchristentums*. 2d ed. Tübingen: Francke, 1995.

Berthelot, K. *Philanthrôpia judaica: Le débat autour de la "misanthropie" des lois juives dans l'Antiquité*. JSJSup 76. Leiden: Brill, 2003.

Betz, H. D. "In Defense of the Spirit: Paul's Letter to the Galatians as a Document of Early Christian Apologetics." Pages 99–114 in *Aspects of Religious Propaganda in Judaism and Early Christianity*. Edited by E. Schüssler-Fiorenza. Notre Dame, Ind.: University of Notre Dame Press, 1976.

Beuken, W. "Does Trito-Isaiah Reject the Temple? An Intertextual Inquiry into Isa. 66.1–6." Pages 53–66 in *Intertextuality in Biblical Writings: Essays in Honour of Bas van Iersel*. Edited by S. Draisma. Kampen, Netherlands: Kok, 1989.

Beyer, H. W. "διακονέω, διακονία, διάκονος." *TDNT* 2:81–93.

Bickerman, E. J. "The Jewish Historian Demetrios." Pages 72–84 in *Christianity, Judaism, and Other Greco-Roman Cults: Studies for Morton Smith at Sixty*. Edited by J. Neusner. Vol. 3. SJLA 12. Leiden: Brill, 1975.

Bihler, J. *Die Stephanusgeschichte im Zusammenhang der Apostelgeschichte*. MTS 1.16. Munich: Hueber, 1963.

Bilde, P. *Flavius Josephus between Jerusalem and Rome*. JSPSup 2. Sheffield: Sheffield Academic Press, 1988.

Binder, D. D. *Into the Temple Courts: The Place of the Synagogues in the Second Temple Period*. SBLDS 169. Scholars Press, 1999.

Blum, R. *Kallimachos: The Alexandrian Library and the Origins of Bibliography.* Madison: University of Wisconsin Press, 1991.
Blundell, M. W. "*Ēthos* and *Dianoia* Reconsidered." Pages 155–75 in *Essays on Aristotle's Poetics.* Edited by A. O. Rorty. Princeton: Princeton University Press, 1992.
———. *Helping Friends and Harming Enemies: A Study in Sophocles and Greek Ethics.* Cambridge: Cambridge University Press, 1989.
Boismard, M.-É., and A. Lamouille. *Les Actes des Deux Apôtres: III Analyses Litteréraires.* EBib ns 14. Paris: Gabalda, 1990.
Bonner, S. *Education in Ancient Rome: From the Elder Cato to the Younger Pliny.* Berkeley: University of California Press, 1977.
Bosworth, A. B. *Alexander the Great and the East: The Tragedy of Triumph.* Oxford: Clarendon, 1996.
———. *From Arrian to Alexander: Studies in Historical Interpretation.* New York: Oxford University Press, 1988.
Bousset, W. *Kyrios Christos: A History of Belief in Christ from the Beginnings of Christianity to Irenaeus.* Translated by J. E. Steely. Nashville: Abingdon, 1970 (1921).
Bowersock, G. W. *Fiction as History: Nero to Julian.* Sather Classical Lectures 58. Berkeley: University of California Press, 1994.
Bowie, E. L. "Apollonius of Tyana: Tradition and Reality." *ANRW* 2.16.2 (1978): 1652–99.
———. "Greeks and Their Past in the Second Sophistic." Pages 166–209 in *Studies in Ancient Society.* Edited by M. I. Finley. London: Routledge, 1974.
Bowker, J. W. "Speeches in Acts: A Study in Proem and Yelamedenu Form." *NTS* 14 (1967/68): 96–111.
Bradley, K. R. *Slaves and Masters in the Roman Empire: A Study in Social Control.* New York: Oxford University Press, 1984.
Braun, M. *History and Romance in Greco-Oriental Literature.* Oxford: Basil Blackwell, 1938.
Braun, W. *Feasting and Social Rhetoric in Luke 14.* SNTSMS 85. Cambridge: Cambridge University Press, 1995.
Brawley, R. L. "Abrahamic Covenant Traditions and the Characterization of God in Luke-Acts." Pages 109–32 in *The Unity of Luke-Acts.* Edited by J. Verheyden. BETL 142. Leuven: Leuven University Press, 1999.
Brehm, H. A. "The Meaning of Ἑλληνίστης in Acts in Light of a Diachronic Analysis of ἑλληνίζειν." Pages 180–99 in *Discourse Analysis and Other Topics in Biblical Greek.* Edited by S. E. Porter and D. A. Carson. JSNTSup 113. Sheffield: Sheffield Academic Press, 1995.
———. "The Role of the 'Hellenists' in Christian Origins: A Critique of Representative Models in Light of an Exegetical Study of Acts 6–8." Ph.D. diss., Southwestern Baptist Theological Seminary (Fort Worth, Texas), 1992.
———. "Vindicating the Rejected One: Stephen's Speech as a Critique of the Jewish Leaders." Pages 266–99 in *Early Christian Interpretation of the Scriptures of*

Israel: Investigations and Proposals. Edited by C. A. Evans and J. A. Sanders. JSNTSup 148. SSEJC 5. Sheffield: Sheffield Academic Press, 1997.

Briant, P. "History and Ideology: The Greeks and 'Persian Decadence.'" Pages 193–210 in *Greeks and Barbarians.* Edited by T. Harrison. New York: Routledge, 2002.

Brodie, T. L. "The Accusing and Stoning of Naboth (1 Kgs 21:8–13) as One Component of the Stephen Text (Acts 6:9–14; 7:58a)." *CBQ* 45 (1983): 417–32.

Bruce, F. F. "Stephen's Apologia." Pages 37–50 in *Scripture: Meaning and Method; Essays Presented to Anthony Tyrell Hanson for His Seventieth Birthday.* Edited by B. P. Thompson. Hull: Hull University Press, 1987.

Bultmann, R. *Theology of the New Testament.* 2 vols. Translated by K. Grobel. New York: Charles Scribner's Sons, 1951.

Burchard, C. *Der dreizehnte Zeuge: Traditions- und kompositions-geschichtliche Untersuchungen zu Lukas' Darstellung der Frühzeit des Paulus.* FRLANT 103. Göttingen: Vandenhoeck & Ruprecht, 1970.

Burgess, T. C. "Epideictic Literature." *Studies in Classical Philology* 3 (1902): 89–261.

Burton, J. B. *Theocritus's Urban Mimes: Mobility, Gender, and Patronage.* HCS 19. Berkeley: University of California Press, 1995.

Buss, M. F. -J. *Die Missionspredigt des Apostels Paulus im pisidischen Antiochien.* FzB 38. Stuttgart: Katholisches Bibelwerk, 1980.

Butts, J. R. "The Progymnasmata of Theon: A New Text with Translation and Commentary." Ph.D. diss., Claremont Graduate School (California), 1986.

Byrskog, S. "History or Story in Acts — A Middle Way? The 'We' Passages," Historical Intertexture and Oral History." Pages 257–83 in *Contextualizing Acts: Lukan Narrative and Greco-Roman Discourse.* Edited by T. Penner and C. Vander Stichele. SBLSymS 20. Atlanta: Society of Biblical Literature, 2003.

———. *Story as History — History as Story: The Gospel Tradition in the Context of Ancient Oral History.* WUNT 123. Tübingen: Mohr Siebeck, 2000.

Cadbury, H. J. "The Hellenists." Pages 59–74 in *The Beginnings of Christianity: The Acts of the Apostles.* Edited by F. J. Foakes Jackson and K. Lake. Vol. 5. London: Macmillan, 1933.

———. *The Making of Luke-Acts.* 2d ed. London: SPCK, 1958.

———. "The Speeches in Acts." Pages 426–27 in *The Beginnings of Christianity: The Acts of the Apostles.* Edited by F. J. Foakes Jackson and K. Lake. Vol. 5. London: Macmillan, 1933.

Calame, C. *The Craft of Poetic Speech in Ancient Greece.* Translated by J. Orion. Ithaca: Cornell University Press, 1995.

Callan, T. "The Preface of Luke-Acts and Historiography." *NTS* 31 (1985): 576–81.

Campbell, R. A. *The Elders: Seniority within Earliest Christianity.* Edited by J. Riches. Edinburgh: T & T Clark, 1994.

Cancik, H. *Mythische und historische Wahrheit.* SBS 48. Stuttgart: Katholisches Bibelwerk, 1970.

Cape, R. W. "Persuasive History: Roman Rhetoric and Historiography." Pages 212–28 in *Roman Eloquence: Rhetoric in Society and Literature*. Edited by W. J. Dominik. New York: Routledge, 1997.

Capper, B. "The Palestinian Cultural Context of Earliest Christian Community of Goods." Pages 323–56 in *The Book of Acts in Its Palestinian Setting*. Edited by R. Bauckham. BAFCS 4. Grand Rapids: Eerdmans, 1995.

Cassells, W. *Supernatural Religion: An Inquiry into the Reality of Divine Revelation*. London: Longmans, 1874 (rev. ed. 1879).

Chance, J. B. *Jerusalem, the Temple, and the New Age in Luke-Acts*. Macon, Ga.: Mercer University Press, 1988.

———. "Talbert's New Perspectives on Luke-Acts: The ABCs of Ancient Lives." Pages 181–201 in *Cadbury, Knox, and Talbert: American Contributions to the Study of Acts*. Edited by M. C. Parsons and J. B. Tyson. Atlanta: Scholars Press, 1992.

Charlesworth, J. H., ed. *The Old Testament Pseudepigrapha*. 2 vols. Garden City, N.Y.: Doubleday, 1983, 1985.

Clark, A. C. *Parallel Lives: The Relation of Paul to the Apostles in the Lucan Perspective*. Carlisle, England: Paternoster, 2001.

Clark, D. L. *Rhetoric in Greco-Roman Education*. New York: Columbia University Press, 1957.

Clauss, J. J. *The Best of the Argonauts: The Redefinition of the Epic Hero in Book 1 of Apollonius's* Argonautica. HCS 10. Berkeley: University of California Press, 1993.

Collins, J. J. *Between Athens and Jerusalem: Jewish Identity in the Hellenistic Diaspora*. New York: Crossroad, 1982.

———. "Judaism as *Praeparatio Evangelica* in the Work of Martin Hengel." *RelSRev* 15 (1989): 226–28.

———. "Reinventing Exodus: Exegesis and Legend in Hellenistic Egypt." Pages 52–62 in *For a Later Generation: The Transformation of Tradition in Israel, Early Judaism, and Early Christianity*. Edited by R. A. Argall, B. A. Bow, and R. A. Werline. Harrisburg, Pa.: Trinity Press International, 2000.

Collins, J. N. *Diakonia: Re-interpreting the Ancient Sources*. New York: Oxford University Press, 1990.

Connolly, J. "Like the Labors of Hercules: *Andreia* and *Paideia* in Greek Culture under Rome." Pages 287–317 in *Andreia: Studies in Manliness and Courage in Classical Antiquity*. Edited by R. M. Rosen and I. Sluiter. MnSup 238. Leiden: Brill, 2003.

———. "Mastering Corruption: Constructions of Identity in Roman Oratory." Pages 130–51 in *Women and Slaves in Greco-Roman Culture*. Edited by S. R. Joshel and S. Murnaghan. London: Routledge, 1998.

———. "Problems of the Past in Imperial Greek Education." Pages 339–72 in *Education in Greek and Roman Antiquity*. Edited by Y. L. Too. Leiden: Brill, 2001.

Connor, W. R. "Historical Writing in the Fourth Century B.C. and the Hellenistic Period." Pages 46–59 in *Cambridge History of Classical Literature*. Edited by P. E. Easterling and B. M. Knox. Vol. 1.3. Cambridge: Cambridge University Press, 1985.

Connors, C. "Field and Forum: Culture and Agriculture in Roman Rhetoric." Pages 71–89 in *Roman Eloquence: Rhetoric in Society and Literature*. Edited by W. J. Dominik. New York: Routledge, 1997.

Conzelmann, H. *Acts of the Apostles*. Edited by E. J. Epp and C. R. Matthews. Translated by J. Limburg et al. Hermeneia. Philadelphia: Fortress, 1987.

———. *Gentiles, Jews, Christians: Polemics and Apologetics in the Greco-Roman World*. Translated by M. E. Boring. Minneapolis: Fortress, 1992.

———. *The Theology of St. Luke*. Translated by G. Buswell. Philadelphia: Harper & Row, 1961.

Cornford, F. M. *Thucydides Mythistoricus*. London: Routledge & Kegan Paul, 1965 (1907).

Cox, P. *Biography in Late Antiquity: A Quest for the Holy Man*. The Transformation of the Classical Heritage 5. Berkeley: University of California Press, 1983.

Cribiore, R. *Gymnastics of the Mind: Greek Education in Hellenistic and Roman Egypt*. Princeton: Princeton University Press, 2001.

Crump, D. *Jesus the Intercessor: Prayer and Christology in Luke-Acts*. Grand Rapids: Baker, 1999 (1992).

Cullmann, O. "L'Opposition contre le Temple de Jerusalem, Motif Commun de la Theologie Johannique et du Monde Ambiant." *NTS* 5 (1959): 157–73.

Cunningham, S. *"Through Many Tribulations": Theology of Persecution in Luke-Acts*. JSNTSup 142. Sheffield: Sheffield Academic Press, 1997.

Dahl, N. A. "The Story of Abraham in Luke-Acts." Pages 139–58 in *Studies in Luke-Acts*. Edited by L. E. Keck and J. L. Martyn. Nashville: Abingdon, 1966.

Dalbert, P. *Die Theologie der hellenistisch-jüdischen Missions-Literatur under Ausschluss von Philo und Josephus*. TF 4. Hamburg: Reich, 1954.

Darr, J. A. *Herod the Fox: Audience Criticism and Lukan Characterization*. JSNTSup 163. Sheffield: Sheffield Academic Press, 1998.

Daube, D. *New Testament and Rabbinic Judaism*. London: Athlone, 1956.

———. "A Reform in Acts and Its Models." Pages 151–63 in *Jews, Greeks, and Christians: Religious Cultures in Late Antiquity; Essays in Honor of William David Davies*. Edited by R. Hamerton-Kelly and R. Scroggs. SJLA 21. Leiden: Brill, 1976.

Dehandschutter, B. "Martyrium und Agon: Über die Wurzeln der Vorstellung vom ΑΓΩΝ im Vierten Makkabäerbuch." Pages 215–19 in *Die Entstehung der jüdischen Martyrologie*. Edited by J. W. van Henten. SPB 38. Leiden: Brill, 1989.

DeSilva, D. A. *Despising Shame: Honor Discourse and Community Maintenance in the Epistle to the Hebrews*. SBLDS 152. Atlanta: Scholars Press, 1995.

———. "Investigating Honor Discourse: Guidelines from Classical Rhetoricians." *SBLSP* 36 (1997): 491–525.

Diamond, F. H. "Hecataeus of Abdera and the Mosaic Constitution." Pages 77–95 in *Essays in Ancient History and Historiography in Honor of T. S. Brown*. Edited by S. M. Burstein and L. A. Orkin. Lawrence: Coronado, 1980.

Dibelius, M. *Geschichtliche und übergeschichtliche Religion im Christentum*. Göttingen: Vandenhoeck & Ruprecht, 1925.

———. *Studies in the Acts of the Apostles*. Edited by H. Greeven. London: SCM, 1956.

Dillon, R. J. *From Eye-Witnesses to Ministers of the Word: Tradition and Composition in Luke 24*. AnBib 82. Rome: Biblical Institute Press, 1978.

Dilts, M. R., and G. A. Kennedy, eds. *Two Greek Rhetorical Treatises from the Roman Empire*. MnSup 168. Leiden: Brill, 1997.

Dominik, W. J. *Speech and Rhetoric in Statius' Thebaid*. ATS 27. Hildesheim, Germany: Olms-Weidmann, 1994.

Donaldson, T. L. "Moses Typology and the Sectarian Nature of Early Christian Anti-Judaism: A Study in Acts 7." Pages 230–52 in *New Testament Backgrounds: A Sheffield Reader*. Edited by C. A. Evans and S. E. Porter. BS 43. Sheffield: Sheffield Academic Press, 1997.

Doran, R. "2 Maccabees and 'Tragic History.'" *HUCA* 50 (1979): 107–14.

———. *Temple Propaganda: The Purpose and Character of 2 Maccabees*. CBQMS 12. Washington: Catholic Biblical Association, 1981.

Dover, K. J. *Greek Popular Morality in the Time of Plato and Aristotle*. Indianapolis: Hackett, 1994 (1974).

Downing, F. G. "Honor among Exegetes." *CBQ* 61 (1999): 53–73.

———. "Theophilus's First Reading of Luke-Acts." Pages 91–109 in *Luke's Literary Achievement: Collected Essays*. Edited by C. M. Tuckett. JSNTSup 116. Sheffield: Sheffield Academic Press, 1995.

Droge, A. J. "Josephus between Greeks and Barbarians." Pages 115–42 in *Josephus' Contra Apionem: Studies in Its Character and Context*. Edited by L. H. Feldman and J. R. Levison. AGJU 34. Leiden: Brill, 1996.

Dschulnigg, P. "Die Rede des Stephanus im Rahmen des Berichtes über sein Martyrium (Apg 6,8–8,3)." *Judaica* 44 (1988): 195–213.

Duff, T. E. *Plutarch's Lives: Exploring Virtue and Vice*. New York: Oxford University Press, 1999.

Dungan, D. L. *A History of the Synoptic Problem: The Canon, the Text, the Composition, and the Interpretation of the Gospels*. ABRL. New York: Doubleday, 1999.

Dupont, J. "Apologetic Use of the Old Testament in the Speeches of Acts." Pages 129–59 in *The Salvation of the Gentiles: Studies in the Acts of the Apostles*. Translated by J. Keating. New York: Paulist, 1979.

———. "La structure oratoire du discours d'Étienne (Actes 7)." *Biblica* 66 (1985): 153–67.

Earl, D. "Prologue-form in Ancient Historiography." *ANRW* 1.2 (1972): 842–56.

Easton, B. S. "The Purpose of Acts." Pages 33–118 in *Early Christianity: The Purpose of Acts and Other Papers*. Edited by F. C. Grant. Greenwich, Conn.: Seabury, 1954.

Eckstein, A. M. *Moral Vision in* The Histories *of Polybius*. HCS 16. Berkeley: University of California Press, 1995.

Eddy, S. K. *The King Is Dead: Studies in the Near Eastern Resistance to Hellenism, 334–31 B.C.* Lincoln: University of Nebraska Press, 1961.

Eden, K. *Poetic and Legal Fiction in the Aristotelian Tradition*. Princeton: Princeton University Press, 1986.

Edmunds, L. *Chance and Intelligence in Thucydides*. Cambridge: Harvard University Press, 1975.

Edwards, C. *The Politics of Immorality in Ancient Rome*. Cambridge: Cambridge University Press, 1993.

Edwards, D. R. *Religion and Power: Pagans, Jews, and Christians in the Greek East*. New York: Oxford University Press, 1996.

Elliott, J. H. "Temple versus Household in Luke-Acts: A Contrast in Social Institutions." Pages 211–40 in *The Social World of Luke-Acts*. Edited by J. H. Neyrey. Peabody, Mass.: Hendrickson, 1991.

Esler, P. F. *Community and Gospel in Luke-Acts: The Social and Political Motivations of Lucan Theology*. SNTSMS 57. Cambridge: Cambridge University Press, 1987.

Evans, C. A. "The Prophetic Setting of the Pentecost Sermon." ZNW 74 (1983): 148–50.

Fantham, E. *Roman Literary Culture: From Cicero to Apuleius*. Baltimore: Johns Hopkins University Press, 1996.

Fearghail, F. Ó. *The Introduction to Luke-Acts: A Study of the Role of Lk 1,1–4—4,44 in the Composition of Luke's Two-Volume Work*. AnBib 126. Rome: Pontifical Biblical Institute, 1991.

Fehling, D. *Herodotus and His "Sources": Citation, Invention, and Narrative Art*. Translated by J. G. Howie. Leeds: Cairns, 1989.

Feldherr, A. *Spectacle and Society in Livy's History*. Berkeley: University of California Press, 1998.

Feldman, L. H. "Cicero's Conception of Historiography." Ph.D. diss., Harvard University, 1951.

———. "Hengel's *Judaism and Hellenism* in Retrospect." JBL 96 (1977): 371–82.

———. *Jew and Gentile in the Ancient World: Attitudes and Interactions from Alexander to Justinian*. Princeton: Princeton University Press, 1993.

———. "The Jews as Viewed by Plutarch." Pages 529–52 in *Studies in Hellenistic Judaism*. AGJU 30. Leiden: Brill, 1996.

———. "Josephus as an Apologist to the Greco-Roman World: His Portrait of Solomon." Pages 69–98 in *Aspects of Religious Propaganda in Judaism and Early Christianity*. Edited by E. Schüssler-Fiorenza. Notre Dame, Ind.: University of Notre Dame Press, 1976.

———. *Josephus' Interpretation of the Bible*. HCS 27. Berkeley: University of California Press, 1998.

———. "Pro-Jewish Intimations in Anti-Jewish Remarks Cited in Josephus' *Against Apion*." Pages 177–236 in *Studies in Hellenistic Judaism*. AGJU 30. Leiden: Brill, 1996.

———. "Pro-Jewish Intimations in Tacitus' Account of Jewish Origins." Pages 377–407 in *Studies in Hellenistic Judaism*. AGJU 30. Leiden: Brill, 1996.

———. "Reading between the Lines: Appreciation of Judaism in Anti-Jewish Writers Cited in *Contra Apionem*." Pages 250–70 in *Josephus' Contra Apionem: Studies in Its Character and Context*. Edited by L. H. Feldman and J. R. Levison. AGJU 34. Leiden: Brill, 1996.

———. *Studies in Josephus' Rewritten Bible*. JSJSup 58. Leiden: Brill, 1998.

Ferguson, E. "The Hellenists in the Book of Acts." *ResQ* 12 (1969): 159–80.

Fitzmyer, J. A. *The Acts of the Apostles*. AB 31. New York: Doubleday, 1998.

———. *The Gospel according to Luke I–IX*. AB 28. New York: Doubleday, 1981.

Flory, S. *The Archaic Smile of Herodotus*. Detroit: Wayne State University Press, 1987.

Flower, M. A. *Theopompus of Chios: History and Rhetoric in the Fourth Century B.C.* New York: Oxford University Press, 1994.

Foakes Jackson, F. J., and K. Lake. "The Internal Evidence of Acts." Pages 121–204 in *The Beginnings of Christianity: The Acts of the Apostles*. Edited by F. J. Foakes Jackson and K. Lake. Vol. 2. London: Macmillan, 1922.

———. "Preface." Pages vii–viii in *The Beginnings of Christianity: The Acts of the Apostles*. Edited by F. J. Foakes Jackson and K. Lake. Vol. 1. London: Macmillan, 1920.

Fornara, C. W. *The Nature of History in Ancient Greece and Rome*. Berkeley: University of California Press, 1983.

Friedländer, M. *Geschichte der jüdischen Apologetik*. Amsterdam: Philo, 1973 (1903).

Frier, B. W. *Libri Annales Pontificum Maximorum: The Origins of the Annalistic Tradition*. Rome: American Academy, 1979.

Fuks, A. *Social Conflict in Ancient Greece*. Edited by M. Stern and M. Amit. Leiden: Brill, 1984.

Fusillo, M. "The Mirror of the Moon: Lucian's *A True Story* — From Satire to Utopia." Pages 351–81 in *Oxford Readings in the Greek Novel*. Edited by S. Swain. New York: Oxford University Press, 1999.

Gabba, E. *Dionysius and* The History of Archaic Rome. Berkeley: University of California Press, 1991.

———. "True History and False History in Classical Antiquity." *JRS* 71 (1981): 50–62.

Gager, J. G. *Moses in Greco-Roman Paganism*. SBLMS 16. Nashville: Abingdon, 1972.

Ganser-Kerperin, H. *Das Zeugnis des Tempels: Studien zur Bedeutung des Tempelsmotivs im lukanischen Doppelwerk*. NTAbh ns 36. Münster: Aschendorff, 2000.

Gasque, W. W. *A History of the Interpretation of the Acts of the Apostles*. Peabody, Mass.: Hendrickson, 1989 (1975).

Gaventa, B. R. "The Peril of Modernizing Henry Joel Cadbury." Pages 7–26 in *Cadbury, Knox, and Talbert: American Contributions to the Study of Acts*. Edited by M. C. Parsons and J. B. Tyson. Atlanta: Scholars Press, 1992.

Georgi, D. *The Opponents of Paul in Second Corinthians*. Philadelphia: Fortress, 1986.

Georgiadou, A., and D. H. J. Larmour. "Lucian and Historiography: 'De Historia Conscribenda' and 'Verae Historiae.' " *ANRW* 2.34.2 (1993): 1448–509.

Gera, D. *Warrior Women: The Anonymous* Tractatus De Mulieribus. MnSup 162. Leiden: Brill, 1997.

Gerber, C. *Ein Bild des Judentums für Nichtjuden von Flavius Josephus: Untersuchungen zu seiner Schrift* Contra Apionem. AGJU 40. Leiden: Brill, 1997.

Gilbert, G. "The List of Nations in Acts 2: Roman Propaganda and the Lukan Response." *JBL* 121 (2002): 497–529.

———. "Roman Propaganda and Christian Identity in the Worldview of Luke-Acts." Pages 233–56 in *Contextualizing Acts: Lukan Narrative and Greco-Roman Discourse*. Edited by T. Penner and C. Vander Stichele. SBLSymS 20. Atlanta: Society of Biblical Literature, 2003.

Glad, C. E. "Frank Speech, Flattery, and Friendship in Philodemus." Pages 21–59 in *Friendship, Flattery, and Frankness of Speech: Studies on Friendship in the New Testament World*. Edited by J. T. Fitzgerald. NovTSup 82. Leiden: Brill, 1996.

———. *Paul and Philodemus: Adaptability in Epicurean and Early Christian Psychagogy*. NovTSup 81. Leiden: Brill, 1995.

Gleason, M. W. *Making Men: Sophists and Self-Presentation in Ancient Rome*. Princeton: Princeton University Press, 1995.

Glombitza, O. "Zur Charakterisierung des Stephanus in Act 6 und 7." *ZNW* 53 (1962): 238–44.

Goodman, M. "Josephus' Treatise *Against Apion*." Pages 45–58 in *Apologetics in the Roman Empire: Pagans, Jews, and Christians*. Edited by M. Edwards et al. New York: Oxford University Press, 1999.

———. *Mission and Conversion: Proselytizing in the Religious History of the Roman Empire*. Oxford: Oxford University Press, 1994.

Gowing, A. M. "Cassius Dio on the Reign of Nero." *ANRW* 2.34.3 (1997): 2558–90.

Graf, F. *Greek Mythology: An Introduction*. Translated by T. Marier. Baltimore: Johns Hopkins University Press, 1993.

Grangaard, B. R. *Conflict and Authority in Luke 19:47 to 21:4*. StBL 8. New York: Peter Lang, 1999.

Gray, V. *The Character of Xenophon's* Hellenica. Baltimore: Johns Hopkins University Press, 1989.

Green, J. B. "Internal Repetition in Luke-Acts: Contemporary Narratology and Lucan Historiography." Pages 283–99 in *History, Literature, and Society in the Book of Acts*. Edited by B. Witherington. Cambridge: Cambridge University Press, 1996.

Green, P. *Alexander to Actium: The Historical Evolution of the Hellenistic Age*. HCS 1. Berkeley: University of California Press, 1990.

———. "Clio Perennis: Aspects of Ancient History." Pages 52–73 in *Essays in Antiquity*. New York: World, 1960.

Grossman, M. "Priesthood as Authority: Interpretive Competition in First-Century Judaism and Christianity." Pages 117–31 in *The Dead Sea Scrolls as Background to Postbiblical Judaism and Early Christianity: Papers from an International Conference at St. Andrews in 2001*. Edited by J. R. Davila. STDJ 46. Leiden: Brill, 2002.

Grube, G. M. A. *The Greek and Roman Critics*. Toronto: University of Toronto Press, 1965.

Gruen, E. S. *Diaspora: Jews amidst Greeks and Romans*. Cambridge: Harvard University Press, 2002.

———. *The Hellenistic World and the Coming of Rome*. 2 vols. Berkeley: University of California Press, 1984.

———. *Heritage and Hellenism: The Reinvention of Jewish Tradition*. HCS 30. Berkeley: University of California Press, 1998.

Grundmann, W. "Das Problem des hellenistischen Christentums innerhalb der Jerusalemer Urgemeinde." ZNW 38 (1939): 45–73.

Gunderson, E. *Declamation, Paternity, and Roman Identity: Authority and the Rhetorical Self*. Cambridge: Cambridge University Press, 2003.

———. *Staging Masculinity: The Rhetoric of Performance in the Roman World*. Ann Arbor: University of Michigan Press, 2000.

Haacker, K. "Stephanus in der Geschichte des Urchristentums." ANRW 2.26.2 (1995): 1515–53.

Habinek, T. H. *The Politics of Latin Literature: Writing, Identity, and Empire in Ancient Rome*. Princeton: Princeton University Press, 1998.

Hadas, M. *Aristeas to Philocrates (Letter of Aristeas)*. New York: KTAV, 1973 (1951).

Haenchen, E. *The Acts of the Apostles: A Commentary*. Translated by R. Mcl. Wilson et al. Philadelphia: Westminster, 1971.

———. "The Book of Acts as Source Material for the History of Early Christianity." Pages 258–78 in *Studies in Luke-Acts*. Edited by L. E. Keck and J. L. Martyn. Nashville: Abingdon, 1966.

Hägg, T., and P. Rousseau. "Introduction: Biography and Panegyric." Pages 1–28 in *Greek Biography and Panegyric in Late Antiquity*. Edited by T. Hägg and P. Rousseau. The Transformation of the Classical Heritage 31. Berkeley: University of California Press, 2000.

Hall, R. G. "Josephus' *Contra Apionem* and Historical Inquiry in the Roman Rhetorical Schools." Pages 229–49 in *Josephus'* Contra Apionem: *Studies in*

Its Character and Context. Edited by L. H. Feldman and J. R. Levison. AGJU 34. Leiden: Brill, 1996.

———. *Revealed Histories: Techniques for Ancient Jewish and Christian Historiography.* JSPSup 6. Sheffield: Sheffield Academic Press, 1991.

Halliwell, S. *Aristotle's Poetics.* 2d ed. London: Duckworth, 1998.

———. "Pleasure, Understanding, and Emotion in Aristotle's *Poetics.*" Pages 241–60 in *Essays in Aristotle's Poetics.* Edited by A. O. Rorty. Princeton: Princeton University Press, 1992.

———. *The Poetics of Aristotle: Translation and Commentary.* Chapel Hill: University of North Carolina Press, 1987.

Hankinson, R. J. *The Sceptics.* New York: Routledge, 1995.

Hansen, W. *Phelgon of Tralles' Book of Marvels.* Exeter: University of Exeter Press, 1996.

Hanson, A. T. *Jesus Christ in the Old Testament.* London: SPCK, 1965.

Hanson, R. P. C. "Studies in Texts (Acts 6.13–14)." *Theology* 51 (1947): 142–45.

Harlow, D. C. *The Greek Apocalypse of Baruch (3 Baruch) in Hellenistic Judaism and Early Christianity.* SVTP 12. Leiden: Brill, 1996.

Harnack, A. von. *The Acts of the Apostles.* Translated by J. R. Wilkinson. New York: Williams & Norgate, 1909.

Hartman, L. *"Into the Name of the Lord Jesus": Baptism in the Early Church.* Edinburgh: T & T Clark, 1997.

Harvey, G. "Synagogues of the Hebrews: 'Good Jews' in the Diaspora." Pages 132–47 in *Jewish Local Patriotism and Self-Identification in the Graeco-Roman World.* Edited by S. Jones and S. Pearce. JSPSup 31. Sheffield: Sheffield Academic Press, 1998.

———. *The True Israel: Uses of the Names Jew, Hebrew, and Israel in Ancient Jewish and Early Christian Literature.* AGJU 35. Leiden: Brill, 1996.

Hata, G. "The Story of Moses Interpreted within the Context of Anti-Semitism." Pages 180–97 in *Josephus, Judaism, and Christianity.* Edited by L. H. Feldman and G. Hata. Detroit: Wayne State University Press, 1987.

Hayward, R. *Divine Name and Presence: The Memra.* Oxford Center for Postgraduate Hebrew Studies. Totowa, N.J.: Allanheld, Osmun & Co., 1981.

Heitmüller, W. "Zum Problem Paulus und Jesus." *ZNW* 13 (1912): 320–37.

Hemer, C. J. *The Book of Acts in the Setting of Hellenistic History.* Edited by C. H. Gempf. WUNT 49. Tübingen: Mohr Siebeck, 1989. Repr., Winona Lake, Ind.: Eisenbrauns, 1990.

Hengel, M. *Acts and the History of Earliest Christianity.* Translated by J. Bowden. Philadelphia: Fortress, 1979.

———. "Between Jesus and Paul: The 'Hellenists,' the 'Seven,' and Stephen (Acts 6:1–15, 7:54–8:3)." Pages 1–29, 133–56 in *Between Jesus and Paul: Studies in the Earliest History of Christianity.* Translated by J. Bowden. Philadelphia: Fortress, 1983.

———. "Der Jakobusbrief als antipaulinische Polemik." Pages 248–78 in *Tradition and Interpretation in the New Testament: Essays in Honor of E. Earle Ellis.* Edited by G. F. Hawthorne and O. Betz. Grand Rapids: Eerdmans, 1987.

———. *Jews, Greeks, and Barbarians: Aspects of the Hellenization of Judaism in the Pre-Christian Period.* Translated by J. Bowden. Philadelphia: Fortress, 1980.

———. *Judaism and Hellenism: Studies in Their Encounter in Palestine during the Hellenistic Period.* 2 vols. Translated by J. Bowden. Philadelphia: Fortress, 1974.

———. "The Origins of the Christian Mission." Pages 48–64, 166–79 in *Between Jesus and Paul: Studies in the Earliest History of Christianity.* Translated by J. Bowden. Philadelphia: Fortress, 1983.

Hengel, M., with C. Markschies. *The "Hellenization" of Judaea in the First Century after Christ.* Translated by J. Bowden. Philadelphia: Trinity Press International, 1989.

Hengel, M., with A. M. Schwemer. *Paul between Damascus and Antioch: The Unknown Years.* Translated by J. Bowden. Louisville: Westminster John Knox, 1997.

Henten, J. W. van, and R. Abusch. "The Jews as Tryphonians and Josephus' Strategy of Refutation in *Contra Apionem.*" Pages 271–309 in *Josephus' Contra Apionem: Studies in Its Character and Context.* Edited by L. H. Feldman and J. R. Levison. AGJU 34. Leiden: Brill, 1996.

Heschel, S. *Abraham Geiger and the Jewish Jesus.* Chicago: University of Chicago Press, 1998.

Hilgert, E. "Speeches in Acts and Hellenistic Canons of Historiography and Rhetoric." Pages 83–109 in *Good News in History: Essays in Honor of Bo Reicke.* Edited by E. L. Miller. Atlanta: Scholars Press, 1993.

Hill, C. C. "Acts 6.1–8.4: Division or Diversity?" Pages 129–53 in *History, Literature, and Society in the Book of Acts.* Edited by B. Witherington. Cambridge: Cambridge University Press, 1996.

———. *Hellenists and Hebrews: Reappraising Division within the Earliest Church.* Minneapolis: Fortress, 1992.

Hinds, S. *Allusion and Intertext: Dynamics of Appropriation in Roman Poetry.* Roman Literature and Its Contexts. Cambridge: Cambridge University Press, 1998.

Hock, R. F. "Homer in Greco-Roman Education." Pages 56–77 in *Mimesis and Intertextuality in Antiquity and Christianity.* Edited by D. R. MacDonald. Harrisburg, Pa.: Trinity Press International, 2001.

Hodgson, P. C. *The Formation of Historical Theology: A Study of Ferdinand Christian Baur.* New York: Harper & Row, 1966.

Holladay, C. R. "Jewish Responses to Hellenistic Culture in Early Ptolemaic Egypt." Pages 139–63 in *Ethnicity in Hellenistic Egypt.* Edited by P. Bilde et al. SHC 3. Aarhus: Aarhus University Press, 1992.

———. *Theios Aner in Hellenistic Judaism: A Critique of the Use of This Category in New Testament Christology.* SBLDS 40. Missoula, Mont.: Scholars Press, 1977.

Hornblower, S. "Narratology and Narrative Techniques in Thucydides." Pages 131–66 in *Greek Historiography*. Edited by S. Hornblower. New York: Oxford University Press, 1994.
———. *Thucydides*. London: Duckworth, 1987.
Horsley, R. A. "Synagogues in Galilee and the Gospels." Pages 46–69 in *Evolution of the Synagogue: Problems and Progress*. Edited by H. C. Kee and L. H. Cohick. Harrisburg, Pa.: Trinity Press International, 1999.
Hübner, H. *Biblische Theologie des Neuen Testaments*. 3 vols. Göttingen: Vandenhoeck & Ruprecht, 1995.
Hunter, R. "History and Historicity in the Romance of Chariton." *ANRW* 2.34.2 (1993): 1055–86.
Hurtado, L. W. *Lord Jesus Christ: Devotion to Jesus in Earliest Christianity*. Grand Rapids: Eerdmans, 2003.
Hyldahl, N. *The History of Early Christianity*. Translated by E. M. Arevad and H. Dyrbye. Frankfurt: Peter Lang, 1997.
Jenkinson, E. M. "*Genus scripturae leve*: Cornelius Nepos and Biography at Rome." *ANRW* 1.3 (1973): 703–19.
Jervell, J. *Die Apostelgeschichte*. KEKNT 3. 17th ed. Göttingen: Vandenhoeck & Ruprecht, 1998.
———. "The Church of Jews and Godfearers." Pages 11–20 in *Luke-Acts and the Jewish People: Eight Critical Perspectives*. Edited by J. B. Tyson. Minneapolis: Augsburg, 1988.
———. "The History of Early Christianity and the Acts of the Apostles." Pages 13–25 in *The Unknown Paul*. Minneapolis: Augsburg, 1984.
———. "The Problem of Tradition in Acts." Pages 19–39 in *Luke and the People of God: A New Look at Luke-Acts*. Minneapolis: Augsburg, 1972.
Jeska, J. *Die Geschichte Israels in der Sicht des Lukas: Apg 7,2b–53 und 13,17–25 im Kontext antik-jüdischer Summarien der Geschichte Israels*. FRLANT 195. Göttingen: Vandenhoeck & Ruprecht, 2001.
Johnson, L. T. *The Acts of the Apostles*. SP 5. Collegeville, Minn.: Liturgical Press, 1992.
———. *The Literary Function of Possessions in Luke-Acts*. SBLDS 39. Missoula, Mont.: Scholars Press, 1977.
———. *The Writings of the New Testament: An Interpretation*. Philadelphia: Fortress, 1986.
Justus, B. "Zur Erzählkunst des Flavius Josephus." Pages 113–22 in *Theokratia: Jahrbuch des Institutum Judaicum Delitzschian (1970–72)*. Vol. 2. Leiden: Brill, 1973.
Kasher, A. "Polemic and Apologetic Methods of Writing in *Contra Apionem*." Pages 143–86 in *Josephus' Contra Apionem: Studies in Its Character and Context*. Edited by L. H. Feldman and J. R. Levison. AGJU 34. Leiden: Brill, 1996.
Kaster, R. A. "Controlling Reason: Declamation in Rhetorical Education at Rome." Pages 317–37 in *Education in Greek and Roman Antiquity*. Edited by Y. L. Too. Leiden: Brill, 2001.

Keaney, J. J., and R. Lamberton, eds. *[Plutarch] Essay on the Life and Poetry of Homer*. ACS 40. Atlanta: Scholars Press, 1996.

Kee, H. C. "Defining the First-Century C.E. Synagogue: Problems and Progress." Pages 7–26 in *Evolution of the Synagogue: Problems and Progress*. Edited by H. C. Kee and L. H. Cohick. Harrisburg, Pa.: Trinity Press International, 1999.

Keitel, E. "Speech and Narrative in *Histories* 4." Pages 39–58 in *Tacitus and the Tacitean Tradition*. Edited by T. J. Luce and A. J. Woodman. Princeton: Princeton University Press, 1993.

Keith, A. M. *Engendering Rome: Women in Latin Epic*. Roman Literature and Its Contexts. Cambridge: Cambridge University Press, 2000.

Kelley, S. *Racializing Jesus: Race, Ideology, and the Formation of Biblical Scholarship*. New York: Routledge, 2002.

Kennedy, G. A. *The Art of Persuasion in Greece*. Princeton: Princeton University Press, 1963.

———. "The Genres of Rhetoric." Pages 43–50 in *Handbook of Classical Rhetoric in the Hellenistic Period 300 B.C.–A.D. 400*. Edited by S. E. Porter. Leiden: Brill, 1997.

———. *New Testament Interpretation through Rhetorical Criticism*. Chapel Hill: University of North Carolina Press, 1984.

———. *Progymnasmata: Greek Textbooks of Prose Composition and Rhetoric*. SBLWGRW 10. Atlanta: Society of Biblical Literature, 2003.

Kidd, I. G. "Posidonius as Philosopher-Historian." Pages 38–50 in *Philosophia Togata I: Essays on Philosophy and Roman Society*. Edited by M. Griffin and J. Barnes. Oxford: Clarendon, 1989.

Kilgallen, J. J. "The Function of Stephen's Speech (Acts 7,2–53)." *Biblica* 70 (1989): 173–93.

———. *The Stephen Speech: A Literary and Redactional Study of Acts 7,2–53*. AnBib 67. Rome: Biblical Institute Press, 1976.

Kirschenbaum, A. *Sons, Slaves, and Freedmen in Roman Commerce*. Washington: Catholic University Press, 1987.

Klein, G. *Der älteste christliche Katechismus und die jüdische Propaganda-Literatur*. Berlin: Reimer, 1909.

———. *Die zwölf Apostel: Ursprung und Gehalt einer Idee*. FRLANT ns 59/77. Göttingen: Vandenhoeck & Ruprecht, 1961.

Kliesch, K. *Das heilsgeschichtliche Credo in den Reden der Apostelgeschichte*. BBB 44. Bonn: Hanstein, 1975.

Klijn, A. F. J. "Stephen's Speech—Acts VII.2–53." *NTS* 4 (1957): 25–31.

Klinghardt, M. *Gesetz und Volk Gottes: Das lukanische Verständnis des Gesetzes nach Herkunft, Funktion, und seinem Ort in der Geschichte des Urchristentums*. WUNT 2.32. Tübingen: Mohr Siebeck, 1988.

Koester, C. R. *The Dwelling of God: The Tabernacle in the Old Testament, Intertestamental Jewish Literature, and the New Testament*. CBQMS 22. Washington: Catholic Biblical Association, 1989.

Konstan, D. "Friendship, Frankness, and Flattery." Pages 7–19 in *Friendship, Flattery, and Frankness of Speech: Studies on Friendship in the New Testament World*. Edited by J. T. Fitzgerald. NovTSup 82. Leiden: Brill, 1996.

———. *Friendship in the Classical World*. Cambridge: Cambridge University Press, 1997.

Koskenniemi, E. *Apollonios von Tyana in der neutestamentlichen Exegese*. WUNT 2.61. Tübingen: Mohr Siebeck, 1994.

Köster, H. "τόπος." *TDNT* 8:187–208.

Kraabel, A. T. "The Disappearance of the God-fearers." Pages 119–30 in *Diaspora Jews and Judaism*. Edited by J. A. Overman and R. S. MacLennan. SFSHJ 41. Atlanta: Scholars Press, 1992.

———. "Immigrants, Exiles, Expatriates, and Missionaries." Pages 71–88 in *Religious Propaganda and Missionary Competition in the New Testament World: Essays Honoring Dieter Georgi*. Edited by L. Bormann, K. Del Tredici, and A. Standhartinger. NovTSup 74. Leiden: Brill, 1994.

———. "*Synagoga Caeca:* Distortion in Gentile Interpretations of Evidence for Judaism in the Early Christian Period." Pages 35–62 in *Diaspora Jews and Judaism*. Edited by J. A. Overman and R. S. MacLennan. SFSHJ 41. Atlanta: Scholars Press, 1992.

Kraus, W. *Zwischen Jerusalem und Antiochia: Die "Hellenisten," Paulus, und die Aufnahme der Heiden in das endzeitliche Gottesvolk*. SBS 179. Stuttgart: Katholisches Bibelwerk, 1999.

Krieger, K.-S. *Geschichtsschreibung als Apologetik bei Flavius Josephus*. TANZ 9. Tübingen: Francke, 1994.

Kümmel, W. G. *The New Testament: The History of the Investigation of Its Problems*. Translated by S. M. Gilmour and H. C. Kee. Nashville: Abingdon, 1972.

Kurz, W. S. "Narrative Models in Luke-Acts." Pages 171–89 in *Greeks, Romans, and Christians: Essays in Honor of Abraham J. Malherbe*. Edited by D. L. Balch et al. Minneapolis: Fortress, 1990.

Larmour, D. H. J. "Making Parallels: *Synkrisis* and Plutarch's 'Themistocles and Camillus.'" *ANRW* 2.33.6 (1992): 4154–200.

Larsson, E. "Die Hellenisten und die Urgemeinde." *NTS* 33 (1987): 205–25.

———. "Temple-Criticism and the Jewish Heritage: Some Reflexions on Acts 6–7." *NTS* 39 (1993): 379–95.

Leeman, A. D. *Orationis Ratio: The Stylistic Theories and Practice of the Roman Orators, Historians, and Philosophers*. 2 vols. Amsterdam: Hakkert, 1963.

Légasse, S. *Stephanos: Histoire et Discours D'Étienne dans les Actes des Apôtres*. LD 147. Paris: Cerf, 1992.

Lentz, J. C. *Luke's Portrait of Paul*. SNTSMS 77. Cambridge: Cambridge University Press, 1993.

Levene, D. S. "Pity, Fear, and the Historical Audience." Pages 128–49 in *The Passions in Roman Thought and Literature*. Edited by S. M. Braund and C. Gill. Cambridge: Cambridge University Press, 1997.

———. "Tacitus' *Histories* and the Theory of Deliberative Oratory." Pages 197–216 in *The Limits of Historiography: Genre and Narrative in Ancient Historical Texts*. Edited by C. Shuttleworth Kraus. MnSup 191. Leiden: Brill, 1999.

Levinskaya, I. *The Book of Acts in Its Diaspora Setting*. BAFCS 5. Grand Rapids: Eerdmans, 1996.

Lévy, E. "L'Art de la Déformation Historique dans les *Helléniques* de Xénophon." Pages 125–57 in *Purposes of History: Studies in Greek Historiography from the 4th to the 2nd Centuries B.C.* Edited by H. Verdin et al. SH 30. Leuven: Orientaliste, 1990.

LiDonnici, L. R. *The Epidaurian Miracle Inscriptions: Text, Translation, and Commentary*. SBLTT 36. Atlanta: Scholars Press, 1995.

Lienhard, J. T. "Acts 6:1–6: A Redactional View." *CBQ* 37 (1973): 228–36.

Lindemann, A. "The Beginnings of Christian Life in Jerusalem according to the Summaries in the Acts of the Apostles (Acts 2:42–47; 4:32–37; 5:12–16)." Pages 202–18 in *Common Life in the Early Church: Essays Honoring Graydon F. Snyder*. Edited J. V. Hills et al. Harrisburg, Pa.: Trinity Press International, 1998.

Long, A. A. *Hellenistic Philosophy: Stoics, Epicureans, Sceptics*. 2d ed. Berkeley: University of California Press, 1986.

Loraux, N. *The Invention of Athens: The Funeral Oration in the Classical City*. Translated by A. Sheridan. Cambridge: Harvard University Press, 1986.

Luce, T. J. *The Greek Historians*. New York: Routledge, 1997.

———. "Tacitus on 'History's Highest Function': *praecipuum munus annalium* (*Ann.* 3/65)." *ANRW* 2.33.4 (1991): 2904–27.

Lüdemann, G. "Acts of the Apostles as a Historical Source." Pages 109–25 in *The Social World of Formative Christianity and Judaism: Essays in Tribute to Howard Clark Kee*. Edited by J. S. Neusner et al. Philadelphia: Fortress, 1988.

———. *Early Christianity according to the Traditions in Acts: A Commentary*. Translated by J. Bowden. Minneapolis: Fortress, 1989.

———. *Opposition to Paul in Jewish Christianity*. Translated by M. E. Boring. Minneapolis: Fortress, 1989.

MacDonald, D. R. *Does the New Testament Imitate Homer? Four Cases from the Acts of the Apostles*. New Haven: Yale University Press, 2003.

Mack, B. L., and V. K. Robbins. *Patterns of Persuasion in the Gospels*. Sonoma, Calif.: Polebridge, 1989.

MacMullen, R. *Paganism in the Roman Empire*. New Haven: Yale University Press, 1981.

Maddox, R. *The Purpose of Luke-Acts*. Edited by J. Riches. Edinburgh: T & T Clark, 1982.

Mader, G. *Josephus and the Politics of Historiography: Apologetic and Impression Management in the* Bellum Judaicum. MnSup 205. Leiden: Brill, 2000.

Malina, B. J. "Understanding New Testament Persons." Pages 141–61 in *The Social Sciences and New Testament Interpretation*. Edited by R. L. Rohrbaugh. Peabody, Mass.: Hendrickson, 1996.

Marguerat, D. "Luc-Actes: Une Unité à Construire." Pages 57–81 in *The Unity of Luke-Acts*. Edited by J. Verheyden. BETL 142. Leuven: Leuven University Press, 1999.

———. "La mort d'Ananias et Sapphira [Ac 5.1–11] dans la stratégie narrative de Luc." *NTS* 39 (1993): 209–26.

Marincola, J. *Authority and Tradition in Ancient Historiography*. Cambridge: Cambridge University Press, 1997.

———. "Genre, Convention, and Innovation in Greco-Roman Historiography." Pages 281–324 in *The Limits of Historiography: Genre and Narrative in Ancient Historical Texts*. Edited by C. Shuttleworth Kraus. MnSup 191. Leiden: Brill, 1999.

Marrow, S. B. "Parrhesia and the New Testament." *CBQ* 44 (1982): 431–46.

Marshall, I. H. *Commentary on Luke*. NIGTC. Grand Rapids: Eerdmans, 1978.

Martin, R. P. "The Seven Sages as Performers of Wisdom." Pages 108–28 in *Cultural Poetics in Archaic Greece: Cult, Performance, Politics*. Edited by C. Dougherty and L. Kurke. New York: Oxford University Press, 1998.

Martin, T. W. "Hellenists." *ABD* 3:135–36.

Mason, S. "*Contra Apionem* in Social and Literary Context: An Invitation to Judean Philosophy." Pages 187–228 in *Josephus' Contra Apionem: Studies in Its Character and Context*. Edited by L. H. Feldman and J. R. Levison. AGJU 34. Leiden: Brill, 1996.

———. *Flavius Josephus on the Pharisees*. SPB 39. Leiden: Brill, 1991.

Matsen, P. P., et al., eds. *Readings from Classical Rhetoric*. Carbondale: Southern Illinois University Press, 1990.

Matthews, S. *First Converts: Rich Pagan Women and the Rhetoric of Mission in Early Judaism and Christianity*. Contraversions. Stanford: Stanford University Press, 2001.

Mattill, A. J. "The Purpose of Acts: Schneckenburger Reconsidered." Pages 108–22 in *Apostolic History and the Gospel: Biblical and Historical Essays Presented to F. F. Bruce on His 60th Birthday*. Edited by W. W. Gasque and R. P. Martin. Grand Rapids: Eerdmans, 1970.

McCullough, H. Y. "The Historical Process and Theories of History in the 'Annals' and 'Histories' of Tacitus." *ANRW* 2.33.4 (1991): 2928–48.

McKnight, S. *A Light among the Gentiles: Jewish Missionary Activity in the Second Temple Period*. Minneapolis: Fortress, 1991.

McLaren, J. S. *Turbulent Times? Josephus and Scholarship on Judaea in the First Century* C.E. JSPSup 29. Sheffield: Sheffield Academic Press, 1998.

Meecham, H. G. *The Oldest Version of the Bible: 'Aristeas' on Its Traditional Origin. A Study in Early Apologetic*. London: Holborn, 1932.

Meijering, E. P. F. C. *Baur als Patristiker: Die Bedeutung seiner Geschichtsphilosophie und Quellenforschung*. Amsterdam: Gieben, 1986.

Mellor, R. *The Roman Historians*. New York: Routledge, 1999.

Mendels, D. "'Creative History' in the Hellenistic Near East in the Third and Second Centuries BCE: The Jewish Case." Pages 357–64 in *Identity, Religion, and*

Historiography: Studies in Hellenistic History. JSPSup 24. Sheffield: Sheffield Academic Press, 1998.

———. "Did Polybius Have 'Another' View of the Aetolian League?" Pages 127–38 in *Identity, Religion, and Historiography: Studies in Hellenistic History.* JSPSup 24. Sheffield: Sheffield Academic Press, 1998.

———. "Hecataeus of Abdera and a Jewish *Patrios Politeia.*" Pages 334–51 in *Identity, Religion, and Historiography: Studies in Hellenistic History.* JSPSup 24. Sheffield: Sheffield Academic Press, 1998.

———. "Pagan or Jewish? The Presentation of Paul's Mission in the Book of Acts." Pages 394–419 in *Identity, Religion, and Historiography: Studies in Hellenistic History.* JSPSup 24. Sheffield: Sheffield Academic Press, 1998.

———. "The Polemical Character of Manetho's *Aegyptiaca.*" Pages 139–57 in *Identity, Religion, and Historiography: Studies in Hellenistic History.* JSPSup 24. Sheffield: Sheffield Academic Press, 1998.

Metzger, B. M. "Ancient Astrological Geography and Acts 2:9–11." Pages 123–33 in *Apostolic History and the Gospel: Biblical and Historical Essays Presented to F. F. Bruce on His 60th Birthday.* Edited by W. W. Gasque and R. P. Martin. Grand Rapids: Eerdmans, 1970.

———. *A Textual Commentary on the Greek New Testament.* New York: United Bible Societies, 1975.

Mitchell, A. C. "'Greet the Friends by Name': New Testament Evidence for the Greco-Roman *Topos* on Friendship." Pages 225–62 in *Greco-Roman Perspectives on Friendship.* Edited by J. T. Fitzgerald. SBLRBS 34. Atlanta: Scholars Press, 1997.

———. "The Social Function of Friendship in Acts 2:44–47 and 4:32–37." *JBL* 111 (1992): 255–72.

Mitchell, M. M. *The Heavenly Trumpet: John Chrysostom and the Art of Pauline Interpretation.* Louisville: Westminster John Knox, 2002.

Moessner, D. P. "And Once Again, What Sort of 'Essence'? A Response to Charles Talbert." *Semeia* 43 (1988): 75–84.

———. "The Appeal and Power of Poetics (Luke 1:1–4): Luke's Superior Credentials (παρηκολουθηκότι), Narrative Sequence (καθεξῆς), and Firmness of Understanding (ἡ ἀσφάλεια) for the Reader." Pages 84–123 in *Jesus and the Heritage of Israel: Luke's Narrative Claim upon Israel's Legacy.* Edited by D. P. Moessner. Harrisburg, Pa.: Trinity Press International, 1999.

———. "'The Christ Must Suffer': New Light on the Jesus-Peter, Stephen, Paul Parallels in Luke-Acts." Pages 117–53 in *The Composition of Luke's Gospel.* Edited by D. E. Orton. Leiden: Brill, 1999.

———. "Dionysius's Narrative 'Arrangement' (οἰκονομία) as the Hermeneutical Key to Luke's Re-Vision of the 'Many.'" Pages 149–64 in *Paul, Luke, and the Graeco-Roman World: Essays in Honour of Alexander J. M. Wedderburn.* Edited by A. Christophersen et al. JSNTSup 217. Sheffield: Sheffield Academic Press, 2003.

———. " 'Eyewitnesses,' 'Informed Contemporaries,' and 'Unknowing Inquirers': Josephus' Criteria for Authentic Historiography and the Meaning of ΠΑΡΑΚΟΛΟΥΘΕΩ." *NovT* 38 (1996): 105–22.

———. *Lord of the Banquet: The Literary and Theological Significance of the Lukan Travel Narrative*. Minneapolis: Fortress, 1989.

———. "The Lukan Prologues in the Light of Ancient Narrative Hermeneutics: Παρηκολουθηκότι and the Credentialed Author." Pages 399–417 in *The Unity of Luke-Acts*. Edited by J. Verheyden. BETL 142. Leuven: Leuven University Press, 1999.

Moessner. D. P., and D. L. Tiede. "Conclusion: 'And some were persuaded...' " Pages 358–68 in *Jesus and the Heritage of Israel: Luke's Narrative Claim upon Israel's Legacy*. Edited by D. P. Moessner. Harrisburg, Pa.: Trinity Press International, 1999.

Momigliano, A. "An Apology of Judaism: The *Against Apion* by Flavius Josephus." Pages 58–66 in *Essays on Ancient and Modern Judaism*. Edited by S. Berti. Translated by M. Masella-Gayley. Chicago: University of Chicago Press, 1994.

Moore, G. F. "Christian Writers on Judaism." *HTR* 14 (1921): 197–254.

Moore, S. D., and J. Capel Anderson. "Taking It like a Man: Masculinity in 4 Maccabees." *JBL* 117 (1998): 249–73.

Moreland, M. "The Jerusalem Community in Acts: Mythmaking and the Socio-Rhetorical Functions of a Lukan Setting." Pages 285–310 in *Contextualizing Acts: Lukan Narrative and Greco-Roman Discourse*. Edited by T. Penner and C. Vander Stichele. SBLSymS 20. Atlanta: Society of Biblical Literature, 2003.

———. "Jerusalem Imagined: Rethinking Earliest Christian Claims to the Hebrew Epic." Ph.D. diss., Claremont Graduate University (California), 1999.

Morgan, J. R. "History, Romance, and Realism in the *Aithiopika of Heliodoros*." *CA* 1 (1982): 221–65.

———. "Make-Believe and Make Believe: The Fictionality of the Greek Novels." Pages 175–229 in *Lies and Fiction in the Ancient World*. Edited by C. Gill and T. P. Wiseman. Austin: University of Texas Press, 1993.

Morgan, M. G. "The Unity of Tacitus, *Histories* 1,12–20." *Athenaeum* 81 (1993): 567–86.

Morgan, T. *Literate Education in the Hellenistic and Roman Worlds*. Cambridge Classical Studies. Cambridge: Cambridge University Press, 1998.

Mosley, A. W. "Historical Reporting in the Ancient World." *NTS* 12 (1965): 10–26.

Moxnes, H. "Conventional Values in the Hellenistic World: Masculinity." Pages 263–84 in *Conventional Values of the Hellenistic Greeks*. Edited by P. Bilde et al. SHC 8. Aarhus: Aarhus University Press, 1997.

Mullen. E. T. *Ethnic Myths and Pentateuchal Foundations: A New Approach to the Formation of the Pentateuch*. SBLSemS. Atlanta: Scholars Press, 1997.

———. *Narrative History and Ethnic Boundaries: The Deuteronomistic Historian and the Creation of Israelite National Identity*. SBLSemS. Atlanta: Scholars Press, 1993.

Murison, C. L. "The Historical Value of Tacitus' 'Histories.' " *ANRW* 2.33.3 (1991): 1686–713.
Murray, O. "Aristeas and Ptolemaic Kingship." *JTS* 8 (1967): 337–71.
Murray, R. "Jews, Hebrews, and Christians: Some Needed Distinctions." *NovT* 24 (1982): 194–208.
Mussner, F. "Καθεξῆς im Lukasprolog." Pages 253–55 in *Jesus und Paulus: Festschrift für Werner Georg Kümmel zum 70. Geburtstag*. Edited by E. E. Ellis and E. Gräßer. Göttingen: Vandenhoeck & Ruprecht, 1975.
Neudorfer, H. -W. "The Speech of Stephen." Pages 275–94 in *Witness to the Gospel: The Theology of Acts*. Edited by I. H. Marshall and D. Peterson. Grand Rapids: Eerdmans, 1998.
———. *Der Stephanuskreis in der Forschungsgeschichte seit F. C. Baur*. Giessen, Germany: Brunnen, 1983.
Neyrey, J. H. "Acts 17, Epicureans, and Theodicy: A Study in Stereotypes." Pages 118–34 in *Greeks, Romans, and Christians: Essays in Honor of Abraham J. Malherbe*. Edited by D. L. Balch et al. Minneapolis: Fortress, 1990.
———. "The Forensic Defense Speech and Paul's Trial Speeches in Acts 22–26: Form and Function." Pages 210–24 in *Luke-Acts: New Perspectives from the Society of Biblical Literature*. Edited by C. H. Talbert. New York: Crossroad, 1984.
———. *Honor and Shame in the Gospel of Matthew*. Louisville: Westminster John Knox, 1998.
———. "Josephus' *Vita* and the Encomium: A Native Model of Personality." *JSJ* 25 (1994): 177–206.
Nickelsburg, G. W. E. *Resurrection, Immortality, and Eternal Life in Intertestamental Judaism*. HTS 26. Cambridge: Harvard University Press, 1972.
———. "Stories of Biblical and Early Post-Biblical Times." Pages 33–87 in *Jewish Writings of the Second Temple Period*. Edited by M. E. Stone. CRINT 2.2. Philadelphia: Fortress, 1984.
Norden, E. *Die antike Kunstprosa*. 2 vols. Stuttgart: Teubner, 1958 (1909).
North, H. F. "Canons and Hierarchies of the Cardinal Virtues in Greek and Latin Literature." Pages 165–83 in *The Classical Tradition: Literary and Historical Studies in Honor of Harry Caplan*. Edited by L. Wallach. Ithaca: Cornell University Press, 1966.
———. *Sophrosyne: Self-Knowledge and Self-Restraint in Greek Literature*. Ithaca: Cornell University Press, 1966.
Oden, R. A. "Philo of Byblos and Hellenistic Historiography." *PEQ* 110 (1978): 115–26.
Økland, J. "Women in Their Place: Paul and the Corinthian Discourse of Gender and Sanctuary Space." Ph.D. diss., University of Oslo (Norway), 2000.
Oliver, J. H. *The Civilizing Power: A Study of the Panathenaic Discourse of Aelius Aristides against the Background of Literature and Cultural Conflict, with Text, Translation, and Commentary*. TAPS 58.1. Philadelphia: American Philosophical Society, 1968.

O'Reilly, L. *Word and Sign in the Acts of the Apostles: A Study in Lucan Theology.* AnG 243. Rome: Editrice Pontificia Università Gregoriana, 1987.

Palmer Bonz, M. *The Past as Legacy: Luke-Acts and Ancient Epic.* Minneapolis: Fortress, 2000.

Parsons, M. C. "Luke and the *Progymnasmata*: A Preliminary Investigation into the Preliminary Exercises." Pages 43–63 in *Contextualizing Acts: Lukan Narrative and Greco-Roman Discourse.* Edited by T. Penner and C. Vander Stichele. SBLSymS 20. Atlanta: Society of Biblical Literature, 2003.

Pearson, L. "Real and Conventional Personalities in Greek History." Pages 136–45 in *Selected Papers of Lionel Pearson.* Edited by D. Lateiner and S. A. Stephens. Chico, Calif.: Scholars Press, 1983.

Pelling, C. "Conclusion." Pages 245–62 in *Characterization and Individuality in Greek Literature.* Edited by C. Pelling. Oxford: Clarendon, 1990.

———. "Epilogue." Pages 325–60 in *The Limits of Historiography: Genre and Narrative in Ancient Historical Texts.* Edited by C. Shuttleworth Kraus. MnSup 191. Leiden: Brill, 1999.

———. *Literary Texts and the Greek Historian.* New York: Routledge, 2000.

———. "Synkrisis in Plutarch's *Lives.*" Pages 349–63 in *Plutarch and History.* London: Duchwork, 2002.

———. "Truth and Fiction in Plutarch's *Lives.*" Pages 19–52 in *Antonine Literature.* Edited by D. A. Russell. New York: Oxford University Press, 1990.

Penner, T. "Civilizing Discourse: Acts, Declamation, and the Rhetoric of *Polis.*" Pages 65–104 in *Contextualizing Acts: Lukan Narrative and Greco-Roman Discourse.* Edited by T. Penner and C. Vander Stichele. SBLSymS 20. Atlanta: Society of Biblical Literature, 2003.

———. "Contextualizing Acts." Pages 1–21 in *Contextualizing Acts: Lukan Narrative and Greco-Roman Discourse.* Edited by T. Penner and C. Vander Stichele. SBLSymS 20. Atlanta: Society of Biblical Literature, 2003.

———. "Early Christian Heroes and Lukan Narrative: Stephen and the Hellenists in Ancient Historiographical Perspective." In *Persuasion and Performance: Rhetoric and Reality in Early Christian Discourse* Edited by W. Braun. SCJ. Waterloo, Ont.: Wilfrid Laurier Press, forthcoming.

———. *The Epistle of James and Eschatology: Re-reading an Ancient Christian Letter.* JSNTSup 121. Sheffield: Sheffield Academic Press, 1996.

———. "Madness in the Method? The Acts of the Apostles in Current Study." *CurBR* 2 (2004): 224–95.

———. "Narrative as Persuasion: Epideictic Rhetoric and Scribal Amplification in the Stephen Episode in Acts." *SBLSP* 35 (1996): 352–67.

———. "Reconfiguring the Rhetorical Study of Acts: Reflections on the Method in and Learning of a Progymnastic Poetics." *PRSt* 30 (2003): 425–39.

———. "*Res Gestae Divi Christi*: Miracles, Early Christian Heroes, and the Discourse of Power in Acts." In *The Role of Miracle Discourse in the Argumentation of the New Testament.* Edited by D. F. Watson. SBLSymS. Atlanta: Society of Biblical Literature, forthcoming.

Penner, T., and C. Vander Stichele. "Gendering Violence: Patterns of Power and Constructs of Masculinity in the Acts of the Apostles." In *Feminist Companion to Acts*. Edited by A.-J. Levine and M. Blickenstaff. FCNT. New York: Continuum, forthcoming.

———. "The Tyranny of the Martyr: Violence and Victimisation in Martyrdom Discourse and the Movies of Lars von Trier." In *Sanctified Aggression: Vocabularies of Violence in Bibles and Cultures*. Edited by Y. Sherwood and J. Bekkenkamp. New York: T & T Clark, forthcoming.

———. "Unveiling Paul: Gendering *Ēthos* in 1 Corinthians 11:2–16." In *Rhetoric, Ethic, and Moral Persuasion in Biblical Discourse*. Edited by T. H. Olbricht and A. Eriksson. T & T Clark, forthcoming.

Perlman, S. "The Historical Example: Its Use and Importance as Political Propaganda in the Attic Orators." *Scripta Hierosolymitana* 7 (1961): 150–66.

Pervo, R. I. "*Panta Koina*: The Feeding Stories in the Light of Economic Data and Social Practice." Pages 163–94 in *Religious Propaganda and Missionary Competition in the New Testament World: Essays Honoring Dieter Georgi*. Edited by L. Bormann, K. Del Tredici, and A. Standhartinger. NovTSup 74. Leiden: Brill, 1994.

———. *Profit with Delight: The Literary Genre of the Acts of the Apostles*. Philadelphia: Fortress, 1987.

Pesch, R. *Die Apostelgeschichte*. 2 vols. EKK 5. Neukirchen-Vluyn: Neukirchener Verlag, 1986–95.

Pesch R., et al. " 'Hellenisten' und 'Hebräer': Zu Apg 9,29 und 6,1." *BZ* 23 (1979): 87–88.

Petzke, G. *Die Traditionen über Apollonius von Tyana und das Neue Testament*. SCHNT 1. Leiden: Brill, 1970.

Philonenko, M. *Joseph et Aséneth: Introduction, Texte Critique, Traduction et Notes*. SPB 13. Leiden: Brill, 1968.

Pichler, J. *Paulusrezeption in der Apostelgeschichte: Untersuchungen zur Rede im pisidischen Antiochien*. ITS 50. Innsbruck: Tyrolia, 1997.

Plümacher, E. *Lukas als hellenistischer Schriftsteller: Studien zur Apostelgeschichte*. SUNT 9. Göttingen: Vandenhoeck & Ruprecht, 1972.

———. "The Mission Speeches in Acts and Dionysius of Halicarnassus." Pages 251–66 in *Jesus and the Heritage of Israel: Luke's Narrative Claim upon Israel's Legacy*. Edited by D. P. Moessner. Harrisburg, Pa.: Trinity Press International, 1999.

Pomeroy, A. J., ed. and trans. *Arius Didymus: Epitome of Stoic Ethics*. SBLTT 44. Atlanta: Scholars Press, 1999.

Porter, S. E. *The Paul of Acts: Essays in Literary Criticism, Rhetoric, and Theology*. WUNT 115. Tübingen: Mohr Siebeck, 1999.

———. "Thucydides 1.22.1 and Speeches in Acts: Is There a Thucydidean View?" *NovT* 32 (1990): 121–42.

Potter, D. S. *Literary Texts and the Roman Historian*. New York: Routledge, 1999.

Poulakos, T. "Towards a Cultural Understanding of Classical Epideictic Oratory." *Pre/Text* 9 (1988): 147–66.
Praeder, S. M. "Jesus-Paul, Peter-Paul, and Jesus-Peter Parallelisms in Luke-Acts: A History of Reader Response." *SBLSP* 23 (1984): 23–39.
———. "Luke-Acts and the Ancient Novel." *SBLSP* 20 (1981): 269–92.
Price, R. M. *The Widow Traditions in Luke-Acts: A Feminist-Critical Scrutiny.* SBLDS 155. Atlanta: Scholars Press, 1997.
Räisänen, H. "Die 'Hellenisten' der Urgemeinde." *ANRW* 2.26.2 (1995): 1468–514.
———. "The 'Hellenists': A Bridge between Jesus and Paul?" Pages 149–202 in *Jesus, Paul, and Torah: Collected Essays*. Translated by D. E. Orton. JSNTSup 43. Sheffield: Sheffield Academic Press, 1992.
Rakotoharintsifa, A. "Luke and the Internal Divisions in the Early Church." Pages 165–77 in *Luke's Literary Achievement: Collected Essays*. Edited by C. M. Tuckett. JSNTSup 116. Sheffield: Sheffield Academic Press, 1995.
Ramsay, W. M. *Was Christ Born at Bethlehem? A Study on the Credibility of St. Luke.* London: Hodder & Stoughton, 1898.
Rappaport, U. "Where Was Josephus Lying — In His *Life* or in the *War*?" Pages 279–89 in *Josephus and the History of the Greco-Roman Period*. Edited by P. Parente and J. Sievers. SPB 41. Leiden: Brill, 1994.
Rau, E. *Von Jesus zu Paulus: Entwicklung und Rezeption der antiochenischen Theologie im Urchristentum.* Stuttgart: Kohlhammer, 1994.
Raubitschek, A. E. "The Speech of the Athenians at Sparta." Pages 32–48 in *The Speeches in Thucydides*. Edited by P. A. Stadter. Chapel Hill: University of North Carolina Press, 1973.
Rawlings, H. R. *The Structure of Thucydides' History.* Princeton: Princeton University Press, 1981.
Rawson, B. "The Roman Family." Pages 1–57 in *The Family in Ancient Rome: New Perspectives*. Edited by B. Rawson. Ithaca: Cornell University Press, 1986.
Reardon, B. P. *The Form of the Greek Romance.* Princeton: Princeton University Press, 1991.
Reitzenstein, R. *Hellenistische Wundererzählungen.* 2d ed. Darmstadt: Wissenschaftliche Buchgesellschaft, 1963.
Reventlow, H. G. *The Authority of the Bible and the Rise of the Modern World.* Translated by J. Bowden. Philadelphia: Fortress, 1984.
Rhodes, P. J. "In Defence of the Greek Historians." *GR* 2 (1994): 156–71.
Richard, E. *Acts 6:1–8:4: The Author's Method of Composition.* SBLDS 41. Missoula, Mont.: Scholars Press, 1978.
———. "The Creative Use of Amos by the Author of Acts." *NovT* 24 (1982): 37–53.
———. "The Divine Purpose: The Jews and the Gentile Mission (Acts 15)." Pages 188–209 in *Luke-Acts: New Perspectives from the Society of Biblical Literature*. Edited by C. H. Talbert. New York: Crossroad, 1984.
———. "The Polemical Character of the Joseph Episode in Acts 7." *JBL* 98 (1979): 255–67.

Richardson, P. "Early Synagogues as Collegia in the Diaspora and Palestine." Pages 90–109 in *Voluntary Associations in the Graeco-Roman World*. Edited by J. S. Kloppenborg and S. G. Wilson. New York: Routledge, 1996.

Richlin, A. "Gender and Rhetoric: Producing Manhood in the Schools." Pages 90–110 in *Roman Eloquence: Rhetoric in Society and Literature*. Edited by W. J. Dominik. London: Routledge, 1997.

Ricoeur, P. *Time and Narrative*. 3 vols. Translated by K. McLaughlin/Blamey and D. Pellauer. Chicago: University of Chicago Press, 1984–88.

Riesner, R. *Paul's Early Period: Chronology, Mission Strategy, Theology*. Translated by D. Stott. Grand Rapids: Eerdmans, 1998.

———. "Synagogues in Jerusalem." Pages 179–211 in *The Book of Acts in Its Palestinian Setting*. Edited by R. Bauckham. BAFCS 4. Grand Rapids: Eerdmans, 1995.

Rist, J. M. *Human Value: A Study in Ancient Philosophical Ethics*. PA 40. Leiden: Brill, 1982.

Robbins, V. K. "The Claims of the Prologues and Greco-Roman Rhetoric: The Prefaces to Luke and Acts in Light of Greco-Roman Rhetorical Strategies." Pages 63–83 in *Jesus and the Heritage of Israel: Luke's Narrative Claim upon Israel's Legacy*. Edited by D. P. Moessner. Harrisburg, Pa.: Trinity Press International, 1999.

———. "Luke-Acts: A Mixed Population Seeks a Home in the Roman Empire." Pages 202–21 in *Images of Empire*. Edited by L. C. A. Alexander. JSOTSup 122. Sheffield: JSOT Press, 1991.

———. "Progymnastic Rhetorical Composition and Pre-Gospel Tradition: A New Approach." Pages 111–47 in *Synoptic Gospels: Source Criticism and the New Literary Criticism*. Edited by C. Focant. BETL 110. Leuven: Leuven University Press, 1993.

———. *The Tapestry of Early Christian Discourse: Rhetoric, Society, and Ideology*. New York: Routledge, 1996.

———. "Writing as a Rhetorical Act in Plutarch and the Gospels." Pages 142–68 in *Persuasive Artistry: Studies in New Testament Rhetoric in Honor of George A. Kennedy*. Edited by D. F. Watson. JSNTSup 50. Sheffield: Sheffield Academic Press, 1991.

Roberts, M. *Biblical Epic and Rhetorical Paraphrase in Late Antiquity*. Liverpool: Cairns, 1985.

Rogers, G. M. *The Sacred Identity of Ephesos: Foundation Myths of a Roman City*. New York: Routledge, 1991.

Roloff, J. *Apostolat-Verkündigung-Kirche: Ursprung, Inhalt, und Funktion des kirchlichen Apostelamtes nach Paulus, Lukas, und den Pastoralbriefen*. Gütersloh: Mohn, 1965.

Romer, F. E. *Pomponius Mela's Description of the World*. Ann Arbor: University of Michigan Press, 1998.

Römer, T., and J.-D. Macchi. "Luke, Disciple of the Deuteronomistic School." Pages 178–87 in *Luke's Literary Achievement: Collected Essays*. Edited by C. M. Tuckett. JSNTSup 116. Sheffield: Sheffield Academic Press, 1995.

Romilly, J. de. *The Great Sophists in Periclean Athens*. Translated by J. Lloyd. New York: Oxford University Press, 1992.

———. *Magic and Rhetoric in Ancient Greece*. Cambridge: Harvard University Press, 1975.

Romm, J. *The Edges of the Earth in Ancient Thought*. Princeton: Princeton University Press, 1992.

———. *Herodotus*. New Haven: Yale University Press, 1998.

Rood, T. "Thucydides' Persian Wars." Pages 141–68 in *The Limits of Historiography: Genre and Narrative in Ancient Historical Texts*. Edited by C. Shuttleworth Kraus. MnSup 191. Leiden: Brill, 1999.

Rorty, A. O. "The Psychology of Aristotelian Tragedy." Pages 1–22 in *Essays on Aristotle's Poetics*. Edited by A. O. Rorty. Princeton: Princeton University Press, 1992.

Russell, D. A. *Greek Declamation*. Cambridge: Cambridge University Press, 1983.

———. "The Panegyrists and Their Teachers." Pages 17–50 in *The Propaganda of Power: The Role of Panegyric in Late Antiquity*. Edited by M. Whitby. MnSup 183. Leiden: Brill, 1998.

Russell, D. A., and N. G. Wilson, eds. and trans. *Menander Rhetor*. Oxford: Oxford University Press, 1981.

Rutherford, R. B. *The Meditations of Marcus Aurelius: A Study*. Oxford: Clarendon, 1989.

Sabbe, M. "The Son of Man Saying in Acts 7,56." Pages 137–78 in *Studia Neotestamentica: Collected Essays*. BETL 98. Leuven: Leuven University Press, 1991.

Sacks, K. S. *Diodorus Siculus and the First Century*. Princeton: Princeton University Press, 1990.

———. "Historiography in the Rhetorical Works of Dionysius of Halicarnassus." *Athenaeum* 61 (1983): 65–87.

———. *Polybius on the Writing of History*. Classical Studies 24. Berkeley: University of California Press, 1981.

———. "Rhetoric and Speeches in Hellenistic Historiography." *Athenaeum* 64 (1986): 383–95.

Sanders, J. T. *The Jews in Luke-Acts*. Philadelphia: Fortress, 1987.

Sandmel, S. *Philo's Place in Judaism: A Study of Conceptions of Abraham in Jewish Literature*. Cincinnati: Hebrew Union College, 1956.

Sandt, H. van de. "Why Is Amos 5,25–27 Quoted in Acts 7,42f.?" *ZNW* 81 (1991): 67–87.

Sandy, G. N. "Apuleius' 'Metamorphoses' and the Ancient Novel." *ANRW* 2.34.2 (1993): 1511–74.

Sawicki, M. *Crossing Galilee: Architectures of Contact in the Occupied Land of Jesus*. Harrisburg, Pa.: Trinity Press International, 2000.

Schäfer, P. "The Exodus Tradition in Pagan Greco-Roman Literature." Pages 9–38 in *The Jews in the Hellenistic-Roman World*. Edited by I. M. Gafni et al. Jerusalem: Zalman Shazar Center for Jewish History, 1996.

———. *Judeophobia: Attitudes towards the Jews in the Ancient World*. Cambridge: Harvard University Press, 1997.

Schiappa, E. *The Beginnings of Rhetorical Theory in Classical Greece*. New Haven: Yale University Press, 1999.

Schimanowski, G. "Der *Aristeasbrief* zwischen Abgrenzung und Selbstdarstellung." Pages 45–64 in *Persuasion and Dissuasion in Early Christianity*. Edited by P. W. van der Horst et al. CBET 33. Leuven: Peeters, 2003.

Schlier, H. "Παρρησία, παρρησιάζομαι." *TDNT* 5:871–86.

Schmidt, D. "Rhetorical Influences and Genre: Luke's Preface and the Rhetoric of Hellenistic Historiography." Pages 27–60 in *Jesus and the Heritage of Israel: Luke's Narrative Claim upon Israel's Legacy*. Edited by D. P. Moessner. Harrisburg, Pa.: Trinity Press International, 1999.

Schmithals, W. *The Theology of the First Christians*. Translated by O. C. Dean, Jr. Louisville: Westminster John Knox, 1997.

Schneckenburger, M. *Über den Zweck der Apostelgeschichte*. Bern: Fischer, 1841.

Schneider, G. *Die Apostelgeschichte*. 2 vols. HTKNT 5. Freiburg: Herder, 1980–82.

———. "Stephanus, die Hellenisten und Samaria." Pages 227–52 in *Lukas, Theologe des Heilsgeschichte: Aufsätze zum lukanischen Doppelwerk*. BBB 59. Bonn: Hanstein, 1985.

———. "Zur Bedeutung von καθεξῆς im lukanischen Doppelwerk." *ZNW* 68 (1977): 128–31.

Scholz, U. "*Annales* or *Historiae*." Pages 205–9 in *Ancient History in a Modern University*. Edited by T. W. Hillard et al. Vol. 2. Grand Rapids: Eerdmans, 1998.

Schürer, E. *The History of the Jewish People in the Age of Jesus Christ (175 B.C.–A.D. 135)*. Revised and edited by G. Vermes et al. 4 vols. Edinburgh: T & T Clark, 1973–1987.

Scott, J. J. "Stephen's Speech: A Possible Model for Luke's Historical Method?" *JETS* 17 (1974): 91–97.

Scott, J. M. *Geography in Early Judaism and Christianity: The Book of Jubilees*. SNTSMS 113. Cambridge: Cambridge University Press, 2002.

———. "Luke's Geographical Horizon." Pages 483–544 in *The Book of Acts in Its Graeco-Roman Setting*. Edited by D. W. J. Gill and C. Gempf. BAFCS 2. Grand Rapids: Eerdmans, 1994.

Scroggs, R. "The Earliest Hellenistic Christianity." Pages 176–206 in *Religions in Antiquity: Essays in Memory of Erwin Ramsdell Goodenough*. Edited by J. Neusner. SHR 14. Leiden: Brill, 1968.

Seccombe, D. "Was There Organized Charity in Jerusalem before the Christians?" *JTS* 29 (1979): 140–43.

Seim, T. K. *The Double Message: Patterns of Gender in Luke and Acts*. Edinburgh: T & T Clark, 1994.

Seland, T. *Establishment Violence in Philo and Luke: A Study of Non-Conformity to the Torah and Jewish Vigilante Reactions.* BibIntS 15. Leiden: Brill, 1995.

———. "Once More—The Hellenists, Hebrews, and Stephen: Conflicts and Conflict Management in Acts 6–7." Pages 169–207 in *Recruitment, Conquest, and Conflict: Strategies in Judaism, Early Christianity, and the Greco-Roman World.* Edited by P. Borgen, V. K. Robbins, and D. B. Gowler. ESEC 6. Atlanta: Scholars Press, 1998.

Sevenster, J. N. *The Roots of Pagan Anti-Semitism in the Ancient World.* NovTSup 41. Leiden: Brill, 1975.

Sherman, N. *The Fabric of Character: Aristotle's Theory of Virtue.* Oxford: Clarendon, 1989.

Shuler, P. L. *A Genre for the Gospels: The Biographical Character of Matthew.* Philadelphia: Fortress, 1982.

Siegert, F. "Early Jewish Interpretation in a Hellenistic Style." Pages 130–98 in *Hebrew Bible/Old Testament; The History of Its Interpretation.* Vol. 1, pt. 1, *Antiquity.* Edited by M. Sæbø. Göttingen: Vandenhoeck & Ruprecht, 1996.

———. "Protreptik und Polemik bei Josephus: Eine Einleitung in sein *Contra Apionem.*" Pages 64–85 in *Persuasion and Dissuasion in Early Christianity.* Edited by P. W. van der Horst et al. CBET 33. Leuven: Peeters, 2003.

Siker, J. S. *Disinheriting the Jews: Abraham in Early Christian Controversy.* Louisville: Westminster John Knox, 1991.

Simon, M. *St. Stephen and the Hellenists in the Primitive Church.* London: Longmans, 1958.

———. *Verus Israel: A Study of the Relations between Christians and Jews in the Roman Empire (A.D. 135–425).* Translated by H. McKeating. Oxford: Oxford University Press, 1986.

Skidmore, C. *Practical Ethics for Roman Gentlemen: The Work of Valerius Maximus.* Exeter: University of Exeter Press, 1996.

Smith, A. " 'Full of Spirit and Wisdom': Luke's Portrait of Stephen (Acts 6:1–8:1a) as a Man of Self-Mastery." Pages 97–114 in *Asceticism and the New Testament.* Edited by L. E. Vaage and V. L. Wimbush. New York: Routledge, 1999.

Soards, M. L. *The Speeches in Acts: Their Content, Context, and Concerns.* Louisville: Westminster John Knox, 1994.

Spencer, F. S. *Acts.* Sheffield: Sheffield Academic Press, 1997.

———. "Neglected Widows in Acts 6:1–7." *CBQ* 56 (1994): 715–33.

———. *The Portrait of Philip in Acts: A Study of Roles and Relations.* JSNTSup 67. Sheffield: Sheffield Academic Press, 1992.

Spilsbury, P. "*Contra Apionem* and *Antiquitates Judaicae*: Points of Contact." Pages 348–68 in *Josephus'* Contra Apionem: *Studies in Its Character and Context.* Edited by L. H. Feldman and J. R. Levison. AGJU 34. Leiden: Brill, 1996.

———. *The Image of the Jew in Flavius Josephus' Paraphrase of the Bible.* TSAJ 69. Tübingen: Mohr Siebeck, 1998.

Squires, J. T. "Fate and Free Will in Hellenistic Histories and Luke-Acts." Pages 131–37 in *Ancient History in a Modern University*. Edited by T. W. Hillard et al. Vol. 2. Grand Rapids: Eerdmans, 1998.
———. "The Function of Acts 8.4–12.25." *NTS* 44 (1998): 608–17.
———. *The Plan of God in Luke-Acts*. SNTSMS 76. Cambridge: Cambridge University Press, 1993.
Stadter, P. A. *Arrian of Nicomedia*. Chapel Hill: University of North Carolina Press, 1980.
Stahl, H.-P. "Speeches and Course of Events in Books Six and Seven of Thucydides." Pages 60–77 in *The Speeches in Thucydides*. Edited by P. A. Stadter. Chapel Hill: University of North Carolina Press, 1973.
Stanton, G. "Stephen in Lucan Perspective." Pages 345–60 in *Studia Biblica 1978: Papers on Paul and Other New Testament Authors*. Edited by E. A. Livingstone. JSNTSup 3. Sheffield: Sheffield Academic Press, 1980.
Steck, O. H. *Israel und das gewaltsame Geschick der Propheten: Untersuchungen zur Überlieferung des deuteronomistischen Geschichtsbild im Alten Testament, Spätjudentum, und Urchristentum*. WMANT 23. Neukirchen-Vluyn: Neukirchener Verlag, 1967.
Ste. Croix, G. E. M. de. "Aristotle on History and Poetry (*Poetics*, 9, 1451a36–b11)." Pages 23–32 in *Essays on Aristotle's Poetics*. Edited by A. O. Rorty. Princeton: Princeton University Press, 1992.
Stemberger, G. "Die Stephanusrede (Apg 7) and die jüdische Tradition." Pages 229–50 in *Studien zum rabbinischen Judentum*. SBAB 10. Stuttgart: Katholisches Bibelwerk, 1990.
Stenschke, C. W. *Luke's Portrait of Gentiles prior to Their Coming to Faith*. WUNT 2.108. Tübingen: Mohr Siebeck, 1999.
Sterling, G. E. "'Athletes of Virtue': An Analysis of the Summaries in Acts (2:41–47; 4:32–35; 5:12–16)." *JBL* 113 (1994): 679–96.
———. *Historiography and Self-definition: Josephos, Luke-Acts, and Apologetic Historiography*. NovTSup 64. Leiden: Brill, 1992.
———. "'Opening the Scriptures': The Legitimation of the Jewish Diaspora and the Early Christian Mission." Pages 199–225 in *Jesus and the Heritage of Israel: Luke's Narrative Claim upon Israel's Legacy*. Edited by D. P. Moessner. Harrisburg, Pa.: Trinity Press International, 1999.
Sternberg, M. *The Poetics of Biblical Narrative: Ideological Literature and the Drama of Reading*. Bloomington: Indiana University Press, 1985.
Stone, A. M. "Was Sallust a Liar? A Problem in Modern History." Pages 230–43 in *Ancient History in a Modern University*. Edited by T. W. Hillard et al. Vol. 2. Grand Rapids: Eerdmans, 1998.
Stowers, S. K. "Romans 7.7–25 as a Speech-in-Character (προσωποποιία)." Pages 180–202 in *Paul in His Hellenistic Context*. Edited by T. Engberg-Pedersen. Minneapolis: Fortress, 1995.
Strange, W. A. *The Problem of the Text of Acts*. SNTSMS 71. Cambridge: Cambridge University Press, 1992.

Strauss, B. S. "The Problem of Periodization: The Case of the Peloponnesian War." Pages 165–75 in *Inventing Ancient Culture: Historicism, Periodization, and the Ancient World*. Edited by M. Golden and P. Toohey. New York: Routledge, 1997.

Stuhlmacher, P. *Biblische Theologie des Neuen Testaments I: Grundlegung, Von Jesus zu Paulus*. Göttingen: Vandenhoeck & Ruprecht, 1992.

Sullivan, J. P. *Literature and Politics in the Age of Nero*. Ithaca: Cornell University Press, 1985.

Surkau, H.-W. *Martyrien in jüdischer und frühchristlicher Zeit*. FRLANT ns 36/56. Göttingen: Vandenhoeck & Ruprecht, 1938.

Swain, S. "Defending Hellenism: Philostratus, *In Honour of Apollonius*." Pages 157–96 in *Apologetics in the Roman Empire: Pagans, Jews, and Christians*. Edited by M. Edwards et al. New York: Oxford University Press, 1999.

———. "Hellenic Culture and the Roman Heroes of Plutarch." Pages 229–64 in *Essays on Plutarch's Lives*. Edited by B. Scardigli. New York: Oxford University Press, 1995.

———. *Hellenism and Empire: Language, Classicism, and Power in the Greek World, A.D. 50–250*. New York: Oxford University Press, 1996.

Sylva, D. D. "The Meaning and Function of Acts 7:46–50." *JBL* 106 (1987): 261–75.

Syme, R. *Tacitus*. 2 vols. London: Oxford University Press, 1958.

Talbert, C. H. "The Acts of the Apostles: Monograph or *Bios?*" Pages 58–72 in *History, Literature, and Society in the Book of Acts*. Edited by B. Witherington. Cambridge: Cambridge University Press, 1996.

———. "Biographies of Philosophers and Rulers as Instruments of Religious Propaganda in Mediterranean Antiquity." *ANRW* 2.16.2 (1978): 1619–51.

———. *Literary Patterns, Theological Themes, and the Genre of Luke-Acts*. SBLMS 20. Missoula, Mont.: Scholars Press, 1974.

———. *Reading Acts: A Literary and Theological Commentary on the Acts of the Apostles*. New York: Crossroad, 1997.

Talbert, C. H., and P. L. Stepp. "Succession in Mediterranean Antiquity, Part 1: The Lukan Milieu; Part 2: Luke-Acts." *SBLSP* 37 (1998): 148–79.

Tannehill, R. C. "The Composition of Acts 3–5: Narrative Development and Echo Effect." *SBLSP* 23 (1984): 217–40.

———. *The Narrative Unity of Luke-Acts: A Literary Interpretation*. 2 vols. Philadelphia: Fortress, 1986–90.

———. "Paul outside the Christian Ghetto: Stories of Intercultural Conflict and Cooperation in Acts." Pages 247–63 in *Text and Logos: The Humanistic Interpretation of the New Testament*. Edited by T. W. Jennings. Atlanta: Scholars Press, 1990.

———. "The Story of Israel within the Lukan Narrative." Pages 325–39 in *Jesus and the Heritage of Israel: Luke's Narrative Claim upon Israel's Legacy*. Edited by D. P. Moessner. Harrisburg, Pa.: Trinity Press International, 1999.

Tatum, J. *Xenophon's Imperial Fiction: On the Education of Cyrus.* Princeton: Princeton University Press, 1989.

Taylor, J. *Les Actes des Deux Apôtres: IV–VI Commentaire Historique.* EBib ns 23, 30, 41. Paris: Gabalda, 1994–2000.

———. "The Community of Goods among the First Christians and among the Essenes." Pages 147–61 in *Historical Perspectives: From the Hasmoneans to Bar Kokhba in Light of the Dead Sea Scrolls. Proceedings of the Fourth International Symposium of the Orion Center for the Study of the Dead Sea Scrolls and Associated Literature, 27–31 January 1999.* Edited by D. Goodblatt, A. Pinnick, and D. R. Schwartz. STDJ 37. Leiden: Brill, 2000.

Taylor, N. "Luke-Acts and the Temple." Pages 709–21 in *The Unity of Luke-Acts.* Edited by J. Verheyden. BETL 142. Leuven: Leuven University Press, 1999.

Tcherikover, V. "Jewish Apologetic Literature Reconsidered." *Eos* 48 (1956): 169–93.

Theissen, G. "Hellenisten und Hebräer (Apg 6,1–6). Gab es eine Spaltung der Urgemeinde?" Pages 323–43 in *Geschichte-Tradition-Reflexion: Festschrift für Martin Hengel zum 70. Geburtstag.* Edited by H. Cancik et al. Vol. 3. Tübingen: Mohr Siebeck, 1996.

———. *The Religion of the Earliest Churches: Creating a Symbolic World.* Translated by J. Bowden. Minneapolis: Fortress, 1999.

———. "Urchristlicher Liebeskommunismus: Zum 'Sitz im Leben' des Topos ἅπαντα κοινά." Pages 689–712 in *Texts and Contexts: Biblical Texts and Their Textual and Situational Contexts: Essays in Honor of Lars Hartman.* Edited by T. Fornberg and D. Hellholm. Oslo: Scandinavian University Press, 1995.

Thomas, C. M. *The Acts of Peter, Gospel Literature, and the Ancient Novel: Rewriting the Past.* New York: Oxford University Press, 2003.

Thomas, R. *Herodotus in Context: Ethnography, Science, and the Art of Persuasion.* Cambridge: Cambridge University Press, 2000.

Thompson, R. P. "Believers and Religious Leaders in Jerusalem: Contrasting Portraits of Jews in Acts 1–7." Pages 327–44 in *Literary Studies in Luke-Acts: Essays in Honor of Joseph B. Tyson.* Edited by R. P. Thompson and T. E. Phillips. Macon, Ga.: Mercer University Press, 1998.

Thornton, C.-J. *Der Zeuge des Zeugen: Lukas als Historiker der Paulusreisen.* WUNT 56. Tübingen: Mohr Siebeck, 1991.

Thyen, H. *Der Stil der jüdisch-hellenistischen Homilie.* FRLANT ns 47/65. Göttingen: Vandenhoeck & Ruprecht, 1955.

Toher, M. "Augustus and the Evolution of Roman Historiography." Pages 139–54 in *Between Republic and Empire: Interpretations of Augustus and His Principate.* Edited by K. A. Raaflaub and M. Toher. Berkeley: University of California Press, 1990.

Tov, E. *Textual Criticism of the Hebrew Bible.* Minneapolis: Fortress, 1992.

Trapp, M. B., ed. and trans. *Maximus of Tyre: The Philosophical Orations.* New York: Oxford University Press, 1997.

Trenkner, S. *The Greek Novella in the Classical Period.* Cambridge: Cambridge University Press, 1958.

Trocmé, E. " 'C'est le ciel qui est mon trône': La polémique contre le Temple et la théologie des Hellénistes." Pages 195–203 in *Le Trône de Dieu.* Edited by M. Philonenko. WUNT 69. Tübingen: Mohr Siebeck, 1993.

Trompf, G. W. *The Idea of Historical Recurrence in Western Thought: From Antiquity to the Reformation.* Berkeley: University of California Press, 1979.

Tyson, J. B. "Acts 6:1–7 and Dietary Regulations in Early Christianity." *PRSt* 10 (1983): 145–61.

———. *The Death of Jesus in Luke-Acts.* Columbia: University of South Carolina Press, 1986.

———. "From History to Rhetoric and Back: Assessing New Trends in Acts Studies." Pages 23–42 in *Contextualizing Acts: Lukan Narrative and Greco-Roman Discourse* Edited by T. Penner and C. Vander Stichele. SBLSymS 20. Atlanta: Society of Biblical Literature, 2003.

———. *Images of Judaism in Luke-Acts.* Columbia: University of South Carolina Press, 1992.

———. *Luke, Judaism, and the Scholars: Critical Approaches to Luke-Acts.* Columbia: University of South Carolina Press, 1999.

Unnik, W. C. van. "Luke-Acts: A Storm Center in Contemporary Scholarship." Pages 15–32 in *Studies in Luke-Acts.* Edited by L. E. Keck and J. L Martyn. Nashville: Abingdon, 1966.

———. "Luke's Second Book and the Rules of Hellenistic Historiography." Pages 37–60 in *Les Actes des Apôtres: Traditions, rédaction, théologie.* Edited by J. Kremer. BETL 48. Leuven: Leuven University Press, 1979.

———. "Remarks on the Purpose of Luke's Historical Writing (Luke I 1–4)." Pages 6–15 in *Sparsa Collecta: Part One; Evangelia, Paulina, Acta.* NovTSup 29. Leiden: Brill, 1973.

Vander Stichele, C. "Gender and Genre: Acts in/of Interpretation." Pages 311–29 in *Contextualizing Acts: Lukan Narrative and Greco-Roman Discourse.* Edited by T. Penner and C. Vander Stichele. SBLSymS 20. Atlanta: Society of Biblical Literature, 2003.

Varneda, V. I. *The Historical Method of Flavius Josephus.* ALGHJ 19. Leiden: Brill, 1986.

Via, E. J. "An Interpretation of Acts 7:35–37 from the Perspective of Major Themes in Luke-Acts." *SBLSP* 14.2 (1978): 209–22.

Vouga, F. *Geschichte des frühen Christentums.* Tübingen: Francke, 1994.

Walbank, F. W. *Polybius.* Sather Classical Lectures 42. Berkeley: University of California Press, 1972.

———. "Profit or Amusement: Some Thoughts on the Motives of Hellenistic Historians." Pages 253–66 in *Purposes of History: Studies in Greek Historiography from the 4th to the 2nd Centuries B.C.* Edited by H. Verdin et al. SH 30. Leuven: Orientaliste, 1990.

Walker, B. *The* Annals *of Tacitus: A Study in the Writing of History.* Manchester: Manchester University Press, 1952.
Walker, P. W. L. *Jesus and the Holy City: New Testament Perspectives on Jerusalem.* Grand Rapids: Eerdmans, 1996.
Wallace-Hadrill, A. "*Civilis Princeps:* Between Citizen and King." *JRS* 72 (1982): 32–48.
———. "The Emperor and His Virtues." *Historia* 30 (1981): 298–323.
Walsh, P. G. "Livy and the Aims of 'historia': An Analysis of the Third Decade." *ANRW* 2.30.2 (1982): 1058–74.
Walter, N. "Apostelgeschichte 6.1 und die Anfänge der Urgemeinde in Jerusalem." *NTS* 29 (1983): 370–93.
———. "Hellenistische Diaspora-Juden an der Wiege des Urchristentums." Pages 37–58 in *The New Testament and Hellenistic Judaism.* Edited by P. Borgen and S. Giversen. Aarhus: Aarhus University Press, 1995.
———. "Jüdisch-hellenistische Literatur vor Philon von Alexandrien (unter Ausschluss der Historiker)." *ANRW* 2.20.1 (1987): 67–120.
———. "Paul and the Early Christian Jesus-Tradition." Pages 51–80 in *Paul and Jesus: Collected Essays.* Edited by A. J. M. Wedderburn. JSNTSup 37. Sheffield: Sheffield Academic Press, 1989.
———. *Der Thoraausleger Aristobulos: Untersuchungen zu seinen Fragmenten zu pseudepigraphischen Resten der jüdisch-hellenistischen Literatur.* TU 86. Berlin: Akademie, 1964.
Wardman, A. *Plutarch's Lives.* Berkeley: University of California Press, 1974.
Watson, F. *Text and Truth: Redefining Biblical Theology.* Grand Rapids: Eerdmans, 1997.
Webb, R. "Imagination and the Arousal of the Emotions in Greco-Roman Rhetoric." Pages 112–27 in *The Passions in Roman Thought and Literature.* Edited by S. M. Braund and C. Gill. Cambridge: Cambridge University Press, 1997.
———. "The *Progymnasmata* as Practice." Pages 289–316 in *Education in Greek and Roman Antiquity.* Edited by Y. L. Too. Leiden: Brill, 2001.
Weber, F. *System der altsynagogalen palästinischen Theologie aus Targum, Midrasch, und Talmud.* Edited by F. Delitzsch and G. Schnedermann. Leipzig: Dörffling & Franke, 1880.
Wedderburn, A. J. M. "Paul and Jesus: Similarity and Continuity." Pages 161–82 in *Paul and Jesus: Collected Essays.* Edited by A. J. M. Wedderburn. JSNTSup 37. Sheffield: Sheffield Academic Press, 1989.
Weinert, F. D. "Luke, Stephen, and the Temple in Luke-Acts." *BTB* 17 (1987): 88–90.
Weiser, A. "Zur Gesetzes- und Tempelkritik der 'Hellenisten.' " Pages 146–68 in *Das Gesetz im Neuen Testament.* Edited by K. Kertelge. QD 108. Freiburg: Herder, 1986.
Welles, C. B. "Isocrates' View of History." Pages 3–25 in *The Classical Tradition: Literary and Historical Studies in Honor of Harry Caplan.* Edited by L. Wallach. Ithaca: Cornell University Press, 1966.

Wendland, P. *Die hellenistisch-römische Kultur in ihren Beziehungen zu Judentum und Christentum.* HNT 1.2. Tübingen: Mohr Siebeck, 1912.

West, M. L. *The East Face of Helicon: West Asiatic Elements in Greek Poetry and Myth.* New York: Oxford University Press, 1997.

Westlake, H. D. "Individuals in Xenophon's *Hellenica.*" Pages 203–25 in *Essays on the Greek Historians and Greek History.* Manchester: Manchester University Press, 1969.

White, H. "The Fictions of Factual Representation." Pages 121–34 in *Tropics of Discourse: Essays in Cultural Criticism.* Baltimore: Johns Hopkins University Press, 1978.

———. *Metahistory: The Historical Imagination in Nineteenth-Century Europe.* Baltimore: Johns Hopkins University Press, 1973.

———. "The Value of Narrativity in the Representation of Reality." Pages 1–25 in *The Content of the Form: Narrative Discourse and Historical Representation.* Baltimore: Johns Hopkins University Press, 1987.

Wiedemann, T. "Rhetoric in Polybius." Pages 289–300 in *Purposes of History: Studies in Greek Historiography from the 4th to the 2nd Centuries B.C.* Edited by H. Verdin et al. SH 30. Leuven: Orientaliste, 1990.

Wiens, D. *Stephen's Sermon and the Structure of Luke-Acts.* N. Richmond Hills, Tex.: BIBAL, 1995.

Wilckens, U. *Die Missionsreden der Apostelgeschichte: Form- und Traditionsgeschichtliche Untersuchungen.* WMANT 5. 3d ed. Neukirchen-Vluyn: Neukirchener Verlag, 1974.

Wilcox, M. "A Foreword to the Study of the Speeches in Acts." Pages 206–25 in *Christianity, Judaism, and Other Greco-Roman Cults: Studies for Morton Smith at Sixty.* Edited by J. Neusner. Vol. 1. SJLA 12. Leiden: Brill, 1975.

———. "The 'God-fearers' in Acts: A Reconsideration." *JSNT* 13 (1981): 102–22.

Williams, C. A. *Roman Homosexuality: Ideologies of Masculinity in Classical Antiquity.* New York: Oxford University Press, 1999.

Williams, G. *Change and Decline: Roman Literature in the Early Empire.* Berkeley: University of California Press, 1978.

Williams, M. H. "Palestinian Jewish Personal Names in Acts." Pages 79–113 in *The Book of Acts in Its Palestinian Setting.* Edited by R. Bauckham. BAFCS 4. Grand Rapids: Eerdmans, 1995.

Wills, L. M. "The Form of the Sermon in Hellenistic Judaism and Early Christianity." *HTR* 77 (1984): 277–99.

———. *The Jewish Novel in the Ancient World.* Ithaca: Cornell University Press, 1995.

Wilson, A. "Reflections on Ekphrasis in Ausonius and Prudentius." Pages 149–59 in *Ethics and Rhetoric: Classical Essays for Donald Russell on His Seventy-Fifth Birthday.* Edited by D. Innes, H. Hines, and C. Pelling. New York: Oxford University Press, 1995.

Wilson, S. G. *The Gentiles and the Gentile Mission in Luke-Acts.* SNTSMS 23. Cambridge: Cambridge University Press, 1973.

———. *Luke and the Law.* SNTSMS 50. Cambridge: Cambridge University Press, 1983.

———. *Luke and the Pastoral Epistles.* London: SPCK, 1979.

Wilson, W. T. "Urban Legends: Acts 10:1–11:18 and the Strategies of Greco-Roman Foundation Narratives." *JBL* 120 (2001): 77–99.

Winkler, J. J. *Auctor and Actor: A Narratological Reading of Apuleius's* The Golden Ass. Berkeley: University of California Press, 1985.

Winter, S. C. "Παρρησία in Acts." Pages 185–202 in *Friendship, Flattery, and Frankness of Speech: Studies on Friendship in the New Testament World.* Edited by J. T. Fitzgerald. NovTSup 82. Leiden: Brill, 1996.

Wiseman, T. P. *Clio's Cosmetics: Three Studies in Greco-Roman Literature.* Leicester: Leicester University Press, 1979.

———. "Crossing the Rubicon." Pages 60–63, 188 in *Roman Drama and Roman History.* Exeter: University of Exeter Press, 1998.

———. "Lying Historians: Seven Types of Mendacity." Pages 122–46 in *Lies and Fiction in the Ancient World.* Edited by C. Gill and T. P. Wiseman. Austin: University of Texas Press, 1993.

———. "Origins of Roman Historiography." Pages 1–22 in *Historiography and Imagination.* Exeter: University of Exeter Press, 1994.

———. "Practice and Theory in Roman Historiography." *History* 66 (1981): 375–93.

Witherington, B. *The Acts of the Apostles: A Socio-Rhetorical Commentary.* Grand Rapids: Eerdmans, 1998.

———. "'Addendum' to W. J. Mccoy, 'In the Shadow of Thucydides.'" Pages 23–32 in *History, Literature, and Society in the Book of Acts.* Edited by B. Witherington. Cambridge: Cambridge University Press, 1996.

———. "Editing the Good News: Some Synoptic Lessons for the Study of Acts." Pages 324–47 in *History, Literature, and Society in the Book of Acts.* Edited by B. Witherington. Cambridge: Cambridge University Press, 1996.

———. "Finding Its Niche: The Historical and Rhetorical Species of Acts." *SBLSP* 35 (1996): 67–97.

Woodman, A. J. *Rhetoric in Classical Historiography: Four Studies.* London: Croom & Helm, 1988.

———. "Self-Imitation and the Substance of History: Tacitus, *Annals* 1.61–5 and *Histories* 2.70, 5.14–15." Pages 143–55 in *Creative Imitation and Latin Literature.* Edited by D. West and T. Woodman. Cambridge: Cambridge University Press, 1979.

———. *Tacitus Reviewed.* New York: Oxford University Press, 1998.

Woodruff, P. "Aristotle on Mimēsis." Pages 73–95 in *Essays on Aristotle's Poetics.* Edited by A. O. Rorty. Princeton: Princeton University Press, 1992.

Worthington, I. "History and Oratorical Exploitation." Pages 109–29 in *Persuasion: Greek Rhetoric in Action.* Edited by I. Worthington. New York: Routledge, 1994.

Zanker, P. *The Power of Images in the Age of Augustus.* Translated by A. Shapiro. Ann Arbor: University of Michigan Press, 1988.

Zeller, E. *Die Apostelgeschichte nach ihrem Inhalt und Ursprung kritisch Untersucht.* Stuttgart: Mäcken, 1854.

Zmijewski, J. "Die Stephanusrede (Apg 7,2–53) — Literarisches und Theologisches." Pages 85–128 in *Das Neue Testament: Quelle christlicher Theologie und Glaubenspraxis.* Stuttgart: Katholisches Bibelwerk, 1986.

Index of Ancient Sources

HEBREW SCRIPTURES

Genesis
15:1–11	308
15:7–11	308
15:13	308
15:13–14	308
15:14	96, 308
15:17–19	308
17:8	308

Exodus
2:11	320
2:11–12	320
2:13	320–21
2:14	320
2:15	321
3:12	96, 308–9
10:1	288
11:9	286
11:10	286
15:17	309
18	74, 266
18:13–26	266
20	90
23:1	294
23:2	294
23:7	294
25:9	311
26:17–27	252
28:3	288
32:1	113
33:7	311

Leviticus
19:10	283
19:11–17	294
19:33–34	283
23:22	283
26:1	317
26:30	317

Numbers
11	74, 266
11:1 (LXX)	266
11:17	266, 288
11:25	288
16–18	252
32	250

Deuteronomy
1	74, 266
1:13	266
4:8	317
4:25–28	317
4:28	311
6:22	288
7:19	288
7:37	98
10:18	265
11	251
11:3	288
12:5	251, 308
12:11	308
12:13–14	308
12:18	308
12:21	308
12:26	308
13–14	251
14:29	265
16:11	265
16:14	265
16:18–20	294
18	90, 251
18:15	90, 98
18:18	90
21	251
21:11	317
23:46	288
24:17	265
24:17–21	283
24:18	265
24:19	265

Deuteronomy (continued)	
24:20	265
26	251
26:12	265
26:13	265
27:15	311
27:19	283
29:2	288
30:17–19	317
31:27–29	317
31:29	311, 317
34:9	288, 311

1 Samuel	
8	322
8:9–18	325

2 Samuel	
2:6	313
6:17	316
7	99
7:1–17	314
7:2	314
7:6	314
7:6–7	314
7:10	314
7:11	314
7:13	314

1 Kings	
2:28	313
5:13	325
8:27	317
8:43	317
9:15	325

2 Kings	
12:4	325
12:14	325

Psalms	
7	316
14	316
77:43 (LXX)	288
77:60 (LXX)	313
110:1	83
131	316
131:5 (LXX)	313–14, 316

Psalms (continued)	
131:7	316
131:8	316
134:9 (LXX)	288

Isaiah	
2:8	312
2:18	317
10:11	317
17:8	312
19:1	317
21:9	317
31:7	317
37:19	312
46:6	317
66	316
66:1	96
66:1–2	98, 309, 316, 322

Jeremiah	
1:16	312
3:4	309
7:3	309
7:6	309
7:6–7	309
7:7	309
7:20	309
14:13	309
16:2	309
16:3	309
19:4	309
19:12	309
22:3	309
24:5	309
25:6	312
28:62	309
29:10	309
32:30	309
33:10	309
35:3	309
35:6	309
36:10	309
39:20	288
39:37	309
40:2	309
42:18	309
51:8	312

Lamentations
2:6	313

Daniel
1–6	237, 241
5:4	317
5:23	317
6:28	317
7:13	83

Joel
2:28–32	277, 280

Amos
5:25–27	95, 312, 316, 323
7:39–48	317
7:41	317
7:42–43	317
7:47	317
7:48	317
9:11–12	283, 314
9:15	314

Zechariah
3:9	285
4:2	285
10	285

NEW TESTAMENT

Matthew
12:45	285
15:34	285
15:36	285
15:37	285
16:10	285
18:22	285
22:25	285
22:26	285
22:28	285
28:19	268

Mark
1:31	75
7:15	30
12:40	265
12:42	265

Mark (continued)
12:43	265
14:56–57	83
14:58	83
14:64	83
16:9	285

Luke
1:1–4	33, 219
2:36	285
2:37	265
4:25	265
4:26	265
7:12	265
8:1	64
9:1	64
9:12	64
10:40	75
18:3	265
18:5	265
18:31	64
20:47	265
21:2	265
21:3	265
21:20–24	323
21:22	323
22:3	64
23:34	290
23:46	290

Acts
1–5	84
1–6	66
1–7	63, 86, 263, 265, 300
1–8	61–62, 64, 269
1:1–2:44	63, 263
1:5	268–69, 308
1:7	308
1:12–26	267
1:14	64
1:15–26	65
1:16	301
1:24	268
1:24–25	64
2	270, 278
2–5	66
2–6	79

Acts (continued)

Reference	Pages
2:1–4	269
2:1–13	277
2:1–8:25	277
2:4	269
2:5	262, 277, 281
2:5–11	279
2:5–12	277
2:8–11	62, 64
2:9–11	62, 68, 279–80, 290
2:14	262
2:14–36	61
2:17–21	277
2:29	301
2:36	279
2:37–42	279, 281
2:38	268
2:41	66, 268
2:42	64, 268
2:42–47	267
2:43	61, 288
2:43–47	61, 63, 66, 263
2:44–45	75
2:45	272
2:46	268
2:47	63, 66
3:1–10	61
3:11–26	64
3:17	301
4	86
4:1	66
4:1–22	61, 296, 317
4:1–31	61, 63, 263
4:3	80
4:5	80
4:5–7	79
4:8	269
4:17–20	64
4:24–31	64
4:30	288
4:32–35	61, 63, 66, 75, 263
4:32–37	74, 267
4:33	79
4:34	272
4:34a	75

Acts (continued)

Reference	Pages
4:34b	75
4:35	74
4:35b	75
4:37	74
5	86, 273
5:1–11	61, 63, 72, 77, 263, 267
5:4	71
5:9	71
5:12	79, 288
5:12–16	61, 63, 66, 263
5:14	63
5:14–15	66
5:16	63
5:17	61, 79
5:17–41	63, 263
5:17–42	296, 317
5:18	80
5:18–42	61
5:21	79–80
5:27	79
5:27–32	64
5:34	79–80
5:40–42	64
5:41	79
5:42	63, 66, 263
6	266, 273
6–8	269
6:1	26, 61, 63–64, 66–68, 70–71, 74–75, 78, 83, 265–66, 276, 279–80
6:1b	67, 76
6:1–6	9, 63, 263, 271, 274
6:1–7	34, 40–42, 60–62, 64–65, 69–70, 72–73, 75–80, 84–85, 262, 267, 273, 285–86, 289, 300–301, 327
6:1–8	34
6:1–15	93
6:1–8:3	7–10, 12, 14–20, 22–23, 26, 29, 32–44, 50–55, 57, 59–61, 69, 72, 78, 84, 90–91, 101–3, 105, 109, 111, 113, 179, 219, 221–23, 260, 262, 265, 285, 301, 303, 325, 327, 329–31, 333

Acts (continued)	
6:1–8:4	93
6:1–15:35	78
6:2	62, 74–76, 274
6:2–4	64, 74
6:2–6	64
6:3	64–65, 76–77, 79–80, 266, 285, 288, 290
6:3a	76
6:3–5	80, 268
6:4	75–76
6:5	64–66, 76–80, 82, 280–81, 285, 288, 290
6:5–6	64, 80
6:5–8:2	83
6:6	62, 65, 77, 81, 269
6:7	62–64, 66, 100, 263, 274, 281
6:8	65, 79, 81–82, 267, 290–91, 320, 322–23
6:8–10	27
6:8–15	32, 42, 63, 287–91, 296, 300–301
6:8–7:1	36, 60, 78–79
6:8–8:3	296
6:9	79, 82, 279, 290–91, 302, 320
6:9–13	297
6:10	27, 33, 79–80, 288, 291, 302, 304, 320, 323
6:10–11	319
6:11	19–20, 33, 80, 83, 85, 289–93, 295, 297, 300, 302, 306, 318, 323
6:11–14	297, 322
6:12	33, 79–81, 297, 302
6:13	19–20, 80, 85, 290, 293, 297, 302, 306
6:13–14	80, 83, 86, 91–92, 96, 289, 291–92, 295, 300, 306, 308, 318, 323
6:14	36, 80, 96, 293, 302, 306
6:15	79–81, 291, 297, 302
6:15–7:1	86
6:27	98
6:35	98
6:59a–60	81

Acts (continued)	
7	20, 51, 87–91, 93–94, 99, 102, 112, 223, 248, 260, 262, 303–4, 306, 308, 311, 314, 319, 323, 325–26, 328, 330
7:1	79
7:1–53	303
7:2	297, 301, 306–7, 319, 321, 324
7:2–8	94, 306–7, 318
7:2–34	85, 87
7:2–53	60, 85
7:4	96, 306–9
7:5	307–8, 310–11
7:6	94, 307–8, 321
7:6–7	94, 96–97, 306, 308, 311, 318–19, 321–22
7:7	96–98, 307, 309–10, 314, 318, 322
7:8	307, 322
7:9	307, 319
7:9–16	94, 319
7:9–29	307
7:10	288, 319
7:11	301, 306
7:11–13	319
7:11–15	319
7:12	301, 306
7:13	10, 319
7:13–14	96, 320
7:15	301, 306, 319
7:16	320
7:17	307
7:17a	320
7:17b–19	320
7:17–22	94
7:17–43	94
7:19	301, 306–7
7:20	307, 320
7:22	288, 320
7:23–24	320
7:23–29	94, 320–21
7:24	317, 320
7:25	94, 307, 320
7:25–29	321
7:26	307, 320–21

Acts (continued)

7:26b	320
7:26–27	324
7:27	320–21
7:27–28	321
7:29	307, 322
7:30	307
7:30–34	321
7:30–36	94
7:30–43	307
7:32	307
7:33	95–96, 307, 309
7:34	307, 321
7:35	94, 307, 321
7:35–43	85
7:35–50	87
7:36	288, 321, 323
7:37	90, 93, 98, 307, 322–23
7:37–41	312
7:37–43	94, 98
7:38	301, 306–7, 322
7:39	301, 306, 312
7:39–42	316, 322
7:39–43	95–96, 307
7:40	100
7:41	98, 312, 316–17
7:42	307, 312
7:42–43	94, 98, 322–23
7:43	307, 311, 322
7:44	85, 301, 306, 310, 313, 322
7:44–45	11, 98, 314
7:44–46	307
7:44–50	44–51, 95, 98, 307
7:44–53	307
7:45	96, 301, 306–7, 310–12, 314, 322
7:46	99, 307, 310–11, 313, 315–16, 322
7:46–47	98, 314
7:46–50	316
7:47	310, 314, 316
7:47–48	316
7:47–50	310, 313, 316–17
7:48	98, 309, 311–12, 314, 316–17
7:48–49	316

Acts (continued)

7:48–53	310
7:49	96, 307, 309, 316
7:49–50	94, 98
7:50	309
7:51	293, 306–7, 323
7:51–53	85, 94, 96–97, 293, 299, 303, 305, 312, 315, 323, 325
7:52	293, 306–7, 322
7:53	293, 307
7:54	291, 297, 302, 304
7:54–55	81, 83
7:54–60	32, 289–90
7:54–8:1	11, 296, 301
7:54–8:2	60, 78–79
7:54–8:3	63, 96, 287–88, 300
7:55	27, 290–91, 293, 297, 302, 307
7:55–56	299, 324
7:56	291, 297, 302, 307
7:56–57	299
7:57	291, 297, 304
7:57–59a	81
7:57–8:1	297
7:58	291, 297, 302
7:58b	82
7:58–59	299
7:59–60	291
7:59	290, 302
7:60	290–91, 297, 302, 320
7:60b	291, 309
8:1	81–82, 291, 294, 296, 301–2, 322
8:1b	83
8:1–2	270
8:1–3	42
8:1–4	40, 68
8:2	294
8:2–3	10
8:2–4	63
8:3	82, 294
8:4	270
8:4–12:5	63
8:5–40	78
8:6	288
8:9–25	289

Acts (continued)		Acts (continued)	
8:13	288	13:46–47	277
8:15–17	269	13:50	263, 281
8:26–40	277	14	88
9:1–28	277	14:1	278
9:11	278	14:1–7	278
9:23	263	14:2	263
9:29	278	14:13	317
9:29–11:18	78	14:13–18	317
9:31	277	14:18	317
9:39	265	14:19	263
9:41	265	14:19–20	278
10	283	15	75, 99, 264, 270, 280, 282, 298, 314
10–11	269, 282	15:1–2	70
10:2	281	15:1–5	68
10:22	281	15:5	70
10:35	281	15:8	269
10:37	268	15:15–17	283
10:44–46	269	15:16	315
11:16	268	15:16–17	314, 325
11:19	68, 270	15:22–35	68
11:19–20	68	15:28	269
11:19–21	35, 38, 269, 278	16–21	270
11:20	68	16:1	285
11:22	270, 278	16:1–3	278
11:26	262, 263	16:14	281
11:27–30	272	16:16–24	289
11:29	75	16:19–24	295
12	270	16:20	263
12:1–14	78	17	88
12:19	29	17:1–9	278
12:25	75	17:4	278, 281
13	91	17:5	263, 319
13–14	269	17:5–9	295
13:1–3	269–70	17:10–14	278
13:2–4	269	17:11–12	278
13:5	278	17:13	263
13:6–12	289	17:14	285, 309
13:9	269	17:17	278, 281
13:14–47	278	17:24–25	317
13:19	285	18:2	263
13:24	268	18:4–8	278
13:26	301	18:5	285
13:38	301	18:5–6	277
13:43	278, 281	18:8	278
13:45	263		

Acts (continued)

Reference	Pages
18:12–17	278, 295
18:14	263
18:17	281
18:19	278
18:19–21	278
18:25	268
18:26–28	278
19:1–6	269
19:1–7	271
19:3	268
19:4	268
19:6	271
19:8–10	278
19:10–18	278
19:11–20	289
19:14	285
19:23–40	296
19:28–41	298
19:29	285
19:33	278
20	286
20:3	278
20:4	285
20:6	285
20:7	268
20:11	268
20:18–21	278
21:4	285
21:8	285
21:11	263, 279
21:20	70, 279
21:24	278
21:27	263, 278–79, 285, 297
21:27–36	317
21:27–23:11	296
21:28	297
21:29	286, 297
21:30	279, 297
21:30–31	297
21:37	70
21:39	278
21:40	70
22:1	297, 301
22:1–21	296
22:2	70

Acts (continued)

Reference	Pages
22:3	278
22:6–10	297
22:16–26	270
22:17–21	297
22:18–21	322
22:20	296
22:22	297
22:23	297
22:30	297
23:1	297, 301
23:1–10	296
23:6	301
23:9	296
23:10	296, 298
23:12	263, 279
23:20	263
23:20–21	279
23:27	279
24:1–21	296
24:5–9	279
24:9	263
24:19	263
24:19–20	279
25:1–12	296
25:2–3	279
25:7	263
25:7–10	279
25:15	279
26:1–32	296
26:2–7	279
26:4	262
26:14	70
26:21	263, 279
26:23	280
26:28	262
27:2	285
27:3	264
27:19	265
27:35	268
28:2	264
28:17	279, 301
28:17–19	279
28:17–24	278
28:25–28	322
28:27–28	277

Romans	
1:1	62
1:16	280
11:13	75
12:7	75
14:14	30
15:25	75
15:31	75
16:1	285
16:21	285
16:23	285

1 Corinthians	
1:1	62
1:14	285
11:23–26	268
12:5	75
15:3–8	62
15:8	62
16:10	285
16:15	75

2 Corinthians	
1:1	285
8:4	75
9:1	75
9:12	75
9:13	75
11:22	68
12:12	62

Galatians	
1:17	62
2:11–14	281

Ephesians	
6:21	286

Philippians	
1:1	286
3:5	68

Colossians	
1:1	286
4:7	286
4:10	285

1 Thessalonians	
1:1	286

2 Thessalonians	
1:1	286

1 Timothy	
4:14	269
5:22	269
16:1	285
17:14	285
18:5	285

2 Timothy	
1:6	269
4:12	286
4:20	286

Titus	
3:12	286

Philemon	
1:1	285
1:24	285

Hebrews	
11:23	320

Revelation	
1:4	285
1:11	285
1:12	285
1:16	285
1:20	285
4:5	285
5:1	285
5:6	285
10:3	285
12:3	285
15:1	285
15:7	285
17:9	285
17:11	285

ANCIENT JEWISH AND CHRISTIAN SOURCES

Aristeas (Letter of)

15–16	237
51	239
56	239–41
70	240
72	240
77	240
83	240
84	240
86	240
87	240
89	240
92	240
99	240
132	238–39
134	239
134–38	238
138	239
139	238
144	239
177–80	237
295–96	238

Artapanus

Frg. 2.1–3	243
Frg. 3.3–6	242
Frg. 3.4–6	243
Frg. 3.7–11	253
Frg. 3.10	243

Aristobulos

Frg. 2	242
Frg. 3	242
Frg. 4	242

Baruch

4:4–5:9	280

Clementine Recognitions

1.38.5–39.1	325

Corpus papyrorum judaicorum

153	226

Eupolemus

Frg. 1	242
Frg. 2.34.1	243

(Ps.)-Eupolemus

8–9	242

Josephus, *Contra Apionem*

1.2	119
1.15	119
1.20	119
1.23–27	147
1.24	119
1.110–27	243
2.77	259
2.157–59	253
2.163	254

Josephus, *Antiquitates judaicae*

1.4	112
1.13	155
1.17	112
1.30	170
2.230–31	252, 320
2.232–35	252
2.238–53	253
2.269	309
2.347–48	253
3.89–101	112
3.99	253
3.123	311
3.179–80	253
3.179–87	312
3.190	253
3.191	256
3.212	254
3.213	254
3.280–81	254
3.322	254
4	264, 266, 273
4.14–66	252
4.196–98	254
8.50–56	243
8.56	118
18.65–84	205

Index of Ancient Sources / 387

Josephus, *Bellum judaicum*
1.1	*111, 219*
1.6	*111*
1.9–11	*111*
1.16	*111*
1.30	*111*

Judith
8:18	*317*

1 Maccabees
13:28	*285*

2 Maccabees
2:19–32	*137*
2:25	*137*
2:29	*137*
4:10	*71*
4:13	*71*
7:1	*285*
15:39	*137*

4 Maccabees
5:1–6:35	*298*
8:8	*71*
17:17	*298*

Philo, *De Abrahamo*
60	*244*
178–99	*244*
183	*244*
185	*244*
191	*244*
199	*244*
217	*244*
225	*245*
262	*245*
263–65	*245*
266	*245*
268	*245*

Philo, *De Iosepho*
54	*246*

Philo, *De migratione Abrahami*
89–93	*238*
128	*244*
179	*244*

Philo, *Quaestiones et solutiones in Exodum*
2.52–53	*311*
2.76	*311*

Philo, *De specialibus legibus*
1.54–57	*33*

Philo, *De vita Mosis*
1.1	*246*
1.21	*250, 320*
1.32	*250, 320*
1.48	*250*
1.63	*250*
1.148–57	*250*
1.157	*250*
1.158	*250*
1.220	*250*
1.237–38	*250*
1.239	*250*
1.251	*250*
1.319	*250*
1.334	*250*
2.2	*246*
2.12	*246, 250*
2.17	*250*
2.18–19	*250*
2.51–52	*251*
2.72	*251*
2.73	*252*
2.74	*252, 311*
2.75	*252*
2.89	*252*
2.159	*252*

Philo, *De virtutibus*
187–89	*245*
219	*245*

Philo, the Epic Poet
Frg. 1	*242*
Frg. 3	*242*

Protoevangelium of James
1.1	*105*

Psalms of Solomon
8:28	280
11:2–6	280
17:26–28	280

Qumran
4Q158	90
4Qtest	90

Sibylline Oracles
3.218–45	243
3.573–85	244

Sirach
24:8–12	311
37:14	285

Targum Neofiti to Exodus
15:17	309

Tobit
3:8	285
3:15	285
6:14	285
7:11	285
12:15	285
14:4b–7	280

Wisdom of Solomon
2:10–21	298
2:12	298, 324
2:14–16	324
2:15	298
2:20	298
3:1–11	298
3:2	298
3:7–8	298
3:10	298
4:17	324
9:6	311

GREEK AND LATIN AUTHORS

Aelius Aristides, *Orations*
23	166

Ammianus Marcellinus
23.6.75–80	201

Aphthonius, *Progymnasmata*
2	189
10	206
11	210

Aristotle, Eudemian Ethics
3.6.4	198

Aristotle, *Poetica*
1448a	149
1449b	190
1450a	187, 190, 196, 208
1450b	187, 208
1451a	187
1451b	116, 148, 164, 187
1452a–b	187
1452b	191
1453b	190–91, 264
1454a	155, 196
1454b	177, 197
1455a	191
1456a	191, 208
1456b	208
1459a	148, 186–87

Aristotle, *Rhetorica*
1.2.4	197
1.3.3–5	230
1.9.3–13	230, 292
1.9.32	230
1.9.33	230–31
1.9.35	127
1.9.38	244
1.9.40	232
2.12–17	197
2.13	197
2.14	197
2.16	198
2.17	198

Aristotle, *Rhetorica* (continued)
2.23	*199*
3.11.1–3	*191*
3.12	*126*
3.12.6	*184*

Aristotle, *Topica*
3.1	*204*

(Ps.)-Aristotle, *On Vices and Virtues*
5.2–3	*198*

Arius Didymus
Frg. 11b	*174*
Frg.11m	*178*

Arrian, *Anabasis*
1.26.1–2	*253*

Cassius Dio, *Roman History*
63.22.3–6	*213*

Cicero, *Epistulae ad familiars*
5.12.3	*126*
5.12.4	*126*
5.12.5–6	*125*

Cicero, *De inventione rhetorica*
1.27	*132, 181*
1.29	*181*
1.31	*183*

Cicero, *De legibus*
1.1.5	*131*
1.2.5	*124*
1.5	*126*

Cicero, *De officiis*
1.55	*275*
1.56	*275*
1.67	*292*
1.86	*294*
1.89	*293*
1.93–94	*292*
1.94	*176*
1.142	*176, 294*
1.142–49	*184*
1.153–59	*294*
1.185	*273*
2.70	*273*

Cicero, *Orator*
37	*126*
66	*126*
207	*126*

Cicero, *De oratore*
2.35	*125*
2.36	*124*
2.51–63	*124*
2.63	*180–81*
2.66–67	*126*
2.206–208	*199*

Demetrius, *De elocutione*
209	*195*
211	*195*
214	*195*
216	*195*
217	*195*
219	*195*
221	*182*

Diodorus Siculus, *Library of History*
1.1.1	*165*
1.1.3–4	*165*
1.1.5	*165*
1.2.2	*166*
1.2.2–8	*127, 164*
1.2.5–6	*166*
1.2.7	*214*
1.2.7–8	*166*
3.57.8	*155*
4.43.2	*155*
8.10.3	*155*
9.1.2	*285*
9.3.3	*285*
9.7.1	*285*
9.28.1	*285*
10.10.1	*285*
12.25–1–2	*274*
13.24.2	*291*
13.24.4–5	*294*
13.25.2–3	*294*
13.33.2	*155*
13.35.5	*155*
14.112.1	*155*

Diodorus Siculus,
Library of History (continued)

15.1.1	*166*
17.27.7	*155*
17.46.6	*155*
17.86.3	*155*
20.1	*180*
20.1.2	*129*
20.1.5	*129*
20.1.5–20.2.2	*214–15*
20.2.2	*129*
31.15.1	*166*
35.1.3	*256*
40.3.1–8	*255*
40.3.3	*255*
40.3.4	*255*
40.3.6–7	*255*

Diogenes Laertius, *De clarorum philosophorum vitis*

7.100	*292, 294*

Dionysius, *Antiquitates romanae*

1.1.1–5	*125*
1.1.2	*164*
1.1.3	*164*
1.4.3	*167*
1.5.2–4	*162*
1.5.3	*164*
1.6.5	*167*
1.8.2	*274*
1.8.2–4	*164*
1.8.3	*221*
1.9–2.29	*235*
1.89.1–3	*284*
1.89.4	*284*
1.90.1	*285*
3.17.1	*185*
3.18.1	*162*
7.66.1–3	*213*
7.65.3	*274*
7.65.5	*274*
7.66.5	*185*
11.1.1–5	*164*
11.1.3	*194*
11.1.4–5	*127, 176*

Dionysius, *De compositione verborum*

3	*184*
12	*184*
18	*194*
20	*184, 194*

Dionysius, *De Lysia*

7	*194*
9	*221*

Dionysius, *Epistula ad Pompeium Geminum*

3	*182, 184–85*
6	*162*

Dionysius, *De Thucydide*

5	*125*
9	*184*
12	*184*
16–18	*129*
19	*184*
34	*184*
37–42	*151, 214*
39	*207*
41	*214*
51	*177*

Duris

FGH 76 F1	*117*

Epictetus, *Dissertationes / Discourses*

2.9.19ff.	*226*

(Aulus) Gellius, *Attic Nights*

5.18.8–9	*125, 185*

Hermogenes, *On Issues*

37	*234*

Hermogenes, *On Types of Style*

408	*115*
412	*115*

Index of Ancient Sources / 391

Herodotus, *Histories*

1.1	106
1.5	114
2.6.3	131
2.113	106
2.118	106
3.70–3.84	285

Horace, *Sermones*

1.4.139–143	227

Isocrates, *Nicocles*

2.48–49	161
2.50–52	151

Isocrates, *Helenae encomium*

14–15	295

Justin, *Epitome*

36.2.15	256

Juvenal, *Satires*

14.96–106	227

Livy, *Ab urbe condita libri*

Preface 9	165
1.10	127

Lucian, *Historia*

2	115
5	148
7	170
8	170, 180
9	147, 170–71
10–14	170
12–13	175
17	170, 175
20	171
20–21	171
24	171
25	171, 207
26	171
28	172
29	172
34	173
37	173
38	173
39	147

Lucian, *Historia* (continued)

39–40	170
41	170, 173
42	147–48, 170–71
43	147
47	147
47–48	170
47–49	173
49	177
50–51	185
51	173, 195, 232
55	190
57	187
58	214
61	173, 175
63	147

Lucian, *Philopseudes*

2	115

Lucian, *Vera historia*

1.3	106
1.4	106, 133

Martial, *Epigrams*

7.82	227
11.94	227

Maximus of Tyre, *Orationes*

14.5	167
22.5	156, 175
22.6	175

Menander Rhetor, *Epideictic Speeches*

2.4	234

Pliny the Younger, *Epistulae*

7.9.3–5	248
7.9.6	248

Plutarch, *Quomodo adulator ab amico internoscatur*

55	167
61	167
66	167
67	167
68	168

Plutarch, *Alexander*
1.2	132

Plutarch, *De Herodoti malignitate*
854f	168
855b–f	168
855e–f	168
856b–c	168
857a–858f	169
859d	169
860d	169, 207
862b–c	169
863b	169
867c–d	169
874a–c	169

Plutarch, *Nicias*
1.5	135

Plutarch, *Theseus*
1.1	162
1.3	162

(Ps.)-Plutarch, *Essay on the Life and Poetry of Homer*
74	181

Polybius, *Histories*
1.1.1	151
1.1.2	152, 155
1.1.2–4	152
1.4.1	152
1.4.2	152
1.4.4–6	152
1.4.11	152
1.11.23–25	156
1.13.11	155
1.87.1	155
2.5b.11	156
2.56.7–8	153
2.56.7–10	116
2.56.9–10	194
2.56.10	153
2.56.11	153
2.56.14	153
2.56.16	153
2.57.8–59.10	153

Polybius, *Histories* (continued)
2.59.7	153
2.60.2	154
2.61.5–6	154
2.61.11	154
2.62.2–3	158
3.20.1–5	154
3.31.7–13	151
3.31.11–13	183
3.33.17	183
3.47.6–48.12	130, 183
3.47.6–49.4	158
3.48.1	158
3.48.8–9	130
3.48.10–12	130
3.48.11	158
3.118.12	151
4.11	176
9.12.6	155
10.2.8–13	205
12.3.2–3	156
12.4b.1–4c.1	156
12.4b.1–12.7.6	183
12.4c.2–5	156
12.6a.3–4	157
12.6b.6–7	157
12.7.2	157
12.7.4	157
12.7.5–6	157
12.8.1–2	157
12.12.2	158
12.12.3	158
12.12.4–5	158
12.13.1–3	158
12.13.4–6	158
12.14.5	158
12.15.7–9	158
12.17–22	158
12.25.5–7	158
12.25.8	164
12.25a.5	159
12.25b1–3	182
12.25b.1–4	159, 212
12.25c.1–5	158
12.25e.1	160
12.25e.1–2	183

Polybius, *Histories* (continued)

12.25e.5	160
12.25e.6–7	159
12.25g.2–3	159
12.25h.1	193
12.25h.1–6	160
12.25h.4–6	193
12.25h.6	160
12.25i.5	183
12.25i.5–6	160
12.25i.6	159
12.25i.8	160, 183
12.25i.9	161, 213
12.25k.1–26a.4	161
12.26c.1	205
12.26c.1–4	161
12.26c.2–3	155
12.27.1	196
12.27.4–7	160
12.27.8–9	160
12.28.5–6	160
12.28.6	160
12.28.7	160
12.28a.6–7	160
12.28a.8–10	160
12.28a.10	160
15.36.1–7	130
15.38.8	130
21.26.16	155
32.8.4	155
32.9.2	155

Quintilian, *Institutio oratoria*

2.4.2–3	132
2.4.22	199
2.17.19–20	129, 162
2.17.26–29	129, 162
3.6.32	234
3.6.80	234
3.7.6	232
3.7.10–11	245
3.7.10–12	232
3.7.14	232
3.7.15	128, 245
3.7.16	233
3.7.18	246
3.7.23	234, 288

Quintilian, *Institutio oratoria* (continued)

3.7.27	240
3.7.28	127, 165, 234
3.8.9	180
3.8.63	126, 129, 162
4.2.45	180
6.2.29–30	192
6.2.31–32	302
6.2.32	192
6.2.35	192
8.3.61–70	192
8.3.67–68	195
10.1.31	127, 162
10.1.32	180
12.2.29–30	128
12.4.1–2	128
12.11.4	124

Rhetorica ad Alexandrum

1440b	304
1441a	305
1441b	201, 305

Rhetorica ad Herennium

1.9.15–16	189
1.13	132
1.16	181
3.10	233
3.13	233
3.14	233

Sallust, *Bellum catalinae*

8.4	119

(Anon.) Seguerianus, *On Narrations*

89–94	189

Seneca, *Epistulae*

114.2–3	164

Sextus Empiricus, *Adversus Grammaticos*

1.252	131
1.253	130
1.258	132
1.263–64	132
1.267–68	132

Strabo, *Geographica*

2.6.3	115
11.5.3	162
16.2.34–46	227
16.2.36	257
16.2.37	257, 310

Suetonius, *De Vita Caesarum: Divus Augustus*

76.2	227

Tacitus, *Annales*

1.1	165
3.65	165

Tacitus, *Historiae*

1.1	165
1.3	127
5.3.2	257
5.4.3	257
5.5.1	227, 257

Theon, *Progymnasmata*

1.13–17	122
1.25–30	122
1.40–42	122
1.43–47	122
1.47–48	122
4.37–43	248
5.1–11	182
5.15–18	182
5.38	248
5.62–71	184
5.195–225	180
5.235–37	248
5.449ff	182
5.471–73	182
6.1–5	199–200
6.11–13	199–200

Theon, *Progymnasmata* (continued)

6.46–56	200
6.71–76	200
6.88–89	192
6.88–97	201, 302
7.1–2	192
7.53–54	192
8.1–3	209
8.16–25	209
9.15–19	233
9.20	233
9.20–24	292
9.21–24	233
9.25	233
9.28–30	233
9.28–31	292
9.78–81	292
9.82–86	295
10.1	204
10.13–15	204
10.27–30	295
10.56–65	204

Thucydides, *History of the Peloponnesian War* (continued)

1.20.2–3	114
1.21.1	115, 148
1.21.2	148
1.22.1	109, 151, 159
1.22.2–3	150
1.22.2–4	147
2.40.3	174

Valerius Maximus, *Memorable Deeds and Sayings*

1.3.3	227
5.4	128

Index of Modern Authors

Abusch, R., 229, 247
Albrect, M. von, 121
Alexander, L. C. A., 4, 131, 133, 141, 163, 166, 219, 279, 282
Allen, J. L., 106
Allen, O. W., 152, 203
Anderson, G., 134, 137, 172, 192
Annas, J., 177, 196
Arai, S., 310
Atkinson, J. E., 135
Atkinson, K., 289
Attridge, H. W., 112, 139, 152, 214, 227–28, 253, 256, 258
Aune, D. E., 4, 133
Avemarie, F., 268
Avenarius, G., 110, 118, 121, 147, 192–93
Aziza, C., 255

Bachmann, M., 99
Bacon, B. W., 15–16
Bakhtin, M. M., 202
Balch, D. L., 129, 135, 163, 204, 235, 258, 273–75, 282–84, 286, 304, 310
Bannon, C. J., 302
Barclay, J. M. G., 95, 227
Bar-Kochva, B., 255–56
Barr, D. L., 4
Barrett, C. K., 20, 51, 63–65, 67, 74, 78–83, 88–89, 96, 99, 313, 316
Bartchy, S. S., 61, 72, 276
Barton, T., 135, 200–201
Bartsch, S., 192, 195
Batstone, W. W., 205
Baumgarten, A. I., 141
Baur, F. C., 8–9, 11–13, 20, 61, 67
Baynham, E., 152, 155
Becker, C., 205
Belfiore, E. S., 178, 191, 197
Berger, K., 11, 29–30
Berthelot, K., 224, 238, 283, 294
Betz, H. D., 224

Beuken, W., 98
Beyer, H. W., 75
Bickerman, E. J., 228
Bihler, J., 29, 50, 268
Bilde, P., 225
Binder, D. D., 290
Blum, R., 133
Blundell, M. W., 191, 206, 208
Boismard, M.-É., 20
Bonner, S., 121, 199
Bosworth, A. B., 210, 249
Bousset, W., 14
Bowersock, G. W., 138
Bowie, E. L., 134, 143
Bowker, J. W., 89
Bradley, K. R., 157
Braun, M., 137
Braun, W., 222
Brawley, R. L., 100, 307
Brehm, H. A., 14, 40, 51, 67–68, 92, 95, 100
Briant, P., 169
Brodie, T. L., 83, 299
Bruce, F. F., 314
Bultmann, R., 15
Burchard, C., 82
Burgess, T. C., 121, 123, 126, 180, 230–32, 234, 295
Burton, J. B., 192
Buss, M. F., 89
Butts, J. R., 122, 199
Byrskog, S., 132–33, 147, 150, 160, 163, 170, 189–90, 196, 210, 216, 219

Cadbury, H. J., 1–2, 46, 67
Calame, C., 107, 178
Callan, T., 109
Campbell, R. A., 65
Cancik, H., 118, 132, 137
Cape, R. W., 124–26
Capel Anderson, J., 298

Capper, B., 64, 276
Cassells, W., 89
Chance, J. B., 4, 51, 99
Charlesworth, J. H., 242–43
Clark, A. C., 222
Clark, D. L., 232
Clauss, J. J., 249
Collins, J. J., 25, 227, 255
Collins, J. N., 64–65, 75
Connolly, J., 144, 166–67, 180,
Connor, W. R., 147
Connors, C., 169
Conzelmann, H., 2, 17, 82, 224
Cox, P., 135
Cribiore, R., 122
Crump, D., 290, 292
Cullmann, O., 67, 89, 99
Cunningham, S., 79, 83

Dahl, N. A., 50, 90, 94, 99, 307–8, 314
Dalbert, P., 225
Darr, J. A., 203
Daube, D., 34, 74, 266, 276
Dehandschutter, B., 299
deSilva, D. A., 143–44
Diamond, F. H., 255
Dibelius, M., 2, 45–49, 56–57, 76–77, 81–82, 85–87, 90–91, 93, 211–12, 334
Dillon, R. J., 87
Dilts, M. R., 189
Dominik, W. J., 211–12
Donaldson, T. L., 99, 315
Doran, R., 118, 133, 136–37, 255
Dover, K. J., 176
Downing, F. G., 143, 221
Droge, A. J., 255
Dschulnigg, P., 32
Duff, T. E., 204
Dungan, D. L., 220
Dupont, J., 90, 92, 307

Earl, D., 137, 165
Easton, B. S., 268
Eckstein, A. M., 154, 159
Eddy, S. K., 143, 228
Eden, K., 148

Edmunds, L., 148, 152, 163–64
Edwards, C., 169, 175
Edwards, D. R., 62, 277
Elliott, J. H., 264
Esler, P. F., 66, 71–72, 75
Evans, C. A., 277

Fantham, E., 235
Fehling, D., 106
Feldherr, A., 178, 191
Feldman, L. H., 25, 112, 118, 125, 135, 139, 225–27, 246, 253
Ferguson, E., 67
Fitzmyer, J. A., 76, 82, 85, 88, 220
Flory, S., 107
Flower, M. A., 120
Foakes Jackson, F. J., 20–21
Fornara, C. W., 110, 113, 120, 210
Friedländer, M., 224–25
Frier, B. W., 125
Fuks, A., 274–75
Fusillo, M., 133

Gabba, E., 108, 147
Gager, J. G., 255–56
Ganser-Kerperin, H., 100
Gasque, W. W., 110, 170
Gaventa, B. R., 2
Georgi, D., 69–70, 225
Georgiadou, A., 121
Gera, D., 128
Gerber, C. C., 206, 253–54, 274, 283, 294
Gilbert, G., 62, 277
Glad, C. E., 166, 169
Gleason, M. W., 144, 169, 201
Glombitza, O., 292
Goodman, M., 225, 283
Gowing, A. M., 213
Graf, F., 130
Grangaard, B. R., 263
Gray, V., 136
Green, J. B., 62
Green, P., 116, 150
Grossman, M., 100
Grube, G. M. A., 180
Gruen, E. S., 143, 226, 229, 239, 254

Grundmann, W., 15
Gunderson, E., 110, 144

Haacker, K., 96, 309–10
Habinek, T. H., 235
Hadas, M., 80, 236–37
Haenchen, E., 3, 17, 50, 56, 67, 72–73, 75, 81, 84, 91, 286
Hägg, T., 234
Hall, R. G., 92, 94, 99, 123, 126, 307
Halliwell, S., 117, 148–49, 152, 155–56, 186, 197, 208–9
Hankinson, R. J., 132
Hansen, W., 133
Hanson, A. T., 311
Hanson, R. P. C., 312
Harlow, D. C., 98
Harnack, A. von, 16, 78
Hartman, L., 268
Harvey, G., 69–70
Hata, G., 224
Hayward, R., 309
Heitmüller, W., 14
Hemer, C. J., 5, 216
Hengel, M., 23–29, 34, 67, 78, 88, 143
Henten, J. W. van, 229, 247
Heschel, S., 12
Hilgert, E., 213–14
Hill, C. C., 14, 17, 33, 40–43, 64, 71–72, 76, 81–83, 86, 90, 269–70, 275–76
Hinds, S., 249
Hock, R. F., 122
Hodgson, P. C., 10, 12–13
Holladay, C. R., 236, 311
Hornblower, S., 104, 150, 205–6, 210, 212
Horsley, R. A., 290
Hübner, H., 99
Hunter, R., 137
Hurtado, L. W., 27
Hyldahl, N., 42, 66, 74

Jenkinson, E. M., 135
Jervell, J., 88, 282, 287, 317
Jeska, J., 93

Johnson, L. T., 66, 74, 76, 93, 95, 220, 228, 265, 267, 271, 277
Justus, B., 206

Kasher, A., 224
Kaster, R. A., 110
Keaney, J. J., 181
Kee, H. C., 80, 289
Keitel, E., 212
Keith, A. M., 144
Kelley, S., 12
Kennedy, G. A., 92, 122, 189, 221, 231, 235
Kidd, I. G., 147
Kilgallen, J. J., 52, 309, 315
Kirschenbaum, A., 157
Klein, G., 62, 225
Kliesch, K., 52, 91
Klijn, A. F. J., 313, 316
Klinghardt, M., 90, 258, 310, 325
Koester, C. R., 80, 98–99, 311, 314, 316
Konstan, D., 166–67
Koskenniemi, E., 134
Köster, H., 80
Kraabel, A. T., 225–26, 282
Kraus, W., 37, 100
Krieger, K. S., 112
Kümmel, W. G., 9
Kurz, W. S., 63, 83, 128

Lake, K., 20–21
Lamberton, R., 181
Lamouille, A., 20
Larmour, D. H. J., 121, 204
Larsson, E., 32, 100
Leeman, A. D., 124
Légasse, S., 67, 314
Lentz, J. C., 222, 278
Levene, D. S., 194–95, 212, 218
Levinskaya, I., 226
Lévy, E., 136
LiDonnici, L. R., 133
Lienhard, J. T., 76
Lindemann, A., 276
Long, A. A., 156
Loraux, N., 175

Luce, T. J., 118, 147, 205
Lüdemann, G., 19–20, 63, 72, 80–82, 91

Macchi, J.-D., 318
MacDonald, D. R., 6
Mack, B. L., 123
MacMullen, R., 135
Maddox, R., 73, 279
Mader, G., 274
Malina, B. J., 202
Marguerat, D., 62, 222
Marincola, J., 111–13, 118, 135, 145, 157, 166, 177, 219
Marrow, S. B., 166, 173
Marshall, I. H., 220
Martin, R. P., 285
Martin, T. W., 57
Mason, S., 112, 225
Matsen, P. P., 189
Matthews, S., 225
Mattill, A. J., 270
McCullough, H. Y., 107
McKnight, S., 225
McLaren, J. S., 112
Meecham, H. G., 225
Meijering, E. P., 12
Mellor, R., 124, 126
Mendels, D., 116, 138–40, 256, 292
Metzger, B. M., 68, 278
Mitchell, A. C., 61, 275
Mitchell, M. M., 192
Moessner, D. P., 4, 58, 62, 93, 118–19, 163, 220, 263, 265, 289, 296
Momigliano, A., 229
Moore, G. F., 12
Moore, S. D., 298
Moreland, M., 6, 235
Morgan, J. R., 137, 192
Morgan, M. G., 205
Morgan, T., 122
Mosley, A. W., 111
Moxnes, H., 144
Mullen. E. T., 146
Murison, C. L., 107
Murray, O., 238
Murray, R., 71

Mussner, F., 220

Neudorfer, H.-W., 7, 32, 82, 89
Neyrey, J. H., 143, 221–22, 230, 234, 245
Nickelsburg, G. W. E., 81, 203, 237, 298
Norden, E., 18
North, H. F., 177, 230, 291–92

Ó Fearghail, F., 220
O'Reilly, L., 92
Oden, R. A., 139
Økland, J., 260
Oliver, J. H., 163–64

Palmer Bonz, M., 56, 249, 280, 334
Parsons, M. C., 122, 220
Pearson, L., 203
Pelling, C., 108, 123, 136, 150, 204, 206, 210
Penner, T., 3, 59, 92, 94, 110, 122, 135, 144, 150, 168, 176, 180, 221, 249, 271, 275, 284, 292, 299, 334–37
Perlman, S., 142
Pervo, R. I., 5–6, 134, 275
Pesch, R., 20, 68
Petzke, G., 134
Philonenko, M., 245
Pichler, J., 89
Plümacher, E., 3, 6, 222, 274
Pomeroy, A. J., 174, 178
Porter, S. E., 109, 150, 210, 269
Potter, D. S., 129, 138, 211, 214
Poulakos, T., 234
Praeder, S. M., 6, 62
Price, R. M., 73

Räisänen, H., 34–37, 51, 76
Rakotoharintsifa, A., 63, 264
Ramsay, W. M., 5
Rappaport, U., 112
Rau, E., 37
Raubitschek, A. E., 109
Rawlings, H. R., 205
Rawson, B., 157
Reardon, B. P., 123, 135, 137

Reitzenstein, R., 132
Reventlow, H. G., 9
Rhodes, P. J., 104
Richard, E., 22, 34, 52, 64, 76, 93, 99, 307, 313, 317, 319
Richardson, P., 226, 289–90
Richlin, A., 144
Ricoeur, P., 188
Riesner, R., 5, 80, 82, 289
Rist, J. M., 176
Robbins, V. K., 123, 219, 283
Roberts, M., 248
Rogers, G. M., 275
Roloff, J., 62
Romer, F. E., 134
Römer, T., 318
Romilly, J. de, 123, 186
Romm, J., 107, 134
Rood, T., 249
Rorty, A. O., 117
Rousseau, P., 234
Russell, D. A., 110, 180, 230, 234
Rutherford, R. B., 127, 201

Sabbe, M., 83
Sacks, K. S., 116, 118, 125, 129, 147, 205, 214
Ste. Croix, G. E. M. de, 117
Sanders, J. T., 99, 135
Sandmel, S., 244–45
Sandt, H. van de, 312
Sandy, G. N., 192
Sawicki, M., 143
Schäfer, P., 224, 226, 255–57
Schiappa, E., 230
Schimanowski, G., 239
Schlier, H., 173
Schmidt, D., 163
Schmithals, W., 38
Schneckenburger, M., 9
Schneider, G., 20, 89, 91, 220
Scholz, U., 154
Schürer, E., 224
Schwemer, A. M., 26
Scott, J. J., 98
Scott, J. M., 62, 277
Scroggs, R., 18, 90

Seccombe, D., 72
Seim, T. K., 74–75
Seland, T., 32–33, 63, 82, 87
Sevenster, J. N., 223
Sherman, N., 197
Shuler, P. L., 230, 232, 234
Siegert, F., 225, 249
Siker, J. S., 308–9
Simon, M., 18, 225
Skidmore, C., 127–28
Smith, A., 222, 292
Soards, M. L., 89, 94, 212
Spencer, F. S., 63, 74, 77, 264, 272, 314
Spilsbury, P., 227, 246, 254
Squires, J. T., 45, 63, 152, 269, 283
Stadter, P. A., 159
Stahl, H.-P., 211
Stanton, G., 50
Steck, O. H., 51, 89, 95, 318
Stemberger, G., 89
Stenschke, C. W., 98, 317
Stepp, P. L., 4
Sterling, G. E., 6, 61, 100, 115, 133, 138–39, 227–28, 236, 282, 300, 315, 322
Sternberg, M., 118, 216
Stone, A. M., 213
Stowers, S. K., 209
Strange, W. A., 67
Strauss, B. S., 184
Stuhlmacher, P., 32
Sullivan, J. P., 235
Surkau, H.-W., 299
Swain, S., 137, 142–43
Sylva, D. D., 313, 315
Syme, R., 107

Talbert, C. H., 4, 62, 135, 317
Tannehill, R. C., 62, 73, 94–96, 99, 296, 307, 309, 323
Tatum, J., 136
Taylor, J., 21, 276
Taylor, N., 99
Tcherikover, V., 228
Theissen, G., 73, 276–77
Thomas, C. M., 120, 132, 285
Thompson, R. P., 63, 265, 273

Thornton, C.-J., 222
Thyen, H., 58
Tiede, D. L., 58
Toher, M., 142
Tov, E., 90
Trapp, M. B., 175
Trenkner, S., 186
Trocmé, É., 99
Trompf, G. W., 128, 152
Tyson, J. B., 12, 53, 67, 73, 86, 263

van Unnik, W. C., 1, 6, 59, 146, 180, 193, 220
Vander Stichele, C., 144, 168, 292, 335, 337
Varneda, V. I., 147, 192
Via, E. J., 94
Vouga, F., 38–39

Walbank, F. W., 118, 147, 156
Walker, B., 202
Walker, P. W. L., 100
Wallace-Hadrill, A., 273, 291–93
Walsh, P. G., 147, 211
Walter, N., 20, 30–31, 73, 77, 225, 239
Wardman, A., 135
Watson, F., 188
Webb, R., 122, 192
Weber, F., 11
Wedderburn, A. J. M., 37
Weinert, F. D., 100
Weiser, A., 29

Welles, C. B., 118
Wendland, P., 46, 85
Wentling, J. L., 4
West, M. L., 146
Westlake, H. D., 202, 211
White, H., 21, 188
Wiedemann, T., 123
Wiens, D., 93
Wilckens, U., 18, 52, 87, 89
Wilcox, M., 46, 86, 281
Williams, C. A., 198
Williams, G., 235
Williams, M. H., 71
Wills, L. M., 89, 136
Wilson, A., 192
Wilson, N. G., 234
Wilson, S. G., 65, 84, 269, 284
Wilson, W. T., 256
Winkler, J. J., 134
Winter, S. C., 273
Wiseman, T. P., 106–7, 125, 132, 137, 163
Witherington, B., 5, 51, 83, 92, 108, 110, 137
Woodman, A. J., 107–8, 124–26, 129, 248
Woodruff, P., 117
Worthington, I., 307

Zanker, P., 175
Zeller, E., 84
Zmijewski, J., 52, 91